OTHER MONOGRAPHS IN THE SERIES,
MAJOR PROBLEMS IN PATHOLOGY

Published

Evans and Cruickshank: *Epithelial Tumours of the Salivary Glands*
Mottet: *Histopathologic Spectrum of Regional Enteritis and Ulcerative Colitis*
Thurlbeck: *Chronic Airflow Obstruction in Lung Disease*
Hughes: *Pathology of the Spinal Cord, 2nd ed.*
Fox: *Pathology of the Placenta*
Striker, Quadracci and Cutler: *Use and Interpretation of Renal Biopsy*
Asbury and Johnson: *Pathology of Peripheral Nerve*
Morson: *The Pathogenesis of Colorectal Cancer*
Azzopardi: *Problems in Breast Pathology*
Hendrickson and Kempson: *Surgical Pathology of the Uterine Corpus*
Katzenstein and Askin: *Surgical Pathology of Non-Neoplastic Lung Disease*
Frable: *Thin-Needle Aspiration Biopsy*

Forthcoming

Burke: *Surgical Pathology of the Spleen*
Finegold: *Pediatric Neoplasia*
Hughes: *Pathology of Muscle, 2nd ed.*
Jaffe: *Surgical Pathology of Lymph Nodes and Related Organs*
LiVolsi: *Pathology of the Thyroid*
Lukeman and Mackay: *Tumors of the Lung*
Mackay, Evans and Ayala: *Soft Tissue Tumors*
Mottet & Norris: *Histopathology of Inflammatory Bowel Disease, 2nd ed.*
Panke and McLeod: *Pathology of Burn Injury*
Phillips: *Pathology of the Liver*
Reagan and Fu: *Pathology of the Uterine Cervix, Vagina and Vulva*
Taylor, Chandor and Nakamura: *Immunomicroscopy*
Variakojis and Vardiman: *Pathology of the Myeloproliferative Disorders*
Whitehead: *Mucosal Biopsy of the Gastrointestinal Tract, 3rd ed.*

JONATHAN S. WIGGLESWORTH, MD., *F.R.C. Path.*

Reader in Paediatric Pathology, Royal Postgraduate
Medical School, University of London; Department of
Paediatrics and Neonatal Medicine, Hammersmith Hospital,
London

PERINATAL PATHOLOGY

Volume 15 in the Series
MAJOR PROBLEMS IN PATHOLOGY
JAMES L. BENNINGTON, M.D., *Consulting Editor*

Chairman, Department of Pathology
Children's Hospital of San Francisco
San Francisco, California

1984
W. B. Saunders Company
Philadelphia, London, Toronto, Mexico City, Rio de Janeiro, Sydney, Tokyo

W. B. Saunders Company: West Washington Square
Philadelphia, PA   19105

1 St. Anne's Road
Eastbourne, East Sussex BN21 3UN, England

1 Goldthorne Avenue
Toronto, Ontario M8Z 5T9, Canada

Apartado 26370—Cedro 512
Mexico 4, D.F., Mexico

Rua Coronel Cabrita, 8
Sao Cristovao Caixa Postal 21176
Rio de Janeiro, Brazil

9 Waltham Street
Artarmon, N.S.W. 2064, Australia

Ichibancho, Central Bldg., 22-1 Ichibancho
Chiyoda-Ku, Tokyo 102, Japan

Library of Congress Cataloging in Publication Data

Wigglesworth, Jonathan S.

Perinatal pathology.

(Major problems in pathology; v. 15)

1. Fetus—Diseases.   2. Fetus—Abnormalities.   3. Infants—Diseases.   I. Title.   II. Series.   [DNLM: 1. Fetal disease—Pathology.   2. Infant, Newborn, Disease—Pathology.   W1
MA492X v.15 / WQ 211 W656p]

RG626.W48 1984   618.3′207   83-20123

ISBN 0-7216-9338-5

Perinatal Pathology   ISBN   0-7216-9338-5

Last digit is the print number: 9   8   7   6   5   4   3   2   1

EDITOR'S FOREWORD

Recent advances in the fields of neonatology and perinatology have brought about a greater understanding of congenital, genetic and metabolic disorders; factors influencing fetal growth and development; and the effects of infection on the fetus. This expanded knowledge of the pathophysiology of disease processes in the fetus along with the advances in the management of the high-risk obstetrical patient and the fetus requiring postnatal intensive care places increasing demands on the pathologist to establish the cause of death and the underlying contributing factors.

In many pathology departments relatively few autopsies are performed on infants who have died in the perinatal period, and as a result fetal autopsies may not be performed in such a way as to obtain the maximum amount of information available. This is unfortunate since details which may be important to the clinician in understanding the cause of death, documenting underlying disease processes, evaluating the treatment provided to the mother, fetus or both, providing genetic counseling or guiding the management of future pregnancies can be obtained from the properly performed fetal autopsy.

In this monograph, Dr. Wigglesworth provides an authoritative, up to date overall review on the subject of the perinatal autopsy. It includes his approach to performing the fetal autopsy based on years of personal experience and research in this field. Of particular interest are the discussions on the approach to the examination of the placenta, the macerated fetus, the lungs, and hemorrhagic lesions of the brain; his recommendation on the handling of specimens for microbiologic or genetic studies; and guidelines for evaluation of pathologic changes secondary to medical treatment and management.

PERINATAL PATHOLOGY offers detailed information on the requirements for and potential of a good perinatal autopsy service and serves as a practical and useful guide to the performance of the perinatal autopsy (the approach, what to suspect, how to make the diagnosis). For clinicians, this monograph provides a basis for determining the potential and limitations of the perinatal autopsy and a foundation for understanding and interpreting the pathologist's autopsy report. Dr. Wigglesworth has managed to compress a great deal of useful information into a small and highly readable text. It should be of paramount interest to perinatologists, neonatologists and obstetricians and gynecologists as well as to anatomic pathologists.

JAMES L. BENNINGTON, M.D.

PREFACE

The pathology of the perinatal period includes a complex mixture of disorders relating to organogenesis, fetal growth, genetic and metabolic defects, problems of maternal illness and obstetric management, problems of immaturity and of neonatal care and a wide range of infectious diseases which produce specific effects in the fetus and newborn infant. Superimposed on this basic complexity there has been an explosion of information on areas such as cytogenetics and biochemistry of inborn metabolic errors and increasing diagnostic and therapeutic possibilities for malformed or immature infants. These advances have changed the perinatal autopsy from an academic observational exercise to one in which the pathologist may be required to provide information which is essential for genetic counseling and planning of future clinical management strategies. Interpretation of the findings often demands knowledge of developmental anatomy and physiology and awareness of current practice in obstetrics and neonatology. However, the small number of fetal and infant deaths occurring in any one institution results in the necessity for a large number of nonspecialist pathologists to perform occasional perinatal autopsies.

The primary purpose of this book is to help the nonspecialist pathologist with the complex sorting process involved in perinatal pathology and to direct that person to the sources of specialized information that may be needed in particular instances. In addition, I have tried to provide enough brief background data on normal structural and functional development and clinical correlations to make the book of value also to other workers in the perinatal field, including obstetricians and neonatologists.

In writing the book an attempt has been made to apportion the space devoted to individual topics in proportion to their clinical importance rather than to their interest as pathological entities. Additional space has been devoted to those areas of perinatal pathology (e.g., examination of the placenta) which pose particular problems for the general histopathologist or currently cause clinical concern (e.g., intraventricular hemorrhage).

As the need to provide a clear overview of perinatal pathology has required that a large subject be compressed into a small space, it has seemed logical that many of the references should be to other books or review articles in which the subjects are handled in greater depth and references to original work may be found.

Thus this volume is in no way intended to supersede any other book on perinatal pathology but to provide a practical working knowledge of the subject and starting point for more academic study.

ACKNOWLEDGMENTS

It is a pleasure to acknowledge the many pathologists and other colleagues who have allowed me to reproduce illustrations from their own published work or unpublished material. The authors and publications concerned are individually acknowledged in the legends to the figures.

I am indebted to Mr. William Hinkes of the Department of Medical Illustrations, Royal Postgraduate Medical School, and to Miss Mahrokh Nohadani of the Department of Paediatrics and Neonatal Medicine who between them prepared most of the photographs. I must also thank Dr. Pamela Davies for giving helpful advice on Chapter 9, and Mrs. Christine White for carrying out a major part of the secretarial work concerned with the book.

Finally my greatest debt is to my wife Joan who typed and corrected the manuscript for me and tolerated my neglect over many months during the gestation period of this work.

CONTENTS

Chapter One

Approach to Perinatal Pathology

The pathology of the perinatal period differs profoundly from that of adult life in both the nature of the pathological processes involved and the complex changing background of growth and development on which they are superimposed and with which they interact. Death in the adult is due to development of a pathological condition in a previously stable organism. In the fetal period death may result from acute or chronic alteration of the uterine environment producing nonspecific changes of acute hypoxia or alteration of the normal processes of growth and development. Intrapartum death may be due to failure of the normal transition from fetus to neonate caused by factors arising acutely de novo or secondary to a prolonged prenatal stress. Neonatal death is most frequently due to inability of the preterm infant to adapt to extrauterine life.

In order to interpret the changes he may find, the pathologist needs to understand the background of normal development upon which pathological changes are superimposed.

This chapter will discuss how the pathologist needs to approach the pathological problems of the perinatal period in order to gain information of both clinical and academic value from the autopsy.

VALUE OF PERINATAL AND INFANT AUTOPSIES

A perinatal autopsy is in many ways of considerably greater importance than one performed on an adult. It is of importance firstly to the family as an aid in genetic counseling or reassurance of the parents. The dead infant may be only the first member of a potential family and to the parents the loss may throw doubt on their ability to have normal healthy children. A properly performed autopsy can be of considerable help either to reassure them as to the good prognosis for further pregnancies or to aid in genetic counseling if the infant proves to be malformed or to have some genetic disorder. The details will also be of value to the obstetrician to aid in management of a subsequent pregnancy. It may be pointed out that negative findings, that is, the absence of congenital anomalies or the absence of evidence of prolonged placental insufficiency, may be of greater importance for these purposes than the demonstration of a pathological cause of death.

The second major reason for performance of perinatal autopsies is to provide a form of quality control on perinatal care. The relative contributions of trauma and asphyxia to perinatal death can be resolved only following skillful performance of a perinatal autopsy. The rapid advances in intensive care of the small preterm infant result in continuing introduction of new and experimental forms of monitoring or treatment. Blood sampling techniques alone may be responsible for hemorrhage, nerve injury, infection or interstitial emphysema.[1] Skin electrodes, oxygen therapy, catheter insertion, mechanical ventilation, use of overhead heaters and intravenous feeding all have recognizable complications referred to at appropriate points in this book. Realistic assessment of the part that such unlooked-for complications of treatment may have played in contributing to an infant's death is an important aspect of the perinatal autopsy. Indeed, the discovery of unexpected hazards of therapy may sometimes throw new light on normal physiological processes (e.g., mask ventilation; see Chapter 12). The recognition that hazards of therapy exist often leads to simple means of avoidance. The rapid time course of perinatal illness ensures that the correct diagnosis of illness (e.g., β-hemolytic streptococcal infection) often cannot be made in life. Moreover, the signs of some potentially fatal conditions (intraventricular hemorrhage) may be quite variable. The ability to make or confirm such diagnoses at autopsy can even stimulate the introduction of improved diagnostic techniques, e.g., real time ultrasound diagnosis of intraventricular hemorrhage in life.

The pathologist can make a valuable contribution to the perinatal team in that the feedback from his work to the obstetrician and neonatologist should influence their management of future cases and thus the development of modern perinatal care.

A final reason for performance of perinatal autopsies is for research purposes. Many aspects of human perinatal physiology and pathophysiology can be understood only by study of human autopsy material. Even if animal models are developed, it is necessary to acquire a thorough knowledge of the human condition in order to establish how appropriate a particular animal model may be.

Epidemiological research into causes of perinatal and infant death is of major concern. It is widely recognized that perinatal mortality rates within any population reflect both background socioeconomic factors and the quality of health care provided. High perinatal mortality rates are no longer considered acceptable in developed countries. Thus there is likely to be continued pressure to explain causes of perinatal death and to introduce effective programs to reduce perinatal mortality in areas where it is unduly high. A high rate of competently performed perinatal autopsies provides an essential background of knowledge on which to base such aims.

THE TIME SCALE OF PERINATAL EVENTS

Pathologists who are used to older children or adults may find it difficult to adjust to the time scale of the perinatal period. The structural and physiological changes occurring over this time are enormous. The brain, for instance, may increase by some 400 per cent in weight between 24 weeks' gestation and term. This is similar to the increase that occurs subsequently between birth and adult life. The differences in structural pattern and physiological function of organs over this period are equally great. The lungs at 24 weeks of gestation may have sufficient development of blood-air barriers to be at the borderline of conferring viability to the fetus; by term they have thinned-out saccular walls with early but regular development of alveoli. The renal glomeruli develop in successive layers until about 36 weeks' gestational age. The cerebral cortex, almost smooth at 24 weeks, has well-developed convolutions and sulci by term. The cerebellum undergoes even more rapid development. Muscle bulk and subcutaneous tissues increase throughout the last trimester.

The pathologist has to understand these changes and must recognize where on the development scale a particular infant fits. In addition to these changes of normal development, comprising both growth and maturation of tissues, he has to recognize the possibility of abnormal development (abnormal growth or maturation) for the stage of pregnancy or the postnatal age of the infant. It is not sufficient to think of a 1500-g infant as premature. It may be either a very well-grown preterm infant of 28 weeks' gestation or a severely growth-retarded infant of 38 weeks' gestation. In order to interpret pathological changes, it is essential to know which.

The effects of delivery are an important additional consideration. Organ maturation may be profoundly influenced by enzymes induced by the process of birth. Enzymes involved in surfactant synthesis in the lungs and those concerned with bilirubin metabolism in the liver are obvious examples. Characteristic pathological lesions induced during birth (intracranial trauma, asphyxial injury) will develop on a time scale related to this occurrence but influenced by the stage of development achieved by the infant when birth took place.

Other pathological lesions may develop only following birth in immature infants. The onset of respiratory distress syndrome caused by surfactant deficiency in the preterm infant is triggered by the birth event. The condition develops fairly rapidly and the appearance of the lungs in a baby who dies will depend on the precise age at death. At 12 hours of age the lungs may be solid and edematous with hyaline membranes lining the respiratory bronchioles but without complete collapse of the periphery of the lobules. This is due to slow clearance of the fetal lung liquid. By 24 hours of age, when the lung liquid is cleared, the hyaline membranes have developed further and the periphery of the lobule is collapsed and intensely congested. By 48 hours there may be early attempts at repair or cellular reaction to methods of treatment. In the brain of such an immature infant a subependymal germinal layer hemorrhage may develop within the first 24 hours of life and expand rapidly to rupture eventually into the ventricular system during the second 24 hours of life.

A LOGICAL APPROACH TO PERINATAL PATHOLOGY

The apparent complexities just discussed can usually be resolved if approached in a logical way. The pathologist has to know or determine the answer to three preliminary questions:

1. What is the gestational age of the infant?
2. Is development normal for this gestational age?
3. When did the infant die in relation to birth?

If the infant died in the neonatal period it is necessary to know at how many minutes (in the first hour), how many hours (in the first 3 days) or how many days (in the first month). The range of likely pathological lesions and their state of development may largely be determined when these preliminary facts are established. The small preterm infant (say 1100 g birth weight at 28 weeks' gestation) who dies with a history of respiratory difficulty on the second or third day of life is likely to have congested airless lungs with histological evidence of respiratory distress syndrome and an intraventricular hemorrhage in the brain.

If the same infant were to die instead at 5 days of age it is likely that secondary problems such as infection, bronchopulmonary dysplasia or necrotizing entero-colitis may have supervened on the original condition.

The mature infant who had a heartbeat but could not be resuscitated at birth may have suffered some acute asphyxial problem during birth and may show evidence of this affecting the internal organs, or may have an unexpected malformation, probably involving severe hypoplasia of the lungs. If such an infant were resuscitated with difficulty but underwent progressive deterioration leading to death at 12 to 24 hours, the combination of asphyxia and intracranial birth trauma might be suspected.

An unusual set of answers to these preliminary questions may suggest the presence of an unusual form of pathology. Normally formed small preterm infants seldom die during labor unless there has been some catastrophic event such as a massive retroplacental hemorrhage. Thus the occurrence of an unexplained anoxic intrapartum death in such an infant has on occasion prompted careful examination of the organs that has revealed a condition such as infection with *Listeria monocytogenes* (see Chapter 9).

As is pointed out in Chapter 3, the inaccessibility of the fetus in utero and the rapidity of the time course of neonatal illness may limit the quantity of laboratory data and background information available to the pathologist. It is therefore very important to be able to make what is essentially a clinical analysis of the case using all available information in order to determine which organs require particularly careful study and which special investigations may be called for.

The perinatal period is a time when biomedical disciplines meet. The background biology of this time of life involves the developmental anatomy and physiology of the fetus and placenta, and the dramatic changes associated with birth. Superimposed on this are the various aspects of medical care, the monitoring and interventions performed by obstetricians, and the techniques of resuscitation and intensive neonatal management practiced by neonatologists. The pathologist working in the perinatal field has to gain some knowledge of all of these events to solve the problems with which he is presented.

NORMAL PERINATAL GROWTH

Although the perinatal pathologist requires a working knowledge of the whole of embryonic and fetal development, his interest in the details of fetal growth commences at the stage when it becomes possible for the fetus to survive following birth. Currently this critical point may be taken as about 24 weeks' gestation (calculated from the first day of the last menstrual period) and is determined largely by the ability of the lungs to support extrauterine respiration. In this brief handling of the subject I will therefore place most emphasis on the period from 24 weeks to term.

Gestational Age Assessment and Its Importance

Age is the independent variable against which growth must always be assessed. A major problem of the perinatal period is that age, in terms of gestational age, is not usually known with accuracy because it depends either on the mother's recollection of her menstrual dates or on some measurement of the fetus or clinical examination of the neonate. All assessment schemata have themselves ultimately been derived from a population in which the clinician has accepted the accuracy of the mother's recollection of her dates. There has been a temptation for pathologists to consider fetuses and infants purely in terms of weight and measurements, as they are more accurate parameters than gestational age. Throughout the perinatal period all such measurements are profoundly influenced by pathological conditions affecting the growth potential and/or nutrition of the fetus. Despite the difficulties, it is therefore essential for the pathologist to try to establish a "best estimate" of gestational age and relate all body measurements and organ sizes to it.

When considering clinical estimates of gestational age, it is important to know the method of assessment which has been used. All assessments quoted in this book, except where otherwise stated, are in completed weeks from the first day of the last menstrual period. Thus an infant born 39 weeks and 5 days after the first day of the last menstrual period will be reckoned as of 39 weeks' gestational age. Assuming a normal menstrual cycle of 28 days, the age of such a fetus from conception would be about 37 to 37½ weeks. In studies on embryos and early fetuses the menstrual history is often ignored and the gestational age is quoted in terms of the figures given in tables derived from measurements of crown-to-rump (CR) length.[2] Obstetricians may correct an inadequate maternal obstetric history on the basis of ultrasound measurement of the fetal biparietal diameter made in the early part of the second trimester. The figures quoted usually come from the data published by Campbell.[3] Assessment of fetal age from crown-rump length measurements and from ultrasound measurements depends on the assumption that all fetuses grow at the same rate in the early part of pregnancy. The sequential measurements possible with the use of ultrasound techniques do give support for this, although there are pathological conditions which retard fetal growth from very early in the second trimester.

In infants who survive birth, the neonatologist may make his own estimate of maturity by assessing a number of external characteristics and neurological signs. The standard scores given to each feature studied (0 to 3 according to its stage of development) are summed to give a total score which is equivalent to a particular gestational age.[4] The accuracy of this type of assessment depends on choosing features which are little affected by nutritional status or state of health of the infant.

The pathologist can make a contribution to gestational age assessment from his observations on convolutional pattern of the brain and histological maturity of organs such as the kidney.

Changes in Weight and Composition of the Body in the Perinatal Period

During the period from 24 weeks to term the fetus increases in weight, on the average, from about 600 g up to 3400 g. From about 32 weeks onward male infants tend to weigh slightly more than female infants and at term the difference is of the order of 200 g. From the mean curves of fetal growth (Fig. 1–1) it can be seen that weight increases at a relatively constant rate until about 36 weeks and then flattens off toward term. Individual fetuses do not necessarily grow along the lines indicated by the cross-sectional data used in compiling birth weight charts. The flattening out of the growth chart near term does appear to indicate that a progressively larger proportion of fetuses are subjected to growth impairment toward the end of pregnancy, as the newborn infant resumes the growth rate characteristic of the period from 30 to 36 weeks for the first 3 months of neonatal life.[5] In fetuses from populations of poor socioeconomic status, and in

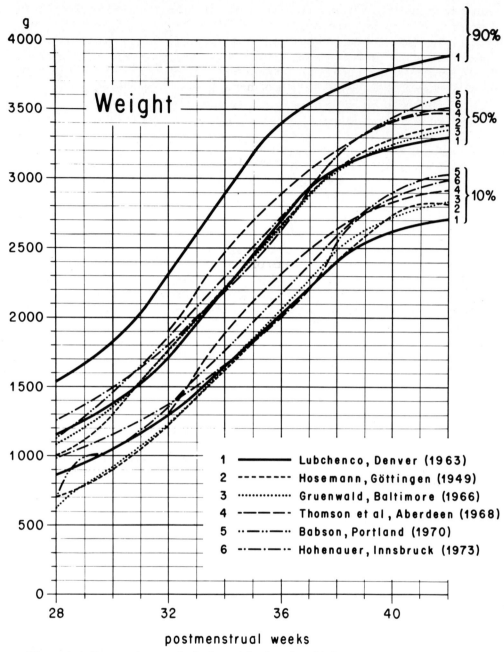

Figure 1–1. Intrauterine standards for weight, based on birth weight measurements of infants born at different postmenstrual ages. Lines indicate percentiles: i.e., 90 per cent of the population has a birth weight which does not exceed the 90th percentile value. (From Brandt, I.: Dynamics of head circumference growth before and after term. In Roberts, D. F. and Thomson, A. M. (eds.): The Biology of Human Fetal Growth. Taylor & Francis Ltd., 1976.)

multiple births, the birth weight curve flattens out at an earlier stage. The true "normal" fetus may be one whose growth carries on along a straight line until term. The fetal growth charts from countries such as Sweden approach this ideal form.[6] Such observations have led to the conclusion that fetal growth in late pregnancy and thus eventual birth weight is limited by the efficiency of the maternal supply line to the fetus.[7]

There is an enormous literature on the relative importance of genetic and environmental factors in determining size at birth in man and many other animal species. Genetic factors are clearly important in determining adult size and body form and might be expected to influence birth weight. Considerable evidence indicates, however, that under normal circumstances, i.e., in the absence of specific pathological conditions, environmental influences are of greater importance than genetic ones in determining birth weight. Such evidence includes the demonstration that birth weight in litter-bearing animals (or multiple births in man) is inversely related to the size of the litter, that birth weight in man and other animals is related more closely to maternal size than to paternal size, and that birth weight in man is powerfully influenced by birth order.[8]

From a biological point of view, this should not be surprising. Species survival clearly depends on adaptability. The ability of the fetus to tailor its growth according to the availability of nutrients with minimal detriment to potential for subsequent growth and development is an essential requirement for survival of any mammalian species. As with all adaptation mechanisms there are limits beyond which it cannot operate effectively. Moderate deviations from the optimal growth pattern may render the baby more susceptible to incidental pathological processes developing at or after birth, while gross ones may cause sufficient disruption of subsequent structural and functional development as to be recognizable as directly damaging to the fetus.

An understanding of the biological spectrum of growth and the arbitrary nature of any line used to distinguish between the normal and pathological is of importance to the perinatal pathologist. The percentile or standard deviation lines on the charts of birth weights for gestation can be useful as indications of the probability of growth being abnormal for a particular stage of gestation but do not clearly delineate those instances in which growth abnormality has been associated with pathological problems. The charts are of particular use to neonatologists in determining which infants should be screened for possible metabolic consequences of fetal nutritional impairment.

Growth in overall size in the perinatal period is accompanied by changes in bodily form and in structure of different organs and tissues. The skin of a very immature infant (28 weeks' gestation or less) appears red because of the ease with which the superficial vessels are seen through the thin gelatinous epidermis. The trunk and limbs appear thin and angular owing to lack of skeletal muscles and subcutaneous fat. With increasing fetal maturity the skin becomes more opaque and the body contours more rounded as the epidermis thickens and skeletal muscles and subcutaneous fat gradually increase.

While these changes in external appearance are widely known and form the basis of some gestational age assessment schemes, the variation in growth rate of individual fetal organs is less widely recognized, although it is readily apparent from fetal organ weight charts derived from selected normally grown singleton infants such as those published by Larroche.[23]

Between 26 to 27 weeks and term most of the major organs, including brain, liver, heart, kidneys and adrenals, increase their weight by 250 to 300 per cent, equivalent to that of the fetus as a whole. The lungs increase their weight by a smaller proportion (about 220 per cent) but the thymus and spleen increase by 460 per cent. Examination of the various organs at macroscopic or histological level may provide clues as to the factors contributing to their different perinatal growth rates. Enlargement of the brain over this period involves considerable growth in the cerebral hemispheres and cerebellum with a regular development of cortical convolutional pattern which provides the pathologist with one of the most useful aids to gestational age assessment (see Chapter 3). There is a continuing change in proportions of different parts of the brain as the basal ganglia and brain stem grow at a slower rate than the cerebral hemispheres and cerebellum during this time. In the kidney, sequential formation of nephrons continues until 36 to 37 weeks and provides a useful histological marker for maturity. Development of the lung in the last trimester is perhaps slower than that of some other tissues because the most extensive development and major preparation for air breathing has already occurred during the period up to 24 weeks of gestation. The major growth in lymphoreticular tissues must indicate a relatively enormous increase in lymphocyte populations.

It is important for the pathologist to recognize that growth and function are as closely related during prenatal development as they are after birth. Much of the normal growth of organs and tissues in the fetus depends on achievement of the levels of function appropriate for that stage of development. Normal development of skeletal muscles and normal joint structure depends on establishment of the spinal reflex arc and the presence of sufficient amniotic fluid to allow the fetus to move its limbs. The ureters will attain a normal caliber only if the kidneys are secreting urine and there is no obstruction at the ureterovesical junction. Elsewhere I outline the importance of fetal pulmonary function (liquid secretion and respiratory movements) for normal lung growth. It follows that abnormal growth of any organ or tissue frequently indicates some subtle failure of function during development. Therefore, the ability to detect slight departures of growth pattern from normal is a useful skill for the perinatal pathologist to cultivate.

PATTERNS OF ABNORMAL GROWTH AND DEVELOPMENT

Most abnormal growth patterns in the perinatal period involve growth retardation rather than growth acceleration. Such impairment in growth may affect the whole body or be limited to specific organs or tissues. I have indicated already how the flattening out of the "normal" growth curve toward term may indicate constraint of fetal growth by the intrauterine environment and the extent to which variations in birth weight may represent a normal physiological adaptation. In this section I will consider the effects of the pathological extremes of this process and other types of growth-retarding stress.

It is now widely recognized that several characteristic patterns of fetal growth impairment may be seen, depending more closely on the time at which a growth-retarding stress developed than on its nature.[3] If fetal growth is impaired at an early stage of development, the effect is relatively uniform throughout the body. Such an infant, if born at term, appears generally small, but with normal bodily proportions. Maturation of different organs is not affected, so at autopsy the convolutional pattern of the brain would reveal that such an infant was mature despite his small size. This type of growth retardation is related to fetal malformation syndromes for a number of reasons. Most teratogenic agents act by inhibiting growth. Any growth inhibition during organogenesis may interrupt some critical phase of organ development in addition to retarding growth throughout the body. Administration of teratogens after the period of organogenesis causes growth retardation only.[9] Quite a brief period of such early growth inhibition causes a permanent defect in growth potential with little chance of any subsequent "catch-up" in growth. A typical example of the relationship between early symmetrical growth retardation and malformation is provided by infection with the rubella virus. This organism is known to impair cell growth in tissue

TABLE 1–1. SOME CAUSES OF DIFFERENT TYPES OF FETAL GROWTH RETARDATION

MALNUTRITION TYPE	HYPOPLASTIC TYPE
Pre-eclampsia	Intrauterine infections (Rubella, toxoplasmosis, CMV)
Multiple pregnancy	Malformation syndromes (trisomies)
Severe maternal malnutrition	
Maternal smoking	

culture; therefore, it is not surprising that symmetrical growth retardation forms part of the syndrome resulting from infection of the fetus within the first 14 weeks of gestation. The characteristic cardiac, auditory and visual lesions are related to specific areas of damage caused by the virus in addition to the generalized growth-retarding effect. A number of other forms of viral and protozoal infection of the fetus in early pregnancy may have a similar growth-retarding influence. Genetic and chromosomal causes of this form of growth retardation are also recognized (Table 1–1).

Numerically more frequent are cases in which growth has been retarded only in the latter part of gestation. Ultrasound evidence suggests that growth impairment in this group is unusual before 20 weeks' gestation.[3] These infants show an asymmetrical form of growth retardation with sparing of brain development at the expense of skeletal tissues and internal organs. The head may appear relatively large; the calvarium is thin and the brain seems tightly packed. The skeletal muscles and subcutaneous tissue are poorly developed; of the internal organs, the liver is unduly small. The ratio of brain weight to liver weight, normally 3:1 throughout the latter part of pregnancy, may be increased to as much as 6:1.[10] This ratio is a useful aid to the recognition and assessment of severity of growth retardation by the pathologist, as it does not require knowledge of the gestational age. Appearance of ossification centers is often delayed in these growth-retarded fetuses.

The appearance of such a growth-retarded infant in life or at autopsy will vary with the timing and severity of the growth-retarding process (Figs. 1–2 through 1–4). The earlier that growth has been retarded the more likely that the infant will show reduction of overall skeletal growth with reduced body length and lack of any obvious wasting. If fetal growth remains normal until a late stage of pregnancy but then becomes severely retarded, the infant will appear long and thin and obviously wasted. The skin may be wrinkled, suggesting an actual loss of previously formed subcutaneous fat, or may be cracked and peeling if the baby is born at or after term. Meconium staining of the nails may indicate episodes of fetal hypoxia.[11, 12]

The pathologist should not be surprised to see such evidence of impaired fetal nutrition in infants who are within the normal body weight range for their gestation. If growth becomes impaired at 35 weeks' gestation in a fetus likely to grow to 4 kg weight by term, the infant eventually born may be 3 kg in weight but show evidence of severe growth retardation.

It has long been recognized that the appearance of many of these babies at birth is characteristic of severe undernutrition. Experimental restriction of the blood supply to the uterus in animals such as rats and monkeys,[13, 14] or restriction of maternal food intake in species such as the sheep,[15] have effects on fetal body weight and organ growth that are similar to those described in preceding paragraphs in human growth retardation (Fig. 1–5). It thus appears that the fetus can be undernourished either by lack of nutrient available to the mother or by

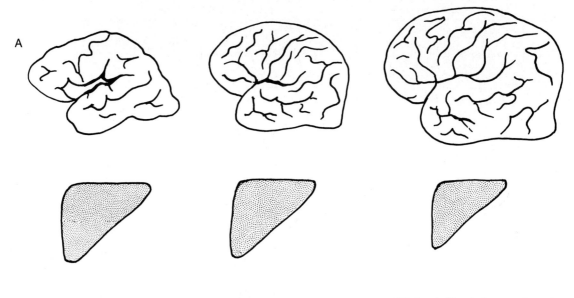

Preterm: Normal Growth   Symmetrical   'Malnutrition' form of
                                Growth Retardation   Growth Retardation

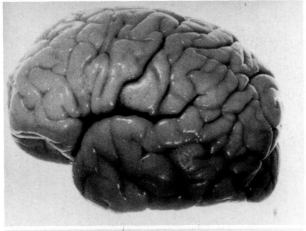

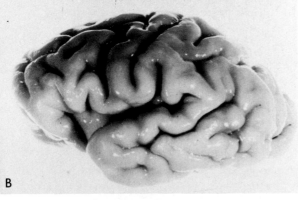

Figure 1–2. *A*, Brain and liver in different types of small infants. *B*, Brain of an infant of 1200 g at 38 weeks' gestation compared with that of an infant of 1470 g at 32 weeks' gestation.

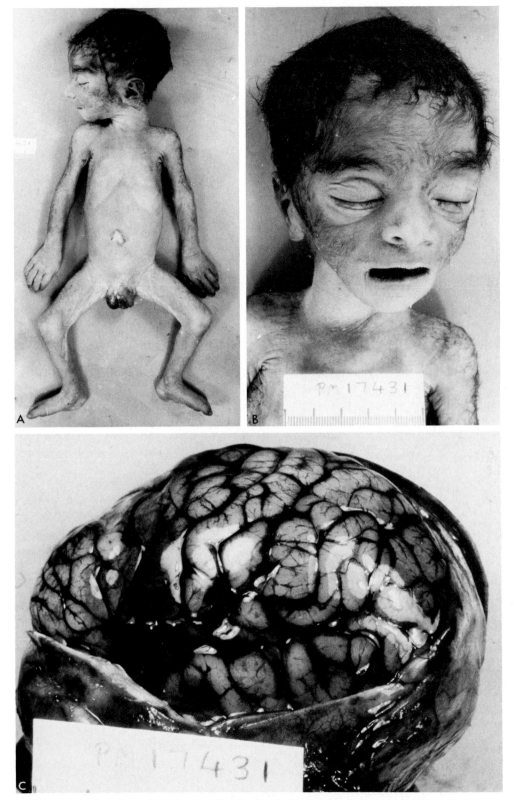

Figure 1–3. *A,* Infant of 1100 g who died during delivery at 34 weeks' gestation (expected weight about 2200 g). *B,* Face of the same infant. Note small face in relation to size of cranium. *C,* Skull of infant opened to show well-developed convolutional pattern of brain, appropriate for 34 weeks' gestation. Ratio of brain weight to liver weight was 6:1.

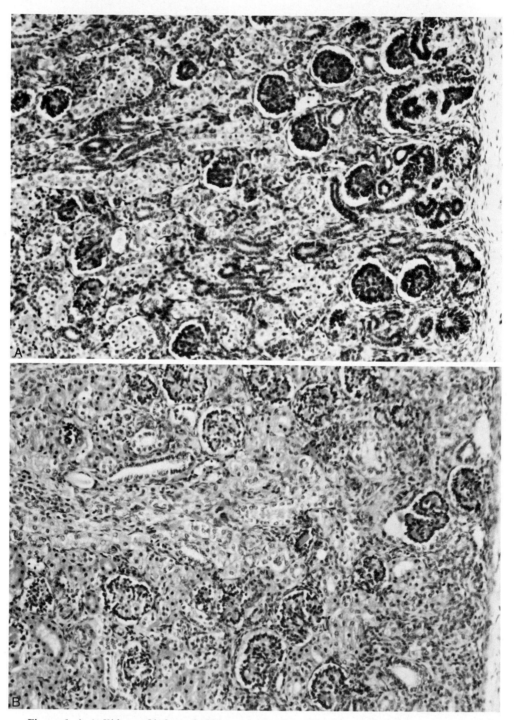

Figure 1–4. *A*, Kidney of infant of 1630 g weight at 30 weeks' gestation. H & E × 150. *B*, Kidney of infant of 1580 g weight at 40 weeks' gestation. H & E × 150. Growth retardation does not affect maturation of the kidney.

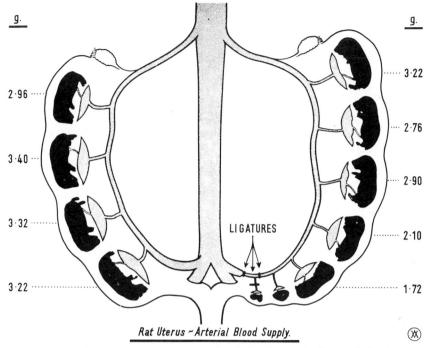

g. **g.**

2·96

3·40

3·32

3·22

LIGATURES

3·22

2·76

2·90

2·10

1·72

Rat Uterus ~ Arterial Blood Supply. ⊗

Figure 1–5. Influence of experimental uterine ischemia on fetal growth in the rat. Figures represent the weight in grams of fetuses in a typical experiment in which vessels had been ligated 4 days earlier. (From Wigglesworth, J. S.: Experimental growth retardation in the foetal rat. J. Pathol. Bacteriol. *88*:1–13, 1964.)

some bottleneck in the supply line by which nutrients are transferred to the fetus. A typical example of the asymmetrical "malnutrition" type of fetal growth retardation is that commonly seen in cases of maternal pre-eclampsia. This condition is associated with obstructive lesions in the spiral arteries supplying the placenta which cause severe reduction in uteroplacental circulation.[16]

There are many situations in which the fetus commonly becomes growth-retarded. The problem is often to determine the point at which physiological adaptation fails and growth retardation becomes a pathological condition. Maternal health and nutrition before and during pregnancy, personal habits during pregnancy, site of implantation and multiple pregnancy are among the many factors that may be responsible.

Although the symmetrical and asymmetrical forms of fetal growth retardation are frequently discussed as if they were totally separate entities, it must be emphasized that the main difference between the two is timing. The earlier that growth becomes retarded, the more symmetrical will be the effect and the poorer the chance for catch-up growth, irrespective of the causal mechanism. However, the pattern of growth impairment may indicate (to the neonatologist in life or the pathologist at autopsy) the most likely underlying cause, such as chronic intra-uterine infection or chromosomal abnormality in the symmetrically retarded fetus. The pattern of growth impairment may also predispose the infant to particular forms of perinatal pathology. Thus the placental vascular damage which causes fetal malnutrition in pre-eclampsia may also place such a growth-retarded fetus at increased risk of asphyxia during birth. The development of asphyxial signs during labor may increase the likelihood of obstetric intervention, but the thin calvarium of such an infant will enhance the risk of intracranial trauma during delivery. The growth-retarded infant is at risk for neonatal hypothermia because he is short of an insulating layer of subcutaneous fat and may also have inadequate stores of the brown fat, which is of particular importance for thermogenesis in the newborn.[17] The lack of glycogen stores in the liver and the inability to carry out normal gluconeogenesis combine to render the infant susceptible to hypoglycemia.[18] Combinations of problems such as birth asphyxia and hypothermia can lead to development of disseminated intravascular coagulation and consequent hemostatic failure.[19]

Thus by recognizing the occurrence and type of fetal growth retardation it is possible to build up a picture of possible underlying pathologic processes, associated clinical problems and secondary pathological lesions. At a practical level this type of analysis may serve to remind the pathologist which organs or tissues require examination with particular care, which further tests may be appropriate and which additional questions should be put to the obstetrician or neonatologist to clarify the clinical background.

Although undernutrition is the most frequent form of fetal malnutrition, it is not the only one. The classic chubby overweight infant of a diabetic mother (IDM) is no less an example of fetal malnutrition than the starved-looking infant of the woman with prolonged pre-eclampsia. Such infants are at increased risk of neonatal respiratory distress at a late stage of gestation and may become severely hypoglycemic. The latter condition is less frequently associated with clinical symptoms and serious sequelae than in growth-retarded infants, possibly because the body stores of these infants enable them to utilize ketone bodies such as β-hydroxybutyrate as an alternate energy source for the brain.

At autopsy the IDM may show obvious differences from other infants who are large for gestational age.[20] The increased body mass affects skeletal tissues and internal body organs, including the liver and heart but not the brain. In an extreme case of an infant examined some years ago, the normal weight relationship between brain and liver was almost reversed. The organ changes contrast markedly with those seen in infants who are unduly large but otherwise normal (Table 1–2). The changes in internal organs and skeletal tissues, almost a mirror image of those seen in fetal growth retardation, appear in part to be caused by increased insulin output by the fetal pancreatic islets (see Chapter 15). Improved control of maternal diabetes in pregnancy has reduced the frequency with which such infants are seen.

The adequacy of postnatal nutrition and the effect of deficiencies on body growth and development are of major concern to the neonatologist. The interactions between nutrition and neonatal illness may have profound influences on fetal growth and thus on findings at autopsy in infants who die following neonatal intensive care. There are difficulties in maintaining adequate nutrition for the healthy preterm infant. Even the most well-maintained incubator environment cannot protect such a baby from thermal stresses which necessitate a high metabolic rate for heat production.[21] The capacity of the gastrointestinal tract for metabolizing milk or formula is severely restricted by the level of maturity of enzyme

TABLE 1–2. ORGAN WEIGHTS IN AN INFANT OF AN UNDIAGNOSED DIABETIC MOTHER COMPARED WITH THOSE OF OTHER LARGE INFANTS*

	BODY WEIGHT (g)	BRAIN (g)	HEART (g)	LIVER (g)
Infant of diabetic mother	5640	377	49	426
Other normally formed large infants (n = 9)	4000–4710 (median 4140)	379–508 (median 443)	21.9–29.5 (median 27.2)	142–255 (median 181)

*Data from Hammersmith Hospital.

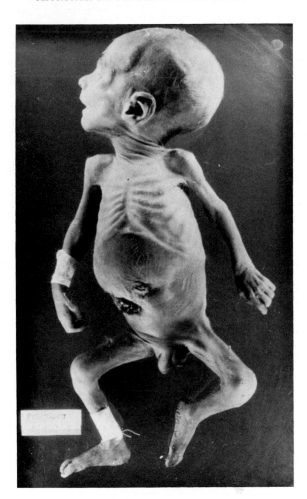

Figure 1–6. Postmortem appearance of an infant of 1475 g birthweight who died at 57 days of age. Postmortem weight 1175 g.

production, and attempts to increase oral feeding to a level sufficient to ensure both energy production and normal growth may have undesirable or fatal consequences.[22] Alternatives such as intravenous feeding have hazards of their own (see Chapter 11). These problems are accentuated in the infant who is ill and requires further increased energy production (e.g., to maintain a high respiratory rate in the respiratory distress syndrome), but whose enzyme function may have been depressed by metabolic acidosis and hypoxia. It is inevitable that the small preterm infant who was of normal weight for gestational age at birth is often severely underweight for his age and maturity when he is discharged from intensive care or dies after several weeks of treatment. At autopsy such infants characteristically show severe loss of subcutaneous and skeletal tissues although not gross abnormality in size of internal organs (Fig. 1–6).

GROWTH VARIATIONS AT ORGAN AND TISSUE LEVEL

I have so far considered how pathological processes may influence body growth as a whole. It is equally important to recognize the ways in which pathological conditions and modes of therapy interact with normal growth processes at the level of individual organs and tissues. The dramatic effects of prolonged mechanical ventilation and increased inspired oxygen level on the lung

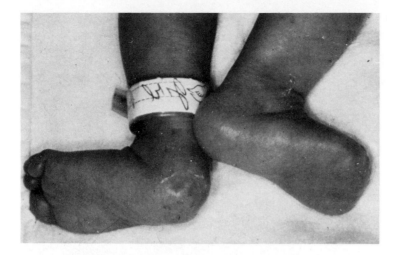

Figure 1–7. The feet of an infant who survived following neonatal intensive care. The toes of the left foot were lost following an ischemic complication of umbilical artery catheterization and there is atrophy of the fat pad of the right heel due to multiple heel stabs. The heel injury proved the more disabling of the two when the child began to walk. (Courtesy of Dr. K. E. Pape, Hospital for Sick Children, Toronto.)

in infants with hyaline membrane disease (see Chapter 10) represent a distortion of the normal growth and maturation process. Such distortions vary from the major ones such as bronchopulmonary dysplasia and retrolental fibroplasia to minor changes recognizable only at the histological level such as irregularities in cartilage formation (see Chapter 19) or in the development of renal glomeruli (see Chapter 21).

Very little is known about the ability of developing tissues to compensate for pathological injury by subsequent remodeling. The possibility of such remodeling needs to be considered when the potential seriousness of any lesion for later function is being assessed (e.g., intracranial hemorrhage in the preterm infant). For practical purposes it is even more important to recognize that apparently trivial forms of injury in the neonatal period may have severe unforeseen long-term sequelae. Two examples may be mentioned. Heel prick sampling of blood in the neonatal period is a minor procedure. On occasion, however, the recurrent

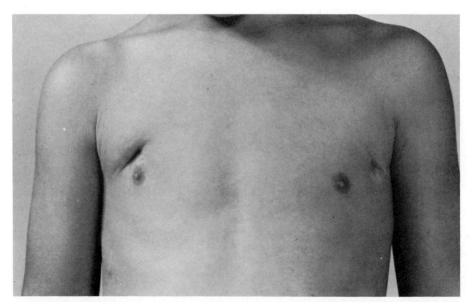

Figure 1–8. Late sequel to neonatal chest drain insertion in a girl aged 8 years. The fibrosis and distortion of the right breast was associated with limitation of shoulder movements and necessitated major surgery. (Courtesy of Dr. K. E. Pape, Hospital for Sick Children, Toronto.)

use of this technique in an infant of very low birth weight has been followed by atrophy of the fat pad of the heel with resultant pain and disability when the child starts walking (Fig. 1–7).

Relief of pneumothorax by insertion of a chest drain may be a necessary life-saving procedure in a sick neonate. If the drain is unthinkingly inserted through the immature breast tissue in a female infant, the extent of the damage may only subsequently become tragically apparent at adolescence when the developing breast becomes distorted by the underlying area of persistent fibrosis (Fig. 1–8).

SUMMARY AND CONCLUSIONS

In this chapter I have attempted to present an overview of what constitutes perinatal pathology. The central theme is the necessity for the pathologist to recognize subtle deviations from the normal pattern of growth and development at both gross and histological levels. The approach to perinatal pathology requires a knowledge not only of normal developmental anatomy and physiology but also of the diagnostic and therapeutic methods currently in use by obstetricians and neonatologists if the pathologist is to interpret adequately the lesions he may find at autopsy.

The pathological findings associated with a perinatal death may be of individual concern to the parents in planning their family and to the obstetrician and neonatologist in assessing standards of perinatal care, in addition to any value for epidemiological and other research purposes.

In the past it has been traditional practice in many pathology departments to regard perinatal autopsies as unimportant and delegate them to the most junior and least experienced staff. From this chapter it should be clear that such an approach is totally unjustified. The performance of a perinatal autopsy and extraction of the maximum information from it is an activity worthy of the attention of an experienced and highly motivated specialist.

REFERENCES

1. Stavis, R. L., and Krauss, A. N.: Complications of neonatal intensive care. Clin. Perinatol. 7:107–124, 1980.
2. Streeter, G. L.: Weight, sitting height, head size, foot length and menstrual age of the human embryo. Contributions to Embryology *11*:143–170, 1920.
3. Campbell, S.: Fetal growth. *In* Beard, R. W., and Nathanielsz, P. W. (eds.): Fetal Physiology and Medicine. London, W. B. Saunders Ltd., 1976, pp. 271–301.
4. Dubowitz, L., Dubowitz, V., and Goldberg, C.: Clinical assessment of gestational age in the newborn. J. Pediatr. 77:1–10, 1970.
5. McKeown, T., and Record, R. G.: The influence of placental size on fetal growth in man, with special reference to multiple pregnancy. J. Endocrinol. 9:418–426, 1953.
6. Lindell, A.: Prolonged pregnancy. Acta Obstet. Gynaecol. Scand. *35*:136–163, 1956.
7. Gruenwald, P.: The supply line of the fetus; definitions relating to fetal growth. *In* Gruenwald, P. (ed.): The Placenta and its Maternal Supply Line. Lancaster, M.T.P., 1975, pp. 1–17.
8. Wigglesworth, J. S.: Foetal growth retardation. Br. Med. Bull. *22*:13–15, 1966.
9. Wilson, J. G.: Current status of teratology: General principles and mechanisms derived from animal studies. *In* Wilson, J. G., and Fraser, F. C. (eds.): Handbook of Teratology. New York, Plenum Press, 1977, pp. 47–74.
10. Gruenwald, P.: Growth and maturation of the foetus and its relationship to perinatal mortality. *In* Butler, N. R., and Alberman, E. D. (eds.): Perinatal Problems. Edinburgh, Livingstone, 1969, pp. 141–161.
11. Clifford, S. H.: Postmaturity. Advanc. Pediatr. 9:13–63, 1957.
12. Gruenwald, P.: Chronic fetal distress and placental insufficiency. Biol. Neonatol. 5:215–265, 1963.
13. Wigglesworth, J. S.: Experimental growth retardation in the foetal rat. J. Pathol. Bacteriol. *88*:1–13, 1964.

14. Hill, D. E., Myers, R. E., Holt, A. B., Scott, R. E., and Cheek, D. B.: Fetal growth retardation produced by experimental placental insufficiency in the rhesus monkey. Biol. Neonatol. *19*:68–82, 1971.
15. Wallace, L. R.: The effect of diet on foetal development. J. Physiol. (Lond), *104*:34P, 1946.
16. Robertson, W. B., Brosens, I., and Dixon, H. G.: The pathological response of the vessels of the placental bed to hypertensive pregnancy. J. Pathol. Bacteriol. *93*:581–592, 1967.
17. Hull, D.: The structure and function of brown adipose tissue. Br. Med. Bull. *22*:92–96, 1966.
18. Warshaw, J. B.: The growth retarded fetus. Clin. Perinatol. *6*:353–363, 1979.
19. Chessels, J. M., and Wigglesworth, J. S.: Coagulation studies in severe birth asphyxia. Arch. Dis. Child. *46*:253–256, 1971.
20. Haust, D. M.: Maternal diabetes mellitus—effects on the fetus and placenta. *In* Naeye, R. L., Kissane, J. M., and Kaufman, N. (eds.): Perinatal Diseases. Baltimore, Williams & Wilkins, 1981, pp. 201–285.
21. Heim, T.: Homeothermy and its metabolic cost. *In* Davis, J. A., and Dobbing, J. (eds.): Scientific Foundation of Paediatrics, 2nd ed. London, Heinemann Medical, 1981, pp. 91–128.
22. Davies, P. A.: Infants of very low birth weight. *In* Hull, D. (ed.): Recent Advances in Paediatrics, Vol. V. London, Churchill-Livingstone, 1976, pp. 89–128.
23. Larroche, J. C.: Developmental Pathology of the Neonate. Amsterdam, Excerpta Medica, 1977.

Chapter Two

Causes and Classification of Perinatal Death

The study and interpretation of perinatal mortality statistics has traditionally been the concern of obstetricians and epidemiologists rather than pathologists. However, there are good reasons why pathologists should be concerned about the causes of perinatal mortality in general, in addition to the more immediate problems posed by individual infants examined at autopsy.

The demonstration that varying perinatal mortality rates are consistently related to socioeconomic factors and incidence of low birth weight may lead to the conclusion that improved medical care has little part to play in increasing perinatal survival or health. It takes the pathologist to reveal the fallacy of such arguments by demonstrating the potentially avoidable nature of many perinatal deaths in low birth weight infants.

Changes in medical practice at a particular institution may be associated with a change in the relative frequency of some conditions at autopsy. The recognition of this type of variation requires knowledge of the nature of the population from which cases are drawn. This may not be easy for the pathologist who examines only deaths in referral neonatal intensive care units, but it is important in relation to any obstetric unit, particularly if this serves a defined area. It is therefore an advantage for the pathologist to be able to think in terms of the population from which his cases are drawn.

This chapter is devoted to a brief consideration of perinatal mortality definitions, causes of perinatal deaths and possible methods of classification.

PERINATAL MORTALITY DEFINITIONS

The study of perinatal mortality involves assessment of deaths in fetuses and infants who have reached a potentially viable stage of maturity. It is therefore essential to make some arbitrary definition of the lower limits of fetal viability in terms of birth weight or gestational age or both. In different countries the lower limit of viability may be defined in terms of the length of gestation (20 or 28 completed weeks) or by weight of the fetus (500 g or 1000 g) or by some combination of the two. Regardless of weight or gestational age, any infant who shows "signs of life" may be included in the neonatal rates. For example, in the United Kingdom a fetus of 28 weeks' gestation is considered to be viable irrespective of birth weight. Thus in a twin birth at 26 weeks' gestation, with each

TABLE 2–1.   DEFINITIONS OF DEATH RATES AND RATIOS

Perinatal death rate: $\dfrac{\text{Fetal deaths + first-week deaths* (both 1000 g or more in weight)}}{\text{Live births and fetal deaths (both 1000 g or more in weight)}} \times 1000$

Perinatal death ratio: $\dfrac{\text{Fetal deaths + first-week deaths* (both 1000 g or more in weight)}}{\text{Live births (1000 g or more in weight)}} \times 1000$

Fetal death rate: $\dfrac{\text{Fetal deaths (1000 g or more in weight)}}{\text{Live births + fetal deaths (both 1000 g or more in weight)}} \times 1000$

First-week death rate:
(Early neonatal
death rate) $\dfrac{\text{First-week deaths* (1000 g or more in weight)}}{\text{Live births (1000 g or more in weight)}} \times 1000$

*7 days are estimated as seven periods of 24 hours.

fetus weighing 800 g, if one twin is stillborn it will be classed as an abortion and not included in the stillbirth rate. The liveborn twin is included in the Office of Population Census and Surveys (OPCS) reports, although it would be excluded from international comparisons as currently recommended by the World Health Organization because these only include infants of over 1000 g (Table 2–1).

Comparison of statistics of this type collected over different periods or in different countries can be of value only if the definitions used and the methods and completeness of data collection are the same in each case.[1] International comparisons may be particularly misleading owing to differences in definitions, birth registration requirements and statistical procedures.[2]

Definitions currently used in the United Kingdom include the following:

$$\text{Perinatal death rate} = \dfrac{\text{No. stillbirths + first week neonatal deaths}}{\text{No. live births and stillbirths}} \times 1000$$

$$\text{Neonatal death rate} = \dfrac{\text{No. deaths up to 28 days of age}}{\text{No. live births}} \times 1000$$

PROBLEMS IN CLASSIFYING PERINATAL DEATHS BY CAUSE

The causes of perinatal death are complex. Death may result from genetic factors causing abnormal development, a range of environmental influences operating through maternal health before and during pregnancy, obstetric factors around the time of birth, or environmental influences operating after birth. In any one case these factors usually operate sequentially so that a single defined "cause" for a perinatal death is the exception rather than the rule. Difficulty in classifying perinatal deaths by cause arises less from a lack of information about causes of perinatal deaths than from the difficulty that medical scientists have in accepting or handling the concept of the multifactorial nature of the causation of death or disease in general and perinatal death in particular.

This difficulty can be illustrated by discussing a characteristic type of case history (Fig. 2–1). A woman of low socioeconomic status may be in poor nutritional state when she becomes pregnant. Such a woman may have inadequate diet during pregnancy, may be a heavy smoker and may develop pre-eclamptic

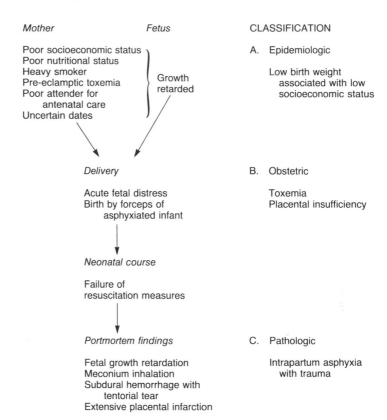

Figure 2–1. A hypothetical case summary showing how the "cause" of death in the perinatal period may be variably classified by different professionals.

toxemia. These factors individually and collectively predispose to impaired fetal growth. There is a high probability that such a patient will not keep appointments for antenatal care (irrespective of free health services available to her) and will be unsure of her menstrual dates.

The obstetrician may be faced with the problem of unexpected severe fetal distress developing during labor at an uncertain time in the gestation. This lack of background data on which to base obstetric decisions increases the risk of severe asphyxia and trauma during delivery. If the baby dies, autopsy might reveal evidence of fetal growth retardation, inhaled meconium and amniotic material in the lungs, a moderate amount of subdural blood clot over the cerebral hemispheres (associated with torn bridging veins and a small tear of the tentorium), and a small flattened placenta containing multiple old and recent infarcts. There is little problem in understanding how fetal death occurred in such a case, although one might be unsure as to the relative importance of the various factors in contributing to death or the precise mechanisms of some of the processes involved, such as how pre-eclamptic toxemia causes vascular damage to the spiral arteries supplying the placenta. However, there are a number of different ways in which the death can be classified according to the purpose of the classification or the individual interest or bias of the person who analyzes the data, as indicated in Figure 2–1.

EPIDEMIOLOGICAL CLASSIFICATION

At an epidemiological level our hypothetical case would be linked to low birth weight associated with poor socioeconomic status. In population terms these are the two constant factors which relate most consistently to the level of perinatal mortality. Over many years in developed countries there has been a rapid and continuing fall in numbers of fetal and neonatal deaths.[3, 4] The rates of fall have been related to the rate of improvement in socioeconomic status of the different countries concerned. Many studies have shown that 60 per cent of neonatal deaths occur in babies below 2500 g birth weight, and variations in neonatal mortality rate may be most clearly related to the incidence of infants below 1500 g.[5] Since so many of the factors associated with increased perinatal mortality are linked to low birth weight, in any comparison of perinatal mortality between different localities or at different times the birth weight distribution of the general population must be taken into consideration.[4-6] This is particularly important if it is desired to separate factors related to the quality of perinatal care from those inherent in the population under consideration.[7] I have pointed out elsewhere precisely how the examination of perinatal mortality rates in terms of birth weight subgroups can provide information of direct relevance for monitoring the efficiency of obstetric and pediatric care.[8]

CLASSIFICATION BY OBSTETRIC AND MATERNAL FACTORS

Classification according to obstetric factors gives a label for the obstetrician to attach to the case, whether or not an autopsy is performed. The definitions used in these classifications, such as the Aberdeen classification (Table 2–2),[9] seem to rely too much on clinical interpretation rather than on objective data and are thus of limited help in assessing potentially avoidable factors.

CLASSIFICATION BY PATHOLOGICAL FINDINGS

Classification by pathological findings can be carried out only in infants examined by autopsy (Table 2–2).[10, 11] The attempt to classify deaths according to causes recorded on birth certificates in cases in which autopsy was not performed is a waste of time for any but grossly obvious malformations (such as anencephaly). Even if a postmortem examination was performed, the demand that the pathologist provide a single cause of death may lead to a loss of information. In the newborn, as in the elderly, multiple factors contributing to death is the rule rather than the exception. The pathologist classifying our hypothetical case may have to decide whether death was caused primarily by birth asphyxia or trauma. In

TABLE 2–2.   PREVIOUS CLASSIFICATIONS OF PERINATAL DEATHS

BY CLINICAL CAUSE[9]	BY PRIMARY AUTOPSY FINDING[11]
Premature, unknown cause	Malformation
Mature, unknown cause	Isoimmunization
Trauma	Antepartum death, no major lesion
Toxemia	Antepartum hypoxia
Antepartum hemorrhage	Intrapartum hypoxia
Maternal disease	Intrapartum hypoxia with cerebral trauma
Fetal deformity	Cerebral birth trauma
Other	Pneumonia
	Hyaline membranes
	Pulmonary hemorrhage
	Intraventricular hemorrhage
	Neonatal death, no major lesion
	Extrapulmonary infection
	Intrapartum death, no major lesion
	Miscellaneous

Reproduced by permission from Lancet *ii*:685, 1980. Wigglesworth, J. S.: Monitoring Perinatal Mortality—A pathophysiological approach.

another instance, such as an infant who died with hyaline membrane disease, intraventricular hemorrhage and necrotizing enterocolitis, the pathologist's decision as to which condition was the cause of death may be as much a matter of guesswork as of knowledge.

DESIGNING A CLASSIFICATION SYSTEM

From the case discussed in the previous section, it can be seen that none of the accepted methods of classifying perinatal deaths can record the full sequence of prenatal and intrapartum events that resulted in the death of this particular infant.

If it is accepted that no classification system can fully describe all characteristics of the cases included, it becomes clear that the information which should be classified routinely is that which most clearly defines subgroups of cases that we may subsequently wish to identify as an index of our population or adequacy of our perinatal care. In addition, we may wish to catalogue our cases according to some recognized clinical or pathological coding system such as the International Classification of Diseases, the Systematized Nomenclature of Pathology, or the Systematized Nomenclature of Medicine.[12–14] In order to decide how perinatal deaths should be classified on a simple basis, it is helpful to consider the major types of pathological findings at autopsy, their relative frequencies and the clinical situations with which they are associated.

PATHOLOGICAL FINDINGS AT AUTOPSY

Pathological findings at autopsy on infants dying in the perinatal period fall into a number of different categories.

A. Signs indicating that the infant has been subjected to some form of generalized stress before death, e.g., poor body and organ growth suggesting impaired placental function, hemorrhages over lungs and heart or inhaled amniotic material in the lungs indicating an acute asphyxial episode.
B. Lesions indicating some specific occurrence during labor or delivery, e.g., tears of the tentorium cerebelli indicating excessive distortion of the cranial bones during birth.
C. Lesions which are related to immature structure and function of different organs and thus develop in small preterm infants after birth, e.g., hyaline membrane disease in the lungs and intraventricular hemorrhage in the brain.
D. Congenital malformations, particularly those involving the central nervous system or heart, and malformation syndromes in which the lungs are hypoplastic.
E. Specific disorders (metabolic, infective, hematological, immunological and so forth) with characteristic pathological findings and often with recognizable modes of transmission or inheritance.
F. Lesions developing as a result of or during the course of treatment of one of the above, e.g., bronchopulmonary dysplasia or pneumothorax in infants treated for hyaline membrane disease using mechanical ventilation.

Most infants who die in the perinatal period have multiple findings, often from several of these categories.

There is currently no up-to-date information on the breakdown of pathological causes of death in the perinatal period. Since the British Perinatal Mortality

TABLE 2–3.   ESTIMATED BREAKDOWN OF U.K. PERINATAL DEATHS IN 1977 INTO MAJOR PATHOLOGICAL SUBGROUPS

	NUMBER	CHARACTERISTICS
Stillbirths—9.4/1000 Total Births		
Congenital malformations	2.4	
Nonmalformed macerated infants	5.0	May show asphyxial signs, growth retardation, infection, etc.
Nonmalformed intrapartum stillbirths	2.0	Most show signs of acute asphyxia, often with preceding growth retardation
First-Week Neonatal Deaths—7.6/1000 Total Births		
Problems of immaturity	3.6	Mainly HMD and IVH
Effects of birth asphyxia	2.0	May show signs of asphyxia, cranial trauma or infection
Congenital malformations	1.5	
Others	0.5	
Late Neonatal Deaths (1–4 Weeks)—1.6/1000 Total Births		
Congenital malformations	1.0	
Late problems of immaturity	0.6	Iatrogenic problems often appear in this group

For the method of arriving at these figures see: Wigglesworth, J. S.: House of Commons second report from Social Services Committee, 1979–80. Vol. 4, London, HMSO, 137–138 (1980). R. Short, Chairman.

Survey of 1958, the perinatal mortality rate in England and Wales fell from 35/1000 to 14.8/1000 (in 1978), and it is probable that different causes of death may have declined at different rates. It is possible to make some approximation to the probable breakdown of pathological causes by examining the results of surveys performed by individual pathologists within the past 10 years and relating them to overall British national figures, and such data as can reasonably be extracted from the OPCS returns. The results of this exercise are shown in Table 2–3.

A PROPOSED SIMPLE CLASSIFICATION OF PERINATAL DEATH

If the slightly artificial separation of stillbirths and neonatal deaths is dispensed with for the purpose of considering deaths from congenital malformations and asphyxial conditions arising during labor, it is possible to classify perinatal death into five major subgroups as shown in Table 2–4. This type of grouping has several practical advantages. It separates out the cases of particular importance in relation to the level of obstetric care, the birth asphyxia group, and the cases which are important in relation to the provision of neonatal care—the deaths associated with immaturity. It is possible in most cases to assign babies on whom postmortem examination was not performed to one of the groups with reasonable confidence. The grouping is not dependent on highly subjective judgments because the asphyxia group will contain all the infants whose deaths may have been associated with trauma.

TABLE 2–4.   SIMPLIFIED CLASSIFICATION OF PERINATAL DEATHS

1. Normally formed macerated stillborn infants
2. Congenital malformations (stillborn or neonatal death)
3. Conditions associated with immaturity (neonatal death)
4. Asphyxial conditions developing in labor (fresh stillbirth or neonatal death)
5. Other specific conditions (e.g., known β-hemolytic streptococcal infection or a fatal inborn error of metabolism)

The linkage of a relatively simple pathological classification of this type with information on birth weight of the dead infants in relation to their background population would combine the virtues of epidemiological and pathological classifications and provide a powerful way of assessing the significance of perinatal mortality trends. A relatively high perinatal mortality rate associated with a high incidence of low birth weight infants may reflect merely the low socioeconomic status of the population served, whereas a similar perinatal mortality rate with deaths affecting large infants may indicate shortcomings in the provision of perinatal care. Such information derived from the birth weight breakdown can be cross-checked against the pathological classification to confirm, for instance, that an unexpectedly high perinatal mortality among babies of over 2.5 kg birth weight was associated with asphyxial conditions at birth rather than a cluster of congenital malformation cases.

This method of classifying perinatal deaths does require that the breakdown of the birth population into birth weight subgroups is known. However, it has already been pointed out that such information is essential for any meaningful comparison of perinatal mortality figures. From what has been said in the previous chapter it might be suggested that a gestational age breakdown would provide the best basis for such comparisons. This undoubtedly is true but would be difficult to achieve for comparisons between hospitals or countries where accuracy of gestational assessment would vary widely.

BASIS FOR VARIABILITY IN PERINATAL MORTALITY STATISTICS

The patterns of mortality within these major groups have been influenced by changes in medical practice over the past few years. The introduction of screening programs for neural tube defects has altered the frequency with which the pathologist encounters anencephaly or meningomyelocele in the strict perinatal period. Other congenital defects may now be diagnosed by realtime ultrasound scan at a time when the pregnancy can be terminated safely. The range of metabolic errors which can be diagnosed by tests on cells cultured from the amniotic fluid is now quite considerable (see Chapter 3). However, these conditions are individually of such rarity that they have little effect on the overall pattern of perinatal mortality. Asphyxial deaths in labor or in the early neonatal period have been considerably reduced by improvements in perinatal care, including use of intrapartum fetal monitoring techniques and more widespread availability of staff skilled in resuscitation and care of the infant at birth. A marked fall in intrapartum deaths associated with asphyxia and trauma was a major feature of the findings of the 1970 British Births Survey as compared with the 1958 British National Perinatal Mortality Survey.[15]

The increasing knowledge and interest in care of the very low birth weight infant has resulted in increased survival in this group.[16, 17] Those preterm infants who die are likely to have received intensive neonatal care and to demonstrate multiple and complex pathological lesions which have advanced to a later stage than described in many texts. The increased survival of low birth weight infants has encouraged obstetricians to consider administration of steroids to advance the maturation of the fetal lung prior to preterm delivery,[18] and to consider performing elective cesarean section to avoid the hazards of premature vaginal breech delivery.[19]

There are enormous regional and national differences in the availability of specialized services of this type. Equally, there are wide differences in the extent to which clinicians are convinced of the value of many of these diagnostic and therapeutic procedures. It is perhaps not surprising that persistent large regional differences exist in perinatal mortality which are not all explicable in terms of variations in socioeconomic status of the population and variations in incidence of low birth weight infants.[7]

REFERENCES

1. Weatherall, J. A. C.: Infant mortality: International differences. Population Trends *1*:9–12, 1976.
2. Pharoah, P. O.: International comparisons of perinatal and infant mortality rates. Proc. Roy. Soc. Med. *69*:335–338, 1976.
3. Alberman, E.: Facts and Figures. *In* Chard, T., and Richards, M. (eds.): Benefits and Hazards of the New Obstetrics. Clinics in Developmental Medicine *64*, London, S.I.M.P. with Heinemann. Philadelphia, J. B. Lippincott Co., pp. 1–17, 1977.
4. Erickson, J. D., and Bjerkedal, T.: Fetal and infant mortality in Norway and the United States. JAMA *247*:987–991, 1982.
5. Lee, K.-S., and Paneth, N.: The very low-birth-weight rate: Principal predictor of neonatal mortality in industrialized populations. J. Pediatr. *97*:759–764, 1980.
6. Chalmers, I., Newcombe, R., West, R., and Campbell, H.: Adjusted perinatal mortality rates in administrative areas of England and Wales. Health Trends *10*:24–29, 1978.
7. Mallet, R., and Knox, E. G.: Standardized perinatal mortality ratios: technique, utility and interpretation. Community Med. *1*:6–13, 1979.
8. Wigglesworth, J. S.: Monitoring perinatal mortality. A pathophysiological approach. Lancet *II*:684–686, 1980.
9. McNay, M., McIlwaine, G. M., Howie, P. W., and Macnaughton, M. C.: Perinatal deaths: analysis by clinical cause to assess value of induction of labour. Br. Med. J. *1*:347–350, 1977.
10. Butler, N. R., and Bonham, D. G.: Perinatal mortality. The first report of the British perinatal mortality survey. London, Livingstone, 1963.
11. Machin, G. A.: A perinatal mortality survey in southeast London, 1970–73: the pathological findings in 726 necropsies. J. Clin. Pathol. *28*:428–434, 1975.
12. International Classification of Diseases: Ninth Revision. Geneva, WHO, 1978.
13. Systematized nomenclature of pathology. Skokie, Ill., College of American Pathologists, 1965.
14. Systematized nomenclature of medicine, 2nd ed. Skokie, Ill., College of American Pathologists, 1979.
15. Chamberlain, R., Chamberlain, G., Howlett, B., and Claireaux, A.: British Births 1970, vol. 1: the first week of life. London, Heinemann Medical Books Ltd., 1975.
16. Stewart, A. L., Reynolds, E. O. R., and Lipscomb, A. P.: Outcome for infants of very low birthweight: survey of world literature. Lancet *1*:1038–1040, 1981.
17. Britton, S. B., Fitzhardinge, P. M., and Ashby, S.: Is intensive care justified for infants weighing less than 801 g at birth? J. Pediatr. *99*:937–943, 1981.
18. Liggins, G. C., and Howie, R. N.: A controlled trial of antepartum glucocorticoid treatment for prevention of the respiratory distress syndrome in premature infants. Pediatrics *50*:515–525, 1972.
19. Goldenberg, R. L., and Nelson, K. G.: The premature breech. Am. J. Obstet. Gynecol. *127*:240–244, 1977.

Chapter Three

Performance of the Perinatal Autopsy

From the previous chapters it should be apparent that most problems in perinatal pathology relate to growth and development. Assessment of the state of growth and development of the infant and his constituent organs and tissues is thus a central aspect of the perinatal autopsy. The information that can be gained from simple weights and measurements is often more important than anything seen under the microscope; the need for the pathologist to be obsessionally concerned with such measurements in the perinatal autopsy constitutes a major difference from the adult autopsy.

The performance of a perinatal autopsy resembles other subspecialist activities in the ease with which it can be made to appear an obscure and difficult art. A comprehensive protocol to cover all eventualities would render the procedure so complex and time-consuming that no general anatomic pathologist could ever carry it out. In order to make this chapter as practical and widely useful as possible, I will stress the relative importance of recording different items of information in particular types of cases, and the acceptable minimum data to be obtained. Each pathologist should in practice establish his own basic protocol according to the facilities and time he has available for perinatal autopsies. However, it is important to be prepared to modify any protocol if new information suggests that important lesions are missed by the standard technique. The performance of the perinatal autopsy has been described in a number of publications which may also be usefully consulted.[1-4]

BACKGROUND INFORMATION

It is important to study clinical information from the maternal and infant case notes before commencing the postmortem examination. However, the notes may give a very incomplete picture because the rapid time course of perinatal illness often results in a lack of laboratory data, as when the infant may have died before a positive bacterial culture report was obtained. As pathological changes in dead infants may be less dramatic than those seen in adults, all possible relevant information is needed. It is advisable whenever possible, and in all complicated neonatal deaths, to discuss the case with the relevant clinician (obstetrician, neonatologist or surgeon) beforehand. Useful information which the clinician may provide includes the following:

1. Desirable studies (blood cultures for chromosomes or microorganisms) not performed in life.

2. The extent of agreement between clinical estimates of gestation and the mother's dates.

3. Diagnoses considered in life (e.g., inborn errors of metabolism) and whether excluded or not.

4. Potential iatrogenic hazards which caused clinical concern.

5. Any atypical clinical features noted in life.

This preliminary discussion can help the pathologist to define the most important areas for study and may allow him to anticipate the possibility of finding an unusual condition and to plan appropriate additional investigations. In certain cases (as when the probability of a rare inborn error of metabolism has been recognized but not fully characterized during life) early performance of an autopsy may be arranged before death occurs in order to allow specific biochemical, histochemical or ultrastructural studies. Such an approach may be acceptable to the parents in order to allow appropriate genetic counseling, particularly if a previous infant has died in a similar manner.

TABLE 3–1.   FOOT LENGTH OF THE FETUS

END OF WEEK	MEAN SITTING HEIGHT (mm)	MEAN FOOT LENGTH (mm)	MINIMUM FOOT LENGTH (mm)	MAXIMUM FOOT LENGTH (mm)	PERCENTAGE MEAN FOOT LENGTH: SITTING HEIGHT
8½	27	4.2	3.8	4.6	15.6
9	31	4.6	4.2	5.0	15.0
10	40	5.5	5.0	6.0	13.8
11	50	6.9	6.0	7.8	13.8
12	61	9.1	7.5	10.8	15.0
13	74	11.4	9.8	13.0	15.4
14	87	14.0	12.5	15.5	16.0
15	101	16.8	15.2	18.5	16.6
16	116	19.9	18.2	21.6	17.0
17	130	23.0	21.0	25.0	17.7
18	142	26.8	24.8	28.8	18.9
19	153	30.7	28.5	33.0	20.0
20	164	33.3	31.0	35.7	20.0
21	175	35.2	32.5	38.0	20.0
22	186	39.5	36.0	43.0	21.0
23	197	42.2	39.0	45.5	21.4
24	208	45.2	42.0	48.5	21.8
25	218	47.7	44.5	51.0	22.0
26	228	50.2	47.0	53.5	22.0
27	238	52.7	49.0	56.5	22.0
28	247	55.2	51.5	59.0	22.3
29	256	57.0	61.0	61.0	22.3
30	265	59.2	55.5	63.0	22.3
31	274	61.2	57.5	65.0	22.3
32	283	63.0	59.0	67.0	22.3
33	293	65.0	61.0	69.0	22.2
34	302	68.2	64.0	72.5	22.6
35	311	70.5	66.0	75.0	22.6
36	321	73.5	69.0	78.0	23.0
37	331	76.5	72.0	81.0	23.0
38	341	78.5	74.0	83.0	23.0
39	352	81.0	76.0	86.0	23.0
40	362	82.5	77.5	87.5	23.0

From Streeter, G. L.: Contributions to embryology, *11*:143–170, 1920.

WEIGHTS AND MEASURES

The size of the body and internal organs of the fetus vary primarily with gestational age (Tables 3–1 through 3–3). They are, however, also affected in characteristic ways by malformation syndromes, placental insufficiency and maternal diabetes as discussed in Chapter 1. A series of basic external measurements and organ weights should be performed in all cases.

Equipment Needed. An essential requirement is a set of scales giving accurate weights to the nearest 1 gram. A measuring board with a fixed head and movable foot is invaluable for measuring crown-heel and crown-rump (sitting height) lengths.

Measurements Made Routinely. Crown-heel (CH) and crown-rump (CR) length should always be measured and should be recorded to the nearest 0.5 cm. Occipital-frontal circumference (OFC) should be measured in all but grossly macerated infants with collapsed heads. This measurement can be made accurately to 1–2 mm. It is worth remembering that the CR length and the OFC are usually

TABLE 3–2 WEIGHTS AND LENGTHS OF NEWBORN INFANTS AND THEIR ORGANS, BY GROUPS OF VARIOUS BODY WEIGHTS

Body Weight	Number of Cases	Body Length	Heart	Lungs, Combined	Spleen	Liver	Adrenal Glands, Combined	Kidneys, Combined	Thymus	Brain	Gestational Age
Gm.		cm.	Gm.	Gm.	Gm.	Gm.	Gm.	Gm.	Gm.	Gm.	Weeks, Days
500	317	29.4	5.0	12	1.3	26	2.6	5.4	2.2	70	23, 5
		±2.5	±1.6	±5	±0.8	±10	±1.7	±2.1	±0.8	±18	±2, 3
750	311	32.9	6.3	19	2.0	39	3.2	7.8	2.8	107	26, 0
		±3.0	±1.8	±6	±1.2	±12	±1.5	±2.6	±1.3	±27	±2, 6
1000	295	35.6	7.7	24	2.6	47	3.5	10.4	3.7	143	27, 5
		±3.1	±2.0	±8	±1.5	±12	±1.6	±3.4	±2.0	±34	±3, 1
1250	217	38.4	9.6	30	3.4	56	4.0	12.9	4.9	174	29, 0
		±3.0	±3.3	±9	±1.8	±21	±1.7	±3.9	±2.1	±38	±3, 0
1500	167	41.0	11.5	34	4.3	65	4.5	14.9	6.1	219	31, 3
		±2.7	±3.3	±11	±2.0	±18	±1.8	±4.2	±2.7	±52	±2, 3
1750	148	42.6	12.8	40	5.0	74	5.3	17.4	6.8	247	32, 4
		±3.1	±3.2	±13	±2.5	±20	±2.0	±4.7	±3.0	±51	±2, 6
2000	140	44.9	14.9	44	6.0	82	5.3	18.8	7.9	281	34, 6
		±2.8	±4.2	±13	±2.7	±23	±2.0	±5.0	±3.4.	±56	±3, 2
2250	124	46.3	16.0	48	7.0	88	6.0	20.2	8.2	308	36, 4
		±2.9	±4.3	±15	±3.3	±24	±2.3	±4.9	±3.4	±49	±3, 0
2500	120	47.3	17.7	48	8.5	105	7.1	22.6	8.3	339	38, 0
		±2.3	±4.2	±14	±3.5	±21	±2.8	±5.5	±4.4	±50	±3, 2
2750	138	48.7	19.1	51	9.1	117	7.5	24.0	9.6	362	39, 2
		±2.9	±3.8	±15	±3.6	±26	±2.7	±5.4	±3.8	±48	±2, 2
3000	144	50.0	20.7	53	10.1	127	8.3	24.7	10.2	380	40, 0
		±2.9	±5.3	±13	±3.3	±30	±2.9	±5.3	±4.3	±55	±2, 1
3250	133	50.7	21.5	59	11.0	145	9.2	27.3	11.6	395	40, 4
		±2.6	±4.3	±18	±4.0	±33	±3.4	±6.6	±4.4	±53	±1, 6
3500	106	51.8	22.8	63	11.3	153	9.8	28.0	12.8	411	40, 4
		±3.0	±5.9	±17	±3.6	±33	±3.5	±6.5	±5.1	±55	±1, 5
3750	57	52.1	23.8	65	12.5	159	10.2	29.5	13.0	413	40, 6
		±2.3	±5.1	±15	±4.1	±40	±3.3	±6.8	±4.8	±55	±2, 3
4000	31	52.4	25.8	67	14.1	180	10.8	30.2	11.4	420	41, 4
		±2.7	±5.3	±20	±4.0	±39	±3.4	±6.2	±3.2	±62	±1, 3
4250	15	53.2	26.5	68	13.0	197	12.0	30.7	11.7	415	41, 2
		±2.5	±5.3	±16	±2.5	±42	±3.7	±5.8	±3.7	±38	±2, 1

From Gruenwald and Minh: Evaluation of body and organ weights in perinatal pathology. Am. J. Clin. Pathol. *34*, 1960.

TABLE 3–3.   WEIGHTS AND LENGTHS OF NEWBORN INFANTS AND THEIR ORGANS BY GESTATIONAL AGE

Gesta-tional Age*	Number of Cases	Body Length	Body Weight	Heart	Lungs, Combined	Spleen	Liver	Adrenal Glands, Combined	Kidneys, Combined	Thymus	Brain
		cm.	Gm.	Gm.	Gm.	Gm.	Gm.	Gm.	Gm.	Gm.	Gm.
24	108	31.3	638	4.9	17	1.7	32	2.9	6.4	2.7	92
		±3.7	±240	±1.6	±6	±1.1	±15	±1.4	±2.6	±1.4	±31
26	143	33.3	845	6.4	18	2.2	39	3.4	7.9	3.0	111
		±3.6	±246	±2.0	±6	±1.5	±15	±1.5	±2.9	±2.3	±39
28	139	36.0	1020	7.6	23	2.6	46	3.7	10.4	3.8	139
		±4.2	±340	±2.3	±7	±1.4	±16	±1.7	±3.6	±2.1	48
30	148	37.8	1230	9.3	28	3.4	53	4.2	12.3	4.6	166
		±3.7	±340	±3.3	±11	±2.0	±19	±2.2	±3.9	±2.3	±55
32	150	40.5	1488	11.0	34	4.1	65	4.3	14.5	5.5	209
		±4.5	±335	±3.7	±11	±2.1	±22	±2.3	±4.8	±2.3	±44
34	104	42.8	1838	13.4	40	5.2	74	5.5	17.7	7.5	246
		±4.5	±530	±3.9	±13	±2.1	±27	±2.3	±5.3	±3.8	±58
36	87	45.0	2165	15.1	46	6.7	87	6.4	21.6	8.1	288
		±4.6	±600	±4.8	±16	±3.0	±33	±3.0	±6.7	±4.2	±62
38	102	47.2	2678	18.5	53	8.8	111	8.4	23.8	9.7	349
		±4.6	±758	±5.5	±15	±4.2	±40	±3.5	±7.0	±4.8	±56
40	220	49.8	3163	20.4	56	10.0	130	8.6	25.6	9.5	362
		±3.9	±595	±5.3	±15	±3.9	±45	±3.4	±6.5	±4.4	±55
42	112	50.3	3263	21.9	56	10.2	139	9.1	25.8	10.4	405
		±3.6	±573	±6.2	±18	±4.3	±45	±4.0	±7.5	±4.4	±54
44	42	52.8	3690	25.8	60	11.2	149	9.3	28.4	10.3	417
		±2.8	±800	±4.5	±17	±4.1	±35	±4.4	±7.5	±4.7	±55

*Gestational age is expressed in weeks from the last menstrual period.
From Gruenwald and Minh: Evaluation of body and organ weights in perinatal pathology. Am. J. Clin. Pathol. *34*, 1960.

very similar during the perinatal period. If they differ by more than 1 cm after the figures are verified, it is necessary to seek the reason for an unusual head size. An unusually large OFC relative to CR may be due to hydrocephalus or to fetal malnutrition: an unduly small OFC may suggest microcephaly or cranial distortion (as by face mask ventilation). Measurements which are not essential but are performed at some centers include shoulder, chest and abdominal circumference and foot length. The last is particularly useful for early fetal studies[5] because it is easier to measure accurately in the small fetus than CR length. It is also said to be relatively little affected by fixation and to be normal for gestational age in anencephalics.

Organ Weights. A minimal selection of internal organs to be weighed includes brain, heart, lungs, liver, spleen, thymus, kidneys and adrenals. Many additional weights and measurements may be performed by pathologists working in specialized centers. For smaller organs such as adrenals, thymus, pancreas and thyroid it is preferable to be able to obtain weights to the nearest 0.1 g.

EXTERNAL EXAMINATION

General features to be looked for and noted include cyanosis, pallor, edema, jaundice and maceration (see Chapter 5). The overall state of nutrition of the infant—whether long and thin, generally plump, or dehydrated—may provide useful information on the time course of perinatal illness. Evidence of trauma should be searched for with reference to the obstetric and neonatal history.

Bruises or petechiae, needle punctures, marks of forceps blades and surgical incisions may all prove of some significance. All drainage tubes, umbilical arterial catheters and so forth should be left in situ until the position of the tip has been checked internally. Because these are usually disposable items, I find it most convenient to cut the protruding end off flush with the skin. This causes minimal interference with dissection and allows the original position of the tube to be reestablished if it becomes partly dislodged before the tip can be checked. External malformations should be looked for. The facial appearance, ears, hands, feet, back, genitalia and orifices should all be examined, not forgetting the choanae and palate. Some characteristic facial appearances and typical abnormalities of the extremities are described and illustrated in Chapter 7. Any limb distortion or unusual position or flexion of hands or feet should also be noted. They may indicate congenital neuromuscular abnormality or prolonged oligohydramnios. If limb distortion is due to the latter cause it is sometimes possible to fold the infant up into the position that was maintained in utero (Fig. 3–1).

Color slides of the external appearance of the whole infant or of relevant details such as facial or limb abnormalities can be extremely useful in cases of malformation, trauma or any instance where medicolegal involvement is likely.

Roentgenographs of the whole infant performed before dissection can provide valuable information on many types of cases, and are essential for diagnosis of certain conditions such as chondrodysplasias (Table 3–4). They also allow recognition of ossification centers as an aid to gestational assessment (Table 3–5).[6] Both anteroposterior and lateral views are needed: the former shows the general

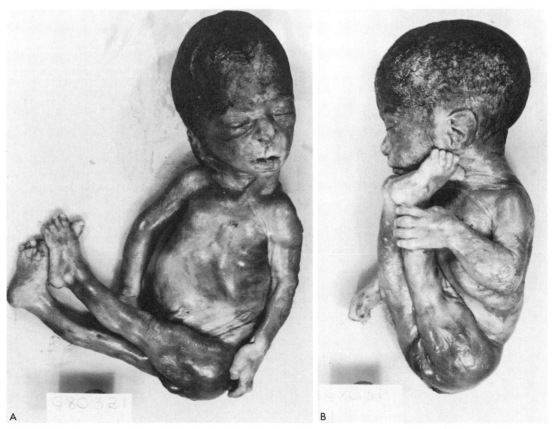

Figure 3–1. A small fetus born after a period of oligohydramnios. *A*, Unfolded, showing an upper abdominal groove. *B*, Folded up into the position adopted in utero.

TABLE 3–4. SOME CONDITIONS THAT CAN BE RECOGNIZED BY POSTMORTEM RADIOGRAPHS IN THE PERINATAL PERIOD

Lethal chondrodysplasias (see Chapter 19)	Classification of these conditions is based on radiological appearances; postmortem diagnosis is possible without internal examination
Other inherited skeletal disorders	Example: osteogenesis imperfecta
Skeletal trauma	Examples: occipital osteodiastasis, fractures of long bones
Skeletal anomalies	Examples: abnormal ribs, vertebrae, long bones
Gas in abnormal sites	Gas embolism, pneumothorax, pulmonary interstitial emphysema, necrotizing enterocolitis
Abnormal calcification	Example: meconium peritonitis

skeletal pattern and some internal abnormalities, while the latter is needed for recognition of cranial trauma and some vertebral abnormalities. In specialized departments such radiologic studies are normally performed routinely on all perinatal autopsies.[4, 7] The films should be available to the pathologist before he begins his examination.

While making his external examination the pathologist should consider whether the infant's maturity is in agreement with that given in the obstetric history or neonatal notes. Pointers to gestational maturity include extent of lanugo hair, length of fingernails and degree of development of breast tissue. These are not precise guides but can contribute to an overall impression, in conjunction with comparison of OFC and CR length, as to whether a small infant is of appropriate maturity for body weight or not. Such an initial impression will be further supported, or refuted, when organ weights and maturities have been evaluated (Fig. 3–2).

Body weight is easy to determine accurately, while gestational age assessment can be difficult. It is important for the pathologist to attempt the latter because it may be a critical indication of the nature of the underlying disorder.

INTERNAL EXAMINATION

Possible incisions are illustrated in Figure 3–3. Dissection of the tongue, larynx and trachea in continuity with the heart and lungs is facilitated by an incision up to the chin, but it may be desired to avoid this if the body is to be viewed after autopsy. In such cases an incision across the chest is adequate, but the neck dissection takes longer. The inverted "V" incision below the umbilicus gives good exposure of the umbilical arteries.

THORACIC CAVITY
The form of the thoracic cage can give useful information on intrathoracic pathology even before the thorax is opened. A narrow chest may suggest the

TABLE 3–5. APPROXIMATE TIME OF APPEARANCE OF OSSIFICATION CENTERS*

Calcaneus	25–26 weeks
Talus	27–28 weeks
Lower femoral epiphysis	36–37 weeks
Upper tibial epiphysis	38–40 weeks

*See Chapter 19.

PROBLEM:
1500 g infant: said to be 32 weeks' gestational age

	Possible Findings	A	B
External	Crown-heel length	37 cm	38 cm
	Crown-rump length	25 cm	25.5 cm
	Occipitofrontal cir-cumference	25 cm	28 cm
	Skin appearance	Rather thin; fingernails not up to tips of fingers	Rather opaque; fingernails to ends of fingers
Internal	Brain	220 g Wide sulci, convolutional pattern = 32 weeks (see Fig. 3–8)	300 g Narrow sulci; little subarach-noid space; convolutional pattern: 37 weeks + (see Fig. 3–8) (insula covered).
	Liver	75 g	60 g
Conclusion		All findings are compatible with a normally developed infant of 32 weeks' gesta-tion; expect lesions related to immaturity—IVH, HMD, etc.	Mature brain pattern com-bined with brain:liver weight ratio of 6:1 indi-cates a severely growth-re-tarded infant of 37 weeks' gestation; expect lesions related to fetal malnutri-tion, evidence of birth as-phyxia, etc.

Figure 3–2. Illustration to show how simple observations combined with a few accurate weights and measurements can clarify the type of pathological lesions to be expected at perinatal autopsy.

possibility of pulmonary hypoplasia, a pale distended chest wall may indicate an underlying tension pneumothorax (Fig. 3–4), or interstitial emphysema may be visible. During the phase of dissection of the skin and muscle off the thorax before it is opened, a useful opportunity is available to assess subcutaneous fat development and to look at the skeletal muscles as represented by the pectorals and intercostals. Neurogenic atrophy may be indicated by pallor and poor muscle development in association with a narrow chest and thin ribs. Apparently abnormal thoracic muscles should prompt sampling of both proximal and distal muscles of upper and lower limbs.

The level of the diaphragm on each side can be checked by inserting a finger into the abdominal cavity before opening the chest. This gives a useful clue to lung hypoplasia or tension pneumothorax if a radiograph is not available.

In all neonatal autopsies, including those of infants with a heartbeat at birth in whom resuscitation attempts failed, the chest should be opened under water to exclude pneumothorax. After cutting through the rib cartilages on each side, the manubrium sterni can be lifted off and the thoracic contents examined in situ. The position of the tips of any chest drains should be located and lung damage

Figure 3–3. Possible skin incisions for examining thoracic and abdominal organs.

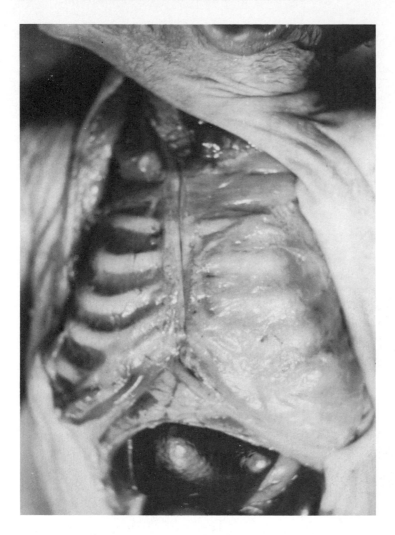

Figure 3–4. A left-sided tension pneumothorax has caused pallor of the overlying chest wall.

from their presence excluded (see Chapter 10). I prefer to dissect the thymus out at this stage, taking care not to damage the innominate vein. The size of the thymus may be of help in assessing the time course of illness. It is normally a rather large bilobed structure overlying much of the heart and the roots of the great vessels and often extending up into the neck, particularly on the right (see Chapter 20). It is less prominent in the immature infant than at term. Severe thymic atrophy is readily recognized, and is a useful indication of prolonged stress such as that associated with intrauterine infection. Other lesions to be seen at macroscopic level are the hemorrhages of acute asphyxia (Chapter 6) and interstitial emphysema extending from the mediastinum (Chapter 10).

Next I open the pericardium and check the shape and size of the heart and the roots of the great vessels, including superior and inferior venae cavae, vena azygos, aortic root, innominate artery, left common carotid artery and left subclavian artery, pulmonary trunk and ductus venosus. At this stage the thoracic contents can be removed in one block unless there is a suspicion of some malformation, such as anomalous pulmonary venous drainage, involving both thoracic and abdominal contents. In fact, if the heart size and form are entirely normal, significant cardiac anomaly is unlikely to be present.

Dissection of the heart is most easily begun from the right side by opening the right atrium between the entries of the superior and inferior venae cavae, cutting through the tricuspid valve and continuing the cut up the anterior wall of the right ventricle just to the right of the ventricular septum and through the pulmonary valve. The normality of the foramen ovale can then be established by pressing on the left atrium and causing the blood trapped within it to press against the septum primum and to occlude the opening (Fig. 3–5). The pulmonary valve, pulmonary trunk, pulmonary arteries and ductus are examined next. The state of patency of the ductus should be assessed, although a ductus which has been functionally closed in life may appear patent at autopsy.

The left atrium can then be opened between the pulmonary veins and the cut carried through the mitral valve up the anterior aspect of the left ventricle to the left of the ventricular septum. The pulmonary veins are most readily checked with a probe. If there is no cardiac malformation, the heart is then dissected free from the lungs and its examination completed by cutting through the aortic valve to allow study of the valve cusps and coronary orifices. If congenital cardiac anomalies are known to be present, or are encountered during dissection, it may be necessary to modify the procedure (see Chapter 11). In many such cases the anatomy is more readily demonstrated to the cardiologists, surgeons and radiologists if the heart is kept attached to the lungs. In some instances additional procedures such as injection of the pulmonary vessels with radiopaque media may be of help. The esophagus is opened and checked for atresia and fistula. The larynx and trachea are opened and examined for evidence of trauma from intubation, or plugging by mucus, meconium or aspirated gastric contents.

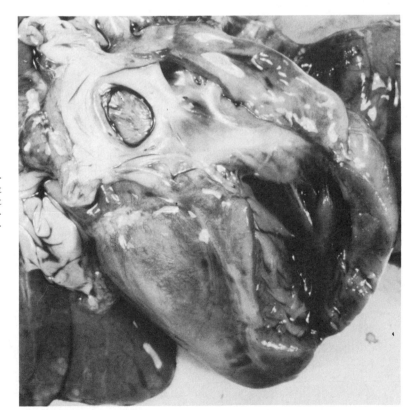

Figure 3–5. Atrial septum viewed from the right side after opening right atrium and ventricle. Foramen ovale occluded by normal septum primum.

The lungs are weighed and carefully examined externally before dissection. The pattern and extent of any expansion with air is noted. It should be considered whether the degree of lung expansion is appropriate in relation to the length of time the infant survived after birth. Interstitial emphysema, petechial hemorrhages or abscesses may be seen. Rarely it is possible to recognize green discoloration by massive meconium inhalation. On cutting into the lung, hemorrhage, edema and plugging of bronchi with mucus or inhaled material may be recognized. It should be remembered, however, that many pathological conditions affecting the newborn lung present at the macroscopic level in the form of airless, congested parenchyma which cannot be diagnosed accurately without histological examination. Gross pulmonary hypoplasia (e.g., in renal agenesis) will usually be obvious. Undersized lungs seen in many other conditions should be recognized as such and not attributed to "atelectasis" (see Chapter 10). The diaphragm should always be examined as part of the respiratory system, particularly in cases of pulmonary hypoplasia.

THE ABDOMEN

After checking the general state of the peritoneal cavity and excluding the obvious conditions such as ascites, hemorrhage, peritonitis or pneumoperitoneum, I always examine for normality of gut rotation and mesenteric attachments. This is readily done by locating the cecum and appendix and following around the colon to the rectum, checking its attachments and then locating the duodenojejunal junction. Any abnormality of intestinal rotation or attachment of large or small gut mesenteries will become apparent during this procedure, which takes only a few seconds. If there is evidence of infarction or necrotizing enterocolitis the abdominal organs should be dissected out in a block to allow study of the mesenteric vessels. Otherwise the intestines can be dissected off the mesentery from the duodenojejunal junction down, divided across the rectum and removed to allow the renal tract and abdominal vessels to be seen in situ.

At this stage the umbilical vein, liver, stomach, pancreas and spleen can conveniently be removed in one block. The umbilical vein should be opened up to the liver and into the portal sinus, and the ductus venosus examined. The stomach and duodenum are opened, the stomach contents noted, and the patency of the common bile duct checked by expressing bile from the gallbladder, if bile-stained content is not readily recognized in the small intestine. After weighing the liver it may be sliced in a coronal plane to reveal any differences between the right and left lobes. The spleen and pancreas are dissected out and studied.

The aorta is then opened, the umbilical arteries examined and if an umbilical artery catheter is in situ the position of the tip is established so that any related thrombus can be recognized. The patency of the renal arteries can be checked and the caliber and course of the ureters and the appearance of the bladder noted.

The normality of the renal tract can readily be established in most instances without recourse to probing of any of the orifices. The ureters usually appear rather dilated, often being 3 to 4 mm in diameter, the bladder wall is soft and pliable, and any urine in the bladder can be expressed through the urethra. A normal appearance provides good evidence for normal function. Any obstruction to the urethra in the presence of continued urine secretion is associated with hypertrophy of the bladder wall, which may be grossly dilated or firm and thick with a rugose lining. Hydroureter and hydronephrosis are obvious if present. Absent urine secretion in infants with severely cystic dysplastic kidneys is associated with narrow thread-like ureters, since normal ureteric growth in utero appears to require urine flow. If there is an obvious abnormality of the renal tract such as a large thick-walled bladder and dilated ureters, the kidneys should be dissected out intact with the lower aorta and inferior vena cava and whole urethra. It is easiest to examine the site of any obstruction after fixing the renal tract in a distended state. Urine may be aspirated and replaced with an equivalent volume of normal saline. If initial observation of the renal tract in situ indicates that ureters and bladder are normal, it is perfectly adequate to remove the kidneys separately. It is normally easiest to take out each one with its associated adrenal and then to dissect off the latter and the excess perirenal brown fat. The relative sizes of adrenals and kidneys are worth noting. The adrenals at birth are normally about one third of the weight of the kidneys. Any gross deviation from this pattern should prompt consideration as to which organ may be abnormal. Lesions readily recognized at macroscopic level in the kidneys include infarcts, cysts and abscesses. The pattern of congestion of cortex and medulla may suggest the presence of tubular or papillary necrosis. The adrenals may show obvious hemorrhage or alteration in the normal pattern of lipid deposition in the cortex (see Chapter 16) in addition to rare occurrences such as congenital infection or tumor.

The bladder with the prostate (or uterus and adnexa) can be removed together with the rectum in most instances. The bladder is opened to check the mucosa. Malformations of the uterus such as bicornuate uterus and the appearance of the fallopian tubes and ovaries are noted. Simple follicular cysts of the ovary are relatively common in the perinatal period. The position of the testes is checked. The scrotum may be distended with air (Chapter 18) or fluid from the peritoneal cavity owing to persistent patency of the processus vaginalis. The testes in cases of breech delivery are often extremely congested and hemorrhagic (Chapter 18).

THE CRANIUM

The traditional coronal scalp incision should be sited just behind the ear in the perinatal case. This minimizes disfigurement after reconstruction in an infant with little hair and allows the posterior flap to be reflected far enough back to expose the suboccipital region. The extent of caput formation or subaponeurotic hemorrhage can be assessed during reflection of the scalp. The shape, mobility and degree of overlap of the cranial bones and size and tension of the anterior fontanelle are then readily studied. Hemorrhage into the temporal or suboccipital muscles is noted.

Dissection of the suboccipital region should then be performed in all cases of fresh stillbirth and neonatal death, particularly infants who have died after vaginal breech, occipitoposterior or forceps delivery, irrespective of gestation. The suboccipital muscles are dissected off the occipital bone to reveal the underlying cartilaginous joints between the squamous and lateral parts. Separation of these joints during birth or a difficult resuscitation (see Chapter 6) is indicated by a projecting ridge on one or both sides where the squamous occipital has been pushed forward, leaving the lateral part in its original position. Although the lesion can often be suspected from an obvious occipital asymmetry or flattening and excessive mobility of the squamous occipital bone, the bulk of the occipital muscles usually prevents confident diagnosis from palpation alone.

Incision of the atlantooccipital membrane reveals herniation of the cerebellar tonsils in some cases of severe birth asphyxia,[3, 8] as well as showing posterior fossa hemorrhage.

A sample of cerebrospinal fluid obtained by sterile needle puncture from the cisterna magna can be useful in many circumstances. It will allow recognition of

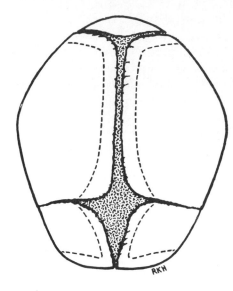

Figure 3–6. The interupted lines indicate the lines of incision when opening the skull. (From Langley F. A.: The perinatal postmortem examination. J. Clin. Pathol. *24*:159–169, 1971.)

hemorrhage before disturbing the anatomy and be available for culture in suspected meningitis or for estimation of abnormal chemical constituents in inborn errors of metabolism.

The skull is opened routinely using a modification of the Beneke technique (Fig. 3–6). A scalpel blade is inserted through the coronal suture and the opening thus made is continued along the lines indicated in the figure using a heavy pair of scissors. The line of incision is kept about one-fourth inch away from the midline in order to avoid damage to the falx and sinuses during the dissection. The two bone flaps are then reflected downward to expose the cerebral hemispheres. The presence of subdural or subarachnoid hemorrhage and the extent of the subarachnoid space can be studied at this stage. The occipital lobe can be gently reflected forward to allow examination of the falx, the tentorium and the great cerebral vein (of Galen). The occipital lobe is then gently replaced within the cranium and the whole procedure is repeated on the opposite side. The anterior end of the falx is then divided and the falx dissected backward.

After this the brain is removed intact by severing the cranial nerves in sequence, cutting through the tentorium on each side along the petrous bone and dividing the brain stem at the level of the foramen magnum. The brain is either supported in one hand while the other is used for dissecting, or it may be gradually poured out onto the dissecting table with the body held upside down during the dissection as shown in Figure 3–7. Removal of the brain intact from infants of all gestational ages is quite easy with a little practice. It is important not to allow the weight of the portion of brain already dissected free to be unsupported at any time and not to allow it to press against dural folds or bone edges. If the brain is very soft, as with massive intracerebral hemorrhage, preservation intact is facilitated by dissecting it directly into a pre-weighed container of fixative. The brain and container are then weighed and the brain weight obtained by subtraction, without further handling. After an initial examination, which should include a preliminary assessment of maturity as indicated by convolutional pattern,[9] the brain is weighed and then fixed by suspension in 10 per cent buffered formalin solution. For this purpose a thread is passed under the basilar artery.

When the brain has been removed, the pituitary can be dissected out and the posterior fossa and dural venous sinuses examined.

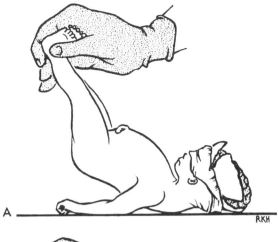

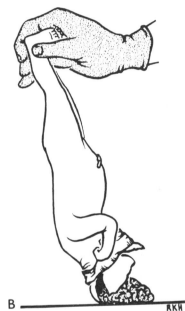

Figure 3–7. One method of avoiding damage to the cerebral hemispheres when removing the brain. (From Langley, F. A.: The perinatal postmortem examination. J. Clin. Pathol., *24*:159–169, 1971.)

It is necessary to use additional or alternative techniques to remove the brains of infants with hydrocephalus or large porencephalic cysts. If it is desired to obtain the brain intact and undistorted, a needle attached to a large syringe with a three-way tap can be inserted into the ventricular system through the fontanelle before the autopsy is begun and a proportion (usually about 50 ml) of the ventricular fluid removed and replaced with concentrated (40 per cent formaldehyde) formalin solution. Within about an hour fixation will be sufficient to allow the brain to be dissected out in the normal manner and to retain its original shape on fixation, even if damaged during removal. The brain of a macerated infant can be dissected out intact inside the dura if the latter is dissected carefully off the cranial bones (see Fig. 5–1).

SPINAL CORD

The vertebral canal is readily opened with bone cutters from the anterior aspect to allow inspection and removal of the spinal cord. After cutting through the vertebral column in the lumbosacral region the neural arches are divided in sequence on each side. Care is needed in order to avoid crushing the cord in the upper cervical region. Posterior root ganglia can be dissected out in continuity with the cord at any desired level. If necessary (as in a suspected high cervical cord injury or a case of myelocele), it is quite easy to remove the cord and brain as a unit, but this may require additional posterior dissection in the upper cervical region. It is helpful to have an assistant to support the head and brain at critical moments. The alternative in such cases is to carry out a complete posterior cord dissection.

Examination of the middle ear in the neonate is a somewhat neglected procedure. It has, however, been suggested that middle ear infection may be a relatively common occurrence in infants treated in neonatal intensive care units, and further studies of the area are needed.[10] I am indebted to Dr. Peter Kelehan for the description of his technique for dissection and examination of the middle and inner ear of the newborn infant (Appendix).

Study of the eyes is occasionally possible, and permission for such examination may be sought in cases of intrauterine infection or suspected retrolental fibroplasia. The latter condition is discussed and illustrated in the textbook of Potter and Craig.[1]

THE LIMBS

Limb dissection is indicated in some instances. Examination of the hip joints may be undertaken in cases of severe talipes to confirm the dislocation that is often associated with this condition. Study of other joints may be necessary to determine the cause of particular joint disorders. Iatrogenic lesions affecting the limbs should be carefully examined at autopsy whenever possible in order to help the neonatologist assess the hazards and likely sequelae of such conditions in life. Postmortem dissection of the cubital fossa has for instance revealed the extensive damage, including traumatic neuroma of the median nerve, that can result from incorrect brachial artery puncture technique.[11] Examination of vessels for thrombosis or embolism may be important if indwelling catheters have been used in life and there has been evidence of consequential circulatory impairment. In suspected congenital neuromuscular disorders the peripheral muscles such as the gastrocnemius and the biceps should always be examined and sampled for histologic examination because they usually show more pronounced changes than the proximal muscles.

PLACENTA

The examination of the placenta is described in Chapter 4.

FURTHER STUDY

Definitive diagnosis of a specific disorder is often not possible on the basis of the macroscopic findings at autopsy. In some cases the clinical history or the autopsy findings suggest the presence of a condition for which diagnostic tests are available. It is important to know which disorders can be diagnosed at autopsy and the specimens needed for the purpose.

Specimens for Microbiology. Postmortem cardiac punctures are performed routinely in some centers. Otherwise heart blood, lung swabs and cultures from any apparently infective lesion can be taken at autopsy. The pathologist should learn the requirements of local viral laboratories for tissue and blood samples and use of specific transport media.

Specimens for Hematology. Hematocrit and analysis of hemoglobins can be performed if the blood is liquid at autopsy. Cell counts and studies of coagulation factors are unreliable.

TABLE 3–6. SOME INBORN ERRORS WHICH MAY PROVE FATAL IN THE PERINATAL PERIOD

CLINICAL PRESENTATION	TYPE OF DEFECT	EXAMPLES	AUTOPSY FINDINGS	TISSUE FOR BIOCHEMICAL DIAGNOSIS*
Vomiting, CNS signs, and acute respiratory failure with hyperammonemia	Urea cycle defect	Ornithine transcarbamylase deficiency, citrullinemia, argininosuccinic aciduria	None specific	Liver; kidney; brain or fibroblast culture
Vomiting, CNS signs and acute respiratory failure with hypoglycemia and acidosis	Disorders of amino acid metabolism	Maple syrup urine disease, Propionic acidemia, Methylmalonic acidemia	None specific	Liver; kidney; brain or fibroblast culture
Vomiting, jaundice, hepatomegaly, hypoglycemia, acute liver failure	Disorders of carbohydrate metabolism	Galactosemia, Hereditary fructose intolerance	Jaundice, hemostatic failure Typical liver pathology (see Ch. 14)	Liver or fibroblast culture
Cardiac failure hypotonia, CNS signs—hepatosplenomegaly	Glycogen storage disease	Type II (Pompe)	Cardiomegaly; excess glycogen storage in liver, heart and muscles	Liver; heart or fibroblast culture
Hepatosplenomegaly Some present with hydrops; some have facial features and x-rays like Hurler's syndrome	Lipid storage diseases	GM, gangliosidosis type 1; Niemann-Pick disease type A;	Storage cells in spleen, liver, bone marrow and placental villi (see Ch. 4)	Spleen; liver; brain or fibroblast culture Spleen; liver; brain or fibroblast culture
	Mucopolysaccharide storage disease	Gaucher's disease; mucopolysaccharidosis VII;		Spleen; liver; brain or fibroblast culture
	Mucolipid storage diseases	mucolipidosis II		Spleen; liver; brain or fibroblast culture; plasma or other body fluids

*Note that frozen tissue samples for enzyme assay may need to be collected immediately after death but material for characterizing storage products or establishing fibroblast cultures can be collected at routine autopsy.

Cytogenetics. Chromosome analysis can be performed on white blood cells if autopsy is carried out within 12 hours of death. Culture of fibroblasts from skin or fascia is possible for periods of up to about 3 days after death.

Immunology. Measurement of immunoglobins can be performed on heart blood (if uncoagulated) within the first 24 hours after death. Other immunological tests, such as for suspected severe combined immunological deficiency (see Chapter 20), depend on the viability of the white cells and require that blood be taken within about 12 hours.

Biochemistry. Most enzyme tests which are performed on blood or tissue specimens require samples to be taken very shortly after death. It may be possible to obtain parental consent for immediate liver or muscle biopsy for this purpose before full autopsy is carried out. Sufficient tissue may be obtainable by needle biopsy for both enzyme studies and electron microscopy. Some tests can, however, be performed usefully on blood or tissues obtained at standard autopsy examination. The galactosemia screening test is reliable if the blood is uncoagulated.[12] Quantitative and qualitative estimation of lipids, carbohydrates and mucopolysaccharides can be carried out on liver, spleen, kidney, heart and muscle tissues. A range of inborn errors of metabolism which may present in the early neonatal period is listed in Table 3–6. It is worth remembering that all these can be diagnosed by enzyme studies on fibroblast cultures. Some abnormal metabolic products can be assessed in samples of urine or body fluids.[13] Further details of autopsy studies on suspected inborn errors of metabolism are given elsewhere.[14–16]

Histochemistry. A wide variety of tests can usefully be performed on tissue obtained at autopsy. These are usually most successful within the first 12 hours after death but may be worth attempting within 24 hours. They include the following:

1. Skeletal muscle—enzymes characteristic of type 1 and type 2 fibers.
2. Pancreas and small intestine—the whole range of gastrointestinal polypeptide hormones.*
3. Liver—α_1 antitrypsin.*
4. Large intestine, colon and rectum—cholinesterases to display neural patterns of Hirschsprung's disease.

RE-EXAMINATION OF FIXED ORGANS

A brief further examination of the organs after fixation can reveal significant lesions (e.g., myocardial necrosis) overlooked in the fresh state. This can conveniently be combined with selection of blocks for histology.

Specimens for Histology. The number of blocks taken and sections cut will inevitably vary according to the facilities available for preparation and study of the materials. As indicated earlier, histological study of the lungs is important because macroscopic diagnosis of pulmonary lesions is particularly difficult in the perinatal period. In the absence of recognizable macroscopic abnormality, sections of other organs seldom yield diagnostic information. They do, however, give useful confirmation of the gestational age of the infant and the time course of perinatal illness. Surveys of normal fetal histology may also be of value to the pathologist inexperienced in perinatal autopsy work in confirming the range of macroscopic appearances compatible with normality.

The selection of blocks I normally take for histology and the information I would hope to get from them are described in the following paragraphs.

LUNGS. At least one block is needed from each of the major lobes for diagnosis of hyaline membrane disease, pneumonia, bronchopulmonary dysplasia, meconium aspiration, massive pulmonary hemorrhage and so forth, and for confirmation of maturity. It is often impossible to assign a cause of death with confidence until the sections of the lung are examined.

BLOCK THROUGH THYROID AND TRACHEA. This can show the presence and extent of tracheal excoriation and infection in relation to use of intubation.

HEART. One section is taken to include left atrium, mitral valve, left ventricle and papillary muscle. This can indicate the presence of unsuspected myocarditis, papillary muscle necrosis or subendocardial or myocardial damage.

LIVER. Blocks of left and right lobes are taken. These show the extent of extramedullary hemopoiesis and the presence and extent of bile stasis. Occasional necrosis, architectural abnormalities or features diagnostic of specific infectious or metabolic disorders are seen.

SPLEEN. One block is taken. This shows the extent of lymphoid development. There is occasionally evidence of excessive hemolysis or a storage disorder.

ADRENALS. One block of each is taken. This shows hemorrhage or necrosis in conditions of shock. Changes in definitive and fetal cortex are characteristic of stress. Lesions related to specific infections, neuroblastoma in situ, and so forth are seen occasionally.

KIDNEYS. One block is needed of each. Maturity of the glomeruli is used as a gestational age marker, and tubular or papillary necrosis as evidence of shock. Confirmation of type and severity of cystic changes is possible. This is a useful site for diagnostic histology of some infections such as candidiasis and CMV.

THYMUS. One block is needed to show the severity of stress reaction if present.

---

*Immunoperoxidase techniques can be applied to formalin-fixed paraffin-embedded tissues.

There is rarely evidence of immunological disorder.

PANCREAS. One block is needed. Islet development can be used as an indicator of normality of gastrointestinal hormones and carbohydrate metabolism. This specimen has occasional diagnostic value, as in cystic fibrosis or specific infections such as CMV, and syphilis.

PLACENTA. Two or three blocks are needed to include the full thickness of the placenta and fetal membranes. They can provide evidence of uteroplacental ischemia, fetal anemia or infections. This is occasionally diagnostic in infections, and in storage diseases.

UMBILICAL CORD. One block is needed. Confirmation of normality of umbilical vessels; assessment of inflammation.

COSTOCHONDRAL JUNCTION. One block is needed; it provides evidence of normality or abnormality of prenatal growth pattern. It has occasional diagnostic value, as in storage diseases.

ANY OTHER ORGAN OR TISSUE THAT APPEARS ABNORMAL. It should be remembered that the quality of postmortem preservation of fetal and neonatal tissues is far better than that of adult organs, presumably because of lower enzyme activities, less likelihood of massive bacterial infection and more rapid cooling down of the small infant body on refrigeration. Details of intestinal epithelium can thus be examined at the histological level many hours after death, and postmortem ultrastructural studies may often reasonably be undertaken if desired.

EXAMINATION OF THE BRAIN AFTER FIXATION

The pathologist has to decide how long to fix the newborn brain before cutting it. Complete fixation may take 4 to 6 weeks, but it may not be possible to assign a cause of death or provide the parents with useful information until the brain has at least been sliced and examined at macroscopic level.

I find that a convenient compromise is to perform an initial examination of the brain after fixation for 4 to 5 days, by which time it is firm enough to handle, slice and photograph if necessary. The presence and extent of most lesions such as malformations, intraventricular hemorrhage, kernicterus and periventricular leukomalacia can be adequately assessed at this time. Small brain blocks for confirmatory histology can be taken at this stage.

If the case is one in which large blocks and detailed neuropathological examination is called for, the brain slices can be re-fixed for a few days before the blocks are taken.

The surface of the cerebral hemispheres, midbrain, cerebellum and brain stem are re-examined for any abnormality, such as herniation at the level of the tentorium or cisterna magna, which may have been overlooked at the fresh stage. Gestational age assessment can be carried out readily by comparison of the convolutional pattern with published illustrations (Fig. 3–8). The cerebellum and midbrain are removed as in an adult neuropathological examination.

The method of dissecting the cerebral hemispheres varies according to the type of case and the information one is hoping to obtain. Most pathologists, particularly if they have had any neuropathological training, will prefer to make the traditional series of 1 cm coronal slices, commencing at the level of the mamillary bodies or just in front of the temporal poles and working forward and backward. I have found it profitable not to adhere rigidly to such techniques but to be prepared to dissect the brain by other methods on occasion. It is much easier to appreciate the nature and extent of subependymal and intraventricular hemorrhage in the preterm infant brain if the hemispheres are separated and the lateral ventricles dissected from the medial aspect. (Many of the illustrations in

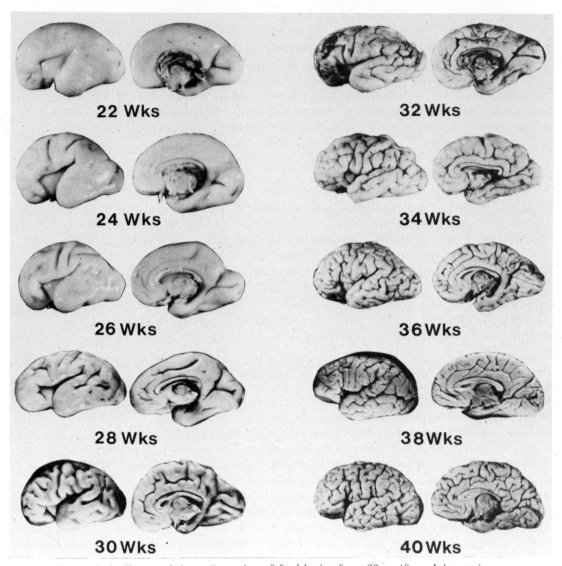

Figure 3–8. Characteristic configuration of fetal brains from 22 to 40 weeks' gestation at two-week intervals. All brains have been brought to the same size. (From Dorovini-Zis, K., and Dolman, C. L.: Gestational development of the brain. Arch. Pathol. Lab. Med., *101*:192–195, 1977.)

Chapter 12 are of brains examined in this way.) The procedure does destroy some tissue on the medial aspect of the hemisphere, but this is seldom of importance in this type of case. It can also be helpful to the neonatologist or radiologist trying to interpret the significance of ultrasound or computed tomographic scans obtained in life if the pathologist is prepared to slice the brain in the planes in which such scans were made. The midbrain, cerebellum and brain stem are examined in the routine manner. Study of the spinal cord is important in cases of death following breech delivery, or if there are limb or muscle abnormalities suggesting neurogenic atrophy, in addition to central nervous system malformation.

We have on occasion recognized the severe atrophy of anterior roots characteristic of spinal muscular atrophy macroscopically within the first month of life.

Selection of blocks of CNS tissue for histology represents a compromise between the minimum with which to avoid overlooking significant lesions and the ideal complete neuropathological survey. Almost all important lesions seen in the perinatal period can be recognized if the following series of blocks is taken.

1. Frontal cortex and white matter. This is taken so as to include the boundary zone between anterior and middle cerebral artery and one of the regions of white matter commonly affected by periventricular leukomalacia.

2. Head of caudate nucleus with lateral ventricle wall and subependymal germinal matrix. This is useful in preterm infants particularly.

3. Thalamus and hippocampus.

4. Midbrain through inferior colliculi.*

5. Medulla at the level of olives.*

6. Cerebellar hemisphere with dentate nucleus.*

If large blocks can be processed readily, numbers 1, 2, and 3 of this list can be combined in one hemispheric section. A similar series of blocks was recommended by Gruenwald and Laurence.[17]

More important than any system for taking specific blocks of tissue for histology is to cut and examine the brain with care and to take histological sections through areas showing unusual consistency (too soft or too firm) or discoloration, particularly in infants subjected to prolonged intensive care.

CONCLUSION

Most of the significant findings in a perinatal autopsy depend on simple but accurate measurements and observations made by gross examination. These allow the pathologist to build a picture of the state of fetal nutrition, severity of stress, occurrence of trauma, or failure of prenatal function of some organ, quite apart from the recognition of any obvious pathological lesions such as gross malformation, hemorrhage or infection. It is critical for the pathologist to get as much information out of this stage of the examination as possible, since anything he misses at this time is permanently lost. The selection of appropriate laboratory investigations to diagnose some uncommon pathological entity may depend on a minor deviation from normal that is recognized during the macroscopic examination.

Performance of the perinatal autopsy may be regarded as a sorting process which can proceed along a number of different pathways, as indicated in Figure 3–9. The level of sophistication of the final answers will be determined by the completeness of the initial data base, the skill and experience of the pathologist in recognizing the clues which point to the correct pathway, and the time and facilities available for performing the appropriate special investigations. If the pathologist is able only to state the type of underlying process involved (e.g., acute asphyxia in a growth-retarded fetus) at the end of his autopsy, this can be of considerable help to obstetricians and neonatologists and does not lessen the value of the procedure.

Histologic examination complements macroscopic observations by giving supporting evidence on gestational age or timing and severity of stress, in addition to any precise pathological diagnosis it may provide. In contrast to macroscopic observations, histological findings can be verified at leisure by comparison with books or papers or reference to the appropriate expert.

---

*These are useful for assessing the distribution and severity of anoxic ischemic damage.

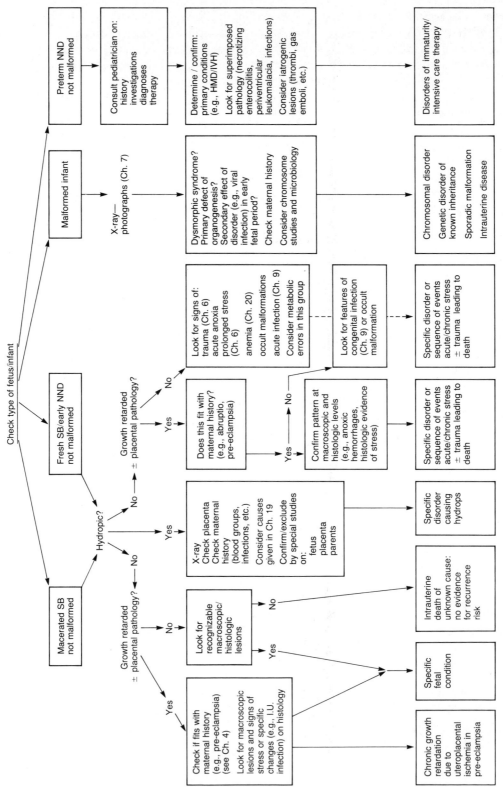

Figure 3–9. A representation of the perinatal autopsy as a sorting process.

REFERENCES

1. Potter, E. L., and Craig, J. M.: Pathology of the fetus and the infant, 3rd ed. Chicago, Year Book Medical Publishers, 1976.
2. Langley, F. A.: The perinatal postmortem examination. J. Clin. Pathol. *24*:159–169, 1971.
3. Barson, A. J.: The perinatal postmortem. *In* Barson, A. J. (ed.): Laboratory Investigation of Fetal Disease. Bristol, John Wright & Sons Ltd., 1981, pp. 476–497.
4. Pryse-Davies, J.: The perinatal autopsy. *In* Anthony, P. P., and MacSween, R. N. M. (eds.): Recent Advances in Histopathology, vol. II. London, Churchill-Livingstone, 1981, pp. 65–82.
5. Berry, C. L.: The examination of embryonic and fetal material in diagnostic histopathology laboratories. J. Clin. Pathol. *33*:317–326, 1980.
6. Russel, J. G. B.: Radiological assessment of age, retardation and death. *In* Barson, A. J. (ed.): Laboratory Investigation of Fetal Disease. Bristol, John Wright & Sons Ltd., 1981, pp. 3–16.
7. Foote, G. A., Wilson, A. J., and Stewart, J. H.: Perinatal postmortem radiography—experience with 2500 cases. Br. J. Radiol. *51*:351–356, 1978.
8. Pryse-Davies, J., and Beard, R. W.: A necropsy study of brain swelling in the newborn with special reference to cerebellar herniation. J. Pathol. *109*:51–73, 1973.
9. Dorovini-Zis, K., and Dolman, C. L.: Gestational development of the brain. Arch. Pathol. Lab. Med. *101*:192–195, 1977.
10. De Sa, D. J.: Polypoidal organization of aspirated amniotic squamous debris (amnion nodosum) in middle-ear cavity of newborn infants. Arch. Dis. Child. *52*:148–151, 1977.
11. Pape, K. E., Armstrong, D. L., and Fitzhardinge, P. M.: Peripheral median nerve damage secondary to brachial arterial blood gas sampling. J. Pediatr. *93*:852–856, 1978.
12. Beutler, E., and Baluda, M. C.: A simple spot screening test for galactosemia. J. Lab. Clin. Med. *68*:137–141, 1966.
13. Haan, E. A., and Danks, D. M.: Clinical investigation of suspected metabolic disease. *In* Barson, A. J. (ed.): Laboratory Investigation of Fetal Disease. Bristol, John Wright & Sons Ltd., 1981, pp. 410–428.
14. Bain, A. D.: Chromosomal and biochemical investigation of the abortus, stillbirth and neonatal death. *In* Barson, A. J. (ed.): Laboratory Investigation of Fetal Disease. Bristol, John Wright & Sons Ltd., 1981, pp. 452–475.
15. Perry, T. L.: Autopsy investigation of disorders of amino-acid metabolism. *In* Barson, A. J. (ed.): Laboratory Investigation of Fetal Disease. Bristol, John Wright & Sons Ltd., 1981, pp. 429–451.
16. Gruenwald, P., and Laurence, K. M.: A method of examining the brain of the newborn. Dev. Med. Child Neurol., *10*:64–68, 1968.

Chapter Four

The Placenta in Perinatal Pathology

The placenta is the organ least well understood by most pathologists. This is a situation for which there are a number of good reasons. Unlike other organs, the placenta is almost never available for study in an intact state in its normal position in the body. The maternal vascular connections are extensively disrupted during delivery so that it is difficult to determine the important spatial relationships between maternal and fetal circulations when the placenta is received in the laboratory. As the human placenta differs radically in structure from that of the commonly available animal species (rats, rabbits, guinea pigs, sheep), there is no readily available experimental model for the study of placental pathology comparable to that of the human placenta.

It is not surprising that there have been continuing arguments over the basic details of anatomy of this organ which have denied the pathologist any logical basis on which to interpret abnormalities. This applies particularly to the common vascular lesions such as infarcts and intervillous thrombi. Moreover, because the placenta becomes available for examination only when the baby is born, its study may be regarded as academic if the baby is alive and healthy. Even if the baby is ill, study of the placenta is usually less informative than direct investigation of the infant. In the United States the obstetrician may be unwilling to have his patient billed for placental examination if he does not feel that this is of direct practical value.

In this chapter I will stress the importance of recognizing the vascular anatomy of the placenta to allow interpretation of the common macroscopic and histological lesions. The value and limitations of placental examination will also be discussed.

DEVELOPMENT OF THE PLACENTA

This brief synopsis can be supplemented by referring to Wynn[1] and Fox,[2] wherein more extensive accounts of placental development and pathology with detailed references can be found.

The major functional part of the human placenta consists of the chorion, which develops from the wall of the primitive blastocyst. By the time implantation is completed at 11 days after conception, the primitive trophoblast has already differentiated into cytotrophoblast and syncytiotrophoblast cell layers. The primitive villi are formed by invasion of the radially orientated trophoblast masses by mesenchyme from the extraembryonic mesoderm. Peripherally, the masses of the cytotrophoblast cell columns expand and fuse with their neighbors to complete the formation of an enclosed lacunar space, the intervillous space.

Development of a fetal circulation and secondary branches to the primitive villi converts them into definitive primary villous stems, and erosion of maternal vessels by the trophoblast allows an intervillous circulation to be established by about 17 days after conception.

The primary villi and intervillous space initially involve the whole surface of the implanted blastocyst, but as growth of the conceptus proceeds the layer of decidua orientated toward the uterine cavity becomes attenuated and the underlying villi degenerate. By the end of the fourth month the villi are restricted to the chorion frondosum, the definitive placenta. There is progressive arborization of the primary villous stems to form the definitive placental lobules. The septa, which partly subdivide the placenta into a number of lobes, are formed by folds of the basal plate that are pulled up into the intervillous space by anchoring villi with a poor growth rate between regions of active placental growth.

From the end of the fourth month on, the placenta shows an increasingly well-developed lobular pattern and progressive changes in villous structure.

CHANGES IN VILLOUS STRUCTURE DURING PLACENTAL DEVELOPMENT

In early pregnancy the villus has a loose edematous stroma and a regular double layer of trophoblast, the inner layer consisting of cytotrophoblast or Langhan's cells and the outer layer of syncytiotrophoblast (Fig. 4–1). Fetal

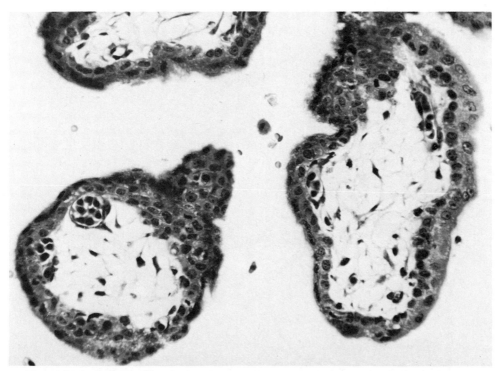

Figure 4–1. Placental villi at 14 weeks' gestation. H and E × 400. (From Wigglesworth, J. S.: Development, anatomy and physiology of the placenta. *In* Fox, M. and Langley, F. A. eds.: Postgraduate Obstetrical and Gynaecological Pathology. Oxford, Pergamon Press, 1973.)

capillaries are small and centrally placed. The stroma contains stellate mesenchymal cells and numerous Hofbauer cells, the latter probably representing placental macrophages. The terminal villi are of very variable size in early pregnancy and may be up to 170μ in diameter.

As pregnancy and placental growth proceed, the villi become more regular in size, the villous stroma is more condensed and the fetal capillaries dilate and come to occupy an increasing proportion of the villous cross-sectional area. New villi are formed by a continuous process of development of trophoblastic sprouts, which become invaded by stroma and fetal capillaries. The trophoblast loses its regular two-layered structure early in the second trimester and the villous cytotrophoblastic cells become isolated into groups. In the third trimester the irregularity of the trophoblast becomes more pronounced and the villous cytotrophoblast less obvious. There is a further increase in the proportion of the stroma of each villus occupied by fetal capillaries.

During the last two months of pregnancy syncytial knots or buds and vasculosyncytial membranes develop. The syncytial knots are regions where the syncytial nuclei are piled up into several layers. Between these regions the syncytium overlying the fetal capillaries becomes attenuated and anuclear. These vasculosyncytial membranes are believed to be important areas for gas transfer, while the trophoblast elsewhere may be more concerned with secretory activities.

STRUCTURE OF THE MATURE PLACENTA

The fetal placenta is divided into 50 to 60 subunits, or cotyledons, each of which arises as a primary stem villus from the chorionic plate and is supplied by primary branches of the umbilical vessels. The primary villi divide to form secondary and tertiary villi. The latter run down through the intervillous space toward the basal plate and are arranged around a central space.[3] The terminal villous network is formed by branches from these tertiary stems, some of which are inserted into the basal plate and recurve into the intervillous space before dividing up into the terminal villi. The definitive vascular unit is the lobule: each cotyledon consists of from one to five lobules.

In order to interpret vascular lesions of the placenta it is important to understand the nature of the intervillous space and the relationship between maternal and fetal circulations.[4] The maternal spiral arteries supplying the intervillous space discharge blood into the central part of the lobules. From these

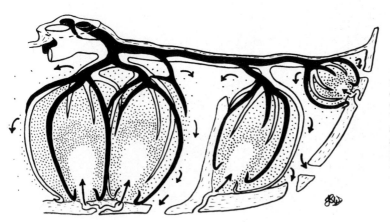

Figure 4–2. Diagram of intervillous space. Arrows indicate direction of maternal blood flow. Compare with Figure 4–5. (From Wigglesworth, J. S.: Vascular anatomy of the human placenta and its significance for placental pathology. J. Obstet. Gynaecol. Br. Cwlth. 76:979–989, 1969.)

sites the blood percolates through the closely packed villi of the periphery of the lobules and drains back to the basally situated decidual veins through subchorial, interlobular and marginal venous lakes (Fig. 4–2).

The intervillous space is nonhomogeneous in two different ways. The caliber of the space itself varies considerably because there are variable-sized spaces at the centers of the lobules, an extensive subchorial lake containing mainly villous stems, and large but irregularly placed regions with sparse villi between the lobules or groups of lobules. The space is nonhomogeneous also from a functional point of view because the spiral arteries discharge into the center of the lobule which is thus arterial in nature, the densely packed villi of the lobule represent a capillary space and the large subchorial and interlobular regions are venous lakes. It is thus not surprising that the structure of villi in the mature placenta differs according to the region of the lobule from which they come. Villi in the center of the lobule often have a relatively immature structure compared with those in the subchorial lake or interlobular regions (Fig. 4–3).

The simplest explanation of how this pattern develops is to postulate that the placental villi grow and branch most actively in regions where there is a good maternal blood supply (Fig. 4–4). The trophoblast may have an active role in obtaining this blood supply as cytotrophoblastic invasion within and around the spiral arteries appears closely related to the dilatation and structural change of these vessels that occurs in early pregnancy.[5]

A completely normal feature of placental development is an increasing deposition of fibrin around the stem villi within the venous areas of the intervillous space.

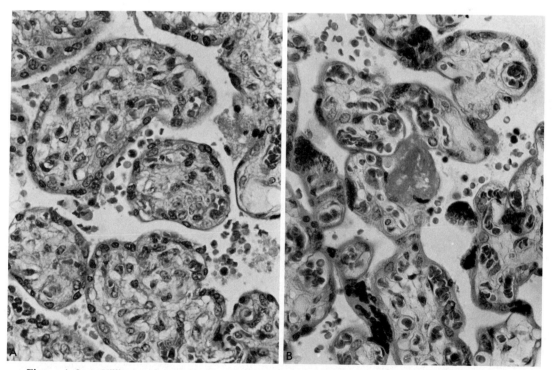

Figure 4–3. *A,* Villi near the center of a lobule at term. *B,* Villi near the periphery of the same lobule, H and E × 370. The central villi have a uniform trophoblast layer and cellular stroma, whereas peripheral villi have syncytial knots, condensed stroma and fibrin deposition. (From Wigglesworth, J. S.: Vascular anatomy of the human placenta and its significance for placental pathology. J. Obstet. Gynaecol. Br. Cwlth. 76:979–989, 1969.)

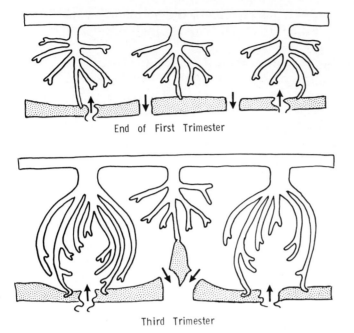

End of First Trimester

Third Trimester

Figure 4–4. Diagrammatic illustration to show how hollow-centered lobular pattern of mature placenta may develop as a result of preferential growth of villi in relation to spiral artery entries. Poor growth of intervening lobules may cause development of septa from folds of decidua pulled into the intervillous space.

EXAMINATION OF THE PLACENTA

GENERAL APPEARANCES

The placenta should initially be examined in an unfixed state, with membranes and related blood clot as little disturbed as possible. The size of the sac relative to the size of the infant and the site at which the sac ruptured are relevant observations to make before membranes and placenta are considered in more detail. The site of rupture of the sac, for instance, is critical if there is a suggestion that fetal bleeding may have occurred as a result of rupture of a fetal vessel in a velamentous cord insertion. The appearance and general features of the amniotic surface of the membranes should be assessed at this stage. In particular it should be noted whether the membranes are clear or cloudy, whether they have an offensive odor and whether they are stained with meconium. The length, site of attachment and general appearance of the umbilical cord should be observed and the length should be measured, particularly if it appears unduly short or long (see p. 77), and the number of vessels should be recorded.

At this stage in order to facilitate more detailed study of the placenta itself I prefer to cut the umbilical cord at about 5 cm from the fetal placental surface and trim off the membranes. The placenta is weighed at this point in the examination. Although Fox[2] has argued vehemently against the value of weighing the placenta as a routine activity, such considerations do not apply if any form of abnormality of the fetus or placenta is in question. The weight of the placenta, like that of any other organ, must relate in some way to its functional mass. Quite apart from the possible significance of relationships between placental and fetal weight, a number of specific conditions are associated with unduly large or unduly small placentae. Two weights of the placenta are obtained: (1) the weight of the organ complete with cord and membranes and (2) the weight of the trimmed placental disc. The former can be related to placental weights as expressed in most series, whereas the latter is the nearest to a functional mass of the organ that can be obtained without recourse to quantitative biochemical or morphometric techniques.

EXAMINATION OF THE FETAL SURFACE

The fetal surface of the placenta displays a number of important features. The umbilical arteries and veins and their branches can be seen clearly over a considerable part of their course, and lesions of the vessels can readily be recognized. The position of cord attachment and the pattern of vessel distribution over the fetal surface show a number of normal variations. The possibility of thrombosis should be considered, particularly if the arteries seem inapparent or the veins congested. As an aid to recognition of the vessel branches it may be remembered that the umbilical artery branches cross superficial to the vein branches at all intersections on the fetal placental surface. Frequently visible beneath the amnion is a small white plaque, the yolk sac remnant. This is of no significance. Multiple plaques or nodules may represent squamous metaplasia (p. 80), amnion nodosum (p. 80) or infection by *Candida albicans* (p. 73). Between the fetal vessel branches, the subchorial lake can be viewed, because the amnion and chorion are thin and relatively translucent. In the placentae of preterm infants, of less than 36 weeks' gestation, the subchorial lake is usually clear. Toward term there is increasing deposition of fibrin in the form of white plaques beneath the chorial plate.

EXAMINATION OF THE MATERNAL SURFACE

The maternal surface of the placenta has a complex appearance that requires some explanation. The surface of most delivered placentae is partly subdivided into about 20 regions of very variable size, the placental lobes. Each of these consists of a group of the true functional units of the placenta discussed earlier, the lobules. Near the periphery of the placenta it is often possible to recognize one or more small lobes that consist of only one lobule (Fig. 4–5). The center of such a peripheral lobule usually shows a slight depression, near which the coils of the terminal part of a spiral artery may be seen if they have not been torn off at delivery. The portions of the spiral arteries within the decidual surface of the placenta have a caliber up to 3 mm but are very thin-walled and usually collapsed. They may be seen most readily if the placenta is gently squeezed to fill them with blood from the intervillous space.[4] Sometimes a considerable length of spiral artery can be seen within a tag of decidual tissue (Streeter's column) remaining attached to the delivered placenta. Little pieces of fresh blood clot are often found within the depressions between the individual lobes or lobules. If these are removed gently it will be seen that they often protrude from round or oval openings into the intervillous space (Fig. 4–5). These openings are the venous exits. A probe or soft catheter introduced through one of the venous exits will pass readily up into the subchorial lake through the loose placental tissue in these regions. The irregularity of the maternal surface of the delivered placenta is due largely to the irregular collapse of the intervillous space as maternal blood is squeezed out of it during birth. The small depressions over the centers of the lobules are caused by collapse of the hollow centers into which the spiral arteries discharge, while the prominent interlobular clefts not only result from the septa but also from collapse of the venous parts of the intervillous space (Fig. 4–5).

There is considerable individual variation in the extent of obvious lobular development of the placenta. The large placentae characteristic of conditions associated with fetal anemia usually show very pronounced lobular formation. Lobular development may appear poor in placentae which are thin and of relatively low weight and may be difficult to recognize in placentae which have a small area of attachment but are thick and thus of average weight. The differences

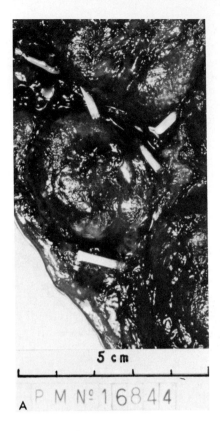

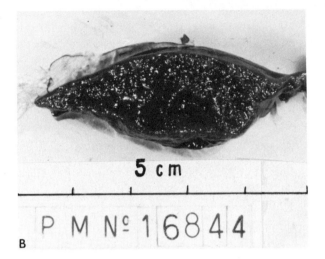

Figure 4–5. *A,* Separate lobule at margin of placenta, viewed from maternal surface. Note the umbilicated appearance. Markers inserted into venous exits. *B,* A slice through the same lobule seen in the fresh state. *C,* Histological appearance of the same slice. H and E × 7. Note the crowded villi around the central spaces in this double lobule. The subchorial lake is not obvious because this has collapsed during delivery.

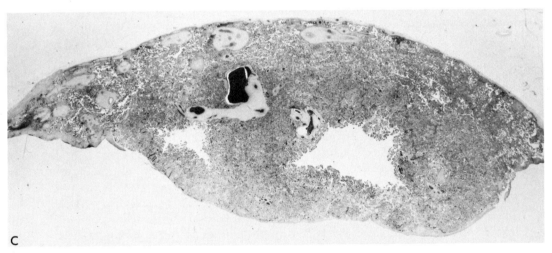

presumably are due to variations in the area over which the chorion frondosum is established and variations in subsequent placental growth rate.

Calcification is an entirely normal feature of the maternal surface of the placenta. It is found with increasing frequency toward term and has been shown to vary according to differences in parity, time of year and maternal vitamin D intake.[2]

THE PLACENTAL SUBSTANCE

Some pathologists prefer to slice the placenta after fixation. If this is done, it is essential that the organ be fixed flat, because interpretation of the appearance of a distorted fixed placenta is virtually impossible. Personally I prefer to slice the organ at about 1 cm intervals in the fresh state. I place the trimmed placenta with the maternal surface upward and cut down to, but not quite through, the fetal surface. Both surfaces of each slice can be examined and, if desired, the placenta can then be fixed with all the slices retained in their normal relationship. Examination of fresh placental slices allows ready confirmation of the normal lobular pattern already described. The hollow centers of many lobules can be seen and appear to be accentuated in the placentae of some stillbirths. The loose structure of the subchorial lake and interlobular or interlobar regions can also be recognized. These regions may appear congested if maternal blood has drained from them less completely than usual.

HISTOLOGICAL SAMPLING

I have stressed how the lobular pattern of the placenta can be recognized during macroscopic examination; this makes interpretation of the common vascular lesions much easier and also allows logical sampling for histological study. Areas of the placenta which should be selected for histology include any lesions that cannot be diagnosed on gross examination or of which it is desired to keep a permanent record and one or two blocks through characteristic lobules. Because it is far easier to cut placental blocks after fixation, I usually fix one or two placenta slices for a day or so and cut appropriate full-thickness blocks from these. Although the placental margin is the easiest site from which to cut blocks, it is not the most suitable region for sampling as there is often an accentuation of conditions such as perivillous fibrin deposition, which render it unrepresentative. In addition to blocks of the placenta itself, a section should be taken through the umbilical cord to check the appearance of the umbilical vessels and to exclude conditions such as thrombosis or infection. The membranes can be conveniently sampled by taking a swiss-roll from the site of rupture up to the edge of the placental disc in the fresh state, and embedding a slice of this after fixation.

ABNORMALITIES OF PLACENTATION

PLACENTAL SHAPE

The final shape of the placenta represents the area where the chorionic villi have obtained sufficient blood supply from maternal vessels to allow development of the definitive lobules. This is usually roughly oval, but may have one of a variety of different forms, for example, bilobate. These are discussed in some detail by Fox and will only be briefly mentioned here.

Accessory Lobe (Succenturiate Lobe). These are common (3 to 6 per cent in the series discussed by Fox) but are of importance only if the accessory lobe is retained within the uterus at delivery.

Bilobate Placenta. In this condition, the two parts are of nearly equal size. It has been suggested that the condition is due to superficial implantation of the ovum, which is thus able to attach to both anterior and posterior walls of the uterus. This is a process which occurs normally in some primates.[6]

Placenta Membranacea. In this rare condition the villi of the chorion laeve fail to regress; therefore, there are villi over the entire surface of the chorion. The etiology is obscure. The condition is associated with poor fetal growth and recurrent antepartum hemorrhage.

Ring-shaped Placenta, Fenestrate Placenta. For a discussion of these rare abnormalities, see Fox.[2]

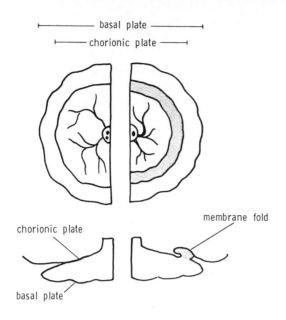

basal plate

chorionic plate

chorionic plate

membrane fold

basal plate

Figure 4–6. Diagram to illustrate features of circummarginate and circumvallate placenta.

Circummarginate   Circumvallate

Placenta Extrachorialis. This is an anomaly in which the chorionic plate of the placenta is smaller than the basal plate. As a consequence there is a transition from membranes to villous chorion at some distance from the margin on the fetal surface of the placenta. The anomaly is of two types, described as *circummarginate placenta* and *circumvallate placenta.* In the former there is a flat transition from villous to membranous chorion, whereas in the latter the membranes are folded or rolled (Fig. 4–6). About 25 per cent of placentae show partial or complete extrachorialis. There is no general agreement on the etiology of this condition; the many theories are reviewed by Fox.[2]

An increased incidence of threatened abortion, antepartum hemorrhage and premature labor has been reported in a number of series of cases of circumvallate placenta, but these problems seem to be related to the complete form of the condition only.[2] It has also been noted that circumvallate placenta is invariably found in cases of extramembranous pregnancy and is a common association of cases of prolonged amniotic fluid leakage.[7] The frequency with which the membranous fold of the circumvallate placenta contains necrotic decidua, ghost villi or blood clot suggests that it may be a secondary, essentially pathological condition. Grosser's theory that reduction of intra-amniotic pressure is an important etiological factor in placenta extrachorialis, as supported by Benirschke and Driscoll,[8] would seem a likely explanation for this group of cases of complete circumvallate placenta.

Placenta Accreta. This is a rare condition in which the decidua basalis is partially or completely missing. Many cases are related to implantation on a previous uterine scar. The villi may be separated from the myometrium by Nitabuch's fibrin layer or they may penetrate into the myometrium. Placenta accreta results in failure of separation of the placenta during the third stage. If the accretion is incomplete, there may be severe postpartum hemorrhage following partial separation.

THE PLACENTA IN MULTIPLE PREGNANCY

Examination of the placenta in twin pregnancy may be an important aid to establishment of zygosity and may reveal specific pathological features related to the condition.[2, 9]

THE PLACENTA OF DIZYGOUS TWINS

Because each of a pair of dizygous twins develops from a different ovum, the placental membranes of each are normally separate. If the ova implant on opposite sides of the uterus, the placentae and membranes remain separate throughout pregnancy. If the ova implant close to each other the placental membranes, although initially separate, will subsequently fuse. However, such secondary fusion does not destroy the separate chorions so that the fused dizygous placentae remain dichorionic.

THE PLACENTA OF MONOZYGOUS TWINS

The form and membrane structure of monozygous twin placentae are determined by the time the single fertilized ovum divides into two individuals. If splitting occurs within the first four days after ovulation—that is, before the chorion has differentiated—each twin will have a separate chorion and amnion, although the placentae may subsequently fuse. If the preimplantation blastocyst splits during the latter part of the first week of gestation, the twins will have a single chorion but separate amniotic sacs. If splitting is delayed until the second week, placentation will be of the monochorionic monoamniotic variety (Fig. 4–7).

EXAMINATION OF TWIN PLACENTAE AS AN AID TO DETERMINING ZYGOSITY

From the foregoing it is apparent that dichorionic fused or separate placentae may be seen with either monozygous or dizygous twins, whereas monochorionic

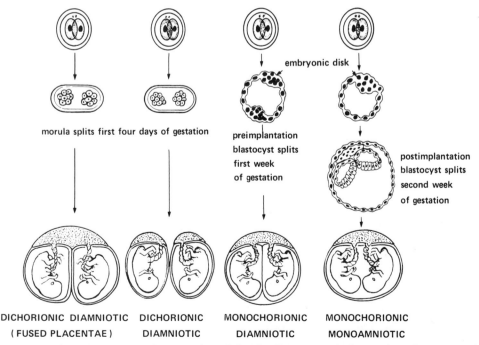

Figure 4–7. Diagrammatic representation of the development and placentation of monozygotic twins. (From Fox, H.: Pathology of the Placenta. W. B. Saunders, Philadelphia, 1978.)

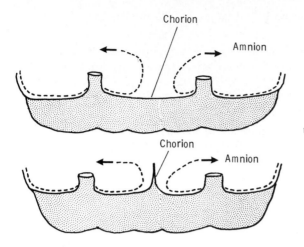

Figure 4–8. Method of testing whether fused twin placentae are monochorial or dichorial.

placentae are seen only with monozygous twins. Thus the one positive statement about zygosity that can be made on morphologic examination of the placenta is that a monochorionic placenta denotes monozygosity.

The only practical problem is to distinguish between a fused dichorionic twin placenta and a monochorionic diamniotic placenta. Examination of the fetal surface will in either case show a double fold of membranes crossing the placenta somewhere between the umbilical cord insertions, and marking the line at which the two sacs were in apposition on the surface of the placenta. If these sacs consist of amnion alone, they can easily be stripped off the placental surface, leaving no visible line of demarcation. If chorion is present, it cannot be stripped off as it is continuous with the underlying chorionic plate (Fig. 4–8). Monochorial, monoamniotic placentae, in which the twins share a common sac, are associated with a high incidence of fetal malformations and stillbirth.[2, 10]

If the facilities of a laboratory that performs enzyme studies are available, zygosity of dichorionic like-sexed twin pairs may be determined to a high degree of probability (although never with certainty) by examination of samples of tissue from each placental disc and of blood from each cord and from both parents.

VASCULAR ANASTOMOSIS AND TWIN-TWIN TRANSFUSION

Nearly all monochorionic twin placentae show anastomoses between the vessels of the two umbilical circulations.[9] These usually involve the major branches of the arteries and veins on the fetal placental surface. Artery-to-artery communications are by far the most common; less frequently, venovenous anastomoses are present.

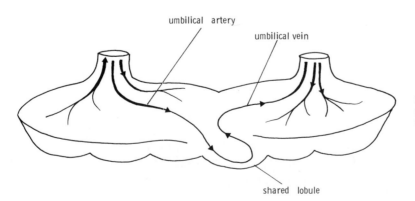

Figure 4–9. Diagram showing one-way flow through shared lobules as basis for twin transfusion syndrome.

Of greater pathological significance are deep arteriovenous communications between the two circulations. These take the form of shared lobules supplied by an umbilical arterial branch from one fetus and drained by an umbilical vein branch into the twin. One-way flow through the shared lobule may be compensated for by reverse flow through superficial arterioarterial or venovenous anastomoses if these coexist. The twin transfusion syndrome is believed to arise when shared lobules causing blood flow from one twin to the other are not compensated for by the presence of such superficial anastomoses or by shared lobules causing flow in the opposite direction (Fig. 4–9).[2, 11] The syndrome occurs in 15 to 30 per cent of cases of monochorial placentation and is defined in terms of a difference in cord hemoglobin between the two twins of > 5 g per cent. The recipient twin of a twin transfusion pair is plethoric and polycythemic and may show cardiomegaly. The donor twin, in contrast, is pale and anemic and may have the organ weight characteristics of the intrauterine malnutrition form of fetal growth retardation.

The placental tissue associated with the donor twin is characteristically pale and bulky, whereas that related to the recipient is of smaller mass but intensely congested. Histological study reveals intense engorgement of the villous capillaries in the recipient. The placental villi of the donor twin resemble those of severe rhesus isoimmunization, being immature and edematous in appearance, with small inconspicuous vessels which contain hemopoietic cells.[12]

VASCULAR LESIONS OF THE PLACENTA

These constitute the macroscopic and histological abnormalities that are most frequently seen by the perinatal pathologist. The form, site and probable significance of these lesions are most readily understood in terms of the vascular pattern of the placental lobules already described.[4]

PLACENTAL INFARCTION

A placental infarct is an area of ischemic necrosis of placental villi; therefore, it should not differ in essentials from infarcts in other organs. The circulation on which survival of the placental trophoblast depends is that through the intervillous space. Placental infarction thus results from obstruction of blood flow through the spiral arteries, usually by thrombosis, and the lesions have a lobular distribution (Fig. 4–10). However, the spiral arteries are not true end arteries. It might be expected that sufficient circulation through a lobule would be maintained following obstruction of the spiral artery supplying it, provided that there was adequate flow through the arteries supplying adjacent lobules. Therefore, ischemic necrosis

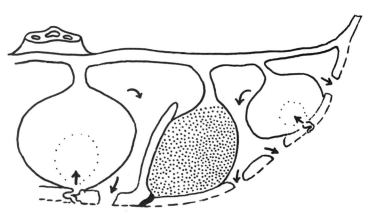

Figure 4–10. Lobular pattern of infarction. (From Wigglesworth, J. S.: Vascular anatomy of the human placenta and its significance for placental pathology. J. Obstet. Gynaecol. Br. Cwlth. 76:979–989, 1969.)

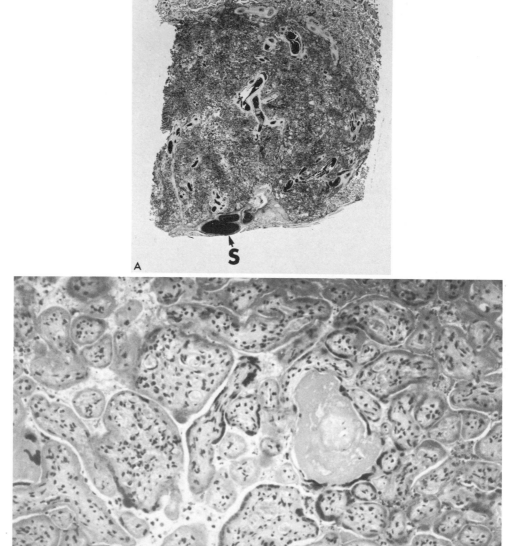

Figure 4–11. Acute infarction. *A*, Photograph of whole section showing engorged spiral artery (s) proximal to site of thrombosis on maternal aspect. H and E × 5. *B*, Villi from a similar infarct showing loss of syncytial nuclear staining. H and E × 300. (*A*, From Wigglesworth, J. S.: Vascular anatomy of the human placenta and its significance for placental pathology. J. Obstet. Gynaecol. Br. Cwlth. *76*:979–989, 1969.)

of one placental lobule probably indicates not only that the spiral artery supplying the infarcted lobule is thrombosed but that flow through adjacent spiral arteries is severely impaired.

In the early stages of their development placental infarcts are red but later turn brown, gray and finally creamy white. On histological examination an early infarct shows engorgement of the fetal capillaries with blood, which has often ruptured into the villous stroma (Fig. 4–11). Loss of staining of syncytial nuclei occurs rapidly. The villi may be pressed together, or the intervillous space may present as a network of fibrin. At a late stage there is total loss of nuclear staining and the infarct appears as a mass of ghost villi variably intermixed with fibrin. The thrombosed spiral artery coils can usually be detected within the decidua overlying an infarct, if they are looked for.

There is often an area of necrotic decidua overlying an infarct. This is probably due to thrombosis of the basal branches of the spiral arteries which supply this tissue.

Placental infarction is characterized by necrosis of the whole villus. It seems surprising that the villous stroma at least cannot be maintained by the fetal placental circulation. Indeed, the histological appearance indicates that cessation of fetal circulation through the lobule is an essential part of the pathological process. This suggests that the villous capillaries are highly responsive to changes in metabolic conditions within the intervillous space. From a teleological point of view there is little advantage to be gained by the fetus from perfusing a portion of the placenta which cannot gain oxygen or nutrients from the maternal blood. Placental infarction may thus serve as a mechanism which allows the fetus to redistribute blood flow to those placental lobules which are adequately supplied by the maternal circulation.

PLACENTAL HEMATOMA

The placental hematoma is closely related to the infarct. It consists of a mass of soft blood clot which usually fills the central space of a lobule and is surrounded by a rim of infarcted villi (Fig. 4–12). Sometimes such hematomas are purely retroplacental and situated within the decidua. Sometimes they protrude into the placental substance with little evidence of placental infarction (Fig. 4–13). They are usually described (Wilkin,[3] Fox[2]) as retroplacental hematomas, although in my experience they are truly retroplacental in a minority of cases. Frequently these lesions are associated with decidual necrosis and liquefaction of the central clot to present as a crater on the maternal surface of the delivered placenta. These localized hematomas are usually (although not invariably) associated with maternal pre-eclampsia. The exact mode of formation of the lesions is not generally agreed

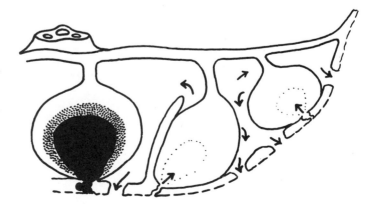

Figure 4–12. Lobular pattern of placental hematoma. (From Wigglesworth, J. S.: Vascular anatomy of the human placenta and its significance for placental pathology. J. Obstet. Gynaecol. Br. Cwlth. 76:979–989, 1969.)

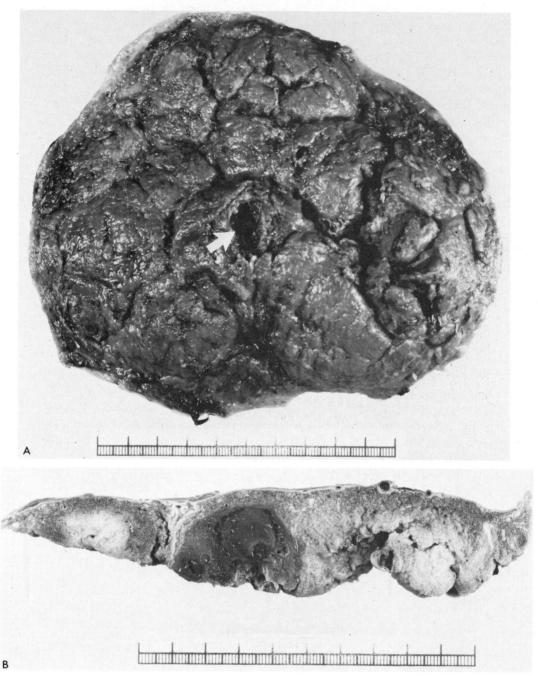

Figure 4–13. *A,* A hematoma presenting as a small mass on the maternal surface of the placenta (arrow). *B,* A slice through the same lesion to show a central mass of clot with a rim of infarcted villi.

on, although they are probably related to rupture of spiral arteries. Some years ago I suggested that the probable mode of origin was by a process of slow aneurysmal dilatation of a spiral artery proximal to a thrombosed segment, as I could trace such aneurysms on serial section of several cases. The occluded vessel would be most likely to dilate and finally rupture into the overlying infarcted lobule. The high blood pressure and damaged spiral artery walls associated with pre-eclampsia make it reasonable to expect such lesions to occur in association with this condition. At the same time the focal spiral artery narrowing resulting from the acute atherosis typical of pre-eclampsia makes it unlikely that eventual spiral artery rupture will be followed by a classic massive placental abruption. Unruptured spiral artery aneurysms can be found not infrequently in placentae, in cases of pre-eclampsia, if they are specifically searched for (Fig. 4–14).

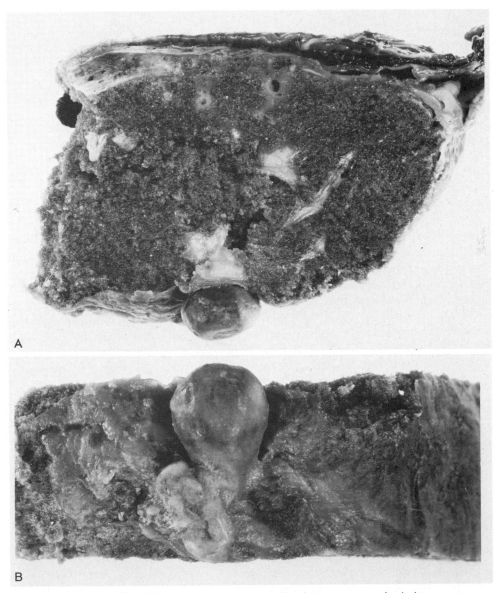

Figure 4–14. *A,* A slice of fixed placenta at margin with a large unruptured spiral artery aneurysm on the maternal surface. *B,* View of slice from maternal aspect showing aneurysm arising from a spiral artery coil.

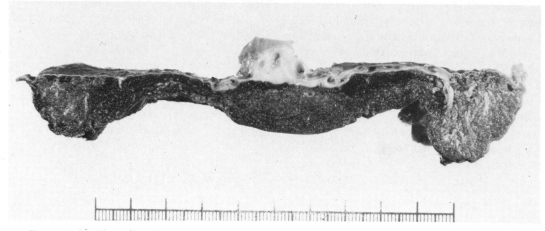

Figure 4–15. Fixed slice of placenta from a case of massive placental abruption. Note extreme congestion of the villi beneath the depression caused by the mass of retroplacental clot (removed) and the darker line representing blood trapped in the subchorial lake.

PLACENTAL ABRUPTION

The classic placental abruption (abruptio placentae) involves massive hemorrhage into the decidua with separation and compression of the central part of the placenta (Fig. 4–15). Although it is not possible to determine the origin of bleeding in such cases, it may be assumed to be derived from spiral artery rupture. Most cases of abruption are not associated with preceding pre-eclampsia, and normal uteroplacental blood flow is usual. Rupture of a spiral artery of normal caliber in such circumstances is likely to be a far more catastrophic event than would be the rupture of a narrowed, partly thrombosed spiral artery in the patient with pre-eclampsia. The placental tissue beneath the mass of retroplacental clot shows obliteration of the intervillous space and acute infarction. The infarction does not show a lobular pattern because there is total disruption of intervillous circulation in this condition. Blood may be trapped in the subchorial lake (Fig. 4–15).

In many cases in which there is a history of severe antepartum hemorrhage with birth of a severely asphyxiated or stillborn infant, it may be difficult to determine the site of bleeding or the extent of placental separation from examination of the placenta. There will be lack of obvious placental compression if blood has been able to escape following separation of the placental margin. Evidence of the extent of placental separation caused by retroplacental hemorrhage in such cases may be obtained by determining the area of the maternal surface affected by bleeding into the decidua (rather than loose fresh clot which can readily be wiped off). Section of the placenta may reveal areas of acute infarction alternating with areas of pallor.

THROMBOSIS WITHIN THE INTERVILLOUS SPACE

Thrombi occur in pre-formed vascular spaces. From consideration of the lobular pattern of the placenta it might be predicted that thrombi would be seen in the centers of the lobules, in the subchorial lake and in the areas between the lobules (Fig. 4–16). Thrombi can indeed be recognized in all these sites. However, the two most frequent and characteristic sites are the centers of the lobules and the subchorial lake. Laminated thrombi within the centers of the lobules are seen in 28 to 48 per cent of cases.[2] When very soft and fresh, they have been called *Kline's hemorrhages.* Like placental infarcts, the lesions undergo the sequence of

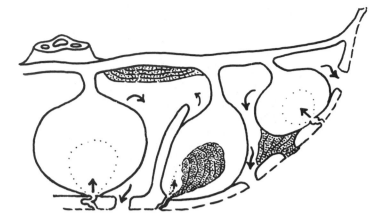

Figure 4–16. Sites of thrombosis within the intervillous space. (From Wigglesworth, J. S.: Vascular anatomy of the human placenta and its significance for placental pathology. J. Obstet. Gynaecol. Br. Cwlth. 76:979–989, 1969.)

change in color from red through brown to gray or creamy white. They often have a narrow rim of infarcted villi around them. This is not surprising since they are within the center of the lobule and must disrupt intervillous flow through it. Sometimes they are associated with partial spiral artery thrombosis. There is considerable speculation in the literature, discussed by Fox,[2] on the possibility that these thrombi are caused by leakage of fetal blood with resultant fetomaternal coagulation.

Thrombi within the subchorial lake are seen in 20 per cent of placentae at term. The lesions usually are seen as pale gray or white layered fibrin masses attached to the chorionic plate. They are sometimes very extensive and may be 1 centimeter or more in thickness, almost filling the subchorial lake on occasion (Fig. 4–17). The layered fibrin structure of these lesions suggests that they must develop gradually. Fox makes the reasonable suggestion that they result from turbulence in the subchorial lake.

A less common variant is *massive subchorial thrombosis,* in which the subchorial lake is distended and distorted by a mass of thrombus containing a high proportion of red cells as well as fibrin. This has most frequently been recognized in cases of abortion during the second trimester, in which it is known as *Breu's mole,* or *fleshy mole.* Although the etiology is obscure, the structure of this type of thrombus indicates that it has developed much more rapidly than the usual type of subchorial fibrin plaque.

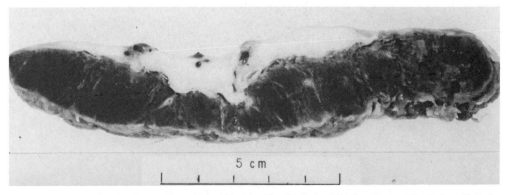

5 cm

Figure 4–17. Massive fibrin deposition filling much of subchorial lake. (From Wigglesworth, J. S.: Vascular anatomy of the human placenta and its significance for placental pathology. J. Obstet. Gynaecol. Br. Cwlth. 76:979–989, 1969.)

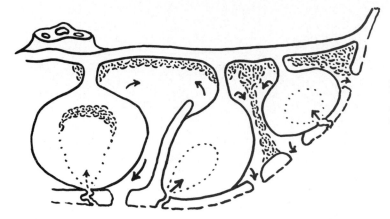

Figure 4–18. Pattern of perivillous fibrin deposition. (From Wigglesworth, J. S.: Vascular anatomy of the human placenta and its significance for placental pathology. J. Obstet. Gynaecol. Br. Cwlth. 76:979–989, 1969.)

PERIVILLOUS FIBRIN DEPOSITION

Perivillous fibrin deposition appears macroscopically as gray or white irregular masses which may be seen near the placental margin, stretching from chorionic to basal plate or outlining one or more of the lobules (Figs. 4–18 and 4–19). The lesion may adjoin an obvious infarct or mass of intervillous thrombus. Placentae from late abortions or early third trimester stillbirths are occasionally seen in which almost the whole placenta has been involved by this process.

Microscopically there is obliteration of the intervillous space by fibrin and necrosis of syncytium with proliferation of large cytotrophoblast cells (X cells of Wilkin[3]). The stroma and villous circulation are preserved in the initial stages of formation of the lesion in contrast to infarction. At a later stage sclerosis of fetal vessels and hyalinization of the stroma may be seen. The caliber of the intervillous space is maintained during the process of fibrin deposition and cannot subsequently be reduced so that the distance which separated the villi in the venous areas in vivo can be appreciated at a histological level (Fig. 4–20).

SIGNIFICANCE OF MACROSCOPIC VASCULAR LESIONS

The significance of vascular lesions of the placenta is related both to their nature and to their extent. Those such as intervillous thrombi and perivillous

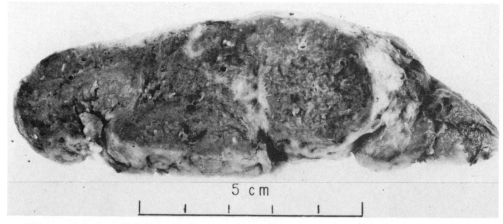

Figure 4–19. Placental slice showing perivillous fibrin deposition as gray or white strands. (From Wigglesworth, J. S.: Vascular anatomy of the human placenta and its significance for placental pathology. J. Obstet. Gynaecol. Br. Cwlth. 76:979–989, 1969.)

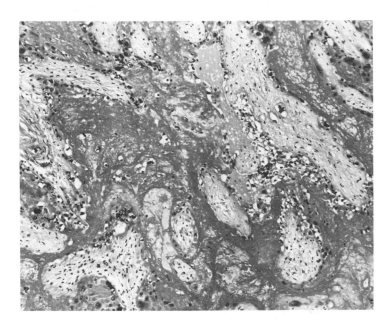

Figure 4–20. Perivillous fibrin deposition. H and E × 100. The intervillous space is obliterated by fibrin, the villi are sclerosed and there is loss of syncytium but preservation of some cytotrophoblast cells. (From Wigglesworth, J. S.: Vascular anatomy of the human placenta and its significance for placental pathology. J. Obstet. Gynaecol. Br. Cwlth. 76:979–989, 1969.)

fibrin deposits that fill up loose venous areas of the intervillous space can appear to involve a large proportion of the placenta on examination after delivery and yet have little effect on intervillous circulation through the placental lobule and thus cause little impairment in placental function. These lesions have not been found to be significantly associated with fetal morbidity.[2] However, massive subchorial lake thrombosis or perivillous fibrin deposition throughout virtually the whole intervillous space is occasionally seen in cases of abortion or fetal death in utero. The florid nature of the lesions in such fatal cases helps to indicate how benign these changes must be in the modest form in which they commonly present.

Relatively small areas of infarction, particularly if they involve the central rather than the marginal region of the placenta, indicate severe impairment in uteroplacental circulation. It is not surprising therefore that infarction is significantly associated with intrauterine fetal death and fetal growth retardation.[2, 13, 14] The closely associated placental hematoma has similar implications and is equally associated with perinatal mortality and morbidity. The pathologist who is unused to examining placentae may have difficulty in recognizing the differences between infarction, intervillous thrombosis and perivillous fibrin deposition at macroscopic level, particularly since they frequently coexist as composite lesions. When they have been present for several weeks these conditions all appear as white masses within the placenta. Identification of the site of each lesion in relation to the lobular architecture is of considerable help. Any doubtful lesions should be submitted to histological section.

HISTOLOGICAL CHANGES OF PLACENTAL HYPOXIA AND ISCHEMIA

The histological changes that have been described as associated with placental hypoxia and ischemia include an excessive number of syncytial knots, proliferation of the villous cytotrophoblast (Langhans) cells, fibrinoid necrosis of villi and thickening of the trophoblastic basement membrane.[2] Proliferation of villous cytotrophoblast cells is readily observed in the placentae of women with preeclampsia (Fig. 4–21).[15, 16] The suggestion that this proliferation is a direct response to hypoxia has been confirmed by culturing villi in hypoxic conditions.[17] Although

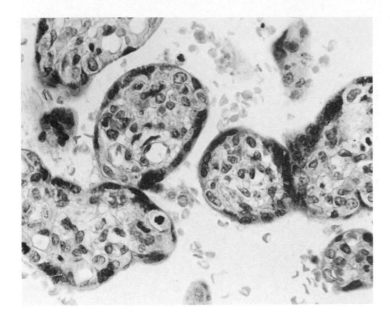

Figure 4–21. Proliferation of Langhans cells in severe pre-eclampsia. H and E × 300. Langhans cells appear as large pale cells within the trophoblast layer. One cell in the center of the field is in mitosis.

there have been a number of claims that syncytial knots are increased in number, in cases of pre-eclampsia this is denied by Fox, who believes that syncytial knots are the result of reduced villous blood flow rather than reduction in blood flow or oxygen tension within the intervillous space. The increase in syncytial knots which is seen in the villi in cases of intrauterine death (see Chapter 5) would fit in with this suggestion. I have been impressed with the essential similarity between syncytial knots and the normal syncytial sprouts which form the first stage of development of new villi. Reduction of fetal villous blood flow might well prevent extension of the villous stroma into the new syncytial sprouts which would continue to develop as long as the intervillous circulation was maintained (Fig. 4–22).

Fibrinoid necrosis of villi and thickening of the trophoblastic basement membrane are both claimed to be more frequent in placentae of patients with pre-eclampsia.[2] Fox discusses evidence that the former condition is due to some immunological reaction.

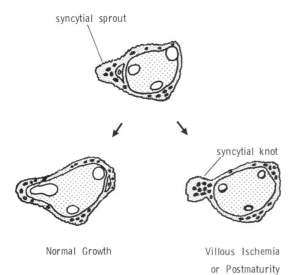

Figure 4–22. A possible mechanism for development of syncytial knots by failure of extension of villous stroma into syncytial sprouts.

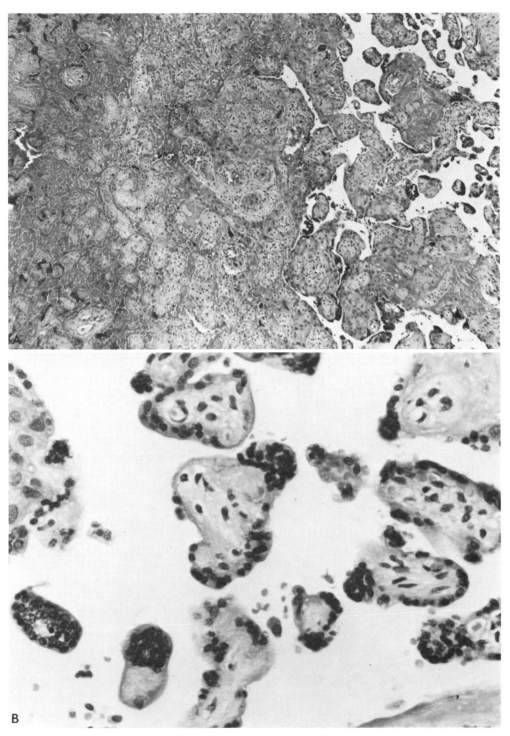

Figure 4–23. *A,* Margin of infarct. H and E × 60. Villi with surviving stroma at the margin of the lesion are enveloped in fibrin, while villi in the adjoining intervillous space show marked syncytial knot formation. *B,* Villi adjacent to infarct from the same case, showing syncytial knot formation. H and E × 600.

If placental histology is assessed in relation to the lobular pattern, the most striking feature of placentae from patients with severe pre-eclampsia is often accentuation of the normal regional variation. Thus the dense areas of the lobule may show marked cytotrophoblast proliferation while the villi in the subchorial lake and interlobular regions show pronounced syncytial knot formation. Surviving villi at the margin of an infarct display a fairly constant pattern of changes. Those directly adjacent to the infarcted tissue are usually enveloped in fibrin and show loss of syncytium, proliferation of cytotrophoblast cells and sclerosis of villous stroma, the usual changes of perivillous fibrin deposition. The surviving villi beyond this region show excessive syncytial knot formation (Fig. 4–23). Such changes can perhaps best be explained on the basis of varying relationships between fetal and maternal placental perfusion in the zone between infarcted and normal placental tissue.

PLACENTAL CHANGES IN SPECIFIC CONDITIONS

FETAL GROWTH RETARDATION

There is no constant pattern of placental abnormality in association with fetal growth retardation. Placentae of cases associated with maternal pre-eclampsia may show infarction, hematomas or the histological changes characteristic of pre-eclampsia such as excessive cytotrophoblast proliferation in the villi.

Many small for dates infants have unduly small placentae. It is a matter for speculation whether and to what extent the placental size has limited fetal growth or whether it is merely a manifestation of a reduced fetal growth potential or fetal malnutrition. In those cases in which an unduly small placenta is associated with a growth-retarded infant of malnourished type, it might be suspected that placental size had become limiting for adequate fetal nutrition. However, it has been argued that the small fetal placenta in such cases is merely a passive victim of an inadequate maternal supply line.[2] The structural relationships between the spiral arteries and the fetal placental lobules discussed earlier in this chapter and the ability of the fetal trophoblast to obtain a blood supply wherever it implants argue against any such passive role for fetal placental growth.

An increased incidence of villitis in the placentae of small for dates infants has been claimed.[18] The association with infection could be either a direct or an indirect one, because women of low socioeconomic status who are likely to have growth-retarded infants may be at greater risk of prenatal infection.

An excess of avascular villi caused by fetal stem artery thrombosis is a not infrequent finding.[19]

RHESUS ISOIMMUNIZATION

The placenta in pregnancies complicated by maternofetal rhesus incompatibility may show a spectrum of changes that relate to the severity of the condition. Placentae from cases involving hydrops are characteristically pale and bulky. In extreme cases the placenta is friable and exudes large quantities of fluid. In severe but nonhydropic cases the placenta has a prominent lobular pattern and may appear pale on section. Intervillous thrombi are commonly seen within the centers of some of the lobules.

On histological examination there is again a spectrum of changes. As Fox has pointed out, different areas of a single placenta may show marked variation in villous histology. The villi may appear markedly edematous with prominent stromal Hofbauer cells and an immature, somewhat regular trophoblast layer with

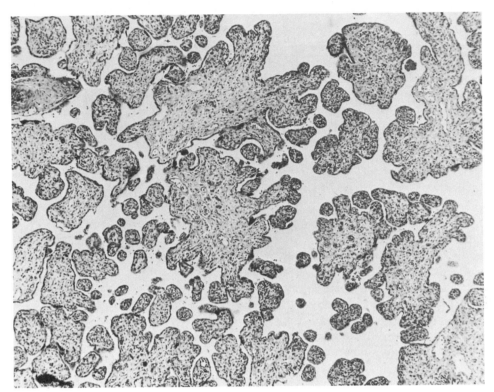

Figure 4–24. Placental villi in Rh hydrops. H and E × 30. Edematous villi with hemopoietic cells in fetal capillaries.

prominent cytotrophoblast cells (Fig. 4–24). Elsewhere, villous edema may be less apparent and the villi may show just a minor degree of structural immaturity. The fetal capillaries contain nucleated red cells and in severe cases may be packed with masses of hemopoietic cells. Specific features claimed to be present in rhesus isoimmunization include thickening of the trophoblastic basement membrane and an increase in fibrinoid necrosis of villi.

The appearance of the villi in rhesus isoimmunization is not specific, and similar changes are seen in fetal anemia of any cause including the donor twin of a transfusion pair and in congenital infections associated with fetal hemolysis such as cytomegalovirus infection. The severity of the change seems related to the degree of extramedullary hemopoietic activity, although Fox may be correct in his contention that it is not merely a response to fetal anemia. Possibly the fetal placenta proliferates in response to the same stimuli that promote fetal hemopoiesis (see Chapter 20).

MATERNAL DIABETES MELLITUS

There is no constant pattern of abnormality in this condition.[2, 20] The placenta may be bulky but is often of normal size: histological changes include villi which may appear either unduly immature or may show accelerated maturation. Thrombosis of fetal stem arteries and proliferative endarteritis of the fetal vessels are among the more commonly recognized abnormalities.

It may be reasonably assumed that the placenta, like the fetus, will show least abnormality in those women with good diabetic control during pregnancy.

PLACENTA IN STORAGE DISORDERS

Inborn errors of metabolism associated with abnormal storage of mucopolysaccharides or lipids (mucopolysaccharidoses, mucolipidoses, lipidoses, gangliosidoses) are associated with characteristic histological appearance of the placental villi, comprising large vacuolated Hofbauer cells in the villous stroma and similar vacuolation of cytotrophoblast cells.[21] Metachromasia may be demonstrable by use of an appropriate technique.[22] This change is sufficiently characteristic to provide a useful clue to the diagnosis in obscure instances of perinatal death (Fig. 4–25).

PLACENTAL INFECTION

The two major routes of infection of the placenta and membranes are by organisms ascending into the amniotic sac from the vagina or cervix and by organisms which reach the placenta in the maternal blood.[2, 23] Uncommon routes include direct spread from a focus of infection in the endometrium, entry into the uterus from the fallopian tube or by introduction from outside during surgical procedures such as amniocentesis. Ascending infections involve organisms which are normal inhabitants of the vagina and thus usually occur in the absence of any infection in the mother. Hematogenous infections, in contrast, are always secondary to an overt or subclinical maternal infection.

ASCENDING INFECTIONS

This is the most common mode of placental infection and usually involves the membranes, with production of a chorioamnionitis.

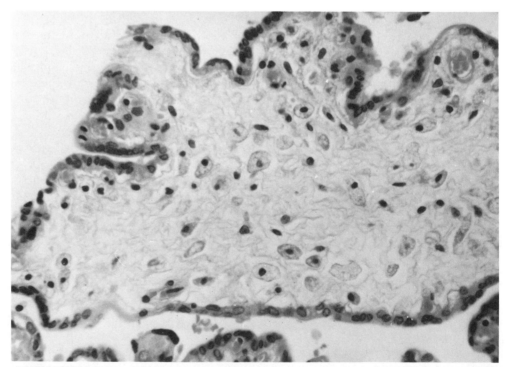

Figure 4–25. Storage cells within placental villi in a case of β-glucuronidase deficiency presenting as fetal hydrops. H and E × 400. Recognition of the significance of this appearance prompted biochemical investigation of frozen tissue and body fluids in an infant whose death would otherwise have been unexplained.

MORPHOLOGICAL CHANGES

The placenta and membranes are often macroscopically normal but may be opaque and foul-smelling on occasion. In chorioamnionitis caused by *Candida albicans* the membranes and umbilical cord may be studded with tiny white or yellow nodules.

Histological polymorphonuclear leukocyte infiltration is seen initially in the extraplacental membranes related to the cervical os. At a late stage the infiltrate involves the chorionic plate and adjacent intervillous space where the polymorphonuclear leukocytes become enmeshed in fibrin (Fig. 4–26). Spread into the vessels and Wharton's jelly of the umbilical cord (funisitis) is seen in the established case.

BACTERIOLOGY

The organisms most frequently cultured in cases of chorioamnionitis include *Escherichia coli*, coagulase-positive staphylococci, *Hemophilus vaginalis*, streptococci, *Proteus mirabilis*, Klebsiella and Pseudomonas. Other bacteria that have been isolated include Clostridia, Pasteurella and gonococci. Nonbacterial agents causing chorioamnionitis include Mycoplasma and *Candida albicans*.

INCIDENCE OF CHORIOAMNIONITIS AND FACTORS INFLUENCING ITS OCCURRENCE

The incidence of chorioamnionitis in different series ranges from 5 to 49 per cent.[2] This wide range may be caused by variations in the criteria used for detection of the condition and a number of other factors which influence the occurrence of infection. The incidence is directly related to the duration of rupture of the membranes before delivery, and may double in cases in which the membranes are ruptured for more than 24 hours. The condition is also known to occur more frequently in populations of low socioeconomic status. Therefore, the incidence of chorioamnionitis reported in a particular study may be influenced by both obstetric and social factors.

The close association between duration of rupture of membranes and incidence of chorioamnionitis emphasizes the important role of the membranes as a physical barrier to ascending infection. Chorioamnionitis does occasionally develop in patients with intact membranes. In such cases infection may have gained entry through an area of devitalized membranes in the region of the cervical os; such areas of degeneration do not always result in premature membrane rupture.[24]

In recent years there has been increasing interest in the possible role of an antibacterial factor in the amniotic fluid as a defense against ascending infections. The phosphate concentration, level of zinc, and an organic component of the amniotic fluid, possibly a peptide, are all concerned in the bacteriostatic effect of normal amniotic fluid.[25] It has been suggested that zinc deficiency could underlie the high incidence of amniotic infection in some low socioeconomic groups.[26]

HEMATOGENOUS INFECTIONS

These are recognized relatively seldom in the human placenta, although infection by this route has been reported for a considerable range of organisms.

MORPHOLOGICAL CHANGES

Hematogenous infections characteristically involve the placental villi rather than the membranes. The usual form of lesion is a villitis. This involves purely the fetal villi, which may show focal infiltration by inflammatory cells with necrosis, granular tissue and fibroblastic proliferation or stromal fibrosis, according to the

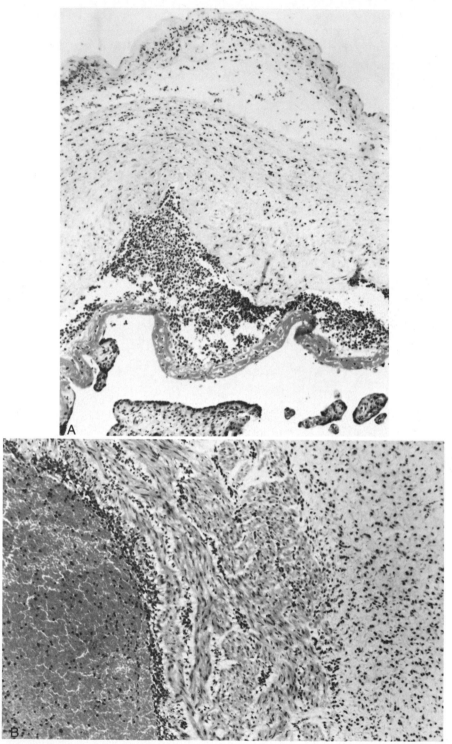

Figure 4–26. *A*, Chorionic plate showing an acute chorioamnionitis. H and E × 150. Masses of polymorphonuclear leukocytes enmeshed in fibrin are present in the intervillous space, in addition to those infiltrating all layers of the chorion and amnion. The amniotic epithelium is partly necrotic. *B*, Umbilical vein wall from the same case, showing polymorphonuclear leukocytes throughout vessel wall and within adjacent Wharton's jelly. H and E × 150.

stage to which the lesion has evolved. Specific features are seen in a number of hematogenous infections. An excellent and well-illustrated review is provided by Blanc.[23]

BACTERIAL INFECTIONS

Pyogenic and Enteric Organisms. In the rare cases in which the common gram-positive or gram-negative organisms reach the placenta by the hematogenous route, they produce septic infarcts and intervillous thrombi with focal perivillous and villous inflammatory changes.

Treponema pallidum. Syphilis is associated with a large placenta with swollen edematous villi, a focal villitis (often containing plasma cells) and proliferative endarteritis and perivasculitis of the fetal stem arteries (Fig. 4–27).

Listeria monocytogenes. This infection may also reach the placenta by the ascending route. Multiple minute white or gray lesions are seen within the parenchyma. These consist of microabscesses with a histological appearance similar to that of the lesions found in other fetal organs (see Chapter 9). Masses of necrotic villi and a meshwork of intervillous fibrin and inflammatory material may be seen in addition.

Mycobacterium tuberculosis. This may present in the form of miliary tubercles or there may be confluent caseous foci.

VIRAL INFECTIONS

Rubella. In the acute stage of the infection there is a focal necrotizing villitis and a necrotizing endarteritis of the fetal vessels. The villous stroma may be edematous or hypercellular with prominent Hofbauer cells which contain eosin-

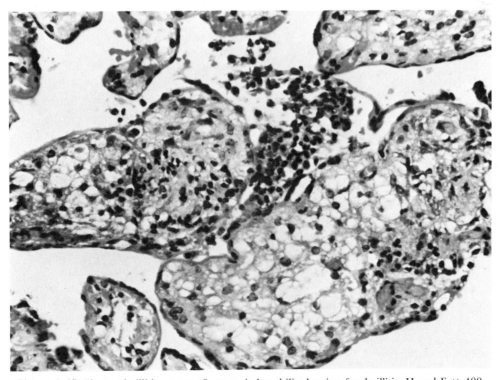

Figure 4–27. Placental villi in a case of congenital syphilis showing focal villitis. H and E × 400.

ophilic granules within their cytoplasm. Eosinophilic inclusion bodies may also be present within the endothelial cells. At a later stage the placenta may show scattered fibrotic villi or may contain a number of persistent active lesions. Many placentae from which rubella virus is isolated show no morphological abnormality.

Cytomegalovirus. Macroscopically the placenta may appear normal, but is sometimes bulky and edematous. At histological level there is a villitis in which lymphocyte or plasma cells infiltrate around the vessels in a characteristic fashion. Focal or generalized villous edema is seen in some instances. Cytomegalovirus inclusion bodies may be found, but seldom in large numbers. If present, they are usually seen in the endothelial cells of the fetal villi.

Other Viral Infections. Recognizable placental abnormalities have been reported in cases of infection by vaccinia, variola minor, varicella and herpes simplex. Details are discussed by Fox[2] and Blanc.[23]

PARASITIC AND PROTOZOAL INFECTIONS

Toxoplasma gondii. The placenta may appear either normal or large. The range of histological appearance of the villi is similar to that seen in infection by cytomegalovirus. The intervillous space may contain nodular masses of histiocytes. Encysted forms of Toxoplasma are seen most frequently in the chorionic plate.

Malaria. The main features include massive numbers of histocytes in the intervillous space, deposition of pigment in the placental parenchyma and sometimes a mild focal lymphocytic and histiocytic villitis (Fig. 4–28). The parasites can often be detected in the maternal blood in the intervillous space.

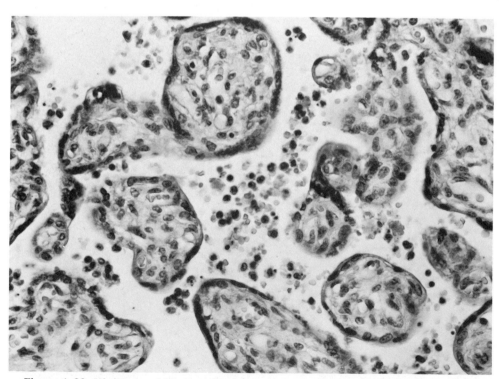

Figure 4–28. Histiocytes within intervillous space in a case of maternal malaria associated with death of the infant. H and E × 400. (Section provided by Dr. H. Platt. Cons. Chem. Path., Basingstoke District Hospital, Basingstoke, Hampshire.)

PLACENTAL TUMORS

PRIMARY TUMORS

TUMORS OF THE TROPHOBLAST

Hydatidiform Mole, Choriocarcinoma. With rare exceptions these are not conditions encountered in perinatal pathology and will not be described here. A good recent account is given by Elston.[27]

NONTROPHOBLASTIC TUMORS

Chorioangioma (Hemangioma). This should probably be regarded as a hamartoma rather than a true neoplasm.[2] The lesions are found in about 1 per cent of placentae. They may appear as single or multiple nodules varying in diameter from a few millimeters to several centimeters. Commonly the tumor appears as a well-circumscribed round red mass abutting the chorionic plate. Larger tumors may protrude from the fetal surface as plum-coloured masses or be separate from the placenta and attached only by a vascular pedicle. On histologic examination, the appearance varies from a cellular mesenchymal pattern with poorly formed vessels through an angiomatous pattern with capilliary-like vessels within a loose fibrous stroma to a degenerated pattern with myxoid, hyalinized or necrotic appearance (Fig. 4–29). Large chorioangiomas are associated with hydramnios and occasionally with fetal cardiomegaly, fetal edema or severe fetal anemia. The fetal edema is apparently due to hypoalbuminemia, resulting from protein leakage from the vessels of the hemangioma, and the fetal anemia has been attributed to damage to the red cells traversing the tumor vessel network. Thrombocytopenia with evidence of disseminated intravascular coagulation has been recorded (see Chapter 20).

Placental Teratoma. This is a very rare condition (see Fox[2]).

SECONDARY TUMORS

Metastases to the placenta have been reported in a number of cases of malignant neoplasms of the mother.[2] The tumor most frequently concerned is malignant melanoma. Others have been carcinomas of breast, bronchus and gastrointestinal tract. In instances of metastasis from a fetal neuroblastoma the placenta may be bulky and the villous vessels plugged by masses of tumor cells, although the villous stroma is not invaded.[2] Placental villous involvement may occur also in fetal leukemia.

THE UMBILICAL CORD

LENGTH OF THE CORD

The average length of the umbilical cord is 54 to 61 cm.[2] Cord lengths of 32 cm or less occur in less than 1 per cent of births and are regarded as abnormally short because they may be expected to interfere with normal vertex delivery. Birth asphyxia developing in such cases is usually attributed to excessive traction on the cord during descent of the fetus. A length of 100 cm is usually regarded as excessively long and is found in approximately 0.5 per cent of births. A very long umbilical cord is thought to predispose to knotting torsion and prolapse. It might also be expected to limit the efficiency of fetal placental perfusion.

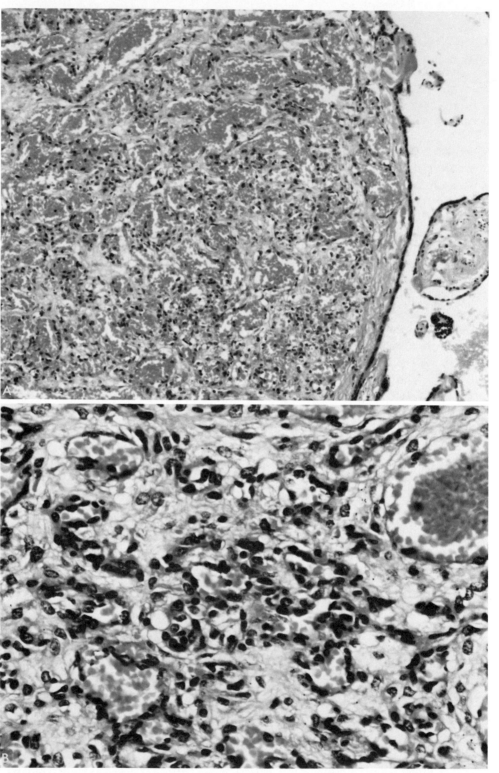

Figure 4–29. *A*, Chorioangioma of angiomatous pattern with dilated vessels within a loose fibrous stroma. H and E × 150. *B*, Another chorioangioma showing thin-walled vessels within a mesenchymal stroma. H and E × 400.

CONSTITUENTS OF THE CORD

The normal cord contains two umbilical arteries and a single umbilical vein. The umbilical arteries regularly communicate with each other close to the placental surface. There may sometimes be supernumerary vessels and the two umbilical arteries occasionally fuse near the cord insertion. In addition, vestigial remnants of allantoic and omphalomesenteric ducts may be found on microscopy. The former appear as a solid cord or duct centrally between the umbilical arteries and the latter as a duct lined by cuboidal or columnar epithelium near the cord margin. A persistent patent urachus may extend into the proximal end of the cord and is occasionally associated with a giant umbilical cord.[28]

SINGLE UMBILICAL ARTERY

This condition occurs in 0.2 to 1.0 per cent of births in different series.[2] An increased frequency is established for cases of maternal diabetes and a lower frequency has been found in United States blacks than in whites. The condition can arise either as a primary aplasia or as a secondary atrophy during development. In the latter instance the second artery is represented by a solid cord. The main importance of single umbilical artery is to heighten suspicion of the possible occurrence of other anomalies in the living infant. The incidence of associated anomalies recognizable at birth is 25 to 50 per cent in most series. The anomalies found may involve any system and are frequently multiple. Occult anomalies may become apparent on follow-up of infants with single umbilical artery thought to be otherwise normal at birth.

VELAMENTOUS INSERTION

In this condition the umbilical vessels are inserted into the membranes and run for a distance between the amnion and chorion before entering the placental tissue. The anomaly carries the danger for the fetus that the unprotected vessels may become torn during delivery with resultant severe fetal hemorrhage. The danger is greatest if the vessels traverse the cervical os (vasa praevia). Tears of the fetal vessels of this type have a perinatal mortality rate of 60 to 70 per cent.[2] However, in most cases of velamentous insertion, labor and delivery are normal and the infant is healthy.

OTHER CORD LESIONS

True knots occur in the cord in less than 1 per cent of cases and must be distinguished from "false knots" caused by local dilatation of umbilical vessels or masses of Wharton's jelly.[2] True knots may cause fetal distress by slow tightening before labor or acute tightening during delivery. Examination of a tight knot should show grooving of the cord and constriction of the umbilical vessels in long-standing cases, and edema, congestion or thrombosis in more acute ones. It is probably not justifiable to attribute fetal asphyxia to the presence of a knot in the absence of such changes.

Umbilical cord torsion has been reported as a cause of fetal death and is seen most frequently at the fetal end of the cord. If the torsion occurred antemortem the cord should remain twisted after separation of the fetus from the placenta and will be congested and edematous. Thrombosis of the cord vessels is rare except as an association of conditions such as knot formation or torsion. Other uncommon lesions include rupture, strictures and hematomas of the cord. These and several rare tumors are discussed by Fox.[2]

LESIONS OF THE PLACENTAL MEMBRANES

SQUAMOUS METAPLASIA OF THE AMNION

This is seen in the form of raised gray or white plaques, usually only a few millimeters in diameter, which can be dislodged from the amnion with difficulty. Histologically the lesions consist of stratified squamous epithelial cells. The only importance of squamous metaplasia is the need to distinguish it from amnion nodosum.

AMNION NODOSUM

This consists of multiple slightly raised round or oval plaques or nodules on the fetal placental surface. They are usually only a few millimeters in diameter, have a shiny surface and leave a depression if picked off. On histologic examination the nodules consist of amorphous granular material containing embedded squamous epithelial cells, cell remnants and sometimes fragments of hair (Fig. 4–30). The lesions are generally accepted as representing deposits of vernix caseosa that have become organized. The condition is seen in cases of oligohydramnios caused by extramembranous pregnancy, renal agenesis or obstruction of the fetal lower urinary tract.

PRACTICAL VALUE OF PLACENTAL EXAMINATION

In theory the placenta provides a large mass of predominantly fetal tissue. This should allow diagnosis of infection or provide an explanation for unexplained asphyxia or impairment in fetal growth.

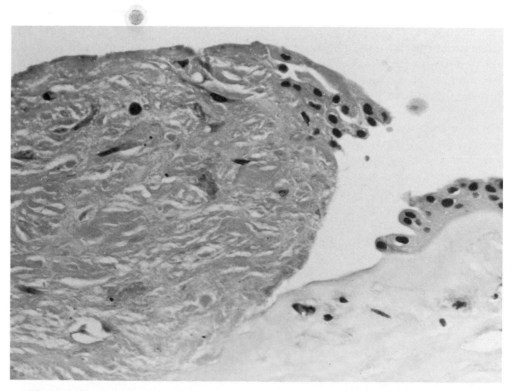

Figure 4–30. Amnion nodosum in a case of severe renal cystic dysplasia, H and E × 400. The lesion is composed of amorphous granular debris with embedded epithelial squames.

If the baby is born dead or dies in the early neonatal period there is no doubt that placental examination is an important part of the autopsy. In this case maximum information is being sought about the pathological factors concerned with perinatal death. Documentation of the presence or absence of almost any of the pathological lesions discussed in this chapter may be essential in the process of unraveling the sequence of events that ended in death of the fetus or infant. The recognition of multiple infarcts and hematomas provides good evidence that death was caused by the effects on uteroplacental circulation of maternal pre-eclampsia. The demonstration of a circumvallate placenta with a small sac and amnion nodosum may provide important evidence for extramembranous pregnancy and explanation for fetal lung hypoplasia in a case in which the history of prolonged amniotic fluid leakage was equivocal. The presence of a completely normal, healthy placenta in association with a well-nourished infant who died during labor may direct attention toward obstetric procedures and modes of acute asphyxia or traumatic injury rather than an underlying defect in placental function. The only diagnosis of a totally unexpected fetal condition I have made as a result of histological examination of the placenta was that of a storage disease (see p. 72 and Chapter 19).

If the baby is born alive, the value of placental examination is by no means so clear-cut; a practical decision has to be made as to how much time should be devoted to this activity in a busy pathology service.

Examination of the placenta of infants recognized to be malformed, edematous or grossly anemic at birth is certainly justifiable. In a significant proportion of such cases a morphological lesion of the placenta can be recognized as a cause—or major indication of the underlying cause—of the infant's condition. In the same group would come placentae of cases recognized as involving grossly abnormal amniotic fluid volumes, polyhydramnios or oligohydramnios.

In the low birth weight infant the practical questions that placental examination might answer include the nature of the process leading to fetal growth retardation and the occurrence of infection in association with preterm birth. However, useful answers will be obtained in relatively few instances. The demonstration of infarcts and histological evidence of villous ischemia in the placenta of a small for dates infant may provide supporting evidence that uteroplacental ischemia was indeed the process which limited fetal growth. The physical characteristics of the infant and the maternal obstetric history would in most cases have already caused this to be accepted as the most likely explanation. The absence of appropriate placental pathology in such a case would be unlikely to influence obstetric decisions on management of a subsequent pregnancy or pediatric handling of the infant.

Evidence of a chronic infective cause for fetal growth failure such as cytomegalovirus or toxoplasmosis may be obtained in a few instances. These diagnoses can normally be made with greater accuracy and as speedily on appropriate samples from the infant as they can from the placenta. If an infant is born unexpectedly and is severely growth retarded or has unusual features such as a purpuric rash, examination of the placenta may be useful. Evidence of ascending infection may be obtained from the placenta in a high proportion of preterm births in some populations but will give little indication as to whether an individual infant is infected and thus requires antibiotic therapy. The same consideration applies to examination of placentae, umbilical cords or membranes from patients with prolonged rupture of the membranes. Chorioamnionitis is too frequent to be used as an indication for antibiotic therapy in the newborn infant.

Examination of the fused twin placenta can allow diagnosis of monozygous twins in those instances in which there is a single chorion (60 to 88 per cent of monozygous twin pairs). Routine determination of the occurrence and type of vascular anastomoses in such placentae seems of little help because the occurrence and severity of twin-twin transfusion is assessed and managed on the basis of the findings in the infants.

Routine placental examination in cases of known maternal disease such as diabetes mellitus or tuberculosis seems of little value; the effects of these conditions on fetal health are more readily assessed by study of the infant directly. The same consideration applies to pre-eclampsia.

In my view, cases in which the placenta should be sent to the pathology laboratory for examination include the following, *in order of priority:*

1. Perinatal deaths.
2. Cases of recognizable malformation, edema or anemia.
3. Extremes of amniotic fluid volume.
4. Severe fetal growth retardation (definition depends on population served).
5. Unexpected severe birth asphyxia.
6. Preterm birth (less than 36 weeks' gestation).
7. Fused placentae from like-sexed multiple pregnancy.
8. Other conditions in which the obstetrician recognizes an abnormal placenta.

Which cases are examined in a particular institution will depend on a number of considerations, including the academic interest and expertise in this field of study and the precise balance between the pathological facilities available and demands on the service.

In order to ensure that most placentae from neonatal deaths will be available for study, a sensible plan used in some centers is for all placentae from other than completely normal spontaneous vertex deliveries to be stored in labeled plastic bags in a special refrigerator for a period of one week (one container for each day) so that they may be retrieved at a later date if needed.

REFERENCES

1. Wynn, R. M.: Principles of placentation and early human placental development. *In* Gruenwald, P. (ed.): The Placenta and its Maternal Supply Line. Lancaster, M.T.P., 1975, pp. 18–34.
2. Fox, H.: Pathology of the placenta. London, W. B. Saunders Ltd., 1978.
3. Wilkin, P.: Pathologie du placenta. Paris, Masson et Cie, 1965.
4. Wigglesworth, J. S.: Vascular anatomy of the human placenta and its significance for placental pathology. J. Obstet. Gynaecol. Br. Cwlth. 76:979–989, 1969.
5. Brosens, I., Robertson, W. B., and Dixon, H. G.: The physiological response of the vessels of the placental bed to normal pregnancy. J. Pathol. Bacteriol. 93:569–579, 1967.
6. Torpin, R., and Hart, B. F.: Placenta bilobata. Am. J. Obstet. Gynecol. 42:38–49, 1941.
7. Kohler, H. G., Peel, K. R., and Hoan, R. A.: Extra-membranous pregnancy and amenorrhoea. J. Obstet. Gynaecol. Br. Cwlth. 70:809–812, 1970.
8. Benirschke, K., and Driscoll, S. G.: The pathology of the human placenta. Berlin, Springer-Verlag, 1967.
9. Strong, J. S., and Corney, G.: The placenta in twin pregnancy. Oxford, Pergamon Press, 1967.
10. Wharton, B., Edwards, J. H., and Cameron, A. H.: Monoamniotic twins. J. Obstet. Gynaecol. Br. Cwlth. 75:158–163, 1968.
11. Conway, C. F.: Transfusion syndrome in multiple pregnancy. Obstet. Gynecol. 23:745–751, 1964.
12. Aherne, W., Strong, J. S., and Corney, G.: The structure of the placenta in the twin transfusion syndrome. Biologia Neonatorum 12:121–135, 1968.
13. Wigglesworth, J. S.: Morphological variations in the insufficient placenta. J. Obstet. Gynaecol. Br. Cwlth. 71:871–884, 1964.
14. Fox, H.: The significance of placental infarction in perinatal morbidity and mortality. Biologia Neonatorum 11:87–105, 1967.
15. Wigglesworth, J. S.: The Langhans layer in late pregnancy: a histological study of normal and abnormal cases. J. Obstet. Gynaecol. Br. Cwlth. 69:355–365, 1962.

16. Fox, H.: The villous cytotrophoblast as an index of placental ischaemia. J. Obstet. Gynaecol. Br. Cwlth. *71*:885–893, 1964.
17. Fox, H.: Effect of hypoxia on trophoblast in organ culture. Am. J. Obstet. Gynecol. *107*:1058–1064, 1970.
18. Altshuler, G., Russell, P., and Ermocilla, R.: The placental pathology of small-for-gestational age infants. Am. J. Obstet. Gynecol. *121*:351–359, 1975.
19. Gruenwald, P.: Abnormality of placental vascularity in relation to intrauterine deprivation and retardation of fetal growth: significance of avascular chorionic villi. N. Y. State J. Med. *61*:1508–1513, 1961.
20. Haust, M. D.: Maternal diabetes mellitus—effects on the fetus and placenta. *In* Naeye, R. L., Kissane, J. M., and Kaufman, N. (eds.): Perinatal Diseases. Baltimore, Williams & Wilkins, 1981, pp. 201–285.
21. Powell, H. C., Benirschke, K., Favara, B. E., and Pflueger, O. H.: Foamy changes of placental cells in fetal storage disorders. Virchows Arch. Pathol. Anat. *369*:191–196, 1976.
22. Haust, M. D., and Landing, B. H.: Histochemical studies in Hurler's disease. A new method for localization of acid mucopolysaccharide, and an analysis of lead acetate "fixation." J. Histochem. Cytochem. *9*:79–86, 1961.
23. Blanc, W. A.: Pathology of the placenta, membranes, and umbilical cord in bacterial, fungal and viral infections in man. *In* Naeye, R. L., Kissane, J. M., and Kaufman, N. (eds.): Perinatal Diseases. Baltimore, Williams & Wilkins, 1981, pp. 67–132.
24. Bourne, G.: The human amnion and chorion. London, Lloyd-Luke, 1962.
25. Schlievert, P., Johnson, W., and Galask, R. P.: Amniotic fluid antibacterial mechanisms: newer concepts. Semin. Perinatol. *1*:59–70, 1977.
26. Applebaum, P. C., Holloway, Y., Ross, S. M., and Dhupelia, I.: The effect of amniotic fluid on bacterial growth in three population groups. Am. J. Obstet. Gynecol. *128*:868–871, 1977.
27. Elston, C. W.: Trophoblastic tumours of the placenta. *In* Fox, H. (ed.): Pathology of the Placenta. London, W. B. Saunders Ltd., 1978, pp. 368–425.
28. Chantler, C., Baum, J. D., Wigglesworth, J. S., and Scopes, J. W.: Giant umbilical cord associated with a patent urachus and fused umbilical arteries. J. Obstet. Gynaecol. Br. Cwlth. *76*:273–274, 1969.

Chapter Five

The Macerated Stillborn Fetus

The macerated stillborn fetus has been a neglected topic in perinatal pathology. Since such fetuses represent at least one third of all perinatal deaths, they clearly deserve more attention than they have been accorded in recent literature on fetal pathology. There are a number of basic practical questions to which clear answers are required. The pathologist needs to decide how much time should be devoted to the study of apparently normally formed macerated stillborn infants, whether anything can be gained from histological studies, whether bacteriology can yield positive information and how much can be learned from study of the placenta.

In fact, the basic problem is the same as that of perinatal pathology in general: to acquire the maximum information, often from minimal lesions, and with limited knowledge of preceding events. The difficulties are compounded in the antepartum stillborn by the delay between fetal death and delivery. In order to determine whether intrauterine growth was normal in such a case it is necessary to relate the pattern of growth and maturation of the fetus to the time of fetal death rather than the time of delivery. This is not an easy task because there may be limited information on the time at which the fetus died, the fetal tissues may have lost weight following fetal death, and the maceration process may obscure structural details on which assessment of maturation might be based. It can also be difficult to distinguish between pathological changes which preceded fetal death and the autolytic changes following death.

Another factor which should not be underestimated is the physically unattractive nature of the macerated fetus. I have always found it easy to devise excellent reasons for not studying such cases with quite as much attention as they merit. It is only by recognizing and overcoming such basic reactions that it is possible to get the most information from autopsies on macerated stillborn infants.

BACKGROUND DATA

The need for full information on the obstetric and medical history, and details of the current pregnancy up to the time of fetal death, is similar to that required for other types of perinatal death. Important additional details needed are the time at which fetal movements ceased and when the fetal heart could no longer be heard. The former is subjective information, but studies on the use of fetal kick charts to provide evidence of severe fetal asphyxia have shown that most pregnant women can recognize fetal movements accurately.[1] Cessation of recognizable fetal movements is usually followed by fetal death within 24 hours. The time at which the fetal heart was no longer heard by medical or nursing staff can sometimes be in error. The error may involve mistaken identification either of a maternal tachycardia as a fetal cardiac impulse or of a fetal bradycardia as a maternal pulse. Problems may also arise in recognition of the time of death of one of a pair of twins. The use of modern electronic recording aids should obviate most of these errors.

THE DEVELOPMENT OF MACERATION

The first sign of maceration is separation of the epidermis from the dermis on applying oblique pressure—skin slipping.[2,3] This may be present by about six hours after death and is to be expected if the infant has been dead in utero for 12 hours or more. By 24 hours after death there may be collection of fluid beneath the epidermis to form bullae. If these bullae are disrupted during birth, or on handling of the dead fetus, large areas of the skin may separate and leave a raw weeping body surface. Progressive hemolysis results in a uniform deep reddish-purple discoloration of all internal tissues. There is exudation of fluid and hemolyzed blood into pleural, pericardial and peritoneal cavities. Similar exudation of fluid into the connective tissues may make the fetus appear generally but variably edematous. These changes are accompanied by progressive softening of all connective tissues and internal organs.

After several days the dura gradually becomes separated from the cranial bones and the fetal skull becomes readily distorted and collapsed. If the fetus has been dead in utero for five to seven days or more, it may be possible to lift one of the parietal bones out cleanly after reflecting the scalp and incising the dura. By this stage the brain is semiliquid and cannot be removed intact from the cranium (unless removed with the dura) (Fig. 5–1). If the dead fetus is retained in utero for more than a week there is gradual fading of the tissue from reddish purple to a yellowish-brown color.

The rate and nature of the process varies with the gestation of the infant and the underlying pathological condition. The tissues of immature growth-retarded infants may change to a brown color and begin to dry up within a few days owing to relatively low soft-tissue mass and low blood volume. The extreme example of this situation is the fetus papyraceous (Fig. 5–2). In the tissue of hydropic infants, on the other hand, the edematous changes of maceration develop early and advance rapidly. Thus it is not possible to time the changes of maceration with any degree of precision. However, it is possible to recognize gross discrepancies between the time at which the fetus was said to have died and the extent of maceration. An infant with skin slipping and normal coloration of internal organs is unlikely to have died more than 48 hours before delivery, whereas an infant with separation of the dura from the cranial bones and hemoglobin-stained effusions of serous cavities is unlikely to have been dead in utero for less than five days.

VALUE OF POSTMORTEM EXAMINATION OF A MACERATED INFANT

Weight and external length measurements can be carried out in the normal way and the figures compared with those expected for the gestational age at which the infant died. The longer the fetus has been dead in utero, the less reliable such figures will be. Head circumference cannot be measured accurately once the cranial bones separate. However, in many macerated infants such measurements can be made satisfactorily and can give useful information on the adequacy of fetal growth for gestation. If both crown-heel length and body weight are low for the gestational age at which the infant died, but head circumference is greater than crown-rump length (see p. 30), the findings are unlikely to be caused by

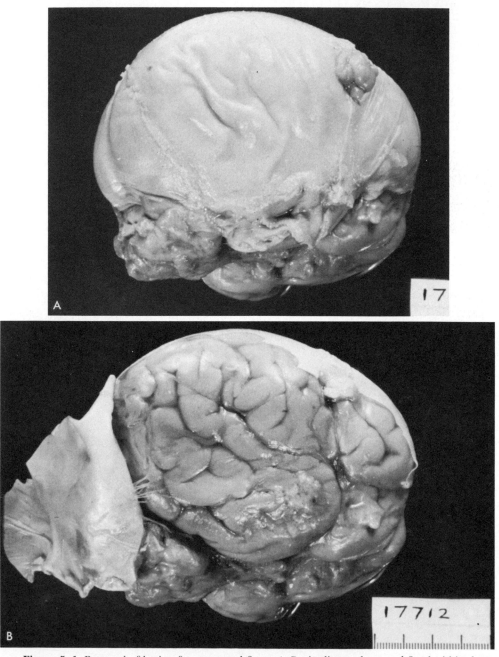

Figure 5–1. Removal of brain of a macerated fetus. *A*, Brain dissected out and fixed within dura; *B*, Convolutional pattern of brain seen on reflecting the dura. This fetus had been dead in utero for about 8 days.

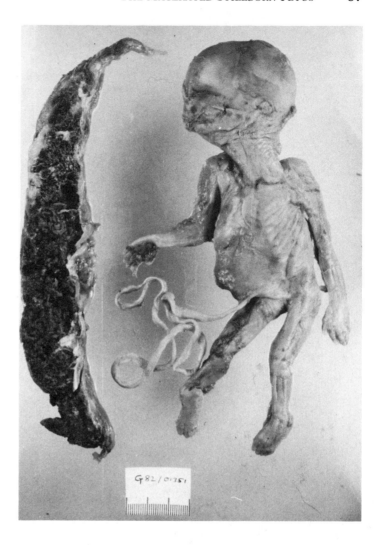

Figure 5–2. Fetus papyraceous, born as a twin to a healthy infant at term. This fetus had been dead in utero for about 4 months.

postmortem autolysis and would suggest the probability of fetal growth retardation (of malnutrition type) or possibly a malformation syndrome involving hydrocephalus.

If the fetus has been dead in utero for less than 48 hours there will usually be little difference in the appearance of the internal organs apart from early softening of the brain and liver. In these infants the entire autopsy can be carried out in the usual way. If there is established maceration it may not be possible to make an exhaustive examination of the brain, since the brain will disintegrate when the attempt is made to remove it. However, it is quite easy in such cases to make a rough assessment of gestational age from the gyral convolutional pattern. This information can be used in conjunction with the external measurements and the weight and appearance of the other internal organs in order to build up a picture of the growth characteristics of the macerated fetus at the time of death. Marked deviation in size of individual organs is readily recognizable in the macerated fetus, as with lung hypoplasia in an infant who dies in utero after prolonged rupture of the membranes. The major internal organs should certainly be weighed whenever possible.

Gross abnormalities which may be associated with intrauterine death can usually be recognized readily on external examination of the fetus. Many are illustrated throughout texts such as Potter and Craig.[2] Occult malformations involving organs such as heart, lungs and kidneys are unlikely to cause intrauterine death, but are easy to diagnose on dissecting the internal organs. Some difficulty may be experienced with the brain or abdominal organs, such as the intestinal tract, which are unduly friable.* It is important not to mistake distortions of the autolyzed fetal tissues for congenital malformations. The collapsed floppy head and distortions of the limbs caused by the lax connective tissues have both been responsible for errors of this type, usually made by staff in the delivery room. Such errors may well go uncorrected in the absence of a formal postmortem examination.

The characteristic features of a number of pathological conditions may be discernible in the macerated fetus. Thus in a pair of twins the differences in growth and hemoglobin level between the donor and recipient of a monozygous twin transfusion syndrome may be recognized if they both die in utero and are examined together. The organ changes of rhesus isoimmunization may be apparent in the macerated infant. When macerated fetuses are examined, chronic intrauterine infection should always be considered. I have diagnosed cases of cytomegalovirus infection and listeriosis which were clinically unsuspected. Enlargement of liver or spleen in association with an atrophic thymus and small adrenals is probably the most useful general indication of such infections.

THE PLACENTA IN INTRAUTERINE DEATH

Following death of the fetus a series of characteristic changes take place in the placental villi owing to cessation of the fetal villous circulation. Trophoblast changes include an increase in the number of syncytial knots, proliferation of the villous cytotrophoblast cells and thickening of the trophoblast basement membrane. At the same time the villous stroma becomes increasingly dense and fibrotic and the villous fetal vessels undergo progressive sclerosis. There is also marked fibromuscular sclerosis of the fetal stem arteries. The changes appear quite rapidly and are advanced by about five days after fetal death (Fig. 5–3). At macroscopic level these alterations are marked only by a variable pallor of the villous parenchyma.

Although it is important to take the changes resulting from fetal death into account when examining the placenta of a stillborn infant, it is equally important to realize that such changes will not influence the appearance or significance of macroscopic lesions such as infarcts and hematomas (p. 61). Indeed the most extreme and extensive examples of placental vascular pathology are to be seen in the macerated stillbirth group. Marked variations in placental size can also be recognized, although the cessation of the fetal villous circulation following intrauterine death may be expected to cause some decrease in placental weight. The various types of cord accident such as tight knots and torsion (p. 79) should be considered as possibilities in this group of cases, although they are not common findings.

If the fetus has been dead for five days or more, the changes of fetal death render interpretation of histology very difficult. Confirmation of macroscopic lesions remains possible, and fetal infections may still present characteristic

---

*In a macerated hydropic infant examined at Hammersmith recently, it was possible to diagnose intrauterine heart failure resulting from arteriovenous aneurysm of the vein of Galen.

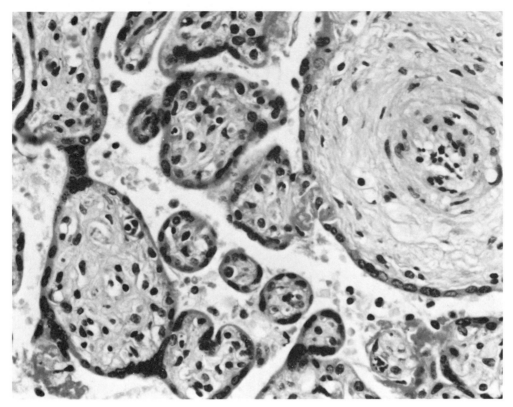

Figure 5–3. Placental villi, showing early sclerosis of fetal vessels in intrauterine death. H and E × 400. This fetus died about 7 days before delivery.

changes. Histological examination of the placenta is unlikely to allow diagnosis of the cause of a macerated stillbirth in which macroscopic study has shown no characteristic abnormality.

MICROBIOLOGY

The idea of screening all macerated stillborn infants for infection does not appeal to me as a worthwhile use of resources, although it may be justifiable for purposes of specific research surveys. In my opinion, bacterial or viral cultures should be carried out only in those cases in which macroscopic study indicates the probability of an infection. I have seldom recognized histological evidence of an infection in cases in which there was no sign of it on gross examination.

HISTOLOGY OF FETAL ORGANS

Histological examination of the lungs should be carried out in all cases. Pulmonary structure is well preserved for several days after fetal death. Evidence of a terminal asphyxial episode with inhalation of meconium or amniotic material is seen in about 50 per cent of intrauterine deaths. It may not have been possible to recognize such changes at gross level. Intrauterine infection may show characteristic lesions in the lungs when the histology of other organs has been obscured by autolytic changes. Examination of other tissues can be helpful but becomes less

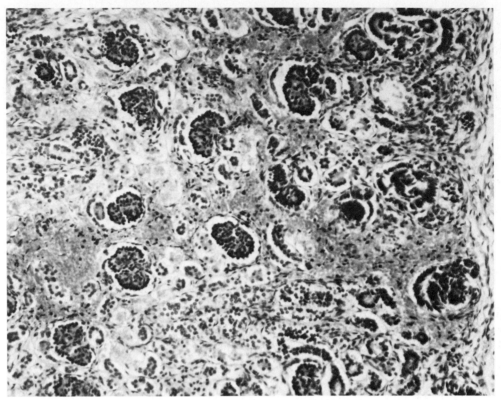

Figure 5–4. Kidney of a fetus of 32 weeks' gestation who had died about 18 hours before delivery. H and E × 120. Focal necrosis with loss of nuclear staining in proximal tubules might be interpreted as an autolytic change, but the characteristic interstitial hemorrhage indicates that this is an early stage of renal cortical necrosis.

so as the maceration process advances after the fetus has been dead for two to three days. It is possible, and may be helpful, to assess renal maturity by the presence or absence of the nephrogenic zone. If the baby has been dead for a relatively short time it is sometimes possible to recognize pathological changes which preceded fetal death, such as renal cortical necrosis (Fig. 5–4), despite the presence of superimposed postmortem autolysis.

The extent to which it is sometimes possible to recognize the characteristic macroscopic and histological patterns of a specific process in the macerated fetus is illustrated with respect to a case of rhabdomyoma (Fig. 5–5). Another example of a rare condition diagnosed on examination of the macerated fetus and placenta is congenital leukemia.[4]

CONCLUSIONS

Macerated stillborn infants should certainly be submitted to postmortem examination. The pathologist must not expect to find a pathological cause for death in all of them. In many he will be able to establish the mode of death or the type of underlying process (e.g., acute asphyxia in a well-grown fetus or severe fetal growth failure). In a few there will be an unsuspected cause of death such as chronic intrauterine infection or a recognizable cord accident or some specific fetal disorder.

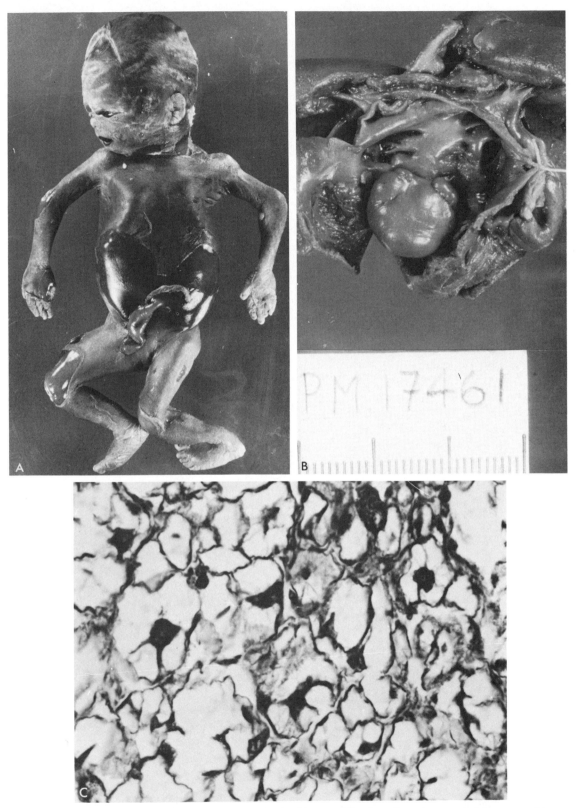

Figure 5–5. *A*, A macerated fetus who had been dead in utero for about 3 weeks. *B*, A large tumor arising from the region on the anterior leaflet of the mitral valve. *C*, Histological appearance of tumor. H and E × 300. The characteristic pattern of congenital rhabdomyoma with spider cells is readily seen despite the advanced autolysis. Permission for examination of this case was sought only because the tumor was seen on ultrasound examination in utero.

Many intrauterine fetal deaths will remain unexplained despite his best efforts. However, as pointed out in the opening chapter, negative findings can be as helpful to parents and clinicians as positive ones, although they appear unexciting to the pathologist.

REFERENCES

1. Pearson, J. F., and Weaver, J. B.: Fetal activity and wellbeing: An evaluation. Br. Med. J. *1*:1305–1307, 1976.
2. Potter, E. L., and Craig, J. M.: Pathology of the Fetus and the Infant. Chicago, Year Book Medical Publishers, 1976, pp. 84–85.
3. Strachan, G. I.: The pathology of foetal maceration. Br. Med. J. *2*:80–82, 1922.
4. Gray, E.: Histochemical and electron microscopy findings in two cases of congenital leukaemia in stillborn infants. Pediatr. Pathol. 1983, in press.

Chapter Six

Intrapartum and Early Neonatal Death: The Interaction of Asphyxia and Trauma

Infants who die during or after asphyxial and traumatic deliveries represent one of the most important types of perinatal deaths to be studied pathologically. The importance is because of the potentially avoidable nature of the lesions rather than their intrinsic pathological interest. Indeed, the organ changes may be banal or difficult to recognize.

Fresh stillborn and neonatal deaths at term are of particular concern to obstetric and pediatric staff. However, it is equally important to recognize the roles of asphyxia and trauma in contributing to mortality and morbidity in preterm infants. Very few of the asphyxial and traumatic lesions seen at autopsy in the perinatal period are necessarily fatal. Similar lesions can be recognized in life or may be assumed to have occurred in a large number of surviving infants. The study of the lesions of perinatal asphyxia or trauma may therefore provide information on the basis of certain types of childhood handicaps.

MECHANISMS OF BIRTH ASPHYXIA

Uteroplacental circulation and fetal oxygenation are directly influenced by the frequency and intensity of uterine contractions. Studies performed on the rhesus monkey have shown that entry of maternal blood into the intervillous space may be cut off at the height of a normal uterine contraction.[1] Any accentuation of this effect by abnormal prolongation or frequency of contractions will cause fetal asphyxia.

Fetal heart rate monitoring during labor shows a number of patterns of fetal heart rate deceleration in relation to uterine contractions.[2] A consistent slowing of fetal heart rate early in the contraction phase (early deceleration pattern) is believed to be caused by fetal head compression and is not associated with any fetal abnormality. Slowing of the fetal heart beginning near the peak of the uterine contraction and recovering slowly (late deceleration) results from impairment in uteroplacental blood flow and indicates fetal hypoxia and acidosis (Fig. 6–1). A further heart rate pattern is recognized, in which the timing of the decelerations varies from one contraction cycle to the next. This pattern, which

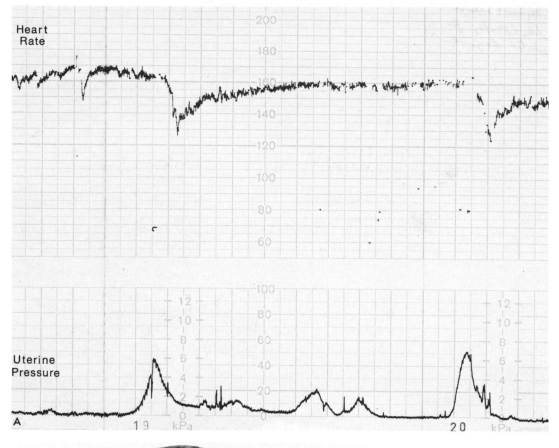

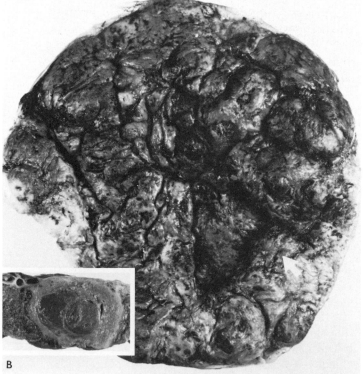

Figure 6–1. *A*, Pattern of late deceleration, recognized on antenatal attendance at 34 weeks' gestation, which prompted cesarean section. *B*, Maternal surface of the placenta (after fixation) showing a crater (arrow) due to recent retroplacental hemorrhage. Slicing the placental substance revealed multiple hematomas (inset). The mother had mild hypertension, but the infant was growth retarded and required intensive care.

has been attributed to umbilical cord compression, may also be of ominous significance for the fetus. In addition to these periodic changes in fetal heart rate occurring in response to the uterine contractions, the baseline fetal heart rate may be an indication of fetal health. In the compromised fetus there is often a loss of the normal beat-to-beat variation in this baseline fetal heart rate.

Experimental studies in the rhesus monkey indicate that maternal hypotension, maternal hypoxia, maternal psychological stress or increased intensity of uterine contractions will all cause a fall in fetal partial arterial oxygen pressure (PaO_2). Abnormal fetal heart rate tracings (late deceleration) are recorded when the PaO_2 falls below 20 mm Hg.[3]

Information about the effects of acute asphyxia on the fetus has been derived mainly from experiments in which fetal animals were studied in a warm saline environment following occlusion of the umbilical cord.[4] There is an initial short period of respiratory efforts which ends abruptly and is followed by a phase of apnea (primary apnea). There is then a period of repeated gasps which become more frequent and weaker before ceasing altogether. During the final phase of secondary or terminal apnea the blood pressure and heart rate fall rapidly and the fetus dies unless revived by mechanical ventilation with oxygen. This sequence may well be influenced in clinical situations by the occurrence of episodes of partial or intermittent prenatal asphyxia in addition to the influence of drugs.

It has been emphasized by Myers that the most important factor determining immediate perinatal survival of the asphyxiated infant is the severity of myocardial damage.[3] A newborn rhesus monkey who apparently recovers well from a prenatal asphyxial insult may go into fatal cardiogenic shock some hours later. Human infants who die in the early neonatal period from the effects of intrapartum asphyxia usually have a very low Apgar score at birth and are assumed to have been born in terminal asphyxia. However, there is an occasional infant who succumbs at some hours of age after having been thought to be entirely normal with an Apgar score of 8 to 10 at birth. These infants may perhaps have suffered myocardial damage during a prenatal asphyxial episode from which they have temporarily recovered at the time of delivery.

MATERIAL AND FETAL CONDITIONS PREDISPOSING TO BIRTH ASPHYXIA

National and local surveys of perinatal mortality and morbidity have shown a number of maternal and fetal conditions which predispose to birth asphyxia. Such factors may be separated into those present before the onset of labor and those that develop during, or in close association with, labor.

FACTORS PRECEDING LABOR

These include the extremes of maternal age or parity, prolonged pregnancy (over 42 weeks), severe maternal pre-eclampsia, the occurrence of maternal illness such as diabetes mellitus, heart disease (congenital or acquired) or severe anemia, bleeding from the placental site, fetal growth retardation, or premature rupture of the membranes.

FACTORS ARISING DURING LABOR

These include the nature of uterine action (as just discussed), drugs administered to the mother (anesthetics, barbiturates, hypotensive narcotic and oxytocic agents), abnormal presentation, prolapse of the cord and bleeding from the placental site (abruptio placentae or placenta previa).

INTERACTION OF DIFFERENT FACTORS

In an individual case a number of these factors may be linked in a variety of ways. A young primigravid mother may be at undue risk of severe pre-eclampsia with resultant fetal growth retardation. The impaired uteroplacental circulation which caused the fetal growth impairment may also place the infant at risk of asphyxia during labor. However, this risk may be enhanced by administration of sedative or antihypertensive drugs to the mother. An abnormal presentation such as transverse lie or breech presentation predisposes to cord prolapse. An increased use of anesthetic or narcotic agents may be needed to allow the obstetrical manipulations required for delivery in such a case.

RELATIONSHIP BETWEEN ASPHYXIA AND TRAUMA

Trauma is revealed in life or at postmortem examination mainly in the group of infants who were admitted to a neonatal intensive care unit with birth asphyxia or were delivered as fresh stillbirths. A primary diagnosis of intracranial birth trauma is very seldom made during life. The pathologist must expect to see infants with gross degrees of birth trauma, readily recognizable at postmortem examination, to which no reference has been made in the clinical records (Fig. 6–2). An important part of the pathologist's role is to attempt to determine the relative importance of trauma and asphyxia in contributing to death in a particular instance. The two conditions can be related in a number of possible ways.

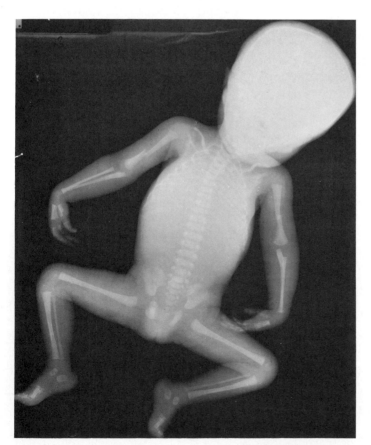

Figure 6–2. Bilateral fractures of the humeri recognized at postmortem in an infant with congenital muscular dystrophy, delivered by the breech, in whom it proved difficult to bring down the arms.

If signs of fetal asphyxia develop during labor they may provoke attempts to hasten delivery by potentially traumatic manipulations such as the application of forceps. The congested organs of the asphyxiated infant may be at increased risk of injury, and the tear of a distended asphyxial vein may cause excessive bleeding. Loss of muscle tone may result in the fetal neck becoming deflexed during descent of the head. Breech or other abnormal presentation may predispose to both asphyxia and injury. The small size of the growth-retarded fetus could predispose to malpresentation, whereas the impaired uteroplacental circulation of some of these fetuses may increase the risk of asphyxia.

It must also be remembered that trauma itself causes shock with resultant anoxic-ischemic damage to the tissues. The failure of an infant to establish respiration at birth may be the result of either severe intrapartum asphyxia with cardiovascular collapse or severe trauma with cardiovascular collapse and brain stem ischemia.

TRAUMATIC LESIONS

Traditionally the classic lesions of intracranial birth trauma such as tentorial tears and subdural hemorrhage have been associated with delivery at term. Progressive improvements in obstetric management have greatly reduced the incidence of these lesions in mature infants so that up to half of the infants who are now found to have fatal birth trauma may be of less than 37 weeks' gestation.[5] It is not possible to quote an incidence for birth trauma because some of the lesions are found only if deliberately searched for. The occurrence and importance of trauma are likely to be underdiagnosed in infants of very low birth weight. Distortion of the head at birth with development of occipital osteodiastasis or a small tentorial tear may cause such an infant to appear asphyxiated at birth. If the baby is resuscitated but subsequently dies at several days of age, the classic lesions associated with prematurity—including hyaline membrane disease of the lungs and intraventricular hemorrhage in the brain—usually overshadow those of trauma. However, it is very likely that the shock caused by the initial trauma in such a case determined the severity of the respiratory and cerebral disorders which eventually resulted in death.

CRANIAL LESIONS

Sites of such hemorrhage are shown in Figure 6–3.

EXTRACRANIAL AND EXTRADURAL HEMORRHAGE

Caput Succedaneum. This is a hemorrhagic edema involving the skin and superficial fascia which results from circulatory stasis caused by compression exerted by the uterus or cervix over the presenting part. The main importance of caput succedaneum at postmortem is to indicate to the pathologist how the infant presented.

Subaponeurotic Hemorrhage. This type of hemorrhage, also known as subgaleal hemorrhage or "severe" caput succedaneum, originates deep to the epicranial aponeurosis, a thin tendinous sheet which covers the scalp and unites the frontal and occipital bellies of the occipitofrontalis muscle. Laterally the epicranial aponeurosis is attached to the zygomatic arch, the auricular muscles and the tissues of the posterior triangle. Hemorrhage into this site occurs into a large potential space with poorly defined margins; blood may spread over the entire scalp and dissect between the muscle fibers into the subcutaneous tissue of the posterior

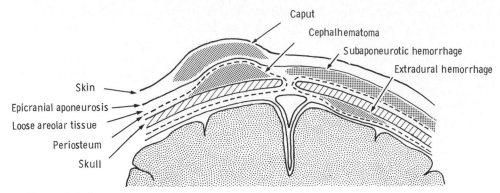

Figure 6–3. Sites of extracranial and extradural hemorrhage in the newborn. (From Pape, K. E. and Wigglesworth, J. S.: Hemorrhage, Ischemia, and the Perinatal Brain. Philadelphia, J. B. Lippincott Co., 1979.)

triangle and suboccipital regions. Massive hemorrhage into this site is occasionally seen at autopsy and may not have been recognized in life. Mild hemostatic abnormalities may be implicated in the etiology.

Cephalhematoma. This is readily distinguished at autopsy from the aforementioned lesions because bleeding in this case occurs beneath the periosteum over the skull surface and is limited peripherally by the periosteal attachments to the bone margins. Usually it involves the parietal bones and is seldom of sufficient extent to be a significant factor in fetal death.

Extradural Hemorrhage. This is usually associated with skull fracture. It is similar to cephalhematoma but involves the plane between the bone and the periosteum on the inner surface of the skull. It is usually of small extent and is not often seen at autopsy.

SKULL FRACTURE

The poorly mineralized bones of the infant skull, separated as they are by membranous sutures, allow considerable cranial distortion without fracture. The major type of fracture which may be seen at postmortem examination is a linear fracture of the parietal bones extending radially along the lines of cleavage. These are not uncommon in infants who have died following difficult breech extraction or cephalic deliveries with forceps, but are readily missed unless the posterior parts of the parietal bones are examined with care. They would be unlikely to be significant in themselves in an infant who survived. A depressed fracture of the parietal bones is occasionally seen in life. I have not encountered such a lesion at postmortem examination.

SEPARATION OF THE SQUAMOUS AND LATERAL PARTS OF THE OCCIPITAL BONE (OCCIPITAL OSTEODIASTASIS)

This is undoubtedly the most important form of disruption of the cranial bones but is consistently missed at autopsy unless specifically looked for, as described in Chapter 2. The squamous and lateral parts of the occipital bone are widely separated by cartilage until about 36 weeks' gestation and do not fuse until the second year of life (Fig. 6–4). The lower margin of the squamous occipital bone forms the posterior boundary of the foramen magnum centrally and is closely related to the occipital sinuses on each side.

Excessive pressure on the suboccipital region during birth causes traumatic separation of the cartilaginous joint between the squamous and lateral parts of the bone on one or both sides. The lower edge of the squamous occipital bone is

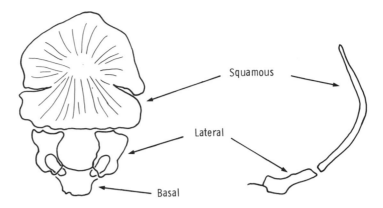

Figure 6–4. Diagram of the occipital bone at term. (From Pape, K. E. and Wigglesworth, J. S.: Hemorrhage, Ischemia, and the Perinatal Brain. Philadelphia, J. B. Lippincott Co., 1979.)

then displaced and rotated forward. In the most severe form of this injury the dura and occipital sinuses are torn, resulting in gross subdural hemorrhage in the posterior fossa, and laceration of the cerebellum (Fig. 6–5). More commonly, particularly in preterm infants, the joint displacement merely causes compression of the posterior fossa without massive subdural bleeding.

The infant is most at risk of this form of injury during vaginal breech delivery, although I have seen it following persistent occipitoposterior presentation or Kielland's rotation for transverse arrest. Occipital osteodiastasis may be seen at all gestations from 27 weeks up until term. As the extent of displacement is variable, the lesion is by no means always fatal and can be recognized on lateral skull radiographs of surviving infants. Indeed, it illustrates the type of problem which the pathologist has to assess in relation to birth trauma in general. A minor separation of the occipital bone with little displacement would be entirely innocuous. A few millimeters' difference in the severity of displacement may result in distortion and obstruction of venous sinuses in the posterior fossa or direct pressure on the cerebellum and brain stem, with rapidly fatal outcome. It has been suggested elsewhere that occipital osteodiastasis is one possible cause of ataxic cerebral palsy in infants who survive vaginal breech delivery.[5] However, no cases diagnosed in the newborn period have yet been followed up for sufficient time to recognize any sequelae.

SUBDURAL HEMORRHAGE: TEARS OF TENTORIUM AND FALX

Subdural hemorrhage usually results from tearing of the unsupported bridging veins passing between the brain and the dural sinuses. Rarely it may result from a tear of the dural folds extending into a sinus, or from laceration of a sinus by the margin of a fractured or separated skull bone.

Anatomy of the Dural Folds. The falx cerebri and the leaves of the tentorium cerebelli are two-layered structures with a radiating pattern of fibers which indicate the normal lines of stress. The dural folds are strengthened with additional bands of fibers at the free margins. It is important to remember that the falx is usually thinner than the tentorium and often has fenestrations anteriorly which should not be confused with traumatic lacerations. The relationships of the cerebral veins and venous sinuses to the dural folds are shown in Figure 6–6. The superior cerebral veins cross the subdural space (marked bridging veins in Figure 6–6) to enter the superior sagittal sinus, and the vein of Galen crosses the space to enter the straight sinus. The details of anatomy and development of these vessels are described elsewhere.[6]

Mechanisms of Injury to Veins and Subdural Folds. The fetal head is well designed to withstand evenly applied compression. Damage to bridging veins or

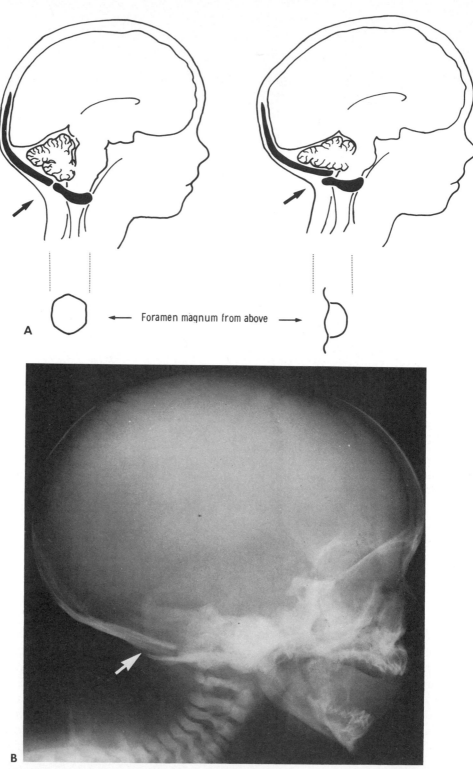

Foramen magnum from above

Figure 6–5. Occipital osteodiastasis. *A*, Mechanism of injury. (From Pape, K. E. and Wigglesworth, J. S.: Hemorrhage, Ischemia and the Perinatal Brain. Philadelphia, J. B. Lippincott Co., 1979.) *B*, Lateral skull radiograph showing occipital osteodiastasis (arrow). (From Wigglesworth, J. S. and Husemeyer, R. P.: Intracranial birth trauma in vaginal breech delivery: the continued importance of the occipital bone. Br. J. Obstet. Gynecol. *84*:684–691, 1977.)

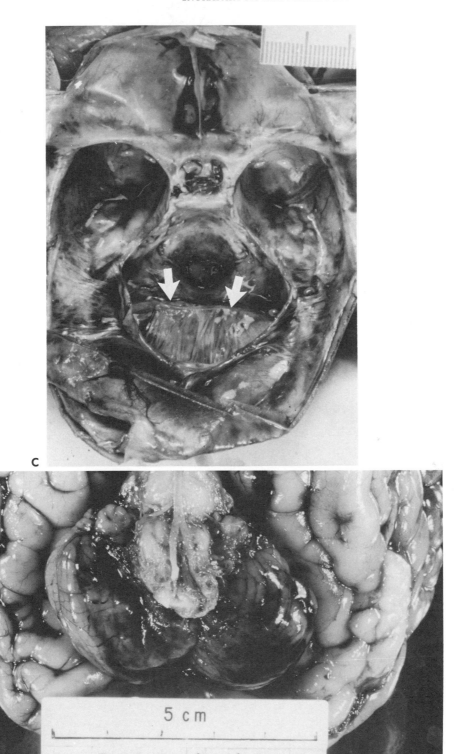

Figure 6–5 *(Continued)*. *C*, Base of the skull after dissection, showing the ridge produced in the posterior fossa (arrow).

D, Inferior surface of hind brain showing laceration of cerebellum. (From Wigglesworth, J. S. and Husemeyer, R. P.: Intracranial birth trauma in vaginal breech delivery: the continued importance of the occipital bone. Br. J. Obstet. Gynecol. *84*:684–691, 1977.)

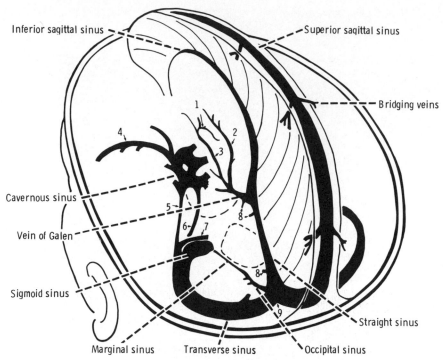

Figure 6–6. Venous sinuses in the newborn: 1, Terminal vein; 2, basal vein; 3, internal cerebral vein; 4, sphenoparietal sinus; 5, superior petrosal sinus; 6, inferior petrosal sinus; 7, petrosal vein of Dandy; 8, superior cerebellar veins; 9, torcula Herophili. (From Pape, K. E. and Wigglesworth, J. S.: Hemorrhage, Ischemia, and the Perinatal Brain. Philadelphia, J. B. Lippincott Co., 1979.)

dural folds usually results from excessive fronto-occipital compression or oblique distortion. Fronto-occipital compression may cause kinking and obstruction of the vein of Galen. This vessel, or the closely related superior cerebellar veins, may be torn by such stresses. Oblique compression, such as may be caused by an incorrect application of forceps, places one tentorial leaf under tension while relaxing the opposite one. Similar uneven pressures are exerted on the bridging veins.

The usual site of origin of subdural hemorrhage is one or more of the groups of superior cerebral bridging veins. The subdural bleed is seen at autopsy as a film of blood or clot over one or both cerebral hemispheres. This may be associated with subarachnoid hemorrhage if the bridging vein has been avulsed at its origin from a cerebral vein. It is seldom possible to demonstrate the ruptured veins at necropsy. I have sometimes been able to show that a particular group of veins was intact over an unaffected hemisphere and missing from the corresponding site over the hemisphere involved in the hemorrhage.

Tears of the tentorium almost invariably involve the free margin close to the junction with the falx. They may be full thickness or may affect only one of the layers of fibers. Extension of such tears medially into the straight sinus or laterally into the lateral sinus is in my experience very rare, although these have been stressed as important occurrences by several authors.[7, 8] Oval tears of the falx may be seen in association with tentorial tears or occasionally as the sole lesion. In cases of vaginal breech delivery it is not unusual to find tentorial tears as an accompaniment to occipital osteodiastasis.

Hemorrhage into the posterior fossa has been regarded as an important cause of death following cranial birth trauma. Sources of such hemorrhage include the superior cerebellar veins which drain into the vein of Galen and straight sinus (Fig. 6–6) and the occipital sinuses. The latter are at risk in severe cases of occipital osteodiastasis.

Relationships Between Tears of Dural Folds, Subdural Hemorrhage and Cerebral Damage. Subdural hemorrhage (from torn bridging veins) and tears of the dural folds are commonly found together because they result from the same type of injury. In some cases the massive nature of the subdural hemorrhage may be considered an adequate cause of death. A more frequent finding is the association of tears of one or both leaves of the tentorium with a trivial subdural bleed. It is often questioned whether the cranial trauma is of any significance in such cases. The older writers recognized that a baby might be born in a state of concussion because of cranial trauma.[9] In recent years it has become customary to ascribe any shock-like state in a newborn baby to birth asphyxia rather than trauma, unless massive subdural hemorrhage develops in life or is revealed at autopsy. Tears of the dural folds can only occur as a result of gross distortion of the cranium. The basic question that the pathologist has to consider is whether the stresses which caused the tears were likely also to have caused damage to the brain in the absence of massive hemorrhage. It seems probable to me that any cranial deformation which was severe enough to damage the dural folds might be expected to cause direct damage to the brain in addition, by a mechanism such as acute brain stem ischemia. I believe that the pathologist should regard any evidence of cranial trauma in an intrapartum or neonatal death as of possible major significance.

EXTRACRANIAL LESIONS

Soft Tissue Injuries. These comprise bleeding from internal organs, including liver, spleen and kidneys, and hemorrhage into skeletal muscles.

One of the most frequently recognized forms of soft tissue trauma is rupture of a subcapsular hematoma of the liver with peritoneal hemorrhage (Fig. 6–7). The risk of this type of trauma is higher if there is enlargement of organs or an operative delivery such as breech extraction. A major peritoneal hemorrhage is readily recognized at autopsy: in most cases the extent of bleeding is such as to suggest that it has been a contributory rather than a primary cause of death. Hemorrhage into the muscles is more readily overlooked at postmortem examination unless the pathologist remembers the possibility. Extensive bruising into muscle tissues may be a major hazard of small preterm infants subjected to vaginal delivery. Massive hemorrhage into the muscles with little or no superficial bruising can be seen infants delivered by the breech. The hemorrhage is particularly severe over the buttocks and may be accentuated in preterm infants. This form of hemorrhage has been reported to cause the renal picture of crush syndrome.[10]

Peripheral Nerve Injuries. These are more likely to be recognized in life than at postmortem examination. If there has been a traumatic delivery or history of an Erb's palsy, diaphragmatic paralysis or Klumpke's paralysis, the nerve roots should be examined with particular care at autopsy.

Bony Injuries. Fractures of long bones are found quite frequently in infants who die following birth trauma (see Fig. 6–2). Common minor lesions such as midshaft fractures of the clavicle can be readily overlooked unless postmortem x-rays are made routinely.

Spinal Injuries. The chief mechanisms postulated as causing spinal injury are most likely to operate during breech delivery. They include excessive longitudinal stretching hyperextension of the head, excessive traction via the brachial plexus

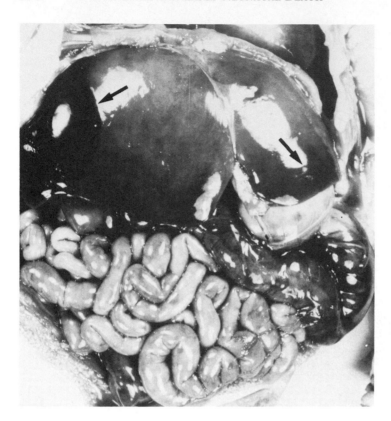

Figure 6–7. Unruptured subcapsular hematomas of the liver (arrow) in a term infant who died following severe birth asphyxia.

and ischemic injury due to narrowing or occlusion of the vertebral arteries. Severe spinal injuries have become relatively infrequent with the use of cesarean section to avoid the need for difficult breech extractions.

The most frequent site of transection is the lower cervical cord. Separation of the vertebrae should be readily apparent on x-ray or dissection, and the cord injury is easily seen on opening the spinal canal at autopsy. More difficult to recognize are the rare instances in which cord transection occurs during a cephalic delivery because in these cases the injury is at the upper end of the cervical cord where it may be obscured by the usual dissection technique.[11] The pathological findings in a case of cord transection which occurred during a difficult midcavity Kielland's rotation at term are illustrated in Figure 6–8. In this instance the infant survived with a heartbeat for six hours despite total transection through the medulla. The lesion was found to be associated with occipital osteodiastasis and a tentorial tear.

ASPHYXIAL LESIONS

A term infant who dies as a result of acute asphyxia during birth may show a number of characteristic features at autopsy. There are often signs that fetal growth has been retarded: a long thin appearance with lack of subcutaneous fat and poor muscle bulk and a relatively large head circumference (OFC more than 1 cm greater than CR length). The skin or fingernails are frequently stained with meconium. All the internal organs are congested: small hemorrhages are seen characteristically over the thymus, lungs and heart. Epicardial hemorrhages are usually distributed along the line of the coronary arteries within the atrioventricular and interventricular grooves. Subcapsular hematomas of the liver are frequent and there may be engorgement of the cerebral veins. Inhalation of meconium may be recognized macroscopically by staining of the larynx and trachea and the presence of meconium-stained mucus in the bronchi. Meconium-stained mucus may also be present within the esophagus and stomach.

Occasionally the lungs may be colored greenish-brown by massive meconium inhalation. In these cases the lungs are at least partly expanded by the inhaled material and are of moderate volume. More frequently the lungs are intensely congested and appear collapsed, although it may be possible to express meconium-stained mucus from the minor bronchi of the cut lung surface by application of gentle pressure. Resorption of the liquid which fills the airways and airspaces in fetal life probably occurs under the influence of circulating catecholamines during normal labor.[12] The process may well be accentuated if there is increased catecholamine production during acute birth asphyxia.

Interstitial emphysema or pneumothorax is seen frequently in infants who die in the early neonatal period following severe birth asphyxia. This is sometimes due to vigorous attempts at resuscitation carried out by staff who are unused to handling ill newborn infants. Also, the condition can develop as a result of the unaided vigorous respiratory efforts of a large term infant because the inspissated mucus and inhaled material forms a ball-valve obstruction in the smaller airways. The same mechanism may result in development of pneumothorax during mechanical ventilation of an asphyxiated infant (see Chapter 10).

The hemorrhagic features of acute intrapartum asphyxia are exaggerated in infants who die as a result of abruptio placentae.[13] These infants have characteristic

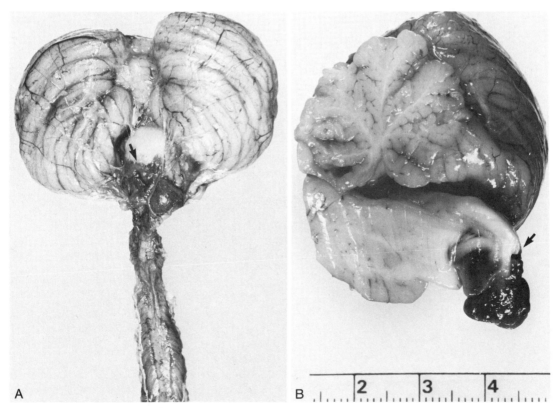

Figure 6–8. Traumatic transection of the medulla (arrow): *A*, posterior view; *B*, sagittal section. (From Pape, K. E. and Wigglesworth, J. S.: Hemorrhage, Ischemia, and the Perinatal Brain. Philadelphia, J. B. Lippincott Co., 1979.)

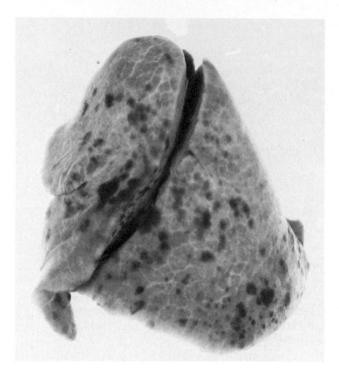

Figure 6–9. Hemorrhages over the lung in a case of abruptio placentae.

large hemorrhages over the lungs and heart which should allow a presumptive diagnosis of abruptio even if the placenta is not available for study (Fig. 6–9). It has been postulated that the florid hemorrhages are the result of a rapid augmentation of fetal blood volume caused by placental compression by the retroplacental clot (Fig. 6–10).

On histology the lungs usually show intense congestion of alveolar capillaries, with a variable degree of hemorrhage into the interstitial tissue and airspaces. The variations in lung volume noted macroscopically are reflected at microscopic level in a variable expansion of the acini. Masses of epithelial squames and granular material are seen commonly both in the bronchi and bronchioles and

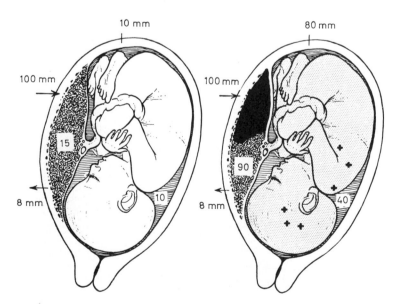

Figure 6–10. Diagram illustrating how pressure changes associated with retroplacental hemorrhage may cause overloading of fetal circulation with accentuation of petechial hemorrhages in viscera. (From Morison, J. E.: Foetal and Neonatal Pathology, 3rd ed. London, Butterworths, 1970.)

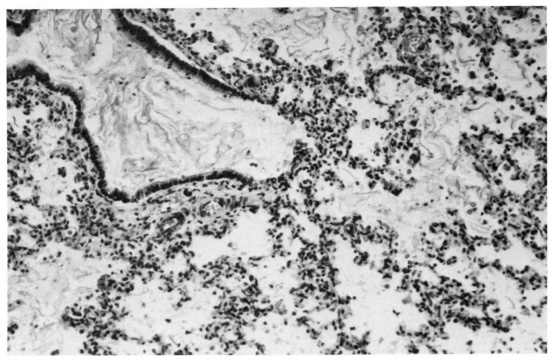

Figure 6–11. Lung from a term infant who died during birth showing masses of epithelial squames plugging a terminal bronchiole and present within the saccules. H and E × 150.

deep within the acini beyond the limits of the bronchiolar epithelium (Fig. 6–11). Use of a specific staining technique, such as Attwood's stain,[14] will show that the epithelial squames are embedded in a mass of inspissated mucus. Fresh meconium appears on histology as yellowish granules. A number of superimposed secondary reactions may be present, particularly if the infant survived for some hours or days after birth. These include hyaline membrane formation, a nonspecific inflammatory reaction or a frank pneumonia, or evidence of milk inhalation.

The appearance of the brain is determined both by the time course of asphyxia and the time of death of the infant in relation to the asphyxial episode. In infants who die during labor following an apparently brief asphyxial episode there is usually intense congestion without much evidence of brain swelling. Brain swelling with tonsillar herniation is sometimes seen in such infants but is more likely in those cases in which there has been a prolonged partial type of asphyxia. If the infant has survived on mechanical ventilation for several days, the brain is usually swollen and has flattened convolutions, obliterated sulci and a pale cortex. There may be evidence of temporal herniation through the incisura of the tentorium into the posterior fossa or tonsillar herniation through the foramen magnum into the cervical canal. On section the brain may show acute congestion of the thalamus, basal ganglia, midbrain and brain stem. Further details of effects of birth asphyxia on the brain are discussed in Chapter 10.

The heart seldom shows specific features other than the characteristic epicardial hemorrhages. In some infants who die following birth asphyxia, acute myocardial necrosis or myocardial fibrosis may be observed (see Chapter 11).

Characteristic changes in the kidneys are seen in some infants who are stillborn (particularly after abruptio placentae) and in many of those who survive for some hours or days after severe birth asphyxia. These changes comprise acute congestion of the medulla, which can be seen at macroscopic level (Fig. 6–12),

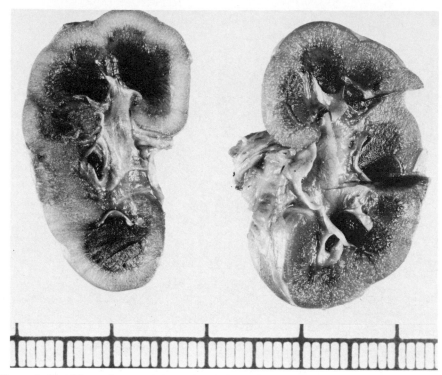

Figure 6–12. Kidneys from an infant who died at 5 days of age following asphyxia. Pallor of the renal cortex and congestion of the medulla was associated with histological evidence of tubular necrosis.

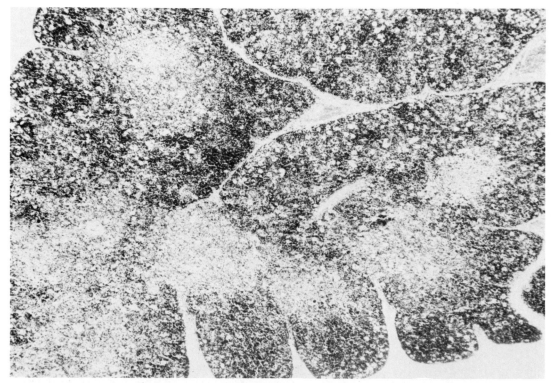

Figure 6–13. Thymus from an infant who died at 20 hours of age following severe birth asphyxia. Loss of lymphocytes in the cortex shows up as a "starry sky" pattern. H and E ×30.

and renal tubular or papillary necrosis recognizable on histology. The occurrence of such changes provides good evidence that the infant has been in a state of shock at some time before death and may help in any attempt to reconstruct the sequence of events.

Other evidence of acute stress which should be looked for is a "starry sky" pattern in the thymus (Fig. 6–13) (see Chapter 20). Prolonged or recurrent antepartum stress may be indicated by irregular cartilage formation and ossification at the costochondral junctions, by evidence of fetal growth retardation or by the changes of uteroplacental ischemia in the placenta.

It is relatively unusual to see a normally formed fresh stillborn preterm infant except in cases of massive antepartum hemorrhage. This is probably due to the resistance of preterm infants to hypoxia. If such an infant is encountered, the possibility of some unusual contributory cause of death, such as intrauterine infection, should be considered.

HEMORRHAGIC LESIONS IN BIRTH ASPHYXIA AND TRAUMA

Many infants who die following an asphyxial birth have hemorrhagic lesions as a prominent finding at autopsy. Several of these, including hemorrhages from ruptured hematomas of the liver and spleen and massive hemorrhage into the muscles in cases of breech delivery, have already been discussed under the heading of traumatic lesions. In many instances, however, the relative contributions of trauma and asphyxia to hemorrhagic lesions may be impossible to assess.

A relatively frequent finding in an infant who dies following an asphyxial birth is massive pulmonary hemorrhage. The condition may develop almost immediately, with blood welling up the endotracheal tube on resuscitation in the

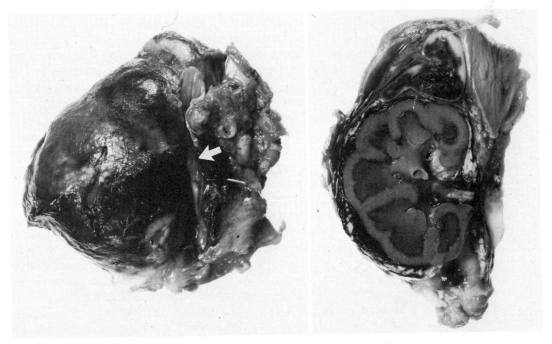

Figure 6–14. Retroperitoneal hemorrhage within adrenal and around the kidney associated with breech delivery: *left*, anterior view showing inferior vena cava (arrow); *right*, coronal section. (From Pape, K. E. and Wigglesworth, J. S.: Hemorrhage, Ischemia, and the Perinatal Brain. Philadelphia, J. B. Lippincott Co., 1970.)

delivery room, or as a secondary phenomenon after several hours. In some of these cases there may be evidence of consumption coagulopathy caused by disseminated intravascular coagulation or there may be one of a number of primary coagulation defects (see Chapter 20). In other instances the condition may perhaps be analogous to the "shock lung" seen in the adult. An outpouring of catecholamines in conditions such as increased intracranial pressure and traumatic shock causes arterial vasoconstriction, which is particularly marked in the pulmonary circulation. Relaxation of this constriction at a later stage leads to flooding of the capillary bed and venules. Damage to the integrity of the microcirculation inflicted during the ischemic phase may result in hemorrhage and edema when the circulation is restored.

Adrenal hemorrhage occurs most frequently in association with breech delivery. There is usually a partial hemorrhagic necrosis of both adrenals without massive blood loss. Occasionally bleeding from this site can present as an expanding mass in the flanks with evidence of insidious blood loss. The specimen shown in Figure 6–14 is from an infant delivered by the breech at term who was thought to have suffered cranial birth trauma but died at two days of age with edema of the extremities. At postmortem examination the cranial structures were found to be intact but there was a massive retroperitoneal hematoma, originating from the right adrenal, which had occluded the inferior vena cava.

Conjunctival and retinal hemorrhages may be recognized in life and are discussed elsewhere.[6]

SUMMARY AND CONCLUSIONS

Throughout this chapter I have emphasized how asphyxia and trauma may interact during the birth process to produce the patterns of lesions which can be recognized at autopsy in fresh stillbirth and early neonatal death. This may be regarded as an unpopular view since many publications in recent years have stressed the rarity of birth trauma as a significant factor in modern perinatal mortality. It is important to point out the extreme care with which a postmortem examination has to be conducted if many of the traumatic lesions described in this chapter are not to be missed (Fig. 6–15). In order to provide the obstetrician and pediatrician with useful information, it is necessary for the pathologist to attempt to reconstruct the series of events which led to the infant's death. Clinical information may be essential in order to carry this out. If, for instance, there is clear evidence that the fetal heart stopped before the onset of the second stage of labor, any cranial birth trauma must have been inflicted after the infant died.

In some cases the mixture of pathological lesions may enable the pathologist to present the obstetrician or pediatrician with a previously unsuspected interpretation of the case. Signs of fetal growth retardation, irregularity of costochondral junctions or presence of a thymic stress reaction may indicate that fetal health was already compromised before the onset of labor. Early renal tubular necrosis provides clear evidence of severe shock which has occurred several hours before death. Signs of trauma and hemorrhage in an infant who was unexpectedly asphyxiated after an apparently uncomplicated instrumental delivery may provide a basis for reconsidering some area of current obstetric practice.

The pathologist needs to cooperate particularly closely with obstetric and pediatric colleagues if a realistic assessment of the relative contributions of trauma and asphyxia is to be made in this group of infants. Such an approach is worth the effort involved if it leads to recognition of areas in which alterations in management may be expected to reduce perinatal mortality and morbidity.

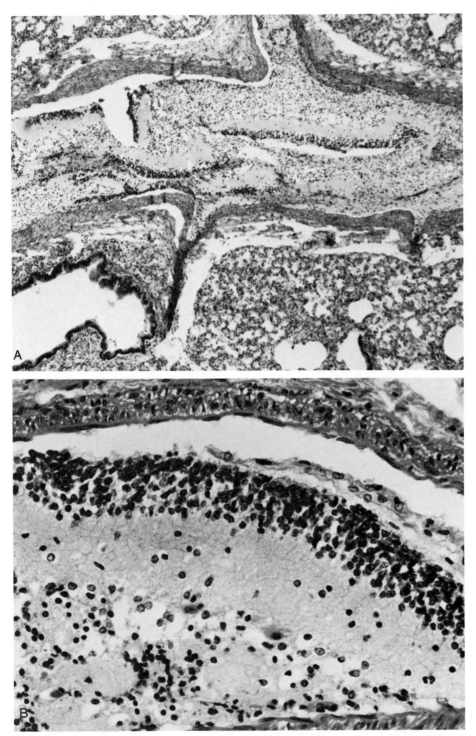

Figure 6–15. Section of lung from an infant who died 20 minutes after a forceps delivery. No abnormality of cranium or brain recognized at autopsy. *A,* H and E ×60 showing masses of fetal cerebellar cortex plugging a pulmonary artery branch. *B,* H and E ×400 showing details of cerebellar histology including external granular layer, molecular layer, and several Purkinje cells. Cerebellar emboli were seen also in sections of liver and adrenal cortex. This condition is rarely reported, but might be caused by occipital osteodiastasis.

REFERENCES

1. Ramsey, E. M., Corner, G. W., and Donner, M. W.: Serial and cineradiographic visualization of maternal circulation in the primate (hemochorial) placenta. Am. J. Obstet. Gynecol. *86*:213–225, 1963.
2. Hon, E. H.: Detection of asphyxia in utero-fetal heart rate. *In* Gluck, L. (ed.): Intrauterine Asphyxia and the Developing Fetal Brain. Chicago, Year Book Medical Publishers, 1977, pp. 167–177.
3. Myers, R. E.: Experimental models of perinatal brain damage: relevance to human pathology. *In* Gluck, L. (ed.): Intrauterine Asphyxia and the Developing Fetal Brain. Chicago, Year Book Medical Publishers, 1977, pp. 37–97.
4. Dawes, G. S.: Fetal and Neonatal Physiology. Chicago, Year Book Medical Publishers, 1968, pp. 141–159.
5. Wigglesworth, J. S., and Husemeyer, R. P.: Intracranial birth trauma in vaginal breech delivery: the continued importance of injury to the occipital bone. Br. J. Obstet. Gynaecol. *84*:684–691, 1977.
6. Pape, K. E., and Wigglesworth, J. S.: Haemorrhage, Ischaemia, and the Perinatal Brain. London, Heinemann, Philadelphia, J. B. Lippincott Co., 1979, pp. 11–38.
7. Morison, J. E.: Foetal and Neonatal Pathology, 3rd ed. London, Butterworths, 1970, pp. 294.
8. Potter, E. L., and Craig, J. M.: Pathology of the Fetus and the Infant, 3rd ed. Chicago, Year Book Medical Publishers, London, Lloyd Luke, 1976, p. 107.
9. Schwartz, P.: Birth Injuries of the Newborn. Basel, S. Karger, 1961.
10. Ralis, Z. A.: Birth trauma to muscles in babies born by breech delivery and its possible fatal consequences. Arch. Dis. Child. *50*:4–13, 1975.
11. Shulman, S. T., Madden, J. D., Esterly, J. R., and Shanklin, D. R.: Transection of the spinal cord: a rare obstetrical complication of cephalic delivery. Arch. Dis. Child. *46*:291–294, 1971.
12. Olver, R. E.: Of labor and the lungs. Arch. Dis. Child. *56*:659–662, 1981.
13. Claireaux, A. E.: Pathology of perinatal hypoxia. J. Clin. Pathol. *30*, suppl. II: 142–148, 1977.
14. Attwood, H. D.: The histological diagnosis of amniotic fluid embolism. J. Pathol. Bacteriol. *76*:211–215, 1958.
15. Valdes-Dapena, M. A., and Arey, J. B.: Pulmonary emboli of cerebral origin in the newborn. Arch. Pathol. *84*:643–646, 1967.

Chapter Seven

Approach to Malformation Syndromes

It is important for any pathologist who carries out perinatal autopsies to be able to recognize the major common malformation syndromes and to record adequately the details of the anomalies present in those syndromes with which he is unfamiliar. An accurate record of the postmortem findings is of considerable help to any clinician to whom the parents are subsequently referred for genetic counseling and is essential in cases with a normal chromosome complement.

The process of analyzing the mixture of gross and subtle variations from normal which may involve face, trunk, limbs and extremities, in addition to multiple internal organ systems, can be difficult and time-consuming. The central theme of this chapter will be a discussion of the practical approach to the malformed baby at autopsy, although other aspects of congenital malformations which are not adequately dealt with under individual organ systems will also be included.

DEFINITIONS OF MALFORMATION AND THE PROBLEM OF THE DEFORMED FETUS

The following definitions are generally useful:[1]

1. Malformation—A primary structural defect that results from a localized error of morphogenesis.
2. Deformation—An alteration in shape or structure or both of a previously normally formed part.
3. Malformation sequence—A malformation together with its subsequently derived structural changes.
4. Malformation syndrome—A recognized pattern of malformations presumed to have the same etiology but not interpreted as the consequence of a single localized error in morphogenesis.

Thus renal agenesis, in which abnormal facial features, limb distortion and lung hypoplasia are secondary to the lack of amniotic fluid, is regarded as a malformation sequence, whereas trisomy 13, in which cerebral, cardiac and renal anomalies may develop as separate consequences of the chromosomal imbalance, is a true malformation syndrome. It is possible to recognize the consequential nature of many of the abnormal features of the infant with renal agenesis because identical features are seen in cases of prolonged amniotic fluid leak dating from early in the second trimester in which there are no primary malformations. This distinction often cannot be made with other "syndromes." It is, for example, usually believed that the defect of the anterior abdominal wall in prune-belly syndrome is due to a primary mesodermal defect. Examination of second trimester abortions suggests that the defect is in fact secondary to abdominal distention by a grossly dilated fetal bladder.[2]

Deformations of growth resulting from tissue destruction during the early fetal period are often confused with malformations. For example, the rubella syndrome is commonly regarded as a malformation syndrome. Yet, of the many features of this syndrome, only septal defects of the heart could be considered malformations in the sense of primary structural defects.

The practical importance of the distinction is that it may aid in determining the etiology and prognosis for future pregnancies in an individual patient. We have seen several infants who died soon after birth with limb deformities, poor muscle development and hypoplastic lungs. It would be easy on a superficial examination to dismiss these defects as multiple congenital malformations. However, dissection of the central nervous system in two such cases revealed evidence of extensive anoxic-ischemic damage that had evidently occurred during the second trimester of pregnancy (Fig. 7–1). In another case, muscle histochemistry led to the diagnosis of congenital dystrophy (see Chapter 19). In each case the pattern of deformity seen at postmortem was the result of an impairment in function during fetal life rather than a localized error of morphogenesis.

CAUSATION OF MALFORMATIONS

Only a brief synopsis will be included. The reader is referred to Warkany (1971)[3] and the *Handbook of Teratology*, Vol. 1 (1977)[4] for more detailed information.

GENETIC CAUSES

There are three accepted patterns of genetic causation for congenital malformations.

GENETIC IMBALANCE DUE TO GROSS CHROMOSOMAL ABNORMALITIES

These abnormalities can arise in a number of ways (Fig. 7–2). A full extra set of chromosomes (triploidy) may be the result of double fertilization of the ovum or failure of the ovum to exclude a polar body during meiosis. An additional full chromosome (trisomy) or absence of a chromosome (monosomy) arises by errors in assortment of chromosomes during meiotic divisions of the gamete or the first mitotic division of the zygote. Chromosomal breakage during cell division may result in partial monosomy if the portion of chromosomal material is lost, or in a duplication deficiency translocation chromosome if there is breakage and rearrangement. Maldivision of a chromosome at the centromere results in a duplication deficiency isochromosome with deficiency of the short arm and the presence of an extra long arm in daughter cells.

These gross chromosomal abnormalities are extremely common during early development and occur in about 4 per cent of recognized pregnancies (Fig. 7–3). The severe effects on morphogenesis of these chromosomal maldistributions

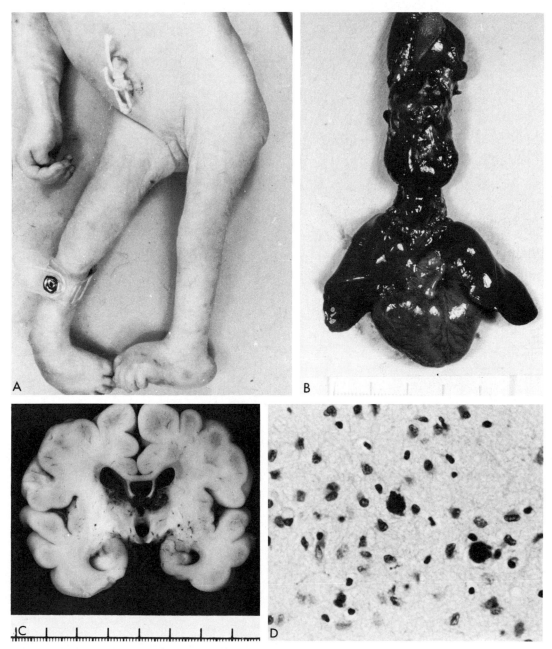

Figure 7–1. *A*, View of right hand and legs of an infant who failed to breathe at birth and died at 2 hours of age. Note bilateral talipes and clenched hand with dorsiflexed wrist. *B*, Heart and lungs of the same infant. Heart is of normal size but lungs are hypoplastic. *C*, Section of brain of a similar infant to that illustrated in *A* and *B*. Ventricles are dilated and there are subependymal pseudocysts. *D*, Thalamus of brain illustrated in *C* showing encrusted neurones and glial proliferation. H and E × 300. Similar features were recognized in the brain of the infant shown in *A* and *B*.

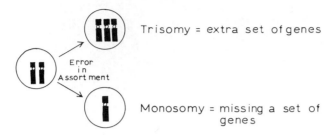

Chromosomal Maldistribution:

Trisomy = extra set of genes

Error in Assortment

Monosomy = missing a set of genes

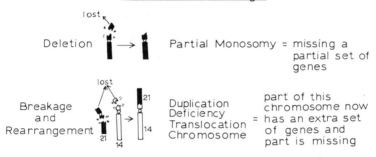

Chromosomal Breakage:

lost

Deletion → Partial Monosomy = missing a partial set of genes

lost

Breakage and Rearrangement

Duplication Deficiency Translocation Chromosome = part of this chromosome now has an extra set of genes and part is missing

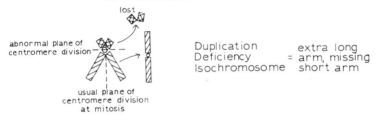

Maldivision at Centromere:

lost

abnormal plane of centromere division

usual plane of centromere division at mitosis

Duplication Deficiency = extra long arm, missing Isochromosome short arm

Figure 7–2. Types of chromosomal abnormality leading to genetic imbalance. (From Smith, D. W.: Recognizable Patterns of Human Malformation, 3rd ed. Philadelphia, W. B. Saunders Co., 1982.)

Figure 7–3. Incidence and types of chromosomal abnormalities. (From Smith, D. W.: Recognizable Patterns of Human Malformation, 3rd ed. Philadelphia, W. B. Saunders Co., 1982.)

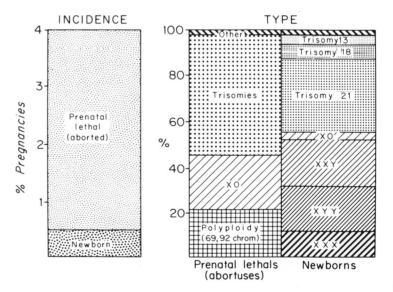

usually result in early death or abortion of the conceptus. As a consequence of the tendency for severe chromosomal abnormalities to lead to early loss of the conceptus, the frequency of different chromosomal abnormalities recognized in aborted fetuses differs markedly from that seen in infants born at a viable stage of development (Fig. 7–3).

The range of chromosomal abnormalities recognized by the neonatologist or perinatal pathologist includes mainly the less severe defects such as trisomy 21, trisomy 13 and trisomy 18.

SINGLE MUTANT GENES

These account for most disorders ordinarily recognized as of genetic origin. The inheritance pattern may be autosomal dominant, autosomal recessive or X-linked (either dominant or recessive). Autosomal dominant disorders tend to show wider variation in expression among affected individuals than autosomal recessive disorders.

POLYGENIC OR MULTIFACTORIAL

In most common malformations it is believed that polygenic inheritance accounts for a significant part of the tendency for recurrence within families, although environmental factors also play a role.

ENVIRONMENTAL CAUSES OF MALFORMATION IN HUMANS

Environmental causes of malformations include drugs, industrial and agricultural chemicals, radiation and infections.

DRUGS

Since the thalidomide disaster, considerable attention has been paid to the potential teratogenic effect of drugs administered to pregnant women. Many drugs have been suspected of causing fetal malformation on the basis of case reports of possible associations, but confirmation of teratogenic activity has been obtained in only a few instances.

There are a number of difficulties in establishing causal relationships between drugs and malformations.[5]

1. It may be difficult to determine whether the malformation is caused by the drug therapy or the disease for which the drug is prescribed.

2. The defect may be the result of synergistic action of two or more drugs.

3. The timing of fetal exposure may be critical.

4. The drug may cause malformation only in genetically predisposed individuals.

5. Drug dosage may be critical in that low doses may be safe but high doses teratogenic.

6. Information on drug dosage may be unreliable because of inadequate clinical records of prescribed drugs, noncompliance in drug taking, the use of nonprescribed drugs by pregnant women and inadequate recollection by the patient as to specific drugs taken and their timing.

Drugs or drug groups for which there is acceptable evidence of teratogenic activity are listed in Table 7–1. In addition, many other groups of drugs have come under suspicion. These include oral hypoglycemic agents used in treatment of diabetes, sex hormones (particularly hormonal pregnancy tests and oral contraceptives), neurotropic anorectics such as amphetamine, tranquilizers, salicylates

TABLE 7–1. TERATOGENIC DRUGS

DRUG (OR DRUG GROUP)	MALFORMATIONS
Thalidomide	Phocomelia Microcephaly; growth deficiency; limb abnormalities

Folate antagonists
  aminopterin
  methotrexate
Alkylating agents
  6 mercaptopurine
  busulphan
  chlorambucil
  cyclophosphamide	

Androgenic steroids	Female virilization

Anticonvulsants
  phenytoin
  phenobarbitone
	Oral clefts; cardiac, skeletal, digital, CNS anomalies;
	  mental deficiency

Warfarin	Nasal hypoplasia; optic atrophy; skeletal abnormalities; mental retardation
Alcohol	Microcephaly; short palpebral fissures; maxillary hypoplasia; joint anomalies; growth deficiency

and antibiotics. The conflicting evidence for teratogenicity of these compounds is reviewed by Smithells[6] and Wilson.[7]

INDUSTRIAL AND AGRICULTURAL CHEMICALS

Many substances have been suspected of teratogenic activity in recent years, but firm evidence has so far been obtained for few.[5]

Methyl mercury poisoning (Minamata disease) in pregnancy causes disturbance in fetal growth, microcephaly and limb deformities.

Lead causes sterility, spontaneous abortion and neonatal death but has not been shown to cause malformation.

Toxic chemicals on which evidence remains conflicting include 2,3,7,8,-tetra chlorodibenzo-p-dioxin (TCDD, a contaminant of the herbicide Agent Orange), polyvinylchloride, insecticides, anesthetic gases and organic solvents.

RADIATION

In utero exposure to large doses of radiation causes microcephaly associated with mental retardation. An absorbed dose of 10 rads to the fetus is considered to be the practical threshold dose for teratogenic effects.[8]

INFECTIONS

A number of infections are known to produce congenital defects if exposure occurs during a critical time in pregnancy.

Rubella. The rubella virus is teratogenic in the first four months after conception, with the highest risk to the fetus at 8 to 10 weeks.[9] Affected infants are frequently growth retarded and may show microcephaly, microphthalmia and cardiac septal defects or patent ductus arteriosus. Many other features which can be recognized include deafness, cataract, glaucoma, chorioretinitis, encephalitis, hepatosplenomegaly, jaundice, thrombocytopenia, anemia, osteolytic lesions of the bone metaphyses and interstitial pneumonia. These may all be regarded as evidence of an infective process rather than congenital malformations (see Chapter 9).

Others. Cytomegalovirus, herpes simplex, varicella and herpes zoster (see Chapter 9) have been responsible for defects. Most of these produce characteristic fetal damage including hydrocephaly, microcephaly and chorioretinitis rather than obvious organ malformation.

POSTMORTEM EXAMINATION OF A MALFORMED OR DEFORMED INFANT

Accurate description of the external appearance of an abnormal infant requires careful analysis of each feature so that it can be appropriately described. This is in practice extremely difficult. We may readily recognize that an infant has an unusual facial appearance but find it difficult to say which parts of the facial structure are abnormal, particularly if the abnormality is one with which we are unfamiliar.

For practical purposes it is better to describe gross features only and to take a series of photographs from which fine detail can be recognized at leisure. These pictures might reasonably include a whole body view, frontal and lateral views of the face and close-ups of any gross deformities of the extremities.

Features that need to be considered during the external examination are discussed in succeeding paragraphs.

HEAD

Hair Pattern. Abnormalities such as variation in the position of the parietal whorl (associated with microcephaly) may not be easy to recognize in the perinatal period. A low posterior hairline in infants with a short neck can sometimes be seen.

Forehead. This can appear prominent or sloping (Fig. 7–4). The former may indicate either a large cranium or hypoplasia of facial structures (e.g., maxilla); the latter is a feature of trisomy 13.

Eyes. Abnormalities may involve the eyes themselves, microphthalmi, colobomata or cataracts. Alternatively, the eyes may be normal in size and form but abnormally positioned, too close (hypotelorism) or too far apart (hypertelorism). The palpebral fissures may be abnormal, slanting up or down from the inner to outer canthus, or there may be epicanthic folds.

Maxilla and Mandible. Malar and maxillary hypoplasia affecting the form of the midfacial region are not immediately obvious at perinatal autopsy and may be recognized only on examination of photographs or radiographs. Maxillary hypoplasia should be looked for if there is a high arched palate. It is seen in some of the chromosomal anomalies. Underdevelopment of the mandible or frank mandibular hypoplasia are more common and should be recognizable by the pathologist.

Occiput. This may be flat (trisomy 21) or prominent (trisomy 18).

Nose. Gross malformations of the nose are seen in cases of alobar holoprosencephaly (Chapter 10). A broad nasal bridge is characteristic of a number of anomalies of skeletal development, including thanatophoric dwarfism. A small or short nose may be a feature of trisomy 18.

Mouth. Cleft lip or palate or both may be seen in a number of trisomic syndromes, including trisomy 13 and trisomy 18. Macrostomia, microstomia or abnormal development of the philtrum can also indicate a chromosomal defect.

Ears. Low-set ears deficient in cartilage are a feature of the oligohydramnios sequence. Low-set or malformed ears are seen also in a number of chromosomal

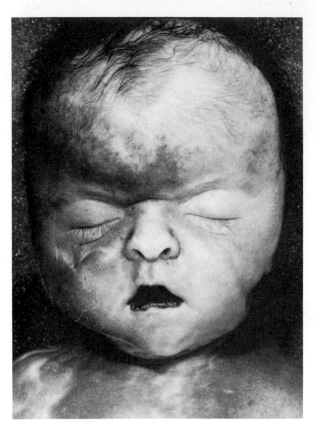

Figure 7–4. Prominent forehead in an infant with Apert syndrome (acrocephalo-syndactyly), who died soon after birth. In this malformation there is irregular synostosis of the coronal suture and hypoplasia of the midfacial region.

anomalies. A low-set ear is defined as one in which the helix meets the cranium at a level below that of a horizontal plane with the corner of the orbit. Such ears are often slanted as well, indicating a delay in morphogenesis.[1]

Neck. This may be short or there may be webbing or redundant skin folds (Turner syndrome, Klippel-Feil syndrome, Meckel-Gruber syndrome).

Thorax. The shape of the thorax may be affected by disorders of skeletal development (e.g., thanatophoric dwarfism) or by abnormalities of fetal neuromuscular formation which have interfered with normal fetal respiratory activity (see Chapter 9). Thus the recognition on external examination that the thorax is narrow with poorly developed ribs may indicate an abnormality affecting the cervical spinal cord, and a broad, "over-expanded" thorax may indicate diaphragmatic maldevelopment (eventration).

Nipple abnormalities which may be recognized include small size and wide spacing (Turner syndrome).

LIMBS

Many malformation syndromes are associated with joint limitation or contractures or both, although these may also be a secondary effect of congenital neuromuscular disorders or prolonged oligohydramnios. The type of underlying abnormality may be suspected from the pattern of distortion and associated external features. The term *arthrogryposis* signifies no more than the presence of joint contractures at birth and does not represent a single entity. A number of characteristic forms of short-limbed dwarfism can be recognized from the external limb appearances (thanatophoric dwarfism, Ellis–van Creveld syndrome, camptomelic dwarfism).

Abnormal crease patterns may be recognized in hands or feet. The most important is a single transverse palmar (simian) crease of the hands or a deep crease between first and second toes of the feet. Other abnormalities include alterations in shape of digits such as clinodactyly (undue curvature), particularly of the fifth finger, and camptodactyly (bent digit).

Characteristic foot abnormalities include rocker bottom foot (Fig. 7–5) and undue prominence of the heel.

Size and shape of nails may reflect the development of the underlying phalanges. Nail hypoplasia is a feature of a number of malformation syndromes.[1]

GENITALIA

Ambiguous external genitalia may indicate abnormal development of the whole genital tract or may represent masculinization of a normal female genital tract by adrenal androgens (congenital adrenal hyperplasia). Abnormalities of the genitalia including hypospadias or cryptorchidism may also be present in a wide variety of chromosomal anomalies.

SEVERE CHROMOSOMAL ANOMALIES OFTEN ASSOCIATED WITH STILLBIRTH OR NEONATAL DEATH

TRISOMY 13[1, 3]

The incidence of this condition is about 1 per 5000 births. These infants characteristically have moderate microcephaly with a sloping forehead (Fig. 7–6), eye defects including microphthalmos or coloboma and cleft lip and/or palate. There is often a capillary hemangioma over the forehead, and localized scalp defects may be present in the parieto-occipital region. The ears may be abnormally formed and low set and frequently there is loose skin over the back of the neck. Polydactyly of the hands is a common feature and there are often simian creases and prominent heels.

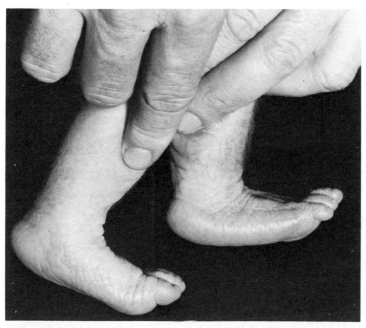

Figure 7–5. Rocker bottom foot in a case of trisomy 18. (Courtesy of Dr. V. Dubowitz.)

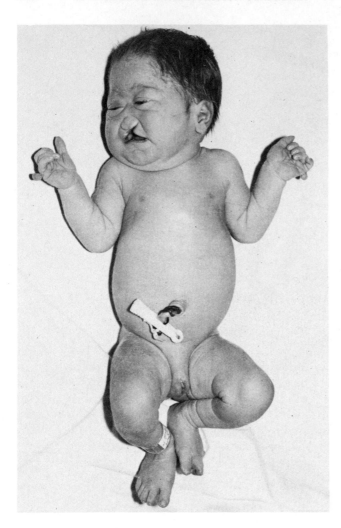

Figure 7–6. Trisomy 13. Note cleft lip and bilateral extra digits. (Courtesy of Dr. V. Dubowitz.)

The most frequent internal abnormalities involve the central nervous system and include arrhinencephaly or holoprosencephaly (see Chapter 10). Other CNS anomalies which have been described are agenesis of the corpus callosum, fusion of basal ganglia, cerebellar hypoplasia and meningomyelocele.

Cardiac anomalies include mitral or aortic atresia, pulmonary stenosis and anomalous venous return. Renal anomalies are frequent. Multiple cysts are present in about 30 per cent of cases, and other anomalies such as horseshoe kidney and hydronephrosis are common. Minor skeletal, genital or intestinal anomalies are often present.

The prognosis for infants with this condition is extremely poor. Death usually occurs within the first month of life.

TRISOMY 18[1, 3]

The incidence of this condition is about 0.3 per 1000 births. The infants are often severely growth-retarded, with a small placenta, single umbilical artery and polyhydramnios. There is hypoplasia of skeletal muscle and subcutaneous tissues. The head shows a prominent occiput and narrow bifrontal diameter; there are low-set, malformed ears, short palpebral fissures, a small mouth and micrognathia (Fig. 7–7). The hands characteristically are clenched, with the index finger overlapping the fourth. The hallux is often short and dorsiflexed. Other external abnormalities include a short sternum, inguinal or umbilical hernia and a small pelvis with limited hip abduction.

The most frequent internal malformations are ventricular septal defects.

Cerebral anomalies include microgyria, cerebellar hypoplasia, defects of the corpus callosum and hydrocephalus.

Renal anomalies, including multiple cysts, are relatively frequent. Many other internal anomalies are described which may involve lung, diaphragm, gastrointestinal tract, skeletal tissues, endocrine organs and genitalia.

The infants usually die within a few weeks of birth.

TRISOMY 21 (DOWN SYNDROME)[1, 3]

This condition has an incidence of about 1 per 660 births. Although it is not usually fatal in the neonatal period, severe cardiac or intestinal anomalies may lead to neonatal or infant death, and the pathologist should be able to recognize the condition.

The infants show brachycephaly with a relatively flat occiput and mild microcephaly (Fig. 7–8). There is a flat face with small nose with a low nasal bridge and inner epicanthic folds. The palpebral fissures slant upward from inner to outer canthus. The ears are small with overfolding of an angulated upper helix. There may be excess skin on the back of a rather short neck. The hands have

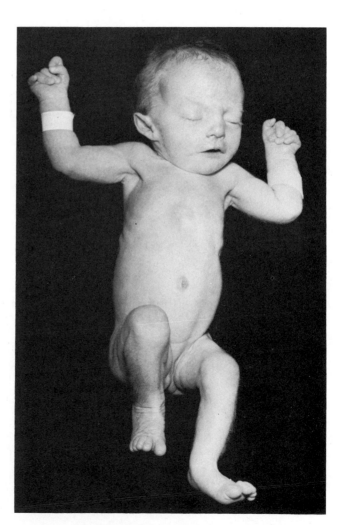

Figure 7–7. Trisomy 18. Note low-set malformed ear and clenched hands with overlapping index finger. (Courtesy of Dr. V. Dubowitz.)

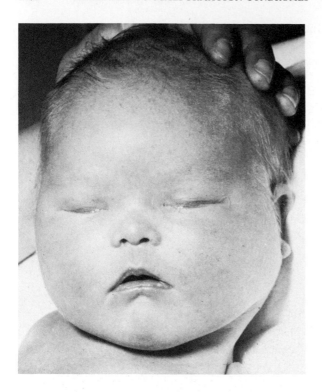

Figure 7–8. Trisomy 21 (Down syndrome) in the newborn. Note the mild microcephaly and flat face with a small nose with low nasal bridge. (Courtesy of Dr. V. Dubowitz.)

short metacarpals and phalanges with hypoplasia of the midphalanx of the fifth finger, which often shows clinodactyly in addition. The short fifth finger may have a single crease and there is often a single transverse palmar crease. There may be a wide gap between first and second toes with a marked plantar crease.

The pelvis is usually hypoplastic with an outward flaring of the iliac wings and shallow acetabular angle.

Cardiac anomalies (present in about 40 per cent of cases) include common atrioventricular canal, ventricular and atrial septal defects, persistent patent ductus arteriosus and tetralogy of Fallot. Gastrointestinal abnormalities include duodenal atresia and tracheoesophageal fistula.

TRIPLOIDY[1, 3]

This is seen relatively seldom as a stillbirth or neonatal death because most affected fetuses are aborted in early pregnancy. The placenta is usually large with partial molar change. There is a variable, sometimes severe, degree of fetal growth retardation. Microphthalmi, colobomata and low-set malformed ears are frequent and there may be hypertelorism and micrognathia. Syndactyly of third and fourth fingers, single transverse palmar crease and talipes are common.

Internal anomalies of the brain include hydrocephalus, and those seen in other organs include congenital cardiac anomalies, adrenal hypoplasia and cystic renal dysplasia or hydronephrosis.

All fetuses with full triploidy are stillborn or die in the early neonatal period. Diploid and triploid mosaics may survive with mental deficiency.

TURNER SYNDROME (XO SYNDROME)[1, 3]

The frequency of Turner syndrome in liveborn female infants is about 1 per 2500 to 5000 total live births. However, this is one of the conditions which is associated with a very high loss rate in early pregnancy and is extremely common in aborted material. It will be seen most frequently by the pathologist who examines early fetal material. Turner syndrome infants with unusually severe cardiac or other malformations may die in the true perinatal period.

Major features are small stature, which may be present at birth, a low posterior hairline, a short neck with webbing or loose skin folds, anomalous ears, a narrow maxilla, a broad chest with widely spaced nipples, cubitus valgus, lymphedema and ovarian dysgenesis (hypoplasia or absence of germinal cells). Renal and cardiac malformations are common. The most frequent cardiac defect is coarctation of the aorta.

OTHER MALFORMATION SYNDROMES COMMONLY RESULTING IN PERINATAL DEATH

SYNDROMES WITH SEVERE CNS MALFORMATION

Anencephaly, meningomyelocele and other common major CNS malformations are discussed in Chapter 12. These may be associated with a variety of other internal malformations. The syndrome in which enterogenous cysts are associated with anterior spina bifida is discussed in Chapter 13.

MECKEL-GRUBER SYNDROME[1]

The main features of this condition are a posterior encephalocele, polydactyly and renal anomalies—usually cystic dysplasia. The lungs are frequently hypoplastic and there may be many other internal anomalies. The infants usually die within a few days of birth. The condition is believed to be of autosomal recessive inheritance.

ZELLWEGER SYNDROME (CEREBRO-HEPATO-RENAL SYNDROME)

These infants have macrogyria or polymicrogyria of the brain, hepatomegaly with dysgenesis and cirrhotic changes and small glomerular cysts in the kidney.

Characteristic external features include a large fontanelle, high forehead with shallow supraorbital ridges and flat occiput. Limb contractures with camptodactyly and simian creases may be present. There are often an elevated serum iron level and evidence of excess tissue iron storage. Absence of peroxisomes in liver and kidney has been reported.[10] The infants usually die within the first few weeks after birth. The condition is of autosomal recessive inheritance.

SYNDROMES ASSOCIATED WITH OLIGOHYDRAMNIOS

All infants with oligohydramnios dating from early in the second trimester present similar external features. These were described originally in infants with renal agenesis (see Chapter 17). There is growth impairment of varying severity. The face shows prominent epicanthic folds, low-set cartilage-deficient ears, a beak-like nose and a small lower jaw. The upper limbs are characterized by large spade-like hands, and the legs show talipes and often distortion and congenital dislocation of the hips. These external features are all evidently the result of lack of amniotic fluid because identical features are seen in cases in which the oligohydramnios is caused by failure of renal output (renal agenesis or cystic renal dysplasia with thread-like ureters and a narrow tubular bladder), lower urinary tract obstruction, or chronic amniotic fluid leakage dating from early in the second trimester (Figs. 7–9 and 7–10). Internally, the syndrome is characterized by hypoplastic lungs. Several cases have been reported in which renal agenesis in one of a pair of monoamniotic twins was associated with normal external features and normal

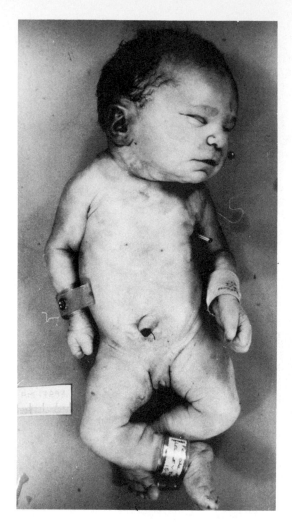

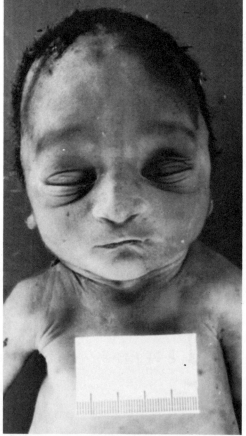

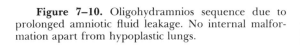

Figure 7–9. Oligohydramnios sequence due to severe renal cystic dysplasia.

Figure 7–10. Oligohydramnios sequence due to prolonged amniotic fluid leakage. No internal malformation apart from hypoplastic lungs.

126

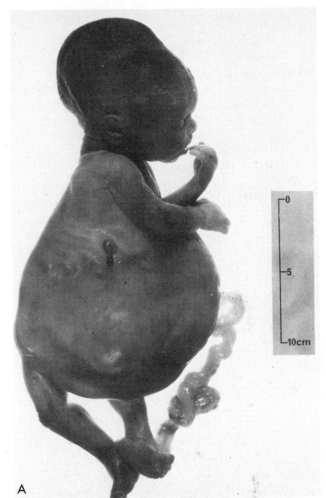

Figure 7–11. *A*, Prune-belly syndrome in a fetus at 26 weeks gestation. *B*, Abdominal wall musculature from the same case showing degenerating muscle fibers. H and E × 30.

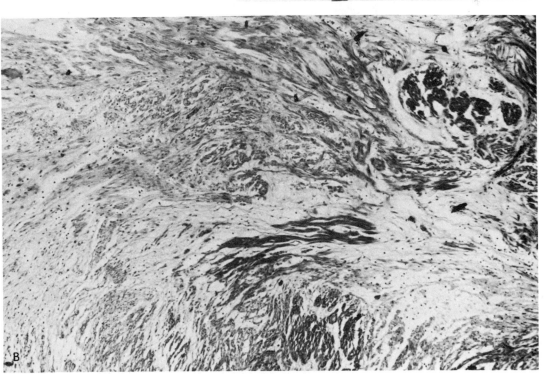

lung growth, resulting from the presence of amniotic fluid associated with the normal twin.[11]

None of the features of the oligohydramnios "syndrome" represent primary defects of organogenesis and are thus not true anomalies. Smith has called the condition "oligohydramnios sequence" (growth retardation, facial abnormality, limb deformity and hypoplastic lungs). It is seen as part of several anomalies.

PRUNE-BELLY SYNDROME

This condition usually occurs in male infants. It is characterized by deficiency of the anterior abdominal wall musculature and bladder outlet obstruction, often associated with absence of the prostate and with cryptorchidism. Although it has been thought that the syndrome represents a defect in formation of mesoderm contributing to both urogenital tract and abdominal wall, study of second trimester fetuses suggests that the abdominal wall muscles may degenerate as a consequence of intrauterine bladder distention (Fig. 7–11). Infants coming to autopsy in the perinatal period usually have total bladder outlet obstruction with features of the oligohydramnios sequence.

THANATOPHORIC DWARFISM AND OTHER FORMS OF LETHAL SHORT-LIMBED DWARFISM

These are described in Chapter 19.

MISCELLANEOUS SYNDROMES

EXOMPHALOS (OMPHALOCELE)

In this condition there is herniation of abdominal viscera through a defect of the anterior abdominal wall in the region of the umbilicus. The wall of the sac consists of peritoneum and the thinned-out wall of the umbilical cord. Large lesions may be associated with marked deficiency of the supraumbilical part of the abdominal wall and contain a large part of the liver in addition to intestines and spleen. Fatalities in this condition are associated with lung hypoplasia, probably due to reduction in thoracic volume resulting from a constant downward tension exerted on the diaphragm by the herniated liver. The abnormality is often associated with other internal anomalies.

BECKWITH-WIEDEMANN SYNDROME[12]

This syndrome is characterized by macrosomia with a particularly large tongue, large kidneys with renal medullary dysplasia, pancreatic hyperplasia including excess islets, and cytomegaly of the fetal adrenal cortex. Many affected infants have a small omphalocele and there is a characteristic crease pattern of the ear lobes. A large number of other defects and associations have been described. The condition is of sporadic occurrence and 60 per cent of infants affected are female. Hypoglycemia and respiratory problems associated with the macroglossia may prove fatal if not recognized in the neonatal period.

PRINCIPLES WHICH DETERMINE THE FATAL NATURE OF MALFORMATIONS

A very large number of malformation syndromes and associated groups of malformations have been described in publications such as Warkany (1971),[3] Smith (1982),[1] and Salmon (1978).[13] Examples of almost any of these syndromes can occasionally be submitted to the pathologist in the neonatal period if, for instance, there is a severe cardiac anomaly. In practice, however, a relatively small number of patterns of malformation syndrome are regularly fatal in the perinatal period. They include those involving severe CNS anomalies, severe cardiac anomalies or hypoplastic lungs, as the reader will discover on looking through all the conditions described in this chapter. Malformed infants who cannot be resuscitated at birth or who die in the first few hours almost invariably have an obstructed airway (e.g., laryngeal atresia [see Chapter 10]) or hypoplastic lungs. Those with cardiac or cerebral anomalies and normally developed lungs usually live for several days or weeks, and the diagnosis will often have been made, or suspected, in life. Thus, in most of the rare malformation syndromes, the pathologist will know the diagnosis before he commences the postmortem examination.

REFERENCES

1. Smith, D. W.: Recognizable Patterns of Human Malformation. 3rd ed. Philadelphia, W. B. Saunders Co., 1982.
2. Pagon, R. A., Smith, D. W., and Shepard, T. H.: Urethral obstruction malformation complex: A cause of abdominal muscle deficiency and the "prune belly." J. Pediatr. 94:900–906, 1979.
3. Warkany, J.: Congenital Malformations. Chicago, Year Book Medical Publishers, 1971.
4. Wilson, J. G., and Fraser, F. C. (eds.): Handbook of Teratology, vol. 1, General Principles and Etiology. New York, Plenum, 1977.
5. Klingberg, M. A., and Papier, C. M.: Teratoepidemiology. J. Biosoc. Sci. II:233–258, 1979.
6. Smithells, R. W.: Environmental teratogens of man. Br. Med. Bull. 32:27–33, 1976.
7. Wilson, J. G.: Embryotoxicity of drugs in man. In Wilson, J. G., and Fraser, F. C. (eds.): Handbook of Teratology, vol. 1, General Principles and Etiology. New York, Plenum, 1977.
8. Brent, R. L.: Environmental factors: Radiation. In Brent, R. L., and Harris, M. I. (eds.): Prevention of Embryonic, Fetal and Perinatal Disease, vol. 3. Bethesda, US Department of Health, Education and Welfare, 1976, pp. 179–197.
9. Rawls, W. E., Desmyter, J., and Melnick, J. L.: Serologic diagnosis and fetal involvement in maternal rubella: Criteria for abortion. JAMA 203:627–631, 1968.
10. Goldfischer, S., Moore, C. L., Johnson, A. B., et al.: Peroxisomal and mitochondrial defects in the cerebro-hepato-renal syndrome. Science 182:62–64, 1973.
11. Fantel, A. G., and Shepard, T. H.: Potter syndrome: Nonrenal features induced by oligoamnios. Am. J. Dis. Child. 129:1346–1347, 1975.
12. Filippi, G., and McKusick, V.: The Beckwith-Wiedemann syndrome. Medicine 49:279–298, 1970.
13. Salmon, M. A.: Developmental Defects and Syndromes. Aylesbury, H. M. & M. Publishers, 1978.

Chapter Eight

Congenital Tumors

Congenital tumors are individually rare and in total contribute little to the workload of the perinatal pathologist. It would clearly be out of place in a work such as this to devote much space to their consideration. The features of the important tumors are described briefly in the chapters on the relevant organs. However, there are some tumors, such as teratomas, which are not precisely limited to a single organ system. In addition, it is important to mention some of the general features of congenital tumors, such as their relationship with malformations, problems in differentiating between neoplasms and hamartomas and the prognosis of apparently malignant tumors in this age group.

TYPES OF CONGENITAL TUMOR

The three major groups of congenital tumors are hamartomas, teratomas and embryomas.

HAMARTOMAS

A hamartoma is a tumor-like mass composed of an excess of tissues which are normal to the site of occurrence. The capacity for growth of a hamartoma normally parallels that of the host and it behaves in a benign fashion. It may be difficult sometimes to differentiate between a hamartoma and a congenital malformation on the one hand or a hamartoma and a neoplasm on the other. Hamartomas may occur at single or multiple sites. In the latter instance they may vary in form at different sites and are sometimes known as hamartoses. They are by far the commonest form of congenital tumor and include relatively banal lesions such as congenital hemangiomas, vascular nevi of the skin and congenital melanotic nevi.

A selection of types of hamartoma which may occur in the perinatal period is listed in Table 8–1. As indicated in the table, some of the syndromes of multiple hamartomas are of autosomal dominant inheritance.

TERATOMAS

These are germ cell tumors of multiple tissues differentiating toward more than one primitive cell layer. The tissues are often foreign to the site of origin of the tumor and show a lack of organization and varying stages of maturation. The

TABLE 8–1. SOME HAMARTOMAS NOTED IN THE PERINATAL PERIOD

SITE	LESION	GENETICS	REFERENCE
Vascular	Hemangiomas; lymphangiomas; cystic hygromas; Angiomatoses (e.g., Sturge-Weber, Von Hippel-Lindau)	Autosomal dominant	Potter and Craig[1] Larroche[2]
Connective tissue	Fibromas, fibromatoses, lipomas		Dehner[3]
Skin	Congenital melanotic nevi		Dehner[3]
Multiple foci	Tuberous sclerosis	Autosomal dominant	Larroche[2]
Neural crest	Neurofibromatosis (von Recklinghausen)	Autosomal dominant	Larroche[2]

tumors are usually at least partly cystic. Histologically, most of the tissues are differentiated and may include organoid structures such as tooth buds. Tissues of ectodermal origin, particularly brain tissue, make up a large proportion of most congenital teratomas. Much of the tissue may resemble glia, but ganglion cells and cavities lined by ependyma are common. Other components regularly found include epidermis and associated structures such as hair and dermal glands and mesodermal tissues including fat, cartilage, bones and muscle. Endodermal components such as intestinal mucosa are less frequent but a very wide variety of structures may be recognized on occasion, including thyroid, pancreas, salivary gland, adrenal and renal tissue.

Increase in size of a teratoma in the neonatal period may be caused by distention of cystic spaces with the products of the lining cells or proliferative activity of the immature constituents. Bolande[4] suggests that the latter form of growth may be limited by the tendency of embryonic tissue to undergo cytodifferentiation into mature structures, although malignant transformation may occur (see later discussion).

In the past there has been discussion and argument over the relationship between teratomas and "parasitic" or "included" twins. In most teratomas there is no vertebral column and the tumor is capable of independent growth. Occasionally, as in several cases described and illustrated by Potter and Craig,[1] the distinction can be extremely difficult.

The most frequent site of teratomas which are noted at birth is the sacrococcygeal region, where they may be attached to the dorsal or ventral surface of the sacrum or coccyx or may arise from the soft tissues of the pelvis (Fig. 8–1). The tumors are often large and may obstruct delivery. Other sites of congenital teratomas include the neck (closely related to the thyroid), the pharyngeal region (from the hard or soft palate, known as epignathi), the mediastinum (sometimes within the pericardium) and the retroperitoneal region.

Teratomas in the infant have a reputation for a high incidence of malignant transformation. Histological evidence of malignant change has been recognized in 11 to 27 per cent of sacrococcygeal teratomas on first resection or biopsy in different published series. Berry and Keeling[5] point out that some of these figures may be influenced by selected late referrals to specializing centers, and Dehner[3] states that malignant transformation is rare in the neonatal period, although it increases rapidly beyond four months age. The most common histological type of malignancy is a large cell adenocarcinoma which resembles the endodermal sinus tumor (yolk sac carcinoma).[3]

EMBRYOMAS

These are tumors arising in organs and tissues which are at a primitive stage of development but are already committed to differentiate into a particular

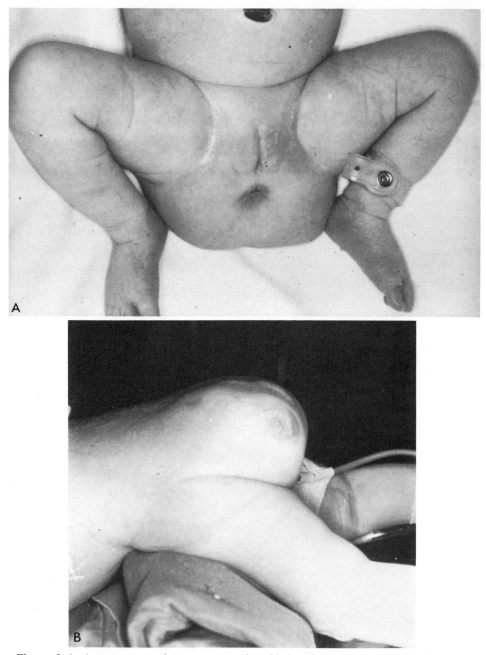

Figure 8–1. A sacrococcygeal teratoma noted at birth. *A* and *B* are external views prior to operative removal. *C,* Glandular epithelium lining cyst wall forming papillary structures resembling choroid plexus. H and E × 150. *D,* Portion of a solid area containing connective tissue, fat, smooth muscle and glial tissue. H and E × 150. This tumor was of benign structure throughout and the child remains well at 6 years of age. (*A* and *B* courtesy of Mr. Pal Singh, Hammersmith Hospital, London, England.)

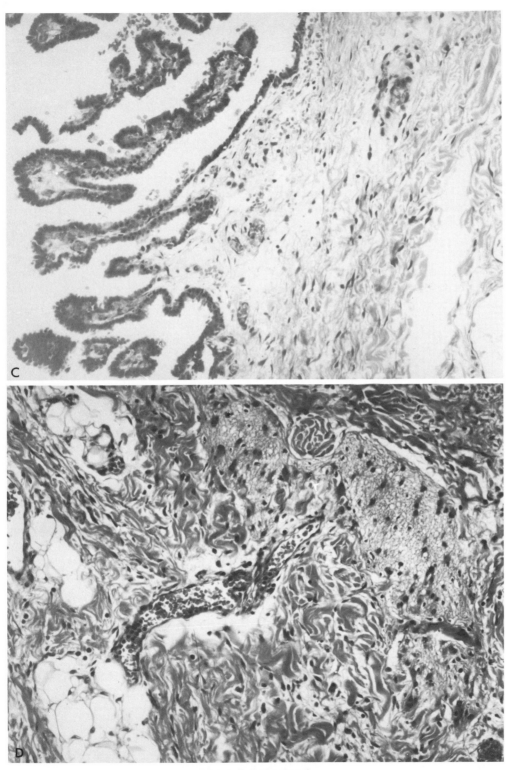

Figure 8–1. *Continued.*

histogenetic type. The tumors are thus restricted either to specific organs or to specific tissues and comprise cells which display features of an early stage of development of the organ or tissue concerned.

A number of types of embryoma may present at birth (Table 8–2). The tumors that are most likely to be encountered are the neuroblastoma and the hepatoblastoma, which are discussed in the appropriate organ system chapters. Others such as rhabdomyoblastoma and retinoblastoma are discussed and illustrated by Dehner.[3]

RELATIONSHIPS BETWEEN CONGENITAL TUMORS AND MALFORMATIONS

A number of associations between malformations and tumors have been reported. In most of these, the tumor developed after birth. Thus Wilms' tumor has been reported to develop with undue frequency in cases of aniridia, congenital hemihypertrophy, the Beckwith-Wiedemann syndrome and a spectrum of genitourinary tract malformations ranging from duplex kidney to male pseudohermaphroditism with hypospadias and cryptorchidism.[4] However, in some series there has been no significant association between these various anomalies and Wilms' tumor.[7] The infantile congeners of Wilms' tumor show a particularly marked association with congenital anomalies. Nodular renal blastoma is seen in cases of trisomy 18 and nephroblastomatosis in association with the Beckwith-Wiedemann syndrome.

Sacrococcygeal teratoma is the one truly congenital tumor associated with malformations. Many of the anomalies reported in conjunction with this tumor are hindgut anomalies—such as imperforate anus, rectovaginal fistula and ectopia vesicae with hypospadias—prompting the suggestion that they result from local growth distortion caused by the tumor in utero.[7] It has also been proposed that the anomalies may be part of the embryopathic process which results in development of the teratoma.[8]

Down syndrome is associated with a greatly increased incidence of leukemia, including both the acute lymphoblastic leukemia and congenital acute myelogenous leukemia.

Other associations between tumors in older infants and children and malformations are discussed by Bolande.[4]

CAUSATION OF CONGENITAL TUMORS

The development of neoplasia during fetal life is clearly relevant to the problem of the etiology of cancer in general. There is little time for environmental

TABLE 8–2.   EMBRYOMAS WHICH MAY BE PRESENT AT BIRTH

TUMOR	COMMENT	REFERENCE
Neuroblastoma	Relatively frequent	See Chap. 16
Hepatoblastoma	Relatively frequent	See Chap. 14
Retinoblastoma	9% recognized at birth— particularly familial or bilateral sporadic tumors	Dehner[3]
Medulloblastoma	Rare in newborn	Dehner[3]
Rhabdomyosarcoma	Most seen in head and neck or genital region	Kauffman and Stout[6]

agents to act, and genetic factors might thus be expected to play a major role. An important hypothesis put forward by Knudson and Strong[9] is that two successive mutations are necessary within a somatic cell for neoplastic change to occur. If the first mutation occurs within a germ cell, only one subsequent mutation during development will lead to tumor formation. In such instances the tendency for neoplasia will be hereditary as is the case with bilateral retinoblastoma. If the first mutation was teratogenic, this would explain the association between teratogenesis and tumor formation.

Population studies which indicate a rather constant rate of occurrence of childhood malignancies in populations of the same racial origin in different parts of the world and at different times tend to support the view that embryonic tumors are genetically determined characteristics.[10] It is pointed out by Berry and Keeling that such hypotheses are not mutually exclusive.

Experimental work indicates that embryonic tissues may be highly susceptible to induction of tumors by certain chemical agents, many of which are also teratogenic, such as urethane and alkylnitrosamines. Agents that have both teratogenic and oncogenic effects tend to cause malformations if administered during organogenesis and tumors if given at a later stage of development. Although the tumors resulting from such experiments are not present at birth, the findings confirm the close relationship between malformations and tumors. The only substance proved to cause tumors in humans following prenatal exposure is diethylstilbestrol. Clear cell vaginal adenocarcinoma has been shown to develop at adolescence in girls whose mothers were given diethylstilbestrol to prevent threatened abortion.[11] Appearance of the tumors is related to the presence of primitive sex duct vestiges (of wolffian or müllerian duct origin) known as vaginal adenosis. These may represent a teratogenic effect of diethylstilbestrol which is known to induce paradoxical masculinization of female fetuses. These observations provide further evidence for an association between teratogenic and oncogenic effects, which may be of relevance to the development of embryonic tumors.

BIOLOGICAL BEHAVIOR OF CONGENITAL TUMORS

As stressed in the opening chapters of this book, it is important for the pathologist to recognize the rapidly changing time course of events in the perinatal period. This applies to tumors as much as to pulmonary or cerebral pathology, although the time course may be a little different.

Most tissues of the infant at birth are undergoing rapid growth and maturation. The most benign tumor may be expected to at least mirror the normal body tissues in this respect. A simple hamartoma such as the capillary hemangioma contains rapidly dividing endothelial cells with multiple mitoses which can be mistaken by the inexperienced pathologist for a malignant vascular tumor. Most of these lesions later undergo spontaneous regression. Histologically malignant congenital embryomas may also undergo spontaneous regression and are less likely to metastasize than apparently identical tumors which present at a later age. This has caused some pathologists to regard the first three months of life as an oncogenic period of grace.[4] The virtual nonoccurrence of classic Wilms' tumor as a congenital neoplasm is a striking distinction from later infancy. Congenital neuroblastoma is the best-known example of a tumor in which regression and cytodifferentiation may occur in both primary and metastatic tumor deposits. Other congenital tumors in which there is a tendency for regression include nodular renal blastoma and nephroblastomatosis. Dehner[3] says of endodermal sinus tumors of the neonatal testis that "like other malignant tumors in the neonate and infant under one year of age, the prognosis is usually much better than the histological features would suggest." Congenital fibrosarcoma-like fibromatosis has a histological appearance identical to that of fibrosarcoma in the adult and yet is usually adequately treated by local excision. Congenital myelogenous leukemia has been claimed to have a high incidence of spontaneous regression, but this may be a result of the difficulty of differentiating true leukemia from other myeloproliferative disorders in the neonatal period.[3]

Rapidly fatal metastasizing tumors may present in the neonatal period, but the pathologist needs to be aware of the potentially benign behavior of many histologically malignant tumors in this age group, as this may modify the extent of treatment which is appropriate.

CONGENITAL SECONDARY TUMORS

These are extremely rare. Malignant melanoma is the best-documented example of a tumor that can spread from mother to fetus across the placenta.[12] Occasional cases of choriocarcinoma have been recorded with spread to both mother and infant.[13]

REFERENCES

1. Potter, E. L., and Craig, J. M.: Pathology of the Fetus and the Infant, 3rd ed. Chicago, Year Book Medical Publishers, 1976, pp. 177–206.
2. Larroche, J. C.: Developmental Pathology of the Neonate. Amsterdam, Excerpta Medica, 1977, pp. 501–504.
3. Dehner, L. P.: Neoplasms of the fetus and neonate. In Naeye, R. L., Kissane, J. M., and Kaufman, N. (eds.): Perinatal Diseases. Baltimore, Williams & Wilkins, 1981, pp. 286–345.
4. Bolande, R. P.: Neoplasia of early life and its relationships to teratogenesis. In Rosenberg, H. S., and Bolande, R. P. (eds.): Perspectives in Pediatric Pathology, Vol 3. Chicago, Year Book Medical Publishers, 1976, pp. 145–183.
5. Berry, C. L., and Keeling, J. W.: Embryonic tumours of children. In Berry, C. L. (ed.): Paediatric Pathology. Berlin, Springer Verlag, 1981, pp. 641–669.
6. Kauffmann, S. L., and Stout, A. P.: Congenital mesenchymal tumors. Cancer 18:460–476, 1965.
7. Berry, C. L., Keeling, J., and Hilton, C.: Coincidence of congenital malformation and embryonic tumors of childhood. Arch. Dis. Child. 45:229–231, 1970.
8. Fraumeni, J. F., Li, F. P., and Dalager, N.: Teratomas in children: Epidemiologic features. J. Natl. Cancer Inst. 51:1425–1430, 1973.
9. Knudson, A. G., and Strong, L. C.: Mutation and cancer: A model for Wilms' tumor of the kidney. J. Natl. Cancer Inst. 48:313–324, 1972.
10. Innis, M. D.: Hereditary theory of childhood oncogenesis. Oncology 26:474–480, 1972.
11. Herbst, A. L., Ulfelder, H., and Poskanzer, D. C.: Adenocarcinoma of the vagina: Association of maternal stilbestrol therapy with tumor appearance in young women. N. Engl. J. Med. 284:878–881, 1971.
12. Freedman, W. L., and McMahon, F. J.: Placental metastasis. Obstet. Gynecol. 16:550–560, 1960.
13. Daamen, C. B. F., Bloem, G. W. D., and Westerbeek, A. J.: Chorionepithelioma in mother and child. J. Obstet. Gynaecol. Br. Cwlth. 68:144–149, 1961.

Chapter Nine

Perinatal Infection

Infections make a major contribution to perinatal mortality and morbidity and may present to clinician or pathologist in many different guises. Specific aspects of infection as they occur in different parts of the body are discussed later in this book under the various organ systems: those relating to the placenta have already been outlined in Chapter 4. This chapter will deal with the general aspects of perinatal infection and the relative importance of different infectious agents as causes of perinatal illness or death.

The fetus and infant are particularly vulnerable to infection because humoral and cellular defense mechanisms are inadequately developed. In this respect the situation resembles that of the immunosuppressed adult. Organisms that would normally be regarded as nonpathogenic in later life may cause life-threatening illness in the perinatal period and such illnesses may progress rapidly. However, the muted reaction of the fetus and neonate to infection can delay diagnosis, and the signs of a rapidly progressing infection may be difficult to distinguish from those of congenital heart disease, birth asphyxia or respiratory distress syndrome.

Infection may be a major cause of preterm birth, particularly in low socioeconomic groups; prematurely born infants are at greater risk of infection than their mature counterparts.

Viral infection of the embryo or fetus may lead to overt malformation or chronic destructive processes in organs such as the brain, as well as severe retardation in fetal growth. Other manifestations of fetal infection may include hepatosplenomegaly, jaundice, purpura or cataracts. Therefore, the pathologist, like the clinician, needs to consider the possibility of infection in infants who come to his attention with a wide variety of signs.

DEFENSE MECHANISMS IN THE FETUS AND NEWBORN INFANT

The fetus enjoys a measure of protection against bacterial infection but has poor defenses against some viruses. The newborn infant, particularly the preterm infant, has rather limited defenses against any form of infection.

DEFENSE MECHANISMS SPECIFIC TO THE FETUS

These relate to the position of the fetus within the amniotic sac. As already mentioned in Chapter 3, the intact placental membranes form a barrier to bacterial infection ascending from the vagina; the barrier may be breeched if the membranes become devitalized over the os, or are prematurely ruptured. In addition, normal amniotic fluid has antibacterial properties apparently related to the phosphate concentration, level of zinc and presence of an organic component.[1] Infection of the fetus from the mother by the hematogenous route requires transfer of organisms across the placental villi, that is, from maternal intervillous space across trophoblast layer, basement membrane and vascular endothelium of the fetal villous capillaries. The villi appear to form an effective barrier to transfer of most bacteria but do not seem to hinder passage of a number of viruses, *Treponema pallidum, Listeria monocytogenes* or toxoplasma.

HUMORAL FACTORS

The fetus acquires maternal IgG antibodies by transfer across the placenta so that by birth it has an IgG level similar to that of the mother.[2] Most of the transfer occurs during the third trimester; therefore the preterm infant may be at a disadvantage from this standpoint. IgM and IgA antibodies do not cross the placenta but can be synthesized by the fetus in response to antigenic stimulation from 20 weeks' gestation on. At birth the infant has greater resistance to infections against which there are effective antibodies within the IgG fraction—that is, many viral and some gram-positive bacterial infections—than to infections against which IgM antibodies are important, such as gram-negative bacterial infections. The fetus will not acquire IgG antibodies to any infection against which the mother herself is not immune. The infant who is exposed to infection in utero may produce specific IgM antibodies. The detection of such antibodies in cord serum can indeed be used as a diagnostic test for a number of congenital infections.[3]

After birth the breast-fed infant may acquire IgA antibodies in the mother's milk. These are important for providing protection to the mucous membranes and may aid in prevention of gastrointestinal infection in young infants.[4]

Nonspecific immune functions may be poorly developed in the fetus and newborn infant. Activation of the complement system is normally associated with production of biologically active products which enhance vascular permeability, chemotaxis and phagocytosis. Complement activity is deficient in the newborn and, as a result, the associated immune functions are impaired.[5, 6]

CELLULAR REACTIONS

The normal inflammatory reaction to injury or infection includes a febrile response related to release of endogenous pyrogens from leukocytes.[7] This reaction is poorly developed in the newborn. Similarly, the raised total neutrophil count characteristic of inflammation in the adult is an inconstant occurrence in the neonate, although a rise in the total number of band cells may be a useful aid to diagnosis of infection in this age group.[8] The profound neutropenia which may be seen in severe neonatal infections is usually associated with a rise in the ratio of immature to total neutrophils. The localized cellular reactions of infection involving a polymorphonuclear leukocyte infiltration followed by a mononuclear response are incompletely developed in the neonatal period.[9] The leukocytes of the newborn may also have deficient bactericidal activity because of inadequacy of the hexose-monophosphate pathway, a situation which persists in infants with chronic granulomatous disease.[10]

ROUTES OF INFECTION OF THE FETUS AND NEONATE

Fetal infection occurs in most cases as a secondary result of maternal infection (Fig. 9–1).

INTRAUTERINE INFECTION

The classic chronic intrauterine infections of the TORCH group and others including those caused by *Treponema pallidum* and *Listeria monocytogenes* affect the fetus by the transplacental route from the maternal bloodstream. Ascending infection from the vagina may involve the fetus in utero in cases of prolonged rupture of the membranes, or by invasion of the amniotic sac through devitalized membranes over the uterine os. This is the presumed method of fetal infection in cases of intrauterine candidiasis.

Another possible route of infection of the fetus from the mother is by way of the uterine wall directly through the chorion and amnion.

In addition, the fetus may be infected directly during the course of procedures such as amniocentesis, intrauterine intraperitoneal transfusion or fetal surgery.

INTRAPARTUM INFECTION

Following the onset of labor, and particularly when the membranes are ruptured, the fetus is most likely to become infected by organisms ascending from the vagina. Obstetric manipulations, including vaginal examination and application of scalp electrodes for monitoring, may promote fetal infection. During the second stage of labor the fetus may acquire organisms during the passage through the birth canal.

Most of the infections acquired by such means are bacterial and are caused by organisms known to colonize the vagina, including β-hemolytic streptococci of group B and *Hemophilus influenzae*, or bowel organisms which readily gain access to the vagina such as *Escherichia coli*.

One form of viral infection which the fetus most often acquires from focal lesions in the birth canal is caused by *Herpesvirus hominis*, and cytomegalovirus may also infect the infant by this route.

ROUTES OF FETAL INFECTION

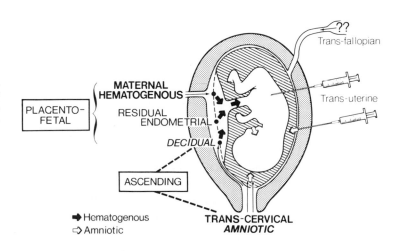

Figure 9–1. Schematic representation of possible routes of infection. (From Blanc, W.: Perinatal Diseases. Baltimore, Williams and Wilkins, 1981.)

NEONATAL INFECTION

Colonization of skin and lower gastrointestinal tract with organisms is a normal neonatal event. Rate and pattern of colonization are affected by a variety of factors, including maturity of the infant at birth, the environment into which the infant is born and maintained in the first days of life (home, hospital nursery or neonatal intensive care unit) and the mode of infant feeding adopted. Normal newborn infants acquire hemolytic streptococci and *Staphylococcus epidermidis* in the nose and throat and on the skin within a few days after birth, whereas ill infants admitted to neonatal intensive care units are more likely to become colonized with gram-negative bacteria.[11] Whether colonization is associated with development of an overt infectious illness will depend on the state of health and maturity of the infant, the level of colonization and virulence of the organism and the sites to which the organisms gain access.

In a hospital environment infants are at risk of acquiring bacterial infections by a variety of means. Organisms may be instilled into the airways during resuscitation with contaminated equipment. They may be transferred from other infected infants on the hands of attendants, inspired from infected humidifier reservoirs or introduced into vessels, airways or body cavities via catheters, endotracheal tubes or drainage tubes.

Viral infections can also be acquired in the neonatal period by such routes and occasionally also from an infected blood transfusion.

The umbilicus of the newborn infant provides a potential site for the entry of microorganisms. Umbilical sepsis is now rare in developed countries; the older literature on the subject is reviewed by Morison.[56]

PATHOLOGY OF INFECTION ACQUIRED IN UTERO

NATURE AND INCIDENCE OF INTRAUTERINE INFECTIONS

The importance of intrauterine infection lies in the persisting handicap characteristic of infants who survive severe infections rather than in the frequency of intrauterine infection. The organisms most often responsible for intrauterine infection have been given the acronym TORCH agents (*T*oxoplasmosis, *R*ubella, *C*ytomegalovirus, *H*erpes simplex).[12] The incidence of detectable congenital infection by cytomegalovirus is of the order of 5 per thousand births (as compared with about 40 maternal infections); that of rubella is only about 5 per ten thousand births (in nonepidemic years). The incidence of toxoplasmosis varies from 0.05 to 6 per thousand births in different countries. Other congenital infections are less frequent.

It is important to recognize that the infant born with obvious stigmata of chronic infection represents only the severe end of a spectrum of intrauterine infection; the effects on the fetus may vary greatly and many infants have no apparent illness. The number of infants found to have viral infections at birth represents a small proportion of cases in which the mother shows evidence of infection during pregnancy. In addition, the range of viruses which can be shown to affect the fetus is but a small proportion of those that affect the mother. This would suggest that the placental villi do provide a significant barrier to the spread of viral infection from mother to fetus but that the barrier is for some reason less effective than normal in the case of a few organisms such as cytomegalovirus and rubella. The method of transfer of viruses across the placenta is not known. Suggestions have included transfer within leukocytes and transfer as a two-stage process with development of a lesion in the placental villus followed by secondary rupture into the vicinity of the fetal vessels. The fetus may not show infection in about half the cases involving placental infection.[13]

SIGNS OF INTRAUTERINE INFECTION

The infant who has suffered chronic intrauterine infection may show a number of characteristic features, some of them nonspecific and others indicative of one or a small group of infectious agents.

Growth retardation is common to all chronic intrauterine infections and the infants are frequently born before term. Gross evidence of damage to the CNS is a characteristic finding: microcephaly may be seen in rubella, whereas hydrocephaly is more frequent in cases of infection with cytomegalovirus or *Toxoplasma gondii*. Petechial hemorrhages are seen in any of the TORCH group while hepatosplenomegaly or jaundice may develop in any of the chronic intrauterine infections. The presence of microphthalmia or cataracts is suggestive of rubella, whereas x-rays may reveal the osteochondritis of syphilis.

Macroscopic pointers to congenital infection are listed in Table 9–1.

VIRAL INFECTIONS

RUBELLA

The frequency of fetal infection and the severity of the effects differ according to the gestational age at which maternal infection occurred. The highest incidence of chronic fetal infection with multiple organ involvement occurs if the mother acquires the illness in the first 8 weeks of pregnancy (Fig. 9–2). Beyond 8 weeks there is a sharp reduction both in the frequency of fetal infection and in the proportion of infected infants who have obvious defects. From Figure 9–2 it can be seen, however, that chronic fetal infection and handicaps can follow maternal rubella infections which develop quite late in the second trimester.

The congenital rubella syndrome as first outlined by Gregg in 1942 was composed of cataracts, deafness and patent ductus arteriosus.[14] Examination of the large number of affected infants born after the rubella epidemic of 1964 allowed recognition of a wide range of additional pathological lesions at autopsy and various forms of handicaps in survivors (the expanded rubella syndrome). Some of the lesions are transient and related to the time during which active viral disease persists in fetus and infant, while others are permanent or may present as delayed effects of viral damage at any time up to puberty.[12]

TABLE 9–1. MACROSCOPIC FEATURES SUGGESTING POSSIBLE CONGENITAL INFECTION

External	Large placenta
	Hydrops
	Fetal growth retardation
	Jaundice
	Purpura
	Skin rashes
	Eye lesions ⟨ Cataracts / Microphthalmia
Internal	Hydrocephaly
	Microcephaly
	Hepatomegaly
	Splenomegaly
	Miliary lesions of liver, lung and other organs

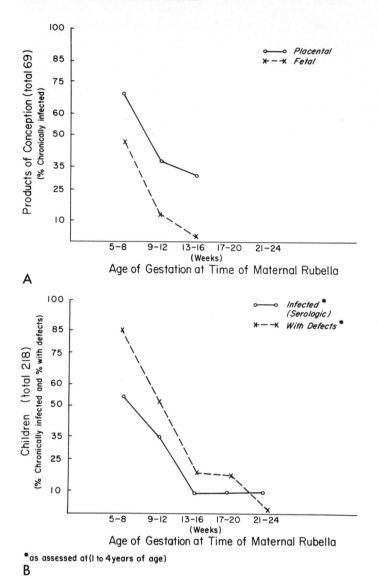

A

B

*as assessed at (1 to 4 years of age)

Figure 9–2. Relationship between gestational age and time of maternal rubella infection and outcome of conceptual infection. *A,* Incidence of chronic placental and fetal infection. *B,* Incidence of infection in newborn and percentage of those with defects detectable in the first years of life. (From Alford, C. A.: Rubella. *In* Remington, J. S. and Klein, J. O. (eds.): Infectious Diseases of the Fetus and Newborn Infant. W. B. Saunders Co., 1976.)

Abortion or fetal death may result from rubella infection, but more often the infant is liveborn and shows evidence of neonatal or delayed disease. The wide spectrum of abnormalities observed results from virally induced mechanisms including inhibition of cell proliferation and direct cytolytic damage.[15] The viral damage preferentially affects vascular walls, causes impairment in blood supply to developing organs and leads to local tissue necrosis, malformation and reduced organ growth. The pattern of damage produced depends on the time of infection. Thus specific cardiac anomalies such as septal defect will only develop following infection within 4 to 6 weeks after conceptional age, whereas retinopathy and deafness may result from rubella infection over a far wider gestational age range.[12]

Specific Pathological Features. FETAL GROWTH RETARDATION. The form of growth retardation observed in congenital rubella syndrome is that referred to in Chapter 1 as "symmetrical" (see p. 8), in which growth of all organs is reduced in proportion, although indices of maturation such as gyral convolutional pattern and histological development of renal glomeruli are appropriate for gestational age. This is presumably due to the inhibition of cell proliferation throughout the tissues of the embryo.

CARDIOVASCULAR SYSTEM. Anomalies recognized most frequently are persistent patency of the ductus arteriosus and stenosis of pulmonary artery branches, although a number of other lesions have been reported, including atrial and ventricular septal defects, stenosis of pulmonary and aortic valves, tetralogy of Fallot, transposition of the great arteries, coarctation of the aorta, persistent atrioventricular canal and tricuspid atresia.[15, 16] A characteristic histological finding is focal fibromuscular proliferation of the intima of artery walls in the absence of significant damage to internal elastic lamina and media. Such changes may involve the pulmonary arteries and aorta and extend into their branches. Focal myocardial necrosis, with or without inflammation, or myocardial scarring and sclerosis of one or more cardiac valves are relatively frequent. The ductus has thin muscle partly replaced by collagen with very little elastic tissue.[17]

THE LUNG. Symptoms of respiratory distress are usually caused by congestive heart failure, but radiological infiltrates are common and are associated with histological evidence of interstitial pneumonitis with patchy collapse, a mononuclear cell infiltrate and occasional interstitial fibrosis. Hyaline membrane formation may be seen in the early stages.[18]

THE LIVER. Hepatomegaly and jaundice are common features of congenital rubella syndrome. There is increased serum alkaline phosphatase and transaminases associated with persistence of rubella virus within the liver.[15] Histological features include parenchymal necrosis, focal extramedullary erythropoiesis, periportal round cell infiltration and bile stasis. The picture of neonatal hepatitis with giant cell transformation (see Chapter 14) is sometimes recognized.

LYMPHORETICULAR SYSTEM. Thrombocytopenia and purpura with anemia and splenomegaly are common, clinically recognized components of the congenital rubella syndrome and are transient phenomena in surviving infants. The anemia is of the hemolytic type and may be associated with histological evidence of erythropoiesis in stomach, intestines, adrenals and kidney. The spleen may show fibrosis and is sometimes shrunken rather than enlarged. Lymph nodes often have precocious development of germinal centers and the thymus is frequently reduced in size with nonspecific lymphopenia on histology.

Disordered immune mechanisms are evidenced by diminished T lymphocytes, proliferation of B lymphocytes and the persistence of virus excretion despite production of rubella antibodies.[12] A number of specific immunological abnormalities have been observed.[19]

PANCREAS. Interstitial pancreatitis has been reported and about 20 per cent of survivors of congenital rubella syndrome develop diabetes mellitus.[20]

CENTRAL NERVOUS SYSTEM. The brain may be small as part of the generalized growth inhibition. Other lesions result from cytolytic damage or from damage to the blood vessels. There is often deposition of calcium and acid mucopolysaccharide in the cerebral vessel walls or focal destruction of vessel walls with disruption of the internal elastic layer and intimal proliferation. Damage involves vessels of all sizes but most frequently the capillaries of the basal ganglia.

EYE AND EAR. Ocular changes include cataracts, microphthalmos, iridocyclitis and retinitis. The latter comprises focal degeneration and proliferation of the pigment epithelium. Deafness in the congenital rubella syndrome is believed caused by damage to the stria vascularis of the cochlea duct with collapse of Reissner's membrane.[15]

BONES. Radiolucencies in the metaphyses of the long bones (celery stalking) correspond to histological findings of increased osteoblastic and osteoclastic activity at the osteochondral junction, with poor development of bone trabeculae.

CYTOMEGALOVIRUS

This is the most frequent cause of perinatal viral infection. It has been estimated to involve 8 per 1000 births in the United States and to be responsible for brain damage in 1 per 1000 births.[12] A high proportion of cases of congenital cytomegalovirus infection are asymptomatic in the neonatal period. It has been estimated that for every infant born with symptoms of cytomegalic inclusion disease there are at least 10 infected infants who do not have abnormalities that suggest such a diagnosis.[21] In the absence of prospective screening for cytomegalovirus, the cases recognized by the neonatologist or pathologist in the perinatal period will therefore represent only the severe end of the spectrum. As infants subjected to neonatal intensive care may also acquire the infection postnatally (e.g., by way of blood transfusion), it will not always be possible for the pathologist to determine which infants were infected in utero.

The infant with severe congenital cytomegalovirus infection may have evidence of growth retardation of the symmetrical form, like that associated with rubella infection. Other features include hepatosplenomegaly, anemia, purpura and jaundice with hydrocephaly or microcephaly. Infants with this infection occasionally have hydrops. Unlike rubella infection, there is little evidence for continued tissue destruction after birth in congenitally affected infants although, like rubella, the virus may persist in the infant in the presence of a high titer of neutralizing antibody.[21] Late development of neurological handicap is likely to be caused by delayed recognition of cerebral damage that occurred in utero rather than continued cerebral damage after birth.

Specific Pathological Features. The most readily recognized morphological feature of cytomegalovirus infection is the presence of the characteristic enlarged cells with large nuclear inclusions, a nucleolus, a perinuclear halo and intracytoplasmic inclusions. The infected cells measure 25 to 40 μ with an intranuclear inclusion of 8 to 10 μ. The inclusions are a mixture of chromatin and virus particles. Intracytoplasmic inclusions measure 2 to 4 μ in diameter and appear late in the life of the infected cell.

The organs most frequently found to be obviously involved at autopsy are kidney, liver and lung. Inclusion-bearing cells are less often found in pancreas, thyroid and brain and may rarely be seen in other organs.

The kidneys may not show any macroscopic abnormality but on histology there is focal replacement of the normal epithelium of the proximal convoluted tubules by the typical inclusion-bearing cells and a mononuclear cell infiltration of the interstitial tissue (Fig. 9–3). Foci of extramedullary hemopoiesis may be prominent. Demonstration of desquamated inclusion-bearing renal tubule epithelial cells in the urine has been used as a diagnostic test.

Enlargement of the liver results mainly from extensive extramedullary hemopoiesis, although other changes including cholestasis, focal necrosis, bile duct proliferation and giant cell transformation (see Chapter 14) may also be present. Inclusions may be seen in bile duct epithelium but are often sparse (Fig. 9–4).

The lungs may be involved in a nodular or diffuse pneumonitis, or there may be occasional inclusion-bearing alveolar epithelial cells with little inflammatory reaction.

The brain is specifically affected in cases involving infection dating from early in gestation.[12] The inclusion-bearing cells are localized to the subependymal region and the virus apparently multiplies within the subependymal germinal matrix cells. Focal necrosis with inflammatory cell infiltration and inclusion-bearing cells in endothelium or neurones is seen in the active stage. Death of the subependymal cells is followed by periventricular calcification and may result in microcephaly or cerebral atrophy with ventricular dilation and focal microgyria or cystic encephalomalacia.

Ocular changes include chorioretinitis, microphthalmos and cataracts.

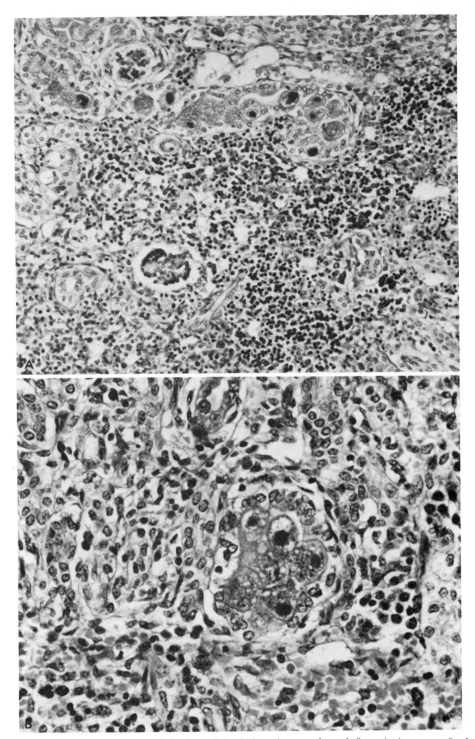

Figure 9–3. Cytomegalovirus infection of the kidney in a newborn infant. *A*, A group of tubule cells containing the typical nuclear inclusions is seen in the upper half of the field. Elsewhere there is extensive extramedullary haemopoietic activity. H and E × 120. *B*, View of a different area of the same section showing cells with both nuclear and cytoplasmic inclusions. H and E × 400.

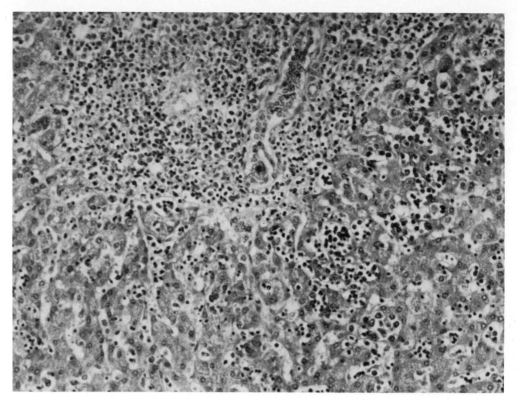

Figure 9–4. Liver in congenital cytomegalovirus infection. H and E × 120. There is excessive extramedullary hemopoiesis and one inclusion-containing cell within the bile duct epithelium.

HERPES SIMPLEX

There are two antigenic strains of *Herpesvirus hominis.* Type 1 infection usually causes "cold sores" in the oral region, while type 2 affects the genitalia and is transmitted venereally. Of herpes simplex infections recognized in the neonate, about 20 per cent are caused by type 1 and 80 per cent by type 2.[12] The incidence of recurrent herpes simplex infections increases in pregnancy, particularly during the latter months. The risk to the infant is said to be about 10 per cent in cases of maternal genital herpes after 32 weeks' gestation, rising to 40 per cent if lesions are present at term. Colonization of the fetus with the virus occurs within about four hours following rupture of the membranes: about half of the infants who acquire the virus in this way become infected. Performance of cesarian section to prevent fetal infection is thus of value only if the membranes are intact or have been ruptured for less than four hours.

Fetal infection may occur early in pregnancy and lead to abortion. Infants born following intrauterine infection may have lesions in skin, CNS, liver, adrenal and eye. Skin lesions are vesicular and have a similar histological appearance to those of varicella-zoster, with balloon cells showing intranuclear inclusions and margination of nuclear chromatin at the periphery of the vesicles. Lesions may be present at birth in infants infected in utero or develop in the neonatal period, often over the presenting part, in infants infected during birth. CNS lesions have areas of liquefactive necrosis or of acute inflammation with impaired brain growth and microcephaly. Liver and adrenals in disseminated herpes simplex have multiple punctate yellow or red lesions which show coagulative necrosis histologically. Typical inclusions may be seen at the margin of the necrotic zones (Fig. 9–5). Eye lesions include conjunctivitis or chorioretinitis.

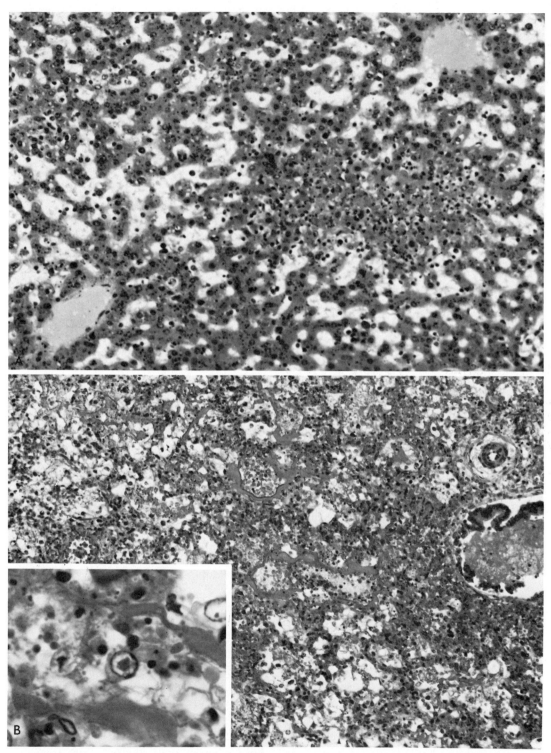

Figure 9–5. Congenital herpes infection in an infant who died at 4 days of age. *A,* Liver showing focal necrosis. H and E × 150. *B,* Lung showing patchy necrosis with hyaline membrane formation. H and E × 150. Inset × 600 shows a cell with a typical nuclear inclusion. (Courtesy of Dr. J. Huber, Pathological Institute, Rijksuniversiteit Utrecht, Utrecht, Belgium.)

ENTEROVIRUSES

The main enteroviruses to infect the fetus and newborn are those of coxsackievirus group B. The infant may become infected in utero shortly before birth, although most infections occur in the early neonatal period, often with onset at about 7 days of age.[12, 22] The affected newborn infant may be asymptomatic or may show a spectrum of conditions including encephalitis and myocarditis.

Pathological findings in the heart include pericardial effusions, cardiac enlargement with dilation of chambers and red and yellow mottling of the flabby myocardium. On microscopy there is focal necrosis with a pleomorphic inflammatory infiltrate (Fig. 9–6). The CNS may show meningitis with mononuclear cell infiltrate and there may be focal hemorrhages and patchy inflammation throughout the brain and brain stem. Inflammatory changes are sometimes seen in pancreas or kidneys and the liver may be congested or show focal necrosis.

HEPATITIS B

The infant of the mother with hepatitis B infection may acquire the antigen transplacentally, but seldom shows signs of infection.[12] Infection of the infant is most likely when the mother has symptomatic disease such as hepatitis in late pregnancy. Transmission in such cases probably occurs during delivery or in the first few days of life with seroconversion at 4 to 6 weeks of age. Few such infants develop symptoms, although some have chronic subclinical hepatitis with raised serum SGPT values and persistent circulating antigen. Acute hepatitis with icterus has been recorded rarely at 2 to 5 months of age.

OTHER VIRUSES

Other viruses including vaccinia, varicella-zoster, rubeola, mumps, polio and western equine encephalitis have also been reported to cause congenital infection.[12]

TOXOPLASMOSIS

Toxoplasma gondii is a protozoan whose main host is the cat. The parasite undergoes two separate life cycles, an enteroepithelial cycle, which can occur only within the cat ileum, and an extraintestinal cycle, which may occur also in alternate hosts such as the pig, sheep and man.[24] The enteroepithelial stage leads to production of massive numbers of oocysts in the feces, which provides one source of human infection. The extraintestinal cycle involves the trophozoite form of the parasite, which can survive and divide only within cells. Endodyogeny of trophozoites within tissue cells may be followed by cell rupture with release of organisms which invade contiguous cells or by the formation of cysts. Consumption of such cysts within undercooked meat is the second main source of human infection; the encysted parasites are resistant to acid-pepsin and tryptic digestion.

Transmission of toxoplasmosis to the fetus occurs during primary infections in pregnancy of seronegative women. It should therefore be preventable if seronegative women avoid contact with cat droppings or consumption of undercooked meat during pregnancy. The severity of the effects on the fetus are related to the time of pregnancy when the maternal infection develops: symptomatic or fatal fetal illness is mainly confined to instances when infection developed in the first and second trimesters. Fetal infection occurs by the transplacental route and cysts may be found within the placenta (see Chapter 4).

The central nervous system is usually severely involved in cases recognized in the neonatal period. Hydrocephaly, chorioretinitis and radiological evidence of intracranial calcification are classic features, but other presentations such as

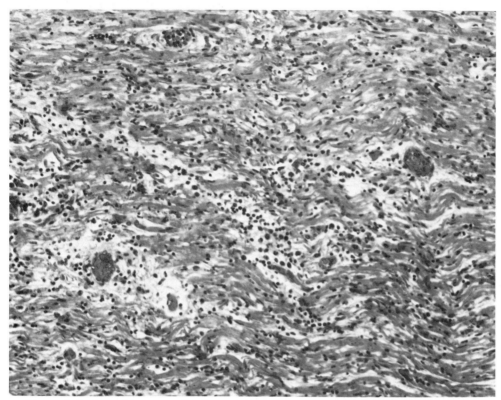

Figure 9–6. Coxsackie myocarditis in an infant who died at 17 days of age. H and E × 150. (Courtesy of Dr. J. Huber, Pathological Institute, Rijksuniversiteit Utrecht, Utrecht, Belgium.)

hydrops fetalis are recognized. Many infants subsequently found to have severe disease appear normal at birth, and severe CNS and eye lesions are not detected for several weeks or months. In some cases this seems attributable to a genuine delayed onset of disease, particularly in preterm infants.

Specific Pathological Features. Histological diagnosis depends on recognition of the parasites. The trophozoites are 2 to 4 μ in diameter and 4 to 8 μ in length, slightly crescentic in form, pointed at one end and rounded at the other with a central nucleus. They may be stained with Wright or Giemsa stains and are characteristic of the acute stage of infection. The cysts are intracellular, may be up to 200 μ in diameter and have a weakly PAS-positive wall. The encysted Toxoplasma have many paraglycogen granules which stain well with PAS.

In infants who die in the neonatal period, there is often extensive cerebral destruction involving cortex, basal ganglia and sometimes the periventricular region. The distribution of lesions relates to the parasitic involvement of the vasculature. There is infiltration of the leptomeninges over affected regions by lymphocytes, plasma cells, macrophages and eosinophils, and parasites may be identified in the intima of the vessels. Periventricular and periaqueductal vasculitis with necrosis leads to development of hydrocephaly. The cerebral lesions are marked by the formation of glial nodules, and necrosis may result in formation of cysts. Extensive calcification often develops in necrotic areas. Toxoplasma cysts and trophozoites may be recognized within or adjacent to areas of necrosis or inflammation, either related to the vessels or in areas of the brain not involved in the inflammatory process. Variable destruction of the spinal cord may be present, and cysts are usually recognized in the white matter.

Chorioretinitis characteristically accompanies the CNS lesions.

The lungs may show widening of alveolar septa with a mononuclear cell infiltrate, and parasites may be found in alveolar epithelial cells and in the endothelium of small vessels. There is sometimes a frank bronchopneumonia.

The heart is nearly always involved. There is focal mononuclear infiltration with patchy hyaline necrosis of myocardial cells, and cysts are found in myocardial fibers with no inflammatory reaction (Fig. 9–7). Myocarditis is thought to be the result of a local reaction to rupture of parasitized cells.

The liver and spleen are enlarged but generally show nonspecific changes related to increased erythropoiesis. Extensive extramedullary hemopoiesis is seen also in the kidney. Focal inflammatory involvement of glomeruli with glomerular and tubular necrosis may occur, and cysts may be recognized in glomeruli and renal tubules of kidneys with no inflammatory involvement. Skeletal muscle, like cardiac muscle, may show focal myositis or merely the presence of multiple parasites or cysts within the muscle fibers. Focal necrosis has been described in adrenal cortex and pancreas, and interstitial inflammation and necrosis can occur in testes and ovaries.

FUNGAL INFECTION: *Candida Albicans*

Oral and perianal thrush are common relatively banal conditions in the newborn and may either result from infection by vaginal organisms during delivery or occur as an environmentally acquired infection.

Intrauterine infection with *Candida albicans* occurs as an ascending infection from the maternal vagina, although the transplacental route has been suggested as a possible alternative.[25, 26] The presence of established fetal infection at birth in cases without a history of prolonged rupture of the membranes indicates that the organism may reach the fetus through intact membranes. Fetal infection is

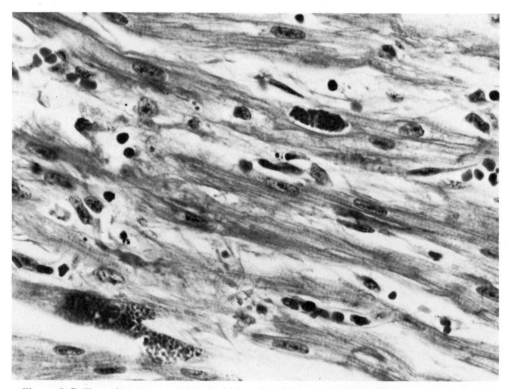

Figure 9–7. Toxoplasma cysts within the heart of an infant one month of age. H and E × 600.

probably most likely to occur during the third trimester when the maternal vagina frequently becomes colonized with *Candida albicans*.

The infant with generalized candidiasis at birth may be growth-retarded and show a skin rash and thus resembles an infant with one of the more common viral or protozoal infections. Subsequent isolation of Candida may be thought to indicate a neonatal infection with the organism. It seems to me probable that the frequency of intrauterine infection with *Candida albicans* is considerably underestimated.

Intrauterine infection may result in massive involvement of the gastrointestinal tract with ulceration and inflammation of the esophagus, stomach and small intestine. Mycelium and spores invade the mucosa and submucosa with penetration into vessels. Cutaneous manifestations may include a diffuse papular and vesicular rash in addition to the common oral and perianal lesions. Pulmonary involvement is frequent in the form of a congenital Candida aspiration pneumonia (Fig. 9–8). The placental lesions are described in Chapter 4.

Cutaneous, gastrointestinal and pulmonary lesions in the fetus could all be expected as a direct result of contamination with infected amniotic fluid which the fetus may aspirate or swallow. Evidence of spread by the fetal bloodstream is provided by cases in which there is involvement of the brain by meningoencephalitis or hydrocephalus,[27] or granulomas within the kidneys. Infants who die within a few days after birth may have lesions within brain, lungs, gastrointestinal tract, kidneys, adrenals, myocardium, liver, spleen, thyroid, pancreas and bone marrow.[28]

BACTERIA: *Listeria monocytogenes*

Listeria monocytogenes is the one bacterium which characteristically causes chronic fetal infection. Although it is a common organism in many farm animals, there seems little evidence that human infection is often acquired directly from animals; most perinatal infections appear to be sporadic.[29] Transmission is usually considered to be transplacental following a minor maternal illness and primary infection of the placenta. Fetal septicemia and involvement of all fetal organs leads to contamination of amniotic fluid with infected urine which may subsequently be aspirated and accentuate the pulmonary changes. It has been suggested that the fetus may form a reservoir of infection which, on reintroduction to the mother, may promote abortion, premature birth or stillbirth.

The infant with congenital listeriosis may be stillborn or may present features indicative of a TORCH infection, including growth retardation, hepatosplenomegaly and a petechial rash. Preterm birth is common and is frequently associated with passage of meconium, which is an unusual feature in uncomplicated preterm birth. Placental changes are described in Chapter 4. The infant sometimes appears normal at birth but develops signs of meningitis at several days of age: on other occasions there is obvious cardiorespiratory disease due to a congenital pneumonia.

At autopsy the internal organs show distinctive changes that should prompt immediate confirmation by bacteriological studies.[28] The liver, lungs, adrenals, brain and almost every other organ are studded with pin-head sized white or gray lesions with little or no surrounding flare (Fig. 9–9). In the liver the lesions may be confluent and up to several millimeters in diameter. In the lung there may be obvious pneumonia. The brain often shows meningitis or meningoencephalitis. The characteristic lesion histologically is a granuloma with necrosis and infiltration with mononuclear cells (Fig. 9–9). The diphtheroid-like organisms are rather weakly gram-positive. Heavy colonization of the intestine is usual and meconium is thus an important material for culture to confirm the diagnosis.

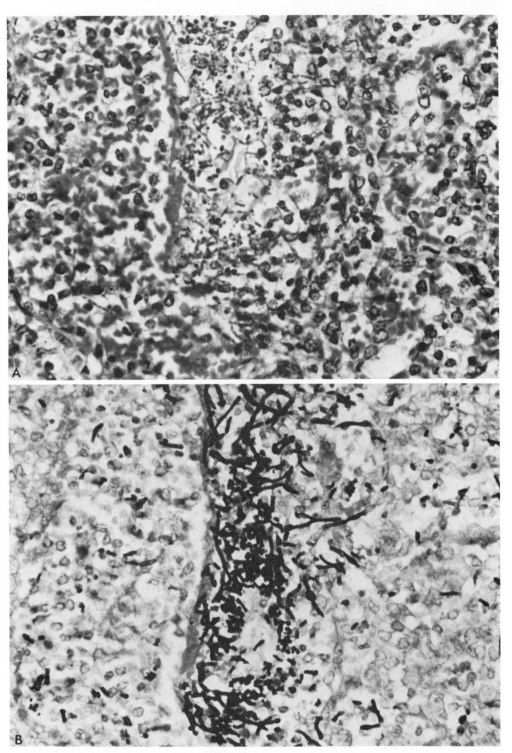

Figure 9–8. Congenital aspiration pneumonia due to *Candida albicans* in an infant who died at 13 hours of age. *A*, H and E × 400. *B*, PAS × 400.

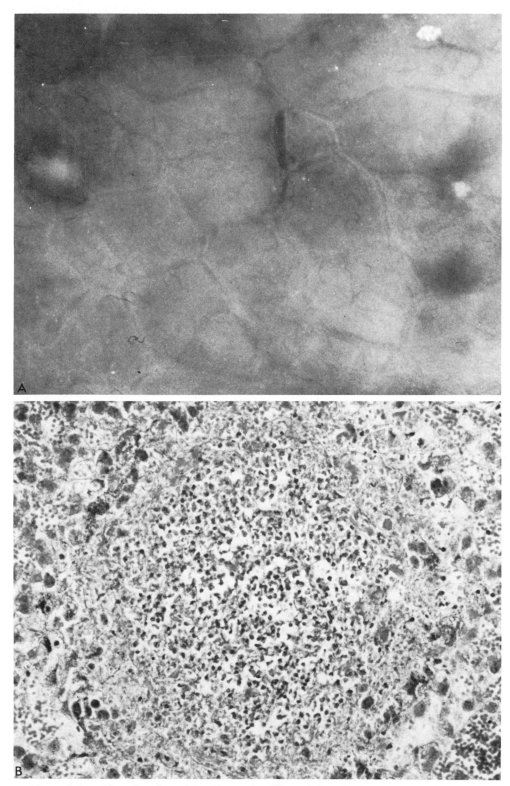

Figure 9–9. *A*, Pleural surface of fixed lung of a stillborn infant infected with *Listeria monocytogenes*. Magnification × 7. Note small, pale lesions. *B*, Adrenal section from the same, slightly macerated, fetus showing a small granuloma. H and E × 120.

Mycobacterium Tuberculosis. Congenital tuberculosis is very rare and is seldom likely to be considered unless the mother is known to have active disease. Transplacental spread will result in infection of the liver, whereas aspiration of infected amniotic fluid results in pulmonary lesions.[30]

SPIROCHETES: TREPONEMA PALLIDUM

Syphilis infects the fetus by the transplacental route but does not produce pathological changes before the fifth month of pregnancy.[31] Despite the fact that fetal infection is almost invariable in women with untreated primary or secondary syphilis, congenital syphilis should be avoidable given maternal VDRL screening and early treatment of the infected mother during pregnancy. However, several factors combine to ensure that congenital syphilis continues to occur even in countries with good antenatal health care services. Mothers with a negative VDRL in early pregnancy may sometimes become infected later during the same pregnancy: mothers in whom the condition was diagnosed may become reinfected following an adequate course of treatment. Women whose lifestyle renders them most at risk of venereal infection are likely to be late in seeking antenatal care, and test results may not have been reported in time if the infant is then born prematurely. Advances in medical care of immature newborn infants of less than 28 weeks' gestation may indeed increase the frequency with which undiagnosed congenital syphilis is seen by the neonatologist or pathologist. It is thus important for the pathologist to be aware of this classic disease as a cause of fetal or early neonatal death.

The stillborn macerated fetus may not show obvious macroscopic features, but hepatosplenomegaly is usually recognizable and the fetus may be hydropic. The placenta is large and pale, resembling that of other conditions which are associated with fetal anemia. See Chapter 4 for further details.

Liveborn infants are often born prematurely and may be growth-retarded. Jaundice is common and osteochondritis can be diagnosed radiologically if sought.

Specific Pathological Features. These can best be illustrated by a case seen in 1981 at Hammersmith Hospital in an infant of 26 weeks' gestation who survived for three days. The maternal VDRL had been discovered to be positive shortly before the infant died. There was gross hepatomegaly (Fig. 9–10), and examination of a wet preparation from the liver under dark ground illumination revealed Treponemata. The liver showed excessive extramedullary hemopoiesis and infiltration of the portal tracts with masses of mononuclear cells. Section of the lower end of the femur showed the ragged yellow metaphyseal line characteristic of syphilitic osteochondritis (Fig. 9–10). A firm gray area of apparent consolidation in the right lower lobe of the lung was characterized by patchy interstitial fibrosis, widening of the alveolar septa and interstitial infiltration by lymphocytes and plasma cells, and a scanty polymorph exudate in the bronchioles (Fig. 9–11). There was marked fibrosis of the pancreas (see Chapter 15), and in the stomach extensive fibrosis of the submucosa had replaced the muscularis mucosae.

In this case careful histological examination confirmed how the infection affects the vascular and connective tissue framework of the organs with onionskin thickening of adventitia of small vessels and chronic inflammatory reaction and advanced fibrosis in involved tissues.[32] It is instructive to recognize how many of the classic features of this disease can develop in utero by such an early stage of gestation and in the absence of compounding factors such as secondary bacterial infection or poor nutrition.

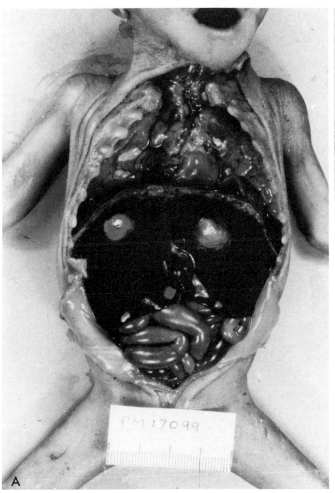

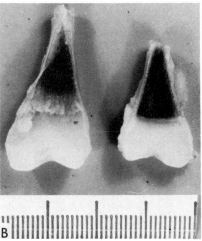

Figure 9–10. Congenital syphilis in a preterm infant. *A,* Gross hepato-megaly. *B,* Lower end of femur (left) shows pale irregular osteochondral junction typical of syphilitic osteo-chondritis as compared with normal femur (right) from another preterm infant.

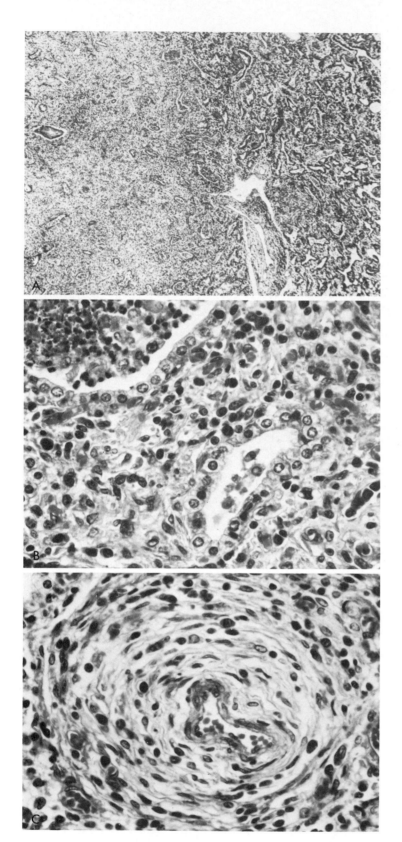

Figure 9–11. Lung in congenital syphilis. *A,* At low magnification the extensive interstitial fibrosis characteristic of pneumonia alba is seen over the left half of the field. H and E × 30. *B,* Chronic inflammatory reaction within interstitial tissue and cellular exudate in bronchioles. H and E × 300. *C,* Small pulmonary artery showing "onion-skin" thickening of adventitia. H and E × 300.

POSTMORTEM DIAGNOSIS OF CONGENITAL INFECTION

In order to make a specific postmortem diagnosis of congenital infection the pathologist needs to suspect the possibility of an infectious etiology at an early stage of the examination and must then institute an appropriate series of further tests.

External and internal features which may indicate the possibility of congenital infection are listed in Table 9–1. Further procedures which the pathologist should then consider undertaking are given in Table 9–2. The selection of investigations performed in an individual case will depend on the circumstances, including the experience of the pathologist and the availability of facilities for the various studies listed. Thus a pathologist who is familiar with the lesions of listeriosis will make a confident macroscopic diagnosis and confirm it by examining fresh material for organisms and by culture, whereas a less experienced pathologist may in addition need to consider the possibilities of herpes simplex or congenital tuberculosis.

TABLE 9–2. PROCEDURE IN CASE OF CONGENITAL INFECTION SUSPECTED AT AUTOPSY

1. Check with case notes or clinicians whether	A. Maternal tests were performed for
	    Syphilis
	    Toxoplasmosis
	    Rubella
	and whether positive or not
	B. Cord sera were taken or available for specific IgM studies; other specimens (blood urine, CSF, stool) sent for bacteriology, virology, etc., in life
	C. Mother has significant lesions (genital herpes or history of recent infection)

2. Consider radiology for	A. Intracranial calcification B. Changes in long bones (syphilitic osteochondritis or "celery stalk" changes of rubella or CMV)
3. Undertake fresh examination of lesions	A. Hanging drop preparation of miliary lesions for Listeria B. Dark ground study of wet preparation from liver for spirochetes C. Frozen section
4. Take specimens for bacteriology	Lung Heart blood Gut contents Lesions Placenta

5. Take specimens for virology	A. *Organs* B. *Fluids*
	    Lung Blood
	    Spleen CSF
	    Kidney Urine
	    Heart Serous effusions
	    Brain
	    Placenta

6. Consider electron microscopy for identification of viral particles	
7. Suggest to clinicians possible further maternal tests (paired sera for rising antibody titers)	
8. Examine histology of organs, including placenta and membranes, with use of special stains as indicated	

It should be stressed that one of the most important procedures, if congenital infection is suspected, is immediate consultation with pediatrician and obstetrician to determine the range of infections which have not been excluded clinically and to set in motion any further studies on the parents that may be indicated.

PATHOLOGY OF INFECTION ACQUIRED DURING OR AFTER BIRTH

NATURE AND INCIDENCE OF INFECTIONS ACQUIRED DURING OR AFTER BIRTH

Many of the infections discussed in the previous section as congenital infections can also be acquired during birth and some of them neonatally. This applies in particular to herpesvirus, Candida, cytomegalovirus, coxsackievirus and hepatitis B infections. The lesions produced following intrapartum or neonatal infection with some of these organisms are less severe than those characteristic of intrauterine infection. Given that there is such an overlap, it may reasonably be stated that most of the infections which characteristically affect the infant during or soon after birth are caused by bacteria. As discussed under route of infection, they include organisms which normally colonize the vagina, those which may contaminate the maternal perineum during delivery and those which may be acquired postnatally from the mother or the environment.

I have stressed in Chapter 1 how the pathologist must continually be aware of the rapid time course of illness in the perinatal period. In the case of bacterial infection it is important to remember that organisms may proliferate and cause death of the infant faster than they can be cultured and categorized by the bacteriologist. Death may indeed have supervened before the diagnosis of infection was suspected by the clinician. The pathologist should therefore be prepared to undertake postmortem microbiological diagnosis in any case when appropriate cultures have not been obtained before or immediately after death.

Two types of disease pattern have been recognized for bacterial infections of the perinatal period, an early-onset disease and a late-onset disease.[33] Early-onset disease typically develops within the first 48 hours of life, usually as an acute multisystem illness, and is often caused by infection with organisms acquired from the vagina during delivery. Respiratory symptoms frequently predominate and the mortality rate is high irrespective of the organism involved. There may be a history of obstetric complications such as prolonged rupture of the membranes, chorioamnionitis or maternal pyrexia, and the infants are often born prematurely. Late-onset disease develops toward the end of the first week of life or later, the illness is less often of a fulminant nature and the mortality rate is lower than that of early-onset disease. Although a number of organisms can be responsible for either disease pattern, the bacteria which cause late-onset disease are commonly acquired from the environment.

The incidence of bacterial infections in the neonatal period cannot be accurately assessed because there is a spectrum that extends from normal asymptomatic bacterial colonization through minor symptoms possibly related to infection to unequivocal sepsis. Septicemia in the newborn may be evidenced by rather indeterminate signs such as respiratory distress, hypothermia, mild jaundice or failure to thrive or by development of hepatosplenomegaly, enlarged kidneys, pallor, cyanosis, apnea or convulsions. Also, it is not possible to give a range of organisms pathogenic for the newborn infant as almost any organism seems capable of causing significant illness at this period of life, particularly in preterm infants.[34] In addition, the organisms predominantly associated with neonatal sepsis change over a period of time and may vary from one unit to another at any one time. Thus in the Hammersmith Hospital NICU over the 9-year period 1967 to 1975 the organism most frequently isolated from blood culture within the first 48 hours of life was the group B hemolytic streptococcus.[35] Over the succeeding 4 years in the same unit *Staphylococcus epidermidis* was the species isolated most often, either early or late in the neonatal period. Changing patterns of perinatal care such as an increasing proportion of tiny infants (below 1000 g birth weight) among those admitted to neonatal intensive care units and increasing use of total parenteral nutrition may be implicated in such alterations,[36] although new strains of bacteria can appear in a nursery without changes in management.[33]

The pathologist no less than the obstetrician and pediatrician needs to remain aware of current local problems in relation to bacterial infection.

In the subsequent pages I will outline details of a few of the more important bacterial pathogens responsible for neonatal sepsis.

GRAM-POSITIVE INFECTIONS

GROUP B β-HEMOLYTIC STREPTOCOCCI

Over the past 20 years the β-hemolytic streptococcus of Lancefield's group B (GBS) has become recognized as the most important gram-positive organism causing perinatal morbidity and death. The organism is present in the vagina of 15 to 25 per cent of pregnant women (and in the throat of 5 per cent) and has been found to colonize about 50 per cent of newborn infants of colonized mothers, where it may be isolated from the upper respiratory tract, external ear or umbilicus.[37] The frequency of proven neonatal infection may be as high as 2.9 per thousand births.

The group B streptococci are differentiated on the basis of type-specific polysaccharides into types Ia, Ib, Ic, II and III. Early-onset disease may be associated with any of the serotypes.

It is not known what determines whether an infant of a mother colonized with GBS will become infected during birth, but it is possible that the mothers are deficient in antibody and the infants lack the protective IgG antibodies they would normally have obtained across the placenta.[38] Most of the infants are preterm and have been born following obstetric manipulations. It may be possible to reduce the incidence of neonatal GBS infection by treatment of carrier mothers with antibiotics if obstetric interventions such as surgical induction of labor become necessary.[39]

The emphasis on the clinical and pathological manifestations of GBS infections in some of the recent literature has given the impression that the disease patterns associated with this organism are of a specific nature. In fact, the clinical and pathological findings described in association with GBS infections can be seen in a wide variety of gram-positive or gram-negative infections at the same period of life.

The infant with early GBS infection often has severe and rapidly progressive respiratory distress associated with apnea and circulatory collapse. In a preterm infant this may initially be mistaken for classic hyaline membrane disease with consequent delay in institution of antibiotic therapy. However, the mortality rate is extremely high even when antibodies are administered within 1 to 2 hours after birth.

Macroscopic findings at autopsy are similar to those of hyaline membrane disease, with congested airless liver-like lungs as the major feature. The microscopic appearances are variable. If death occurred within 10 to 12 hours there may be extreme congestion and collapse, with poorly developed, rather fluffy hyaline membranes lining respiratory bronchioles and masses of cocci with relatively little inflammatory reaction (Fig. 9–12). It has been shown by use of fluorescein-labeled antisera that cocci can form a considerable part of the membranes, and it has been postulated that the organisms may promote membrane formation by damaging the alveolar epithelium.[40] In many cases, however, the lungs show a characteristic widespread neonatal pneumonia, particularly if the infant survived for more than 12 hours (Fig. 9–13) (see also Chapter 10). Cocci can usually be seen in the lungs at autopsy if the infant received less than 6 hours of antibiotic therapy.[35]

Meningitis frequently develops in neonatal GBS infections and is a major feature of late-onset disease. Meningitis developing soon after birth may be associated with any serotype, but that characteristic of late-onset disease is usually of type III.[41] (For details of the pathology of meningitis see Chapter 10.) Other manifestations of neonatal infection due to GBS include facial cellulitis, conjunctivitis, osteomyelitis, suppurative arthritis and impetigo.[33] We have seen late-onset GBS sepsis present as bacterial endocarditis (see Chapter 11).

STAPHYLOCOCCAL INFECTION

Staphylococci are separated into *S. aureus* strains (usually coagulase-positive) and *S. epidermidis*.[42] Most of the classic forms of staphylococcal disease in the newborn mentioned in the following discussion are attributable to *S. aureus*, although *S. epidermidis* is pathogenic in the newborn and in some neonatal intensive care units may now be an important cause of neonatal illness. Staphylococcal

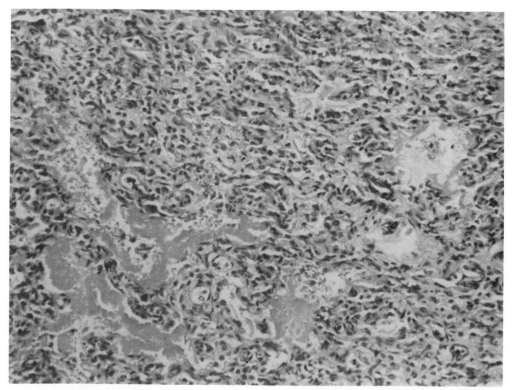

Figure 9–12. Lung of an infant of 27 weeks' gestational age who died at 29 hours of age with β-hemolytic streptococcal sepsis. H and E × 120. Poorly developed hyaline membranes are present.

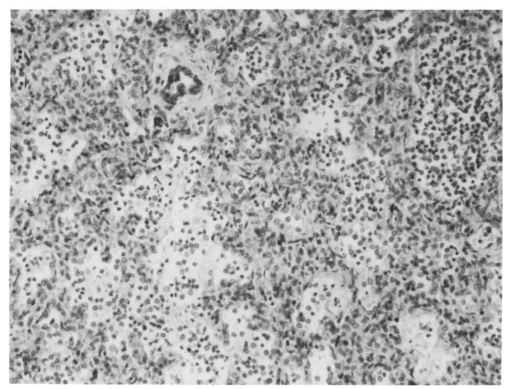

Figure 9–13. Lung of an infant of 29 weeks' gestational age who died at 13 hours of age with β-hemolytic streptococcal sepsis. H and E × 120. This lung shows an obvious neonatal pneumonia.

infections are usually acquired postnatally from the environment, but *S. epidermidis* can frequently be isolated from the blood within 48 hours of birth, according to our recent experience.[36]

Severe epidemics of staphylococcal infection with phage types 80 and 81 occurred in nurseries during the 1950's. In recent years nursery epidemics of severe staphylococcal infection have been infrequent.

Skin diseases are prominent among the manifestations of staphylococcal infection. These include bullous impetigo, toxic epidermal necrolysis (scalded-skin syndrome) and furunculosis.

Purulent conjunctivitis, cervical lymphadenitis and ethmoiditis with periorbital cellulitis may result from staphylococcal infection. Staphylococcal otitis media is common in preterm infants and may lead to recurrent purulent or serous otitis.[43]

Breast abscesses in the newborn are commonly due to staphylococcal infection.

Staphylococcal septicemia is similar to that caused by other organisms.

Staphylococcal pneumonia is a florid and characteristic form of infection, usually associated with pleurisy or empyema and characterized by the presence of microabscesses which occlude the terminal bronchioles with formation of pneumatoceles (see Chapter 10).

Osteomyelitis may occur during severe staphylococcal infection. Staphylococcal arthritis may be secondary to osteomyelitis but has also been described as a complication of femoral venipuncture.[44]

OTHER GRAM-POSITIVE ORGANISMS

These include hemolytic streptococci of groups D and G, nonhemolytic streptococci and Clostridia. The latter organisms, particularly *Clostridium butyricum*, may be associated with development of necrotizing enterocolitis, as discussed in Chapter 13.

GRAM-NEGATIVE INFECTIONS

ESCHERICHIA COLI

This organism is a frequent cause of neonatal illness and may be associated with both early- and late-onset disease patterns. Intrapartum infection with *E. coli* may result in early pneumonia and septicemia, while late infection of the infant already colonized with the organism may develop at any time in the neonatal period. *E. coli* is one of the major causes of neonatal meningitis; the condition is particularly associated with those strains which have the K1 antigen.[33] Meningitis due to *E. coli* is difficult to treat effectively and frequently results in long-term handicap. Also, *E. coli* is the organism most often implicated in neonatal urinary tract infections.

HEMOPHILUS INFLUENZAE

This organism is being increasingly recognized in our own unit as a cause of overwhelming early neonatal infection in preterm infants. The clinical picture of early-onset disease is indistinguishable from that described as typical of GBS infection. Macroscopic and histological findings at autopsy are also identical to those seen in GBS infection, including the appearance of pulmonary hyaline membranes infiltrated with masses of microorganisms.

PSEUDOMONAS AERUGINOSA

Constant vigilance is required to keep neonatal intensive care units free of this organism, which thrives in moist conditions such as those provided by sink traps or the humidifiers of mechanical ventilators. The infant is most likely to become infected from the environment during resuscitation or later treatment, although occasional instances of infection with Pseudomonas at birth have been reported in association with maternal infection.[28]

The major features of infection with *P. aeruginosa* in the newborn are similar to those of infections in debilitated adult patients. Pseudomonas septicemia may be associated with development of severe diffuse lesions. A skin rash may commence as erythema multiforme but there may later be local ulceration and necrosis. A typical site for such local lesions is the tongue and buccal cavity, where dark red or black necrotic ulcers may develop (Fig. 9–14). On histological study the most striking feature is the extensive nature of the hemorrhage and necrosis in relation to a rather poor polymorphonuclear response. Masses of microorganisms may be seen throughout the affected tissues. Larroche describes and illustrates lesions within the salivary glands and mentions the middle ear as a readily overlooked site of involvement.[28]

The lungs are nearly always affected and are usually the most obvious focus of infection at autopsy. The characteristic feature of Pseudomonas pneumonia is the presence of necrotic and hemorrhagic areas. The small gray necrotic zones may allow a presumptive diagnosis on macroscopic examination. Histologically there is extensive necrosis with massive infiltration with organisms in the affected region of lung, although intervening parenchyma may be relatively normal (Fig. 9–15). Destruction of mucosae with infiltration of submucosa by organisms is a typical finding in Pseudomonas infection.

The gastrointestinal tract may be involved at any level by similar hemorrhagic necrotic lesions, as illustrated by Larroche.[28] Other internal organs which may be

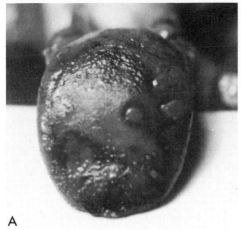

A

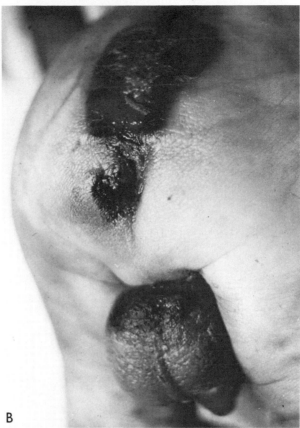

Figure 9–14. Septicemia due to *Pseudomonas aeruginosa* with death at 19 days of age. *A*, Early necrotic lesions on tongue. *B*, Large necrotic areas in sacral and perianal regions.

B

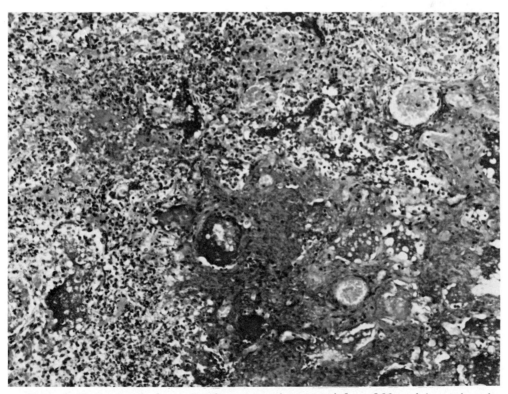

Figure 9–15. Pneumonia due to *Pseudomonas aeruginosa* in an infant of 26 weeks' gestation who died at 3 weeks of age. H and E × 150. There is an area of necrosis with a surrounding inflammatory reaction.

163

affected include adrenals, spleen, kidneys, pancreas and muscle tissues. Meningitis and meningoencephalitis are additional complications.

The extensive necrosis characteristic of the Pseudomonas lesions may be explicable on the basis of a predilection of the organism for vessel walls with a resultant vasculitis. Both artery and vein walls are often massively infiltrated by organisms with surrounding edema and necrosis but little inflammatory response. Vessel lumina may be thrombosed.[45]

KLEBSIELLA-ENTEROBACTER-SERRATIA GROUP

Infection with these organisms is usually environmentally derived and most frequently occurs after the first 48 hours. This group of bacteria may cause meningitis associated with an unusual form of hemorrhagic necrotic encephalomyelitis (see Chapter 10).[46]

NEISSERIA GONORRHOEAE

This organism remains a potential cause of serious morbidity (ophthalmia neonatorum), although it is seldom associated with generalized or fatal sepsis.[47]

OTHER ORGANISMS WHICH CAN CAUSE PERINATAL INFECTION

PARASITIC INFECTIONS

These include malaria, African trypanosomiasis and Chagas' disease, and have been reviewed by Reinhardt.[48]

CAMPYLOBACTER

Campylobacter species (formerly Vibrio) are an important cause of diarrhea which may develop in the newborn infant of an infected mother.[49] Meningoencephalitis has caused death in the perinatal period.[50]

CHLAMYDIA

Chlamydia trachomatis (TRIC agent) is probably the most frequent cause of ophthalmia neonatorum.[47] In addition, this organism causes a form of afebrile pneumonia in young infants, although symptoms often develop after the first month of age.[51] Maternal chlamydial infection has recently been linked to an increased perinatal mortality.[52]

MYCOPLASMA

Mycoplasma is not infrequently cultured in cases of chorioamnionitis, and has been reported in association with abortion or fetal death. It is not clear to what extent the organism is a cause of perinatal mortality, although mycoplasma T strains have been isolated as the sole organisms in cases of congenital pneumonia,[53] and *Mycoplasma hominis* has been shown to cause infection of the central nervous system in the newborn infant.[54]

PERINATAL INFECTION AS A COMPLICATION OF INVESTIGATION AND THERAPY

Infection is a significant risk of almost all procedures involved in perinatal care, as has been stressed throughout this chapter. Infection can be introduced in utero by surgical procedures such as amniocentesis or intrauterine transfusion. Ascending infection from the vagina or introduction of organisms from the exterior may result from any obstetric manipulation.

At birth the infant is at risk from contaminated resuscitation equipment. The mucosal damage to the upper airways inseparable from intubation provides a site of entry for bacteria if, for instance, the suction apparatus is contaminated with Pseudomonas or *E. coli.*

In the neonatal period all forms of handling will put the ill preterm infant at risk of acquiring infection. The less mature or more severely ill an infant is, the greater is the need for interference and thus the greater the hazard of infection. For instance, procedures such as endotracheal suction may cause transient bacteremia.[55] Introduction of indwelling catheters is associated with infection; the greater risk appears to be related to venous catheters which are now seldom used.[11] Blood sampling procedures carry their own risks. Osteomyelitis and septic arthritis have been reported as complications of femoral vein puncture, and osteomyelitis of the calcaneum has occurred following repeated heel punctures. Total parenteral nutrition is associated with development of chronic infections such as disseminated candidiasis. A possible reason for a high incidence of infection when Intralipid is included in the infusion fluid is reticuloendothelial blockade; the lipid may overwhelm the reticuloendothelial system and prevent subsequent phagocytosis of bacteria.

REFERENCES

1. Schlievert, P., Johnson, W., and Galask, R. P.: Amniotic fluid antibacterial mechanisms: Newer concepts. Semin. Perinatol. *1*:59–70, 1977.
2. Adinolphi, M.: The development of lymphoid tissues and immunity. *In*: Davis, J. A., and Dobbing, J. (eds.): Scientific Foundations of Paediatrics, 2nd ed. London, Heinemann, 1981, pp. 525–544.
3. Monif, G. R. G., and Harty-Golder, B. J.: Intrauterine infections. *In*: Barson, A. J. (ed.): Laboratory Investigation of Fetal Disease. Bristol, John Wright & Sons Ltd., 1981, pp. 363–386.
4. Hanson, L. A., Carlson, B., Dahlgren, U., Mellander, L., and Svanborg-Eden, C.: The secretory IgA system in the neonatal period. *In*: Ciba Foundation Symposium 77, Perinatal Infections. Amsterdam, Excerpta Medica, 1980, pp. 187–204.
5. Kohler, P. F.: Maturation of the human complement system. J. Clin. Invest. *52*:671–677, 1973.
6. Miller, E. M., and Stiehm, E. R.: Phagocytic, opsonic and immunoglobulin studies in newborns. Calif. Med. *119*:43–63, 1973.
7. Atkins, E., and Bodel, P.: Fever. N. Engl. J. Med. *286*:27–34, 1972.
8. Akenzua, G., Saigal, S., Hui, Y. T., and Zipursky, A.: Neutrophil and band counts in the diagnosis of neonatal infections. Pediatrics *54*:38–42, 1974.
9. Eitzman, D. V., and Smith, R. T.: The nonspecific inflammatory cycle in the neonatal infant. Am. J. Dis. Child. *97*:326–334, 1959.
10. Bellanti, J. A., Cantz, B. E., and Maybee, D. A.: Defective phagocytosis by newborn leukocytes: A defect similar to that in chronic granulomatous disease? (Abstr.) Pediat. Res. *3*:376, 1969.
11. Marks, M. I., and Welch, D. F.: Diagnosis of bacterial infections of the newborn infant. Clin. Perinatol. *8*:537–558, 1981.
12. Rosenberg, H. S., Kohl, S., and Vogler, C.: Viral infections of the fetus and the neonate. *In* Naeye, R. L., Kissane, J. M., and Kaufman, N. (eds.): Perinatal Diseases. Baltimore, Williams & Wilkins, 1981, pp. 133–200.
13. Alford, C. A., and Pass, R. F.: Epidemiology of chronic congenital and perinatal infections of man. Clin. Perinatol. *8*:397–414, 1981.
14. Gregg, N. M.: Congenital cataract following German measles in the mother. Trans. Ophthalmol. Soc. Aust. *3*:35–46, 1942.
15. Esterly, J. R., and Oppenheimer, E. H.: Intrauterine rubella infection. *In* Rosenberg, H. S., and Bolande, R. P. (eds.): Perspectives in Pediatric Pathology. Chicago, Year Book Medical Publishers, 1973, vol. 1, pp. 313–338.
16. Way, R. C.: Cardiovascular defects and the rubella syndrome. Can. Med. Assoc. J. *97*:1329–1334, 1967.
17. Campbell, P. E.: Vascular abnormalities following maternal rubella. Br. Heart J. *27*:134–138, 1965.
18. Phelan, P., and Campbell, P.: Pulmonary complications of rubella embryopathy. J. Pediatr. *75*:202–212, 1969.
19. South, M. A., Montgomery, J. R., and Rawls, W. E.: Immune deficiency in the congenital rubella and other viral infections. Birth Defects, Original Article Series, *11*:234–238, 1975.

20. Merser, M. A., Forest, J. M., and Bransby, R. A.: Rubella infection and diabetes mellitus. Lancet *1*:57–60, 1978.

21. Hanshaw, J. B.: Cytomegalovirus. *In* Remington, J. S., and Klein, J. O. (eds.): Infectious Diseases of the Fetus and Newborn Infant. Philadelphia, W. B. Saunders Co., 1983, pp 104–143.

22. Cherry, J. D.: Enteroviruses. *In*: Remington, J. S., and Klein, J. O. (eds.): Infectious Diseases of the Fetus and Newborn Infant. Philadelphia, W. B. Saunders Co., 1983, pp. 290–334.

23. Dupuy, J. M., Frommel, D., and Alagille, D.: Severe viral hepatitis type B in infancy. Lancet *1*:191–194, 1975.

24. Remington, J. S., and Desmonts, G.: Toxoplasmosis. *In* Remington, J. S., and Klein, J. O. (eds.): Infectious Diseases of the Fetus and Newborn Infant. Philadelphia, W. B. Saunders Co., 1983, pp. 144–263.

25. Lopez, E., and Aterman, K.: Intra-uterine infection by Candida. Am. J. Dis. Child. *115*:663–670, 1968.

26. Miller, M. J.: Fungal infections. *In*: Remington, J. S., and Klein, J. O. (eds.): Infectious Diseases of the Fetus and the Newborn Infant. Philadelphia, W. B. Saunders Co., 1983, pp. 464–506.

27. Burry, A. F.: Hydrocephalus after intrauterine fungal infection. Arch. Dis. Child. *32*:161–163, 1957.

28. Larroche, J. C.: Developmental pathology of the neonate. Amsterdam, Excerpta Medica, 1977, pp. 243–282.

29. Seeliger, H. P. R., and Finger, H.: Listeriosis. *In* Remington, J. S., and Klein, J. O. (eds.): Infectious Diseases of the Fetus and Newborn Infant. Philadelphia, W. B. Saunders Co., 1983, pp. 264–289.

30. Voyce, M. A., and Hunt, A. C.: Congenital tuberculosis. Arch. Dis. Child. *41*:299–300, 1966.

31. Ingall, D., and Norins, L.: Syphilis. *In* Remington, J. S., and Klein, J. O. (eds.): Infectious Diseases of the Fetus and Newborn Infant. Philadelphia, W. B. Saunders Co., 1983, pp. 335–374.

32. Oppenheimer, E. H., and Hardy, J. B.: Congenital syphilis in the newborn infant: Clinical and pathological observations in recent cases. Johns Hopkins Med. J. *129*:63–82, 1971.

33. Klein, J. O., and Marcy, S. M.: Bacterial infections. *In* Remington, J. S., and Klein, J. O. (eds.): Infectious Diseases of the Fetus and Newborn Infant. Philadelphia, W. B. Saunders Co., 1983, pp. 782–819.

34. Davies, P. A.: Pathogen or commensal? (Annotation). Arch. Dis. Child., *55*:169–170, 1980.

35. Jeffery, H., Mitchison, R., Wigglesworth, J. S., and Davies, P. A.: Early neonatal bacteraemia: Comparison of group B streptococcal, other gram-positive and gram-negative infections. Arch. Dis. Child. *52*:683–686, 1977.

36. Battisti, O., Mitchison, R., and Davies, P. A.: Changing blood culture isolates in a referral neonatal intensive care unit. Arch. Dis. Child. *56*:775–778, 1981.

37. Baker, C. J., and Barrett, F. F.: Transmission of group B streptococci among parturient women and their neonates. J. Pediatr. *83*:919–925, 1973.

38. Baker, C. J., and Kasper, D. L.: Correlation of maternal antibody deficiency with susceptibility to neonatal group B streptococcal infection. N. Engl. J. Med., *294*:753–756, 1976.

39. Yow, M. D., Mason, E. O., Leeds, L. J., Thompson, P. K., Clark, D. J., and Gardner, S. E.: Ampicillin prevents intrapartum transmission of group B streptococcus. JAMA *241*:1245–1247, 1979.

40. Katzenstein, A.-L., Davis, C., and Braude, A.: Pulmonary changes in neonatal sepsis due to group B β-hemolytic streptococcus: Relation to hyaline membrane disease. J. Infect. Dis. *133*:430–435, 1976.

41. Baker, C. J., and Barrett, F. F.: Group B streptococcal infections in infants. The importance of the various serotypes. JAMA *230*:1158–1160, 1974.

42. Shinefield, H. R.: Staphylococcal infections. *In* Remington, J. S., and Klein, J. O. (eds.): Infectious Diseases of the Fetus and Newborn Infant. Philadelphia, W. B. Saunders Co., 1983, pp. 882–916.

43. Warren, W. S., and Stool, S. E.: Otitis in low birth weight infants. J. Pediatr. *79*:740–743, 1971.

44. Chacha, P. B.: Suppurative arthritis of the hip joint in infancy. A persistent diagnostic problem and possible complication of femoral vein puncture. J. Bone Joint Surg. *53*A:538–544, 1971.

45. Teplitz, C.: Pathogenesis of pseudomonas vasculitis and septic lesions. Arch. Pathol *80*:297–307, 1965.

46. Cussen, L. J., and Ryan, G. B.: Hemorrhagic cerebral necrosis in neonatal infants with enterobacterial meningitis. J. Pediatr. *71*:771–776, 1976.

47. Holmes, K. K.: Gonococcal infection. *In* Remington, J. S., and Klein, J. O. (eds.): Infectious Diseases of the Fetus and Newborn Infant. Philadelphia, W. B. Saunders Co., 1983, pp. 619–635.

48. Reinhardt, M. C.: Effects of parasitic infections in pregnant women. *In* Ciba Foundation Symposium 77: Perinatal Infections. Amsterdam, Excerpta Medica, 1980, pp. 149–163.

49. Mawer, S. L., and Smith, B. A. M.: Campylobacter infection of premature baby. Lancet *1*:1041, 1979.

50. Eden, A. N.: Perinatal mortality caused by vibrio fetus. Review and analysis. J. Pediatr. *68*:297–304, 1966.

51. Tipple, M. A., Beem, M. O., and Saxon, E. M.: Clinical characteristics of the afebrile pneumonia associated with chlamydia trachomatis infection in infants less than 6 months of age. Pediatrics *63*:192–197, 1979.
52. Martin, D. H.: Prematurity and perinatal mortality in pregnancies complicated by maternal chlamydia trachomatis infections. JAMA *247*:1585–1588, 1982.
53. Tafari, N., Ross, S., Naeye, R. L., Judge, D. M., and Marboe, C.: Mycoplasma T strains and perinatal death. Lancet *1*:108–109, 1976.
54. Siber, G. R., Alpert, S., Smith, A. L., et al.: Neonatal central nervous system infection due to mycoplasma hominis. J. Pediatr. *90*:625–627, 1977.
55. Storm, W.: Transient bacteremia following endotracheal suctioning in ventilated newborn. Pediatrics *65*:487–490, 1980.
56. Morison, J. E.: Foetal and Neonatal Pathology. 3rd ed. London, Butterworths, pp. 583–586.

Chapter Ten

The Respiratory System

The frequency with which the respiratory system is affected by perinatal disease processes reflects the importance of lung development and function as the major determinants of infant viability. The ability of the infant to begin breathing air at birth has been the traditional criterion for live birth, since this ability, rather than mere presence of a heartbeat, is the essential prerequisite for independent existence. Thus a high proportion of the disorders which the pathologist may recognize in the perinatal period represent some failure of normal development of the respiratory system. Immaturity of functional maturation is represented by the idiopathic respiratory distress syndrome with surfactant deficiency. Failure of normal fetal lung growth due to prenatal functional impairment is represented by a wide variety of conditions associated with lung hypoplasia. In addition to conditions which influence its growth or biochemical maturation, the lung may be a primary target for generalized disease processes. Prenatal or intrapartum asphyxial changes produce characteristic lung lesions. Most perinatal infections present as pneumonia. The airways and lung parenchyma are at risk for a variety of hazards of neonatal care.

Many of the conditions which are seen in the fetal or neonatal lung can be diagnosed by the traditional pattern recognition techniques of histopathology. Some knowledge of structural development of the lung, fetal lung function and biochemical maturation are of considerable value in aiding interpretation of the range of lesions seen. Throughout this chapter I will stress how the interaction between structure and function may help to account for many of the characteristic pathological changes in this organ.

DEVELOPMENT OF THE RESPIRATORY SYSTEM

The human lung develops as an outgrowth from the ventral aspect of the primitive foregut during the fourth week after conception. The initial epithelial tubule, representing the trachea, undergoes a series of divisions to form the major bronchial branches. This sequential branching has been shown to be under the control of the adjacent mesenchyme.[1] Indeed, it seems probable that mesenchyme-epithelial reciprocal induction processes may control a large proportion of basic pulmonary development.[2]

The postembryonic phase of lung development is traditionally subdivided into three separate stages: pseudoglandular, canalicular and terminal sac (Fig. 10–1).[3]

168

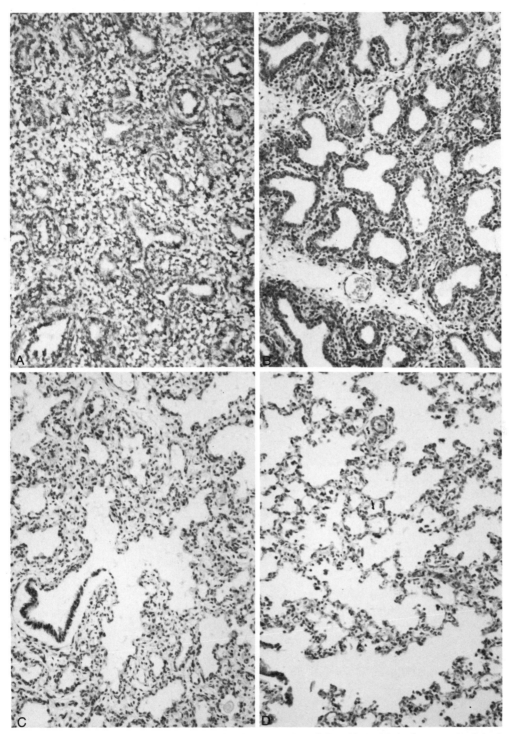

Figure 10–1. Lung at various stages of development. H and E × 80. A, 16 weeks (menstrual age). Pseudoglandular stage of development. B, 20 weeks. Canalicular stage. C, 26 weeks (partly inflated with fixative). Saccular stage. D, 36 weeks (partly inflated with fixative). Alveolar formation is recognizable.

PSEUDOGLANDULAR PHASE: 7 TO 17 WEEKS

During this stage the airways consist of simple epithelial tubules within a loose mesenchymal stroma. The epithelium is of low columnar form with basal nuclei and can be shown to contain abundant glycogen. The mesenchyme shows condensations around the primitive bronchial tubules. The major bronchial generations develop during this period.

CANALICULAR PHASE: 17 TO 24 WEEKS

This stage is characterized by the enlarging caliber of the peripheral airways and the thinning out of the peripheral epithelium to a simple cuboidal form. At the same time the pulmonary capillaries become intimately associated with the epithelium to form the first blood-air barriers. Condensation of elastic tissue around the airways appears during this stage.

TERMINAL SAC PHASE: 24 WEEKS TO TERM

This stage is characterized by differentiation of the lining epithelium into types I and II pneumonocytes and the consequent appearance of surfactant within the peripheral airways. The blood-air barriers develop progressively and a supporting network of elastic fibers becomes increasingly prominent around the airways and within the alveolar septa.

Although the infant may sometimes be able to establish extrauterine respiration from as early as 24 weeks' gestation, there is an enormous difference in lung structure between this time and term. A progressive branching of respiratory bronchioles and increase in complexity of the terminal sacs occurs throughout this period, and development of shallow cup-shaped alveoli can be recognized by term.

DEVELOPMENT OF THE LUNG AS A HOLLOW FLUID-FILLED ORGAN

From the start of the canalicular phase up to term, the lung has hollow fluid-filled airways of progressively increasing structural complexity. From animal studies performed mainly on the lamb, it is known that the chloride-rich fluid which fills the airways is secreted by a halide pump mechanism analogous to that involved in similar secretory activities within the intestine.[4] At term the rate of liquid secretion in the lamb is of the order of 10 per cent of the lung volume per hour. Thus lung liquid may contribute significantly to the amniotic fluid. There is evidence that this lung liquid secretion is important for fetal lung growth. Chronic drainage of the fluid through a tracheal cannula significantly retards lung growth in the fetal lamb.[5] The cellular origin of the fluid is not yet known but is presumably the respiratory epithelium of the airways. There are a number of different cell types within the developing respiratory epithelium, including ciliated and nonciliated (Clara) cells, basal cells, goblet cells and Kulchitsky's cells. The last-named, which are present as scattered single cells and as groups of cells with related nerve fibers (neuroepithelial bodies), produce a number of peptide hormones which may well prove to be of considerable importance for fetal lung development. The process of lung liquid secretion can be abolished experimentally by infusion of catecholamines or β-adrenergic agonists, suggesting that sympathetic stimulation may play a role in switching off lung liquid secretion at birth.[6]

The fetus undertakes respiratory movements from early in the second trimester. These are recognized as bursts of high frequency low amplitude movement involving the diaphragm and to a lesser extent the chest wall. In lambs it can be shown that these movements cause little net flux of tracheal fluid, although they are associated with significant transthoracic pressure gradients. Respiratory movements are readily abolished by CNS depressants such as barbiturates and by hypoglycemia or hypoxia.[7] Experimental evidence suggests that these respiratory movements are also important for normal fetal lung growth (see p. 180). We have suggested that respiratory movements aid retention of liquid within the fetal lung and allow it to exert a molding influence.[8] Thus normal fetal lung growth appears dependent on development of appropriate forms of functional activity.

DEVELOPMENT OF SURFACTANT SECRETION

The ability of the lung of the newborn infant to retain air, even at the low transpulmonary pressure of end-expiration, depends on rapid adsorption to the alveolar surface of a material with surface tension–lowering properties, pulmonary surfactant. This material, as isolated from mammalian lungs, is a complex water-insoluble particulate material consisting principally of phospholipids, neutral lipids and proteins, although its composition and molecular structure are not yet fully known.[4] The production of surfactant is linked temporally with the appearance of the osmiophilic lamellar bodies within the type II cells of the alveolar epithelium. These structures are 0.2 to 0.5 μ in diameter and consist of stacks of membranous material. They are believed to represent an intracellular store of surfactant. It is in fact probable that surfactant is normally secreted in a dry particulate form because this can be shown to allow efficient maintenance of a monomolecular surface-active lining layer.[9]

The maturation of the enzyme pathways for surfactant synthesis by the respiratory epithelium is associated with the appearance in the amniotic fluid of increasing quantities of lecithin. This is presumably derived from lung liquid that has entered the amniotic fluid from the respiratory tract. The measurement of lecithin/sphingomyelin ratios in amniotic fluid has become a useful method for prenatal assessment of maturity of the fetal lung and the potential risk of respiratory distress syndrome (RDS).[10]

Both structural maturation of the lung and secretion of surfactant can be promoted by injection of glucocorticoids into the fetus.[11] Administration of dexamethasone to pregnant women in threatened preterm labor is used to advance lung maturation in the fetus in order to prevent development of RDS. Thyroxine may also have an influence on surfactant production. A rise in endogenous cortisol production occurs just before the onset of normal labor. Thus the therapeutic administration of steroids to women in whom the danger of premature labor exists may mimic a normal process by which maturation of the pulmonary epithelium and secretion of surfactant are enhanced shortly before the infant is born. Subsequent resorption of lung liquid under the influence of raised circulating catecholamine levels during labor may ensure that the normal infant is born with the lungs fully adapted for extrauterine respiration.

MALFORMATIONS OF THE RESPIRATORY SYSTEM

PULMONARY AGENESIS

Bilateral pulmonary agenesis is a rare condition in which the trachea ends blindly and the pulmonary artery joins the aorta. In effect the condition represents a defect in organogenesis of both respiratory and cardiovascular systems.[12]

Unilateral pulmonary agenesis is less rare and is compatible with survival. The single lung is hypertrophied and extends into the opposite half of the thoracic cavity.[13]

LARYNGEAL ANOMALIES

Laryngeal Atresia. In this condition the larynx is usually occluded by a mass of cartilage just below the vocal cords, although several different types have been described.[14] A narrow channel often connects pharynx and trachea, but this is insufficient to allow postnatal respiration. The lesion is relatively uncommon but can cause clinical consternation because the larynx appears relatively normal when viewed from above but attempts at intubation are unsuccessful (Fig. 10–2). The lungs are heavy with rather dilated but otherwise relatively normal saccules. Immediate tracheostomy would offer the only hope for infant survival.

Other Laryngeal Anomalies Involving Respiratory Obstruction at Birth. These include laryngeal webs, papillomas (Fig. 10–3) and mucus-secreting cysts. Although these are not common, they can present as acute emergencies at birth and are treatable if recognized.

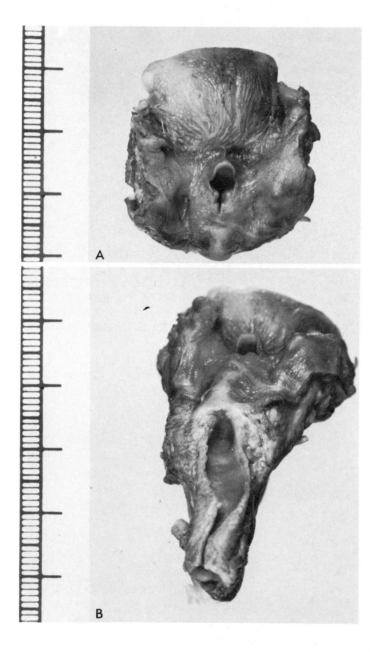

Figure 10–2. Laryngeal atresia: *A,* Larynx viewed from above. *B,* Upper end of trachea. A mass of cartilage occludes the lower part of the larynx.

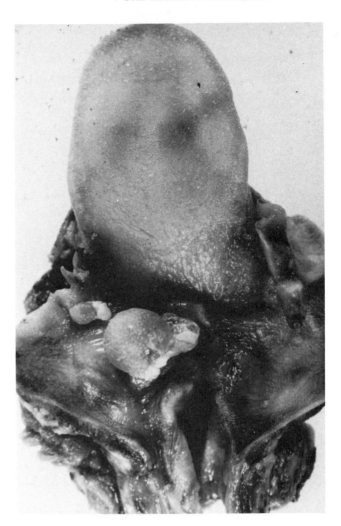

Figure 10–3. Papilloma occluding larynx in an infant with multiple anomalies.

OTHER MALFORMATIONS

Tracheal Agenesis. This is a rare condition in which the trachea is absent, despite presence of the larynx, and the bronchi originate from the esophagus (Fig. 10–4). Several types are described according to the pattern of origin of the bronchi.[14, 15]

Tracheal and Bronchial Malacias. These are not commonly recognized at perinatal autopsy. However, bronchomalacia may be an important lesion underlying development of congenital lobar emphysema, and is a significant factor in camptomelic syndrome (Chapters 7, 19).

Tracheo-esophageal Fistula. This is described in Chapter 13.

Congenital Diaphragmatic Hernia. This abnormality most frequently comprises a large defect of the posterolateral aspect of the left leaf of the diaphragm (foramen of Bochdalek) with persistence of the left pleuroperitoneal canal, which should normally close at 45 to 50 days after ovulation. There is usually herniation of small intestine, stomach, spleen and left lobe of the liver into the thoracic cavity, with shift of the mediastinum to the right. The left lung is compressed and hypoplastic and the right lung may be similarly but less severely affected. The primary defect is on the right side in a smaller proportion of cases (5 of 14 studied by Larroche).[16] In some cases one leaf of the diaphragm is represented by a thin membrane, with virtually no muscle, which forms a sac for the abdominal contents which have herniated into the thoracic cavity (eventration).

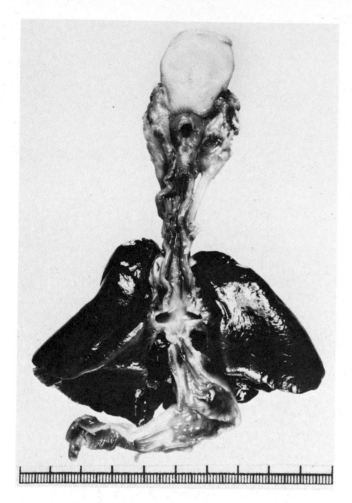

Figure 10–4. Tracheal agenesis. The bronchi arise directly from the esophagus.

Studies of the hypoplastic left lung in fatal cases of congenital diaphragmatic hernia have shown a variable reduction of bronchial branching, although this does not relate well to the severity of lung hypoplasia.[17, 18] The peripheral parts of the acinus show development of terminal sacs, but biochemical indices of maturation show relative immaturity of the left lung as compared with the right lung and unilateral hyaline membrane disease may develop (Fig. 10–5). It is of interest to note that in this condition, in which abnormality of lung growth has been induced at a very early stage of development, the periphery of the lung may be relatively mature.

About half of all cases of diaphragmatic hernia are associated with other abnormalities.[19] However, the condition does commonly present as the sole abnormality in well-grown infants at term. The possibility of survival following operative repair of the defect is primarily dependent on the severity of lung hypoplasia, and in particular the extent to which the contralateral lung is affected. The hypoplastic lung may not expand if there is severe impairment in maturation. A persistently high pulmonary artery pressure (persistent fetal circulation) is a frequent postoperative problem.

BILATERAL PULMONARY HYPOPLASIA

I have pointed out in an earlier chapter that the presence of pulmonary hypoplasia is one of the most crucial factors which determine that an infant with a malformation syndrome will die at birth or soon after.

Definition of Lung Hypoplasia. The external form of the lung at postmortem examination is usually quite normal with normal lobation. A practical problem for the pathologist is how he should define lung hypoplasia in infants of varying size and maturity. There has undoubtedly been a tendency for pathologists to overlook the condition and to regard small but apparently normally formed lungs as atelectatic. In the recent literature, lung hypoplasia has been defined in terms of the ratio of lung weight to body weight: a lung-to-body weight ratio of 0.012 to 1 or less is taken to denote lung hypoplasia.[20] From our own studies on lung size it is apparent that the weight of the lungs relative to that of the body as a whole alters during fetal life.[21] Lungs of fetuses in the early second trimester are relatively much heavier than those of infants at term (Fig. 10–6). Definition of lung hypoplasia in terms of lung-to-body weight ratio should therefore change according to gestational age. As an interim measure until sufficient figures for the normal range, with confidence limits, are available, we have accepted a figure of 0.012 for infants of 28 weeks' gestation or more, and 0.015 for those of lower gestational age. Wet weight might not be an accurate means of assessing lung mass in the perinatal period because the lung may contain variable volumes of blood, lung liquid or edema fluid. However, measurement of lung DNA as an index of cell population does show similar relationships and confirms that a low lung-to-body weight ratio is indicative of a low lung cell population.[21]

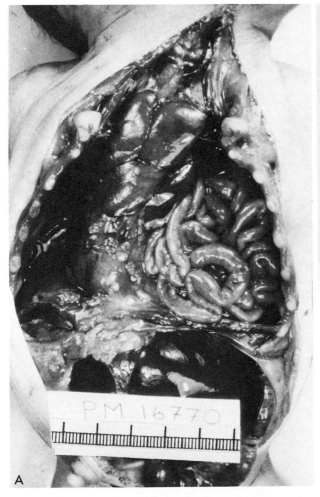

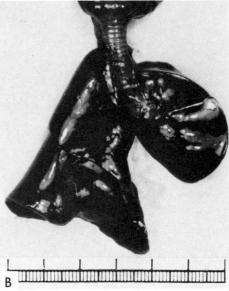

Figure 10–5. Congenital diaphragmatic hernia in an infant of 30 weeks' gestation who died at 4 hours age before operation could be undertaken. *A,* View of small intestine within left pleural cavity. Note shift of mediastinum into right pleural cavity. *B,* Lungs on removal. The left lung is more hypoplastic than the right and is distorted in form.

Illustration continued on following page

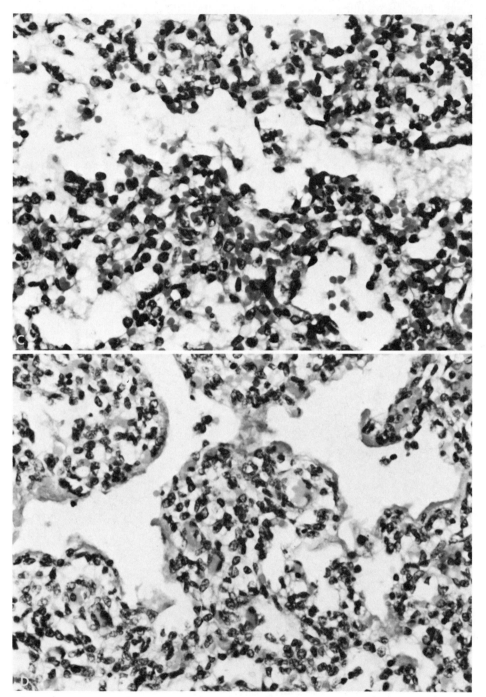

Figure 10–5 *Continued. C,* Section of right lung showing immature structure but no hyaline membranes. H and E × 400. *D,* Section of left lung showing early, but definite HMD. H and E × 400.

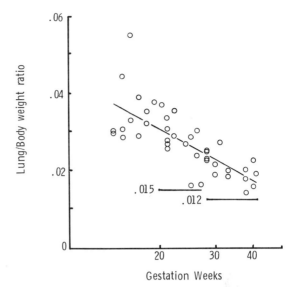

Figure 10–6. Lung/body weight ratios. (From Wigglesworth, J. S., and Desai, R.: Use of DNA estimation for growth assessment in normal and hypoplastic fetal lungs. Arch. Dis. Child. *56*:601–605, 1981.)

Different Forms of Bilateral Lung Hypoplasia. A large range of conditions is regularly associated with hypoplastic lungs.[22–24] These can be broken down into a number of groups as shown in Table 10–1. The major subdivisions of lung hypoplasia are cases associated with oligohydramnios and cases associated with normal or increased amniotic fluid. Many of the structural and functional features of these various forms of hypoplastic lung have remained poorly defined despite an increasing interest in the condition. Morphometric studies suggest that an important component in several forms of bilateral lung hypoplasia is a reduction in the number of generations of bronchial branching as is seen in cases of diaphragmatic hernia.[25, 26] There is less agreement about other aspects of lung structure and development. It is stated by Potter and Craig that hypoplastic lungs occurring in conditions with reduced intrathoracic space show decrease in lung parenchyma and closely packed normal bronchi, whereas those associated with

TABLE 10–1. CONDITIONS ASSOCIATED WITH LUNG HYPOPLASIA

MAJOR CAUSAL OR ASSOCIATED FEATURE		PATHOLOGICAL CONDITION
Prolonged oligohydramnios	Failure of fetal urine production or outlet obstruction	Renal agenesis; severe renal cystic dysplasia; prune-belly syndrome
	Prolonged rupture of membranes	
Abnormalities of thoracic cage		Congenital thoracic dystrophy; thanatophoric dwarfism
Abnormalities of diaphragm		Aplasia of diaphragm; eventration of diaphragm
CNS anomalies		Anencephaly (if medulla involved); iniencephaly; Meckel-Gruber syndrome (but may also have severe renal cystic dysplasia)
Congenital neurological or neuromuscular disorders		Congenital muscular dystrophy; Werdnig-Hoffmann disease with onset from birth; intrauterine anoxic-ischemic damage to CNS
Severe polyhydramnios		Many of above neurological or muscular disorders; cases of fetal hydrops of any cause resulting in pleural effusions

renal agenesis may show generalized maturation arrest.[27] Other studies on the lungs of infants with renal agenesis or dysplasia have found them to be structurally mature with normal surface properties,[26] or not to differ from those associated with other malformations.[28]

Our studies on the structural and biochemical aspects of human fetal lung hypoplasia showed that the lungs from all conditions associated with oligohydramnios dating from earlier than 20 weeks' gestational age show a similar defect.[29] This involves failure of growth and maturation of the peripheral parts of the acinus with delay in development of blood-air barriers, delay in epithelial maturation, lack of elastic tissue development and low concentrations of lung phospholipids (Fig. 10–7). In contrast, the hypoplastic lungs of infants with normal or increased amniotic fluid usually have a structure which is appropriate for the gestational age (Fig. 10–8) and normal phospholipid content. The latter group has included cases involving a variety of abnormalities affecting thoracic volume or neuromuscular activity.

Time of Onset of Lung Hypoplasia. The lung DNA content in hypoplastic fetal lungs of infants born near term is often similar to that of normally developed fetal lungs at about 20 weeks' gestational age (Fig. 10–9). This implies that fetal lung growth must have been retarded in such infants from before 20 weeks' gestation. The reduction in generations of bronchial branching noted by Hislop et al.[26] in several forms of lung hypoplasia suggests an onset before 17 weeks' gestation when bronchial branching is complete. However, the lesion associated with retardation of fetal lung growth can sometimes be ascertained to have developed during the fetal period. Thus rupture of fetal membranes with loss of amniotic fluid may have been observed and recorded in the mother's case notes.

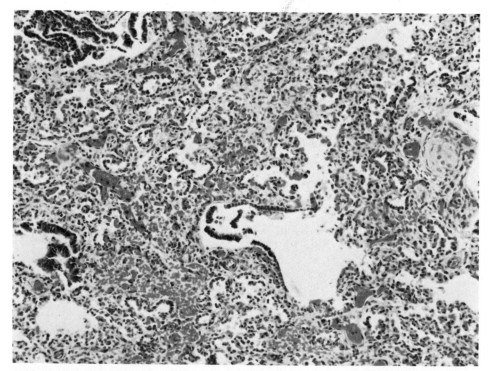

Figure 10–7. Hypoplastic lung from an infant with severe renal cystic dysplasia born at 38 weeks' gestation. There is extensive persistence of cuboidal alveolar epithelium and interstitial hemorrhage. H and E × 150. (From Wigglesworth, J. S., Desai, R. and Guerrini, P.: Fetal lung hypoplasia: biochemical and structural variations and their possible significance. Arch. Dis. Child. 56:606–615, 1981.)

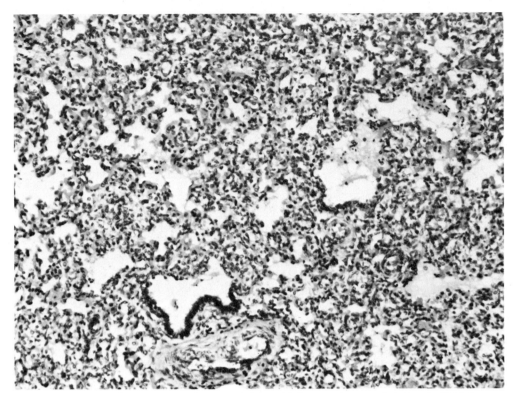

Figure 10–8. Hypoplastic lung from an infant with intrauterine anoxic-ischemic CNS damage (brain illustrated in Chapter 7) born at 34 weeks' gestation. Histological structure appears normal and relatively mature. H and E × 150.

Anoxic-ischemic damage to the CNS may be present in association with a relatively normally developed brain (Chapter 7), indicating that damage has occurred well after the period of organogenesis. These observations suggest that the early part of the second trimester may be a vulnerable period for human fetal lung growth.

Cause of Fetal Lung Hypoplasia. It has usually been considered that fetal lung hypoplasia is caused by a physical compression effect. However, as mentioned earlier (p. 172), it has been shown that chronic drainage of fetal lung liquid via

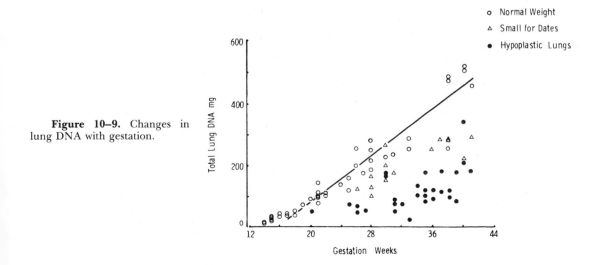

Figure 10–9. Changes in lung DNA with gestation.

the trachea will impair fetal lung growth in the lamb. We have demonstrated that sectioning of the spinal cord above the level of the phrenic nucleus in the fetal rabbit causes severe lung hypoplasia without impairing development of the diaphragm or thoracic wall musculature, whereas sectioning at lower levels of the cord has little effect.[8] If high cord transection is combined with ligation or transection of the trachea, the lungs become large and fluid-filled. These experiments suggest that lung hypoplasia caused by CNS injury or abnormality may be the result of a loss of the ability to retain fluid within the lung, probably as a result of impairment in fetal respiration. This is supported by experiments in lambs in which the damping of fetal respiratory movements by insertion of a flexible Silastic window in the chest wall caused similar impairment in lung growth.[30]

If indeed the secretion of lung liquid and its retention by fetal respiratory activity are important for normal lung growth (p. 170), the effects of CNS lesions or physical reduction in thoracic volume can be interpreted as limiting these functions. It is not clear why lack of amniotic fluid should be associated with such severe impairment in both growth and maturation of the lung. If this is purely a pressure effect it is clearly a rather subtle one that differs in some way from those induced by influences affecting thoracic volume in the presence of normal amniotic fluid.

Fetal respiratory activity and retention of fluid within the airways both become apparent early in the second trimester. Fetal respiratory movements are readily depressed by a wide range of influences, including maternal hypoglycemia, smoking or ingestion of CNS depressants such as alcohol or barbiturates.[31] Lung liquid secretion can be readily abolished experimentally by infusion of catecholamines or β_2-adrenergic agents. It thus seems likely on theoretical grounds that significant impairment of fetal lung growth could be caused by any nonspecific stress which acted between the time of onset of these functional activities and midway through the canalicular phase of development, that is, between 12 and 20 weeks' gestational age in the human. Gross lung hypoplasia as recognized by the pathologist at autopsy may represent one end of a spectrum of changes resulting from impairment in fetal lung function. The mild end of this spectrum may involve minor impairment in structural and biochemical maturation leading to neonatal respiratory distress syndrome. The increased incidence of neonatal respiratory problems in infants born to women subjected to amniocentesis in the second trimester as reported in a British multicenter trial[32] provides one possible example of such an effect.

OTHER LUNG ANOMALIES

Abnormal Lobation and Sequestration. Incomplete separation of the lobes of either lung is sufficiently common to be considered a normal variation. Accessory lung lobes with normal structure and normal bronchial relationships are not associated with any pathological problems.

Sequestered lung lobes are characterized by a lack of communication with the normal bronchial tree. Two forms of sequestered lobe are recognized, extralobar and intralobar. The extralobar form is usually located in the left thoracic cavity and has an arterial supply from the descending aorta and venous drainage into the inferior vena cava, hemiazygos or azygos venous systems (Fig. 10–10). The intralobar variety forms part of a normal lung lobe but usually also receives an arterial supply from the aorta, although venous drainage is into the pulmonary veins. Occasionally, sequestered lobes may be found outside the thoracic cavity.[33]

Segments of sequestered lung tissue—either intralobar or extralobar—may communicate with the alimentary tract, particularly the esophagus. These have been given the name *bronchopulmonary foregut malformations* and are seen more frequently on the right side than on the left.

In all instances the structure of the pulmonary tissue is abnormal, with cystic cavities lined by cuboidal or columnar epithelium, or large alveolar duct–like structures. There is a lack of normal alveolar development. Intralobar sequestered lung masses and bronchopulmonary foregut malformations may be a site of infection (see case described in Chapter 21). Theories of origin of sequestration are discussed by Stocker et al.[33]

Congenital Lobar Emphysema. This condition of congenital overexpansion of the lung appears to result from some form of bronchial obstruction by extrinsic vessels or intrinsic bronchial abnormality.[33] Most cases involve evidence of bronchial cartilage deficiency. The main histological feature is overdistension of alveoli, although some cases are described with an increase in alveoli or alveolar fibrosis.

Congenital Cystic Adenomatoid Malformation. Congenital cystic adenomatoid malformation is a hamartomatous condition which is usually symptomatic within the first few days of life or may be an unexpected finding at autopsy in infants who die at birth or soon after. Three morphologically distinct types have been described by Stocker et al.[33] and correlated with various clinical and radiographic features (Fig. 10–11). This classification is modified from that of Van Dijk and Wagenwoort.[34] Histological features common to all include:

1. An adenomatoid increase in structures resembling terminal bronchioles
2. A polypoid configuration of the cuboidal to columnar epithelial lining of the cystic structures
3. An increase in elastic tissue in areas lined by cuboidal to columnar epithelium
4. An absence of inflammation

The large cysts of type I lesions are lined by ciliated columnar and pseudostratified epithelium, often with segments of mucus-secreting cells (Fig. 10–12). The cysts communicate with the bronchi. The epithelium overlies a well-developed fibromuscular layer of up to 300 μ in thickness. Small cysts surround the large ones as illustrated in Figures 10–11 and 10–12. Type II lesions comprise multiple medium-sized cysts which resemble dilated terminal bronchioles and are lined by ciliated cuboidal to columnar epithelium over a fibromuscular layer which does not exceed 100 μ in thickness. Increased elastic tissue is present beneath the epithelium. These bronchiole-like cysts communicate with structures resembling distended respiratory bronchioles, alveolar ducts and alveoli (Fig. 10–13). Mucus-secreting cells are not seen, but groups of smooth muscle fibers are sometimes present. The type III lesions form a firm mass which may be of considerable weight (average 83 g in the patients described by Stocker et al.) and commonly causes a mediastinal shift. Evenly spaced cysts lined by ciliated cuboidal epithelium communicate with intermediate channels resembling bronchioles, which in turn lead into alveolar duct–like structures lined by cuboidal epithelium and surrounded by mesenchyme. The appearance resembles the early canalicular stage of fetal development (17 to 20 weeks). The type III lesions are sometimes associated with anasarca.

The large cysts of the type I lesions frequently expand within a few days after birth and cause increasing respiratory distress. The type II and type III lesions are probably encountered most frequently at perinatal autopsy because type II lesions are often associated with other anomalies and type III lesions are usually fatal within a short time after birth.

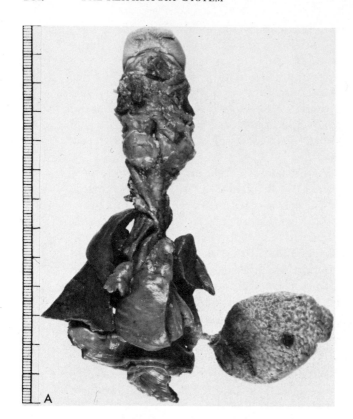

Figure 10–10. A large sequestered left lung lobe, with arterial supply from the descending aorta. This was associated with massive pleural effusions and hydrops. The "normal" lungs are hypoplastic in this case. *A*, Macroscopic appearance. *B*, Histologic appearance: H and E × 150. The lung comprises mainly alveolar duct–like structures that resemble the appearance seen in solid areas of congenital cystic adenomatoid lung (Type III).

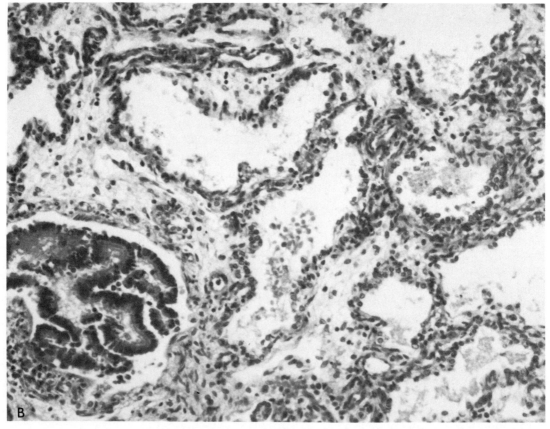

TYPE I   TYPE II   TYPE III

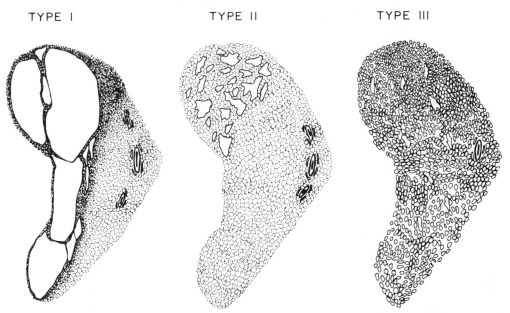

Figure 10–11. Classification of congenital cystic adenomatoid malformation. Type I is composed of a small number of large cysts with thick smooth muscle and elastic tissue walls. Relatively normal alveoli are seen between and adjacent to these cysts. Mucous glands may be present. Type II contains numerous smaller cysts (< 1 cm in diameter) with a thin muscular coat beneath the ciliated columnar epithelium. The area between the cysts is occupied by large alveolus-like structures. The lesion blends with the normal parenchyma. Type III occupies the entire lobe or lobes and is composed of regularly spaced bronchiole-like structures separated by masses of cuboidal epithelium lined alveolus-like structures. (From Stocker, J. T., Madewell, J. E., and Drake, R. M.: Congenital cystic adenomatoid malformation of the lung. Hum. Pathol. *8*:155–171, 1977.)

It has been suggested that the large area of involvement and poor differentiation of type III lesions indicate an insult related to the time of appearance of the primary branches of the lung bud (26 to 28 days) and that the association between type II lesions and anomalies such as renal agenesis and syrenomelia supports an origin during the third week. The well-differentiated state of type I lesions would indicate a rather later origin for this group. This unified view is not universally agreed upon, and some authors believe that only the type III lesions should be called *cystic adenomatoid lungs*.[35]

Congenital Pulmonary Lymphangiectasis. This condition is usually associated with stillbirth or early neonatal death. Most infants have rapidly progressive respiratory distress, although some live for several weeks, and survival up to the age of 5 years has been reported.[16, 33, 36, 37] At autopsy the lungs are firm and have an irregular surface with a prominent, slightly depressed network of thick interlobular septa (Fig. 10–14). On cut section the dilated cystic lymphatics are seen within the septa, in the subpleural region and in close association with the bronchi. On microscopy the walls of the dilated lymphatics are seen to have a thin endothelial cell lining over a network of elastin, collagen and sometimes muscle fibers.

The condition is most frequently seen in congenital anomalies of the cardiovascular system involving obstruction to pulmonary venous drainage. Cases that I have encountered have been associated with total anomalous pulmonary venous drainage, cor triatriatum, and premature closure of the foramen ovale. Rarely, pulmonary lymphangiectasis forms part of a generalized lymphangiectasis or develops as an isolated lesion.

Text continued on page 186

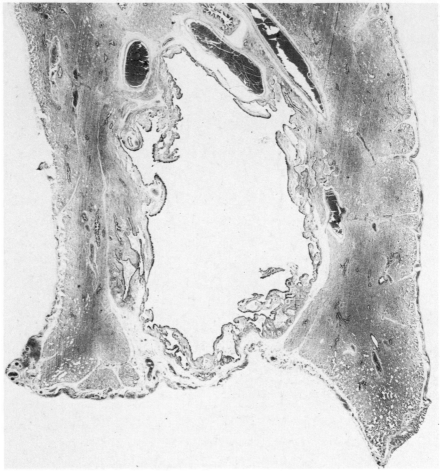

Figure 10–12. Section of a left lower lobe excised in the neonatal period showing Type I CCAM. H and E × 5.5.

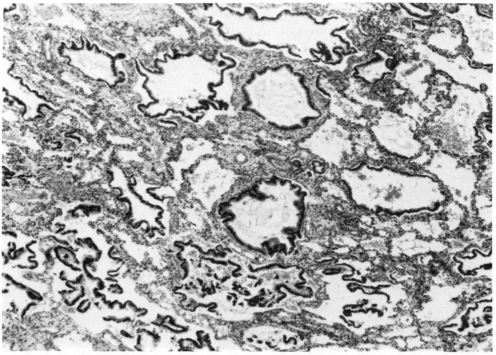

Figure 10–13. Type II CCAM. There are multiple cysts resembling dilated terminal bronchioles. H and E × 60.

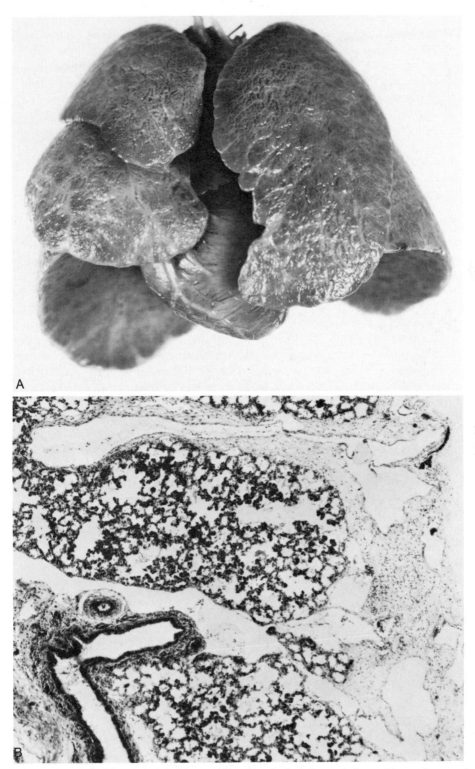

Figure 10–14. *A,* Congenital pulmonary lymphangiectasis in an infant with total anomalous pulmonary venous drainage. The network of thick interlobular septa is characteristic. *B,* Section of lung from the same case showing dilated lymphatic channels within subpleural and interlobular connective tissue. H and E × 60.

HYALINE MEMBRANE DISEASE AND ITS SEQUELAE

It has been known since the 1920's that infants who die in the early neonatal period may show solid airless lungs with hyaline-like membranes lining the peripheral parts of the airways on microscopic study. The postmortem findings have been recognized to develop most frequently in preterm infants and to be associated with a group of clinical signs known as the *respiratory distress syndrome*. These include a rapid respiratory rate with sternal and subcostal chest wall recessions, cyanosis, an expiratory grunt and a characteristic chest radiograph. Since the demonstration by Avery and Mead[38] that the lungs of preterm infants who died with respiratory distress syndrome and had hyaline membrane disease exhibited abnormal surface properties, it has become widely assumed that respiratory distress syndrome (RDS), hyaline membrane disease (HMD) and surfactant deficiency are synonymous. For a proper understanding of this major area of developmental pathology it is important that pediatricians and pathologists recognize that this unifying view is a considerable oversimplification.

The findings at autopsy are best explained if one thinks of RDS and HMD as involving separate but overlapping groups of infants (Fig. 10–15). All the clinical features of RDS can be present in infants who do not have HMD. In our own case material we found that some 25 per cent of infants with RDS who died did not have HMD at autopsy.[39] This incidence may of course vary from one unit to another according to the stringency of the criteria used for establishing a clinical diagnosis of RDS. Major pathological findings in infants in our study who died with clinical RDS not associated with HMD are shown in Table 10–2. In addition, some infants are found to have HMD at autopsy but have not been recognized to have clinical RDS in life. This might for instance be the case in infants who required mechanical ventilation from the time of birth.

There is a similar imperfect association between HMD and evidence of surfactant deficiency in the lungs of infants studied postmortem. Another study we carried out on infants who died in our own unit showed that 69 per cent of those who died with pulmonary hyaline membranes were immature and had lungs deficient in surfactant as assessed by performance of pressure volume loop measurements and measurements of surface properties of lung extracts on the Whilhelmy balance.[40] Of the 31 per cent of infants with pulmonary hyaline membranes in whom pressure volume loop measurements and the surface properties of lung extracts indicated the presence of surfactant, one in four was

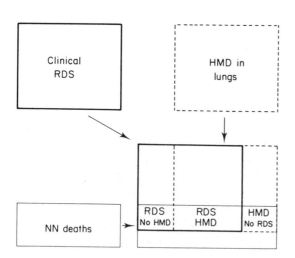

Figure 10–15. Diagram to illustrate the relationship between the clinical diagnosis of RDS and the presence of pulmonary HMD that best explains the findings at autopsy in neonatal deaths. (From Wigglesworth, J. S.: Pathology of neonatal respiratory distress. Proc. Roy. Soc. Med. *70*:861–863, 1977.)

TABLE 10–2. MAJOR FINDINGS IN 82 CASES OF RESPIRATORY DISTRESS SYNDROME NOT ASSOCIATED WITH HYALINE MEMBRANE DISEASE*

PATHOLOGY	NO. AND PERCENTAGE OF CASES	
Intraventricular hemorrhage	17	(21%)
Birth asphyxia (e.g., aspiration of meconium and epithelial squames)	14	(17%)
Infections	10	(12%)
Massive pulmonary hemorrhage	9	(11%)
Extreme immaturity only	7	(8.5%)
Hypoplastic lungs	6	(7.25%)
Intracranial hemorrhage other than IVH	6	(7.25%)
Pneumothorax	5	(6%)
Other, including congenital heart disease; necrotizing enterocolitis; rhesus isoimmunization; multiple malformations	8	(10%)

*From Wigglesworth, J. S.: Pathology of neonatal respiratory distress. Proc. Roy. Soc. Med. 70:861–863, 1977.
Hammersmith Hospital, 1970–75. Although diagnostic accuracy in life is now considerably greater for many of these conditions, confusion still arises, particularly in infants who die before they can be fully assessed in a neonatal intensive care unit.

recovering from HMD and showed return of surfactant on that basis. The rest showed a variety of findings, including massive pulmonary hemorrhage and evidence of severe birth asphyxia. As will be discussed later, hyaline membranes are composed mainly of extravasated blood constituents with degenerated bronchiolar epithelium. It is not perhaps surprising that they can develop in any respiratory illness in the newborn which is associated with increased capillary permeability. Surfactant deficiency in the preterm infant lung is the most frequent but not the only cause of this pathological appearance. Thus any discussion of the pathology of HMD requires separate consideration of the causes of surfactant deficiency and of the process of hyaline membrane formation.

FACTORS ASSOCIATED WITH SURFACTANT DEFICIENCY

The development of the enzyme pathways for synthesis of surfactant in sufficient quantities to maintain a stable alveolar lining layer is a function of maturity.[11] Thus there is a close correlation between gestational age and the incidence of respiratory distress associated with surfactant deficiency.[4] Amniotic fluid lecithin/sphingomyelin ratios usually indicate lung maturity from about 35 weeks' gestational age, and most infants who die with surfactant deficiency will be at a lower gestational age than this. However, the relationship between gestational age and surfactant deficiency is complicated by the range of stimuli which can advance maturation of surfactant synthetic pathways and probably by stresses which can depress surfactant production or hasten the destruction of the formed alveolar lining layer.[11] Inhibition of surfactant synthetic activities would be expected at a low pH as might be caused by an asphyxial episode, but enhancement of synthesis will result from any intrinsic rise in glucocorticoid production as induced by stress. Sexual differences in the ease with which surfactant synthesis can be induced in the preterm human fetal lung have been reported.[41]

A number of clinical situations are recognized in which there may be an increased or decreased incidence of RDS presumed (or proved) to be caused by surfactant deficiency. There is a significantly increased risk of RDS in the second as compared with the first of twin pairs.[42] This is usually assumed to be caused by inhibition of surfactant synthesis by the increased asphyxia to which the second twin is likely to be subjected. An alternative explanation is that maturation of the surfactant synthetic pathways is enhanced in the first twin. There is claimed to be a lower incidence of RDS (than expected for gestation) because of advanced maturation of the surfactant synthetic pathways in infants born to women with pre-eclampsia and recurrent bleeding episodes.[43, 44] These are presumably conditions of increased stress.

Considerable argument has arisen over the influence of cesarean section on the incidence of RDS.[4] It is clearly important to allow for possible effects on lung maturation of the conditions for which cesarean section is performed before the effects of the operation itself can be established. From studies in which these influences have been fully allowed for on a matched gestational age basis, it would appear that cesarean section performed before the onset of labor may increase the risk of RDS at certain gestational ages. The increased risk may well be accounted for by absence of the rise in glucocorticoid production and absence of the raised circulating catecholamine levels that are associated with the onset of labor.

There has been conflicting evidence on the influence of a prolonged interval after rupture of the membranes on the incidence of RDS. From some studies it has been concluded that premature membrane rupture increases the risk of RDS, whereas from others it appears that this decreases the risk of RDS.[44, 45] This is perhaps not surprising because rupture of the membranes may have a number of different effects. To the extent that rupture of the membranes may constitute a stress, it may induce increased fetal secretion of glucocorticoids and catecholamines. This may promote maturation of the surfactant synthetic pathways, resorption of fetal lung liquid and increased surfactant release. Moreover, there is an increased risk of fetal infection following premature membrane rupture and this may constitute an additional stress. However, it is now clear, as discussed earlier in this chapter, that premature membrane rupture dating from the second trimester causes impairment both in lung growth and in epithelial and connective tissue maturation. Thus the net effect of premature membrane rupture on fetal lung development, surfactant synthesis and the consequential risk of RDS may depend on factors such as the gestational age at which membrane rupture occurred, the interval between the time the membranes were ruptured and delivery and, possibly, how much fluid was lost.

Infants of diabetic mothers have been said to have an increased incidence of RDS for their gestation.[46] This tendency is seldom observed now that most infants of diabetics are born at 38 weeks' gestation or later, whereas in the past many of the infants were born by preterm cesarean section.

PATHOLOGY OF HYALINE MEMBRANE DISEASE

The macroscopic and microscopic appearances of the lungs in the preterm infant with surfactant deficiency vary according to the age at which death occurs.[47] If the infant dies within the first 12 hours, the lungs may appear no more than moderately congested, although they are usually uniformly airless. Sometimes there is minimal aeration of the anterior parts, for instance, of the right middle lobe. On histological examination at this early stage the acini appear moderately expanded, but there is evidence of the acidophilic membrane material lining the respiratory bronchioles. There may be visible accumulation of basophilic material related to the site of hyaline membrane formation (Fig. 10–16). This represents necrotic bronchiolar epithelium. It can be seen regularly as the first stage of HMD in experimental animals such as the 125-day lamb.[48] The interlobular septa at this stage are broad, with obvious distension of the lymphatic vessels.

Between 12 and 24 hours of age the infant lung develops the classic

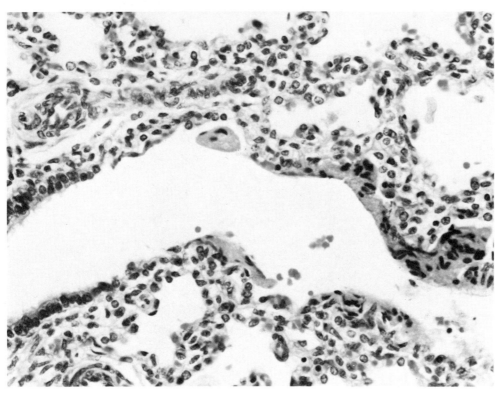

Figure 10–16. Very early hyaline membrane formation in a respiratory bronchiole of the lung of an infant of 30 weeks' gestation who died at 1 hour of age following vigorous attempts at resuscitation. H and E × 400. The membranes contain basophilic material representing necrotic bronchiolar epithelium. The terminal sacs are not collapsed at this stage; they still contain lung liquid.

appearance of HMD. If an infant dies at this stage the lungs are found to be acutely congested, totally airless and of liver-like consistency on section (Fig. 10–17). A presumptive diagnosis of HMD can readily be made on macroscopic examination alone. The histological appearance differs in several ways from that of cases seen at the earlier stage. The hyaline material lining the respiratory bronchioles has become more prominent and uniform and the bronchioles may be obviously dilated (Fig. 10–17). Basophilic material is no longer seen within the membranes. The terminal sacs are completely collapsed and the membrane-lined bronchioles thus appear to be separated by thick, intensely congested cellular septa. The pulmonary arterioles may appear constricted and many of them may be occluded by fibrin thrombi. The interlobular septa are less wide than in the early stages but may still appear relatively broad, with dilated lymphatics. The main change that occurs to present this altered appearance is a gradual removal of much of the lung liquid. If the serum bilirubin level is raised, hyaline membranes are often stained yellow. The cause of the raised serum bilirubin in such cases would seem of more significance than the color of the membranes, although the latter has provoked interest in some quarters.[49]

At an ultrastructural level there is loss of the osmiophilic lamellar bodies from the type II pneumonocytes at this stage of the process. If static pressure volume loop determinations are performed, the lungs hold a low maximal volume of air and deflate almost totally at low transpulmonary pressure (Fig. 10–18).

By 48 hours of age a cellular reaction to the hyaline membranes may take place. Histiocytes may be applied to the surface of the membranes. These have

Text continued on page 192

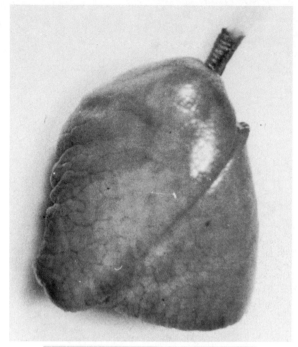

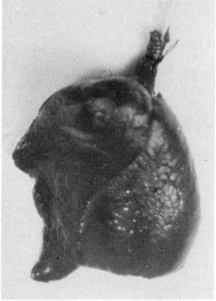

A

Figure 10–17. *A*, Left lungs of a pair of twins of 29 weeks' gestation and 1100 g birth weight who both died at about 30 hours of age (in 1967). Twin I died of IVH and twin II of severe RDS. The lungs have been inflated to 40 cm H_2O pressure and then deflated stepwise to 5 cm H_2O transpulmonary pressure. The lung of twin I (top) retains 80 per cent of its maximal volume, while that of twin II (bottom) is completely collapsed. (From Reynolds E.O.R., et al.: Hyaline membrane disease, respiratory distress, and surfactant deficiency. Pediatrics *42*:758–768, 1968. Copyright American Academy of Pediatrics 1968.)

Illustration continued on opposite page

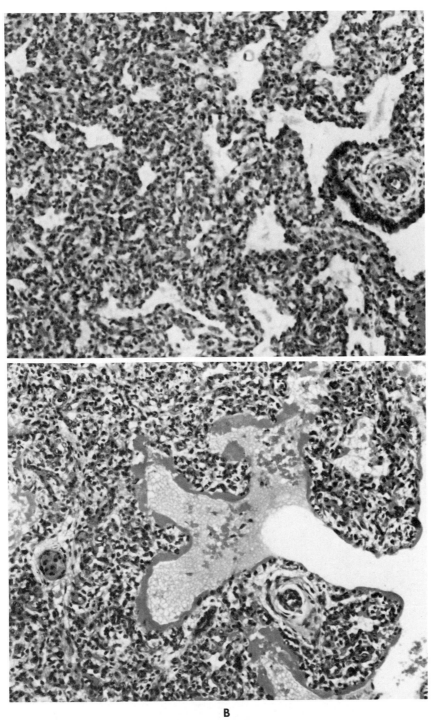

B

Figure 10–17 *Continued. B*, Section of the opposite (uninflated) lungs of the same twins. H and E × 150. The section of the lung of twin I (top) shows an immature pattern only, while that of twin II shows dilated respiratory bronchioles containing red cells and proteinaceous material, lined with well-developed hyaline membranes, and collapse with congestion of terminal sacs.

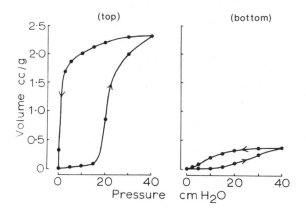

Figure 10–18. Static pressure volume loops performed on the lungs of the twins illustrated in Figure 10–17. (From Reynolds E.O.R., et al.: Hyaline membrane disease, respiratory distress, and surfactant deficiency. Pediatrics *42*:758–768, 1968. Copyright American Academy of Pediatrics 1968.)

been called membranophages by Larroche (Fig. 10–19).[16] Osmiophilic lamellar bodies may be seen reappearing within the type II cells from 48 hours on,[47] and by 3 to 5 days they may be present in greater numbers than in the normal preterm infant lung. This is paralleled by return of normal surface characteristics. Removal of the membrane material is accompanied by regeneration of bronchiolar epithelium. Focal edema and a fibroblastic reaction around the respiratory bronchioles may be regarded as a normal part of the repair process. Total disappearance of hyaline membranes is usually achieved by about a week of age in infants who have not required mechanical ventilation and high inspired oxygen concentrations, although the histological pattern of the lung with a persisting cellular reaction around the respiratory bronchioles may indicate a "recovered" HMD.

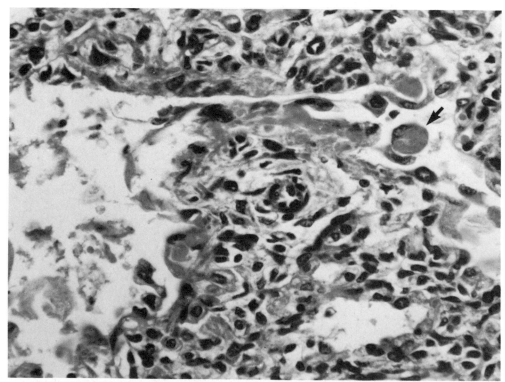

Figure 10–19. Resolving HMD at 6 days. H and E × 400. Histiocytes are applied to the membrane lining a respiratory bronchiole, and one lying free contains engulfed hyaline material (arrow).

**HYALINE MEMBRANE FORMATION IN THE PRESENCE OF NORMAL
SURFACTANT**

As has been pointed out earlier, hyaline membranes are not confined to instances of surfactant deficiency. Infants with massive pulmonary hemorrhage may have obvious hyaline material lining the respiratory bronchioles, although often it is less regular in appearance than that associated with surfactant deficiency. Surface properties are characteristically normal.[40] Term infants who die as a result of severe birth asphyxia may have well-developed pulmonary hyaline membranes (Fig. 10–20) despite normal surface properties. The histological appearance of these lungs differs from that seen in lungs with surfactant deficiency only in the greater maturity of the underlying lung structure. Sometimes aspirated epithelial squames can be recognized embedded within or deep to the membrane material. Intensely lipid-staining membranes may be seen in the lungs of infants who have died in circumstances which suggest that milk aspiration may have occurred.

COMPONENTS OF HYALINE MEMBRANES

Histochemical and ultrastructural studies on hyaline membranes have shown that they consist primarily of plasma constituents mixed with products of degenerated bronchiolar epithelium.[50, 51] The demonstration that fibrin could be detected within the membranes by ultrastructural and immunofluorescent methods was interpreted by many to imply that the membranes consist of fibrin.[52, 53] The membranes of surfactant-deficient HMD do not stain for fibrin using conventional histological stains, although those associated with massive pulmonary hemorrhage do. Lauweryns has pointed out that even at an ultrastructural level fibrin is a relatively minor component of most hyaline membranes.[51]

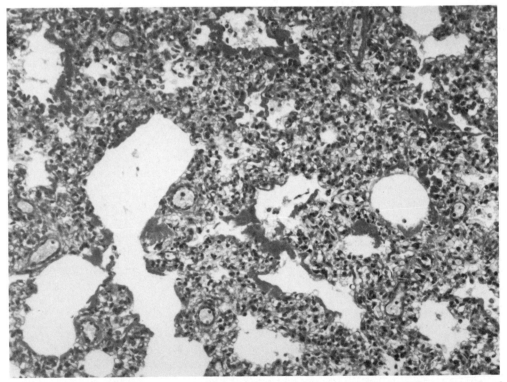

Figure 10–20. Hyaline membrane formation in the lung of a term infant who died at 9 hours of age following severe birth asphyxia. H and E × 150.

ETIOLOGY OF HYALINE MEMBRANE DISEASE

HMD was previously ascribed to aspiration of amniotic material, particularly vernix caseosa, as implied by the term vernix membranes, which was in frequent use. The recognition of the association between HMD and immaturity and the evidence of surfactant deficiency in these cases has caused attention to be focused almost exclusively on this group of infants. Hyaline membranes are not seen in the lungs of stillborn infants and are thus clearly related to air breathing. The frequency with which hyaline membranes are seen in the newborn infant lung in circumstances other than surfactant deficiency indicates that exudation of blood constituents occurs readily as a result of a number of different forms of stress. Following resorption of the fluid, the solid material appears to be plastered around the walls of the respiratory bronchioles in all cases. The pressures set up across the respiratory bronchiolar wall during inspiratory efforts in the face of a high surface tension tending to collapse the airspaces would be a potent cause of plasma exudation.

Thus HMD can be regarded as a nonspecific result of exudation of plasma constituents into the acinus in the newborn. However, surfactant deficiency in the preterm infant lung is the most frequent and important cause of this pathological appearance.

The reasons why there should be such a wide gestational age range at which the preterm infant lung may be stable or unstable have not, to my mind, yet been fully explained, despite the enormous volume of work that has been performed on the biochemistry of surfactant synthesis and the factors that may advance or retard maturation of the enzyme pathways.

BRONCHOPULMONARY DYSPLASIA

This condition was first recognized and described by Northway and colleagues soon after the introduction of mechanical ventilation for treatment of severe RDS in preterm infants;[54] since then it has presented a significant problem in neonatal intensive care units throughout the world. The earliest changes appear as an accentuation of the normal repair process involving the walls of the bronchioles affected by HMD. The lung may appear quite solid as if involved in a pneumonic process, even in infants who die as early as 5 to 7 days of age. There is edema around the bronchioles and throughout the saccular septa associated with fibroblast proliferation (Fig. 10–21). Luxuriant hyaline membrane persists in the respiratory bronchioles for up to 2 weeks. The lumina of many bronchioles may be occluded, with secretions which become organized by fibroblast invasion. The saccules distal to such obstructed bronchioles appear to regress in structure, with loss of blood-air barriers and reappearance of a cuboidal epithelium. There is hyperplasia and squamous metaplasia of bronchial epithelium (Fig. 10–21). Foci of distorted proliferated capillaries may be seen and may be the site of focal hemorrhages. Elsewhere there may be a relative lack of a capillary bed. The lung at a late chronic stage of the condition (3 to 5 weeks) macroscopically appears irregular, with areas of overdistention alternating with areas of collapse. On microscopic examination the edematous areas around the bronchioles and in the saccular septa have become the site of fibrosis, and the bronchiolar walls may show considerable muscular hypertrophy (Fig. 10–22).

The early papers on the subject stressed the importance of oxygen toxicity as the primary etiological factor and emphasized the similarity of the findings to those resulting from oxygen toxicity in experimental animals.[54, 55] Some groups of workers have subsequently claimed that the major factor is high pressure ventilation and that high inspired oxygen concentrations have only a limited role.[56]

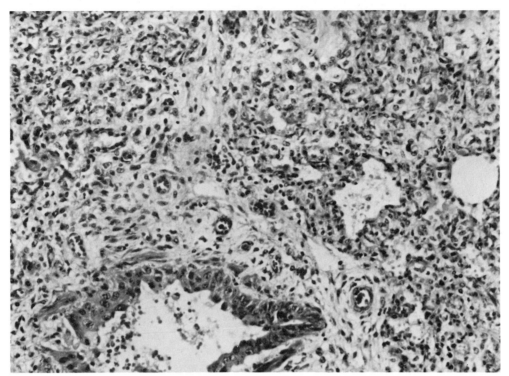

Figure 10–21. Early bronchopulmonary dysplasia (BPD) in an infant who died at 4 days of age. There is interstitial edema with fibroblast proliferation and hyperplasia of bronchial epithelium. H and E × 150.

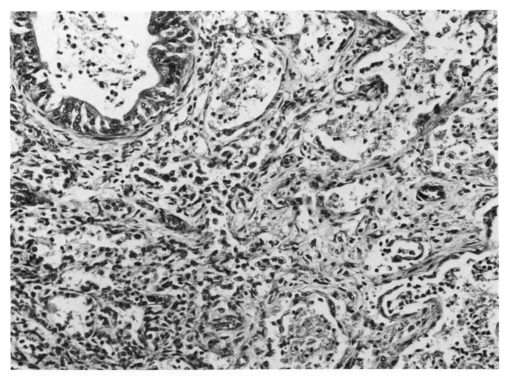

Figure 10–22. Late changes of BPD in an infant who died at 5 weeks of age. Patchy fibrosis of alveolar septa and persistent bronchial epithelial hyperplasia. H and E × 150. (From Banerjee, C. K. et al.: Pulmonary fibroplasia in newborn babies treated with oxygen and artificial ventilation. Arch. Dis. Child. *47*:509–518, 1972.)

Statistical evidence adduced in support of one or the other view is not entirely convincing, because prolonged use of high pressure ventilation and prolonged administration of oxygen in high concentration usually involve the same infants. In fact, one of the most striking features of bronchopulmonary dysplasia is the range of changes seen and their patchy distribution throughout the lung. Damage to bronchial and bronchiolar ciliary structure has been stressed by one group.[57]

Some of the changes would seem to be a logical consequence of high pressure ventilation. These include in particular the hypertrophy of bronchiolar walls and bronchial epithelial hyperplasia. The obstruction of bronchiolar lumina, which was a pronounced feature in many of the early reports, is almost certainly due to impaction of secretions caused by poor humidification. We saw this form of change in the cases of severe bronchopulmonary dysplasia which developed during initial attempts at ventilator management in the late 1960's but have not observed it since effective humidification techniques were introduced. The edema and fibroblast proliferation around the bronchioles and within the saccular septa does indeed seem likely to be a result of high inspired oxygen concentrations. Quite apart from the similarity of the changes to those seen in other species and in other areas (e.g., the retina) in human oxygen toxicity, there is a close relationship between chronic pulmonary interstitial emphysema and local development of bronchopulmonary dysplasia.

ACUTE PULMONARY INTERSTITIAL EMPHYSEMA

Before the use of modern resuscitation techniques interstitial emphysema occurred mainly in term infants as a consequence of meconium inhalation. The unaided respiratory efforts of these infants could cause interstitial emphysema if the inhaled mucus and meconium led to a ball-valve type of obstruction. The condition has now become a major problem in neonatal intensive care units since the introduction of mechanical ventilation for treatment of severe RDS and other forms of respiratory failure in the newborn. The high pressures which may be required for mechanical ventilation of infants with surfactant deficiency render this group of preterm infants at particular risk of interstitial emphysema and its sequelae.

The condition is classically envisaged as resulting from a disturbance in equilibrium between the pressure within the alveolar and vascular compartments of the lung.[58] Rupture of the saccular wall results in entry of air to the perivascular, peribronchial and subpleural connective tissues. Air readily dissects along the lymphatic channels within the connective tissue compartment and may present as a line of bubbles or large bullae at the lung surface. The adjacent lung parenchyma is often collapsed and pulmonary veins within the interlobular septa may be compressed. The cut surface of a lung which is involved by severe interstitial pulmonary emphysema may have a Swiss cheese appearance (Fig. 10–23).

PNEUMOTHORAX

This results when air within the interstitial tissues ruptures into the pleural cavity. At autopsy it may be suspected, in the absence of any history, when the chest appears expanded or if there is pallor or visible interstitial emphysema affecting the thoracic wall. Large pneumothoraxes will be seen readily if a radiograph of the chest is taken before the autopsy is begun (Fig. 10–24). Testing for pneumothorax by opening the chest under water must be carried out carefully to avoid missing small collections of air (Chapter 3). A tension pneumothorax may displace the mediastinum, depress the diaphragm and cause the ipsilateral lung to collapse. The collapse will not be complete in cases of severe HMD as the

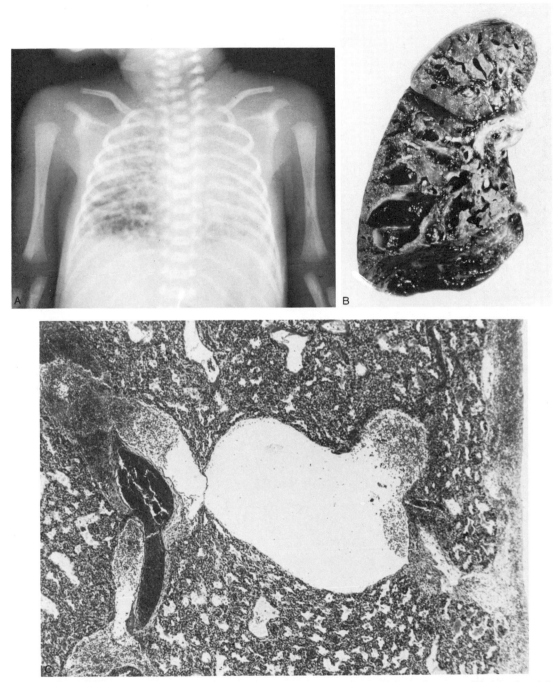

Figure 10–23. *A*, Postmortem x-ray showing acute pulmonary interstitial emphysema affecting the right lung in particular. *B*, Cut surface of the right lung of the same case showing the "swiss cheese" appearance. *C*, Section of the same lung showing an emphysematous bulla in the interobular septum. H and E × 30.

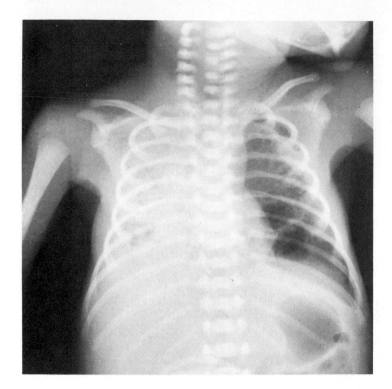

Figure 10–24. Postmortem x-ray showing a left-sided pneumothorax in addition to bilateral acute pulmonary interstitial emphysema.

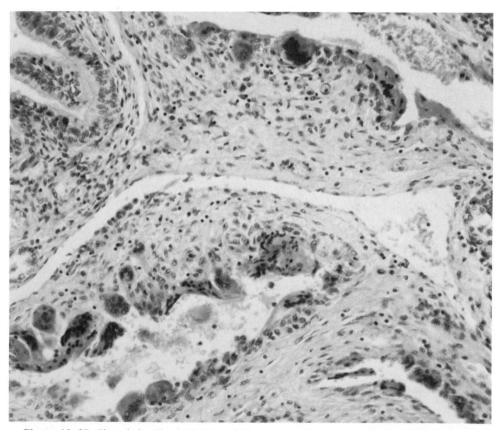

Figure 10–25. Chronic localized PIPE in a lobectomy specimen from an infant of 5 weeks of age. H and E × 150. Spaces in the interlobular septa are lined by histiocytes and foreign body giant cells.

lung is splinted by fluid. If the infant was on treatment with a high inspired oxygen concentration at the time of death, the oxygen within the pneumothorax will prevent reduction of the oxyhemoglobin within the red cells in the adjacent tissues. The bright red lung underlying the pneumothorax will contrast at autopsy with the dark red of the opposite lung.

PNEUMOMEDIASTINUM AND PNEUMOPERITONEUM

These are possible sequelae of acute interstitial pulmonary emphysema as the connective tissue space around the bronchi and pulmonary vessels is continuous with that of the mediastinum and retroperitoneal tissues. Pneumopericardium is described in Chapter 11 and other causes of pneumoperitoneum in Chapter 13.

CHRONIC PERSISTENT INTERSTITIAL PULMONARY EMPHYSEMA (PIPE)

This has become a well-recognized entity since widespread use of mechanical ventilation procedures in the newborn. Two forms are described, localized and diffuse.[33] Localized PIPE develops usually in infants who have had RDS with a period of mechanical ventilation and is seen as a multicystic mass which involves the left upper lobe in 50 per cent of cases[33] and may require surgical excision at several weeks or months of age. Irregular cysts are present within the affected lobe, with fibrous connective tissue walls which contain hemosiderin pigment and are partially lined by multinucleated cells of foreign body giant cell type (Fig. 10–25). The intervening lung parenchyma is usually collapsed and may show changes of bronchopulmonary dysplasia. In diffuse PIPE the cysts are more uniform and smaller in size and the lung parenchyma usually shows severe bronchopulmonary dysplasia.

WILSON-MIKITY SYNDROME

This condition has been described mainly by neonatologists and radiologists rather than pathologists.[59, 60] It consists of late respiratory distress developing within the first month of life in small preterm infants and involving tachypnea, cyanosis and chest retractions. Rales and cough may be present. Chronic pulmonary insufficiency with repeated chest infections and failure to thrive are later features. Radiological findings include streaky infiltrates and scattered lucencies. Recovery is said to occur in most cases. In those infants who come to autopsy the lungs show cystic emphysematous areas interspersed with areas of collapse. On histological examination there is cellular thickening of the alveolar septa, increase in fibroelastic tissue and patchy emphysema. Possible causes for this condition include localized pulmonary collapse owing to hypersecretion, aspiration or immature structure with localized air trapping. In common with many other pediatric pathologists I have yet to see a case in my autopsy material.

PNEUMONIA

The respiratory tract constitutes the most frequent site for localization of infection during the perinatal period. Many instances of respiratory infection will not have been diagnosed in life and will present as a macroscopic or histological abnormality at postmortem examination. It is usually not possible to make a confident diagnosis of pneumonia on macroscopic examination in the perinatal period because many of the other conditions described in this chapter, including HMD, bronchopulmonary dysplasia and massive pulmonary hemorrhage, are associated with firm lungs which are readily confused with pneumonia. The distribution of the cellular reaction in neonatal pneumonia is that of bronchopneumonia. However, the reaction of a newborn lung to infection is somewhat different from that of the adult lung, and most intrapartum and neonatal pneumonias are characterized by a cellular reaction with little evidence of the fibrin network typical of pneumonic consolidation in the adult.

CLASSIFICATION OF PERINATAL PNEUMONIAS

It has been suggested that pneumonia in the fetus and newborn infant can be classified into four categories according to the time and mode of acquisition of the infection.[61]

1. Pneumonia acquired by the transplacental route. The pneumonia in these cases is part of a generalized infection.
2. Congenital or intrauterine pneumonia. This is an inflammatory condition of the lungs found in stillborn infants or infants who die in the first few days of life.
3. Pneumonia acquired during birth. The signs of pneumonia develop during the first week of life and infection is caused by microorganisms that colonize the maternal birth canal.
4. Pneumonia acquired after birth. The microorganisms come from the environment, often from human contacts or equipment.

In practice it may often be difficult to distinguish between these categories, particularly categories 2 and 3, but the classification is of value as an aid to thinking how timing and route of infection may be linked with the type of infecting microorganism. (There is further discussion of this in Chapter 9.)

TRANSPLACENTALLY ACQUIRED PNEUMONIA

The organisms responsible include cytomegalovirus, rubella, herpes simplex, the enteroviruses, *Toxoplasma gondii*, genital mycoplasmas, *Mycobacterium tuberculosis*, *Listeria monocytogenes* and *Treponema pallidum*. Details of these infections are given in Chapter 9.

INTRAUTERINE PNEUMONIA

The airways of the fetal lung are in direct communication with the amniotic fluid. In the event of chorioamnionitis, the lungs may be directly infected by inhalation of infected amniotic fluid.[62, 63] It is also possible that polymorphonuclear leukocytes can be inhaled from the fluid in the absence of a true bacterial infection. In many stillborn infants or those who die shortly after birth at an extremely immature stage of development, often well before 26 weeks' gestation, the lungs show a uniform infiltration of polymorphonuclear leukocytes throughout the airways and airspaces (Fig. 10–26). It is difficult to determine whether or not this condition always represents a genuine bacterial infection.

A form of intrauterine pneumonia which is occasionally encountered is that caused by *Candida albicans* (Chapter 9).

BACTERIAL PNEUMONIA IN THE NEWBORN

Both gram-positive and gram-negative infections are common as a cause of bacterial pneumonia in the newborn period (see Chapter 9). The clinical diagnosis of pneumonia may be difficult in life. In small preterm infants the clinical picture

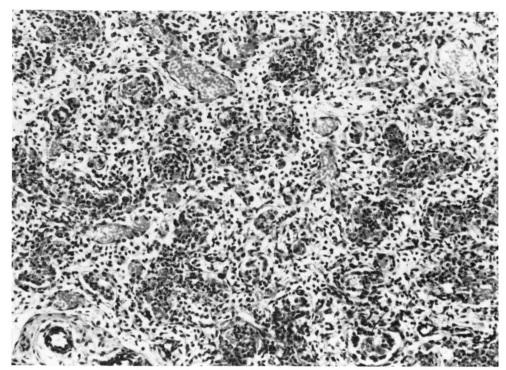

Figure 10–26. Intrauterine pneumonia in a fetus aborted at 24 weeks' gestation. H and E × 150. In this case heavy growth of *E. coli* and Bacteroides sp. was obtained on culture.

may resemble that of RDS. In the term infant, infection may be associated with evidence of birth asphyxia and with inhalation of amniotic material. Infection acquired prenatally, or during passage through the birth canal, may progress so rapidly that the infant dies before a diagnosis is possible.

Pneumonia Due to Gram-Positive Organisms. Of these, the most common and important is that caused by infection with β-hemolytic streptococci of Lancefield's group B. These organisms form a normal part of the vaginal flora in about 20 to 25 per cent of women. General aspects of infections caused by this important organism are discussed in Chapter 9. The infants may show severe respiratory distress at birth, and an initial diagnosis of RDS caused by surfactant deficiency may only be revised on recognition that the infant has profound toxemia. Death often occurs within a few hours after birth. At autopsy the lungs may have a macroscopic appearance resembling HMD, although sometimes there is an obvious pinkish discoloration similar to the appearance of early maceration. This is presumably due to the hemolysins produced by the organisms.

On histological examination there may be a characteristic neonatal pneumonia (Chapter 9). In some instances, particularly in preterm infants, there is hyaline membrane formation within the respiratory bronchioles in addition to a polymorphonuclear cell reaction. In these cases the organisms may be seen to infiltrate the hyaline membranes in large numbers. It has been suggested that this appearance is a result of some specific effect of the organisms and that the membranes differ from those of classical HMD caused by surfactant deficiency.[64] Although the appearance is seen most frequently in cases of infection with β-hemolytic streptococci of group B, I have seen a similar picture in cases in which the lung was infected with streptococci and *Hemophilus influenzae*.

The most florid form of gram-positive pneumonia, with abscesses, bullae (pneumatoceles) and fibrinous pleurisy, is that caused by infection with *Staphylococcus aureus*. This is most likely to be seen in infants who die at several weeks of age.

Pneumonia Due to Gram-Negative Organisms. Gram-negative microorganisms commonly responsible for pneumonia in the perinatal period include *E. coli*, Klebsiella and *Pseudomonas aeruginosa*. Infections due to gram-negative organisms characteristically produce less of a polymorphonuclear reaction in the newborn lung than do those due to gram-positive organisms. This may be typified by Pseudomonas infections, which are characteristically associated with areas of hemorrhage and necrosis in the lung. The latter often present as small gray areas on macroscopic examination, which allows a presumptive diagnosis to be made before culture and microscopy. The lack of an infiltrate by neutrophils may be noted, as in other gram-negative infections (Chapter 9).

MASSIVE PULMONARY HEMORRHAGE

Small hemorrhages into interstitial tissue and alveoli are a common finding in most of the conditions discussed in this chapter. In some instances, however, an infant may be seen at autopsy to have hemorrhage throughout the airways and airspaces of most or all of each lung (Fig. 10–27).[65–67] One of the clinical associations of this condition is birth asphyxia; in such cases the infant very shortly after birth may be seen to have blood welling up the trachea. In some there is evidence of a consumption coagulopathy caused by disseminated intravascular

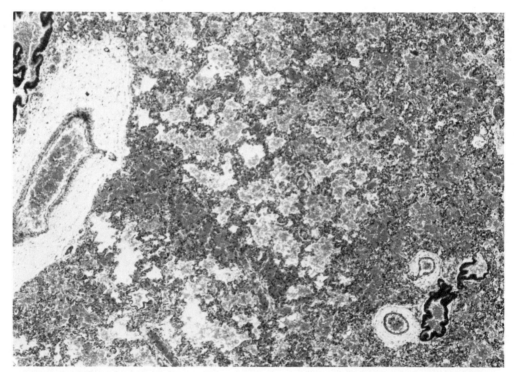

Figure 10–27. Massive pulmonary hemorrhage in the lung of an infant of 34 weeks' gestation who died at 4 days of age with β-hemolytic streptococcal meningitis. H and E × 30. Hemorrhage involves the terminal sacs and bronchioles but not the interstitial tissue.

coagulation or a primary coagulation defect.[68] In other cases, as described in Chapter 6, the condition may be regarded as analogous to shock lung in the adult.

Another group of infants who may develop massive pulmonary hemorrhage are those with severe fetal growth retardation. In these circumstances the bleeding may not develop until the second or third day of life. Once the condition becomes recognizable at clinical level it usually proves fatal.[65]

Examination of the hematocrit of the blood welling up the trachea in cases of massive pulmonary hemorrhage revealed that in many of them the liquid was a heavily blood-stained edema fluid rather than pure blood.[66] This indicates that the bleeding might be a manifestation of acute left heart failure. In this particular study there was not the characteristic excess of growth-retarded and male infants in the hemorrhage group, which suggests that the cases might not be typical of those with massive pulmonary hemorrhage at autopsy. In a different study the frequency of pulmonary hemorrhage at autopsy was linked to the concentration of oxygen used for management in life.[69]

It seems likely that massive pulmonary hemorrhage in the newborn is not a single entity. In some instances it may represent a hemorrhagic edema resulting from acute heart failure, but in others there is a genuine massive bleeding. Some of the possible underlying mechanisms have been pointed out, but in many instances the pathogenesis remains obscure.

INFLUENCE OF MANAGEMENT ON THE PATHOLOGY OF THE RESPIRATORY SYSTEM IN THE NEWBORN

Since a major part of neonatal intensive care is concerned with respiratory management, it is perhaps only to be expected that an equally large proportion of all iatrogenic problems in the newborn are related to the respiratory system.[70]

Obstetric activities such as artificial rupture of the membranes may increase the likelihood of pulmonary infection. Performance of cesarean section on the basis of a mistaken estimate of maturity has in the past been responsible for cases of severe or fatal RDS due to surfactant-deficient HMD. This should be avoidable by performance of lecithin/sphingomyelin ratio studies on the amniotic fluid. Resuscitation at birth may cause direct introduction of infection (Chapter 7).

Intubation may present a variety of hazards. Use of an indwelling nasotracheal tube may cause choanal damage with subsequent stenosis of the anterior naris. Endotracheal tubes of all types may cause laceration of the larynx or excoriation of the trachea. In a small sick preterm infant the latter may develop within 6 to 8 hours (Fig. 10–28). A common sequel to such damage is secondary infection; less frequently stenosis of the trachea may develop within a few weeks.

Mechanical ventilation may predispose to a number of problems in addition to those resulting from intubation. The use of high pressure ventilation for management of RDS due to surfactant deficiency increases the risk of pneumothorax. This risk may be enhanced by the application of continuous positive airway pressure. An almost equal risk is posed by the confident clinical diagnosis of pneumothorax prompting exploratory needling of the chest in infants with RDS whose condition undergoes a sudden deterioration. By the time the chest radiograph taken to confirm the diagnosis is processed and found to be clear, the infant may have air bubbling from bilateral chest drains. It is important that residents in neonatal intensive care units be made aware how soft and friable the lung of the preterm infant may be. The noncompliant lung of an infant with RDS is readily pierced by a relatively soft plastic catheter, and the "lung kebab"

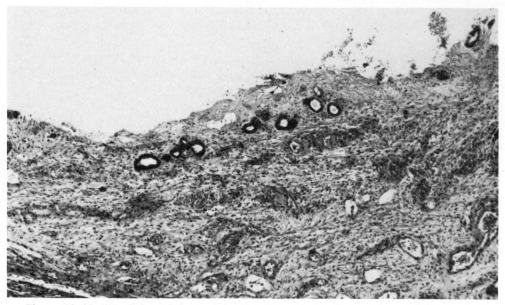

Figure 10–28. Excoriation of the trachea in an infant maintained on the ventilator for 7 days. There is loss of epithelium and a mild inflammatory reaction. H and E × 30.

syndrome in which the infant lung is transfixed by a drainage cannula is familiar to most pediatric pathologists who perform autopsies on infants from neonatal intensive care units (Fig. 10–29). Such trauma inevitably results in development of a bronchopleural fistula and may be a major factor determining eventual death of the infant.

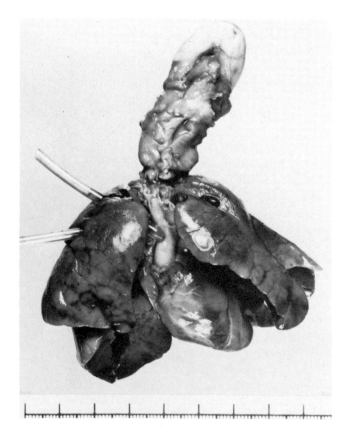

Figure 10–29. Heart and lungs of an infant of 29 weeks' gestation who died at 6 days age. The right lung has been transfixed by one plastic cannula and impaled by another. A groove on the upper surface of the left lung marks the site of a third cannula.

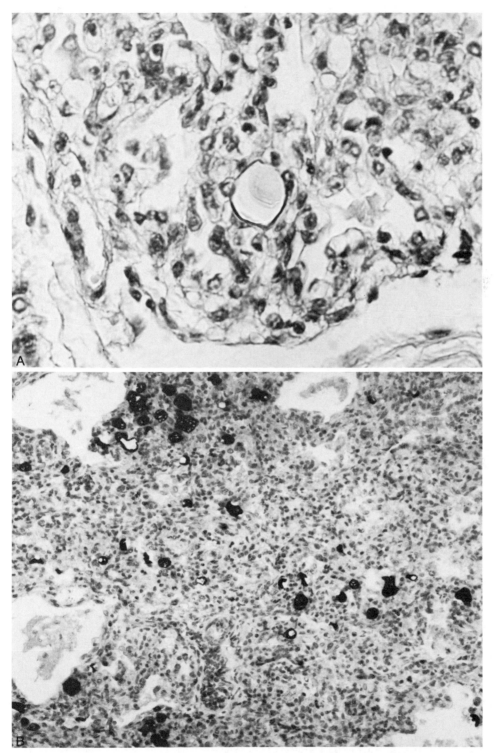

Figure 10–30. *A,* Lung of an infant who received prolonged intravenous feeding including Intralipid. H and E × 400. A dilated capillary presents with a refractile halo in the center of the field. *B,* Another paraffin section from the same case stained with Sudan black B. × 150. The altered lipid emboli within the pulmonary capillaries stain readily by this method in routine sections and present as prominent black masses.

The possible relationships between the features of bronchopulmonary dysplasia and high inspired oxygen concentration, use of high ventilatory pressures and inadequate humidification and clearance of secretions have been discussed earlier in the chapter.

In addition to the effects of management directed toward the respiratory system, the lungs are a frequent site of problems related to intravenous feeding. Intralipid embolization may be prominent in the lungs of small preterm infants infused during life with 10 to 20 per cent Intralipid mixtures.[71, 72] On routine paraffin-embedded sections, distended "empty" capillaries can be seen which often present a refractile halo (Fig. 10–30). Lipid stains are strongly positive on frozen sections and Sudan black gives a positive stain on the paraffin sections (Fig. 10–30). This indicates that part of the lipid has been oxidized to a ceroid-like material.[73] We have recently found that the preservation of Intralipid in lung vessels in paraffin sections may depend on the use of a short (12-hour) processing schedule. The presence of Intralipid within the lungs can be confirmed by biochemical analysis. Lipid emboli can be detected within the lungs of infants who die at up to 15 days after cessation of intravenous therapy, but there is evidence of gradual breakdown and removal of the lipid material by phagocytic activity. There is no direct evidence that lipid emboli are harmful in the lung, but they could be expected to contribute to any ventilation-perfusion imbalance. Prolonged intravenous feeding may be associated with development of chronic systemic infections caused by organisms such as cytomegalovirus and *Candida albicans*. These frequently localize in the lungs.

REFERENCES

1. Wessels, N. K.: Mammalian lung development: Interactions in formation and morphogenesis of tracheal buds. J. Exp. Zool. *175*:455–466, 1970.
2. Franzblau, C., Hayes, J. A., and Snider, G. L.: Biochemical insights into the development of connective tissue. *In* Hodson, W. A. (ed.): Development of the Lung. New York, Marcel Dekker, 1977, pp. 367–397.
3. Inselman, L. S., and Mellins, R. B.: Growth and development of the lung. J. Pediatr. *98*:1–15, 1981.
4. Strang, L. B.: Neonatal respiration: Physiological and clinical studies. Oxford, Blackwell, 1977.
5. Alcorn, D., Adamson, T. M., Lambert, T. F., Maloney, J. E., Ritchie, B. C., and Robinson, P. M.: Effects of chronic tracheal ligation and drainage on the fetal lamb lung. J. Anat. *123*:649–660, 1977.
6. Brown, M. J., Olver, R. E., Ramsden, C. A., Strang, L. B., and Walters, D. V.: Effects of adrenaline infusion and of spontaneous labour on lung liquid secretion and absorption in the fetal lamb. J. Physiol. *313*:13P–14P, 1981.
7. Boddy, K., and Dawes, G. S.: Fetal breathing. Br. Med. Bull. *31*:3–7, 1975.
8. Wigglesworth, J. S., and Desai, R.: Effects on lung growth of cervical cord section in the rabbit fetus. Early Hum. Dev. *3*:51–65, 1979.
9. Morley, C. J., Bangham, A. D., Johnson, P., Thorburn, G. D., and Jenkin, G.: Physical and physiological properties of dry lung surfactant. Nature *271*:162–163, 1978.
10. Harvey, D., and Parkinson, C. E.: Prediction of the respiratory distress syndrome. *In* Barson, A. J. (ed.): Laboratory Investigation of Fetal Disease. Bristol, John Wright & Sons, 1981, pp. 267–298.
11. Taeusch, H. W., Jr., and Avery, M. E.: Regulation of pulmonary alveolar development in late gestation and the perinatal period. *In* Hodson, W. A. (ed.): Development of the Lung. New York, Marcel Dekker, 1977, pp. 399–418.
12. Östör, A. G., Stillwell, R., and Fortune, D. W.: Bilateral pulmonary agenesis. Pathology *10*:243–248, 1978.
13. Maltz, D. L., and Nadas, A. S.: Agenesis of the lung: Presentation of eight new cases and review of the literature. Pediatrics *42*:175–188, 1968.
14. Landing, B. H., and Dixon, L. G.: Congenital malformations and genetic disorders of the respiratory tract (larynx, trachea, bronchi and lungs). Am. Rev. Respir. Dis. *120*:151–185, 1979.
15. Cox, J. N.: Respiratory system. *In* Berry, C. L. (ed.): Paediatric Pathology. Berlin, Springer-Verlag, 1981, pp. 299–394.

16. Larroche, J. C.: Developmental pathology of the neonate. Amsterdam, Excerpta Medica, 1977, pp. 23–79.
17. Kitagawa, M., Hislop, A., Boyden, E. A., and Reid, L.: Lung hypoplasia in congenital diaphragmatic hernia. A quantitative study of airway, artery and alveolar development. Br. J. Surg. *58*:342–346, 1971.
18. Boyden, E. A.: Structure of compressed lungs in congenital diaphragmatic hernia. Am. J. Anat. *134*:497–507, 1972.
19. Butler, N., and Claireaux, A. E.: Congenital diaphragmatic hernia as a cause of perinatal mortality. Lancet *1*:659–663, 1962.
20. Askenazi, S. S., and Perlman, M.: Pulmonary hypoplasia: Lung weight and radial alveolar count as criteria of diagnosis. Arch. Dis. Child. *54*:614–618, 1979.
21. Wigglesworth, J. S., and Desai, R.: Use of DNA estimation for growth assessment in normal and hypoplastic fetal lungs. Arch. Dis. Child. *56*:601–605, 1981.
22. Mendelsohn, G., and Hutchins, G. M.: Primary pulmonary hypoplasia. Am. J. Dis. Child. *131*:1220–1223, 1977.
23. Goldstein, J. D., and Reid, L. M.: Pulmonary hypoplasia resulting from phrenic nerve agenesis and diaphragmatic amyoplasia. J. Pediatr. *97*:282–287, 1980.
24. Page, D. V., and Stocker, J. T.: Anomalies associated with pulmonary hypoplasia. Am. Rev. Respir. Dis. *125*:216–221, 1982.
25. Chamberlain, D., Hislop, A., Hey, E., and Reid, L.: Pulmonary hypoplasia in babies with severe rhesus isoimmunization: A quantitative study. J. Pathol. *122*:43–52, 1977.
26. Hislop, A., Hey, E., and Reid, L.: The lungs in congenital bilateral renal agenesis and dysplasia. Arch Dis. Child. *54*:32–38, 1979.
27. Potter, E. L., and Craig, J. M.: Pathology of the fetus and the infant, 3rd ed. Chicago, Year Book Medical Publishers, London, Lloyd-Luke, 1976, pp. 302–303.
28. Reale, F. R., and Esterly, J. R.: Pulmonary hypoplasia: A morphometric study of the lungs of infants with diaphragmatic hernia, anencephaly, and renal malformations. Pediatrics *51*:91–96, 1973.
29. Wigglesworth, J. S., Desai, R., and Guerrini, P.: Fetal lung hypoplasia: Biochemical and structural variations and their possible significance. Arch. Dis. Child. *56*:606–615, 1981.
30. Liggins, G. C., Vilos, G. A., Campos, G. A., Kitterman, J. A., and Lee, C. H.: The effect of bilateral thoracoplasty on lung development in fetal sheep. J. Dev. Physiol. *3*:275–282, 1981.
31. Wigglesworth, J. S., and Desai, R.: Is respiratory function a major determinant of perinatal survival? Lancet *1*:264–267, 1982.
32. Report by M. R. C. working party on amniocentesis: An assessment of the hazards of amniocentesis. Br. J. Obstet. Gynaecol. *85*:suppl. 2, 1978.
33. Stocker, J. T., Drake, R. M., and Madewell, J. E.: Cystic and congenital lung disease in the newborn. *In* Rosenberg, H. S., and Bolande, R. P. (eds.): Perspectives in Pediatric Pathology, vol. 4. Chicago, Year Book Medical Publishers, Inc., 1978, pp. 93–154.
34. Van Dijk, C., and Wagenvoort, C. A.: The various types of congenital adenomatoid malformation of the lung. J. Pathol. *110*:131–134, 1973.
35. Östör, A. G., and Fortune, D. W.: Congenital cystic adenomatoid malformation of the lung. Am. J. Clin. Pathol. *70*:595–604, 1978.
36. Laurence, K. M.: Congenital pulmonary lymphangiectasis. J. Clin. Pathol. *12*:62–69, 1959.
37. Esterly, J. R., and Oppenheimer, E. A.: Lymphangiectasis and other pulmonary lesions in the asplenia syndrome. Arch. Pathol. *90*:553–560, 1970.
38. Avery, E. M., and Mead, J.: Surface properties in relation to atelectasis and hyaline membrane disease. Am. J. Dis. Child. *97*:517–523, 1959.
39. Wigglesworth, J. S.: Pathology of neonatal respiratory distress. Proc. Roy. Soc. Med. *70*:861–863, 1977.
40. Reynolds, E. O. R., Roberton, N. R. C., and Wigglesworth, J. S.: Hyaline membrane disease, respiratory distress and surfactant deficiency. Pediatrics *42*:758–768, 1968.
41. Ballard, P. L., Ballard, R. A., Granberg, J. P., Sniderman, S., Gluckman, P. D., Kaplan, S. L., and Grumbach, M. M.: Fetal sex and prenatal betamethasone therapy. J. Pediatr. *97*:451–454, 1980.
42. Rokos, J., Vaeusorn, O., Nachman, R., and Avery, M. E.: Hyaline membrane disease in twins. Pediatrics *42*:204–205, 1968.
43. Gluck, L., and Kulovich, M. V.: Lecithin/sphingomyelin ratios in amniotic fluid in normal and abnormal pregnancy. Am. J. Obstet. Gynecol. *115*:539–546, 1973.
44. Chiswick, M. L.: Prolonged rupture of membranes, pre-eclamptic toxaemia, and respiratory distress syndrome. Arch. Dis. Child. *51*:674–679, 1976.
45. Jones, M. D., Burd, L. I., Bowes, W. A., Battaglia, F. C., and Lubchenco, L. O.: Failure of association of premature rupture of membranes with respiratory-distress syndrome. N. Engl. J. Med. *292*:1253–1257, 1975.
46. Farrell, P. M., and Avery, M. E.: Hyaline membrane disease. Am. Rev. Respir. Dis. *111*:657–688, 1975.
47. Gandy, G., Jacobson, W., and Gairdner, D.: Hyaline membrane disease. I. Cellular changes. Arch. Dis. Child. *45*:289–310, 1970.
48. Reynolds, E. O. R., Jacobson, H. N., Motoyama, E. K., Kikkawa, Y., Craig, J. M., Orzalesi, M. M., and Cook, C. D.: The effects of immaturity and prenatal asphyxia on the lungs and pulmonary

function of newborn lambs: The experimental production of respiratory distress. Pediatrics *35*:382–392, 1965.

49. Valdes-Dapena, M. A., Nissim, J. E., Arey, J. B., Godleski, J., Schaaf, H. D., and Haust, M. D.: Yellow pulmonary hyaline membranes. J. Pediatr. *89*:128–130, 1976.

50. Gajl-Peczalska, K.: Plasma protein composition of hyaline membranes in the newborn. Arch. Dis. Child. *39*:226–231, 1964.

51. Lauweryns, J. M.: "Hyaline membrane disease" in newborn infants. Macroscopic, radiographic and light and electron microscope studies. Hum. Pathol. *1*:175–204, 1970.

52. Gitlin, D., and Craig, J. M.: The nature of the hyaline membrane in asphyxia of the newborn. Pediatrics *17*:64–71, 1956.

53. Van Breeman, V. L., Neustein, H. B., and Bruns, P. D.: Pulmonary hyaline membranes studied with the electron microscope. Am. J. Pathol. *33*:769–789, 1957.

54. Northway, W. H., Jr., Rosan, R. C., and Porter, D. Y.: Pulmonary disease following respirator therapy of hyaline membrane disease. Bronchopulmonary dysplasia. N. Engl. J. Med. *276*:357–368, 1967.

55. Banerjee, C. K., Girling, D. J., and Wigglesworth, J. S.: Pulmonary fibroplasia in newborn babies treated with oxygen and artificial ventilation. Arch. Dis. Child. *47*:509–518, 1972.

56. Taghizadeh, A., and Reynolds, E. O. R.: Pathogenesis of bronchopulmonary dysplasia following hyaline membrane disease. Am. J. Pathol. *82*:241–264, 1976.

57. Bonikos, D. S., Bensch, K. G., Northway, W. H., Jr., and Edwards, O. K.: Bronchopulmonary dysplasia: The pulmonary pathologic sequel of necrotizing bronchiolitis and pulmonary fibrosis. Hum. Pathol. 7:643–666, 1976.

58. Macklin, M. T., and Macklin, C. T.: Malignant interstitial emphysema of the lungs and mediastinum as an important occult complication in many respiratory diseases and other conditions—an interpretation of the clinical literature in the light of laboratory experiment. Medicine *23*:281–358, 1944.

59. Wilson, M. G., and Mikity, V. G.: A new form of respiratory disease in premature infants. Am. J. Dis. Child. *99*:489–499, 1960.

60. Hodgmann, J. E., Mikity, V. G., Tatter, D., and Cleland, R. S.: Chronic respiratory distress in the premature infant—Wilson-Mikity syndrome. Pediatrics *44*:179–195, 1969.

61. Klein, J. O., and Marcy, S. M.: Bacterial infections. *In* Remington, J. S., and Klein, J. O. (eds.): Infectious Diseases of the Fetus and Newborn Infant. Philadelphia, W. B. Saunders Co., 1976, pp. 747–891.

62. Naeye, R. L., Dellinger, W. S., and Blanc, W. A.: Fetal and maternal features of antenatal bacterial infections. J. Pediatr. *79*:733–739, 1971.

63. Blanc, W.: Pathology of the placenta, membranes, and umbilical cord in bacterial, fungal, and viral infections in man. *In* Naeye, R. L., Kissane, J. M., and Kaufman, N. (eds.): Perinatal Diseases. Baltimore, Williams & Wilkins, 1981, pp. 67–132.

64. Ablow, R. C., Driscoll, S. G., Effmann, E. L., Gross, I., Jolles, C. J., Uauy, R., and Warshaw, J. B.: A comparison of early-onset group B streptococcal neonatal infection and the respiratory distress syndrome of the newborn. N. Engl. J. Med. *294*:65–70, 1976.

65. Fedrick, J., and Butler, N. R.: Certain causes of neonatal death IV. Massive pulmonary hemorrhage. Biol. Neonat. *18*:243–262, 1971.

66. Cole, V. A., Normand, I. C. S., Reynolds, E. O. R., and Rivers, R. P. A.: Pathogenesis of hemorrhagic pulmonary edema and massive pulmonary hemorrhage in the newborn. Pediatrics *51*:175–187, 1973.

67. Trompeter, R., Yu, V. Y. H., Aynsley-Green, A., and Roberton, N. R. C.: Massive pulmonary hemorrhage in the newborn infant. Arch. Dis. Child. *50*:123–127, 1975.

68. Chessells, J. M., and Wigglesworth, J. S.: Haemostatic failure in babies with rhesus iso-immunization. Arch. Dis. Child. *46*:38–45, 1971.

69. Boothby, C. B., and De Sa, D. J.: Massive pulmonary hemorrhage in the newborn. A changing pattern. Arch. Dis. Child. *48*:21–30, 1973.

70. Valdes-Dapena, M.: Iatrogenic disease in the perinatal period as seen by the pathologist. *In* Naeye, R. L., Kissane, J. M., and Kaufman, N. (eds.): Perinatal Diseases. Baltimore, Williams & Wilkins, 1981, pp. 387–418.

71. Barson, A. J., Chiswick, M. L., and Doig, C. M.: Fat embolism in infancy after intravenous fat infusions. Arch. Dis. Child. *53*:218–223, 1978.

72. Levene, M. I., Wigglesworth, J. S., and Desai, R.: Pulmonary fat accumulation after Intralipid infusion in the preterm infant. Lancet *II*:815–818, 1980.

73. Fagan, D. G.: Iatrogenic problems in neonatal intensive care. *In* Barson, A. J. (ed.): Fetal and Neonatal Pathology. Eastbourne, Praeger, 1982, pp. 239–246.

Chapter Eleven

The Cardiovascular System

Abnormalities of cardiovascular function play a major role throughout the field of perinatal pathology. Cardiac malformations remain an important cause of neonatal death, although skilled diagnosis of such lesions in life now allows many of them to be surgically corrected. The increased possibility of therapeutic intervention means that analysis of cardiac anomalies at autopsy is no longer merely an academic exercise but one that is of practical concern to radiologists, physicians and cardiac surgeons.

Major changes in the circulation occur as a necessary part of the adaptation of the fetus to extrauterine life. The smooth transition of the pulmonary circulation from a high pressure low flow system to a low pressure high flow system may be impaired in a variety of situations from congenital malformation to perinatal hypoxia, with serious consequences to the infant.

Impaired function of the myocardium itself may result from inborn errors of metabolism, intrauterine or perinatal infection, and ischemic damage incurred during hypoxic episodes at any time during the perinatal period. Ischemic myocardial damage is increasingly recognized as an important problem in infants subjected to neonatal intensive care and may underlie lesions in other organs such as brain and kidneys.

In this chapter I will consider how far it may be possible to assess these functional problems by simple pathological means at autopsy.

DEVELOPMENT OF THE HEART

In the sixth week the future heart consists of a straight tube. By a process of differential growth the heart tube becomes looped so that there is a right-angled flexure between the atrial and ventricular segments and a second flexure between the inlet and outlet parts of the ventricular segment (Fig. 11–1). This looping normally occurs to the right (dextro- or d-ventricular looping). Septation then occurs within the atrial, ventricular and truncal segments.[1]

Atrial septation is dependent on extensive reorganization of the venous system, which results in persistence of the right cardinal vein as the superior vena cava and the right vitelline vein as the inferior vena cava so that all systemic blood drains to the right side of the primitive atrium (Fig. 11–2). The left side of the sinus venosus persists only as the coronary sinus and oblique vein. The primary pulmonary vein develops as a new vessel from the left side of the primitive atrium.

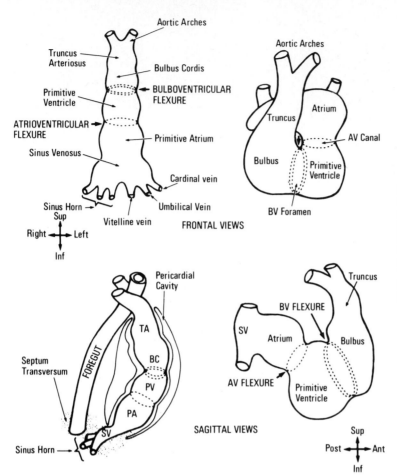

Figure 11–1. Diagram illustrating the relationship of the segments of the primary heart tube before (left) and after (right) bulboventricular looping. (From Shinebourne, E. A. and Anderson, R. H.: Congenital heart disease. *In* Scott, R. B. (ed.): Price's Textbook of the Practice of Medicine. Oxford, Oxford University Press, 1978.)

At a later stage this vessel and the first pair of its branches from each lung bud become absorbed into the atrial wall to form the main pulmonary veins.

The atrial septum is formed from three structures in three recognizable stages. First, the septum primum grows down toward the atrioventricular junction where the superior and inferior endocardial cushions are developing. Second, the lower edge of the septum primum fuses with the endocardial cushions while its upper part breaks down to form the ostium secundum. Third, the septum secundum develops to the right of the septum primum to leave a functional opening, the foramen ovale.

Development of the ventricular septum, and definitive alignment of the atrioventricular communications with the ventricles and the ventricles with their respective outflow tracts, involves a further series of stages (Fig. 11–3). Pouches develop within the ventricular segment with growth of an intervening trabecular segment, which partly divides it into inflow (left ventricular) and outflow (right ventricular) portions. At this stage both atria open to the future left ventricle and all outflow is from the right ventricle. Subsequent stages involve development of an inlet septum between left and right atrioventricular orifices, septation of the conus and truncus, development of a definitive infundibular septum by coalescence of the walls of the left and right outflow tracts, shift of the aortic outflow tract to the left ventricle and development of the membranous septum to close the interventricular communication. The definitive ventricular septum thus has four parts—inlet, trabecular, infundibular (or outlet) and membranous.

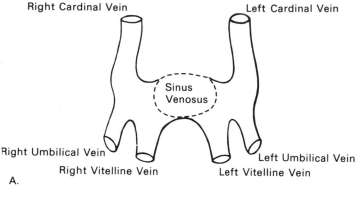

A.

Figure 11–2. Diagram illustrating the development of definitive systemic venous channels. (From Shinebourne, E. A. and Anderson, R. H.: Congenital heart disease. *In* Scott, R. B. (ed.): Price's Textbook of the Practice of Medicine. Oxford, Oxford University Press, 1978.)

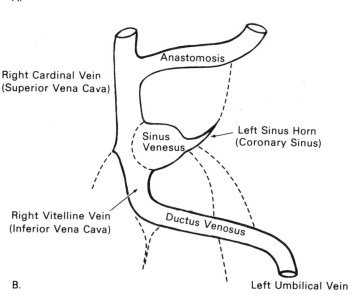

B.

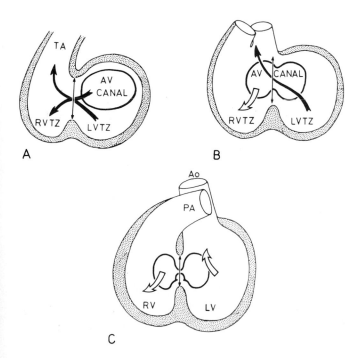

A

B

C

Figure 11–3. *A,* The initial interventricular foramen represents the primitive ventricular constriction and carries hypothetical right ventricular inlet and left ventricular outlet streams. *B,* After shift of the atrioventricular canal, a new interventricular foramen is formed that carries only the left ventricular outlet stream. *C,* After the presumptive aorta has become committed to the developing left ventricle, a new interventricular foramen which does not carry an important stream of blood is formed. This latter interventricular window closes to become the membranous septum. Key: TA, truncus arteriosus; RVTZ, right ventricular trabecular zone; AV, atrioventricular; LVTZ, left ventricular trabecular zone; PA, pulmonary artery; Ao, aorta. (From Anderson, K. R. and Anderson, R. H.: Growth and Development of the Cardiovascular System: Anatomical Development. Scientific Foundations of Paediatrics. London, William Heinemann Medical Books Ltd., 1981.)

Formation of the aorticopulmonary septum results in the aortic outflow tract becoming connected to the fourth aortic arch while the pulmonary outflow tract becomes attached to the sixth arch. During fetal life the latter connects to the descending aorta as the ductus arteriosus.

FETAL CIRCULATION AND THE CHANGES AT BIRTH

In the fetus, oxygenated blood returning from the placenta through the umbilical vein enters the right atrium through the inferior vena cava. Most of this flow passes through the foramen ovale into the left atrium and ventricle and is directed to the coronary arteries and head and neck structures. Flow entering the right atrium through the superior vena cava is nearly all directed to the right ventricle and thence to the ductus arteriosus. Resistance in the pulmonary arteries is high in fetal life while that in the ductus is low, so that a relatively small proportion of right ventricular output goes to the lungs.

It has been estimated that in late fetal life 40 per cent of cardiac output enters the ascending aorta from the left ventricle, while 60 per cent is from the right ventricle.[2] Of the 40 per cent of cardiac output which enters the ascending aorta, half goes to the head and neck, while another 4 per cent of total cardiac output supplies the coronary arteries. This leaves only 16 per cent to traverse the isthmus between left subclavian artery and ductus. Although 60 per cent of output enters the pulmonary trunk, only 8 per cent goes to the lungs, while the remainder passes into the descending aorta through the ductus. The descending aorta thus receives 68 per cent of total cardiac output. Most of this flow goes to the low pressure placental circulation.

As the caliber of blood vessels in fetal life reflects the flow through them, the isthmus of the aortic arch between the left subclavian artery and the entry of the ductus is normally rather narrow in the newborn infant, particularly in comparison with the width of the descending aorta. It is important not to mistake this appearance for coarctation.

At birth there is a sharp rise in peripheral vascular resistance as the umbilical arteries constrict and the placental blood flow falls. At the same time the rising oxygen tension within the pulmonary trunk which follows the onset of extrauterine respiration causes a fall in pulmonary artery resistance and an increase in pulmonary blood flow. The cessation of umbilical venous return leads to a fall in right atrial pressure while the increase in pulmonary flow causes left atrial pressure to rise. Thus the foramen ovale closes and interatrial flow ceases. The rising oxygen tension in the pulmonary trunk after birth also stimulates closure of the ductus arteriosus.

The most critical feature of this sequence is the progressive fall in pulmonary resistance. This resistance is located mainly in the small pulmonary arteries and arterioles. In fetal life these vessels have a small caliber and thick media, which are readily recognized on histological study. The medial layer thins out rapidly after birth as the pulmonary vessel resistance falls toward adult levels.

CONGENITAL HEART DISEASE

NOMENCLATURE AND ANALYSIS OF CONGENITAL CARDIAC ANOMALIES

The traditional method of describing congenital cardiac anomalies has been in the form of malformation patterns, hypoplastic left heart syndrome, tetralogy of Fallot, Taussig-Bing complex, and so forth. However, a relatively large proportion of cardiac defects recognized at autopsy in the perinatal period are of a complex nature and do not fit precisely into one of the named patterns. The advent of corrective surgery for many cardiac defects has necessitated the development of accurate diagnostic methods in life and the ability to describe any malformation in consistent terms which can be applied both in the living patient and at autopsy. The simplest and most logical method of analyzing and describing congenital cardiac anomalies is the sequential chamber localization method developed by Shinebourne and colleagues from the segmental approach first suggested by Van Praagh.[3, 4] This depends on establishing the morphology and connections of the cardiac chambers and great arteries and determining the spatial relationships of these structures to each other.

The first step is to establish atrial positions (situs). At postmortem this is done by examining the morphology of the atria. Morphological features of left and right atria are detailed in Figure 11–4. The normal heart with the left atrium on the left is said to show *situs solitus*. In *situs inversus* the morphologically left atrium is on the right and the morphologically right atrium on the left. In *situs ambiguus* both atria may be morphologically right atria (*dextroisomerism*) or morphologically left atria (*levoisomerism*). In life, where atrial morphology is difficult to visualize, the pattern of the bronchi is a useful guide, as a morphological left (hyparterial) bronchus occurs on the same side as a morphological left atrium, and a morphological right (eparterial) bronchus is seen on the same side as a morphological right atrium. Several anomalies of abdominal organs are characteristically found in cases of situs ambiguous. Thus situs ambiguous of bilateral right lung type is usually associated with a central liver and absent spleen, while situs ambiguous of left lung type is characteristically associated with central liver and polysplenia.

The next stage is to ascertain the atrioventricular connections. This requires recognition of the morphological features of the left and right ventricles as indicated in Figure 11–5. If the morphological right atrium connects with the morphological right ventricle and the morphological left atrium connects with the morphological left ventricle, *atrioventricular concordance* is present. If the morphological right atrium connects with the morphological left ventricle and the morphological left atrium with the morphological right ventricle, *atrioventricular discordance* is present. These connections apply regardless of the positions of the cardiac chambers within the thoracic cavity. The terms concordance and discordance cannot be used if there is situs ambiguous, if both atrioventricular valves enter the same chamber (univentricular heart) or if there is tricuspid or mitral atresia (absence of right or left atrioventricular connection).

The third stage is to establish the ventriculoarterial connections. The four possible connections are as follows:

1. *Arterial concordance.* The aorta arises from morphological left ventricle and the pulmonary trunk from morphological right ventricle.

2. *Arterial discordance (transposition).* The aorta arises from the morphological right ventricle and the pulmonary trunk from the left ventricle. In *d*-transposition the aortic valve is to right and in *l*-transposition to the left of the pulmonary valve.

3. *Double-outlet connection.* This is one in which more than half of both great arteries arise from the same ventricle. All arterial connections in univentricular hearts fall into this category.

4. *Single-outlet connection.* This may be a truncus arteriosus, an aorta or a pulmonary trunk. Each of these may arise from the right ventricle, the left ventricle or over-riding a septal defect.

Text continued on page 216

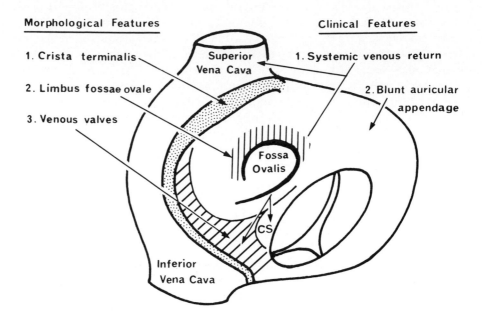

Morphological Features

1. Crista terminalis

2. Limbus fossae ovale

3. Venous valves

Clinical Features

1. Systemic venous return

2. Blunt auricular appendage

Superior Vena Cava

Fossa Ovalis

CS

Inferior Vena Cava

a) Morphologically Right Atrium

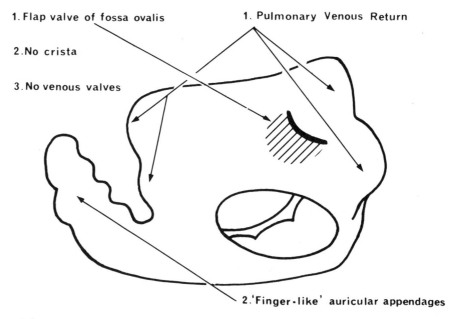

1. Flap valve of fossa ovalis

2. No crista

3. No venous valves

1. Pulmonary Venous Return

2.'Finger·like' auricular appendages

b) Morphologically Left Atrium

Figure 11–4. Diagram illustrating the distinguishing features of the morphologically right and left atria. Features of morphological significance are shown to the left-hand side; those of clinical value to the right-hand side (CS, coronary sinus). (From Anderson, R. H., and Shinebourne E. A. (eds.): Paediatric Cardiology 1977. Edinburgh, Churchill Livingstone, 1978.)

Morphological Features

Clinical Features

1. Trabecula septomarginalis

1. Semilunar·Atrioventricular
   Discontinuity

2. Coarse apical
   trabeculations

3. Pointed shape

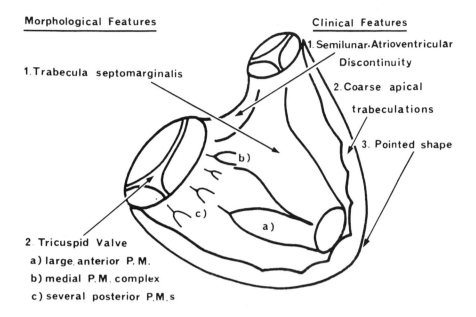

2. Tricuspid Valve
   a) large anterior P. M.
   b) medial P. M. complex
   c) several posterior P.M.s

a) Morphologically Right Ventricle

1. Smooth septal surface

1. Semilunar · Atrioventricular Continuity

2. Fine apical
   trabeculations

2. Mitral valve
   a)
   b) } Paired P.M.

3. Ellipsoidal shape

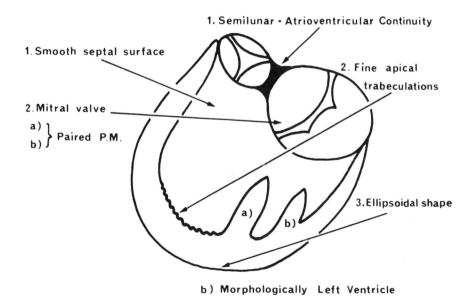

b) Morphologically Left Ventricle

Figure 11–5. Diagram illustrating the morphological and clinical features which permit differentiation of the right and left ventricles (compare with Fig. 11–4). (PM, papillary muscle). (From Anderson, R. H., and Shinebourne, E. A. (eds.): Paediatric Cardiology 1977. Edinburgh, Churchill Livingstone, 1978.)

The fourth stage is to ascertain the relationships, such as the right ventricle to the right or left of the left ventricle and the aortic valve to the right or left of the pulmonary valve.

Finally, it is necessary to determine the associated anomalies present:

1. Anomalies of venous return.
2. Anomalies of atrial anatomy.
3. Anomalies of the atrioventricular junction.
4. Anomalies of ventricular anatomy.
5. Anomalies of infundibular anatomy.
6. Anomalies of the aortic arch and its derivatives.

This may at first seem a cumbersome way to describe a congenitally malformed heart, and some of the terms, such as situs solitus and atrioventricular discordance, can seem threatening. In fact, the time taken to check the relevant features in a heart with a simple form of anomaly (e.g., *d*-transposition) is very brief and the exercise prevents the possibility that subsidiary anomalies may be overlooked. The real value of the method comes when it is necessary to analyze and describe a complex malformation with which the pathologist is totally unfamiliar. It will be found that a highly complex malformation can be analyzed as readily and almost as quickly by this method as can a simple one.

PRACTICAL HINTS FOR EXAMINING MALFORMED HEARTS

In Chapter 2 it was stressed that the anatomy of the great arteries and veins should be checked before removal of the heart and lungs from the thorax, and that most congenital cardiac anomalies would be indicated on external examination by some abnormality of cardiac shape or position. Because the majority of cardiac anomalies which are seen in the perinatal period involve defects of the conotruncus or great arteries, some abnormality of this area will usually be apparent. There may, for instance, be gross disparity in size between aortic and pulmonary roots, an abnormal relationship between them, or the presence of an indeterminate vessel arising from the ventricles. In such cases the later establishment of precise ventriculoarterial connections and relations between pulmonary and aortic valves is facilitated if the ventricular outflow tracts are retained intact until the heart has been fixed, if only for a few hours. The need for this should be explained to surgeons, physicians, radiologists and neonatologists who may wish to have the anatomy displayed to them at the time of autopsy, and a convenient later time arranged for full demonstration and discussion.

Personally I prefer to make separate small openings into atria and ventricles in the fresh state, remove internal blood clot, probe the interior carefully to establish the major type of anomaly and then fix the specimen with lungs attached for 24 hours or more before complete dissection and analysis. Small pieces of absorbent material can be introduced into the cardiac chambers to aid fixation. Injection of pulmonary arteries, if desired, is performed before immersion in fixative. Once the specimen is fixed, the important ventriculoarterial connections and their relationships can be demonstrated by any desired means of dissection, and the recognition of features such as double-outlet ventricle presents no problem.

ABNORMALITIES OF VENOUS RETURN

ANOMALOUS SYSTEMIC VENOUS RETURN

A persistent left superior vena cava is common and seldom of clinical importance. It results from failure of involution of the intrathoracic part of the

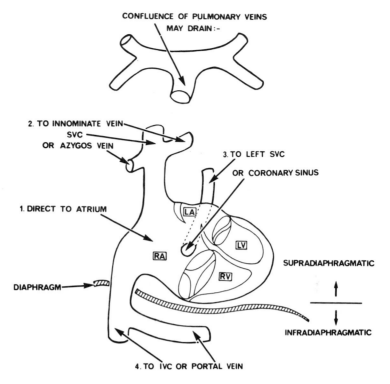

Figure 11–6. Diagram to illustrate the possible sites of drainage of the pulmonary veins in total anomalous pulmonary venous drainage. (From Shinebourne, E. A. and Anderson, R. H.: Congenital heart disease. *In* Scott, R. B. (ed.): Price's Textbook of the Practice of Medicine, 12th ed. Oxford, Oxford University Press, 1978.)

left superior cardinal vein and is associated with absence of the innominate vein. The vessel usually opens into the coronary sinus but sometimes directly into the left atrium.[5]

A number of abnormalities of the inferior vena cava are described, including direct entry of the hepatic vein into the right atrium or replacement of the inferior vena cava by the azygos systems.[6]

ANOMALOUS PULMONARY VENOUS RETURN

Total anomalous pulmonary venous drainage occurs when, during the course of development, the common pulmonary vein arising from the left side of the primitive atrium fails to make contact with the confluence of intrapulmonary veins formed in situ.[6, 7] As a result, the confluence of pulmonary veins may unite with one of a number of other venous channels (Fig. 11–6). Possible anomalous sites of pulmonary venous drainage are:

1. Above the diaphragm: into the innominate vein, superior vena cava, azygos vein, left superior vena cava, coronary sinus or directly into the right atrium.

2. Below the diaphragm: into the inferior vena cava or portal vein (Fig. 11–7).

The final common pulmonary venous channel in such cases is often partly obstructed with a resultant raised pulmonary venous pressure. Development of such a raised pressure in utero may well be the cause of the pulmonary lymphangiectasis which is seen at autopsy in many cases of total anomalous pulmonary venous drainage.

ABNORMALITIES OF ATRIAL CHAMBERS

These include atrial septal defects,[5, 8] cor triatriatum[9] and premature closure of the foramen ovale.[10]

Figure 11–7. Total anomalous venous drainage into a vein passing down towards the diaphragm. This vessel entered the portal vein system.

ATRIAL SEPTAL DEFECTS

On examining the heart of the fetus dying in the perinatal period it is important for the pathologist to be able to distinguish between a normal patent foramen ovale and a true atrial septal defect. If the procedure described in Chapter 3 is followed this should present no problem. Most atrial septal defects are of the ostium secundum type—that is, they are caused by imperfect development of the definitive septum which thus fails to occlude the ostium secundum when the foramen ovale closes after birth.

The other two types of atrial septal defect are rare. One is the ostium primum type of defect caused by failure of normal fusion of the septum primum and the endocardial cushions. The other is the sinus venosus defect, in which a defect of the atrial septum is associated with anomalous drainage of the upper right pulmonary vein to the superior vena cava or the lower right pulmonary vein to the inferior vena cava.

Ostium primum defects are mainly associated with a cleft mitral valve leaflet.

None of these defects are likely to cause death in the perinatal period but may well be found as part of more complex anomalies or in association with malformations of other systems.

COR TRIATRIATUM

This is a rare condition in which the pulmonary veins enter a chamber behind the true left atrium with which it communicates through a pinhole orifice.[9] The anomaly results from failure of reincorporation of the common pulmonary vein into the left atrium. In the only neonatal case I have seen there was pulmonary lymphangiectasis presumably caused by the prolonged high venous pressure during fetal life.

PREMATURE CLOSURE OF THE FORAMEN OVALE

This is a very rare condition which leads to failure of the left atrium to receive blood from the inferior vena cava during intrauterine life with consequent underdevelopment of the left ventricle. The infants are born in congestive heart failure and die soon afterward.[10]

ABNORMALITIES OF THE ATRIOVENTRICULAR JUNCTION

The most important defects are common atrioventricular canal,[5, 8] atresia of atrioventricular valve (absent atrioventricular connection) and double-inlet ventricle.

COMMON ATRIOVENTRICULAR CANAL

This condition is common in association with trisomy 21 (Chapter 7) but is otherwise rare. There is a septal defect which appears to involve the lower part of the atrial septum and the upper part of the ventricular septum. The atrioventricular valves are distorted and have abnormal anterior and posterior leaflets which bridge the septal defect (Fig. 11–8). Several types of this anomaly are recognized according to the mode of attachment of the bridging leaflets.[11] A constant feature is the disproportionately short inlet length of the ventricles as compared with the outlet length. This feature provides the clue to the mode of development of this lesion as a consequence of failure of normal development of the inlet septum rather than from failure of fusion of the endocardial cushions, the traditional explanation.[12]

ATRIOVENTRICULAR VALVE ATRESIA: ABSENT ATRIOVENTRICULAR CONNECTION

Atresia of tricuspid or mitral valves is associated with a univentricular heart.[5] Atresia of the tricuspid valve is usually associated with a large univentricular heart of left ventricular type and a rudimentary outlet chamber below the pulmonary orifice. Atresia of the mitral valve is most often seen in association with aortic atresia as an extreme form of the hypoplastic left heart syndrome, but may also be seen with a univentricular heart of right ventricular type and a rudimentary outlet chamber related to the aortic orifice. When there is atresia of an atrioventricular valve the corresponding atrium is poorly developed and the venous return passes to the opposite atrium through a large patent foramen ovale or atrial septal defect.

DOUBLE-INLET VENTRICLE

This is usually a univentricular heart of indeterminate form.

EBSTEIN ANOMALY

This comprises displacement of the orifice of the tricuspid valve to the junction of the inlet and trabecular portions of the right ventricle, with inclusion of the inlet portion of the ventricle into the right atrium. It may coexist with pulmonary atresia and a ventricular septal defect.[13]

ABNORMALITIES OF THE VENTRICULAR CHAMBERS

Apart from ventricular septal defect, abnormalities of the ventricular chambers are commonly associated with abnormal atrioventricular or ventriculoarterial connections.

VENTRICULAR SEPTAL DEFECT

Defects may involve any of the four constituent parts of the ventricular septum—inlet, trabecular, infundibular and membranous. Failure of development

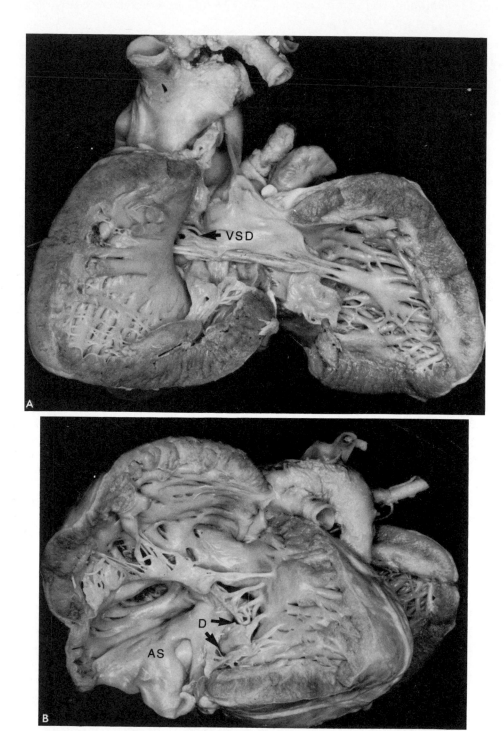

Figure 11–8. Common atrioventricular canal in a case of trisomy 21 associated with death in the neonatal period. *A,* View with left ventricle opened. The anterior leaflet of the "mitral" valve continues through a ventricular septal defect (VSD). *B,* View of right atrium and right ventricle. Abnormal atrioventricular valve leaflets continue through the septal defect. The atrial septum (AS) is well formed but there is a defect (D) above the valve leaflets, usually regarded as the atrial component of the canal.

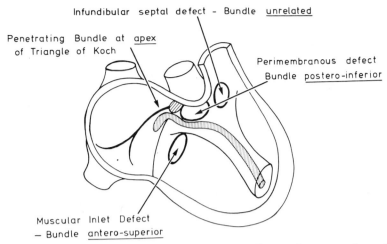

Infundibular septal defect - Bundle <u>unrelated</u>

Penetrating Bundle at <u>apex</u>
of Triangle of Koch

Perimembranous defect
Bundle <u>postero-inferior</u>

Muscular Inlet Defect
— Bundle <u>antero-superior</u>

Figure 11–9. The relationships of the atrioventricular bundle to various types of ventricular septal defect. (From Shinebourne, E. A. and Anderson, R. H.: Current Paediatric Cardiology. Oxford, Oxford University Press, 1980.)

of the membranous septum results from inadequate formation of the muscular components and the resulting defect has a fibrous rim. These defects are now usually known as perimembranous.[5, 14] Small isolated defects of the trabecular septum often close spontaneously and may be of little functional significance.

Determination of the site of a ventricular septal defect in life is of considerable importance to the surgeon because it may have a close relationship with the conducting tissue (Fig. 11–9). The atrioventricular bundle runs posteroinferior to a perimembranous defect but anterosuperior to an inlet defect and is unrelated to defects involving the trabecular or infundibular parts of the septum.

Ventricular septal defects seen by the pathologist in the perinatal period are usually part of a complex cardiac anomaly or are associated with a multiorgan malformation syndrome.

SINGLE VENTRICLE

As explained earlier, univentricular heart may be of left or right ventricular morphology in association with absence of right or left atrioventricular connections, respectively, or of indeterminate morphology with a double inlet.

HYPOPLASIA OF LEFT OR RIGHT VENTRICLE

These are usually associated with aortic and pulmonary atresia, respectively, and are described later. A rare form of hypoplasia of right ventricular muscle is known as Uhl's anomaly.[15]

ABNORMALITIES OF THE GREAT ARTERIES AND CONOTRUNCUS

The majority of the severe congenital cardiac anomalies which the pathologist will see in the perinatal period have obvious major defects of the great arteries and conotruncus, although all segments of the heart may be involved. The common lesions include aortic atresia (hypoplastic left heart syndrome), pulmonary atresia and transposition of the great arteries. Less common anomalies include coarctation, truncus arteriosus, double-outlet right ventricle and interrupted aortic arch.

AORTIC ATRESIA: HYPOPLASTIC LEFT HEART SYNDROME[16]

The great arteries are normally related in this anomaly, but the aortic root ends blindly within the cardiac muscle just below the coronary arteries without formation of valve tissue. The arch of the aorta is hypoplastic but expands gradually toward the junction with the enlarged pulmonary trunk and ductus arteriosus. During life all blood flow to the body traverses the ductus arteriosus with supply to the head, neck, right arm and coronary arteries by a reverse flow through the aortic arch and supply to the rest of the body through the descending aorta. There are two types of left ventricular structural alterations associated with this syndrome. In one there is a small left ventricular chamber with a thick white lining caused by endocardial fibroelastosis associated with a stenosed but patent mitral valve (Fig. 11–10). In the other, the left ventricular chamber can be discovered only on dissection as a blind slit-like pouch within the myocardium, because the mitral valve is atretic (Fig. 11–11). This second variety constitutes one form of univentricular heart with absent atrioventricular connections.

Infants with hypoplastic left heart syndrome go into severe heart failure and shock within 2 to 3 days of birth and usually die during the first week. They are often well-grown term infants with no other abnormalities. The rapidity with which severe heart failure and death occur may partly be accounted for by the disadvantage suffered by the cardiac muscle itself in obtaining its coronary supply.

PULMONARY ATRESIA

The main subdivision of pulmonary atresia is into those with an intact ventricular septum and those with a septal defect. In pulmonary atresia with an

Figure 11–10. Hypoplastic left heart syndrome. An example of the type with a small left ventricular chamber with marked endocardial thickening.

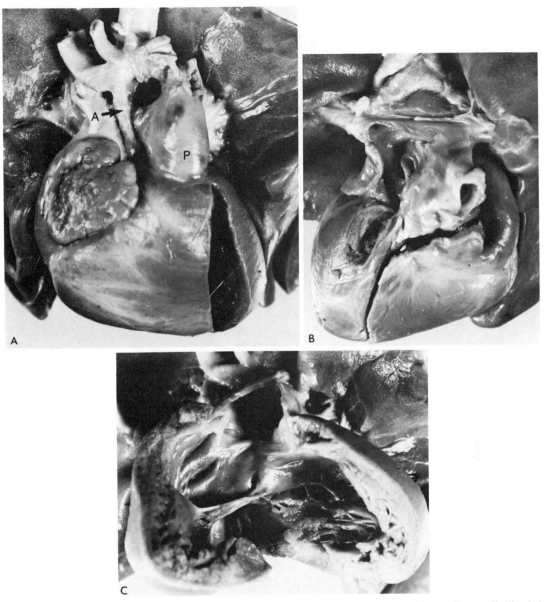

Figure 11–11. An example of hypoplastic left heart syndrome of the type with a minute, slit-like left ventricle. *A*, View of anterior aspect. Note the narrow ascending aorta 'A" and the wide pulmonary trunk "P." *B*, View of posterior aspect showing slit-like left ventricle. *C*, Anterior view, opened to show hypertrophied right ventricle.

intact septum the pulmonary trunk is represented by a fibrous remnant arising from the right ventricular myocardium. There is a large aortic arch and the pulmonary arteries are supplied by reverse flow through the ductus arteriosus (Fig. 11–12). The right ventricular cavity is small but usually thick-walled and the tricuspid valve is often dysplastic. The right atrium may be either undersized or hypertrophied and dilated according to the extent of flow and regurgitation through the tricuspid valve. The infants are severely cyanosed and usually die within the first week or two of life.

Pulmonary atresia with a ventricular septal defect is, in its most common form, an extreme variant of tetralogy of Fallot, with the aorta over-riding the septal defect and a well-developed right ventricular cavity. These infants are

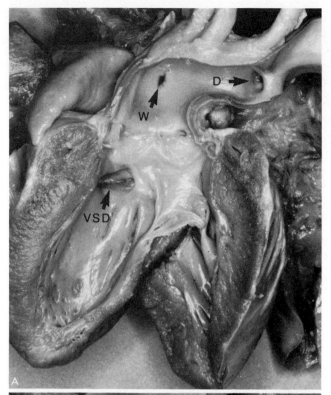

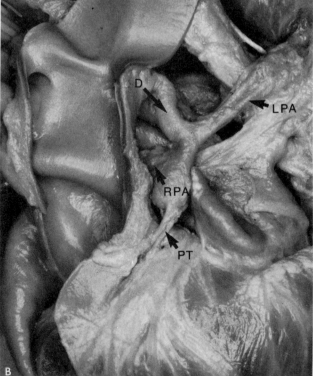

Figure 11–12. Pulmonary atresia in the newborn. *A*, Left ventricle and aortic arch. VSD, ventricular septal defect; W, site of Waterston shunt (side-to-side connection of right pulmonary artery and ascending aorta); D, ductus arteriosus. Note how easy it is to mistake this for truncus arteriosus (Fig. 11–14). *B*, Close-up view of same specimen to show how the ductus arteriosus feeds into the pulmonary arteries, and the presence of an atretic pulmonary trunk. D, ductus arteriosus; LPA, left pulmonary artery; RPA, right pulmonary artery; PT, pulmonary trunk The swelling at the beginning of the right pulmonary artery is due to thrombosis of the lumen.

Illustration continued on opposite page.

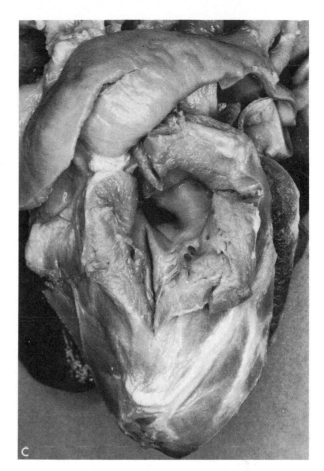

Figure 11–12 *Continued. C,* Close-up view of same specimen to show hypoplastic right ventricle despite the presence of a VSD in this case. This specimen, which also showed tricuspid atresia, should probably be classified as a univentricular heart of left ventricular type with absent right atrioventricular connection, right ventricular outlet chamber and pulmonary atresia.

characterized by the presence of major aortopulmonary collateral arteries that probably represent persistent segmental arteries.[5] Lung growth and infant survival after birth depend on the size and continued patency of these vessels.

TRANSPOSITION OF THE GREAT ARTERIES

In the common form of transposition of the great arteries there is situs solitus with atrioventricular concordance and ventriculoarterial discordance (Fig. 11–13). Blood entering the right atrium passes to the right ventricle and out into the aorta, whereas that returning to the left atrium from the lungs passes to the left ventricle and into the pulmonary arteries. Oxygenation of systemic blood is totally dependent on mixing of pulmonary and systemic flow at atrial level through the foramen ovale and at arterial level through the patent ductus arteriosus. The usual relationship of aortic to pulmonary valves is for the aortic valve to be to the right of the pulmonary valve (*d*-transposition), although a number of other relationships are possible.

This is the commonest form of cyanotic congenital heart disease seen in the neonatal period. In the absence of an atrial or ventricular septal defect, the untreated condition is usually fatal within the first 2 weeks of life. Despite the advent of highly effective surgery in the form of balloon atrial septostomy in the neonatal period, followed by performance of the Mustard procedure in later infancy, the pathologist will still see examples of this condition.

Figure 11–13. D-transposition of the great arteries. Note the aorta arising from the right ventricle. The heart has a characteristic form of a blunt cone lying on its side.

TETRALOGY OF FALLOT

Classic tetralogy of Fallot comprising ventricular septal defect, aortic overriding, pulmonary infundibular stenosis and right ventricular hypertrophy is rarely seen at autopsy in the perinatal period except in infants with other fatal conditions such as trisomy 21 with duodenal atresia.

COARCTATION OF THE AORTA

Coarctation may be caused by a localized constriction at the entrance of the ductus (juxtaductal coarctation) or a narrowing of the isthmus.[17] Most examples of coarctation which are seen by the pathologist in the perinatal period involve severe narrowing of the isthmus and some degree of hypoplasia of the whole aortic arch in association with intracardiac anomalies resulting in preferential pulmonary arterial flow. As stressed earlier (p. 212), it is important not to mistake the relatively narrow aortic isthmus which occurs as a normal feature in the newborn infant for coarctation.

TRUNCUS ARTERIOSUS

This comprises a single arterial trunk which gives rise to ascending aorta, pulmonary arteries and the coronary arteries. The condition is caused by failure of septation of the primitive truncus during the embryonic period. Several types are described by Collet and Edwards,[18] according to the mode of origin of the pulmonary arteries from the trunk (Fig. 11–14). In type 1 a single pulmonary artery arises from the posterior aspect of the trunk and subsequently divides to supply the lungs. In type 2 the pulmonary arteries arise separately but close together from the posterior aspect. In type 3 the pulmonary arteries arise from opposite lateral aspects of the trunk. If the pulmonary arteries are supplied by a ductus arising from the "trunk" (type 4 in the original classification), this represents pulmonary atresia rather than truncus arteriosus, and a fibrous cord, representing the atretic main pulmonary artery, will normally be found on careful dissection. If pulmonary artery and aorta arise side by side from a common origin (type 5), this would now be classified as aorticopulmonary window. The trunk over-rides a ventricular septal defect and has a variable number of valve cusps (from two to six). Infants with truncus arteriosus are cyanotic, and some will die in the perinatal period.

DOUBLE-OUTLET RIGHT VENTRICLE

A double-outlet ventricle is defined as one giving rise to more than one and a half valves.[5] There is a ventricular septal defect which is subaortic or subpulmonary according to the relationship of the pulmonary and aortic orifices. The defect is caused by failure of the normal process of transfer of the aortic origin to the left ventricle during development.

INTERRUPTED AORTIC ARCH

This anomaly is usually associated with other defects. It is classified according to the site of interruption of the arch.[19] The two major types are Celoria and Patton type A, in which interruption is distal to the origin of the left subclavian artery, and type B, in which the arch is interrupted between the left common carotid and left subclavian arteries. Interruption proximal to the left common carotid artery (type C) is extremely rare. In all cases blood flow to the trunk and lower limbs is dependent on a large patent ductus arteriosus which continues into the descending aorta.

Surgical correction of this lesion is difficult, and a high proportion of affected infants die in the neonatal period or early infancy.

OTHER AORTIC ARCH ANOMALIES

Anomalous Origin of the Right Subclavian Artery. This arises from the arch distal to the left subclavian artery orifice and passes behind the trachea and esophagus. It is said to be a cause of tracheal compression.

Right-Sided Aortic Arch. This is a harmless anomaly, but may be seen as part of a serious malformation complex such as tetralogy of Fallot or truncus arteriosus.

Double Aortic Arch. This forms a vascular ring around the esophagus and trachea. It is usually associated with other anomalies.

OTHER ANOMALIES OF THE HEART

ACARDIA

Acardiac monsters are rare. An acardiac monster can survive only to birth as a member of a monozygous twin pair in which the co-twin supports the circulation of both.

ECTOPIA CORDIS[5]

This condition occurs in several forms and is compatible with prolonged survival following surgery if not associated with other fatal anomalies.

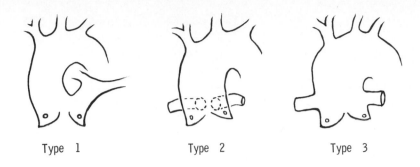

Type 1   Type 2   Type 3

Presence of coronary arteries and at least one pulmonary artery arising from truncus distinguishes the condition from:

a.   b.

A   Aortic Atresia   Pulmonary Atresia

Figure 11–14. *A,* Diagram illustrating the various forms of truncus arteriosus. *B,* Truncus arteriosus Type 2 to show right ventricle and truncus, with pulmonary arteries arising side by side from its posterior wall.

OTHER CONGENITAL CARDIAC LESIONS

HYPERTROPHY OF THE NORMALLY FORMED HEART

The recognition of a hypertrophied but normally formed heart at autopsy in the perinatal period should prompt search for causes of increased cardiac output. These include lesions such as placental chorioangiomas (Chapter 4) or arteriovenous aneurysms of the vein of Galen (Fig. 11–15). Angiography may have been performed in life to investigate the possibility of congenital cardiac anomalies in such cases.

An unduly large heart may be one feature of the macrosomia seen in occasional infants born to women with poorly controlled or undiagnosed diabetes.[20]

Cardiac hypertrophy is a feature of glycogenosis II (Pompe's disease). This is seldom a cause of death in the perinatal period. If the diagnosis is suspected, it may be supported by characteristic histochemical and ultrastructural findings in skeletal and cardiac muscle tissue. Definitive diagnosis requires demonstration of the absence of the enzyme alpha-1:4-glucosidase in biopsy tissue taken in life or immediately after death. Partial deficiencies in the heterozygote parents can also be recognized. For further information the reader should consult Howell[21] and McAdams et al.[22]

CONGENITAL RHABDOMYOMA

This is a rare "tumor" consisting of large muscle cells with glycogen-containing vacuoles. It is often associated with tuberous sclerosis of the brain. The hemodynamic disturbances caused by the tumor mass within the left ventricular myocar-

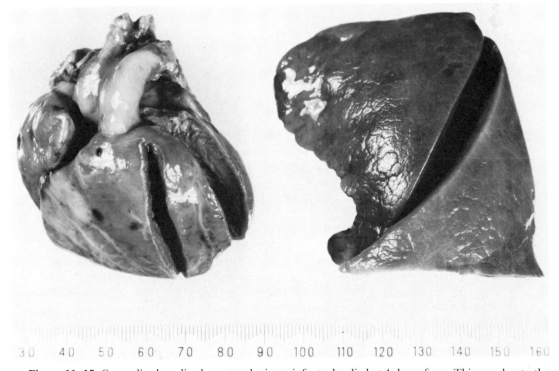

Figure 11–15. Generalized cardiac hypertrophy in an infant who died at 4 days of age. This was due to the aneurysm of the vein of Galen illustrated in Chapter 12. Epicardial hemorrhages indicate acute terminal anoxia (see Chapter 6). Growth of the left lung has been distorted by the enlarged heart.

dium and ventricular septum may lead to death in the neonatal period. The lesion is regarded as a dysplasia rather than a true neoplasm.[23] (See Chapter 5 for illustration.)

MYOCARDITIS

Myocarditis in the perinatal period may result from viral, bacterial, protozoal or fungal infection.

VIRAL MYOCARDITIS

Most reports of fatal viral myocarditis in the newborn relate to coxsackievirus group B,[24] although myocarditis may be present in congenital rubella infection (Chapter 9). In fatal cases the heart is usually enlarged with dilated chambers and flabby, pale or variegated myocardium. On microscopy the myocardium is congested with edema and eosinophilic degeneration of the muscle and a mixed inflammatory infiltration with an excess of mononuclear cells. Other organs involved in coxsackievirus B infections include the brain (meningoencephalitis), adrenals, liver and lungs.

OTHER FORMS OF MYOCARDITIS

The myocardium is a frequent site for localization of the lesions of congenital toxoplasmosis. Multiple cysts may be seen throughout the myocardium, with a variable inflammatory reaction (Chapter 9). A myocarditis associated with invasion of the cardiac muscle by mycelium and spores in septicemia caused by *Candida albicans* has been reported by Larroche.[25] Abscesses may develop within the myocardium in cases of bacterial sepsis (Fig. 11–16).

ENDOCARDITIS

Small blood-filled cysts on the valve cusps are a relatively common finding in the perinatal period and are of no significance.[26] Bacterial endocarditis is uncommon at this time of life: most reported cases involve small verrucous lesions situated on the mitral valve leaflets.[27] In 1982, I examined one infant in whom a massive bacterial vegetation on the posterior leaflet of the mitral valve had caused death by occlusion of the mitral orifice at 17 days of age. In this case, as in one previously reported,[28] the organism responsible was the β-hemolytic streptococcus of Lancefield group B.

ENDOCARDIAL FIBROELASTOSIS

This condition comprises gross endocardial and subendocardial thickening with increase in collagen and elastic fibers that are evident microscopically. It is seen in two forms which should be clearly distinguished. Localized areas of fibroelastosis are seen in the chambers of congenitally malformed hearts in which valvar stenosis with incompetence may have been expected to cause increased turbulence (hemodynamic effect). The example most frequently seen is the endocardial fibroelastosis of the left ventricle in cases of aortic atresia associated with a patent but stenosed mitral valve.[5]

Primary endocardial fibroelastosis is a condition in which myocardial failure

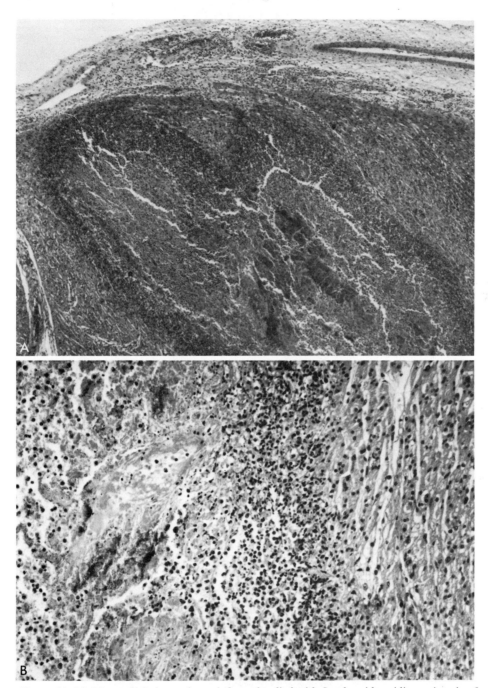

Figure 11–16. Myocardial abscess in an infant who died with Staph-epidermidis septicemia after prolonged neonatal intensive care. *A*, Left ventricle. H and E × 30. *B*, Margin of abscess. H and E × 150.

develops in association with gross cardiac hypertrophy resulting in death within the first few weeks or months of life.[29] The endocardium of the left atrium and dilated globular left ventricle is thickened and opaque (Fig. 11–17). The endocardial thickening characteristically envelops the papillary muscles. The right ventricle is variably affected. Most cases are sporadic but some are familial.[5] The condition may be a late reaction to recovering viral myocarditis but there is little evidence for this in most of the primary cases.

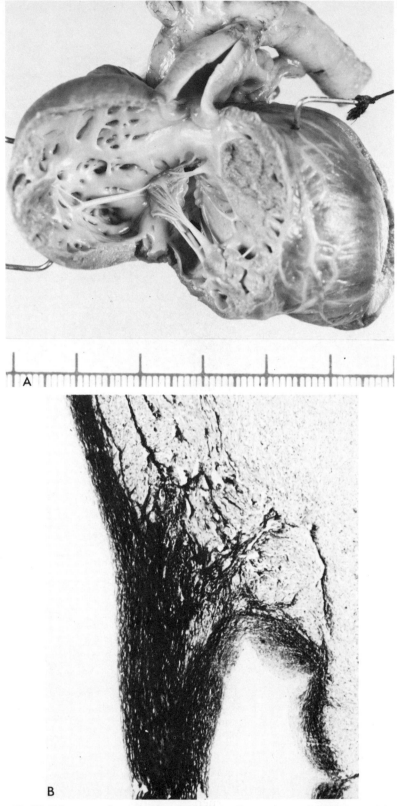

Figure 11–17. Primary endocardial fibroelastosis in the newborn. *A,* Right ventricle opened to show thickened glistening endocardium with involvement of papillary muscles. *B,* Section showing endocardium and papillary muscle. Elastic-Van Gieson × 30. Note the dense elastin staining of the papillary muscle.

MYOCARDIAL ISCHEMIA

Myocardial infarction has been regarded as a relatively uncommon lesion in the perinatal period,[25] although it has long been recognized that infants with cardiac anomalies may be unduly susceptible to developing focal myocardial necrosis.[30, 31]

Detailed study of the coronary arterial tree and myocardium in perinatal and infant deaths[32] has recently shown that myocardial necrosis occurs far more frequently than hitherto appreciated. Myocardial lesions vary from small zones of subendocardial damage to larger "geographic" areas of necrosis scattered haphazardly through the myocardium and a small group with massive necrotic lesions of myocardium or the papillary muscles (Figs. 11–18 through 11–20). Coronary artery lesions described in association with these forms of necrosis range from focal medial necrosis to intramural thrombosis and severe proliferative intimal lesions. The hearts of infants who die after prolonged neonatal intensive care and recurrent severe hypoxic episodes frequently show old myocardial scars. De Sa has suggested that the epicardial hemorrhages along the lines of the coronary vessels, which are such a characteristic feature of acute perinatal hypoxia, may mirror similar changes in the vasa vasorum of the coronary vessels. He argues that rupture of the vasa vasorum resulting from reactive hypertension during hypoxic episodes may be the underlying mechanism for the focal myocardial necrosis and resultant scarring.

It can be difficult to recognize early myocardial necrosis, either on gross examination or in routine histological preparations, from the newborn infant heart because the myocardial fibers are small and the normal nuclei may appear

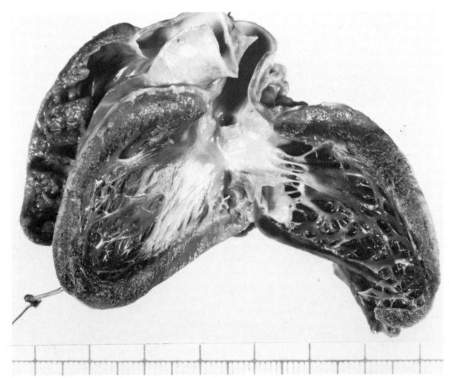

Figure 11–18. Massive myocardial infarction in a term infant who died at 38 hours of age following severe birth asphyxia. Infarction involves the left ventricle and much of the ventricular septum but is not associated with coronary artery thrombosis.

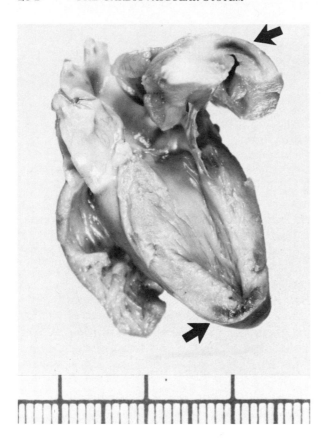

Figure 11–19. Focal myocardial infarction (arrow) in an infant of 25 weeks' gestation who died at 7 days of age.

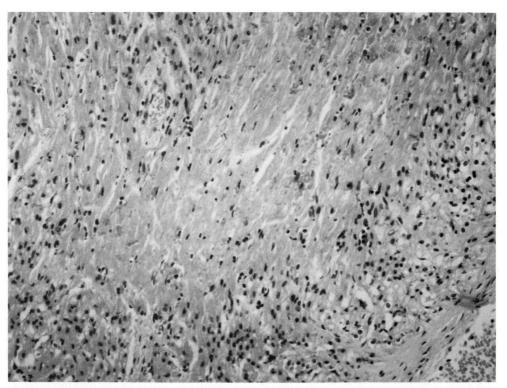

Figure 11–20. Focal ischemic necrosis of myocardial fibers in an infant who suffered severe birth asphyxia and died at 8 days of age. H and E × 150. There is loss of nuclear staining in necrotic fibers in center of field.

pyknotic. Sampling problems may also result in many focal lesions being missed. It thus seems probable that ischemic myocardial necrosis is indeed a common occurrence in the perinatal period. If so, the extent to which an initial hypoxic episode has damaged the myocardium may be a major factor in determining the adequacy with which other organs such as brain, kidney, adrenals and intestine are subsequently perfused.

The scarring which may be seen in the hearts of infants subjected to prolonged mechanical ventilation could be regarded merely as a result of maintaining moribund infants alive by artificial means. However, similar lesions are seen in infants who die at some months of age having been relatively well following discharge from the neonatal intensive care unit. These form part of the spectrum of lesions dating from the neonatal period which can be recognized in cases of sudden infant death (Chapter 21). It must be assumed that many infants with focal myocardial necrosis and scarring survive the neonatal period, either with or without the aid of intensive care facilities. The extent to which such myocardial damage contributes to morbidity and mortality in later life remains to be assessed.

PERICARDIUM

ANOMALIES

Pericardial defects are rare. They are seen more often in male infants and are usually left-sided. There is often associated deficiency of the pleura with heart and left lung lying in a common pleuropericardial cavity.[33]

PNEUMOPERICARDIUM

This develops as an occasional sequel to interstitial emphysema if the air travels along the adventitia of the pulmonary vessels and ruptures through the pericardial serosa. The condition may accompany pneumothorax and pneumoperitoneum or develop as an isolated event.[34] In most instances pneumopericardium is associated with mechanical ventilation but can occur spontaneously.

PERICARDIAL EFFUSIONS AND HEMOPERICARDIUM

An increase in pericardial fluid is seen in any condition with anasarca, including rhesus isoimmunization, vascular anomalies leading to intrauterine heart failure, and some fetal infections.

Hemopericardium is rare. It has been reported as a spontaneous occurrence,[35] and may result from trauma during attempted atrial balloon septostomy or angiography in the newborn infant.[36]

PERICARDITIS

This may occasionally be seen in severe perinatal infections (e.g., staphylococcal septicemia) but is uncommon in the perinatal period.

DUCTUS ARTERIOSUS

During fetal life about 50 per cent of total cardiac output goes through the ductus into the aorta while only 8 per cent perfuses the pulmonary circulation (p. 212). The functional closure of the ductus after birth partly results from the rise in pulmonary artery oxygen tension following onset of air breathing but is itself important in maintaining the increased circulation through the lungs.[2] The perinatal relationships between the ductus and the pulmonary circulation are of considerable importance in determining neonatal cardiorespiratory function.

STRUCTURE OF DUCTUS

The ductus at term has a thick and partly disrupted internal elastic lamina and an unusual media composed of smooth muscle cells separated by clear spaces containing a metachromatic ground substance and scattered elastic fibers (Fig. 11–21). Intimal cushions protrude into the lumen of the vessel and give the intimal surface a corrugated appearance on macroscopic examination. These corrugations run along the length of the vessel and increase in prominence with length of neonatal survival.

POSTNATAL CLOSURE OF THE DUCTUS

Functional closure of the ductus postnatally is a biochemical phenomenon which is now known to involve changes in local prostaglandin activity. The muscle tone of the fetal ductus is apparently controlled by endogenous production of prostaglandin E compounds (PGE).[37] Administration of prostaglandin synthetase-inhibitors such as indomethacin causes intense and persistent contraction of the ductus in the fetal animal and is used in the medical treatment of persistent patent ductus arteriosus.[38] The synthesis and functional activity of PGE occurs mainly under hypoxic conditions. Thus the increase in oxygenation of the arterial blood after birth inhibits production and function of PGE and leads to closure of the ductus.

Infusion of PGE is used to maintain patency of the ductus prior to surgery in infants with cardiac anomalies and ductus dependency (e.g., interrupted aortic arch).

Anatomical closure proceeds from the midpoint toward the pulmonary artery; the aortic end is normally the last part to close. Anatomical closure is usually observed by about 10 days of age. In immature infants, below 32 weeks' gestational age, the endothelial cushions are underdeveloped and closure is achieved mainly by contraction of the wall, often with trapping and organization of blood clot within the lumen.[25]

PATENT DUCTUS ARTERIOSUS (PDA)

A large PDA is a feature of many cardiac anomalies and is a frequent finding in the rubella syndrome (Chapters 6, 7). In such cases the ductus may lack development of the normal endothelial cushions. If an infant dies within the first week of life with a normally formed ductus, it is not usually possible for the pathologist to say whether it was functionally patent during life or not. The effects of the terminal hypoxia will in most cases result in relaxation and functional re-opening of the ductus.

In ill preterm infants with prolonged hypoxia and acidosis associated with respiratory distress syndrome, patent ductus arteriosus is a frequent clinical problem in life. It may be accentuated by fluid overload and has been reported as unduly frequent in infants treated with some forms of artificial surfactant.[39] The immature structure of the ductus may compound the problems resulting from hypoxia and acidosis in such cases.

PERSISTENT FETAL (TRANSITIONAL) CIRCULATION

This term was coined to describe a clinical syndrome in which the pulmonary vascular resistance fails to fall after birth and foramen ovale and ductus arteriosus remain patent, resulting in left-to-right shunting at atrial and ductal levels. The infants are cyanotic, but no structural defects of the heart can be demonstrated

Figure 11–21. *A*, Ductus at term. H and E × 60. There is a relatively thick tunica intima and the media consists of small muscle cells separated by clear spaces. *B*, Junction between pulmonary trunk and ductus in an infant aged 7 days. Elastic-Van Gieson × 60. The pulmonary trunk (left) has a regular pattern of elastic fibers throughout the media that includes most of the vessel wall, whereas the media of the ductus (right) contains scattered elastic fibers only and the intima is thick.

on investigations such as angiography. In many cases there may be a history of severe birth asphyxia. Other associations include maternal diabetes and a high hematocrit.[40]

In those cases that come to autopsy this does not, in my experience, seem to represent a single discrete condition. In some instances there is evidence of severe birth asphyxia with massive inhalation of amniotic material. In others there may be unexplained hypertrophy or underdevelopment of the heart without any recognizable local malformation.

It is probably most logical to think of persistent fetal circulation as a functional result of a whole range of conditions which encompass a number of structural abnormalities of the heart or pulmonary vessels in addition to the group of cases in which no structural abnormality is detectable. In severe birth asphyxia, pulmonary vasoconstriction and dilatation of the ductus result from the hypoxia and acidosis. This is little different from the effects of respiratory distress syndrome in the preterm infant. There may be a similar effect if the pulmonary circulation does not have the capacity to accept the full right ventricular output, as may be the case if the infant has hypoplastic lungs. Finally, pulmonary arterial pressure may have become fixed at a high level in utero owing to a cardiac anomaly such as transposition of the great arteries or hypoplastic left heart syndrome.

Most of the structural causes of persistent fetal circulation are readily evident at postmortem examination. However, it is important, when assessing the state of the pulmonary circulation at a histological level, to distinguish between persistence of the normal constricted fetal pulmonary arteries and the development in utero of a genuine hypertrophy of the pulmonary arterial media, indicating a prenatal pulmonary hypertension (Fig. 11–22).

PERIPHERAL VESSELS

Thrombosis and embolism of almost any vessel can occur as an apparently spontaneous event in the perinatal period. Frequently seen are thrombi of small pulmonary vessel branches in association with hyaline membrane disease (p. 189). I have occasionally seen spontaneous thromboembolism with acute ischemia of limbs or massive infarction of one or other internal organ as a prenatal event, or developing during, or shortly after, birth. The placenta has been suggested as a possible source for emboli or thromboplastins in such cases. In practice the most frequent and important forms of peripheral vessel obstruction are those that develop as complications of investigation or treatment.

EFFECTS OF MANAGEMENT ON THE CARDIOVASCULAR SYSTEM

Damage to blood vessels represents one of the most frequent forms of hazard arising during neonatal management.

Indwelling umbilical catheters are used for sampling and monitoring in many ill newborn infants. The types of lesion which may arise following the use of umbilical catheters have been documented and illustrated extensively by Larroche.[25] Indwelling venous catheters are now seldom used, and the hazards largely affect the liver and intestine rather than the vascular tree itself, although thrombi might develop within the portal sinus and its branches.

Mural thrombosis affecting the abdominal aorta or iliac vessels is a frequent finding at autopsy in infants who have had an indwelling umbilical arterial catheter.

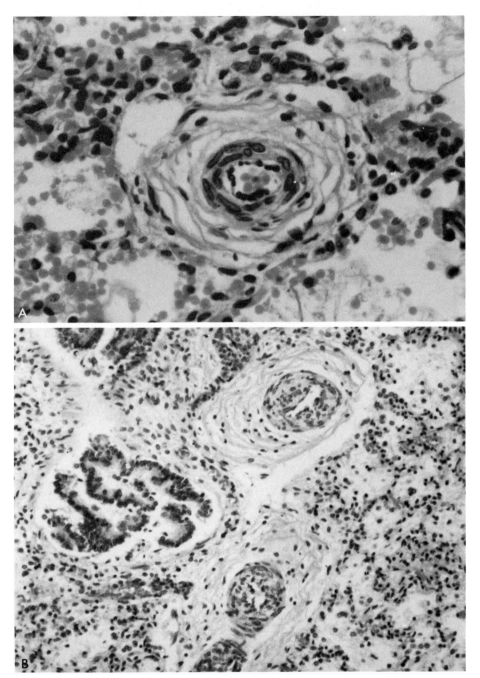

Figure 11–22. *A,* Normal pulmonary artery branch in a term infant who died during birth. H and E × 350. *B,* Intimal and medial proliferation in small pulmonary artery branches in a case of transposition of the great arteries in which death occurred at 2 days of age. H and E × 150.

The thrombus may form a sheath around the catheter tip and remain in situ attached to the aortic wall after the catheter is removed (Fig. 11–23). Physical occlusion of one external iliac artery often causes a "white leg" in vivo. Failure to remove the catheter rapidly in such a case, or formation of thromboemboli, may result in gangrene and loss of toes. If aortic mural thrombi extend to the renal or mesenteric arteries or a catheter occludes the orifice of one of these vessels, there may be infarction of kidneys or intestine. Infusion of hyperosmolar solutions through the catheter is likely to increase the risk of such forms of damage.

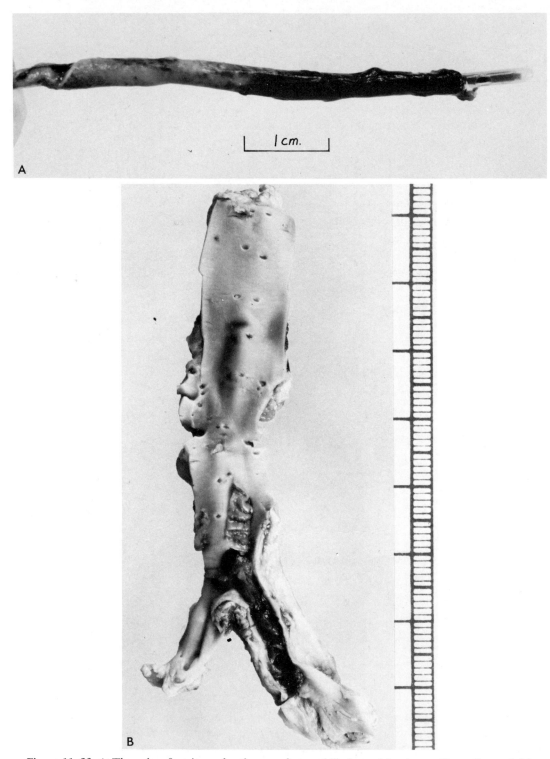

Figure 11–23. *A,* Thrombus forming a sheath around an umbilical arterial catheter. (From Gupta, J. M., et al.: Umbilical artery catheterization in the newborn. Arch. Dis. Child. *43*:382–387, 1968.) *B,* Mural thrombus in lower aorta and left common iliac artery in an infant who died at 7 days age. This type of thrombus develops as a sleeeve around an arterial catheter as shown in *A* and may remain, as in this case, when the catheter is removed.

Ischemia and gangrene may follow the use of peripheral arteries for blood sampling (e.g., gangrene of the hand following repeated radial artery puncture in an infant with no ulnar artery). We have seen gangrene of the leg following an attempt at angiography via the femoral veins in a very small infant. Cerebral infarction was reported as a specific hazard following the use of temporal artery catheterization.[41]

Hemorrhage following perforation of a vessel may have a direct effect such as massive abdominal hemorrhage resulting from perforation of an umbilical artery by a catheter. However, the effects of vessel damage are sometimes rather indirect. Use of the brachial artery for multiple blood sampling in small preterm infants was associated with subsequent development of median nerve palsies which were apparently caused by hematoma formation within the cubital fossa.[42]

Direct damage to the heart may result from angiographic studies or during attempts at balloon septostomy. Bruising and laceration of the myocardium are not uncommon and cardiac perforation is reported.[36]

The occurrence of many of these hazards will have been recognized in life. However, it is important that the exact mode of development of any such lesions be established by the pathologist and discussed with the clinicians as an aid to improving methods of management. Any new or unsuspected lesion should be examined with particular care.

CONCLUSIONS

From the content of this chapter it will be seen that cardiac anomalies tend to dominate descriptive cardiovascular pathology of the perinatal period. Such lesions should not in fact present the pathologist with any great problem, provided that the specimen is appropriately handled before fixation, as the anatomical defects can be analyzed at leisure.

The links between abnormal cardiac anatomy and pulmonary vessel structure should always be remembered. In infants subjected to birth asphyxia or neonatal intensive care it may be more important to recognize the possibility of ischemic myocardial damage and the range of lesions related to methods of investigation and management. Pathological lesions within the heart may determine the range of pathology in other organs in the perinatal period or may reflect primary lesions elsewhere. The ability of the pathologist to analyze the status of the cardiovascular system can thus provide a central basis for understanding the pattern of lesions seen throughout the rest of the body.

REFERENCES

1. Anderson, K. R., and Anderson, R. H.: Growth and development of the cardiovascular system. (A) Anatomical development. *In* Davis, J. A., and Dobbing, J. (eds.): Scientific Foundations of Paediatrics, 2nd ed. London, Heinemann, 1981, pp. 342–372.
2. Dawes, G. S.: Fetal and Neonatal Physiology. Chicago, Year Book Medical Publishers, 1968, pp. 91–105.
3. Shinebourne, E. A., Macartney, F. J., and Anderson, R. H.: Sequential chamber localisation—logical approach to diagnosis in congenital heart disease. Br. Heart J. *38*:327–340, 1976.
4. Van Praagh, R.: The segmental approach to diagnosis in congenital heart disease. Birth Defects, Original Article Series *8*:4–23, 1972.
5. Becker, A. E., and Anderson, R. H.: Pathology of Congenital Heart Disease. London, Butterworths, 1981.
6. Anderson, R. C., Heilig, W., Novick, R., and Jarvis, C.: Anomalous inferior vena cava with azygous drainage: So-called absence of the inferior vena cava. Am. Heart J. *49*:318–322, 1955.
7. Berry, C. L.: Congenital heart disease. *In* Pomerance, A., and Davies, M. J. (eds.): The Pathology of the Heart. Oxford, Blackwell Scientific Publications, 1975, pp. 533–578.
8. Goor, D. A., and Lillehei, C. W.: Atrial septal defects. *In* Congenital Malformations of the Heart. New York, Grune & Stratton, 1975, pp. 103–111.
9. Van Praagh, R., and Corsini, I.: Cor triatriatum: Pathologic anatomy and consideration of

morphogenesis based on 13 postmortem cases and a study of normal development of the pulmonary vein and atrial septum in 83 human embryos. Am. Heart J. *78*:379–405, 1969.

10. Brody, H.: Antenatal occlusion of foramen ovale; report of two cases. Am. J. Clin. Pathol. *23*:37–40, 1953.

11. Piccoli, G. P., Wilkinson, J. L., Macartney, F. J., Gerlis, L. M., and Anderson, R. H.: Morphology and classification of complete atrioventricular defects. Br. Heart J. *42*:633–639, 1979.

12. Allwork, S. P.: Anatomical-embryological correlates in atrioventricular septal defect. Br. Heart J. *47*:419–429, 1982.

13. Zuberbuhler, J. R., Allwork, S. P., and Anderson, R. H.: The spectrum of Ebstein's anomaly of the tricuspid valve. J. Thorac. Cardiovasc. Surg. *77*:202–211, 1979.

14. Soto, B., Becker, A. E., Moulaert, A. J., Lie, J. T., and Anderson, R. H.: Classification of ventricular septal defects. Br. Heart J. *43*:332–343, 1980.

15. Vecht, R. J., Carmichael, D. J. S., Gopal, R., and Philip, G.: Uhl's anomaly. Br. Heart J. *41*:676–682, 1979.

16. Lev, M.: Pathologic anatomy and interrelationship of hypoplasia of the aortic tract complexes. Lab. Invest. *1*:61–70, 1952.

17. Edwards, J. E.: Aortic arch system. *In* Gould, S. E. (ed.): Pathology of the Heart and Blood Vessels, 3rd ed. Springfield, Charles C Thomas, 1968, pp. 416–454.

18. Collett, R. W., and Edwards, J. E.: Persistent truncus arteriosus. A classification according to anatomic types. Surg. Clin. North Am. *29*:1245–1270, 1949.

19. Celoria, G. C., and Patton, R. B.: Congenital absence of the aortic arch. Am. Heart J. *58*:407–413, 1959.

20. Haust, M. D.: Maternal diabetes mellitus: Effects on the fetus and placenta. *In* Naeye, R. L., Kissane, J. M., and Kaufman, N. (eds.): Perinatal Diseases. Baltimore, Williams & Wilkins, 1981, pp. 201–285.

21. Howell, R. R.: The glycogen storage diseases. *In* Stanbury, J. B., Wyngaarden, J. B., and Fredrickson, D. S. (eds.): The Metabolic Basis of Inherited Disease. 4th ed. New York, McGraw-Hill, 1978, pp. 137–159.

22. McAdams, A. J., Hug, G., and Bove, K. E.: Glycogen storage disease, types I to X. Criteria for morphologic diagnosis. Hum. Pathol. *5*:463–487, 1974.

23. Fenoglio, J. J., McAllister, H. A., and Ferrans, V. J.: Cardiac rhabdomyoma: A clinicopathologic and electron microscopic study. Am. J. Cardiol. *38*:241–251, 1976.

24. Cherry, J. D.: Enteroviruses. *In* Remington, J. S., and Klein, J. O. (eds.): Infectious Diseases of the Fetus and Newborn Infant. Philadelphia, W. B. Saunders Co., 1976, pp. 366–413.

25. Larroche, J. C.: Developmental Pathology of the Neonate. Amsterdam, Excerpta Medica, 1977, pp. 257–258.

26. Begg, J. G.: Blood-filled cysts in the cardiac valve cusps in foetal life and infancy. J. Pathol. Bacteriol. *87*:177–178, 1964.

27. Johnson, D. H., Rosenthal, A., and Nadas, A. S.: Bacterial endocarditis in children under 2 years of age. Am. J. Dis. Child. *129*:183–186, 1975.

28. Lewis, I. C.: Bacterial endocarditis complicating septicemia in an infant. Arch. Dis. Child. *29*:144–146, 1954.

29. McKinney, B.: Endocardial fibroelastosis. *In* Pathology of the Cardiomyopathies. London, Butterworths, 1974, pp. 11–28.

30. Franciosi, R. A., and Blanc, W. A.: Myocardial infarcts in infants and children. I. A necropsy study in congenital heart disease. J. Pediatr. *73*:309–319, 1968.

31. Esterly, J. H., and Oppenheimer, E. H.: Some aspects of cardiac pathology in infancy and childhood, IV. Myocardial and coronary lesions in cardiac malformations. Pediatrics *39*:896–903, 1967.

32. De Sa, D. J.: Coronary arterial lesions and myocardial necrosis in stillbirths and infants. Arch. Dis. Child. *54*:918–930, 1979.

33. Moore, R. L.: Congenital deficiency of the pericardium. Arch. Surg. *11*:765–777, 1925.

34. Pomerance, J. J., Weller, M. H., Richardson, C. J., Soule, J. A., and Cato, A.: Pneumopericardium complicating respiratory distress syndrome: Role of conservative management. J. Pediatr. *84*:883–886, 1974.

35. Potter, E. L., and Craig, J. M.: Pathology of the Fetus and the Infant, 3rd ed. Chicago, Year Book Medical Publishers, 1976, p. 251.

36. Stanger, P., Heymann, M. A., Tarnoff, H., Hoffman, J. I., and Rudolph, A. M.: Complications of cardiac catheterization of neonates, infants and children. A three-year study. Circulation *50*:595–608, 1974.

37. Olley, P. M., Coceani, F., and Bodach, E.: E-type prostaglandins. A new emergency therapy for certain cyanotic congenital heart malformations. Circulation *53*:728–731, 1976.

38. Heymann, M. A., Rudolph, A. M., and Silverman, N. H.: Closure of the ductus arteriosus in premature infants by inhibition of prostaglandin synthesis. N. Engl. J. Med. *295*:530–533, 1976.

39. Fujiwara, T., Maeta, H., Morita, T., Watabe, Y., Chida, S., and Abe, T.: Artificial surfactant therapy in hyaline membrane disease. Lancet *1*:55–59, 1980.

40. Brown, R., and Pickering, D.: Persistent transitional circulation. Arch. Dis. Child. *49*:883–885, 1974.

41. Simmons, M. A., Levine, R. L., Lubchenco, L. O., and Guggenheim, M. A.: Warning: Serious sequelae of temporal artery catheterization. J. Pediatr. *92*:284, 1978.

42. Pape, K. E., Armstrong, D. L., and Fitzhardinge, P. M.: Peripheral median nerve damage secondary to brachial arterial blood gas sampling. J. Pediatr. *93*:852–856, 1978.

Chapter Twelve

The Central Nervous System

Cerebral pathology is of major importance as a cause of perinatal death or persistent handicap in both preterm and term infants. Many of the malformation syndromes which prove fatal in the perinatal period involve the central nervous system, as do a range of inborn errors of metabolism and cytogenetic abnormalities that are compatible with prolonged survival. The forms of cerebral damage recognized most frequently at autopsy in the perinatal period and diagnosed most often in life are those in the spectrum of hemorrhagic and ischemic lesions. The extreme frequency of some types of cerebral vascular damage has been appreciated only since the advent of diagnostic techniques, such as real-time ultrasound, which can be applied to the ill newborn infant. It has become apparent that the patterns of damage seen at autopsy are linked to the problems of maintaining an appropriate circulation to the developing brain in the face of dramatic changes in systemic blood pressure, intracranial pressure and blood gas tensions. The malleable nature of the cranium of the fetus and newborn infant ensures that external pressures may affect the brain and that cerebral pathology may be reflected in alterations of the extracerebral cerebrospinal fluid space and the cranial bones. It is thus critical to observe the brain carefully in relation to the cranial cavity at the time of postmortem examination, even if a specialist neuropathologist is available to help examine it in detail after fixation.

Throughout this chapter I will stress that a knowledge of the vascular patterns of the developing brain may be more important than detailed understanding of cerebral cellular structure for interpretation of perinatal cerebral pathology because so many of the lesions are of vascular origin.

DEVELOPMENT OF THE BRAIN

EMBRYOLOGY OF THE CENTRAL NERVOUS SYSTEM

The neural tube develops from the neural plate ectoderm during the third and fourth weeks after conception. A neural groove first becomes visible at about 18 days after ovulation when the embryonic disc is 1 to 1.5 mm in length.[1] Closure of the groove to form the neural tube begins at about 22 days and is completed by closure of the caudal neuropore at 26 days. The different regions of the brain are indicated by a series of flexures, all of which can all be recognized by the end of the fifth postovulatory week (Fig. 12–1). The right and left cerebral vesicles appear at 32 to 33 days, by which time the right and left cerebellar plates also can

243

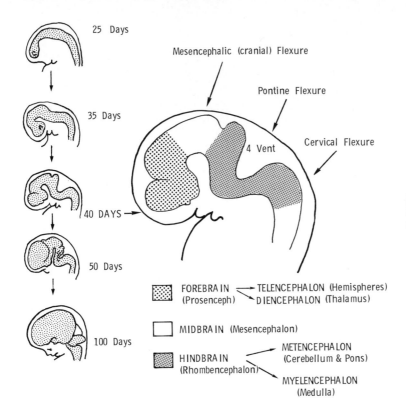

25 Days

Mesencephalic (cranial) Flexure

Pontine Flexure

Cervical Flexure

35 Days

4 Vent

40 DAYS

50 Days

100 Days

FOREBRAIN (Prosenceph) → TELENCEPHALON (Hemispheres)
↘ DIENCEPHALON (Thalamus)

MIDBRAIN (Mesencephalon)

HINDBRAIN (Rhombencephalon) → METENCEPHALON (Cerebellum & Pons)
↘ MYELENCEPHALON (Medulla)

Figure 12–1. Diagram to illustrate regions of the brain as indicated by flexures at about 40 days postconceptional age.

be identified at the rhombic lip of the hind brain (Fig. 12–2). The cerebellar primordia do not fuse in the midline until about nine postovulatory weeks. Throughout prenatal life development of the cerebellar hemispheres and cerebellum continues to lag behind that of the basal ganglia, thalamus, midbrain and brain stem. However, during the fetal period the cerebral hemispheres and cerebellum grow faster than the midbrain and brain stem and thus gradually reduce the disparity.

LATER DEVELOPMENT OF THE BRAIN

The macroscopic and histological appearances of the fetal brain from 10 to 40 weeks menstrual age are illustrated and described by Larroche.[2] The cerebral hemispheres in the early second trimester are thin-walled structures with a relatively large ventricular cavity and a smooth external surface. The sylvian fissure on the lateral aspect of the brain and the calcarine and cingulate sulci on the medial aspect develop by 18 weeks and the central sulcus by 20 weeks. All the major primary sulci can be recognized by 28 weeks. Development of secondary sulci occurs progressively throughout the remainder of intrauterine life.

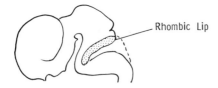

Rhombic Lip

Figure 12–2. Diagram to illustrate origin of cerebellum in an embryo at 8 weeks postconceptional age.

DEVELOPMENT OF THE CEREBRAL CORTEX

The cortical plate first can be recognized during the eighth postovulatory week. Neurons develop by mitotic activity within the ventricular zone of the cerebrum and migrate out along radially orientated glial fibers to reach their appointed positions within the cortical plate—a remarkable process that has been described in detail by Sidman and Rakic.[3] The layered pattern of the cortex is built up by groups of neurons that successively take up positions external to those that have migrated earlier. The maximal rate of neuronal proliferation within the cerebrum has been shown to occur at 12 to 18 weeks.[4] After this initial phase of neuronal proliferation and migration, further growth within the cerebral hemispheres is associated with proliferation of cells of the subependymal germinal matrix beneath the wall of the lateral ventricle and migration of these cells into the widening cerebral hemisphere. Most of the subependymal cells are probably destined to form the supporting glial elements. Throughout the latter half of pregnancy the axons and dendritic spines and processes of the cortical neurons are progressively elaborated and myelination commences according to a regular sequence. This rapid increase in the number of neuronal connections in the latter part of gestation is associated with a steady increase in cortical area and thus an increasing complexity in convolutional pattern.

BLOOD SUPPLY TO THE DEVELOPING BRAIN

This is described in detail elsewhere,[5] and only a brief description is given here. The mammalian central nervous system has evolved from a basic tubular structure with a blood supply in the form of a surface capillary network. The evolution of the mammalian brain with its specialized regions, including the cerebral hemispheres and cerebellum, has required considerable modifications of the original simple pattern. The patterns of blood supply change throughout development in parallel with the marked regional variation in growth rate and in relation to regional differences in metabolic activity.

The basic cranial arterial pattern is recognizable by the end of the embryonic stage but, as explained earlier, the cerebral vesicles are still small and the cerebellar processes barely formed by this time. As the cerebral hemispheres develop, the vascular pattern becomes elaborated within the thickening mass of tissue. By the latter part of the second trimester there is a very well-developed arterial supply to the central regions of the brain, including brain stem, midbrain, basal ganglia and thalamus. Branches of anterior and middle cerebral arteries supply basal ganglia and thalami and feed into the microcirculation of the rapidly proliferating subependymal cell matrix (Fig. 12–3). In the last third of gestation, as the connections of the cortical neurons increase in number and myelination begins, there is progressive increase in complexity of the vascular bed within the cortex and white matter of the cerebral hemispheres. At the same time the subependymal matrix cells are migrating out to their final position, and the subependymal microcirculation is gradually remodeled (Fig. 12–4). The net result is a change in the pattern of circulation from a central to a cortical and white matter orientation. The most marked difference in blood supply between the immature and mature organ is seen in the fetal cerebellum. Neuronal proliferation in the cerebellum occurs throughout fetal life within the temporary external granular layer just beneath the surface pial membrane. The blood supply to these proliferating cells is derived from the rich capillary bed within the pia, as the outer layers of the cerebellum are almost totally avascular. In the rat, which has a cerebellum similar to that of the human, development of a mature capillary bed can be traced within the outer part of the cerebellum as the external granular layer disappears.[6]

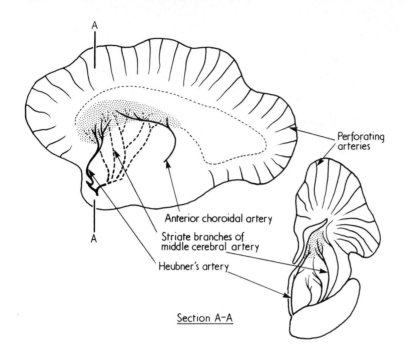

Figure 12–3. Arterial supply to the basal ganglia at 29 weeks' gestation. (From Hambleton, G. and Wigglesworth, J. S.: Origin of intraventricular hemorrhage in the preterm infant. Arch. Dis. Child. *51*:651–659, 1976.)

The venous drainage pattern of the developing brain is notable for the large, prominent thin-walled vessels of the galenic vein system, which drains a major part of the future white matter of the hemispheres (Fig. 12–5). Part of the subependymal matrix microcirculation drains directly into the terminal vein and its major branches. However, much of the subependymal venous drainage occurs by way of the basal vein system which enters the vein of Galen near its junction with the straight sinus. The pattern of the sinuses, and the important bridging veins draining into them from the cerebral veins, is illustrated in Chapter 6.

MALFORMATIONS OF THE CENTRAL NERVOUS SYSTEM

Neural tube defects, including anencephaly and spina bifida, constitute the commonest group of fatal malformations in some parts of the world such as the north and west parts of Britain and Northern Ireland.[7] Many epidemiological studies have been performed in the attempt to discover environmental causes in

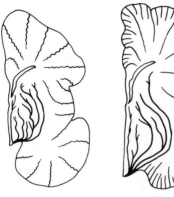

24 weeks   34 weeks

Figure 12–4. Change in arterial pattern of cerebellum between 24 and 34 weeks' gestation. (From Wigglesworth, J. S., and Page, K. E.: An integrated model for hemorrhagic and ischemic lesions in the newborn brain. Early Hum. Develop. *2*:179–199, 1978.)

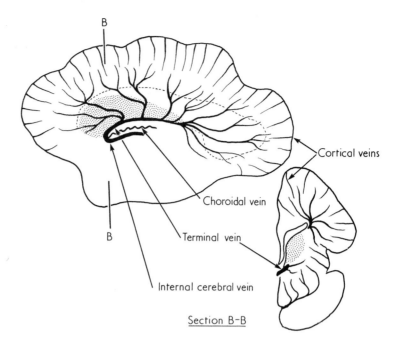

Figure 12–5. Veins related to caudate nucleus at 30 weeks' gestation. (Modified from Hambleton, G. and Wigglesworth, J. S.: Origin of intraventricular hemorrhage in the preterm infant. Arch. Dis. Child. *51*:651–659, 1976.)

Cortical veins

Choroidal vein

Terminal vein

Internal cerebral vein

Section B-B

the high-risk areas. Among the many associations reported have been poor maternal nutrition, deficiencies in minerals such as iron, calcium and zinc, epidemics of potato blight, and consumption of tea. In experimental animals teratogens which cause anencephaly and hydrocephalus include dyes, salicylates, rifampicin and hypoglycemic sulfonamides. Deficiencies in certain vitamins, excess vitamin A, anoxia, carbon dioxide narcosis and zinc deficiency may also cause anencephaly and hydrocephalus. Genetic factors have been implicated also in a range of human studies.

Many open neural tube defects are now detected by alpha-fetoprotein (AFP) determinations on maternal blood and amniotic fluid. Screening programs have been set up in many areas. These mainly involve measurement of maternal blood AFP as a first step.[8] Patients in whom maternal serum AFP at 16 to 19 weeks is above 120 μg/L have amniocentesis to check amniotic AFP level. Termination of pregnancy is offered to those patients with high amniotic AFP levels.

Some investigators have advocated widespread use of antenatal screening of this type. However, there are a number of difficulties. The process of amniocentesis carries a small but distinct risk of fetal loss (about 1 per cent). There is also evidence that fetal lung development may be impaired if amniotic leakage is prolonged (Chapter 10). The cases most readily diagnosed are those involving fetuses with potentially fatal defects such as anencephaly. Hence the scope for prevention of handicap is strictly limited. Therefore, the value of antenatal screening programs may be questioned. In addition, religious, moral or legal considerations may influence the extent to which antenatal screening is performed at a particular center.

ANENCEPHALY

The appearance of the anencephalic fetus is distinctive (Fig. 12–6). The crown of the head is flat and consists of a vascular mass of tissue without skin or cranial vault. There are bulging eyes, a broad nose, malformed ears, a large tongue and a short neck. The defect may involve the whole spine (craniorachischisis). Notable associated features are a large thymus and extremely small adrenals

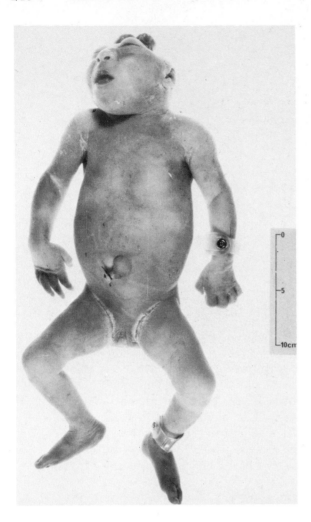

Figure 12–6. Term fetus with anencephaly.

with almost total lack of a fetal cortex. Many anencephalic fetuses have hypoplastic lungs, and a high proportion have associated polyhydramnios.

The forebrain and midbrain are represented by the area cerebrovasculosa, a mass of thin-walled vascular channels distended with blood, and underlying remnants of necrotic nervous tissue over the base of the skull. In some cases medulla may be present and allow survival of the infant for several days. All the cranial nerves are present but may be poorly developed and end blindly in the area cerebrovasculosa. The anterior lobe of the pituitary can usually be recognized readily as a small bright-red structure sitting on the flattened pituitary fossa. Histologically, the cell composition usually appears normal. The posterior lobe is very poorly developed and lacks signs of neurosecretion.

Whether anencephaly arises from primary failure of closure of the anterior end of the neural tube (Giroud)[7] or from a secondary rupture of the primitive brain (Gardner) is unsettled.[9]

ENCEPHALOMYELOCELE

The encephalomyelocele develops secondary to midline defects of the cranial bones. The most common form is a defect of the occipital bone with an occipital encephalomyelocele.[10] Other typical, but less frequent, sites are interparietal and frontonasal. Occurrence of an occipital encephalomyelocele in association with splanchnic defects is known as the Meckel-Gruber syndrome (Chapter 7).

INIENCEPHALY

In this condition there is abnormal development of the occipital region of the skull and the cervical vertebrae with absence of the neck and extreme retroflexion of the spine.[11] In some cases it is associated with an occipital encephalocele. The less severe forms of this condition merge into the Klippel-Feil syndrome, in which there is shortening of the neck due to abnormalities of the cervical vertebrae. Iniencephaly, like encephalomyelocele, is commonly associated with hypoplastic lungs and often with many other internal anomalies.

Despite the fact that the cranium is intact, the condition may be mistaken for anencephaly by the inexperienced observer.

HYDROCEPHALUS DUE TO AQUEDUCTAL MALFORMATIONS

Obstructive hydrocephalus is commonly caused by narrowing or occlusion of the aqueduct.[12, 13] The abnormality may involve stenosis of the lumen without surrounding gliosis, forking of the aqueduct with two abnormal channels, complete or partial occlusion by a septum, or gliotic stenosis. One form of hydrocephalus associated with aqueduct stenosis is of recessive sex-linked inheritance affecting mainly males, and accounts for about 2 per cent of cases of uncomplicated hydrocephalus.

DANDY-WALKER SYNDROME

This is a congenital anomaly of the cerebellum characterized by six major features: hydrocephalus, defective development of the vermis of the cerebellum, cyst-like enlargement of the fourth ventricle, enlargement of the posterior fossa, elevated location of the transverse sinuses and the tentorium, and in many cases lack of patency of one or more of the foramina of the fourth ventricle.[13, 14] The mechanism responsible for the anomaly is uncertain but involves failure of fusion of the cerebella primordia in the midline and probably inadequate escape of cerebrospinal fluid from the ventricular system. This latter state may be a result of either overproduction of cerebrospinal fluid or failure (or delay) of opening of the foramina of the fourth ventricle. Some cases may be genetically determined, possibly by an autosomal recessive form of inheritance. The condition presents usually as a progressive hydrocephalus in infancy. The frequent accompaniment of other anomalies may result in death during the perinatal period.

HOLOPROSENCEPHALY

This term denotes failure of normal division of the prosencephalic structures, telencephalon and diencephalon, into separate cerebral hemispheres.[15] The defect is of variable severity. In the most complete form, alobar holoprosencephaly (Fig. 12–7), the cerebrum has no lobes and no interhemispheric fissure. Arhinencephaly (absence of the olfactory bulbs and tracts) is usually present. In semilobar holoprosencephaly the interhemispheric fissure is indicated posteriorly. At the mild end of the spectrum there may only be arhinencephaly or midline continuity of the cingulate gyrus within the interhemispheric fissure.

Certain characteristic facial appearances indicate the presence and severity of holoprosencephaly. These are, in descending order of severity, as follows:

1. Cyclops, in which the infant has a central eye and a proboscis.
2. Ethmocephaly, characterized by hypoplastic eyes and a proboscis.
3. Cebocephaly, in which there is hypotelorism and a rudimentary nose with single nostril.
4. Midline cleft lip with hypotelorism.
5. Intermaxillary rudimentary facies.

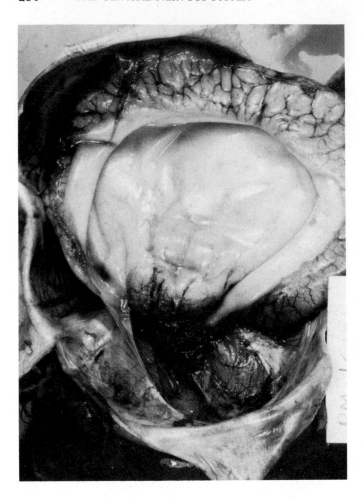

Figure 12–7. Holoprosencephaly. In the alobar variety seen here, the hemispheres are fused to form a single "holosphere," which is open caudally.

The most abnormal facies are associated with alobar holoprosencephaly and often with absence of the pituitary, while the milder facial defects indicate less severe cerebral abnormality. Alobar holoprosencephaly can, however, be seen in infants without diagnostic facies.

Several chromosomal defects are linked with holoprosencephaly. Infants with trisomy 13 may display any of the variants of the condition. Trisomy 18 and deletion of the short arm of chromosome 18 are often associated with arhinencephaly but not the more severe varieties of holoprosencephaly.

Most cases of alobar holoprosencephaly are microcephalic.

OTHER CEREBRAL MALFORMATIONS

These include schizencephaly (cleft brain), agenesis of the corpus callosum and a range of abnormalities including microgyria, lissencephaly, pachygyria and status verrucosus, which may be described as "abnormalities of cell migration." The last group are well discussed and described by Larroche.[16]

SPINAL CORD MALFORMATIONS

The important group of spinal cord malformations comprises the various forms of myelodysplasia associated with spina bifida.[13]

Myelocele. This is the most severe form of malformation in which the neural tube has failed to close. The defect consists of an exposed area of granulation tissue overlying the abnormal cord tissue and continuous peripherally with the skin. Cerebrospinal fluid exudes from the spinal canal, which opens onto the deficient area (Fig. 12–8).

Meningomyelocele. The spinal lesion involves a bluish sac of arachnoid and dura. Within the CSF-filled sac the central canal of the cord is usually grossly dilated and the cord elements mingled with the membranes form a cyst wall.

Meningocele and Spina Bifida Occulta. These less severe forms of myelodysplasia seldom achieve importance in the perinatal period.

This simple traditional classification does not adequately express the variations in abnormal structures that may be found on detailed examination of these cases.[17] The spinal cord is often abnormal above the level of the spina bifida. Lesions that are frequently found include diastematomyelia, hydromyelia and syringomelia. Duplication of the cord or central canal may be present below the lesion.

The common type of spina bifida, as seen in infants who die in the perinatal period, involves a characteristic association of lumbosacral myelocele or meningomyelocele with hydrocephalus and the Arnold-Chiari malformation (Fig. 12–9).

The Arnold-Chiari malformation is characterized by an elongated medulla and fourth ventricle extending down through the foramen magnum into the upper cervical canal with a tongue of cerebellar tissue derived from the vermis on the dorsal aspect. The elongated medulla may be kinked at its junction with

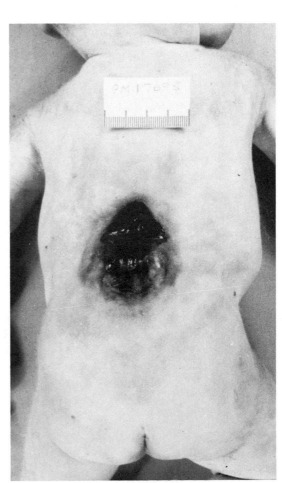

Figure 12–8. A lumbar myelocele in a term infant.

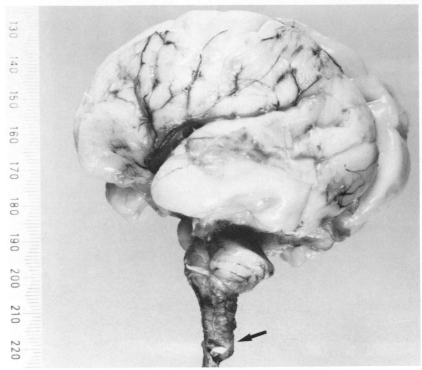

Figure 12–9. Lateral view of the brain and cervical cord of an infant of 28 weeks' gestation who died at 8 hours of age with myelocele and mild hydrocephalus. The temporal lobe has been somewhat damaged during dissection. Note the tongue of cerebellum extending down the posterior aspect of the cervical cord (arrow): the Arnold-Chiari malformation.

the spinal cord. A number of variations in the basic pattern are described.[18] The posterior fossa is small, the tentorium and falx are hypoplastic and the bones of the skull vault are usually thin and may be fenestrated. Hydrocephalus has developed by birth in most cases. The spinal cord defect is often associated with talipes.

The Arnold-Chiari malformation and hydrocephalus usually are assumed to be secondary results of spina bifida, and have been ascribed by different authors to fluid distention from above, traction from below, or overgrowth of neural tissue in early development.[13]

VASCULAR MALFORMATIONS OF THE BRAIN

These are rare. The malformation which is seen most often is an arteriovenous aneurysm of the vein of Galen.[19] The grossly dilated vein is fed by aberrant arterial branches from the posterior or middle cerebral arteries (Fig. 12–10). The infant may be born in congestive cardiac failure with a marked cardiomegaly (Chapter 11).

PRENATAL DEGENERATIONS OF THE CENTRAL NERVOUS SYSTEM

These should be differentiated from anomalies arising during the embryonic phase because there may sometimes be evidence of an underlying etiological agent (e.g., an infective process). Ruling out a hereditary form of malformation is important in providing genetic counseling to the parents.

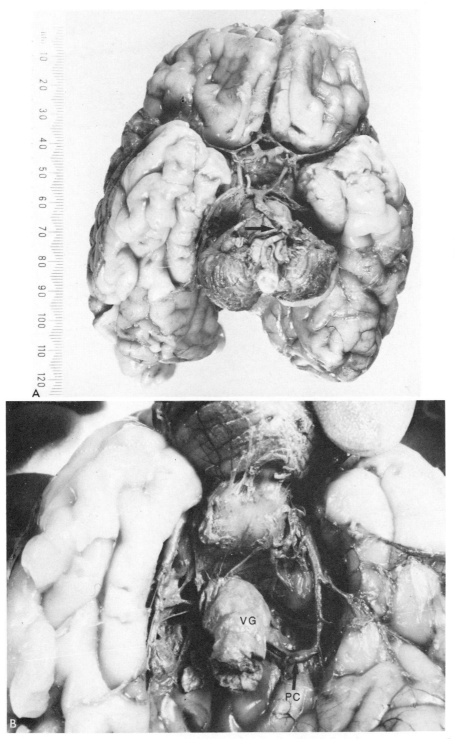

Figure 12–10. Arteriovenous aneurysm, vein of Galen. Vessels injected after fixation. *A*, Inferior surface of brain showing tortuous basilar artery (arrow). *B*, Close-up after reflection of cerebellum to show dilated posterior cerebral artery branches (PC) feeding into the vein of Galen (VG).

HYDRANENCEPHALY, PORENCEPHALY

In hydranencephaly the major part of the cerebrum has been destroyed prenatally, and the brain appears as a fluid-filled membranous sac within a cranium of relatively normal capacity. The sac comprises meninges with islands of gliosed cortical tissue. The destroyed regions of cerebrum are those supplied by the carotid arteries. Regions supplied through the vertebral system, including the basal parts of the occipital and temporal poles, hippocampi, amygdaloid nuclei, brain stem and cerebellum, usually remain intact (Fig. 12–11). The pattern of destruction suggests that blood flow to the areas supplied by the internal carotid arteries has been severely impaired during prenatal life. However, angiographic studies have given conflicting results.[13]

Porencephaly is now generally used as a nonspecific term to describe any cystic cavity within the developing brain. Some of these represent local destructive processes while others are abnormalities of development dating from the embryonic period. Most discussions of these lesions relate to the appearances of the brain in older infants and children, and fail to distinguish the effects of prenatal insults from those that may occur during or after birth.

MICROENCEPHALY AND HYDROCEPHALY

Either of these may be the result of destructive processes which have developed prenatally. Intrauterine infections with agents such as cytomegalovirus or *Toxoplasma gondii* are sometimes responsible. The small shrunken brain in such conditions is readily differentiated from that seen in the classic forms of microcephaly; these infants survive the perinatal period to die later.[13]

HEMORRHAGIC LESIONS OF THE BRAIN

Nontraumatic hemorrhage may develop at virtually any site within and around the infant brain. However, there are a number of characteristic patterns of bleeding which can be recognized by the pathologist at autopsy. Indeed some of these patterns can now be diagnosed in life with the use of computerized tomography or real-time ultrasound scanning techniques. The purpose of this section is to discuss the nature and significance of some of the more typical bleeding patterns which may be observed.

SUBARACHNOID HEMORRHAGE

Bleeding into the subarachnoid space can arise in three separate ways:

1. Leakage of blood from the fine vessels of the leptomeningeal plexus.
2. Rupture of bridging veins within the subarachnoid space.
3. Secondary spread from the ventricular system by leakage through the foramina of Luschka and Magendie.

At this point we are only concerned with leptomeningeal bleeding because rupture of bridging veins has been considered in Chapter 6 and secondary spread of hemorrhage from the ventricles is related to the problem of intraventricular hemorrhage, which is discussed later in the chapter. Two patterns of primary subarachnoid hemorrhage from the leptomeningeal vessels can be recognized. In one form the bleeding is generalized throughout the subarachnoid space, while in the other the hemorrhage is localized over the surface of the hemisphere as a convexity hemorrhage.

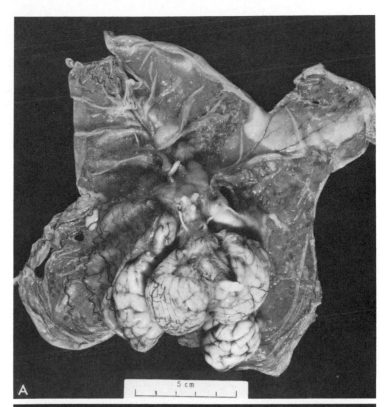

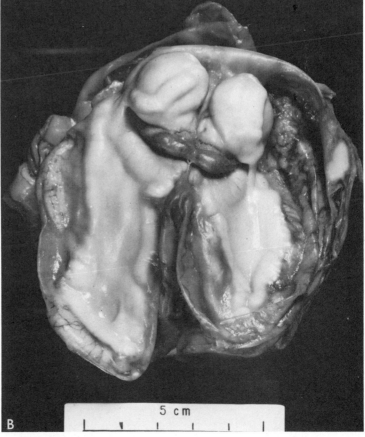

Figure 12–11. Hydranencephaly. *A*, Remnants of brain viewed from below to show preservation of inferior parts of occipital and temporal lobes and cerebellum. *B*, Viewed from above to show basal ganglia.

GENERALIZED SUBARACHNOID HEMORRHAGE

A spectrum of subarachnoid bleeding may be seen in the brains of infants who die in the neonatal period. It ranges from multiple discrete petechial hemorrhages through patchy areas of subarachnoid bleeding to masses of liquid blood throughout the subarachnoid space with pooling within the sulci (Fig. 12–12). In most instances the quantity of blood is insufficient to provide an explanation for the infants' death. The bleeding is usually attributed to anoxia and is probably very common in preterm infants who survive, as well as in those who die.[20, 21] Subarachnoid bleeding of this type may well account for many of the bloody or xanthochromic CSF samples obtained in preterm and term infants. Massive generalized subarachnoid hemorrhage is sometimes a manifestation of hemostatic failure.[22]

CONVEXITY SUBARACHNOID HEMORRHAGE (SUBARACHNOID HEMATOMA)

These are thick, localized masses of clot with a sharply defined border which are seen commonly over the temporal and occipital lobes (Fig. 12–13). Of 33 cases studied by Larroche,[23] two thirds were located over the temporal lobe and the lesions were seen twice as frequently on the left side as the right side. I have found it difficult to take histological sections through convexity hemorrhages because the blood is always firmly clotted and the underlying brain is usually very soft. However, it has been shown that some of these hemorrhages are subpial in origin.[24]

Convexity hemorrhage is often associated with hemostatic failure such as that caused by consumption coagulopathy, and there may be coexistent cerebellar hemorrhages. At autopsy in infants with hemostatic failure the firm blood clot over the brain may present a striking contrast to the liquid blood oozing from venipuncture sites and from other organs of the body.[25] The solid clot over the

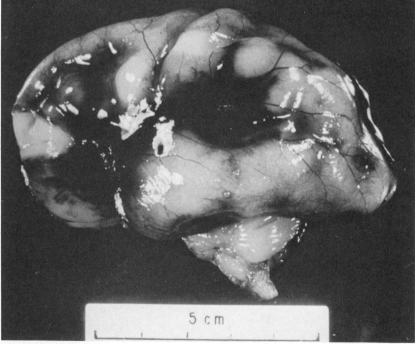

5 cm

Figure 12–12. Brain of an infant of 27 weeks' gestation showing massive primary subarachnoid hemorrhage. Death occurred at 5 hours of age with early HMD.

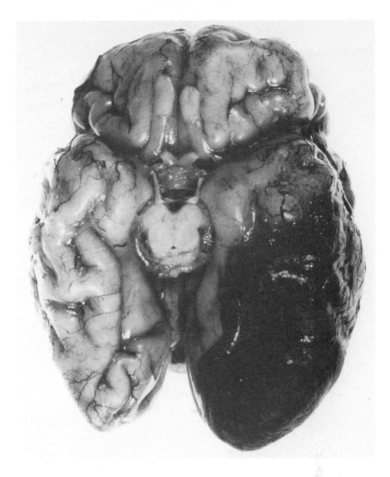

Figure 12–13. Basal view of cerebrum of an infant of 38 weeks' gestation, showing a massive convexity hemorrhage. Death occurred at 2 days of age with severe rhesus isoimmunization and evidence of disseminated intravascular coagulation. (From Pape, K. E., and Wigglesworth, J. S.: Haemorrhage, Ischaemia and the Perinatal Brain. London, Spastics International Medical Publications, 1979.)

brain can be explained in cases of subpial origin on the basis of thromboplastin release from damaged brain tissue. If this hemorrhage does indeed occur into the subarachnoid space, the event must take place before the coagulation mechanism fails.

It is not clear how these lesions develop. The lack of any association with arterial infarction of the underlying cortex has led Larroche to argue that they are of venous origin.[23] In her series of 33 patients, 20 had been given exchange transfusions for treatment of hyperbilirubinemia, sepsis or coagulation disorders. It was hypothesized that a transient rise in venous pressure could have caused the bleeding. However, I have observed such lesions in infants with coagulation disorders who have not had exchange transfusion.

Convexity hemorrhage still seems to be a postmortem diagnosis, and I am not aware of cases that have been recognized during life. It is thus not possible to give an account of the evolution or long-term effects of this type of hemorrhage.

INTRACEREBRAL HEMORRHAGE

Hemorrhage can arise from virtually any site within the cerebral tissue. However, several characteristic patterns may be recognized. These are cortical hemorrhage, white matter hemorrhage and subependymal hemorrhage. The last is discussed later in the chapter with intraventricular hemorrhage. Because intracerebral hemorrhage is frequently caused by cerebral vessel occlusion, the subject is discussed in this section.

CORTICAL HEMORRHAGE

This form of bleeding is not very common. It is usually seen in term infants who have a history of severe birth asphyxia (Fig. 12–14). The bleeding develops within areas of cerebral necrosis, and the basic lesion should in most cases probably be regarded as arterial infarction.[26] Very similar lesions can be seen in term monkey fetuses subjected to prolonged partial asphyxia.[27] Cortical hemorrhage may also result from hemorrhagic venous infarction of cortex and subcortical white matter following obstruction of the superior sagittal sinus or its tributary veins. Larroche states that the region of the parietal lobes drained by the anastomatic vein of Trolard is particularly vulnerable.[23] I have seen this form of hemorrhagic cerebral damage only in infants who have become dehydrated during the course of acute infections, an association referred to in the older literature by the term *marantic thrombosis*.

WHITE MATTER HEMORRHAGE

This is most often seen in preterm infants. The hemorrhage usually occurs in association with, or as a sequel to, subependymal hemorrhage. The introduction of real-time ultrasound scanning has allowed the development of this type of bleeding to be observed during life (Fig. 12–15). Such observations coupled with the appearances at postmortem examination support the suggestion that the hemorrhage represents secondary bleeding into an area of periventricular leukomalacia.[28, 29]

CEREBRAL VESSEL OCCLUSION

Occlusion of Cerebral Arteries. The anatomical findings in cerebral artery thrombosis or embolism vary with the time before birth, or death, at which the

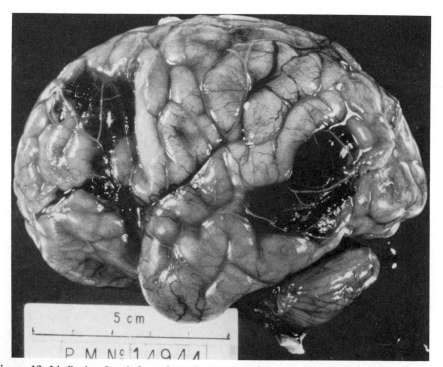

Figure 12–14. Brain of an infant of 1200 g birth weight at 38 weeks' gestation, showing multiple hemorrhagic cortical infarcts. The cerebral arteries have been injected with barium gelatin. (From Pape, K. E., and Wigglesworth, J. S.: Haemorrhage, Ischemia and the Perinatal Brain. London, Spastics International Medical Publications, 1979.)

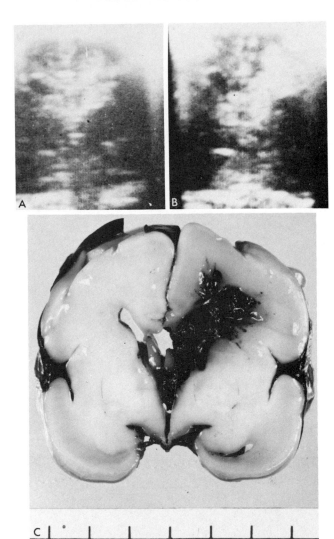

Figure 12–15. White matter "spread" from subependymal hemorrhage in an infant of 28 weeks' gestation. *A,* Ultrasound scan at 4 hours age showing subependymal hemorrhage. *B,* Ultrasound scan at 4 days of age showing extensive spread. *C,* Coronal section through brain of the infant who died a few hours after the second scan. The presence of congested veins at the margin of the lesion suggests that the "spread" represents secondary hemorrhage into an area of venous infarction. (*A,* and *B* courtesy of Dr. M. I. Levene, University of Leicester.)

lesion occurred. A recent thrombosis of the middle cerebral artery may occur with cortical necrosis and hemorrhagic infarction of the underlying white matter. Thrombi or emboli dating from several weeks before death are associated with cerebral softening and cyst formation. Of the series of cases described by Larroche,[23] two were attributed to thrombosis or embolism of the middle cerebral artery associated with exchange transfusion and intravenous bicarbonate infusion, respectively. The possibility of cerebral artery occlusion as an iatrogenic hazard has been emphasized by the report of cortical infarction following the use of indwelling temporal artery catheters.[30]

Venous Infarction of the Cerebrum. This is seen occasionally as a primary condition in stillbirths and early neonatal deaths. It usually involves obstruction of the deep vein system, often with thrombosis of the vein of Galen. There is dilatation of the deep vein tributaries with surrounding hemorrhages and necrosis. The hemorrhage may be accentuated within the subependymal layer in the immature infant. Rupture of this type of subependymal hemorrhage into the ventricular system is one mode of development of intraventricular hemorrhage. The alternative form of venous infarction caused by thrombosis of the sagittal sinus and its tributaries was discussed earlier.

CEREBELLAR HEMORRHAGE

Several forms of hemorrhage may be seen within the cerebellum of the newborn infant. Massive cerebellar hemorrhage develops occasionally as a result of birth trauma, as illustrated in Chapter 5. Localized cerebellar hemorrhage may be a typical finding in low birth weight infants with a bleeding diathesis.[25] The lesion is a raised mass of solid clot beneath the pia arachnoid, usually over the inferior surface of the cerebellar hemisphere (Fig. 12–16). As mentioned earlier, this lesion is often associated with convexity hemorrhages of the cerebrum. An occasional source of hemorrhage within the cerebellum is the subependymal zone in the roof of the fourth ventricle.[31]

A particular type of cerebellar hemorrhage has been reported in small preterm infants who were ventilated by a face mask.[32] The hemorrhage developed predominantly in infants in whom the mask was firmly attached by a 1-inch velcro band around the head. This apparatus caused marked head molding with tower-skull deformity. The cerebellar hemorrhages had the characteristics of venous infarcts, hemorrhagic lesions involving a large proportion of the cerebellum in some instances, but containing persisting necrotic cerebellar tissue. Dr. Pape and I recognized similar cerebellar venous infarcts in infants who died following mask ventilation in which a netting support was used around the head.[33] The anatomical sites of cerebellar hemorrhages and venous infarcts are illustrated in Figures 12–17 and 12–18. Hemorrhages are seen commonly within the cerebellar cortex in the form of petechiae in the external granular or molecular layers. We have suggested that the frequency of hemorrhage in the cerebellar cortex is related to the poorly formed capillary bed in this region, which is in a continual process of remodeling during the rapid cerebellar growth continuing throughout the peri-

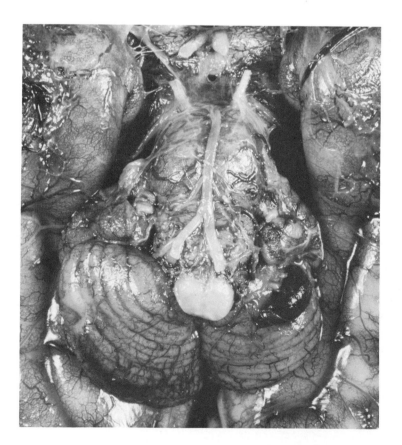

Figure 12–16. Superficial cerebellar hemorrhage in an infant of 34 weeks' gestation who died at 35 hours of age with severe rhesus isoimmunization. (From Pape, K. E., and Wigglesworth, J. S.: Haemorrhage, Ischaemia and the Perinatal Brain. London, Spastics International Publications, 1979.)

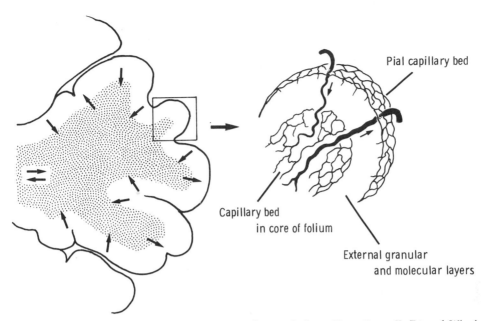

Figure 12–17. Vascular anatomy of the developing cerebellum. (From Pape, K. E., and Wigglesworth, J. S.: Haemorrhage, Ischaemia and the Perinatal Brain. London, Spastics International Medical Publications, 1979.)

natal period.[33] The capillaries readily break down following stress, but the extent of bleeding is small. The cerebellar infarcts associated with mask ventilation may be confined to the central portions of the cerebellar folia if the hemorrhage is small (Fig. 12–19) but may involve all layers if large (Fig. 12–20). Venous obstruction causes blood to pool in the capillary bed within the center of the folia and this may result in a central hemorrhagic lesion. We have suggested that these cerebellar infarcts are due to the combined effects of generalized impairment in cerebral blood flow caused by raised intracranial pressure and localized obstruction to posterior fossa venous drainage caused by cranial distortion.

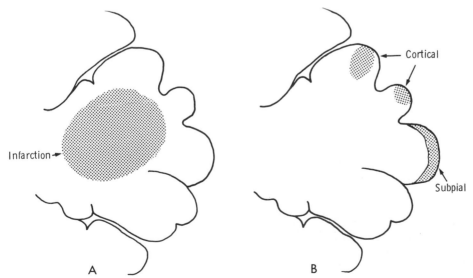

Figure 12–18. Common sites of origin of hemorrhagic cerebellar lesions. *A*, Venous infarction; *B*, hemorrhages. (From Pape, K. E., and Wigglesworth, J. S.: Haemorrhage, Ischaemia and the Perinatal Brain. London, Spastics International Medical Publications, 1979.)

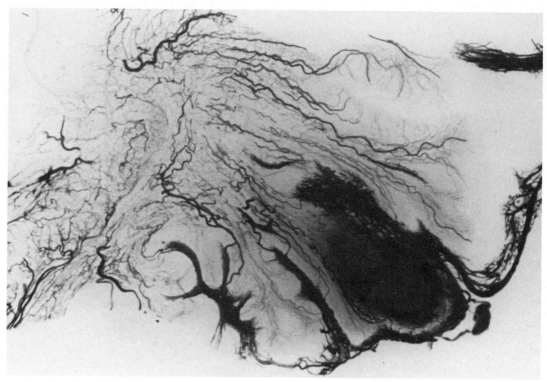

Figure 12–19. Cleared barium-gelatin injected cerebellum showing small venous infarct in the core of the folium. (From Pape, K. E., and Wigglesworth, J. S.: Haemorrhage, Ischaemia and the Perinatal Brain. London, Spastics International Medical Publications, 1979.)

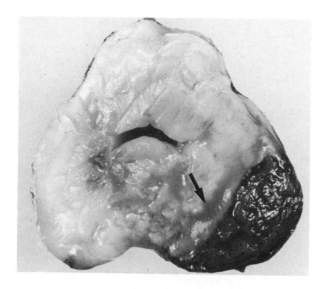

Figure 12–20. Venous infarction involving the right cerebellar hemisphere in an infant of 27 weeks' gestation who died at 25 days following prolonged mask ventilation. Necrotic cerebellar tissue (arrow) extends beyond the haemorrhagic area. (From Pape, K. E., and Wigglesworth, J. S.: Haemorrhage, Ischaemia and the Perinatal Brain. London, Spastics International Medical Publications, 1979.)

INTRAVENTRICULAR HEMORRHAGE

This condition has become recognized in recent years as one of the major causes of death and neurological handicap in preterm infants. The development of computerized axial tomography and, more recently, of real-time ultrasound scanning as methods for diagnosis of this form of hemorrhage in life has revealed that the condition occurs in 40 to 50 per cent of infants below 1500 g in birth weight who are admitted to neonatal intensive care units.[34, 35] Many of these infants do not die, and some do not show obvious clinical symptoms and may not require major supportive therapy in the newborn period. It has thus become an important concern of neonatologists to determine how the site and size of subependymal and intraventricular hemorrhages influence subsequent cerebral development.

PATHOLOGICAL ANATOMY OF INTRAVENTRICULAR HEMORRHAGE

Intraventricular hemorrhage arises most frequently from rupture of a subependymal hemorrhage over the lower part of the head of the caudate nucleus directly opposite the foramen of Monro (Fig. 12–21). Less often the hemorrhage arises over the body or tail of the caudate. Our studies show a relationship between site of origin and gestational age.[36] In infants of 28 weeks' gestation or less, subependymal hemorrhage occurs usually over the body of the caudate nucleus, while the head of the caudate nucleus becomes the most common site of origin at more advanced gestational ages. Subependymal hemorrhage can develop and give rise to intraventricular hemorrhage in any site where germinal matrix tissue occurs, including the lateral aspect of the lateral ventricle in the region of the trigone, the lateral aspect of the occipital or temporal horns and the roof of the fourth ventricle.[31] Subependymal hemorrhage is equally frequent in both hemi-

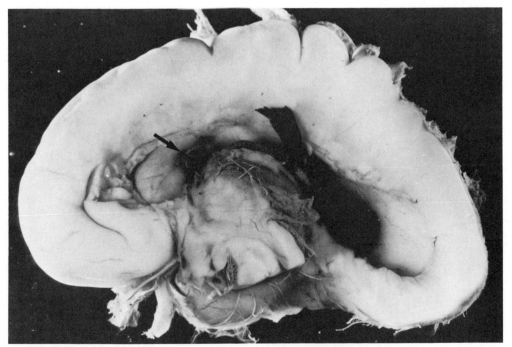

Figure 12–21. Sagittal section of the brain of an infant of 29 weeks' gestation dissected from the medial aspect to show subependymal hemorrhage over the head of the right caudate nucleus (arrow) and a mass of clot within the ventricle extending into the occipital horn. (From Hambleton, G. and Wigglesworth, J. S.: Origin of intraventricular hemorrhage in the preterm infant. Arch. Dis. Child. *51*:651–659, 1976.)

spheres and is found to be bilateral in about half the cases diagnosed in life or at autopsy. There are often multiple hemorrhages over one caudate nucleus (Fig. 12–22).

Following rupture of a subependymal hemorrhage the spread of blood through the ventricular system is quite variable as judged by autopsy findings in infants who die in the first few days after birth. There is usually a mass of clot loosely attached to the choroid plexus and to the site of rupture with spread through the foramen of Monro to the opposite lateral ventricle and to the third ventricle, aqueduct and fourth ventricle. Sometimes the blood clot may form a complete cast of the ventricular system. However, in many cases there is no spread of clot beyond the ventricle into which the subependymal hemorrhage originally ruptured. The lateral ventricle or ventricles which contain clot are distended in addition by bloodstained CSF. The hemorrhage apparently causes obstruction to drainage of CSF from the lateral ventricles, possibly by mechanical plugging of the foramen of Monro. In cases in which hemorrhage is limited to one ventricle, the obstruction may be caused by the enlarging subependymal hematoma before rupture occurs, since the usual site of subependymal hemorrhage is directly opposite the foramen of Monro.

Externally the brain may show either pallor or congestion of the leptomeninges. There is sometimes visible flattening of convolutions over one or both hemispheres. A characteristic finding is a mass of clot within the subarachnoid

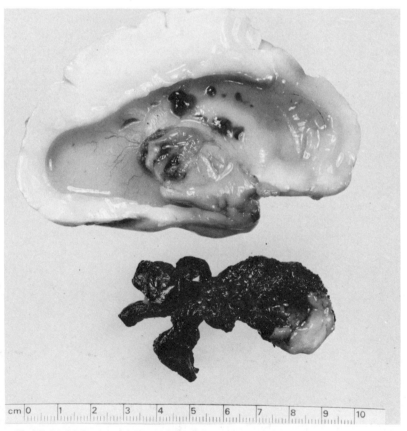

Figure 12–22. Multiple sites of SEH in the left lateral ventricle wall at 31 weeks' gestation. The mass of clot removed from the ventricle is seen below the brain specimen. (From Pape, K. E., and Wigglesworth, J. S.: Haemorrhage, Ischaemia and the Perinatal Brain. London, Spastics International Medical Publications, 1979.)

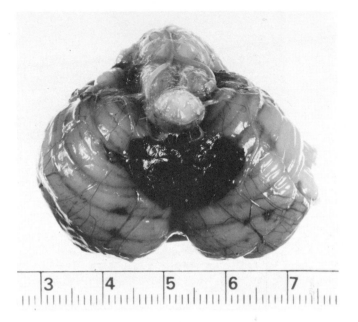

Figure 12–23. Cerebellum from a case of SEH/IVH showing the characteristic localized mass of clot within the cisterna magna. (From Pape, K. E. and Wigglesworth, J. S.: Haemorrhage, Ischaemia and the Perinatal Brain. London, Spastics International Medical Publications, 1979.)

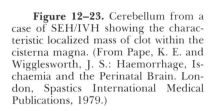

space of the cisterna magna with a very limited spread over the inferior surface of the cerebellum (Fig. 12–23). There may be extension of subarachnoid hemorrhage over the midbrain, over the lower surface of the cerebral hemispheres and into the sylvian fissures, or evidence of one or more separate sites of subarachnoid bleeding. There is intrathecal hemorrhage along the length of the spinal cord irrespective of the extent to which blood has spread through the subarachnoid space over the brain. The extent of subarachnoid spread is not obviously related either to the severity of the intraventricular hemorrhage or to the length of survival of the infant.

This variable appearance is probably caused by the very variable pattern of ventricular distention and consequent brain swelling. The normal preterm infant brain has wide sulci and a large extracerebral CSF space (Fig. 12–24). The acute brain swelling resulting from obstruction of CSF drainage allows blood to pass from the ventricular system through the foramina of Luschka and Magendie into the cisterna magna, but usually prevents spread throughout the remainder of the subarachnoid space over the cerebral hemispheres. It may be difficult for the pathologist to appreciate that these immature brains are swollen because there is such a wide variation in the size of the extracerebral CSF space according to the pressures to which the head has been subjected in life and variations in fetal nutrition and maturity.

Elsewhere we have pointed out that a considerable degree of hydrocephaly can occur without any lasting rise in intracranial pressure or increase in head circumference, if the increase in ventricular volume is balanced by resorption of the extracerebral CSF (Fig. 12–25).[37] It is only when the limit of this form of compensation is reached that a sustained rise in intracranial pressure develops and leads to an increasing head circumference.

Since the introduction of real-time ultrasound for diagnosis and monitoring of cerebral pathology in the newborn it has become apparent that the subependymal and intraventricular hemorrhage may develop and extend over a period of hours or days.

The subsequent course is largely related to the extent of the fully developed lesion. At postmortem examination, small subarachnoid hemorrhages may be

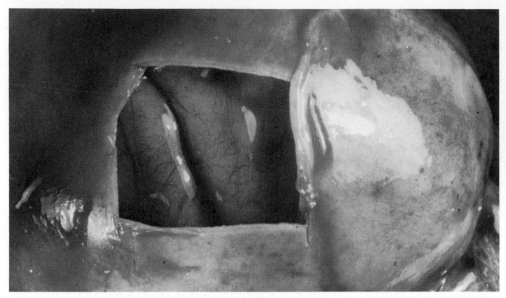

Figure 12–24. View of right cerebral hemisphere through a small cranial window in an infant of 28 weeks' gestation showing the large extracerebral CSF space. (From Pape, K. E. and Wigglesworth, J. S.: Haemorrhage, Ischaemia and the Perinatal Brain. London, Spastics International Medical Publications, 1979.)

macroscopically recognizable merely as areas of yellow staining up to two weeks after the hemorrhage. Masses of clot in the cisterna magna and in the ventricular system are more slowly broken down. The clot changes from a glossy black to a dull brown and is recognizable as old within about four days. However, a shrunken greenish-gray mass may still be present up to 6 weeks after the hemorrhage; flakes of old clot can be seen adhering to the lateral ventricle wall, particularly in the occipital and temporal horns (Fig. 12–26). An unruptured subependymal hemorrhage is rather indolent and remains full of apparently fresh liquid blood for up to 3 weeks. At the microscopic level, however, the contents of such a hematoma include hemosiderin-packed macrophages, indicating that the blood has been present for some time (Fig. 12–27). A reactive gliosis develops around the hemorrhage which persists indefinitely as a subependymal pseudocyst.

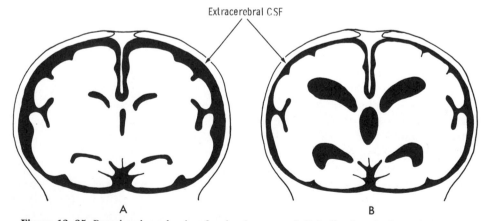

Figure 12–25. Postulated mechanism for development of clinically silent hydrocephalus following IVH. *A,* Normal preterm brain; *B,* developing hydrocephalus compensated by resorption of extracerebral CSF. (From Pape, K. E. and Wigglesworth, J. S.: Haemorrhage, Ischaemia and the Perinatal Brain. London, Spastics International Medical Publications, 1979.)

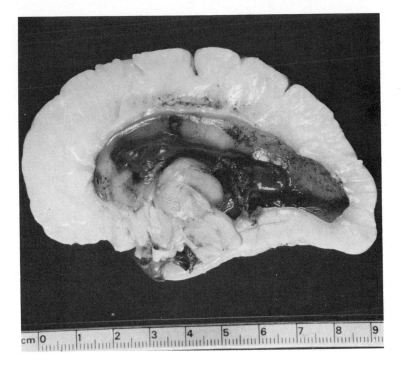

Figure 12–26. Old IVH in the brain of an infant born at 29 weeks' gestation who died at 19 days of age. (From Wigglesworth, J. S. and Pape, K. E.: An integrated model for haemorrhagic and ischaemic lesions in the newborn brain. Early Hum. Develop. 2:179–199, 1978.)

With modern neonatal intensive care an increasing number of infants with massive intraventricular hemorrhage survive for a prolonged period. In such infants the development of frank hydrocephalus with an increasing head circumference may be noted from the second week of life. Ultrasound studies have shown that persistent ventricular dilatation develops in many infants who do not have an obvious increase in head circumference.

The pathological findings in posthemorrhagic hydrocephalus have been described by Larroche[23, 38] and Deonna et al.[39] The meninges around the brain stem are thickened and may show a persistent rusty-brown discoloration owing to infiltration with hemosiderin-laden macrophages. The foramina of Luschka and Magendie are often occluded and the entire ventricular system dilated. In cases in which the fourth ventricle is not enlarged the aqueduct of Sylvius is obstructed with nuclear material and old red cells. There is often an irregular hemorrhagic destruction of much of the white matter related to the original site of bleeding (Fig. 12–28). If the infant survives long enough, the white matter sometimes becomes largely replaced by a group of smooth-walled cysts which communicate with the main ventricular cavity. The overlying cortex may show the pseudomicropolygyria seen in other forms of hydrocephalus.

CLINICOPATHOLOGICAL ASSOCIATIONS OF SUBEPENDYMAL AND INTRAVENTRICULAR HEMORRHAGE

Subependymal and intraventricular hemorrhage is a condition of immature infants and particularly of those below 32 weeks' gestation. The hemorrhages are most frequent and most severe in the least mature infants. The bleeding develops most commonly after birth but can sometimes be recognized in stillborn fetuses. Many of the other associations noted in the literature between these hemorrhages and various conditions such as fetal growth retardation and sex differences are derived from populations of dead infants and probably need to be confirmed by infant populations in whom real-time ultrasound has been used for diagnosis.

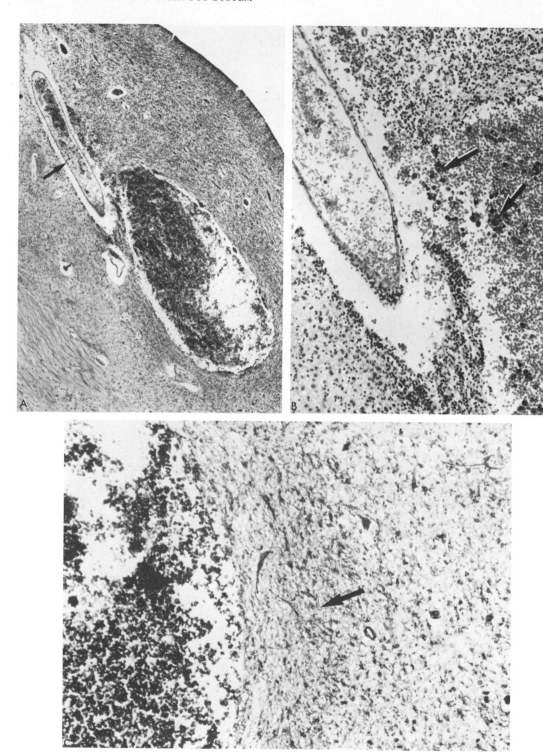

Figure 12–27. *A,* Section through an old unruptured SEH in an infant of 24 weeks' gestation who died at 33 days of age. The hemorrhage is close to an intact terminal vein branch (arrow). H and E × 40. *B,* Part of the section shown in *A* at higher magnification. Hemosiderin-laden macrophages (arrow) are present within the SEH, but there is no visible fibrin. H and E × 150. *C,* Section through the wall of another SEH from the same brain showing reactive gliosis (arrow). Holzer × 150. (From Pape, K. E. and Wigglesworth, J. S.: Haemorrhage, Ischaemia and the Perinatal Brain. London, Spastics International Medical Publications, 1979.)

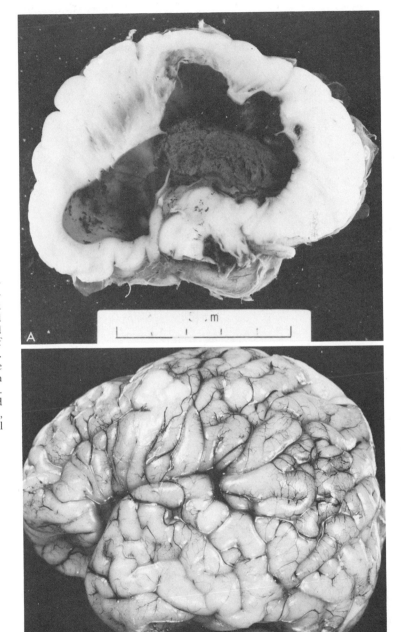

Figure 12–28. *A,* Posthemorrhagic hydrocephalus in a 31-week-gestation infant who died at 40 days of age. A mass of old clot overlies the basal ganglia and there is irregular destruction of the periventricular white matter. *B,* External appearance of the hemisphere shown in *A.* (From Pape, K. E. and Wigglesworth, J. S.: Haemorrhage, Ischaemia and the Perinatal Brain. London, Spastics International Medical Publications, 1979.)

However, an association between subependymal and intraventricular hemorrhage and hyaline membrane disease has been noted frequently and can be confirmed on a population studied in life by ultrasound.[40]

There has been clinical concern over the possible relationship between the use of alkaline buffer therapy for respiratory distress syndrome and the development of intraventricular hemorrhage following the suggestion that sodium bicarbonate–induced hypernatremia might cause intracranial hemorrhage.[41] Significant associations between total dosage of sodium bicarbonate solutions by intravascular infusion during life and autopsy findings of intraventricular hemorrhage have been confirmed by some groups but not by others. It is probable that any relationship between intraventricular hemorrhage and alkaline therapy depends more on the concentration and rate of infusion than on the total quantity of buffer given. Most neonatologists currently favor correction of acidosis by slow intravenous infusion of alkali solutions rather than by rapid bolus injection.

Abnormalities of hemostasis are common in infants with intraventricular hemorrhage but there is no evidence that they are causal. There is also no evidence that infusion of coagulation factors can prevent intraventricular hemorrhage.

ETIOLOGICAL ASPECTS OF SUBEPENDYMAL AND INTRAVENTRICULAR HEMORRHAGE

Until recently all theories on the etiology of these hemorrhages have centered on the veins draining through the subependymal germinal matrix tissue.[42] Several authors have stated that the bleeding originates from the terminal (thalamostriate) vein, which emerges from the subependymal matrix tissue near the ganglionic eminence. Others have claimed that bleeding in the region of periventricular venous drainage was caused by venous stasis related to pressures on the fetal head during birth, postnatal asphyxia with venous thrombosis or venous infarction of the subependymal matrix. Even those authors who have found that the terminal vein was intact in the majority of cases of subependymal and intraventricular hemorrhage have concluded that the hemorrhage was derived from smaller vein branches. The sharp angle at which the terminal veins join the internal cerebral vein at the foramen of Monro has been implicated as causing a point of vulnerability in the deep vein drainage system.

Our studies on the vascular anatomy of the immature fetal brain have shown that the arteries to the basal ganglia are unduly large relative to those supplying the cortex. From this we have inferred that a relatively large proportion of total cerebral blood flow supplies the basal ganglia and periventricular subependymal matrix. This vascular bed within the germinal matrix tissue has the form of an irregular rete system rather than a mature capillary bed and may allow a preferential route for arteriovenous flow in the fetal brain. Dissection and microscopy of our injected material has demonstrated disruption of the microcirculation rather than rupture of the terminal vein or its branches.[36] We have suggested that this might result from transient rises of arterial pressure associated with apneic attacks in preterm infants. Such an effect would be accentuated by the cerebral vasodilation caused by the hypercapnia and hypoxia of the respiratory distress syndrome. The soft cranium of the preterm infant allows increases in arterial pressure to be accompanied by more pronounced changes in transmural pressure than would be the case with a rigid skull.

Indirect estimations of cerebral blood flow in infants with respiratory distress have confirmed an increased cerebral blood flow prior to the development of subependymal and intraventricular hemorrhage.[43] Experimental induction of hypertension or hypercapnia has been shown to cause intraventricular hemorrhage in the newborn beagle.[44] Nuclear scanning studies on cerebral blood flow using the Xe[133] method have documented decreased flow in asphyxiated preterm infants.[45] These studies have been interpreted as indicating that a subsequent restoration of flow to an ischemic brain may result in subependymal and intraventricular hemorrhage. Thus the initial event may be either hyperperfusion or hypoperfusion of the brain.

The occurrence of intraventricular hemorrhage may cause shock and falling blood pressure resulting in secondary ischemic damage to the periventricular region. The frequent coexistence of hemorrhagic and ischemic lesions in newborn infant brains at varying maturities and consideration of anatomical and physiological aspects of the cerebral circulation have allowed us to develop a theoretical model for hemorrhagic and ischemic lesions of the newborn brain which expresses the variety of possible sequences (Fig. 12–29).[46]

SOURCES OF INTRAVENTRICULAR HEMORRHAGE OTHER THAN SUBEPENDYMAL HEMORRHAGE

These include (1) bleeding from the choroid plexus, (2) spread from an intracerebral hemorrhage away from the subependymal layer and (3) venous infarction.

The most frequent of these is choroid plexus hemorrhage. This has been found in up to 25 per cent of cases of intraventricular hemorrhage by Larroche,[23] although it usually occurs in addition to subependymal hemorrhage and the extent of the choroid plexus bleeding is small. In my experience the choroid plexus is most often recognized as the primary site of bleeding in relatively mature infants of 36 weeks' gestation or more. This observation is supported by the infrequent recognition of subependymal hemorrhage in cases of intraventricular hemorrhage diagnosed by real-time ultrasound in infants of this maturity. Intraventricular spread from an intracerebral hemorrhage arising away from the subependymal layer is an occasional autopsy finding.

Venous infarction occurs in most instances as a secondary result of massive subependymal hemorrhage with obstruction to the tributaries of the terminal vein. On the rare occasions when deep vein obstruction develops as a primary event in an immature infant, venous infarction and subependymal hemorrhage are inevitable consequences.

ISCHEMIC LESIONS OF THE BRAIN

Ischemic lesions of the developing brain are of major concern from clinical, social and economic points of view because they contribute significantly to neurological handicap in children who survive. Such lesions may be responsible for mental retardation, seizures or the various forms of cerebral palsy (spasticity, choreoathetosis or ataxia). The pathologist who examines brains in the perinatal period is in a position to assess the structural basis for these various forms of handicap at a time near their inception. Correlations of findings with the immediate clinical background and with the classic findings in brains of older children who have died with established symptomatology should provide a logical basis for efforts to prevent these forms of brain damage.

The pattern of ischemic lesions seen within the brain varies with gestational age, although certain forms of damage may occur in both preterm and term infants. Periventricular leukomalacia may be regarded as the characteristic lesion

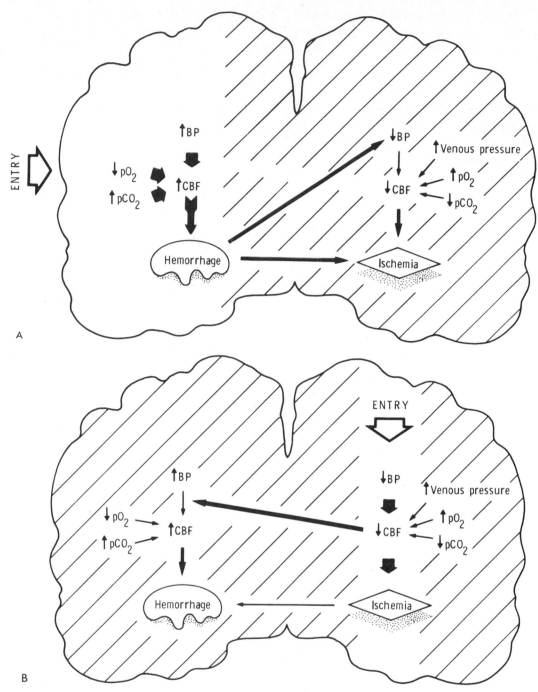

Figure 12–29. Two possible sequences leading to hemorrhage and ischemia in the preterm infant brain. *A,* Hypoxia and hypercapnia associated with respiratory distress are visualized as causing cerebral vasodilation and increased cerebral blood flow. Temporary rises in arterial pressure may readily be transmitted to the microcirculation and lead to hemorrhage. Ischemia will be caused by hemorrhagic disruption of the periventricular circulation or by posthemorrhagic shock. *B,* Hypotension following birth asphyxia or prolonged apnea causes ischemic damage to the periventricular microcirculation. Subsequent reperfusion at normal or increased blood pressure results in bleeding. Persistent hypoperfusion causes periventricular leukomalacia. It is not yet clear which of these sequences may be more common, but the major problem expressed by both is poor control of cerebral blood flow in the sick preterm infant. (From Wigglesworth, J. S. and Pape, K. E.: An integrated model for haemorrhagic and ischaemic lesions in the newborn brain. Early Hum. Develop. *2:*179–199, 1978.)

of the preterm infant brain, whereas anoxic and ischemic damage to the cerebral cortex is characteristic of the term infant. Ischemic damage to the basal ganglia, thalamus and nuclei of midbrain and brain stem may be seen in infants of any gestational age.

PERIVENTRICULAR LEUKOMALACIA

This is the common ischemic lesion of the preterm infant brain, although it may also occur at term and is reported occasionally in adults. Friede has pointed out that the condition represents nothing more than infarction of the periventricular white matter.[26]

The traditional macroscopic appearance of periventricular leukomalacia is that of white spots located in the periventricular white matter of the centrum semiovale and in the auditory and optic radiations.[29] A series of histological changes may be seen depending on the severity and stage of evolution of the condition. The earliest stage is that of coagulation necrosis (Fig. 12–30), characterized by a homogeneous appearance of the tissue with loss of nuclear staining which is shown up well by periodic acid–Schiff (PAS) or Luxol fast blue techniques. The boundary between normal and affected tissue may be sharply defined. At a slightly later stage there is axonal degeneration with the appearance of the characteristic "retraction balls" representing swollen and disintegrated axis cylinders. A cellular reaction consisting of lipid-filled microglial cells develops rapidly, and within a few days there may be a reactive astrocytosis. The central areas of large lesions may liquefy and disappear, leaving multiple cavities (Fig. 12–31).

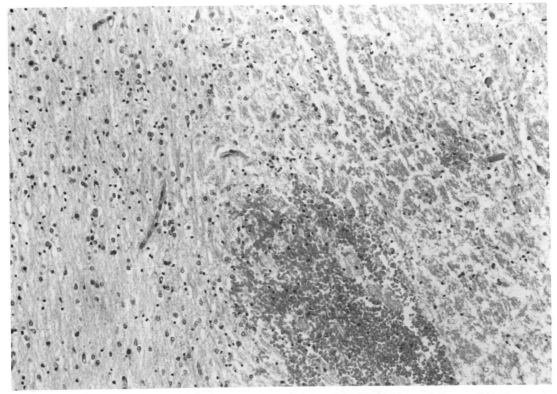

Figure 12–30. Early periventricular leukomalacia. Coagulation necrosis and patchy hemorrhage is seen in the right half of the field. H and E × 150. (From Pape, K. E. and Wigglesworth, J. S.: Haemorrhage, Ischaemia and the Perinatal Brain. London, Spastics International Medical Publications, 1979.)

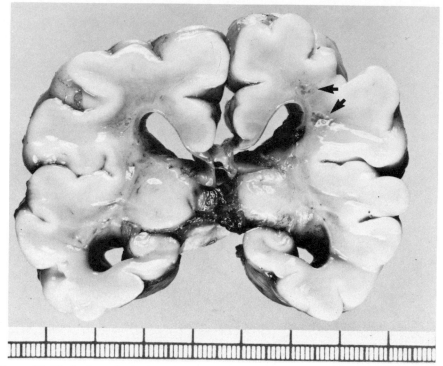

Figure 12–31. Perivascular leukomalacia. Multiple small cavities (arrow) in the brain of an infant of 34 weeks' gestation who died at 11 days of age.

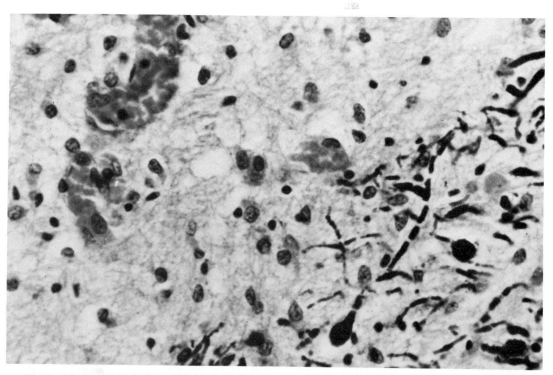

Figure 12–32. Multiple basophilic degenerated neurones and axons at the periphery of an area of long-standing PVL. H and E × 400.

There are often small areas of hemorrhage in recent lesions and groups of macrophages containing hemosiderin in old ones. Basophilic stick-like structures may be prominent at the periphery of necrotic areas of long-standing PVL (Fig. 12–32). These are thought to represent either broken-down axons or small calcified capillaries.[47]

The advent of neonatal intensive care has been associated with the recognition of variants of periventricular leukomalacia in which the infarction is far more extensive than that described in the early literature on this lesion. The necrosis may be so gross that the pathologist is tempted to dismiss it as an artefact of postmortem autolysis (Fig. 12–33). In some instances re-perfusion of the ischemic periventricular tissue causes it to be transformed into a massive hemorrhagic infarct.[28]

An important difference between periventricular leukomalacia in preterm and term infant brains has been pointed out by Larroche.[47] In preterm infants it is often the only brain lesion present, but in term infants it is usually associated with evidence of neuronal necrosis.

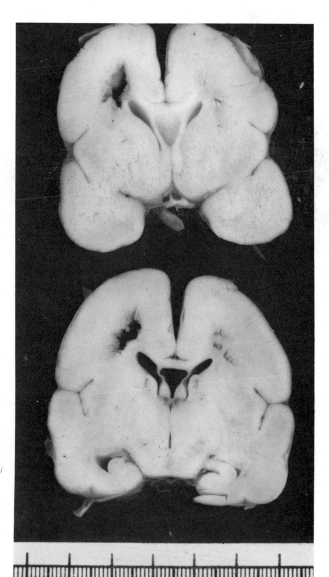

Figure 12–33. Massive cystic PVL in the brain of an infant of 26 weeks' gestation who died at 20 days of age.

The sites typically involved in periventricular leukomalacia represent the boundary zones between the ventriculopetal and ventriculofugal arteries within the brain. The condition is widely accepted as caused by failure of perfusion at these boundary zones during episodes of hypotension. It has been suggested that the poor development of ventriculofugal arteries may predispose to the occurrence of periventricular leukomalacia in preterm infants.[48]

The usual clinical presentation involves recurrent apnea but there is as yet no method of diagnosing the early stages of periventricular leukomalacia during life. However, late cystic lesions can be recognized by real-time ultrasound. The difficulty of diagnosis during life means that it is not possible to quote an incidence of this condition.

The sequence of events leading to this condition can be illustrated in terms of the diagram of Figure 12–29B used in discussing the etiology of subependymal and intraventricular hemorrhage. Prolonged hypotension and reduced cerebral blood flow, as shown on the right of the diagram, will result in ischemic necrosis. Restoration of normal or increased cerebral blood flow following improvement in blood pressure may be expected to cause subependymal and intraventricular hemorrhage or, if the periventricular tissue is already undergoing necrosis, may lead to massive hemorrhagic infarction.

Although this type of analysis may be regarded as unduly speculative, it may perhaps help in indicating why hemorrhagic and ischemic lesions are so frequently combined and why it can be difficult to determine at autopsy which was the primary event.

Periventricular leukomalacia is an important form of cerebral damage which may lead to spastic hemiplegia and quadriplegia. The characteristic lesion involves the area of white matter through which the long descending tracts pass from the motor cortex. The leg distribution is closer to the ventricles and is thus most likely to be damaged. Any lateral extension of the lesion would affect the arms as well. With upper limb involvement there tends to be a greater incidence of intellectual deficits, as might be expected with larger lesions involving association and commissural fibers. Pathological evidence linking cerebral palsy to this lesion is provided from the study of the CNS in infants who die at several months of age.[28, 58] In such cases there is a demonstrable association between periventricular leukomalacia involving the internal capsule and atrophy of the related corticospinal tract. Severe periventricular leukomalacia involving the occipital lobe and optic radiation might be expected to lead to impaired visual function.

ANOXIC-ISCHEMIC NECROSIS OF GRAY MATTER

This is a subject on which there has been much confusion in the literature relating to perinatal and pediatric neuropathology. There are several problems in interpreting the effects of anoxic-ischemic injury of the brain in the perinatal period. The first of these is the time required before the neurons show any changes that are histologically recognizable. It may take 36 to 48 hours following experimental circulatory arrest before classic anoxic neuronal changes can be distinguished in material prepared by routine histological methods. It is thus not possible to map out the pattern of CNS damage in infants who die within the first 48 hours after birth. In those infants who survive for a long period of time there may be secondary changes, such as those resulting from poor cerebral perfusion during maintenance on a ventilator, or from transneuronal degeneration, which obscures the patterns of initial injury. The variable pattern of pathological changes and of clinical syndromes in infants who survive following severe birth asphyxia has also been puzzling. The various patterns of lesion recognizable at autopsy and the nature of the underlying processes that determine each pattern are gradually becoming apparent as a result of experimental studies combined with observations on human material from cases in which there is knowledge of the clinical background.

The mechanisms leading to cessation of function and ultimate death of an individual cell in the CNS are similar, regardless of whether the initial event is pure ischemia or pure hypoxia. In either case there will be failure of oxidative phosphorylation with increased anaerobic glycolysis, resulting in a local increase in lactic acid concentration and decreasing pH until cellular activities are inhibited. If there is reduction or cessation of circulation, the failure of removal of metabolites will inhibit cellular activity more rapidly than if circulation is maintained. It might therefore be expected that total failure of circulation would have the most rapidly damaging effect on cells of the CNS. Because inhibition of cell activity results from local accumulation of metabolic products it might also be expected that the most metabolically active cells would suffer most rapidly. In prolonged partial asphyxia of experimental fetuses, failure of perfusion of the cerebral cortex and white matter develops after a variable period and is associated with irregular neuronal necrosis of the cortex.[49] The damage is of more rapid onset and appears more severe if there is plentiful carbohydrate substrate to allow anaerobic glycolysis with production of excessive lactic acid. The pattern of damage thus appears largely determined by attempts at compensation during asphyxia. In experimental total anoxia resulting from umbilical cord occlusion there is irreversible damage within a few minutes with necrosis of cells of the nuclei of brain stem and thalamus. The necrosis of brain stem and thalamic nuclei has been related to the high metabolic rate of these cells as compared with the lower rate of those of the cortex. Similar patterns of damage can be recognized in human infants.[50]

PATHOLOGICAL ANATOMY OF ANOXIC-ISCHEMIC DAMAGE

If the infant dies a few days after birth, there may be obvious brain swelling due to edema with flattening of the cerebral convolutions and compression of the ventricles.[47] The central parts of the brain, including thalami and basal ganglia and sometimes the periventricular white matter, are often intensely congested (Fig. 12–34). There may be evidence that the brain swelling has caused part of the temporal lobe to be herniated through the tentorial notch into the posterior fossa or that the tonsils of the cerebellum have been herniated through the foramen magnum into the cervical canal. However, often there is no cerebral swelling and merely evidence of intense central congestion.

Histological Changes of Anoxic-Ischemic Damage.[29,47] Histological changes in the early stages include shrinkage of neurons with acidophilic cytoplasm and pyknosis or karyorrhexis of nuclei (Fig. 12–35). Sometimes there is ballooning and vacuolation of the cytoplasm of the degenerating neurons. Those neurons that do not disappear often shrivel up or become encrusted (Fig. 12–36). Neuronal bodies and sometimes processes may become amphophilic or basophilic and may give a positive stain for PAS, calcium or iron. Microglia appear within 2 to 3 days after a hypoxic episode, and hypertrophied astrocytes can be seen within 3 to 5 days (Fig. 12–37). A dense feltwork of fine glial fibers develops within a few weeks. In the immature infant brain the early changes of neuronal damage are difficult to recognize because the neurons are small and have little cytoplasm.

Patterns of Brain Damage. These are most readily recognized in infants who have survived sufficiently long for the extent of the primary lesion to become

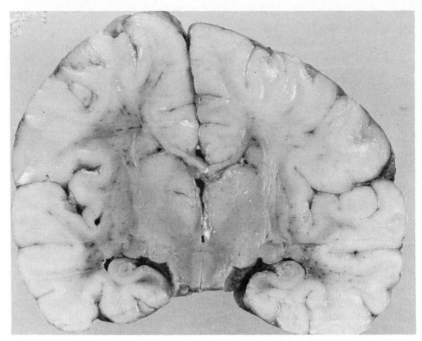

Figure 12–34. Coronal section through a term infant brain showing compression of the ventricles and congestion of basal ganglia and white matter. (From Pape, K. E. and Wigglesworth, J. S.: Haemorrhage, Ischaemia and the Perinatal Brain. London, Spastics International Medical Publications, 1979.)

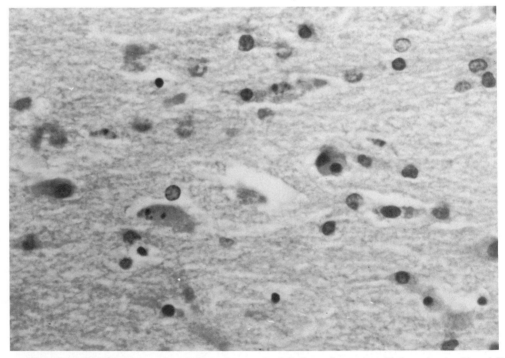

Figure 12–35. Thalamus of an infant who survived 7 days after severe birth asphyxia. H and E × 300. There is extensive loss of neurones. A few remaining neurones show karyorrhexis of the nucleus.

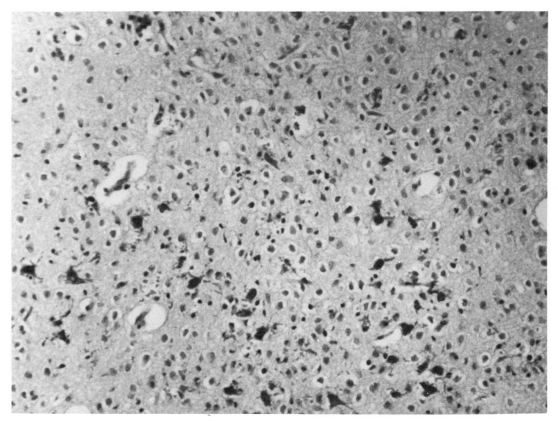

Figure 12–36. Encrusted neurones in the thalamus of an infant who died at 8 weeks of age after severe birth asphyxia. H and E × 120.

established, but in whom secondary lesions, such as those resulting from persistent seizures, have not yet developed. Although the patterns of damage can be subdivided in a number of different ways,[29] I will mention here only two subgroups that should be differentiated from each other.

CORTICAL DAMAGE. This may involve the classic boundary zone between the territories of the different cerebral arteries, the whole of the region supplied by a single artery, or may affect an even wider area.

DEEP GRAY MATTER, INCLUDING NUCLEI OF BASAL GANGLIA, THALAMUS, MIDBRAIN AND BRAIN STEM. Lesions may involve the thalamus or basal ganglia alone, or develop in association with damage to the reticular formation, substantia nigra, red nucleus, periaqueductal gray matter, tegmentum, colliculi, pontine nuclei, inferior olivary nuclei, gracile and cuneate nuclei, and cranial nerve nuclei including dorsal vagal nuclei and auditory nuclei.

In long-term survivors with damage to basal ganglia there is formation of aberrant bundles of myelinated glial fibrils that give the nuclei a marbled appearance—*status marmoratus.*

MECHANISMS UNDERLYING DIFFERENT PATTERNS OF CEREBRAL DAMAGE

The lesions of cortical boundary zones in the newborn, as in the adult, are considered to be caused by the effects of hypotension on cerebral perfusion, as in the periventricular boundary zone lesions typical of the preterm infant. More widespread cortical necrosis is analogous to the changes seen in prolonged partial

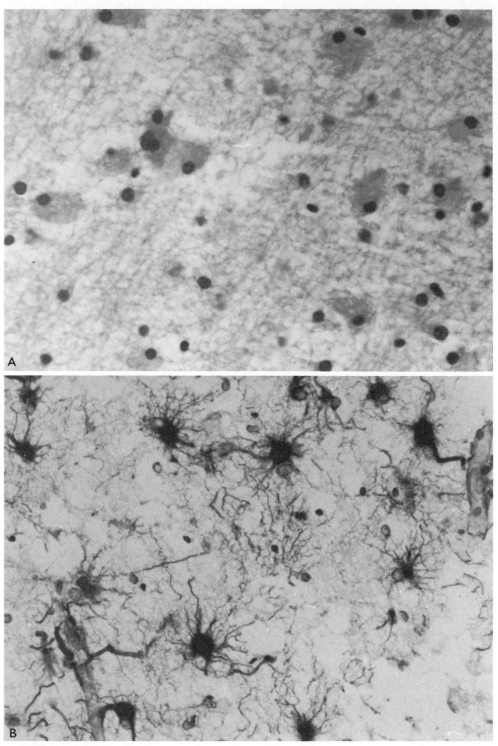

Figure 12–37. Hypertrophied astrocytes in the perivascular white matter of the same brain shown in Figure 12–35. *A*, H and E × 300. *B*, Immunoperoxidase stain for glial fibrillary acidic protein × 300.

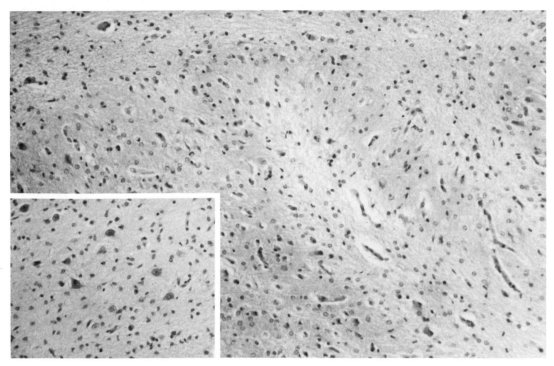

Figure 12–38. Dentate nucleus of infant who had a cardiac arrest during resuscitation from severe birth asphyxia but survived 7 days. H and E × 150. There is almost complete loss of neurones. Inset shows part of normal dentate nucleus at same magnification for comparison.

asphyxia in the experimental fetus, in which it seems related to a widespread reduction in cerebral perfusion. Cerebral edema and brain swelling may well result in obstruction of individual vessels such as the posterior cerebral arteries by compression against the tentorial margin.

The pattern of thalamic and brain stem necrosis is seen particularly in infants who have suffered acute severe anoxic episodes such as a prolapsed umbilical cord or cardiac arrest in the neonatal period (Fig. 12–38).[50] These insults could be expected to cause total failure of cerebral circulation, as does umbilical cord occlusion in the experimental fetus. In general terms it seems that cortical and white matter lesions are likely to be prominent in cases in which prolonged asphyxia occurred before circulatory failure, whereas brain stem and thalamic damage results from total cessation of flow to the metabolically active nuclei in these regions.

As the circulation may fail at any time in an asphyxiated fetus, any variety of lesions can be seen at postmortem examination in individual cases. The variable pattern of lesions is reflected in the clinical symptomatology of surviving infants. Athetoid cerebral palsy may be seen in those with predominant thalamic injury, while those in whom the range of cortical and white matter lesions has developed may be expected to display seizures, spasticity or mental retardation. The difficulties in feeding and swallowing associated with brain stem lesions often lead to early death.

KERNICTERUS

This term refers to bilirubin staining of the deep gray matter nuclei of the brain and brain stem. As such it may, like hyaline membrane disease of the lungs, be regarded as a postmortem diagnosis. The intensity of staining varies from a pale lemon to a bright yellow color. In the classic condition the nuclei affected include the lateral thalamic nucleus, hippocampus, globus pallidus, subthalamic nucleus, geniculate bodies, colliculi, nuclei of brain stem and floor of the fourth ventricle, dentate nucleus, inferior olive, cuneate and gracile nuclei and anterior horn cells of spinal cord. In unstained frozen sections bilirubin is seen as golden-yellow granules within the neurons and glia. Changes of the various stages of neuronal necrosis may be seen on routine paraffin sections. In infants who survive the acute stage but die later, widespread neuronal loss with gliosis and poor myelination in the regions of affected nuclei have been described.[51]

The original description referred to the brain changes seen in relatively mature infants who had died following severe rhesus isoimmunization. The pathological findings were recognized in those cases in which the serum bilirubin level had exceeded 20 to 30 mg/dl. The early clinical signs were hypotonia, lethargy and poor sucking with development of spasticity, while long-term sequelae include deafness and athetosis.[52]

Following the widespread introduction of exchange transfusion for treatment of neonatal hyperbilirubinemia and, more recently, the use of anti D immuno-globulin prophylaxis to prevent rhesus isoimmunization, these cases are now rarely seen. However, kernicterus is seen quite frequently at autopsy in small preterm infants who die in neonatal intensive care units.[53] In this group the serum bilirubin may not have risen above 8 to 9 mg/dl and there are seldom clinical signs attributable to kernicterus in life. The affected infants have all been severely hypoxic and acidotic and often hypoglycemic during life (Fig. 12–39). Low plasma albumin or displacement of bilirubin from albumin by certain drugs may increase the proportion of bilirubin which circulates in a free form, in which it can enter the brain. It is difficult in such cases to decide whether the bilirubin staining seen at autopsy is merely a terminal event in an infant with anoxic-ischemic damage to deep gray matter nuclei, or whether the bilirubin caused, or accentuated, the nuclear damage. Bilirubin depresses cell respiration, uncouples oxidative phos-phorylation in mitochondria and inhibits incorporation of amino acids into proteins. Therefore, it is perhaps reasonable to assume that entry of bilirubin into the nuclei would enhance any preceding anoxic-ischemic damage. It may be difficult in surviving preterm infants to determine whether deafness or athetosis was caused by bilirubin toxicity or anoxic-ischemic damage. Hyperbilirubinemia may also be a hazard of some antibiotics that may be prescribed to ill preterm infants who are at risk of developing kernicterus.

Thus the precise role of kernicterus in causing CNS damage to preterm infants treated by intensive care currently remains in doubt. The recognition of a rising number of such cases among preterm infants submitted to autopsy at a particular center could reasonably be taken as an indication to reconsider methods of clinical management, such as feeding practices and guidelines for use of phototherapy or exchange transfusion.

INFECTIVE LESIONS OF THE BRAIN

INTRAUTERINE INFECTION

Intrauterine infections involving the CNS are those of the TORCH group. The effects of intrauterine infections include microcephaly, cerebral atrophy with ventricular dilatation and microgyria, cystic encephalomalacia and hydrocephaly. The changes characteristic of each of the major infective agents are described in

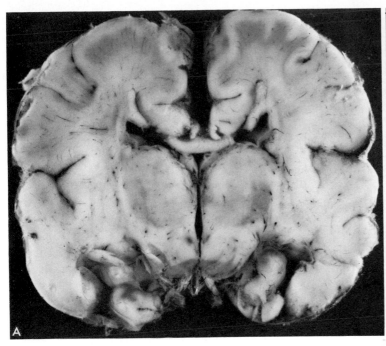
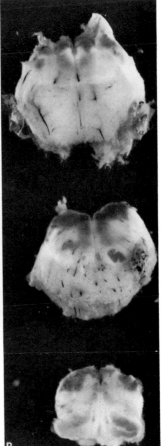

Figure 12–39. Coronal slice of cerebrum *A* and slices through brain stem *B* photographed with blue filter to show mild bilirubin staining of subcortical white matter, thalamus and hippocampus, and marked staining of nuclei in floor of 4th ventricle and olivary nuclei, from an infant of 29 weeks' gestation who died at 4 days of age following severe hypoglycemic episodes. Maximum serum bilirubin 345 iu (20 mg/dl).

Chapter 9. Many of the lesions caused by organisms such as the rubella virus are due to a vasculitis and may therefore sometimes resemble those caused by the anoxic-ischemic or hemorrhagic lesions already discussed. It may often be difficult to determine whether an infant who dies in the perinatal period with partly calcified necrotic cerebral lesions has suffered an intrauterine infection or an episode of severe intrauterine cerebral anoxia. The miliary granulomas over the meninges in cases of listeriosis are quite characteristic and may be recognized at a macroscopic level.

NEONATAL INFECTIONS

The most common form of infection of the CNS seen in the neonatal period is bacterial meningitis.

MENINGITIS

Meningitis may develop during the course of sepsis caused by any of the bacterial pathogens discussed in Chapter 9. The incidence of meningitis in the newborn is about 0.4 per 1000 births in most series.[54, 55] Meningitis and meningoencephalitis are not often seen in infants who die in the first 48 hours after birth but may be well developed by 4 to 5 days. In the early stages of meningitis the meninges over the base of the brain may appear opaque, whereas in established meningitis there is a yellow exudate which may fill the sulci and basal cisterns.

The exudate is often most marked over the inferior surface of the cerebellum (Fig. 12–40). The polymorphonuclear exudate with a fibrin meshwork, characteristic of the acute phase of the infection, gradually gives way to a mononuclear cellular infiltrate in infants who survive for 2 to 3 weeks, and an acute hydrocephalus may develop as a result of occlusion of the foramina of the fourth ventricle by purulent exudate. Hydrocephalus of the communicating variety may be seen at a late stage if CSF, circulation or resorption is impaired by a chronic inflammatory reaction.

Meningitis is commonly accompanied by an ependymitis and the choroid plexus may be enveloped in purulent exudate. Obstruction of the aqueduct by purulent or necrotic material is an additional cause of hydrocephalus.[55]

HEMORRHAGIC MENINGOENCEPHALITIS

Thrombosis of cerebral veins may occur, particularly in infections due to gram-negative organisms, giving rise to a hemorrhagic meningoencephalitis. Hemorrhagic and necrotic features are particularly marked in cases of infection with *P. aeruginosa*, Proteus and *Serratia marcescens*.[56, 57] At autopsy the brain may appear swollen and edematous, with extensive purplish discoloration or frank hemorrhagic necrosis. Histological study shows widespread necrosis with masses of organisms around the vessels and infiltrating the cerebral substance.

OTHER CONDITIONS

Many other conditions can occasionally be recognized in the central nervous system in the perinatal period.

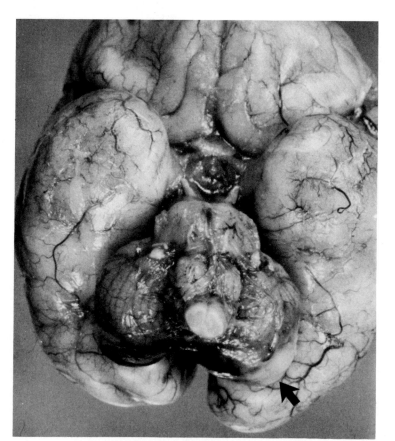

Figure 12–40. Brain of an infant of 28 weeks' gestation who died at 6 days of age with meningitis due to *E. coli*, despite intraventricular antibiotic therapy. Exudate over cerebellum is arrowed.

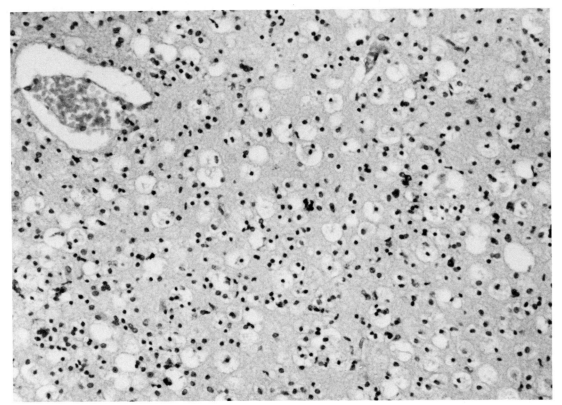

Figure 12–41. Storage cells in periventricular region of cerebrum in an infant with mucopolysaccharidosis VII. H and E × 150.

INBORN LYSOSOMAL ENZYME DEFICIENCIES

These conditions, including lipidoses, mucopolysaccharidoses, mucolipidoses and a variety of other disorders, are usually recognized after the neonatal period. Many of them can now be diagnosed in early pregnancy from culture of fetal cells obtained at amniocentesis. Fetuses obtained by therapeutic abortion may be available for pathological studies. Occasionally they come to the pathologist undiagnosed in the perinatal period. The precise diagnosis in such cases usually requires biochemical studies on fresh tissues or fibroblast cultures (Chapters 3 and 19) but characteristic storage cells may sometimes be seen within the CNS if they are sought (Fig. 12–41).

NEUROMUSCULAR DISORDERS

Infants with disorders such as spinal muscular atrophy may die in the early neonatal period. The combination of muscle wasting, limb distortion and lung hypoplasia may suggest a multiorgan malformation syndrome but may result from a primary neurological abnormality. The CNS should therefore be studied with particular care in any infant who dies with arthrogryposis or muscle wasting.

INFLUENCE OF MEDICAL CARE ON THE DEVELOPING BRAIN

Iatrogenic influences have been suggested as playing a role in production of many of the lesions described in this chapter. These include the possible involvement of alkali therapy in the genesis of subependymal and intraventricular hemorrhage, the cerebral infarction arising as a complication of temporal artery catheterization, mask ventilation causing cerebellar venous infarction and drugs causing deafness or increasing susceptibility of the preterm infant to kernicterus.

However, the gravest concern is that the progressive extension of neonatal intensive care methods to infants of ever lower birth weight and gestational age will lead to an increasing population of neurologically handicapped survivors. The technical ability to maintain life in very small preterm infants is far ahead of the ability to maintain an appropriate cerebral circulation or even to detect severe ischemic cerebral damage in the living newborn infant. Assessment by the pathologist of the extent of cerebral damage in small preterm infants who die following neonatal intensive care should help the neonatologist formulate appropriate policies for the institution or maintenance of intensive care support.

It will be apparent from this, and from the balance of the chapter as a whole, that in my view the pathologist can use his time more profitably in recognition and accurate assessment of the various forms of ischemic cerebral damage than in detailed description of cerebral anomalies for which the genetic basis is well established.

REFERENCES

1. O'Rahilly, R., and Gardner, E.: The developmental anatomy and histology of the human central nervous system. *In* Vinken, P. J., and Bruyn, G. W. (eds.): Handbook of Clinical Neurology, vol. 30. Amsterdam, North Holland Publishing Co., 1977, pp. 15–40.
2. Larroche, J. C.: Development of the central nervous system. *In* Developmental Pathology of the Neonate. Amsterdam, Excerpta Medica, 1977, pp. 319–353.
3. Sidman, R. L., and Rakic, P.: Neuronal migration, with special reference to developing human brain: A review. Brain Res. *62*:1–35, 1973.
4. Dobbing, J., and Sands, J.: Timing of neuroblast multiplication in developing human brain. Nature *226*:639–640, 1970.
5. Pape, K. E., and Wigglesworth, J. S.: Blood supply to the developing brain. *In* Haemorrhage, Ischaemia and the Perinatal Brain. London, Heinemann, Philadelphia, J. B. Lippincott Co., 1979, pp. 11–38.
6. Koppel, H., Lewis, P. D., and Wigglesworth, J. S.: A study of the vascular supply to the external granular layer of the postnatal rat cerebellum. J. Anat. *134*:73–84, 1982.
7. Giroud, A.: Anencephaly. *In* Vinken, P. J. and Bruyn, G. W. (eds.): Handbook of Clinical Neurology, vol. 30. Amsterdam, North Holland Publishing Co., 1977, pp. 173–208.
8. Laurence, K. M.: Antenatal detection of neural tube defects. *In* Barson, A. J. (ed.): Fetal and Neonatal Pathology. Eastbourne, Praeger Scientific, 1982, pp. 75–102.
9. Gardner, W. J.: Dysraphic states. From syringomyelia to anencephaly. Amsterdam, Excerpta Medica, 1973.
10. Emery, J. L., and Kalhan, S. C.: The pathology of exencephalus. Dev. Med. Child. Neurol. *12*, Suppl. *22*:51–64, 1970.
11. Nishimura, H., and Okamoto, N.: Iniencephaly. *In* Vinken, P. J., and Bruyn, G. W. (eds.): Handbook of Clinical Neurology, vol. 30. Amsterdam, North Holland Publishing Co., 1977, pp. 257–268.
12. De Lange, S. A.: Progressive hydrocephalus. *In* Vinken, P. J., and Bruyn, G. W. (eds.): Handbook of Clinical Neurology, vol. 30. Amsterdam, North Holland Publishing Co., 1977, pp. 525–563.
13. Urich, H.: Malformation of the nervous system, perinatal damage and related conditions in early life. *In* Blackwood, W., and Corsellis, A. N. (eds.): Greenfield's Neuropathology. London, Edward Arnold, 1976, pp. 361–469.
14. Brown, J. R.: The Dandy-Walker syndrome. *In* Vinken, P. J., and Bruyn, G. W. (eds.): Handbook of Clinical Neurology, vol. 30. Amsterdam, North Holland Publishing Co., 1977, p. 623–646.
15. Demyer, W.: Holoprosencephaly (cyclopia-arhinencephaly). *In* Vinken, P. J., and Bruyn, G. W. (eds.): Handbook of Clinical Neurology, vol. 30. Amsterdam, North Holland Publishing Co., 1977, pp. 431–478.
16. Larroche, J. C.: Cytoarchitectonic abnormalities. *In* Vinken, P. J., and Bruyn, G. W. (eds.): Handbook of Clinical Neurology, vol. 30. Amsterdam, North Holland Publishing Co., 1977, pp. 479–506.
17. Emery, J. L., and Lendon, R. G.: The local cord lesion in neurospinal dysraphism (meningomyelocele). J. Pathol. *110*:83–96, 1973.

18. Variend, S., and Emery, J. L.: The pathology of the central lobes of the cerebellum in children with myelomeningocele. Dev. Med. Child. Neurol. *16*: Suppl. 32, 99–106, 1974.

19. Norman, M. G., and Becker, L. E.: Cerebral damage in neonates resulting from arteriovenous malformation of the vein of Galen. J. Neurol. Neurosurg. Psychiatr. *37*:252–258, 1974.

20. Haller, E. S., Nesbitt, R. E. L., and Anderson, G. W.: Clinical and pathologic concepts of gross intracranial hemorrhage in perinatal mortality. Obstet. Gynecol. Surv. *11*:179–204, 1956.

21. Morison, J. E.: Foetal and Neonatal Pathology, 3rd ed. London, Butterworths, 1970.

22. Courville, C. B.: Birth and Brain Damage. Pasadena, Courville, M. F., 1971.

23. Larroche, J. C.: Lesions of haemorrhagic type; mainly venous. *In* Developmental Pathology of the Neonate. Amsterdam, Excerpta Medica, 1977, pp. 355–398.

24. Friede, R. L.: Subpial hemorrhage in infants. J. Neuropathol. Ext. Neurol. *23*:548–556, 1972.

25. Chessells, J. M., and Wigglesworth, J. S.: Secondary haemorrhagic disease of the newborn. Arch. Dis. Child. *45*:539–543, 1970.

26. Friede, R. L.: Developmental Neuropathology. Vienna, Springer-Verlag, 1975.

27. Myers, R. E.: Two patterns of perinatal brain damage and their conditions of occurrence. Am. J. Obstet. Gynecol. *122*:246–276, 1972.

28. Armstrong, D., and Norman, M. G.: Periventricular leukomalacia in neonates. Complications and sequelae. Arch. Dis. Child. *49*:367–375, 1974.

29. Norman, M. G.: Perinatal brain damage. *In* Rosenberg, H. S., and Bolande, R. P. (eds.): Perspectives in Pediatric Pathology, vol. 4. Chicago, Year Book Medical Publishers, 1978, pp. 41–92.

30. Simmons, M. A., Levine, R. L., Lubchenco, L. O., and Guggenheim, M. A.: Warning: Serious sequelae of temporal artery catheterization. J. Pediatr. *92*:284, 1978.

31. Leech, R. W., and Kohnen, P.: Subependymal and intraventricular hemorrhages in the newborn. Am. J. Pathol. *77*:465–475, 1974.

32. Pape, K. E., Armstrong, D. L., and Fitzhardinge, P. M.: Central nervous system pathology associated with mask ventilation in the very low birth weight infant: A new etiology for intracerebellar hemorrhages. Pediatrics *58*:473–483, 1976.

33. Pape, K. E., and Wigglesworth, J. S.: Specific haemorrhagic lesions of the newborn brain. *In* Haemorrhage, Ischaemia and the Perinatal Brain. London, Heinemann, Philadelphia, J. B. Lippincott Co., 1979, pp. 85–99.

34. Papile, L. A., Burstein, J., Burstein, R., and Koffler, H.: Incidence and evolution of subependymal and intraventricular hemorrhage: A study of infants with birth weights less than 1,500 g. J. Pediatr. *92*:529–534, 1978.

35. Levene, M. I., Wigglesworth, J. S., and Dubowitz, V.: Cerebral structure and intraventricular hemorrhage in the neonate: A real-time ultrasound study. Arch. Dis. Child. *56*:416–424, 1981.

36. Hambleton, G., and Wigglesworth, J. S.: Origin of intraventricular hemorrhage in the preterm infant. Arch. Dis. Child. *51*:651–659, 1976.

37. Pape, K. E., and Wigglesworth, J. S.: Pathological anatomy of intraventricular haemorrhage. *In* Haemorrhage, Ischaemia, and the Perinatal Brain. London, Heinemann, Philadelphia, J. B. Lippincott Co., 1979, pp. 118–132.

38. Larroche, J. C.: Post-haemorrhagic hydrocephalus in infancy: Anatomical study. Biol. Neonat. *20*:287–299, 1972.

39. Deonna, T., Payot, M., Probst, A., and Prod'hom, L. S.: Neonatal intracranial hemorrhage in premature infants. Pediatrics *56*:1056–1064, 1975.

40. Levene, M. I., Fawer, C. L., and Lamont, R. F.: Risk factors in the development of intraventricular hemorrhage in the preterm neonate. Arch. Dis. Child. *57*:410–417, 1982.

41. Volpe, J. J.: Neurology of the Newborn. Philadelphia, W. B. Saunders Co., 1981, p. 270.

42. Pape, K. E., and Wigglesworth, J. S.: The clinico-pathological relationship and aetiological aspects of intraventricular haemorrhage. Haemorrhage, Ischaemia and the Perinatal Brain. London, Heinemann, Philadelphia, J. B. Lippincott Co., 1979, pp. 133–148.

43. Cooke, R. W. I., Rolfe, P., and Howat, P.: Apparent cerebral blood-flow in newborns with respiratory disease. Dev. Med. Child. Neurol. *21*:154–160, 1979.

44. Goddard, J., Lewis, R. M., Armstrong, D. L., and Zeller, R. S.: Moderate, rapidly induced hypertension as a cause of intraventricular hemorrhage in the newborn beagle model. J. Pediatr. *96*:1057–1060, 1980.

45. Lou, H. C., Lassen, N. A., and Friis-Hansen, B.: Impaired autoregulation of cerebral blood flow in the distressed newborn infant. J. Pediatr. *94*:118–121, 1979.

46. Wigglesworth, J. S., and Pape, K. E.: An integrated model for haemorrhagic and ischaemic lesions in the newborn brain. Early Hum. Develop. *2*:179–199, 1978.

47. Larroche, J. C.: Lesions of ischaemic type, mainly arterial. *In* Developmental Pathology of the Neonate. Amsterdam, Excerpta Medica, 1977, pp. 399–445.

48. Takashima, S., and Tanaka, K.: Development of cerebrovascular architecture and its relationship to periventricular leukomalacia. Arch. Neurol. *35*:11–16, 1978.

49. Myers, R. E.: Experimental models of perinatal brain damage: Relevance to human pathology. *In* Gluck, L. (ed.): Intrauterine Asphyxia and the Developing Fetal Brain. Chicago, Year Book Medical Publishers, 1977, pp. 37–97.

50. Leech, R. W., and Alvord, E. C.: Anoxic-ischemic encephalopathy in the human neonatal period: The significance of brain stem involvement. Arch. Neurol. *34*:109–113, 1977.

51. Norman, R. M.: Malformations of the nervous system, birth injury and diseases of early life. *In* Blackwood, W., McMenemey, W. H., Meyer, A., Norman, R. M., and Russell, D. S. (eds.): Greenfield's Neuropathology, 2nd ed. London, Edward Arnold, 1963, pp. 324–440.
52. Van Praagh, R.: Diagnosis of kernicterus in the neonatal period. Pediatrics *28*:870–876, 1961.
53. Gartner, L. M., Snyder, R. N., Chabon, R. S., and Bernstein, J.: Kernicterus: High incidence in premature infants with low serum bilirubin concentrations. Pediatrics *45*:906–917, 1970.
54. Klein, J. O., and Marcy, S. M.: Bacterial infections. *In* Remington, J. S., and Klein, J. O. (eds.): Infectious Diseases of the Fetus and Newborn Infant. Philadelphia, W. B. Saunders Co., 1976, pp. 747–891.
55. Larroche, J. C.: Bacterial meningo-encephalitis. *In* Developmental Pathology of the Neonate. Amsterdam, Excerpta Medica, 1977, pp. 455–463.
56. Ragazzini, F., La Cauza, C., and Ferrucci, I.: Infection by serratia marcescens in premature children. Ann. Pediatr. *205*:289–300, 1965.
57. Cussen, L. J., and Ryan, G. B.: Hemorrhagic cerebral necrosis in neonatal infants with enterobacterial meningitis. J. Pediatr. *71*:771–776, 1967.
58. De Reuck, J., Chattha, A. S., and Richardson, E. P., Jr.: Pathogenesis and evolution of periventricular leukomalacia in infancy. Arch. Neurol. *27*:229–236, 1972.

Chapter Thirteen

The Alimentary Tract

The alimentary tract is an important site of congenital anomalies that may produce symptoms soon after birth. In addition, it is subject to a number of characteristic ischemic, metabolic and infective conditions in the perinatal period.

DEVELOPMENT OF THE INTESTINAL TRACT

The foregut and hindgut form as invaginations of the yolk sac in association with development of the head and tail folds of the embryo about the twentieth day of development. The communication of the midgut with the extraembryonic portion of the yolk sac via the body stalk gradually reduces as the primitive endodermal tube increases in length. The stomach appears initially as a dilation of the tube during the fourth week. The cranial part of the foregut gives rise to the endodermal part of the mouth and much of the pharynx. The outgrowth of the ventral part of the foregut that is due to develop into the respiratory tract (Chapter 10) appears also during the fourth week.

During the fifth week the rapidly growing midgut herniates out into the body stalk as a loop that has at its apex the attachment of the yolk sac (vitellointestinal duct). In the subsequent 4 to 5 weeks the herniated loop rotates counterclockwise through 180 degrees before returning into the abdomen (Fig. 13–1). The proximal limb of the loop forms the duodenum, jejunum and upper ileum, while the distal limb forms the terminal ileum, ascending colon and part of the transverse colon. The hindgut gives rise to the descending colon and rectum. In the early stages of development the hindgut communicates with the allantois above the cloacal membrane. During the seventh week, these structures become separated by downgrowth of the urorectal septum into the ventral urogenital sinus and the dorsal rectum (Fig. 13–2). The latter remains closed by the anal membrane until the twelfth week.

MALFORMATIONS OF THE INTESTINAL TRACT

ESOPHAGEAL ATRESIA

This anomaly occurs with a frequency of 1:1 to 2000 births; a number of forms are described (Fig. 13–3).[1] In the common type of this anomaly the upper part of the esophagus forms a dilated, rather thick-walled blind pouch, while the lower part is relatively narrow and has a fistulous communication with the dorsal

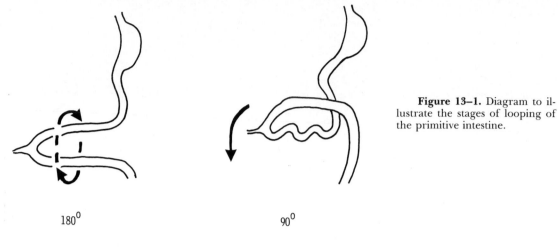

Figure 13–1. Diagram to illustrate the stages of looping of the primitive intestine.

180°   90°

aspect of the trachea just above the bifurcation. At least 80 per cent of instances of esophageal atresia are of this type.[2, 3] The second most frequent type (7 to 8 per cent of cases) is that in which no fistula is present. Other variations are very rare. The anomaly is believed to result from failure of the tracheal groove on the ventral aspect of the foregut (fourth postconceptional week) to separate fully from the esophagus.

The condition is commonly associated with polyhydramnios, as indeed are other disorders in which the fetus is unable to swallow amniotic fluid (anomalies or intrauterine damage involving the brain stem, congenital muscular dystrophy and so forth). The volume of amniotic fluid may be rather finely balanced in relation to fetal functions that tend to increase or decrease it.

Esophageal atresia is frequently associated with other anomalies (Table 13–1), particularly those involving the anorectal region. The name VATER association has been applied to one group of anomalies comprising *V*ertebral anomalies, *A*nal atresia, *T*racheo-*E*sophageal fistula and *R*enal anomalies.[4]

INTESTINAL ATRESIAS AND REDUPLICATIONS

Atresia of the small intestine may involve duodenum, jejunum or ileum. Atresia of the large intestine is rare. A common site for intestinal atresia is the junction of the second and third parts of the duodenum (Fig. 13–4). About 20 to 30 per cent of cases of duodenal atresia are associated with Down's syndrome.

Three types of atresia may be recognized:

1. A diaphragm is formed across the gut.
2. An interruption in gut continuity with an intervening fibrous cord.
3. A missing segment of gut with no fibrous cord but a defect in the mesentery at the site of atresia.

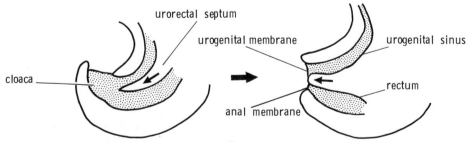

Figure 13–2. Diagram to show development of rectum from primitive cloaca.

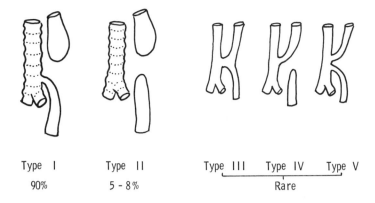

Figure 13–3. Different types of esophageal atresia and tracheo-esophageal fistula.

Type I Type II Type III Type IV Type V

90% 5 - 8% Rare

Intestinal atresias are often multiple and may be of mixed types. The traditional explanation for intestinal atresia has been on the basis of the classic embryological concept that there is a period during embryogenesis when the intestinal lumen becomes occluded by epithelial cells. Intestinal atresia was thought to result from failure of recanalization of a part of the intestine (see discussion in Morison[1]). Recognition that a phase of intestinal occlusion may occur only in the duodenum has cast doubt on this concept. It also has been pointed out by Santulli and Blanc[5] that meconium and amniotic squames may be found in the bowel distal to the site of congenital atresia, indicating occlusion later than the postulated recanalization stage. Studies involving experimental intrauterine surgery have suggested that intestinal atresias may result from vascular impairment during development of the gut.[6]

Enteric reduplications arise dorsal to the intestine within the small gut mesentery or in the thorax (Fig. 13–5). The reduplicated segments of bowel have well-developed muscle layers; the lining epithelium is often partly of gastric type. These reduplications are believed to be derived from endodermal cells of the foregut that become displaced posteriorly and adherent to the notochord. Enteric cysts may rarely be found within the vertebral canal; they communicate through

TABLE 13–1. ANOMALIES ASSOCIATED WITH ESOPHAGEAL ATRESIA IN INFANTS WHO DIED IN THE NEONATAL PERIOD

SYSTEM INVOLVED	NUMBER	ANOMALIES PRESENT (No.)
None	2	
Cardiovascular system	9	VSD (4)
		ASD
		Truncus arteriosus
		Pulmonary atresia with transposition
		Coarctation (preductal)
		Hypoplastic left heart
Renal tract	4	Cystic dysplasia (3)
		Absent kidney
Gastrointestinal tract	3	Imperforate anus (2)
		Duodenal atresia
		Absent gallbladder
Skeletal system	2	Absent digits
		Talipes
Respiratory system	2	Pulmonary hypoplasia
		Bronchopulmonary-foregut malformation
Others	3	Ocular hypoplasia
		Unilateral cerebellar hypoplasia
		Hypospadias

Hammersmith Hospital. Total number of infants: 14.

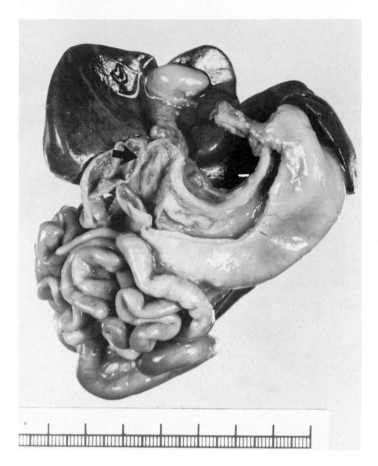

Figure 13–4. Duodenal atresia in a newborn infant with multiple anomalies. The stomach and upper duodenum are thick-walled and dilated. The site of atresia is arrowed.

an anterior spina bifida with the small intestine. The subject of intestinal atresias and reduplications is dealt with at length by Berry and Keeling.[7]

MALROTATION

Malrotation may be complete or incomplete. Incomplete rotation associated with an unfixed mesentery predisposes to volvulus (see later discussion).

MECKEL'S DIVERTICULUM

The Meckel's diverticulum represents persistence of a portion of the vitellointestinal duct and is usually without significance. Rarely there may be a fibrous cord attaching the diverticulum to the umbilicus which predisposes to development of volvulus. A persistent patent vitellointestinal duct is uncommon. See Berry and Keeling[7] for references.

IMPERFORATE ANUS

The imperforate anus in its simplest form represents persistence of the anal membrane. A partial persistence of the anal membrane is associated with anal stenosis. Instances in which there is a high defect are frequently associated with more extensive anomalies of the urogenital sinus region or other internal anomalies (e.g., VATER association).[7, 8]

THE BUCCAL CAVITY

A number of abnormalities of the oropharynx and tongue are described and illustrated in texts such as Potter and Craig[9] and Berry.[7] Apart from the gross

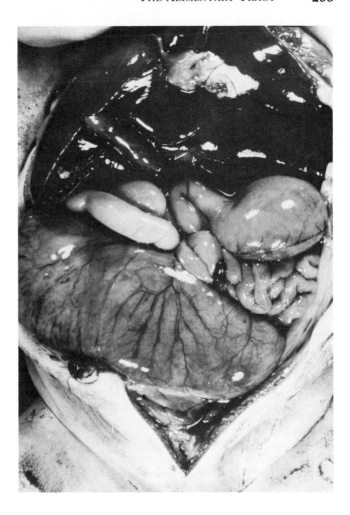

Figure 13–5. A reduplication of the small intestine at autopsy in a newborn infant with multiple anomalies. A separate enteric cyst was associated with an anterior spina bifida in this case.

maxillofacial anomalies associated with conditions such as holoprosencephaly (see Chapter 10), the most likely feature of the buccal cavity for the pathologist to note in the perinatal period is marked variation in size of the tongue.

MACROGLOSSIA

Macroglossia is a feature of the Beckwith-Weidemann syndrome (Chapter 7) and may be noted also in Down syndrome, glycogen storage disease type 2 and lymphangiectasis.

MICROGLOSSIA

Failure of normal tongue development in the form of microglossia may be seen in association with undergrowth of the mandible as part of a first arch syndrome (Fig. 13–6) (see also p. 387). It may also be a sign of a congenital neuromuscular disorder.

STOMACH

MUCOSAL EROSIONS

Mucosal erosions are a frequent finding at autopsy in the perinatal period and are probably related to ischemia as discussed later in connection with necrotizing enterocolitis.

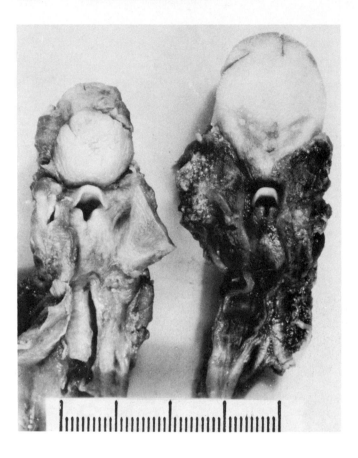

Figure 13–6. Microglossia occurring as part of a first arch syndrome is seen on the left as compared with a normal tongue and larynx on the right.

GASTRIC PERFORATION

In autopsies on infants from neonatal intensive care units the most frequent cause of gastric perforation is pressure from the tip of a plastic feeding tube. The condition can also occur as a result of overdistension of the stomach with gas during resuscitation procedures. Spontaneous perforation of the stomach in association with deficiencies in the muscle layers has been described by a number of authors.[10]

HYPERTROPHIC PYLORIC STENOSIS

The condition of hypertrophic pyloric stenosis involves hypertrophy of the circular muscle fibers of the pylorus with secondary thickening and dilation of the stomach. It characteristically affects first-born male infants and symptoms become apparent within the first two weeks of life. It will seldom be recognized at perinatal autopsy but is illustrated by Berry and Keeling.[7]

INTESTINE

MECONIUM ILEUS

This disorder is commonly associated with cystic fibrosis of the pancreas (Chapter 15) but also has been described in infants with a normal pancreas.[11] The inspissated meconium resulting from abnormal pancreatic secretion causes high intestinal obstruction. The characteristic features at surgery or autopsy include a relatively normal jejunum, dilated coils of ileum and a collapsed empty colon.

The meconium within the ileum is gray and sticky, with hard pellets of mucus obstructing the distal portion. Histological features include distension of mucosal glands with inspissated secretions and distortion of the villi by the impacted meconium (Fig. 13–7).

MECONIUM PERITONITIS

Meconium peritonitis is a sterile peritonitis resulting from leakage of meconium into the peritoneal cavity following bowel rupture in utero. The most frequent cause is meconium ileus associated with fibrocystic disease of the pancreas, but similar changes develop following intrauterine bowel rupture of any other etiology. Calcification is usually apparent radiologically and may allow the diagnosis to be made in utero. Adhesions are often well developed. A foreign body reaction may be recognizable histologically.

INTESTINAL INFARCTION AND NECROTIZING ENTEROCOLITIS

Intestinal infarction in the perinatal period can result from the classic forms of mechanical obstruction such as volvulus, strangulation in a hernia, and intussusception. Progressive obstruction of the local blood vessels is caused in these conditions by twisting or compression against the neck of a hernial orifice. Volvulus can occur in utero[12] and is most likely to occur in fetuses with incomplete gut rotation and an abnormal mesentery. The bowel may become infarcted following incarceration in an external or internal hernia or an omphalocele, but obstruction is uncommon in the usual form of congenital diaphragmatic hernia. The possibility of development of one of these surgical emergencies in the neonatal period is stressed at this point because signs of intestinal obstruction developing in the

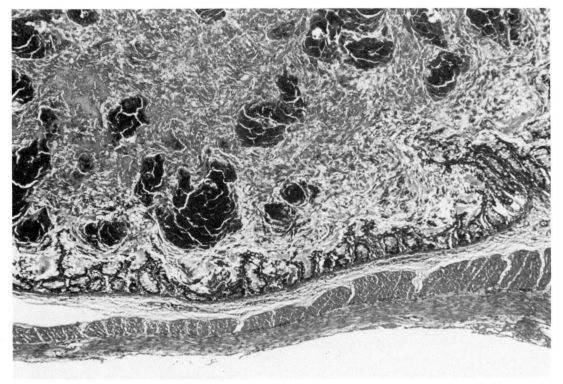

Figure 13–7. Ileum in meconium ileus showing distortion of villi by the inspissated secretions and impacted meconium. × 30.

newborn infant may be incorrectly attributed to necrotizing enterocolitis with resultant delay in surgical consultation and exploration.

A variety of patterns of ischemia and inflammatory bowel disease have been recognized since modern, relatively invasive methods of neonatal care were first introduced in the early 1960's. Perforation of the colon was described as a sequel to exchange transfusion for rhesus incompatibility or placement of indwelling umbilical venous catheters. Infarction of the small intestine from superior mesenteric artery thrombosis is an occasional complication of the use of indwelling umbilical arterial catheters. A number of other conditions have been described in which there may be localized bowel injury or perforation in the perinatal period. These include the ischemic necrosis occasionally seen in Hirschsprung's disease (see later discussion), bowel infarction caused by spontaneous perinatal aortic thrombosis,[13] bowel infarction due to obstruction of small vessels in homocystinuria, and perforation of the bowel (usually lower ileum) following obstruction by a milk plug.[14] Meconium peritonitis caused by intrauterine bowel rupture is most likely to develop on an ischemic basis.[12]

Necrotizing enterocolitis now is seen characteristically as a condition arising in infants of very low birth weight and is not confined to those in whom arterial or venous catheters have been inserted. The terminal ileum is the most frequent site of involvement, but the colon is often affected and multiple lesions are common.[12]

Signs of the condition develop usually at several days of age in the form of ileus and abdominal distension, often preceded by passage of blood in the stools. In fatal cases this may be associated with circulatory collapse. Abdominal radiographs may show evidence of gas within the intestinal wall. Up to 27 per cent of infants below 1200 g weight have been reported to develop this condition. The incidence varies from one intensive care unit to another.[15] In part this difference may be related to variation in the strictness of criteria used for clinical diagnosis in different units but may also reflect genuine differences in incidence, as evidenced by the frequency of the lesion at autopsy.

The pathological findings are variable and probably reflect the size and rate of progression of lesions, different underlying pathogenetic factors and the stage of development at which the infant may die or come to surgery. In rare cases when an infant dies from a cause other than necrotizing enterocolitis at an early stage in the development of necrotizing enterocolitis, the bowel may be distended and congested with gas bubbles clearly visible beneath the serosa along the mesenteric border (Fig. 13–8). A more frequent appearance is of a segment of distended, intensely congested bowel with no recognizable gas bubbles. Grossly, the bowel wall may be frankly gangrenous with dulling of the normal glistening sheen of the peritoneum,[12] and a perforation may be present. The necrotic areas vary considerably in size and may involve several centimeters of intestine at any one site. The lesions are asymmetric, showing accentuation of necrotic changes on the antimesenteric border, and if multiple, they often vary in severity from one site to another (Fig. 13–9). A thinned-out gray necrotic central area may protrude above the adjacent congested bowel, resembling the center of a pointing abscess. If signs of necrotizing enterocolitis have been present for several days before death, the affected segments of bowel appear thick-walled and there is often a localized or generalized fibrinous peritonitis associated with perforation. Healing lesions are characterized by fibrous adhesions or local areas of bowel thickening or stenosis.

The earliest histological evidence of bowel ischemia is mucosal congestion with hemorrhage into the lamina propria. The established lesions show hemor-

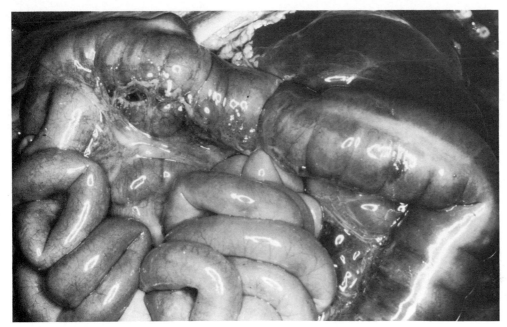

Figure 13–8. Very early necrotizing enterocolitis with subserosal gas bubbles along the mesenteric border of the colon.

rhagic infarction of mucosa and submucosa, which may extend to involve the muscle layers and serosa. Gas bubbles often can be seen within the submucosa, and bacterial colonies are sometimes a prominent feature. In some cases there is marked hemorrhagic edema of submucosa and muscularis with an associated inflammatory reaction throughout the bowel wall (Figs. 13–10 and 13–11).

The spectrum of appearances probably is related to the severity of the initiating episode of bowel ischemia and rapidity with which the lesions develop.

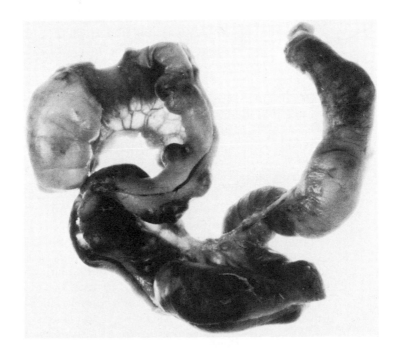

Figure 13–9. Resected segment of bowel showing asymmetric pattern of lesions of necrotizing enterocolitis.

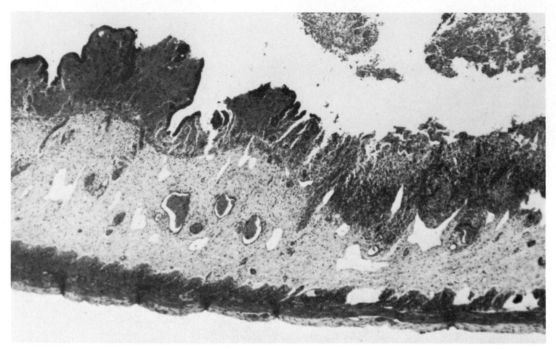

Figure 13–10. Section from the segment of bowel illustrated in Figure 13–9 showing hemorrhagic infarction of mucosa and lamina propria. H and E × 30.

Severe and extensive bowel ischemia will lead to a rapidly progressive hemorrhagic infarction with little time for development of an inflammatory response. A more localized bowel ischemia may result in a slowly developing lesion in which there is time for an inflammatory response to become apparent.

The condition is not entirely confined to infants of very low birth weight under intensive care. It is occasionally seen in full-term infants. Epidemics of necrotizing enterocolitis in newborn nurseries have been reported in association with infection by Salmonella sp.[16] or *Clostridium butyricum.*[17] The condition has also been described in infants subjected to angiocardiography for investigation of congenital heart disease.[18] In this group of infants necrotizing enterocolitis was associated with the use of hypertonic contrast media.

Three factors have been suggested as being important in the pathogenesis of necrotizing enterocolitis: (1) bowel ischemia, (2) infections of the bowel wall, and (3) mucosal damage. Bowel ischemia is probably the primary factor in most instances. In conditions of acute perinatal asphyxia it is probable that a severe reduction of the splanchnic circulation serves as a mechanism for conserving blood flow to the heart, lungs, brain and (before birth) the placenta,[19] as has been shown for hypoxic animals in utero.[20] The cardiorespiratory problems of the very low birth weight infant or the infant with congenital heart disease would be expected to predispose to such a splanchnic ischemia, while thromboembolic complications of umbilical vessel catheterization or disseminated intravascular coagulation might enhance the effect. As supporting evidence for the occurrence of generalized splanchnic ischemia in these cases, De Sa has reported a high frequency of ischemic lesions in other splanchnic organs, including adrenals, kidneys and liver, of infants found to have bowel ischemia at necropsy.

The occurrence of necrotizing enterocolitis in epidemic form in association with gut colonization by specific bacterial strains indicates some role for bacterial infection in the pathogenesis of the condition. De Sa argues strongly that bacterial invasion is a secondary event consequent upon prior ischemic damage to integrity

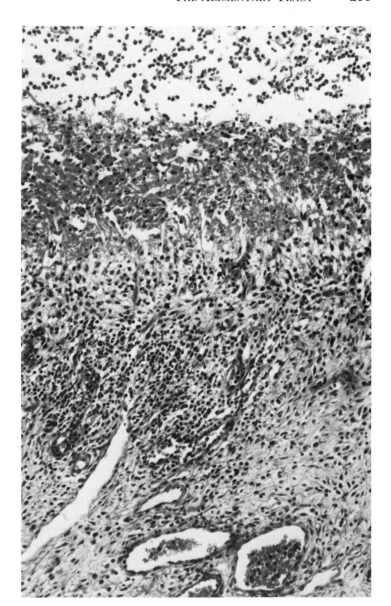

Figure 13–11. Section of a different area of the same case showing superficial necrosis associated with an inflammatory reaction in the submucosa. H and E × 120.

of the bowel wall. It is possible that subclinical episodes of perinatal bowel ischemia are common in relatively mature infants but cause little harm unless there is heavy gut colonization with an appropriate bacterial strain. It has been suggested that some forms of infant feeding may predispose to necrotizing enterocolitis by providing a medium which supports heavy bacterial growth.[21]

Mucosal damage may be an essential prerequisite for bacterial invasion. Such damage probably occurs in most instances as a result of ischemia. However, a dramatic increase in the frequency of necrotizing enterocolitis in infants of very low birth weight fed a hyperosmolar artificial formula prompted the suggestion that hypertonic feedings might impair mucosal integrity and allow subsequent bacterial invasion.[15]

HIRSCHSPRUNG'S DISEASE

Hirschsprung's disease is caused by a failure of the normal migration of neuroblasts derived from the neural crest down the gut to form the myenteric plexus during the fifth to twelfth weeks of gestation. The submucosal plexus, which is derived by secondary migration of cells from the myenteric plexus (third to fourth month), is also abnormal. This condition occurs in about 1 in 2000 live births and is strongly associated with Down's syndrome.[22] Hirschsprung's disease characteristically presents in the neonatal period with signs of intestinal obstruction. In 80 to 90 per cent of cases involvement does not extend more proximally than the sigmoid colon (short-segment disease). In 10 to 20 per cent, aganglionosis does extend proximal to the sigmoid colon and may rarely involve the entire colon or extend into the small intestine. Occasional cases of ultrashort-segment disease are recognized in which aganglionosis involves merely the distal rectum and anus. Diagnosis in such cases is often delayed beyond the neonatal period. The classic pathological appearance in the short-segment disease is of a dilated and hypertrophied proximal segment of colon, an intermediate conical zone and a narrowed distal segment. Total lack of ganglion cells from the myenteric and deep and superficial submucosal plexuses is found within the distal segment. Large longitudinally oriented nerve trunks can be seen in the myenteric and deep mucosal plexuses (Fig. 13–12). Between normal and aganglionic segments there is usually a short zone containing few ganglion cells. However, this does not correspond to the cone seen macroscopically.

This condition represents an important diagnostic problem to the surgical pathologist. The diagnostic techniques and difficulties have been well reviewed and discussed by Weinberg,[23] so only a brief outline is given here. Currently the diagnosis is generally made on the basis of clinical signs combined with radiology, rectal manometry and the histological and histochemical appearance in rectal biopsies.

Rectal Biopsy. This should be taken 2 to 3 cm above the anal valves (mucocutaneous junction or pectinate line) because there is an intervening hypoganglionic region in normal children. A full-thickness longitudinal biopsy should readily allow diagnosis on the basis of absence of ganglion cells on serial sections.

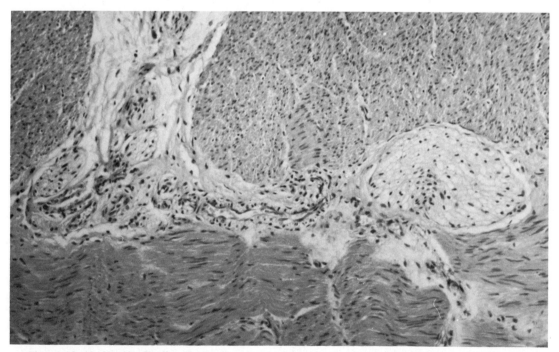

Figure 13–12. Longitudinally orientated nerve trunks in the myenteric plexus of the rectum in a case of Hirschsprung's disease. H and E × 150.

Suction mucosal biopsy has largely replaced full-thickness or submucosal biopsy for diagnosis in many centers following the work of Aldridge and Campbell[24] and Campbell and Noblett.[25] Because these workers showed that the distance between groups of ganglion cells in the submucosal plexus never exceeded 1 mm, it was possible to confirm a diagnosis of aganglionosis by evaluating serially sectioned 2-mm biopsies of submucosa.

The use of acetylcholinesterase techniques shows up the abnormal nerve trunks in the myenteric and submucosal plexuses and reveals many additional nerve fibers extending into the lamina propria (Fig. 13–13). This procedure has formed the basis of histochemical methods for diagnosis of Hirschsprung's disease. In many centers acetylcholinesterase histochemistry is now used as the standard method of diagnosis; it requires examination of fewer sections than routine hematoxylin- and eosin-stained sections but is claimed to have equal diagnostic reliability.[26, 27] Some pediatric pathologists still consider that histochemical findings should be confirmed by full-thickness biopsy demonstrating aganglionosis at operation before bowel resection is undertaken.[7] As pointed out by Weinberg,[23] the main difficulty with any of the rectal biopsy techniques lies not in confirmation of the diagnosis in the typical case but in failing to establish the diagnosis in the face of atypical disease such as ultrashort-segment disease or hypoganglionosis.

Complications. The main serious complication of Hirschsprung's disease is a form of enterocolitis with infarction of areas of mucosa in the ileum and colon. The lesion is apparently related to delay in institution of treatment and is of obscure pathogenesis, although an allergic vasculitis has been suggested as a

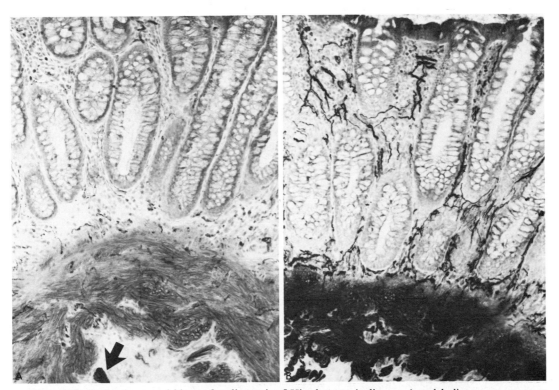

Figure 13–13. Suction rectal biopsy for diagnosis of Hirschsprung's disease. Acetylcholinesterase preparations in cryostat sections of snap frozen tissue. *A*, Normal biopsy. A few fine nerve fibers are present in the lamina propria and muscularis mucosae. Ganglion cells (arrowed) are present in the submucosa. *B*, Hirschsprung's disease. A marked increase in thickened nerve fibers is present in the muscularis mucosae and in the lamina propria. Nerve fibers and nerve trunks are also present in the submucosa. Magnification × 130. (Courtesy of Dr. B. D. Lake, The Children's Hospital, Great Ormond Street, London.)

possible cause.[28] Perforation due to stercoral ulceration or surgical manipulation constitutes the second major complication. These complications are seldom encountered in the neonatal period and are rare with modern diagnostic and treatment facilities.

NEONATAL SMALL LEFT COLON SYNDROME

In infants having neonatal small left colon syndrome, failure to pass meconium, abdominal distension and vomiting are noted within 2 to 3 days after birth. Radiographs of the abdomen show dilated loops of small intestine, right colon and transverse colon with an abrupt transition at the splenic flexure to a left-sided microcolon. Normal bowel activity follows the diagnostic barium enema, so it is important not to confuse this entity with Hirschsprung's disease. Small left colon syndrome is seen in a high proportion of infants of diabetic mothers. There is morphological evidence that the colonic myenteric plexuses are immature in this condition. It has been suggested that a neurohumoral imbalance may be involved in its etiology. See discussion in Haust.[29]

REFERENCES

1. Morison, J. E.: Foetal and Neonatal Pathology, 3rd ed. London, Butterworths, 1970, pp. 341–343.
2. Holder, T. M., Cloud, D. T., Lewis, J. E., and Pilling, G. P.: Esophageal atresia and tracheoesophageal fistula. Pediatrics *34*:542–549, 1964.
3. Holder, T. M., and Ashcraft, K. W.: Esophageal atresia and tracheoesophageal fistula. Ann. Thorac. Surg. *9*:445–467, 1970.
4. Smith, D. W.: Recognizable Patterns of Human Malformation, 3rd ed. Philadelphia, W. B. Saunders Co., 1982.
5. Santulli, T. V., and Blanc, W. A.: Congenital atresia of the intestine: Pathogenesis and treatment. Ann. Surg. *154*:939–948, 1961.
6. Louw, J. H., and Barnard, C. N.: Congenital intestinal atresia: Observations on its origin. Lancet *II*:1065–1067, 1955.
7. Berry, C. J., and Keeling, J. W.: Gastrointestinal system. *In* Berry, C. J. (ed.): Paediatric Pathology. Berlin, Springer Verlag, 1981, pp. 209–265.
8. Bill, A. H., and Johnson, R. J.: Failure of migration of the rectal opening as a cause for most cases of imperforate anus. Surg. Gynecol. Obstet. *106*:643–651, 1958.
9. Potter, E. L., and Craig, J. M.: Pathology of the Fetus and the Infant. Chicago, Year Book Medical Publishers, 1976, pp. 355–360.
10. Purcell, W. R.: Perforation of the stomach in a newborn infant. Am. J. Dis. Child. *103*:66–71, 1962.
11. Oppenheimer, E. H., and Esterly, J. R.: Pathology of cystic fibrosis: Review of the literature and comparison with 146 autopsied cases. *In* Rosenberg, H. S., and Bolande, R. P. (eds.): Perspectives in Pediatric Pathology, vol. 2. Chicago, Year Book Medical Publishers, 1975, pp. 241–278.
12. De Sa, D. J.: The spectrum of ischemic bowel disease. *In* Rosenberg, H. S., and Bolande, R. P. (eds.): Perspectives in Pediatric Pathology, vol. 3. Chicago, Year Book Medical Publishers, 1976, pp. 273–309.
13. Bjarke, B., Herin, P., and Blombäck, M.: Neonatal aortic thrombosis: A possible manifestation of congenital antithrombin III deficiency. Acta Paediatr. Scand. *63*:297–301, 1974.
14. Cook, R. C. M., and Rickham, P. P.: Neonatal intestinal obstruction due to milk curds. J. Pediatr. Surg. *4*:599–605, 1969.
15. Book, L. S., Herbst, J. J., Atherton, S. O., and Jung, A. L.: Necrotizing enterocolitis in low-birth-weight infants fed an elemental formula. J. Pediatr. *87*:602–605, 1975.
16. Stein, H., Beck, J., Solomon, A., and Schmaman, A.: Gastroenteritis with necrotising enterocolitis in premature babies. Br. Med. J. *II*:616–619, 1972.
17. Howard, F. M., Flynn, D. M., Bradley, J. M., Noone, P. E., and Szawatkowski, M.: Outbreak of necrotising enterocolitis caused by *Clostridium butyricum*. Lancet *2*:1099–1102, 1977.
18. Cooke, R. W. I., Meradji, M., and De Villeneuve, V. H.: Necrotising enterocolitis after cardiac catheterisation in infants. Arch. Dis. Child. *55*:66–68, 1980.
19. Lloyd, J. R.: The etiology of gastrointestinal perforations in the newborn. J. Pediatr. Surg. *4*:77–84, 1969.
20. Dawes, G. S.: The umbilical circulation. Am. J. Obstet. Gynecol. *84*:1634–1648, 1962.
21. Book, L. S., Herbst, J. J., and Jung, A. L.: Comparison of fast- and slow-feeding rate schedules to the development of necrotizing enterocolitis. J. Pediatr. *89*:463–466, 1976.

22. Graivier, L., and Sieber, W. K.: Hirschsprung's disease and mongolism. Surgery *60*:458–461, 1966.
23. Weinberg, A. G.: Hirschsprung's disease—A pathologist's view. *In* Rosenberg, H. S., and Bolande, R. P. (eds.): Perspectives in Pediatric Pathology, vol. 2. Chicago, Year Book Medical Publishers, 1975, pp. 207–239.
24. Aldridge, R. T., and Campbell, P. E.: Ganglion cell distribution in the normal rectum and anal canal. J. Pediatr. Surg. *3*:475–490, 1968.
25. Campbell, P. E., and Noblett, H. R.: Experience with rectal suction biopsy in the diagnosis of Hirschsprung's disease. J. Pediatr. Surg. *4*:410–415, 1969.
26. Lake, B. D., Puri, P., Nixon, H. H., and Claireaux, A. E.: Hirschsprung's disease. An appraisal of histochemically demonstrated acetylcholinesterase activity in suction rectal biopsy specimens as an aid to diagnosis. Arch. Pathol. Lab. Med. *102*:244–247, 1978.
27. Patrick, W. J. A., Besley, G. T. N., and Smith, I. I.: Histochemical diagnosis of Hirschsprung's disease and a comparison of the histochemical and biochemical activity of acetylcholinesterase in rectum mucosal biopsies. J. Clin. Pathol. *33*:336–343, 1980.
28. Berry, C. L., and Fraser, G. C.: The experimental production of colitis in the rabbit with particular reference to Hirschsprung's disease. J. Pediatr. Surg. *3*:36–42, 1968.
29. Haust, M. D.: Maternal diabetes mellitus—Effects on the fetus and placenta. *In* Naeye, R. L., Kissane, J. M., and Kaufman, N. (eds.): Perinatal Diseases. Baltimore, Williams & Wilkins, 1981, pp. 201–285.

Chapter Fourteen

The Liver and Biliary System

In the perinatal period the liver may show characteristic manifestations of altered nutritional or hemopoietic status, circulatory impairment, trauma or metabolic or infectious disease. Recognition of some abnormality in hepatic size or appearance can provide the pathologist with important clues in the diagnosis of a range of pathologic alterations. Conversely, the demonstration of a completely normal liver at autopsy can help to exclude a number of abnormalities. Jaundice is discussed in Chapter 20; it may be associated with conditions other than hepatic disease, particularly in the neonatal period.

DEVELOPMENT OF THE LIVER AND BILIARY SYSTEM

The liver primordium appears at about the twenty-fifth day as a tubular evagination from the ventral aspect of the future duodenal segment of the foregut endoderm. Initial development is by dichotomous branching after a diverticulum representing the future gallbladder has been formed. Hepatic parenchymal cells and bile ducts are formed from the endodermal component while the interstitial tissues and capsule are derived from the mesoderm of the septum transversum, which is invaded by the developing parenchymal tissue at an early stage. The definitive vascular pattern of the liver is achieved by a complex series of modifications of the primitive paired umbilical and vitelline veins. The vitelline veins are broken up into sinusoids by the developing parenchymal cell cords, and eventually the proximal portion of the right vitelline vein persists as the hepatic vein. The right umbilical vein and part of the left umbilical vein disappear, and the persisting portion of the (left) umbilical vein establishes a communication with the right vitelline vein, the ductus venosus. The S-shaped portal vein is derived from part of both left and right vitelline veins and anastomatic channels between them (Fig.14–1).

The blood supply of the developing liver and changes in blood flow to left and right lobes in the perinatal period are responsible for differences in macroscopic and histological appearance of the lobes.[1] In fetal life the left lobe of the liver is supplied mainly by oxygenated blood from the portal vein. The parenchyma of the left lobe is thus less likely than that of the right lobe to suffer ill effects from fetal hypoxia. At birth the left and right lobes are of nearly equal size. Cessation of umbilical flow at birth results in a marked reduction of blood flow to the left lobe, which may undergo partial atrophy in the first few days of neonatal life. In the newborn period the right lobe of the liver tends to show more hemopoiesis and the parenchymal cells contain more lipid, glycogen and iron than those of the left lobe. Not infrequently a sharp demarcation line may be visible between left and right lobes in the neonatal period due to a congested left lobe and a pale right lobe. Subsequent limitation in growth of the left lobe as a result of its restricted postnatal blood supply presumably accounts for the different sizes of left and right lobes in later life.

304

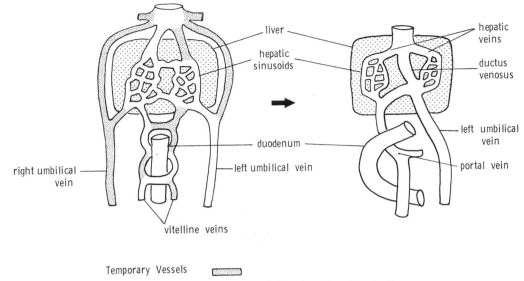

Temporary Vessels ▭

Figure 14–1. Development of the veins related to the liver.

VARIATIONS IN LIVER HISTOLOGY WITH MATURITY

In the preterm infant the lobular structure of the liver is poorly defined. The parenchymal cell plates are irregular, and the sinusoids are wide and packed with erythropoietic cells (Fig. 14–2). The portal tracts have relatively wide zones of connective tissue containing immature leukocytes and often including prominent eosinophil myelocytes. By term there is usually a marked reduction in the extent of extramedullary hemopoiesis, although it is occasionally prominent in large infants. In routine sections stained with hematoxylin and eosin the parenchymal cells of the mature fetal liver often appear clear and empty with little cytoplasm (Fig. 14–3). This is due to the high glycogen content of the parenchymal cells. The appearance is seen only in infants who die as a result of acute intrapartum asphyxia or trauma as the liver glycogen is rapidly depleted under conditions of stress and as a normal process after birth. Postnatally and particularly during stress the parenchymal cells around the portal tracts become depleted of glycogen before those around the central veins, giving a variation in staining reaction in different parts of the lobule. This has in the past sometimes led to a misdiagnosis of anoxic damage to the centrilobular parenchymal cells.

ABNORMALITIES OF POSITION, SHAPE AND SIZE OF THE LIVER

In situs inversus the liver lies on the left, and the left lobe is larger than the right. A central liver is characteristic of the asplenia syndrome (Chapter 11). Abnormal forms may result from malformations affecting the normal integrity of the peritoneal cavity. In the usual form of congenital left diaphragmatic hernia, the left lobe is often large and congested, with a fissure marking the site of compression by the margin of the diaphragm. Extreme distortion associated with bilateral diaphragmatic hernia is illustrated in Figure 14–4. In cases of exomphalos, the liver, if it extends into the hernial sac, is usually large and distorted and often of globular form.

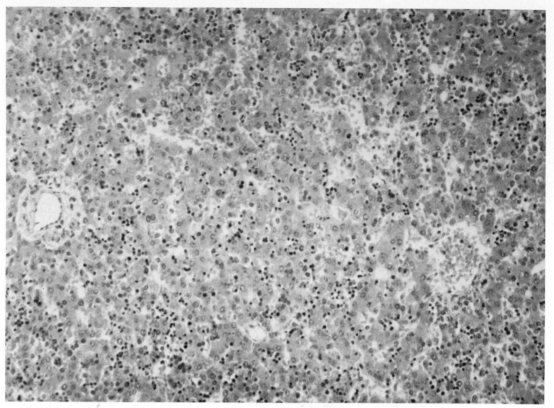

Figure 14–2. Liver at 20 weeks' gestation showing extensive extramedullary hemopoiesis. H and E × 150.

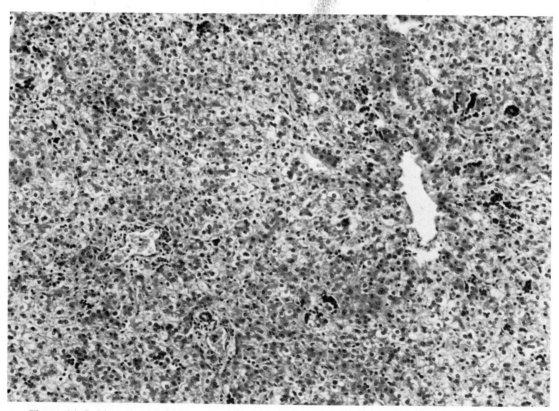

Figure 14–3. Liver at term from a case of intrapartum asphyxia. Vacuolation of parenchymal cells due to glycogen content. H and E × 150. Extramedullary hemopoiesis is prominent also in this case.

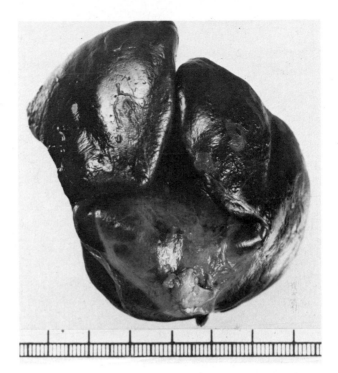

Figure 14–4. Liver from a case of bilateral diaphragmatic hernia, viewed from anterior aspect, showing extreme distortion, as portions of both left and right lobes have separately herniated into the thorax during development.

HEPATOMEGALY

An unduly large liver that is otherwise grossly normal should cause the pathologist to think of a number of possibilities.

Extreme Congestion. Apparent enlargement of the fetal liver may represent merely a terminal anoxic congestion, with dilatation of sinusoids by blood entering through the umbilical vein from the placenta (Fig.14–5).

Increased Hemopoietic Activity. This is characteristic of erythroblastosis fetalis but may be a reason for hepatomegaly in other infective processes associated with fetal hemolytic anemia. These include cytomegalovirus infection, congenital rubella and congenital syphilis.

Inborn Errors of Metabolism. Possibilities include many of the conditions discussed in succeeding paragraphs, although very few of them are manifested by hepatomegaly in the first month of life.

SMALL LIVER

An unduly small liver is seen in infants who have suffered chronic intrauterine malnutrition, as in prolonged maternal pre-eclampsia with uteroplacental ischemia.

INBORN ERRORS OF METABOLISM

It is relatively uncommon for the pathologist to be able to make a firm diagnosis of an inborn metabolic error at autopsy in the perinatal period. For the specific enzyme assays to be undertaken, it is usually necessary for the diagnosis to be considered in life so that appropriate samples can be obtained before or immediately after death. However, the pathologist should be aware of the range of defects that may occasionally be encountered because some of them have characteristic histological or ultrastructural appearances, and abnormal storage

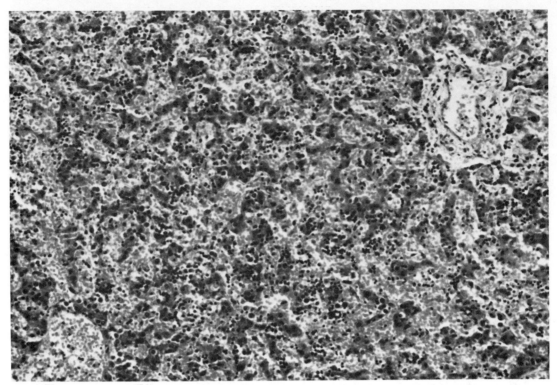

Figure 14–5. Extreme congestion of hepatic sinusoids due to transfusion from the placenta during birth of an acutely asphyxiated fetus. H and E × 150.

products may be detectable. Recognition of the nature of the disease process will allow investigation and precise diagnosis in a subsequent pregnancy, although postmortem diagnosis can be made in a clinically unsuspected case if frozen tissue is available or fibroblast cultures are established at the time of autopsy (Chapter 3). Discussion and detailed references to these conditions are to be found in Stanbury et al.,[2] and hepatic manifestations in infancy are described and referenced by Hardwick and Dimmick.[3]

GLYCOGEN STORAGE DISEASE

Of the variety of forms of this condition known, the only ones that might occur occasionally in the neonatal period are (1) type I glycogenosis (von Gierke's disease, glucose phosphorylase defect) and (2) type II glycogenosis (Pompe's disease, α-1,4-glucosidase defect). Type I is characterized by gross enlargement of liver and kidneys; the liver parenchyma contains massive increase in glycogen and lipid. Type II involves most organs, including heart, skeletal muscle, tongue, liver, adrenals and kidneys. In the liver, glycogen is present in large lysosomal masses.

NIEMANN-PICK DISEASE

The infantile form of Niemann-Pick disease is associated with massive hepatosplenomegaly and progressive mental and motor retardation caused by sphingomyelin deposition within the reticuloendothelial system and neurons. Jaundice may be an early feature. Parenchymal cells appear vacuolated, and large foamy cells with lipid vacuoles in the cytoplasm are prominent within the hepatic sinusoids and in the spleen.

WOLMAN'S DISEASE

Wolman's disease is a rare systemic inborn error of lipid metabolism, associated with deficiency of acid esterase, which usually is manifested in early infancy with vomiting, diarrhea and failure to thrive. There is hepatosplenomegaly and large calcified adrenals. The liver shows portal and periportal fibrosis with foamy histiocytes containing triglyceride and cholesterol esters in periportal and centrilobular zones.

GAUCHER'S DISEASE

Gaucher's disease results from deficiency of β-glucosidase with consequent accumulation of glucocerebrosides in reticuloendothelial cells. An acute variant of the disease may be fatal in infancy, and some infants have at birth had the clinical picture of hydrops fetalis. The typical Gaucher cells may be seen in the liver of affected newborn infants.

MUCOPOLYSACCHARIDOSES

Mucopolysaccharidoses include Hurler syndrome and Hunter syndrome. These may show liver enlargement but usually are diagnosed after the neonatal period.

GALACTOSEMIA

Galactosemia comprises a group of conditions of autosomal recessive inheritance caused by deficiency of one of the two enzymes involved in the metabolism of galactose to fructose-I-phosphate. The classic form of the condition, due to deficiency of galactose-1-phosphate uridyl transferase, is associated with vomiting, diarrhea and failure to thrive on administration of lactose-containing feeds. Death may occur in the neonatal period. Jaundice develops early, but classic signs such as hepatomegaly, lenticular cataracts, mental retardation and hepatic cirrhosis will appear only at a later stage in cases in which the diagnosis is missed in the neonatal period. Histological features of the liver that may be seen within the first month of life include generalized fatty infiltration, bile duct proliferation in the portal tracts and cholestasis. Pseudoglandular transformation of hepatocytes and development of cirrhosis are seen at a later stage. Milder variants of the transferase deficiency form of galactosemia and cases of galactokinase deficiency are unlikely to be encountered by the pathologist in the newborn period.

HEREDITARY FRUCTOSE INTOLERANCE

Hereditary fructose intolerance is a rare inborn error of metabolism of autosomal recessive inheritance due to deficiency of fructose-1-phosphate aldolase. The disorder has a dramatic onset following introduction of fructose-containing feeds (e.g., cow's milk formula with added sucrose) with vomiting, failure to thrive and sometimes evidence of acute hepatic failure, including a bleeding diathesis.

Findings in the liver are almost identical to those seen in galactosemia, but in acute cases there may be extensive hepatic parenchymal necrosis. The liver shown in Figure 14–6 is from an infant who became moribund at 9 days of age with massive intracranial and gastrointestinal hemorrhage. Failure to recognize this picture as caused by an inborn error of metabolism might have resulted in a repeat tragedy had the parents not sought immediate medical advice when their next child began to vomit at 5 days of age. The disorder is readily treated by withdrawal of fructose from the diet.

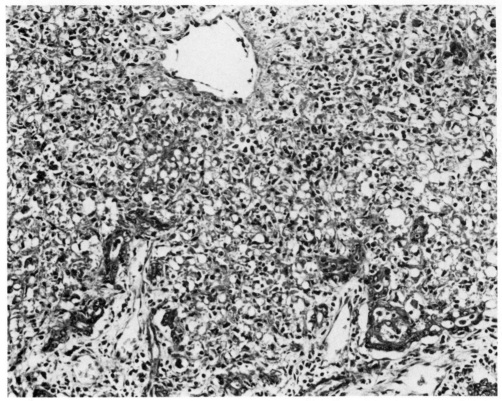

Figure 14–6. Hereditary fructose intolerance in an infant who died at 9 days of age. H and E × 150. There is extensive parenchymal cell necrosis with fatty infiltration of surviving parenchymal cells and early bile duct proliferation.

HEREDITARY TYROSINEMIA

Hereditary tyrosinemia is of autosomal recessive inheritance and may become manifested in an acute form in infancy with vomiting, diarrhea and abdominal distension. Enlargement of liver, spleen and kidneys is characteristic. Pathological changes in the liver are very similar to those of galactosemia and hereditary fructose intolerance.

α_1-ANTITRYPSIN DEFICIENCY

The protease inhibitor α_1-antitrypsin is synthesized in the liver and accounts for about 90 per cent of serum α_1-globulin. In α_1-antitrypsin deficiency the material accumulates within the hepatocytes.

The protease inhibitor system has at least 24 alleles, and most of the affected infants have the protease inhibitor ZZ phenotype, although 80 to 90 per cent of individuals with this phenotype are normal. Affected infants may develop conjugated hyperbilirubinemia and evidence of hepatocellular damage in the first month of life. In the early stages the hepatic changes are those of a nonspecific hepatitis with parenchymal cell necrosis and bile duct proliferation. By three months of age the characteristic PAS–positive diastase-resistant globules of 3 to 40μ diameter can be recognized in periportal hepatocytes. Immunofluorescent and immunoperoxidase techniques can be used to confirm their identity.[4]

FATTY INFILTRATION IN THE NEWBORN LIVER

The depletion of glycogen in the periportal region of the liver lobule that occurs under conditions of perinatal anoxic stress (p. 305) may be associated with fatty infiltration of a similar distribution. These changes are usually more pronounced in the right lobe of the liver, which in utero is supplied with less well-oxygenated blood than the left lobe (p. 304). Fatty infiltration is also commonly found as a concomitant of hepatic parenchymal necrosis in conditions such as congenital heart disease and neonatal cardiovascular collapse associated with severe birth asphyxia or respiratory disease (e.g., RDS) and forms one of the changes seen in many of the inborn errors of metabolism already mentioned. A rare condition of familial steatosis has been described in which massive fatty infiltration of the liver is a major feature,[5] and Reye's syndrome has occasionally been recognized in the neonatal period (see p. 424).

HEPATIC NECROSIS IN THE PERINATAL PERIOD

Areas of ischemic or hemorrhagic necrosis are a relatively common finding at autopsy in the perinatal period (Fig. 14–7). Irregular areas of old necrosis and fibrosis are occasionally seen in the liver of stillborn fetuses or in cases of early neonatal death (Fig. 14–8). These suggest that an episode of cardiovascular collapse may have occurred in utero. Foci of parenchymal cell necrosis have been described in infants dying with hyaline membrane disease.[6] This may be one feature of disseminated intravascular coagulation in the newborn but is an inconstant one because both fibrinogen and fibrin thrombi may be broken down by the enhanced fibrinolytic activity seen in this condition. The placental vessels have been implicated as a possible source for fibrin emboli in the fetal liver.

The most striking examples of neonatal hepatic necrosis are seen in infants with congenital heart disease, particularly those with hypoplastic left heart syndrome or coarctation of the aorta.[7] In such cases the distribution of necrosis is often predominantly midzonal, suggesting that it has resulted from a poor hepatic arterial supply. Similar changes may develop in very low birth weight infants who are maintained alive in neonatal intensive care units following episodes of severe cardiovascular collapse.

Umbilical venous catheterization has in the past provided a possible iatrogenic cause for portal sinus thrombosis and consequent hepatic necrosis. The effect may be due to the placement of the catheter itself or to its use for infusion of hyperosmolar solutions such as THAM or bicarbonate.[8] Hepatic fibrosis and portal hypertension have been reported as sequelae in infants who survived the neonatal period. Indwelling umbilical venous catheters have been employed less frequently since these dangers were recognized.

Extensive hepatic necrosis has also been described in association with viral and bacterial infections of the newborn[9] and could be a result of direct infection of hepatic parenchyma or a nonspecific effect of acute cardiovascular collapse.

HEPATIC LESIONS IN PERINATAL INFECTION

Perinatal infections often cause nonspecific changes in the liver that suggest the possibility of infection but not its precise nature. Occasionally, however, there

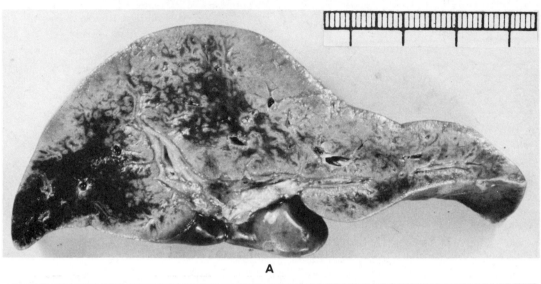

A

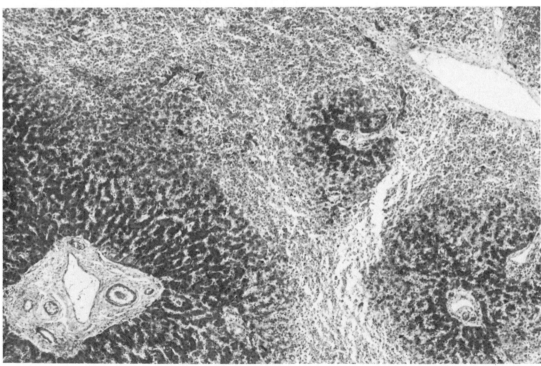

B

Figure 14–7. *A,* Liver slice from a term infant who died of acute intrapartum asphyxia, showing irregular areas of hemorrhagic necrosis. *B,* Section from the margin of an area of necrosis in the same case. H and E × 30.

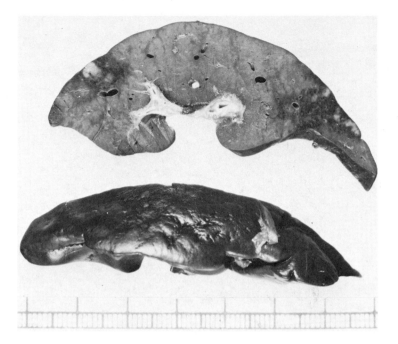

Figure 14–8. Sections of liver of a newborn infant showing old necrosis and fibrosis dating from intrauterine life.

are characteristic hepatic lesions that allow the pathologist to make a presumptive diagnosis on the basis of the macroscopic or histological appearance at autopsy.

NONSPECIFIC HEPATIC CHANGES IN INFECTION

Foremost among nonspecific changes is hepatomegaly. This is often, but not invariably, associated with splenomegaly and is usually attributable to increased extramedullary hemopoietic activity and the presence of hemolytic anemia. The change is thus most frequently seen in congenital infections such as cytomegalovirus infection, rubella and toxoplasmosis. Other nonspecific hepatic changes include cholestasis, lymphocyte infiltration of portal tracts, periportal fibrosis and fatty infiltration. Giant cell transformation of hepatic cells may be seen in many viral infections. Congenital enterovirus infections due to coxsackievirus or echoviruses may be associated with massive central and midzonal hepatic necrosis without a significant inflammatory response. Similar changes can be seen in any infection that is associated with profound cardiovascular collapse and impaired hepatic circulation.

SPECIFIC HEPATIC CHANGES IN INFECTION

Cytomegalovirus Infection. In addition to the nonspecific changes already described, the typical cytomegalic inclusions may be seen in bile duct epithelium (Chapter 9).

Herpes Simplex. This infection is associated with characteristic multiple discrete white or yellow foci, usually 1 to 3 mm in diameter, scattered throughout the liver substance.[10] Individual lesions have a peripheral hemorrhagic zone that, with their larger size, helps to differentiate them from those of *Listeria monocytogenes*. On microscopy the center of each lesion consists of necrotic parenchyma with little inflammatory reaction, whereas the surviving hepatocytes at the periphery contain large, irregularly staining nuclei, including some with intranuclear inclusions typical of herpes simplex (Chapter 9).

Chickenpox (Varicella Zoster). The lesions are similar to those seen in herpes simplex.

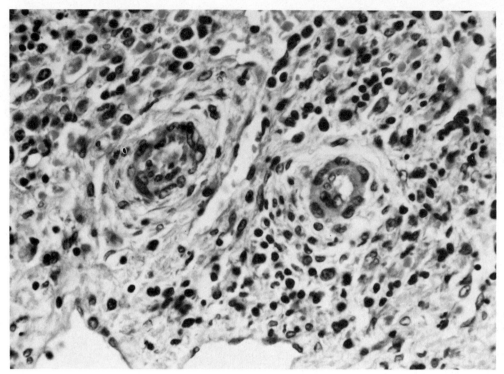

Figure 14–9. Liver in congenital syphilis showing adventitial thickening of arterioles in the portal tracts with chronic inflammatory cell infiltration. H and E × 300.

Listeriosis. Miliary granulomas may be seen in many organs in this condition, but are usually easy to recognize in the liver. They appear as multiple well-demarcated gray spots of about 1 mm diameter (Chapter 9). On microscopy there is a central zone of necrosis with surrounding inflammatory reaction involving polymorphonuclear leukocytes, histiocytes and lymphocytes. The organisms can be demonstrated as short gram-positive rods within the lesions in tissue from abortion as well as in stillborn infants and neonates. Listeriosis has been suggested as a causal factor in some cases of extrahepatic biliary atresia.[11]

Tuberculosis. Congenital tuberculosis is rare, but as a blood-borne transplacental infection it is likely to involve the liver.[10] Microscopic miliary lesions may be found predominantly within the well-oxygenated left lobe.

Syphilis. The liver is enlarged and may show diffuse inflammation involving portal tracts and parenchyma with periportal and interstitial fibrosis. Scarring and fissuring of the liver occur in some cases. In a fetus that died at 27 weeks' gestation (Chapter 9) the liver showed mild chronic inflammation and fibrosis in the periportal regions with adventitial thickening of the arterioles but no parenchymal fibrosis (Fig. 14–9).

NEONATAL HEPATOCELLULAR GIANT CELL TRANSFORMATION

Neonatal hepatocellular giant cell transformation, which was originally considered to be a form of hepatitis,[12] is now recognized as a nonspecific morphological response to hepatic damage associated with conjugated hyperbilirubinemia. Giant cells containing at least three or four nuclei are seen on microscopy and are associated with cholestasis within canaliculi, tubular transformation of hepatocytes and a mild mononuclear infiltrate. The giant cells contain hemosiderin, bilirubin and lipofuscin within the cytoplasm (Fig. 14–10).

The appearance may result from viral hepatitis due to rubella, cytomegalovirus, herpesvirus, coxsackievirus and hepatitis B virus infections. It is also seen in about half of all cases of extrahepatic biliary obstruction. In many cases the diagnosis remains obscure.[10, 13]

ATRESIA OF BILE DUCTS

Atresia of the bile ducts has traditionally been subdivided into intrahepatic and extrahepatic forms of atresia. Intrahepatic biliary atresia is very uncommon,[14] although series of cases have been reported with a spectrum of extrahepatic abnormalities, including odd facies and cardiovascular anomalies.[15] Most cases of extrahepatic biliary obstruction are caused by extrahepatic biliary atresia, but choledochal cyst is a rare and surgically treatable cause.

Atresia of the bile ducts usually is manifested as conjugated hyperbilirubinemia with acholuric stools from birth. The etiology of extrahepatic biliary atresia is uncertain but is now generally considered most likely to be a secondary result of some process causing damage to the biliary tree during the fetal period.[10] The observation that biliary obstruction may occur in some cases of congenital listeriosis[11] suggests that infective processes could provide one such form of prenatal injury. Further evidence that biliary atresia is an acquired disorder is

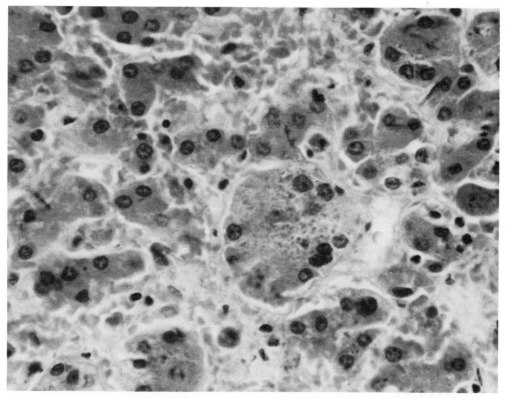

Figure 14–10. Giant cell transformation in the newborn liver. H and E × 300. The change was associated with prolonged intravenous feeding in an infant who died at 8 weeks age.

presented by Rushton.[10] As the hepatic parenchymal cells, which are initially normal in biliary atresia, are assumed to be derived from the primitive bile duct system, it follows that the latter must have developed normally. Other factors suggesting that atresia of the bile ducts is a secondary phenomenon include the variability in the extent of the extrahepatic lesion, the occurrence of cases in which jaundice is of late onset, and the histological appearance of the atretic extrahepatic bile ducts, which present an intense inflammatory reaction with destruction of epithelium and fibrosis.

The differentiation between extrahepatic biliary atresia and neonatal hepatitis by liver biopsy is of considerable practical importance, and is discussed by Rushton[10] and Berry and Keeling.[16] The main feature of extrahepatic biliary atresia is uniform proliferation of bile ducts in the interlobular portal tracts (Table 14–1).

THE LIVER IN PARENTERAL NUTRITION

Infants maintained on total parenteral nutrition (TPN), particularly preterm infants, frequently develop conjugated hyperbilirubinemia and sometimes other evidence of hepatic damage, such as elevated serum glutamic pyruvic transaminase levels.[17] The earliest evidence of hepatic complications may appear as soon as 5 days after institution of TPN, although a longer period is usually required. The earliest and most frequent morphological alterations are fatty change within the hepatocytes and bile stasis within both hepatocytes and canaliculi. The hepatocytes may show tubular transformation and minimal giant cell transformation. In infants who die after maintenance on TPN for several weeks, the liver may be dark greenish-brown in color and show extensive cholestasis with portal fibrosis, bile duct proliferation and a mild portal inflammatory reaction (Fig. 14–11). Occasionally with prolonged TPN the lesion progresses to a diffuse hepatic fibrosis with development of liver failure.[17] If Intralipid has been a component of the TPN regimen, the Kuppfer cells may appear large and pigmented, with Sudan black–positive material within the cytoplasm.

The hepatic damage is usually attributed to the amino acid component of the intravenous feeds; a hepatotoxic peptide has been suggested as one possibility.[18] Ultrastructural changes, including giant mitochondria, indicate hepatotoxic damage. One group has questioned whether the lesion may be caused by lack of oral feedings rather than by the toxicity of intravenous feedings.[19]

TABLE 14–1. DISTINGUISHING FEATURES OF EXTRAHEPATIC BILIARY ATRESIA AND NEONATAL HEPATITIS

EXTRAHEPATIC BILIARY ATRESIA	NEONATAL HEPATITIS
Widened portal tracts	Hepatocellular necrosis
Distorted, angular, elongated bile ducts	Disturbed hepatic architecture
Fibrosis of portal tracts	Giant cell transformation
Inflammation of portal tracts	Inflammation of portal tracts
Normal hepatic architecture	Inflammation of parenchyma
Cholestasis (canalicular and ductular)	Cholestasis (particularly intracellular)
Bile lakes	
Giant cell transformation (50%)	

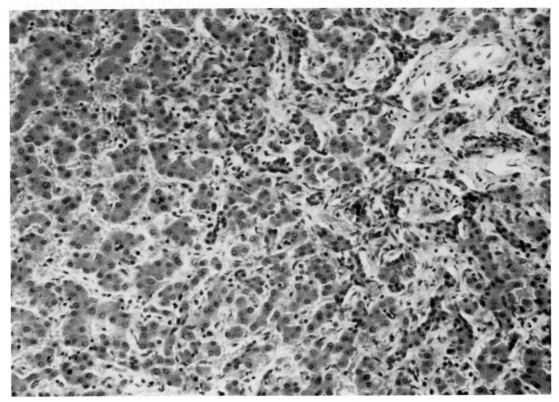

Figure 14–11. Liver in prolonged parenteral nutrition. H and E × 150. There is early portal fibrosis with tubular transformation of hepatocytes and bile stasis.

CIRRHOSIS AND FIBROSIS

True cirrhosis is rare in the perinatal and neonatal periods. Occasional instances have been recorded in which cirrhosis developed in utero.[10]

Congenital hepatic fibrosis is one feature of infantile polycystic disease. In those cases observed in the neonatal period the renal disease is of greater importance.[20] Prominent portal triads can be seen on macroscopic examination of the cut liver surface. On histologic examination there are multiple dilated bile ducts within the luxuriant fibrous stroma of the portal tracts (Fig. 14–12).

Hepatic fibrosis with increased numbers of bile ducts in the portal tracts has been described in some chromsomal anomalies, of which the most common is trisomy 18.

Hepatic vein walls may show fibrous thickening in infants with congenital heart disease who are born in cardiac failure.[3]

ERYTHROBLASTOSIS

The liver of the infant with severe Rh isoimmunization syndrome is enlarged and, if death occurs in the first 2 to 3 days, is usually brick-red in color. Microscopically the most striking feature is massive extramedullary erythropoiesis (Fig. 14–13). The parenchymal cell plates may appear disrupted by the masses of hemopoietic cells. An excess of iron can usually be demonstrated within the parenchymal cells. The livers of infants who die at several days of age sometimes

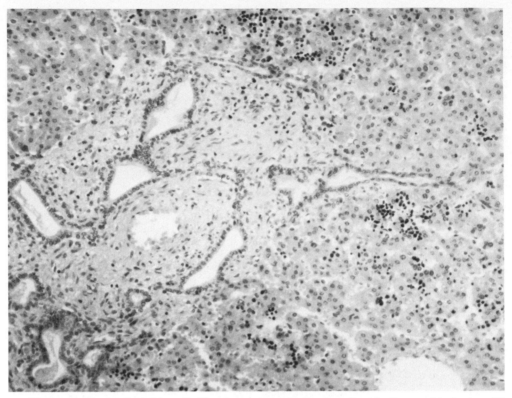

Figure 14–12. Congenital hepatic fibrosis in a case of infantile polycystic disease with death at 18 hours of age. H and E × 150. There are multiple dilated bile ducts within the prominent fibrous stroma of the portal tracts.

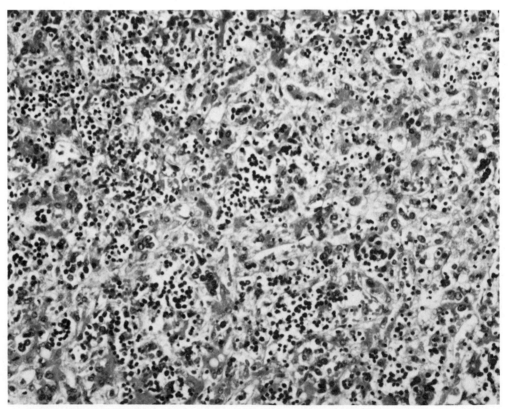

Figure 14–13. Liver from an infant of 31 weeks' gestation who developed hydrops due to rhesus isoimmunization and had a heartbeat at birth but could not be resuscitated. H and E × 150. The cell plates are distorted by the massive extramedullary hemopoiesis.

TABLE 14–2. CONGENITAL TUMORS OF THE LIVER

TUMOR	CHARACTERISTIC FEATURES
Mesenchymal hamartoma	Large pedunculated mass up to 1000 g, mainly affecting right lobe
Hemangioendothelioma	Asymptomatic hepatomegaly with congestive heart failure and thrombocytopenia
Hepatoblastoma	Raised serum α-fetoprotein. May be associated with hemihypertrophy or Beckwith-Wiedemann syndrome

appear green with marked bile stasis within hepatocytes and canaliculi in association with conjugated hyperbilirubinemia.

Other conditions associated with fetal hemolytic anemia, including infections such as cytomegalovirus, may cause similar liver appearances.

HEPATIC TRAUMA

This is described and illustrated in Chapter 6.

TUMORS

Primary tumors of the liver are rare but may be recognized at birth or in the neonatal period. They include the mesenchymal hamartoma, hemangioendothelioma and hepatoblastoma (Table 14–2).

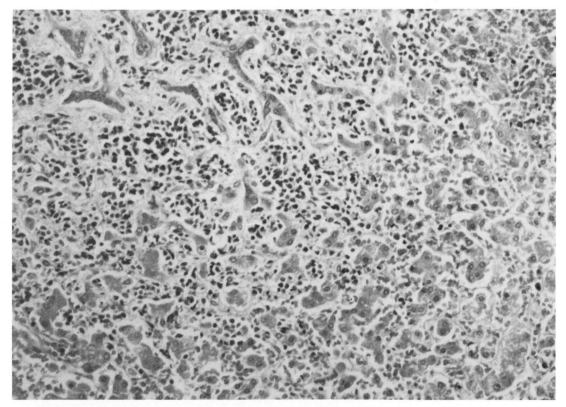

Figure 14–14. Neuroblastoma: secondary deposit within the liver in a term infant who died at 28 hours of age following intracranial birth associated with vaginal breech delivery. H and E × 150.

For descriptions of these tumors see Dehner.[21, 22] The main tumor that produces metastases to the liver in the newborn is neuroblastoma (Fig. 14–14) (see Chapter 8).

GALLBLADDER

Abnormalities of the gallbladder are very rare; the two most common are septation and duplication. The gallbladder is usually hypoplastic in extrahepatic biliary atresia but may sometimes be of normal size. The content in such cases is clear mucus.

Choledochal cysts arise as localized dilatations of the common bile duct and are thought to occur as a result of obstruction to bile flow. They are fusiform or saccular, vary considerably in size and may appear as palpable abdominal masses. They are a rare cause of obstructive jaundice in the neonatal period. The cyst wall consists of smooth muscle and fibrous tissue with a lining of biliary epithelium. The epithelium may be destroyed by an inflammatory reaction.

REFERENCES

1. Emery, J. L.: The functional symmetry of the liver. Ann. N. Y. Acad. Sci. *III*:37–42,1963.
2. Stanbury, J. B., Wyngaarden, J. B., and Fredrickson, D. S. (eds.): The Metabolic Basis of Inherited Disease, 4th ed. New York, McGraw-Hill, 1978.
3. Hardwick, D. F., and Dimmick, J. E.: Metabolic cirrhoses of infancy and early childhood. *In* Rosenberg, H. S., and Bolande, R. P. (eds.): Perspectives in Pediatric Pathology, vol. 3. Chicago, Year Book Medical Publishers, 1976, pp. 103–144.
4. McPhie, J. L., Birnie, S., and Brunt, P. W.: α_1–Antitrypsin deficiency and infantile liver disease. Arch. Dis. Child. *51*:584–588, 1976.
5. Suprun, H., and Freundlich, E.: Fatal familial steatosis of myocardium, liver and kidneys in three siblings. Acta Paediatr. Scand. *70*:247–252, 1981.
6. Wade-Evans, T.: Thrombi in the hepatic sinusoids of the newborn and their relation to pulmonary hyaline membrane formation. Arch. Dis. Child. *36*:286–292, 1961.
7. Shiraki, K.: Hepatic cell necrosis in the newborn. Am. J. Dis. Child. *119*:395–400, 1970.
8. Larroche, J. C.: Developmental pathology of the neonate. Amsterdam, Excerpta Medica, 1977, pp. 233–241.
9. Potter, E. L., and Craig, J. M.: Pathology of the Fetus and the Infant. Chicago, Year Book Medical Publishers, 1976, p. 402.
10. Rushton, D. I.: Fetal and neonatal liver disease. Diagn. Histopathol. *4*:17–48, 1981.
11. Becroft, D. M. O.: Biliary atresia associated with prenatal infection by *Listeria monocytogenes*. Arch. Dis. Child. *47*:656–660, 1972.
12. Craig, J. M., and Landing, B. H.: A form of hepatitis in the neonatal period simulating biliary atresia. Arch. Pathol. *54*:321–333, 1952.
13. Montgomery, C. K., and Ruebner, B. H.: Neonatal hepatocellular giant cell transformation. A review. *In* Rosenberg, H. S., and Bolande, R. P. (eds.): Perspectives in Pediatric Pathology, vol. 3. Chicago, Year Book Medical Publishers, 1976, pp. 85–101.
14. Mowat, A. P., Psacharopoulos, H. T., and Williams, R.: Extrahepatic biliary atresia versus neonatal hepatitis. Review of 137 prospectively investigated patients. Arch. Dis. Child. *51*:763–770, 1976.
15. Alagille, D., Odievre, M., Gautier, M., and Dommergues, J. P.: Hepatic ductular hypoplasia associated with characteristic facies, vertebral malformations, retarded physical, mental, and sexual development, and cardiac murmur. J. Pediatr. *86*:63–71, 1975.
16. Berry, C. L., and Keeling, J.: Liver and gallbladder. In Berry, C. L. (ed.): Paediatric Pathology. Berlin, Springer Verlag, 1981, pp. 267–298.
17. Witzleben, C. L.: Neonatal liver disease. *In* Naeye, R. L., Kissane, J. M., and Kaufman, N.: Perinatal Diseases. Baltimore, Williams & Wilkins, 1981, pp. 346–368.
18. Bernstein, J., Chang, C. H., Brough, A. J., and Heidelberger, K. P.: Conjugated hyperbilirubinemia in infancy associated with parenteral alimentation. J. Pediatr. *90*:361–367, 1977.
19. Rager, R., and Finegold, M.: Cholestasis in immature newborn infants: Is parenteral alimentation responsible? J. Pediatr. *86*:264–269, 1975.
20. Blyth, H., and Ockenden, B. G.: Polycystic disease of kidneys and liver presenting in childhood. J. Med. Genet. *8*:257–284, 1971.
21. Dehner, L. P.: Hepatic tumors in the pediatric age–group: A distinctive clinicopathologic spectrum. *In* Rosenberg, H. S., and Bolande, R. P. (eds.): Perspectives in Pediatric Pathology, vol. 4. Chicago, Year Book Medical Publishers, 1978, pp. 217–268.
22. Dehner, L. P.: Neoplasms of the fetus and neonate. *In* Naeye, R. L., Kissane, J. M., and Kaufman, N. (eds.): Perinatal Diseases. Baltimore, Williams & Wilkins, 1981, pp. 286–345.

Chapter Fifteen

The Pancreas

DEVELOPMENT

The pancreas develops as two outgrowths from the duodenum that appear during the fourth week after conception. The dorsal bud forms the body and tail of the organ while the ventral bud moves around dorsally when the duodenal loop rotates to the right and fuses with the dorsal bud (at the end of the sixth week) to form a major part of the head of the pancreas. The early pancreatic ducts undergo repeated branching within a mesenchymal stroma. Acini first appear early in the third month and continue to proliferate up to and following birth (Fig. 15–1). By term the pancreas consists of compact lobules with little intervening connective tissue (Fig. 15–2).

The islets of Langerhans develop in two phases. Small clusters of cells appear on the outer surface of the ducts at about 10 weeks and develop into large islets within the interlobular connective tissue but then degenerate toward the end of gestation. The definitive islets appear in the fourth month from the duct walls in the centers of the lobules and increase in size throughout the rest of intrauterine life. The development of the pancreas was described in detail by Liu and Potter[1] and is illustrated in Potter and Craig.[2] A neural crest origin of pancreatic endocrine cells has been claimed by Pearse et al.[3] but has not been supported by other workers.[4]

PANCREATIC ANOMALIES

AGENESIS

This is a very rare abnormality of the pancreas but has been described as a familial condition.[5]

ANNULAR PANCREAS

If the ventral part of the pancreas fails to migrate dorsally, a mass of pancreatic tissue remains surrounding the second part of the duodenum. The anomaly is frequently associated with neonatal intestinal obstruction (Fig. 15–3), although it is by no means certain that stenosis or atresia of the duodenum in such cases is necessarily a result rather than an association of the pancreatic anomaly.[6]

PANCREATIC ENDOCRINE TISSUE AND THE HORMONES OF THE GASTROINTESTINAL TRACT

The pancreatic islets are now known to include at least four separate cell types.[7] Glucagon and insulin, secreted by the A (α) and B (β) cells, respectively,

321

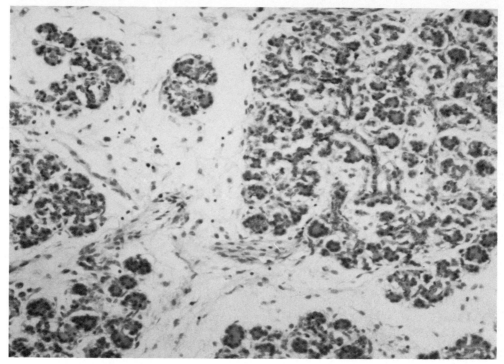

Figure 15–1. Pancreas at 20 weeks' gestation. H and E × 150.

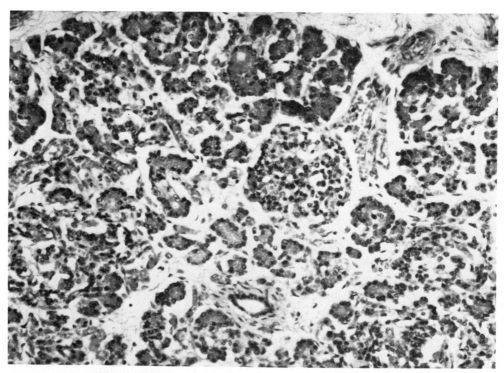

Figure 15–2. Pancreas at 40 weeks' gestation. H and E × 150.

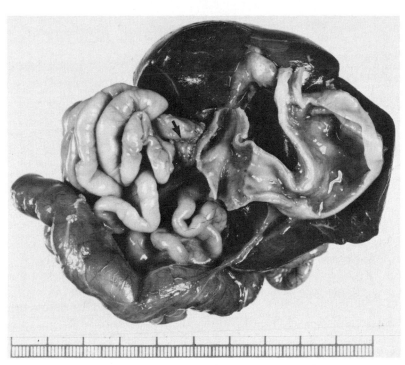

Figure 15–3. Annular pancreas (arrowed) in an infant of 33 weeks' gestation who died with multiple congenital anomalies. The stomach and upper duodenum are thick-walled and dilated as in duodenal atresia.

can be detected by about 20 weeks' gestation. The D (δ) cells secrete somatostatin, a potent inhibitor of insulin and glucagon release, while an additional hormone, pancreatic polypeptide, whose function remains to be determined, has been localized to the D_1 cells. Both these additional hormones are detectable within the fetal and neonatal pancreas by immunocytochemical techniques.[8] Additional polypeptide hormones, including vasoactive intestinal peptide and gastrin, are also present within the fetal and neonatal pancreas. It is not certain that substances such as somatostatin and pancreatic polypeptide act as circulating hormones; they may have a local paracrine rather than endocrine function. It has been shown that gap junctions are present between the different types of endocrine cell within the pancreatic islet,[9] offering support to the concept that direct interactions between the cell types may be of importance in maintaining normal hormonal regulation of gastrointestinal function.

The pancreatic hormones do not exist in isolation from those of the remainder of the gastrointestinal tract. The glucagon-like peptide enteroglucagon is present in specific cells within the intestine, particularly the distal small intestine and large intestine, while in the dog (but not in man), true "pancreatic" glucagon is found within the gastric fundus.[8] Somatostatin and vasoactive intestinal peptide are present widely throughout the intestine and other tissues, including the brain, as are a number of other peptides with known or putative hormonal activity, including bombesin and substance P. Development of normal gastrointestinal function postnatally may depend both on the normality of prenatal gastrointestinal hormone development and on the stimulus to gastrointestinal hormone production provided by enteral feeding.[10]

VARIATIONS IN ISLET MORPHOLOGY IN THE PERINATAL PERIOD

Variations in pancreatic endocrine morphology and function recognized in the perinatal period may reflect either a prenatal or postnatal impairment in gastrointestinal or general metabolic function, and do not necessarily imply a primary defect in cellular differentiation.

Infants of diabetic mothers characteristically have increased islet tissue throughout the pancreas (Fig. 15–4). The islets are increased both in size (up to twice the normal diameter or greater) and in number.[11] Because there seems to be no consistent enlargement of the pancreas as a whole, the proportion of the organ represented by islet tissue is considerably increased, to two to three times the normal figure. There is a higher ratio of B cells to A cells than normal, and the B cells may show pleomorphism, hyperchromasia or hypertrophy of the nuclei and hypertrophy of the cytoplasm. A mixed cellular infiltrate of lymphocytes, histiocytes and neutrophils, most often containing many eosinophils, is sometimes seen within the peri-insular or intrainsular connective tissue. This inflammatory infiltrate may be the morphological expression of the reaction between maternal anti-insulin antibodies and fetal insulin in the B cells. Islet hypertrophy and hyperplasia are not seen in all these infants. If hypertrophy and hyperplasia relate to the blood sugar level to which the fetus is exposed, it would be expected that these features, like the external appearances and macrosomia of the classic infant of a diabetic mother, would seldom develop in the face of modern exacting chemical control of diabetes in pregnancy.

Other conditions in which large islets with hypertrophy of individual islet cells is seen include erythroblastosis fetalis (Fig. 15–5) and hereditary tyrosinemia (see Hardwick and Dimmick).[12] We noted hypertrophic islets and an increase in pancreatic polypeptide in the pancreas of preterm infants who died at a week or more of age and had been fed by the nasogastric route, but normal-appearing islets in those who were intravenously fed.[13] On quantitative immunocytochemistry the latter group were found to have an increase in insulin-containing tissue. This suggested that the mode of feeding of preterm infants in the neonatal period might exaggerate some aspect of endocrine development and lead to hormonal imbalance at a later stage of infancy.

Neonatal hypoglycemia occurs characteristically in preterm and in particular in growth-retarded neonates in whom it is not associated with any consistent histological abnormality of the islets. Other causes include hepatic enzyme defects (e.g., galactosemia, hereditary fructose intolerance), growth hormone and glucocorticoid deficiency and inappropriate insulin secretion. Inappropriate insulin secretion may be associated with hyperplasia of the islets as already discussed, with B cell proliferation or with B cell tumor.[14]

The condition of nesidioblastosis has been recognized with increasing frequency as a cause of severe hypoglycemia in early infancy.[15, 16] Superficially the pancreas shows a lack of normal discrete islets. More detailed study reveals continued proliferation of endocrine cells from the pancreatic ductules and infiltration of the acinar tissue by groups and sheets of endocrine cells (Fig. 15–6). As studied with the aid of immunocytochemistry the proportions of different cell types are relatively normal.[15] Nesidioblastosis has been recognized in some cases of sudden infant death as well as in clinically recognized instances of acute hypoglycemia.[17, 18] The etiology of the condition remains obscure.

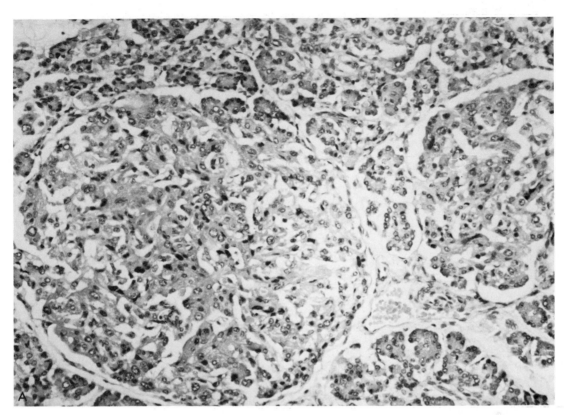

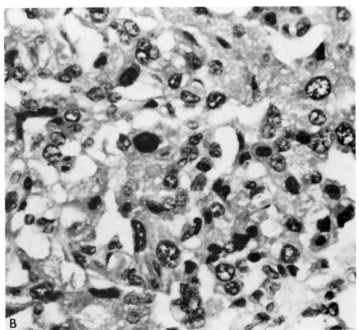

Figure 15–4. Islet cell hyperplasia and hypertrophy in the pancreas of an infant of a diabetic mother. *A,* H and E × 150. Note the enormous diameter of the islets in comparison with the normal appearance seen in Figure 15–2. *B,* Part of an islet (H and E × 350) showing variation in nuclear size and staining.

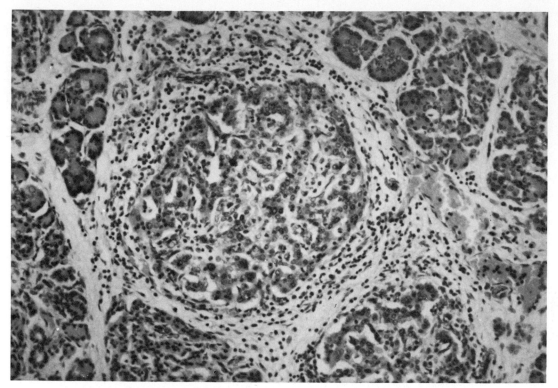

Figure 15–5. Islets in rhesus isoimmunization. H and E × 150. Note the similarity in appearance to that sometimes seen in association with maternal diabetes with infiltration by eosinophil leukocytes.

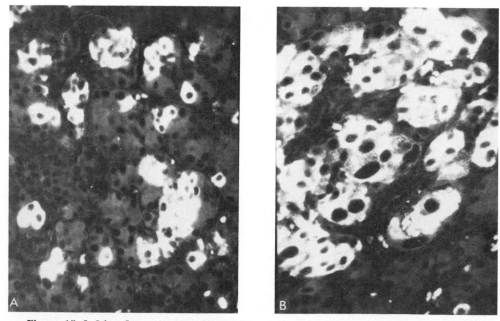

Figure 15–6. Islets from *(A)* normal neonatal pancreas and *(B)* pancreas of infant with nesidio-blastosis (referred with untreatable hypoglycemia) stained by the indirect immunofluorescence method for insulin, × 300. The irregular cell morphology and increased insulin staining are apparent in *B*. (Courtesy of Dr. J. M. Polak, Dept. of Histochemistry, Royal Postgraduate Medical School, London.)

CONDITIONS AFFECTING THE EXOCRINE PANCREAS

Relatively few perinatal diseases are associated with abnormality of the exocrine pancreas.

CYSTIC FIBROSIS

Cystic fibrosis is the most characteristic disorder that is known to affect the pancreas in the perinatal period. The pathological findings in infancy and childhood are well reviewed by Oppenheimer and Esterly.[19] The disease is inherited as an autosomal recessive; about 5 per cent of the population carry the gene. Homozygous individuals have increased secretion of sodium and chloride in sweat, saliva and other secretions. Infants who die with cystic fibrosis in the neonatal period commonly present with meconium ileus or peritonitis (see p. 294), but cystic fibrosis may occasionally be recognized at autopsy in infants who die (e.g., of an acute infection) without the diagnosis being made during life.

Usually it is not possible to recognize the pancreas as macroscopically abnormal in the neonatal period. By microscopy the distended mucus-plugged ducts may readily be seen, with periductal and interacinar fibrosis (Fig. 15–7). However, the extent of pancreatic involvement is variable, and the absence of classic pancreatic changes does not exclude the diagnosis.[19] The viscid nature of mucous secretions throughout the body in cystic fibrosis causes recognizable changes within the lungs and liver as well as in the pancreas and intestinal tract. Hyperplasia and obstruction of submucosal glands of the trachea and bronchi may be seen in the neonatal period. Repeated pulmonary infection with development of bronchiectasis is the major cause of morbidity and mortality in older children. Hepatic changes,

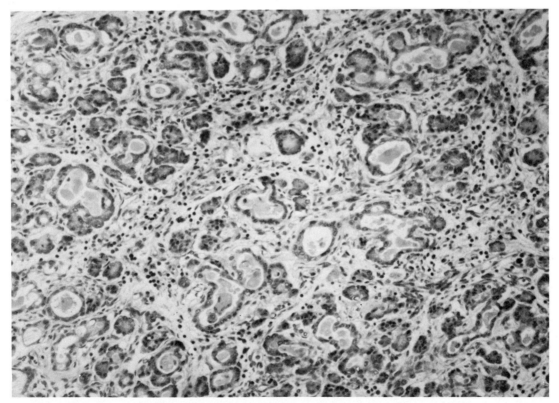

Figure 15–7. Pancreas in an infant with cystic fibrosis who died at 8 days of age. H and E × 150. Dilated acini are plugged with inspissated secretions and there is an early increase in connective tissue with chronic lymphocytic infiltration. Compare with Figure 15–8.

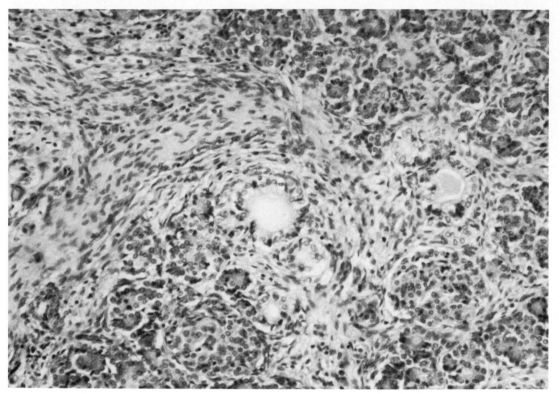

Figure 15–8. Pancreas in congenital syphilis. H and E × 150. Note the broad bands of fibrous tissue separating groups of acini.

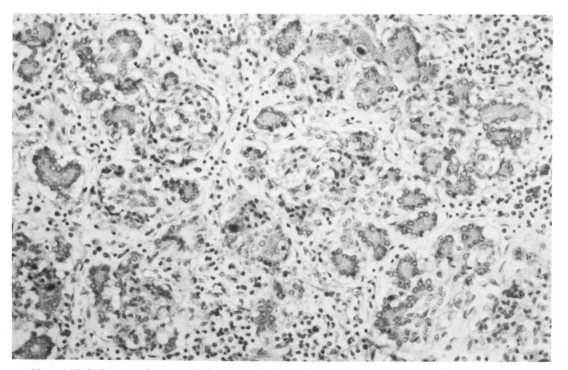

Figure 15–9. Pancreas in congenital cytomegalovirus infection. H and E × 150. There is a mononuclear cell infiltration and typical cytomegalic cells with nuclear inclusions in some acinar cells.

including obstruction of small bile ducts with bile duct proliferation and portal fibrosis, may be seen from birth onward. Obstruction of the vas deferens by abnormal secretion results in dilatation of the epididymal ducts and eventual destruction of the sperm transport system with subsequent sterility in the affected male.

OTHER DISORDERS INVOLVING THE EXOCRINE PANCREAS

Congenital syphilis is associated with gross increase in the interacinar connective tissue and a typical chronic inflammatory reaction involving lymphocytes, plasma cells and macrophages. The reaction was already well developed in a case seen at 27 weeks' gestation (Fig. 15–8) and is worth remembering as a possible indication of diagnosis in an obscure case. Cytomegalic inclusion disease may involve the pancreas with development of typical owl-eyed cells in both exocrine tissue and islet cells (Fig. 15–9). Disorders involving the hemopoietic tissues often involve the pancreas. Thus erythroblastosis fetalis resulting from Rh isoimmunization may be associated with extensive extramedullary hemopoiesis throughout the pancreas in addition to the islet changes described earlier. Pancreatic involvement is said to be frequent in cases of congenital leukemia.[2]

REFERENCES

1. Liu, H. M., and Potter, E. L.: Development of the human pancreas. Arch. Pathol. *74*:439–452, 1962.
2. Potter, E. L., and Craig, J. M.: Pathology of the Fetus and the Infant. Chicago, Year Book Medical Publishers, 1976, pp. 344–354.
3. Pearse, A. G. E., Polak, J. M., and Heath, C. M.: Development, differentiation and derivation of the endocrine polypeptide cells of the mouse pancreas. Diabetologia *9*:120–129, 1973.
4. Pictet, R. L., Rall, L. B., Phelps, P., and Rutter, W. J.: The neural crest and the origin of the insulin-producing and other gastrointestinal hormone-producing cells. Science *191*:191–192, 1976.
5. Sherwood, W. G., Chance, G. W., and Hill, D. E.: A new syndrome of pancreatic agenesis. The role of insulin and glucagon in somatic and cell growth. Pediatr. Res. *8*:360, 1974.
6. Elliott, G. B., Kliman, K. R., and Elliott, K. A.: Pancreatic annulus: A sign or a cause of duodenal obstruction? Can. J. Surg. *11*:357–364, 1968.
7. Hirsch, H. J., Loo, S. W., and Gabbay, K. H.: The development and regulation of the endocrine pancreas. J. Pediatr. *91*:518–520, 1977.
8. Polak, J. M., Bloom, S. R., and Pearse, A. G. E.: Gut endocrinology: Correlation of physiology and morphology. Clin. Endocrinol. *5*(Suppl.):2055–2165, 1976.
9. Orci, L.: A portrait of the pancreatic B-cell. Diabetologia *10*:163–187, 1974.
10. Lucas, A.: Gut hormones and infant feeding. *In* Davis, J. A., and Dobbing, J. (eds.): Scientific Foundations of Paediatrics. London, William Heinemann, 1981, p. 87–91.
11. Haust, M. D.: Maternal diabetes mellitus—Effects on the fetus and placenta. *In* Naeye, R. L., Kissane, J. M., and Kaufman, N. (eds.): Perinatal Diseases. Baltimore, Williams & Wilkins, 1981, pp. 201–285.
12. Hardwick, D. F., and Dimmick, J. E.: Metabolic cirrhoses of infancy and early childhood. *In* Rosenberg, H. S., and Bolande, R. P. (eds.): Perspectives in Pediatric Pathology, vol. 3. Chicago, Year Book Medical Publishers, 1976, pp. 103–144.
13. Wigglesworth, J. S., Polak, J. M., and McCrossan, M. V.: Effects of neonatal feeding in development of the endocrine pancreas: Possible relevance to sudden infant death. Arch. Dis. Child. *53*:434 (Abstract), 1978.
14. Fischer, G. W., Vazquez, A. M., Buist, N. R. M., Campbell, J. R., McCarty, E., and Egan, E. T.: Neonatal islet cell adenoma: Case report and literature review. Pediatrics *53*:753–756, 1974.
15. Heitz, P. U., Klöppel, G., Häcki, W. H., Polak, J. M., and Pearse, A. G. E.: The pathologic basis of persistent hyperinsulinemic hypoglycemia in infants. Diabetes *26*:632–642, 1977.
16. Aynsley-Green, A., Polak, J. M., Bloom, S. R., Gough, M. H., Keeling, J., Ashcroft, S. J. H., Turner, R. C., and Baum, J. D.: Nesidioblastosis of the pancreas: Definition of the syndrome and the management of the severe neonatal hyperinsulinaemic hypoglycaemia. Arch. Dis. Child. *56*:496–508, 1981.
17. Polak, J. M., and Wigglesworth, J. S.: Islet-cell hyperplasia and sudden infant death. Lancet *2*:570–571, 1976.
18. Cox, J. M., Guelpa, G., and Terrapon, M.: Islet-cell hyperplasia and sudden infant death. Lancet *2*:739–740, 1976.
19. Oppenheimer, E. H., and Esterly, J. R.: Pathology of cystic fibrosis. Review of the literature and comparison with 146 autopsied cases. *In* Rosenberg, H. S., and Bolande, R. P. (eds.): Perspectives in Pediatric Pathology, vol. 2. Chicago, Year Book Medical Publishers, 1975, pp. 241–278.

Chapter Sixteen

The Endocrine Organs

The fetal endocrine organs in a number of animal species have been shown to have a major role in controlling fetal development and determining the timing of birth. The wide species differences make it unjustifiable to assume that the same is true for the human fetus. There is evidence that most human fetal hormonal requirements can be met by transplacental transfer.

This is a difficult area to study in the human, and there is a lack of data on normal endocrine function at birth, particularly in preterm infants. Probably as a consequence of this, relatively few endocrine abnormalities are recognized in life during the perinatal period. With a few notable exceptions, the pathology of endocrine organs in the fetus and newborn infant is mainly descriptive of lesions discovered incidentally at autopsy by the pathologist.

DEVELOPMENT OF ENDOCRINE FUNCTION IN THE FETUS

The subject of fetal endocrinology is well covered by Silman et al.[1] The human fetus has a functioning endocrine system from early in gestation. Production of testicular hormones during the first trimester is essential for determination of the male genitalia (Chapter 18). In the rabbit this testicular development requires production of follicle-stimulating hormone and luteinizing hormone by a functional fetal pituitary. The human male anencephalic has normal genitalia, but both male and female anencephalics have poor gonadal development. This has prompted the suggestion that HCG from the placenta may promote sufficient testicular development to allow normal genital differentiation, but that later gonadal growth requires a functional anterior pituitary.

The human fetal thyroid secretes thyroxine from seven weeks on. At term the circulating fetal levels may be higher than those in the mother. In the athyroid human infant fetal growth is relatively normal, implying that in the absence of fetal production of thyroid hormones in utero, transplacental transfer of thyroid hormones can supply fetal requirements.

Human growth hormone is detectable in the circulation by 10 weeks and attains levels well above those in the mother by the middle of the second trimester. However, the hormone is not essential for fetal growth, and fetuses without pituitaries or with familial hypopituitarism may show normal body growth in utero. Swaab and colleagues have nevertheless presented evidence that fetal growth in both rats and humans is influenced by neuropeptides such as α-melanocyte-stimulating hormone produced by the pars intermedia of the pituitary.[2]

It has been suggested that insulin is the most important growth hormone of the fetus[3] and is present within the fetal pancreas from 11 weeks after conception.[4] Increased insulin production by the fetal pancreas in response to high maternal blood sugar levels is thought to be the major mechanism underlying the somatic changes in infants of diabetic mothers (Chapter 15). Insulin production by the human fetal pancreas appears more responsive to changes in amino acid concentration than to changes in glucose,[4] an observation in accord with its primary role as a growth hormone.

Both epinephrine and norepinephrine are secreted by the adrenal medulla, norepinephrine being converted to epinephrine under the influence of pituitary ACTH. The relatively high circulating norepinephrine levels in the fetus may be of importance in maintaining fetal vascular tone.

Secretion of parathyroid hormone by the fetus may be stimulated by changes in fetal calcium level secondary to untreated maternal parathyroid disease.

The fetal adrenal is a highly active organ and secretes large quantities of steroids that are further metabolized in the fetal liver and the placenta before transfer to the maternal bloodstream. This is discussed in more detail later in the chapter. In the sheep, fetal adrenal cortisol is responsible for initiation of labor under the influence of fetal pituitary ACTH, but no such clear relationship is demonstrable in man. It has, however, been suggested that the pituitary-adrenal axis may modulate the timing of onset of labor because anencephalics show a wide variation in length of gestation if spontaneous delivery is allowed.[5] Fetal cortisol may be important in ensuring organ maturation prior to birth, particularly maturation of the surfactant synthetic pathways within the alveolar epithelium of the lungs. This effect may again represent only a fine-timing control; anencephalics born at term often have normal mature lungs and the appearance of surfactant within the lungs of rabbit fetuses is retarded but not prevented by decapitation.[6]

Fetal endocrine function thus seems to provide an important background to normal human fetal development, but it has not yet been possible to establish a critical role for any endocrine function in the human fetus such as those demonstrable for the pituitary-adrenal axis and thyroid in the fetal lamb.

PITUITARY

DEVELOPMENT

The pituitary originates from two separate parts. The anterior lobe develops from Rathke's pouch, an evagination of the stomodeum just anterior to the buccopharyngeal membrane, which appears at the start of the fourth postconceptional week. The posterior lobe is formed from a downward extension of the diencephalon, the infundibulum. Fusion of the two parts occurs by the end of the second month when the gland becomes functional. The intermediate lobe develops from the posterior wall of Rathke's pouch. At term the anterior lobe of the pituitary contains many acidophilic cells, a few basophilic cells and a large number of undifferentiated cells without specific granules. A colloid-filled cleft, the residual lumen of Rathke's pouch, separates it from the narrow intermediate lobe, which contains a group of gland-like cavities. The posterior lobe is composed of cells and fibers resembling neuroglia.

PATHOLOGICAL CHANGES

Most abnormalities recognized in the pituitary in the perinatal period are developmental. In anencephaly the posterior lobe fails to develop and the anterior

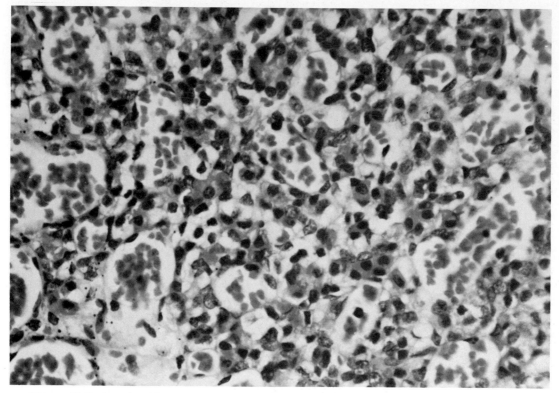

Figure 16–1. Anterior lobe of the pituitary in an anencephalic. H and E × 350. The cellular pattern appears normal but there is intense congestion.

lobe is of variable size. However, often it is easily seen as a prominent cherry-red structure and the cells are remarkably well differentiated on microscopy (Fig. 16–1).

Pituitary hypoplasia or aplasia is common in cases of alobar holoprosencephaly (Chapter 12). Occasional cases of pituitary aplasia in the absence of other abnormalities have been reported.[7] All cases of absence of the pituitary or hypothalamus are associated with adrenal hypoplasia.

THYROID

DEVELOPMENT

The thyroid first appears during the third postconceptional week as a diverticulum from the floor of the pharynx. The gland forms a solid bilobed mass which descends in the neck but remains attached to the floor of the pharynx by a hollow stalk, the thyroglossal duct. The solid cell cords of the embryonic thyroid become hollowed out to form the colloid-filled follicles of the functional gland. The parafollicular or "C" cells, which produce calcitonin, have been shown in lower animals to be derived from the neural crest and to migrate to the thyroid via the ultimobranchial bodies.[8] A similar origin is likely in man.

STRUCTURE

The thyroid gland of the newborn infant has a variable histological appearance. Many show colloid-filled follicles and characteristically have a vascular intervening stroma (Fig. 16–2). In the preterm infant, the follicles are irregular in

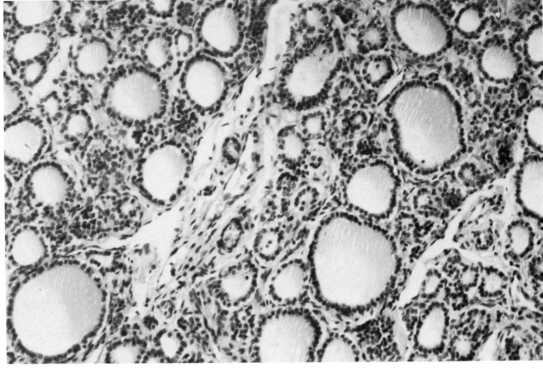

Figure 16–2. Thyroid from an infant of 28 weeks' gestation who died at 5 days of age. H and E × 150. Many of the thyroid follicles are packed with colloid.

size and the stroma is prominent. The thyroid of many infants shows a totally different appearance, with lack of colloid, desquamation of epithelium and often masses of pyknotic aggregated nuclei between and within the follicles (Fig. 16–3). This appearance has puzzled pathologists. Some, such as Potter and Craig,[9] are satisfied that the change is caused by autolysis. Others interpret the change as due to hyperactivity of the gland at the time of birth.[10, 11] Larroche discusses studies that indicate that the newborn infant has an acute rise in output of thyroxine and triiodothyronine in the first 48 hours of life with return to normal levels on the third or fourth day. In a large autopsy series, Larroche found that thyroid glands from infants who died within the first 24 hours after vaginal delivery had empty follicles, whereas those who died later showed increased colloid content. Delivery by cesarean section and fetal growth retardation were associated with the presence of colloid within the thyroid follicles.

PATHOLOGICAL CHANGES

Absence of the thyroid is the most common cause of sporadic cretinism. Some thyroid tissue may be present in such fetuses along the track of descent of the thyroid, either at the base of the tongue or above the cricoid cartilage. Congenital goiter is most often associated with hypothyroidism. In some instances there is hyperplasia of the epithelium lining the follicles, with lack of colloid. In others the gland contains large follicles lined with a flattened epithelium and distended by colloid.

Congenital goiter may be caused by administration of drugs to the mother, particularly those containing iodine. In such cases the gland shows irregular elongated follicles with a columnar epithelium and virtually no colloid.[11]

Congenital goiter with thyrotoxicosis is seen in infants of thyrotoxic mothers and is ascribed to transplacental transfer of long-acting thyroid stimulator (LATS).

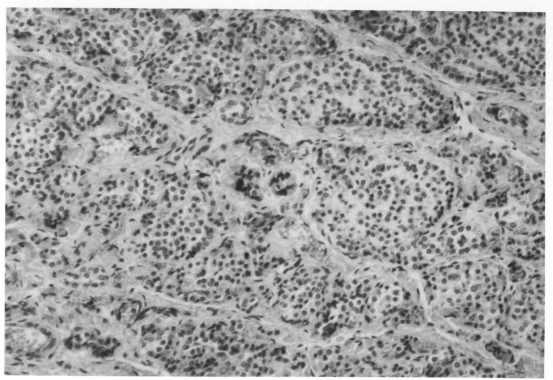

Figure 16–3. Thyroid from a term infant who died a few minutes before birth. H and E × 150. The epithelium is desquamated and small nuclear aggregates are present.

PARATHYROIDS

DEVELOPMENT AND STRUCTURE

The parathyroids develop as outgrowths of the third and fourth pair of pharyngeal pouches. The parathyroids derived from the fourth pouches remain related to the lateral lobes of the thyroid while those from the third pouches are associated with the thymus as it migrates and usually lie near the inferior poles of the thyroid.

In the newborn infant the parathyroid glands are composed of interlacing cords of chief cells separated by connective tissue and blood vessels (Fig. 16–4). Oxyphil cells and fat are not seen in the parathyroid in infancy.

PATHOLOGICAL CHANGES

The parathyroids are absent or hypoplastic in DiGeorge syndrome (absence of thymus, absence or hypoplasia of parathyroids and conotruncal anomalies) (Chapter 15). The parathyroid abnormality in this disorder is manifested by hypocalcemia with development of tetany in the neonatal period. Hypocalcemic tetany in the newborn is more often caused by other conditions such as a high phosphate intake from cow's milk feedings. The diagnosis of DiGeorge syndrome may be overlooked until the signs of congenital heart disease and development of recurrent infection caused by immunological deficiency become apparent.

Both primary hyperparathyroidism and hyperparathyroidism secondary to maternal hypoparathyroidism may rarely present in the neonatal period.[12]

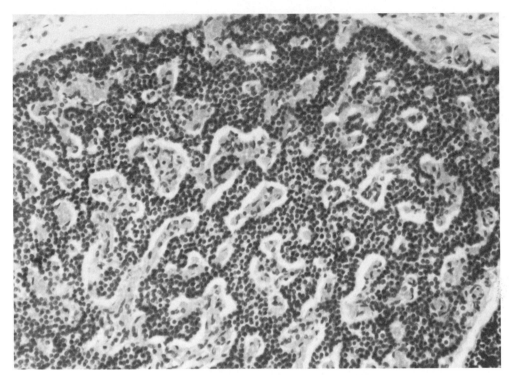

Figure 16—4. Normal parathyroid in a term infant. H and E × 150.

ADRENALS

DEVELOPMENT

The adrenal cortex develops during the fifth postconceptional week from the mesenchyme of the coelomic wall. By 8 weeks the cortex shows differentiation into a broad fetal zone and a narrow peripheral zone, the definitive adult cortex. The fetal cortex, which constitutes the major part of the gland throughout fetal life, consists of large polyhedral cells with acidophilic cytoplasm and abundant lipid. The definitive cortex consists of small cells with a dense nucleus and vacuolated cytoplasm containing lipid droplets. It is generally agreed that the definitive cortex develops into the zona glomerulosa and outer zona fasciculata of the mature gland, but it has been claimed that the inner fasciculata and the zona reticularis are derived from the fetal cortex.[11]

The cells of the adrenal medulla are derived from the sympathetic nervous system and are thus of neural crest origin. The cells migrate from the neural crest at about the seventh week and congregate at the center of the adrenal, where they develop into characteristic chromaffin cells. However, during the fetal period the cells of the adrenal medulla appear as groups of undifferentiated neuroblasts near the central vein. Throughout fetal life about three fourths of the width of the adrenal consists of the fetal cortex.

FUNCTIONS OF THE ADRENAL CORTEX IN THE PERINATAL PERIOD

The fetal and adult zones of the adrenal cortex are involved in different forms of steroid biosynthesis and secretion.[1, 13]

The fetal cortex forms part of the fetoplacental unit and is concerned in the metabolic pathways for estrogen synthesis. In particular, pregnenolone sulfate, formed in the placenta, is converted to dehydroepiandrosterone (DHA) in the fetal adrenal cortex and may then pass to the fetal liver, where it is hydroxylated to 16-α-hydroxydehydroepiandrosterone before return to the placenta for conversion to estriol. The fetal zone cannot synthesize cortisol, corticosterone and aldosterone because it lacks essential enzymes such as 3-β-hydroxydehydrogenase. However, it is able to convert progesterone formed in the placenta into these steroids. The fetal zone of the cortex is stimulated by the peptides of the intermediate lobe of the fetal pituitary, corticotrophin-like intermediate lobe peptide (CLIP) and α-melanocyte-stimulating hormone (αMSH).

The adult zone of the adrenal cortex has developed the ability to synthesize both mineralocorticoids and glucocorticoids by the third trimester; preterm infants do not normally show evidence of an impaired reaction to stress in the early neonatal period. The adult zone is stimulated by ACTH production from the fetal anterior pituitary.

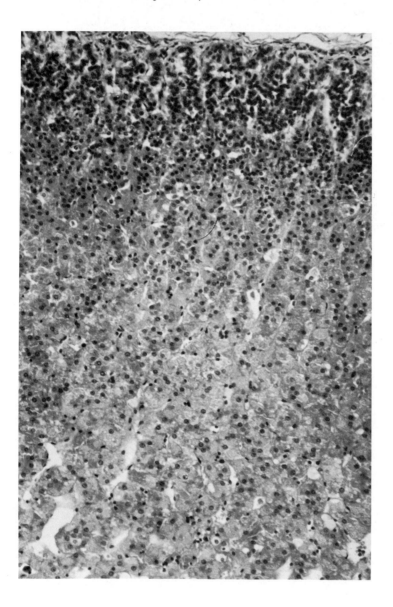

Figure 16–5. Adrenal at term showing that the organ is composed mainly of fetal cortex, with the definitive cortex limited to a small subcapsular zone. H and E × 150.

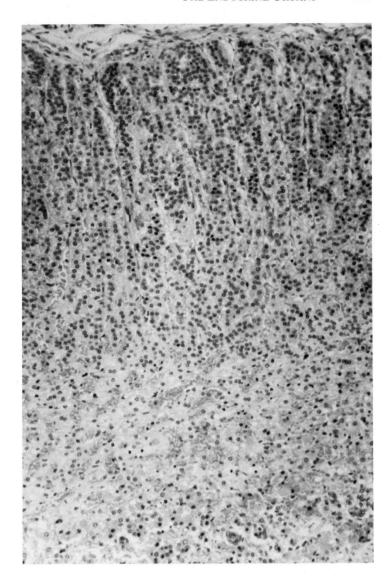

Figure 16–6. Adrenal at 4 weeks of age showing development of definitive cortex and atrophy of fetal cortex. H and E × 150.

There is some evidence that growth-retarded infants have smaller adrenals and may respond less well to stress in the neonatal period than infants with normal growth.[13, 14]

CHANGES IN THE ADRENAL AFTER BIRTH

The fetal zone of the adrenal cortex atrophies rapidly during the first month after birth, irrespective of the time of gestation at which the infant was born (Figs. 16–5 and 16–6). At the same time the adult cortex differentiates into the normal definitive zones. However, the growth and development of the adult cortex is considerably less rapid than the atrophy of the fetal cortex. Thus there is a fairly rapid decrease in adrenal weight after birth from about 8 to 10 gm (combined weight) in the 3 kg infant at term to about 3 gm in the 5 kg infant at 3 months of age.

The collapsed stroma of the fetal cortex contributes to the connective tissue around the adrenal medulla.

However, in infants who die in the neonatal period, there is considerable variation in the extent to which the fetal cortex has atrophied and the adult cortex has developed at a particular age. This variation apparently reflects variations in the type and severity of stress to which the infant was subjected during life.

ABNORMALITIES OF FORM AND POSITION

Anomalies of the renal tract may be associated with abnormal adrenal form. In renal agenesis the adrenals are flat, discoid structures on the posterior abdominal wall. In cases in which the kidneys are fused the adrenals may also be fused in the midline.

Accessory nodules of adrenal cortical tissue are common and of no functional significance. Such nodules may be attached to or embedded within the normal adrenal or related to other organs such as the testis or inferior pole of the kidney or even located within the thoracic cavity.[11]

ADRENAL HYPOPLASIA

Anencephaly is associated with severe adrenal hypoplasia. The combined weight of the adrenals in this condition is well below 1 gm at term. On histological examination the adult cortex appears relatively well developed, but the fetal zone is almost completely absent (Fig. 16–7). This finding is in accord with the lack of the intermediate lobe of the pituitary and its hormones (CLIP and MSH) in the anencephalic fetus.

The fetal zone of the cortex is relatively well developed in anencephalics examined in the early second trimester but degenerates during the latter part of

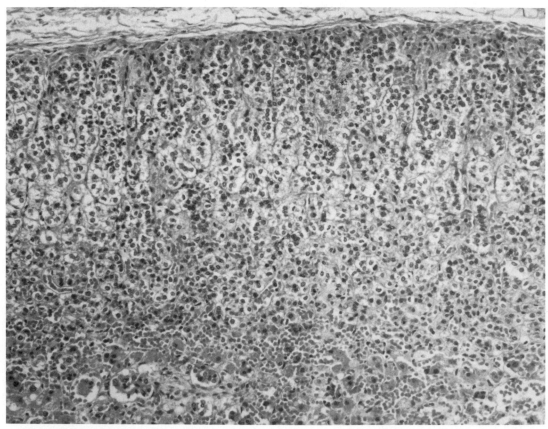

Figure 16–7. Adrenal in anencephaly, showing well-developed definitive cortex and almost total lack of fetal cortex. H and E × 150.

gestation.[15] Pituitary aplasia or hypoplasia occasionally occurs in infants without anencephaly. All such infants, as well as those with hypothalamic malformations associated with lack of hypothalamic-pituitary connections, have adrenal hypoplasia of a form identical to that seen in anencephaly.[11]

Idiopathic adrenal hypoplasia is recognized as occurring in several different forms.[11, 16, 17] In one, the adrenals are similar to those of infants with anencephaly or pituitary aplasia, with virtual absence of fetal cortex. Death occurs within a few days of birth if the condition is not recognized. In a second distinctive form of adrenal hypoplasia the adrenal cortex is composed of large pale cells without organization into the normal cortical layers. This form has been called the *cytomegalic* type of adrenal hypoplasia. In the third form of adrenal hypoplasia, seen in 15 of 20 cases recognized by Larroche, the histological appearance is that of a miniature of the normal fetal gland, with gross reduction in overall adrenal size but a normal ratio of adult cortex to fetal cortex. Pseudocysts of the adult cortex are characteristic of this form of adrenal hypoplasia.

Idiopathic adrenal hypoplasia is more common in the male and is often familial. Several modes of genetic inheritance have been suggested, including autosomal recessive and X-linked. It is possible that inheritance may vary accoriding to the type of hypoplasia.

The diagnosis of adrenal hypoplasia is seldom made in life unless a previous sibling has been affected or the infant survives the early neonatal period. Thus of the 20 affected infants recognized by Larroche, 18 died in the first 48 hours after birth. These were mainly preterm infants with respiratory distress. Clinical signs of hypoadrenalism, including circulatory collapse, hyponatremia, hyperkalemia, and hypoglycemia, may develop within the first 2 weeks. If the condition is recognized clinically, replacement therapy may be successful.

The relatively small adrenals of growth-retarded infants have been mentioned earlier (Fig. 16–8).

CHANGES ATTRIBUTED TO ADRENAL STRESS

A number of variations in the appearance of the adrenal in the perinatal period have been observed and have been suggested to indicate preceding episodes of stress.

The amount and distribution of lipid in the adrenal of the macerated stillborn fetus has been classified into several different types by Becker and Becker.[18] In some instances lipid is confined to the adult cortex (type 1), whereas in others it is present throughout the fetal cortex (type 2) and in a third group there is massive fatty change throughout the fetal cortex (type 3). It has been claimed that type 1 change is associated with an acute mode of death, type 2 with a more prolonged illness and type 3 with a chronic illness such as that due to preeclamptic toxemia and placental infarction.

In fresh stillborn infants the histological features of stress as recorded in adult adrenals have been recognized by De Sa.[19] These include:

1. A diffuse compact cell change, with plump eosinophilic cells in the cortex instead of the normal pale cells with foamy cytoplasm
2. Reduction of stainable and refractile lipid in the cortex
3. Increased pyroninophilia of the adrenal cortical cells
4. Degeneration, with or without cytolysis, of the cortical cells.

Lipid depletion commonly affects most of the fetal cortex with sparing of the definitive cortex and outer fetal cortex only, with persistence of clear, lipid-filled cells in the inner fetal cortex (clear cell reversal).

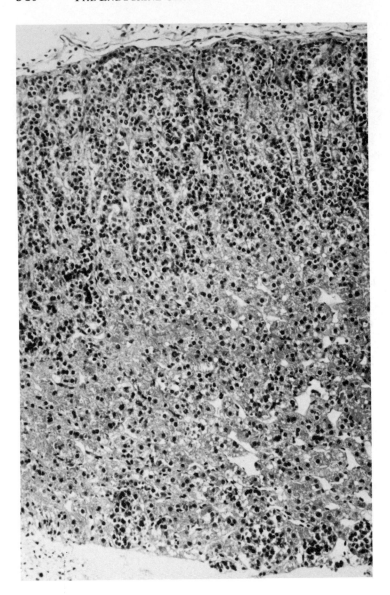

Figure 16–8. Adrenal of a severely growth-retarded infant born at 28 weeks' gestation who died at 4 days of age. H and E × 150. There is a poorly developed fetal cortex but a far more prominent definitive cortex that is commonly seen at term. Compare with Figure 16–5.

The adrenals of preterm infants often show a cystic pseudofollicular change of the definitive cortex (Fig. 16–9). The cystic spaces may be filled with blood. This appearance has been attributed to prenatal stress with focal degeneration of the adrenal cortical cells.[19, 20]

HEMORRHAGE AND INFARCTION

The fetal cortex is often congested, with grossly dilated sinusoids. This appearance may be mistaken for hemorrhage.

Adrenal hemorrhage is seen in cases of birth asphyxia and trauma most often, but not exclusively, in association with breech delivery. The lesions usually take the form of partial hemorrhagic necrosis, but there is sometimes massive bleeding, as illustrated in Chapter 5. Adrenal hemorrhage in breech delivery is often attributed to trauma incurred during manipulation of the infant's trunk by the obstetrician, but, as stressed by De Sa and Nicholls, may well be caused by asphyxia.[21]

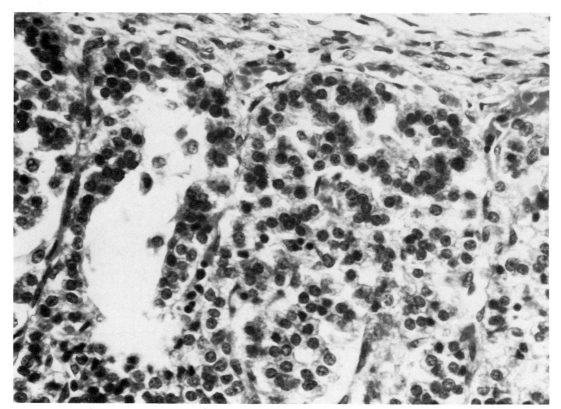

Figure 16–9. Adrenal of a preterm infant showing pseudofollicular change of the definitive cortex. H and E × 300.

Adrenal infarction is often ischemic rather than hemorrhagic, or both forms of change may be present in the same organ. Patchy adrenal infarction is seen relatively frequently in preterm infants dying during intensive care and may be associated with infarction of other splanchnic organs such as the kidneys, intestine and liver (Fig. 16–10). Thrombosis of the central vein of the adrenals is a relatively common autopsy finding and is linked with adrenal infarction.[21]

The adrenals of infants who die following neonatal intensive care but do not show frank infarction may display an accelerated degeneration of the fetal cortex.

ADRENALS IN ERYTHROBLASTOSIS

In severe erythroblastosis due to Rh isoimmunization the adrenals are large with pronounced lipid streaking of the fetal cortex, which can be seen to run from center to periphery. On histological examination, many of the cortical cells are ballooned and foamy in appearance because of gross lipid infiltration (Fig. 16–11). I have seen similar changes in other conditions in which the fetus is severely anemic at birth.

ADRENAL CYTOMEGALY

In adrenal cytomegaly there are abnormally large cells within the fetal cortex. The nuclei are densely basophilic and several times larger than normal, and the cytoplasm appears granular and eosinophilic (Fig. 16–12). A few such cells scattered throughout the fetal cortex are seen relatively frequently. However, the most dramatic examples are seen as part of the Beckwith-Wiedemann syndrome (Chapter 7). The significance of the large cells is unclear.

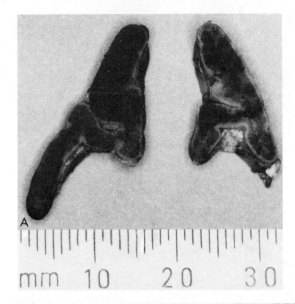

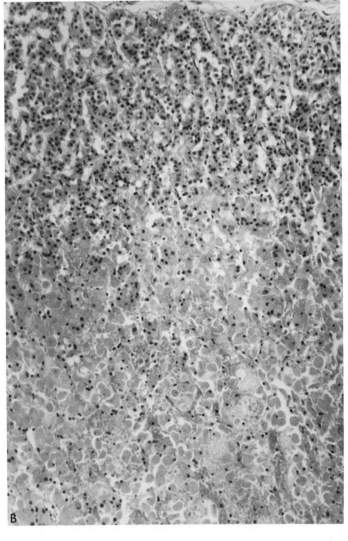

Figure 16–10. Adrenals of an infant who died of septicemia at 4 days of age, showing extensive infarction. *A*, Macroscopic view showing areas of hemorrhagic infarction. *B*, Histologic section showing early ischemic necrosis of the fetal cortex. H and E × 150.

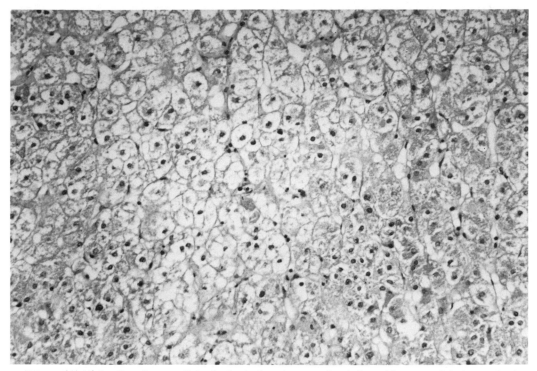

Figure 16–11. Swollen, foamy cells in the fetal adrenal cortex of an infant with severe Rh isoimmunization. H and E × 150. These groups of foamy lipid-filled cells tend to be orientated at right angles to the surface of the adrenal giving a streaky appearance to the cut surface.

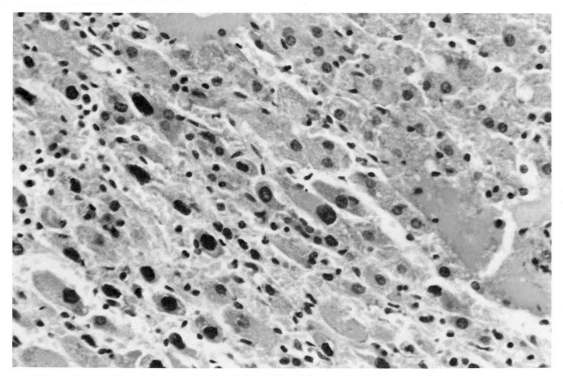

Figure 16–12. Adrenal cytomegaly. H and E × 600. This was an incidental finding in the fetal cortex of a fresh stillborn term infant. The appearance has little resemblance to that of cytomegalovirus infection.

ADRENALS IN INFECTION

The adrenals show characteristic changes in a number of infections. They are a frequent site of the granulomas of listeriosis (Chapter 9), may harbor Toxoplasma cysts within the endothelial cells and may show fibrosis beneath the capsule in congenital syphilis (see Potter and Craig).[9] Coagulative necrosis affecting the adrenals and liver is a leading feature of disseminated herpes simplex infection in the newborn.

CONGENITAL ADRENAL HYPERPLASIA

The various forms of congenital adrenal hyperplasia are caused by enzyme deficiencies in the metabolic pathways for adrenal steroid production with resulting increased ACTH output by the pituitary leading to adrenal hypertrophy and excessive production of abnormal androgenic and aldosterone-like steroids.[9, 11, 22]

The most frequent abnormality is a deficiency of 21-hydroxylase. If the deficiency is partial, there is virilization of the female fetus at birth with an enlarged clitoris, which is often associated with fusion of the labia and a vagina that opens into the posterior urethra. The male infant may show little external abnormality apart from increased scrotal pigmentation and a slightly enlarged penis. An incomplete 21-hydroxylase deficiency in the male may not be recognized in the neonatal period. Complete 21-hydroxylase deficiency (salt-losing form of 21-hydroxylase deficiency) is associated with lack of aldosterone secretion leading to hyponatremia, hyperkalemia and death in adrenal crisis within a few days or weeks of birth if the diagnosis is missed. Both forms of 21-hydroxylase deficiency are of autosomal recessive inheritance.

A rare form of adrenal cortical hyperplasia is caused by an 11-hydroxylation defect. This hyperplasia is associated with development of hypertension and cardiac hypertrophy owing to salt retention resulting from secretion of desoxycorticosterone.

The adrenals in all these forms of congenital hyperplasia are grossly enlarged (up to several times normal weight) and have an excessively convoluted (cerebriform) surface (Fig. 16–13). The latter feature is particularly prominent on cut section. There is increase in both fetal and adult cortex on histological examination.

ADRENAL TUMORS

Tumors of the adrenal cortex are exceedingly rare in the perinatal period. Neuroblastoma, in contrast, is one of the most common malignant embryomas that may be seen in the newborn infant.

Congenital Neuroblastoma. Neuroblastoma represents 15 to 50 per cent of all neonatal malignant tumors.[23] The incidence in United States cases in children less than 29 days of age has recently been quoted as 19.7 per million live births per year.[24] The condition usually is detected as an abdominal mass, although cases in which extensive metastatic spread has occurred may involve unusual features such as hepatomegaly or paralysis with a neurogenic bladder. A characteristic pattern of metastatic neuroblastoma in neonates known as stage IVs involves microscopic bone marrow infiltration with hepatic and cutaneous metastases. The gross and histological features of congenital neuroblastoma are otherwise identical to those of neuroblastoma appearing in older infants and children (Fig. 16–14).

There is a high incidence of spontaneous regression in congenital neuroblastoma, which usually commences 2 to 6 months after the initial diagnosis with diminution in size of the liver. The primary tumor and its metastases undergo a process of maturation and come to resemble a ganglioneuroma.

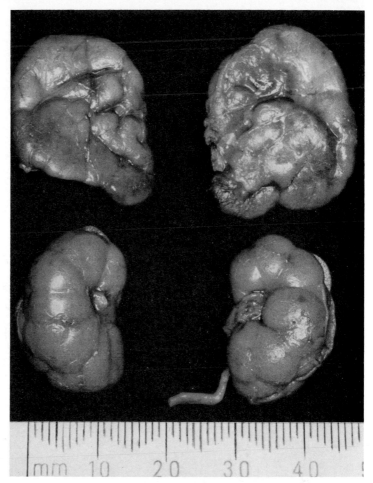

Figure 16–13. Adrenals in congenital adrenal hyperplasia. This was an incidental finding in an infant aborted spontaneously at 24 weeks' gestation. The adrenals already have a cerebriform pattern, but this is less marked than at term.

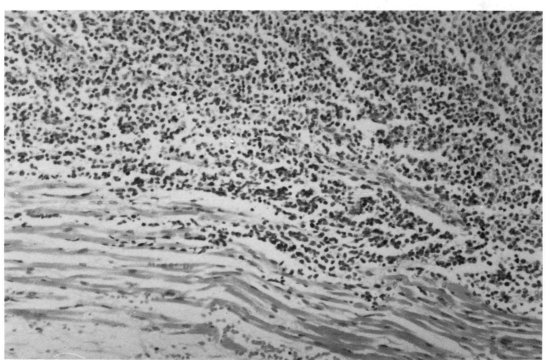

Figure 16–14. Congenital neuroblastoma invading the psoas muscle. H and E × 150. The section is from a term infant who died at 30 hours of age following severe birth asphyxia with intracranial trauma.

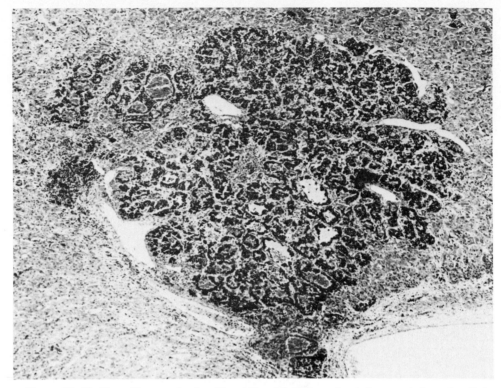

Figure 16–15. Neuroblastoma in situ. H and E × 30. This section is from an infant who died as a result of severe Rh rhesus isoimmunization.

NEUROBLASTOMA IN SITU

Neuroblastoma in situ comprises nodular aggregates of primitive neuroblasts in the center of the adrenal glands recognized as an incidental finding at perinatal autopsy (Fig. 16–15). The quoted frequency of the condition varies from 1 in 10 to 1 in 500 perinatal autopsies according to the minimum size of nodules accepted and the effort made to find them.[25, 26] There is some evidence that the appearance of such nodules may represent a normal stage of development in early fetal life.[27] Although the larger aggregates probably represent a precursor of metastasizing neuroblastoma, it is clear that most of them regress spontaneously.

PANCREATIC ISLETS

These are discussed in Chapter 15 along with the exocrine pancreas.

REFERENCES

1. Silman, R. E., Chard, T., and Boyd, N. R. H.: Fetal endocrinology. *In* Philipp, E. E., Barnes, J., and Newton, M. (eds.): Scientific Foundations of Obstetrics and Gynaecology, 2nd ed. London, William Heinemann, 1977, pp. 359–375.
2. Swaab, D. F., Boer, G. J., and Visser, M.: The fetal brain and intrauterine growth. Postgrad. Med. J. *54* (Suppl. 1):63–73, 1978.
3. Liggins, G. C.: The drive to fetal growth. *In* Beard, R. W., and Nathanielsz, P. W. (eds): Fetal Physiology and Medicine. London, W. B. Saunders, Ltd., 1976, pp. 254–270.
4. Milner, R. D. G.: Growth and development of the endocrine pancreas. *In* Davis, J. A., and Dobbing, J. (eds.): Scientific Foundations of Paediatrics, 2nd ed. London, William Heinemann, 1981, pp. 701–713.

5. Honnebier, W. J., and Swaab, D. F.: The influence of anencephaly upon intrauterine growth of fetus and placenta and upon gestation length. J. Obstet. Gynaecol. Br Cwlth. *80*:577–588, 1973.
6. Chiswick, M. L., Ahmed, A., Jack, P. M. B., and Milner, R. D. G.: Control of fetal lung development in the rabbit. Arch. Dis. Child. *48*:709–713, 1973.
7. Sadeghi-Nejad, A., and Senior, B.: Familial syndrome of isolated aplasia of the anterior pituitary. J. Pediatr. *84*:79–84, 1974.
8. Pearse, A. G. E., Polak, J. M., and Van Noordan, S.: The neural crest origin of the C cells and their comparative cytochemistry and ultrastructure in the ultimobranchial gland. *In* Talmage, R. V., and Munson, P. L. (eds.): Calcium, Parathyroid Hormone and Calcitonins. Amsterdam, Excerpta Medica, 1972, pp. 29–40.
9. Potter, E. L., and Craig, J. M.: Pathology of the Fetus and the Infant, 3rd ed. Chicago, Year Book Medical Publishers, 1976, pp. 317–343.
10. Sagreiya, K., and Emery, J. L.: Perinatal thyroid discharge. A histological study of 1225 infant thyroids. Arch. Dis. Child. *45*:746–745, 1970.
11. Larroche, J. C.: Developmental Pathology of the Neonate. Amsterdam, Excerpta Medica, 1977, pp. 225–231.
12. Rhone, D. P.: Primary neonatal hyperparathyroidsm. Report of a case and review of the literature. Am. J. Clin. Pathol. *64*:488–499, 1975.
13. Forsyth, C. C.: Growth and development of the adrenal cortex. *In* Davis, J. A., and Dobbing, J. (eds.): Scientific Foundations of Paediatrics, 2nd ed. London, William Heinemann, 1981, pp. 660–691.
14. Anderson, A. B. M., Laurence, K. M., Davies, K., Campbell, H. and Turnbull, A. C.: Fetal adrenal weight and the cause of premature delivery in human pregnancy. J. Obstet. Gynaecol. Cwlth. *78*:481–488, 1971.
15. Sucheston, M. E., and Cannon, M. S.: Microscopic comparison of the normal and anencephalic human adrenal gland with emphasis on the transient-zone. Obstet. Gynecol. *35*:544–553, 1970.
16. Kerenyi, N.: Congenital adrenal hypoplasia. Report of a case with extreme adrenal hypoplasia and neurohypophyseal aplasia, drawing attention to certain aspects of etiology and classification. Arch. Pathol. *71*:336–343, 1961.
17. Sperling, M. A., Wolfson, A. R., and Fisher, D. A.: Congenital adrenal hypoplasia: An isolated defect of organogenesis. J. Pediatr. *82*:444–449, 1973.
18. Becker, M. J., and Becker, A. E.: Fat distribution in the adrenal cortex as an indication of the mode of intrauterine death. Hum. Pathol. *7*:495–504, 1976.
19. De Sa, D. J.: Stress response and its relationship to cystic (pseudofollicular) change in the definitive cortex of the adrenal gland in stillborn infants. Arch. Dis. Child. *53*:769–776, 1978.
20. Oppenheimer, E. H.: Cyst formation in the outer adrenal cortex. Studies in the human fetus and newborn. Arch. Pathol. *87*:653–659, 1969.
21. De Sa, D. J., and Nicholls, S.: Haemorrhagic necrosis of the adrenal gland in perinatal infants: A clinicopathological study. J. Pathol. *106*:133–149, 1972.
22. Visser, H. K. A.: The adrenal cortex in childhood, Part II: Pathological aspects. Arch. Dis. Child. *41*:113–136, 1966.
23. Dehner, L. P.: Neoplasms of the fetus and neonate. *In* Naeye, R. L., Kissane, J. M., and Kaufman, N.: Perinatal Diseases. Baltimore, Williams & Wilkins, 1981, pp. 286–345.
24. Bader, E. L., and Miller, R. W.: U. S. cancer incidence and mortality in the first year of life. Am. J. Dis. Child. *133*:157–159, 1979.
25. Bolande, R. P.: Neoplasia of early life. *In* Rosenberg, H. S., and Bolande, R. P. (eds.): Perspectives in Pediatric Pathology, vol. 3. Chicago, Year Book Medical Publishers, 1976, pp. 145–183.
26. Beckwith, J. B., and Perrin, E. V.: In situ neuroblastomas: A contribution to the natural history of neural crest tumors. Am. J. Pathol. *43*:1089–1104, 1963.
27. Turkel, S. B., and Itabashi, H. H.: The natural history of neuroblastic cells in the fetal adrenal gland. Am. J. Pathol. *76*:225–244, 1974.

Chapter Seventeen

The Kidneys and Urinary Tract

There are few diseases that primarily affect the kidneys and urinary tract during the perinatal period. However, this system is an important site of congenital anomalies, ranging from the inevitably fatal renal agenesis and the severe forms of renal cystic dysplasia to obstructive lesions of the lower urinary tract. Major renal or urinary anomalies form a component of many multiorgan malformation syndromes, and microcystic renal lesions occur in a number of inborn errors of metabolism. In addition, the kidney is rapidly and severely affected by episodes of circulatory collapse in the perinatal period. Histological examination of the organ can provide the pathologist with useful evidence of such events.

DEVELOPMENT AND FUNCTION OF THE KIDNEYS IN THE FETUS

RENAL DEVELOPMENT

Development of the definitive kidney is preceded by appearance and regression of primitive and nonfunctional systems, the pronephros and mesonephros. The latter is of importance in that the mesonephric (wolffian) duct develops from it and persists in the male as the ductus deferens. The definitive kidney first appears during the fifth postconceptional week. The ureteric bud forms as an outgrowth of the mesonephric duct and extends into the metanephric mesenchyme of the lower end of the urogenital ridge. The terminal end of the ureteric bud, the ampulla, undergoes a series of dichotomous divisions. The first few generations form the renal pelvis and calyces while subsequent divisions form the collecting tubules. The tips of the ampullae induce formation of nephrons from the adjacent metanephric blastema. The nephrons appear initially as solid masses of cells that develop slit-like cavities and then elongate into an S shape before attaching at one end to the ampulla (Fig. 17–1). By this means a continuous lumen becomes established between nephron and collecting tubule. The distal end of the nephron develops a concavity around the capillaries that form the glomerular tuft and differentiates into the epithelial cells of the glomerulus and the lining cells of Bowman's capsule.

The sequential formation of nephrons throughout fetal life was described in a series of papers by Osathanondh and Potter and is summarized in Potter and Craig (1976).[1] Nephron induction ceases at between 32 and 36 weeks' gestation, and beyond this time the nephrogenic zone beneath the renal capsule disappears (Fig. 17–2). Following preterm birth, glomerular formation continues until the normal complement of glomeruli is achieved.

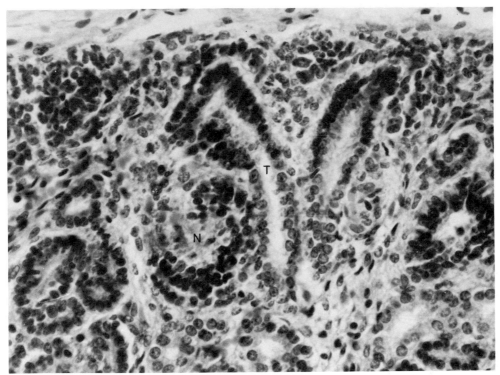

Figure 17–1. Renal cortex at 20 weeks' gestation. H and E × 300. A developing nephron, "N," is seen closely related to the ampulla of a collecting tubule, "T."

PRENATAL RENAL FUNCTION

Urine secretion commences from the time when the first differentiated nephrons are formed. The gross bladder distension that can be observed early in the second trimester in some cases of bladder outlet obstruction indicates that there is significant urinary output early in fetal life. However, the quantitative aspects of fetal urine production are unknown. Urine is discharged into the amniotic cavity, and some will subsequently be swallowed by the fetus, although it is believed that some fetomaternal transfer of urea and water can take place directly from the amniotic sac across the uterine wall.[2] The consistent development of oligohydramnios in cases of renal agenesis and urinary outlet obstruction indicates that fetal urine forms a major constituent of amniotic fluid in the latter half of pregnancy.

Uric acid is present in considerable amounts in the urine of the newborn infant. The kidneys of infants who die at a few days of age often show prominent orange-yellow streaking of the renal medulla caused by the presence of urate deposits within the collecting tubules. These deposits are of no pathological significance.

MALFORMATIONS OF THE KIDNEYS

BILATERAL RENAL AGENESIS (POTTER'S SYNDROME)

This condition is ascribed to failure of development of the ureteric bud from the mesonephric duct or to degeneration of the ureteric bud at an early stage. It is said to occur with an incidence of about 1 in 4000 births. The infants show the

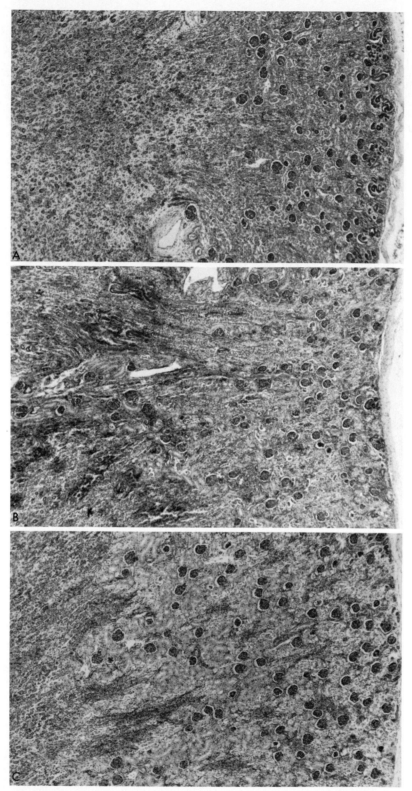

Figure 17–2. Kidney at different stages of gestation. H and E × 30. *A*, 28 weeks; *B*, 36 weeks; *C*, 40 weeks. Note the disappearance of the subcapsular layer of newly forming glomeruli at 36 weeks and the increasing number of layers of developed glomeruli with advancing gestation.

external features characteristic of oligohydramnios dating from early in pregnancy (Chapter 7) and normally die at a few hours of age as a result of lung hypoplasia. Rare cases have been reported in which renal agenesis in one of a pair of monoamniotic twins without oligohydramnios was associated with a normal external appearance and normally developed lungs, and death has been delayed until renal failure supervened.[3]

On dissection, the kidneys and ureters are absent and the bladder is represented by a narrow tubular structure. The adrenals are discoid in form because of lack of molding by the renal tissue during development (Chapter 16). Bilateral renal agenesis is seen in all cases of sirenomelia and is often associated with abnormalities of the genital tract such as absent uterus and vagina or of the lower intestine or heart.[1]

UNILATERAL AGENESIS

Unilateral agenesis is seen only incidentally in the perinatal period. In females with unilateral renal agenesis the fallopian tube on the affected side is usually absent.

OTHER VARIATIONS IN FORM AND POSITION

Variations are common but are of little functional significance in the perinatal period. One or both kidneys may be situated either abnormally close to the midline or near the brim of the pelvis. They are usually rounded in form and often have the pelvis directed anteriorly. Fusion of the kidneys characteristically involves the lower poles and presents as the horseshoe kidney in which the ureters pass anterior to the fused portion (Fig. 17–3). Sometimes the ureter from one kidney crosses the midline to enter the bladder on the opposite side, a condition known as crossed ectopia. Other abnormalities of form are illustrated in Potter and Craig.[1] These minor anomalies are all compatible with normal survival but may assume importance in chronically ill infants in whom the distorted pelvicalyceal system forms a nidus for ascending infection with organisms such as *Candida albicans* (Fig. 17–3*B*).

RENAL HYPOPLASIA

Since renal development is dependent on induction of nephron formation within the metanephric blastema by the ureteric bud, normal renal tissue cannot develop in the absence of a ureter, although occasional instances of a small mass of cysts in the position of the kidney may be observed with no apparent ureter. In the presence of a ureter some form of renal tissue is virtually always present. Grossly undersized kidneys are most often associated with cystic dysplastic change. In older infants, unduly small kidneys (< 2 standard deviations below mean for body weight) often have evidence of secondary pathology such as pyelonephritis, which may obscure the underlying primary hypoplasia. A condition of congenital bilateral oligonephronic renal hypoplasia is recognized in which the few nephrons present are hypertrophied and the infants suffer from anemia and growth failure.[4] In the neonatal period extremely small kidneys without cystic change can sometimes be seen.

RENAL CYSTS AND CYSTIC DISEASE

In recent years the subject of renal cysts and cystic disease in infancy has been dominated by the studies of Osathanondh and Potter,[5] which are summarized

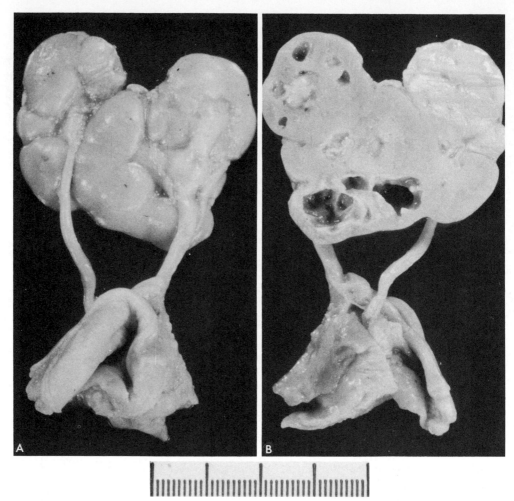

Figure 17–3. Horseshoe kidney·from an infant of 27 weeks' gestation who died at 5 weeks of age. *A*, Anterior surface showing relation of ureters to fused lower poles. *B*, Cut section with multiple abscesses due to infection with *Candida albicans*.

by Potter and Craig. As a result of studies on over 300 kidneys, including a large number of microdissections, these workers developed a classification of renal cystic conditions and propounded theories of origin for each variety. It is important that this classification be understood because it has been widely adopted, although I do not find the approach used fully satisfying at an intellectual level for reasons to be explained.

INFANTILE POLYCYSTIC DISEASE (TYPE I CYSTIC KIDNEY OF OSATHANONDH AND POTTER)

In infantile polycystic disease, which is of autosomal recessive inheritance, the kidneys are grossly and uniformly enlarged but appear superficially of normal form (Fig. 17–4). On external examination the cortex is seen to be speckled with multiple minute cysts. The cut surface of the kidney presents a characteristic uniform spongy appearance with fusiform, radially oriented cysts that represent cystic dilations of the collecting tubules. Normal glomeruli are present throughout the cortex. Microdissection studies show that the nephrons are normally attached. The condition thus appears to result from a secondary dilation of the collecting tubules. Cystic dilations of intrahepatic bile ducts are always present (Chapter 14).

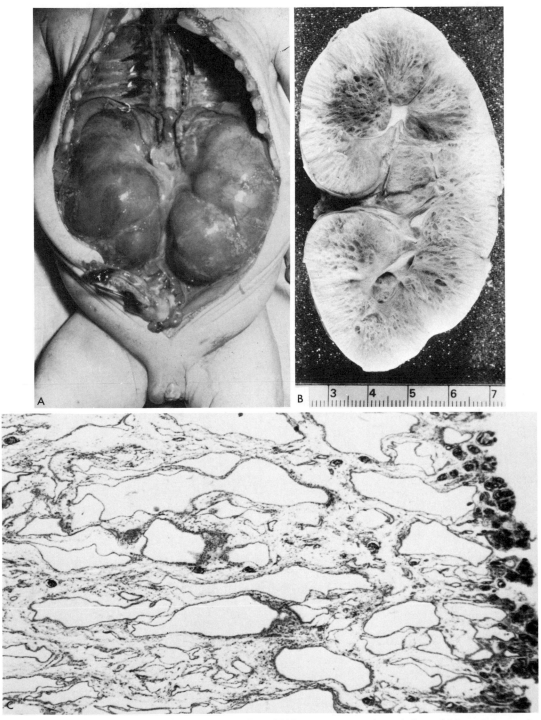

Figure 17–4. Infantile polycystic disease. *A,* View of kidneys at autopsy in an infant of 30 weeks' gestation who died at 18 hours of age of severe respiratory distress associated with hypoplastic lungs. *B,* Cut surface of kidney showing the characteristic spongy appearance. *C,* Histologic appearance. H and E × 30. There is generalized fusiform dilatation of the tubules, accounting for the spongy appearance seen at macroscopic level. Glomeruli are present beneath the capsule.

The condition is of variable expression. In some families the infants do not die in the neonatal period but later have manifestations of infantile hepatic fibrosis, although both kidneys and liver are always affected.[6] In those cases I have seen, the infants had hypoplastic lungs and died in respiratory failure within a few hours of birth.

CYSTIC DYSPLASTIC KIDNEYS (TYPE II CYSTIC KIDNEY OF OSATHANONDH AND POTTER)

This is the form of cystic kidney that is seen most frequently at autopsy in the perinatal period. The kidney may be represented by small masses of cysts associated with thread-like ureters and a narrow tubular bladder, or may be large, with multiple cysts of varying size. Sometimes one kidney is large and the other small (Fig. 17–5), and occasionally the cystic change affects part of a kidney only.

Microdissection has shown reduction in both collecting tubules and nephrons, the cysts being derived from terminal parts of the few collecting tubules. If the cysts are large the kidneys are enlarged (Potter type IIA); if they are small or absent the kidneys are small (Potter type IIB). With either type the renal calyces are absent and the pelves and ureters are usually narrow, indicating lack of urine production. On section the kidneys appear to consist entirely of connective tissue and cysts.

Microscopy shows a considerable increase in connective tissue with thick-

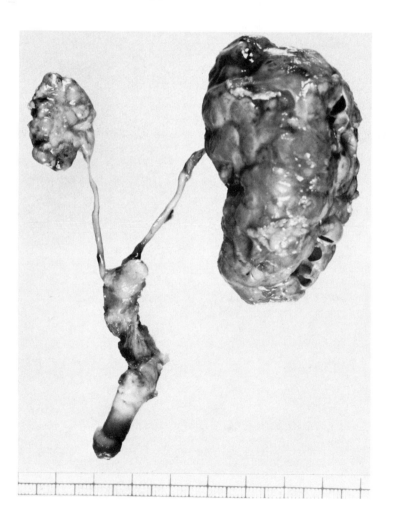

Figure 17–5. Cystic dysplastic kidneys associated with threadlike ureters and a narrow tubular bladder. One kidney is markedly enlarged (Potter type 11A) and the other is extremely small (Potter type 11B).

walled cysts, small groups of tubules and scanty, poorly developed glomeruli (Fig. 17–6). Areas of undifferentiated mesenchyme may be seen and islands of cartilage and thick nerve trunks are often present. There is an absence of normal glomeruli and collecting tubules. Cystic kidneys of this type are said to be characteristic of cases in which there is total urinary outflow obstruction due to agenesis or atresia of the urethra.[1]

POLYCYSTIC KIDNEYS OF ADULT TYPE (TYPE III CYSTIC KIDNEYS)

In polycystic kidneys of adult type, which are infrequently seen in the newborn, normal and abnormal nephrons are intermingled. The condition affects both kidneys symmetrically, and cysts involve any part of the collecting tubules or Bowman's capsule. Although this condition is similar to the autosomal dominant form of polycystic disease as recognized in adults, it is not clear whether the condition as seen in the newborn is indeed the same. Infant deaths are not characteristic of families with the dominant form of polycystic disease.[7]

PARTIAL OR INTERMITTENT URINARY OUTFLOW OBSTRUCTION
(TYPE IV CYSTIC KIDNEY)

In cases in which urinary obstruction develops late or is incomplete, such as that caused by valvular obstruction in the posterior urethra, cysts are present in the outer cortex and there is usually hydronephrosis and hydroureter with a thickened, trabeculated bladder (Figs. 17–7 and 17–8). According to Potter, the initial stages of tubule and nephron development are normal, but increased pressure associated with outflow obstruction damages the ampullae, prevents induction of further nephrons and causes the nephrogenic zone to disappear. The level of renal function that is retained by the infant is determined by the nephron population induced before development of outflow obstruction.

COMMENT ON THE CLASSIFICATION OF CYSTIC KIDNEYS IN THE
NEWBORN

The painstaking studies of Osathanondh and Potter have considerably added to our knowledge of cystic disease of the kidneys. The classification into types as outlined earlier was clearly a useful way of sorting the findings on microdissection of kidneys, but it obscures the varying significance of the differences between types. Thus type I cystic kidneys represent a specific inherited disorder that is not explained on any simple embryological basis. In contrast, it appears that types II and IV kidneys may result from a similar defect (i.e., obstruction to urine outflow) and differ from each other only in the stage of development at which the defect becomes operative. Type III kidneys are again the result of a mechanism or a number of mechanisms that affect some nephrons while leaving others intact.

It is probably better, as suggested by Risdon,[8] to think of renal aplasia or dysplasia and the common forms of cystic displasia or multicystic kidney (Potter types II and IV) as variants on a continuum rather than a series of rigidly separated types of abnormality.

OTHER CONDITIONS ASSOCIATED WITH RENAL CYSTS

A large number of other conditions are associated with renal cysts of various types.[7] Renal cystic dysplasia with either large or small kidneys is a feature of Meckel-Gruber syndrome (Chapter 7). Dysplastic cystic changes of a diffuse nature are seen in Jeune's asphyxiating thoracic dystrophy, and a characteristic form of renal cyst lined with hyperplastic epithelium may be seen in tuberous sclerosis. Renal cortical cysts are seen as a minor component of a number of congenital

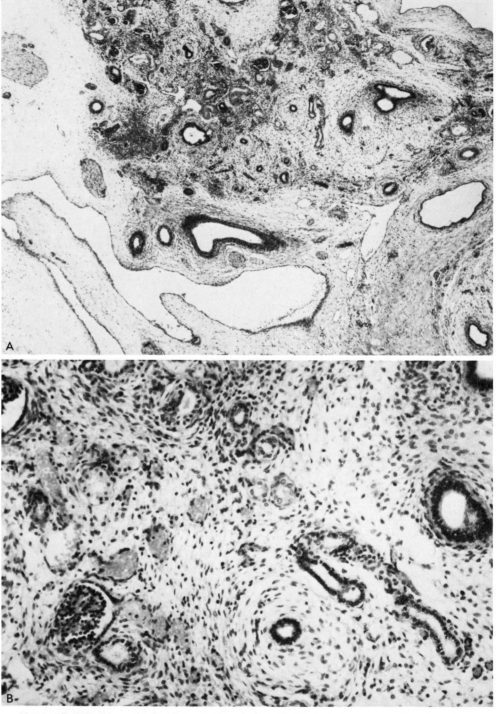

Figure 17–6. Cystic renal dysplasia. *A*, H and E × 30. There is loose connective tissue between the cysts containing nerve trunks and blood vessels and areas of mesenchyme containing renal tubular structures and occasional, poorly formed glomeruli. *B*, Detail of the same section (× 150), to show tubules and glomeruli within mesenchymal stroma.

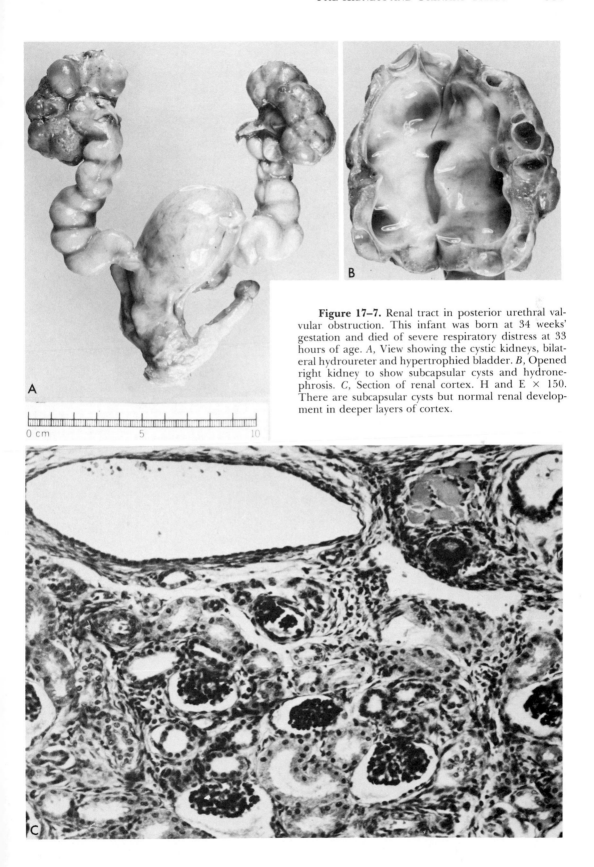

Figure 17–7. Renal tract in posterior urethral valvular obstruction. This infant was born at 34 weeks' gestation and died of severe respiratory distress at 33 hours of age. *A*, View showing the cystic kidneys, bilateral hydroureter and hypertrophied bladder. *B*, Opened right kidney to show subcapsular cysts and hydronephrosis. *C*, Section of renal cortex. H and E × 150. There are subcapsular cysts but normal renal development in deeper layers of cortex.

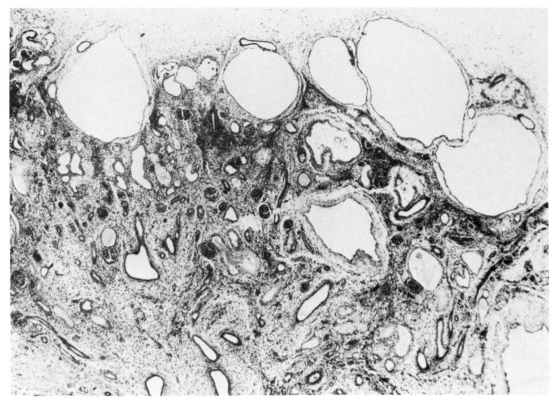

Figure 17–8. Kidney in prune-belly syndrome associated with urethral atresia at 26 weeks' gestation. H and E × 30. Cysts are most prominent in the subcortical region but there is evidence of severe disruption of nephrogenesis throughout the cortex as urinary obstruction has been present from early development. Compare with Figure 17– 7C.

malformation syndromes, including Zellweger syndrome and the autosomal trisomy syndromes trisomy 13 and 18.

KIDNEYS IN BECKWITH-WIEDEMANN SYNDROME

The kidneys in Beckwith-Wiedemann syndrome are often grossly enlarged and markedly lobulated. There is disorganization of medullary development with dilated collecting ducts and presence of primitive ducts, but cortical structure is normal. Nodular renal blastema and nephroblastoma have been reported to develop in these kidneys.[9]

RENAL LESIONS OF ASPHYXIA AND ISCHEMIA

A range of renal lesions may develop in the perinatal period in association with renal ischemia. The pattern of damage is quite variable, and both cortical and medullary lesions may be seen in the same infant. The susceptibility of the fetus and newborn infant to this form of damage is probably another manifestation of the shutdown of the splanchnic circulation in response to asphyxia or hypotension that also causes ischemic lesions of the intestine and adrenals (Chapters 13 and 16).[10, 11] The development of renal cortical or papillary necrosis in association with acute intrapartum asphyxia has already been mentioned in Chapter 6. Abruptio placentae is often associated with cortical necrosis. I have recognized necrosis of tubules within the cortex in a fetus aborted as early as 22 weeks' gestation in association with severe pre-eclampsia and placental infarction (Fig. 17–9). In other instances there may be extensive hemorrhage at the corticomed-

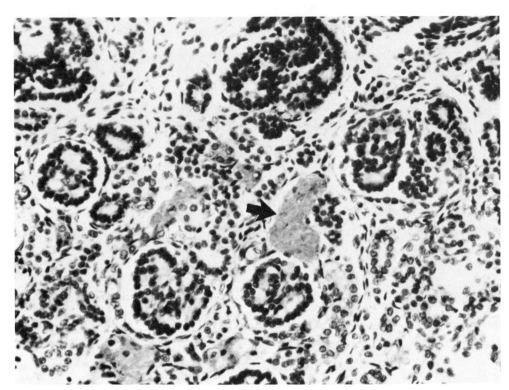

Figure 17–9. Renal cortex in a fetus stillborn at 22 weeks' gestation in association with severe maternal pre-eclampsia. H and E × 400. Established renal tubular necrosis is present (arrowed) indicating an episode of shock in utero.

ullary junction. Infants who die following severe birth asphyxia frequently have evidence of necrosis within the renal medulla. The demonstration of recovering tubular necrosis within such kidneys confirms the occurrence of an asphyxial or hypotensive episode (Fig. 17–10).

Vascular lesions seen in the kidneys of infants who die following neonatal intensive care include cortical and medullary necrosis, renal tubular necrosis and infarction (Figs. 17–10 and 17–11), associated with either arterial or venous thrombosis. The lesions are most often related to recurrent episodes of severe hypotension, and affected infants often have necrotizing enterocolitis or adrenal or myocardial necrosis in addition. Other etiological factors include congenital cardiac anomalies, severe anemia, disseminated intravascular coagulation and acute bacterial or viral infections. Of the last-named, echovirus infections have been incriminated in some cases of combined renal and adrenal infection.[12] Renal vein thrombosis is particularly likely to develop in newborn infants who become dehydrated and results in a swollen kidney with acute hemorrhagic infarction. Renal artery thrombosis is an occasional complication of umbilical artery catheterization.

In infants who survive renal infarction, foci of calcification may be recognizable within the necrotic tissue on radiological examination. Medullary infarction may lead to pelvicalyceal deformity in survivors, which can be visualized on intravenous or retrograde urography.[13]

RENAL INFECTIONS

Bacteriological infection of the kidney is rare in the perinatal period, although congenital pyelonephritis has been described.[14] Occasionally the kidney may be

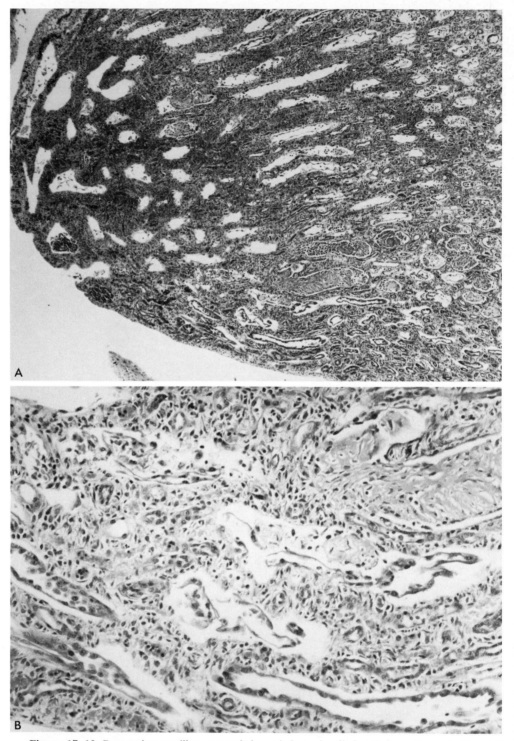

Figure 17–10. Recovering papillary necrosis in an infant who died at 6 days of age. *A,* H and E × 30. There is interstitial hemorrhage at the tip of the papilla and plugging of collecting tubules by desquamated epithelium. *B,* Detail of same section (× 150). Some of the tubules are lined by regenerating epithelium.

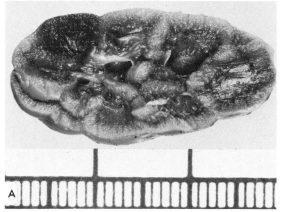

Figure 17–11. Renal infarction in an infant of 25 weeks' gestation who died at 7 days of age. *A*, Macroscopic view of cut kidney. *B*, Histologic section showing acute infarction. H and E × 30.

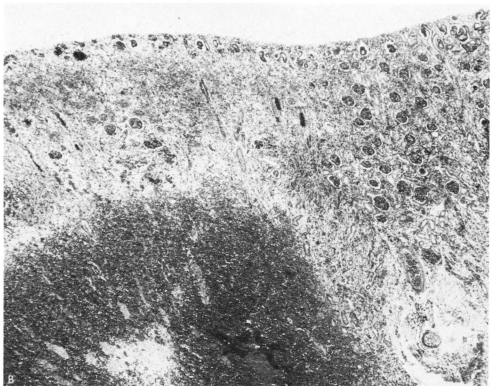

the site of abscess formation in a generalized septicemia. In later infancy bacterial infection is a frequent complication of renal anomalies such as cystic renal dysplasia and obstructive uropathy.

Viral infections may involve the kidneys in the perinatal period. Echovirus infection has been mentioned already as a cause of renal infarction. Cytomegalovirus infection often involves the kidney, and the typical owl-eyed cells are readily recognized in the proximal convoluted tubules in association with interstitial extramedullary hemopoietic activity (Chapter 9).

Fungal infection is a recognized complication of prolonged intravenous feeding of sick neonates. Such infections not infrequently localize in the kidneys, particularly if there is a minor underlying anomaly (Fig. 17–12).

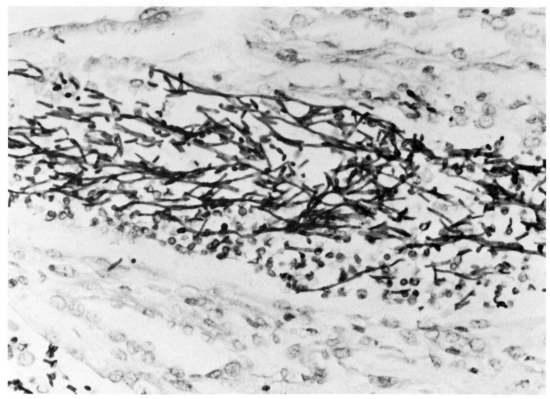

Figure 17–12. Medulla of horseshoe kidney illustrated in Figure 17–3 showing *Candida albicans* within the renal tubules. PAS × 400.

CONGENITAL NEPHROTIC SYNDROME

Congenital nephrotic syndrome is of autosomal recessive inheritance and has been recognized most often in families of Finnish origin. The infants are normal at birth, but the placenta is usually large and there may be polyhydramnios. Edema develops within the first few days of life with massive proteinuria and with red cells and red cell casts on urine microscopy. The proteinuria is unresponsive to corticosteroids and immunosuppressive therapy, and death from renal failure is usual within the first 2 years.

Early in the disease the glomeruli may appear normal on light microscopy, although nonspecific fusion of epithelial foot processes may be recognized on electron microscopy. Hypercellularity and hyalinization of glomeruli develop at a later stage, and at death there is widespread nonspecific glomerulosclerosis. Atrophy and focal cystic dilation of proximal tubules are sometimes prominent features.

No consistent pattern of immune complex deposition has been recognized.[8, 15]

CONGENITAL TUMORS

CONGENITAL MESOBLASTIC NEPHROMA

Since this tumor was clearly separated from nephroblastoma by Bolande,[16] it has become recognized as the most frequent renal tumor to present in the neonatal period. The tumor usually behaves as a benign neoplasm and is adequately treated by surgery. If it is incorrectly diagnosed as nephroblastoma, the child will be subjected to unnecessary additional treatment with radiation and chemotherapy, which carries its own significant risk of mortality and morbidity.

The tumor is usually unilateral and is most often recognized at birth or in the early neonatal period. It is a large tumor that may be several hundred grams in weight and has been reported as causing dystocia. The tumor is smooth-surfaced, being covered by the expanded renal capsule, but is poorly demarcated from the normal renal parenchyma. On section the tumor has a rubbery consistency and trabeculated appearance similar to that of a uterine fibroid and may contain a few cystic cavities, but it does not show hemorrhage or necrosis. The usual microscopic appearance is of interlacing sheets and bundles of spindle-shaped cells with entrapped tubular and glomerular remnants of normal kidney. Other histological patterns are described and illustrated by Bolande.

NODULAR RENAL BLASTEMA

Nodular renal blastema consists of microscopic clusters of immature meta-nephric blastema usually situated beneath the capsule of the kidney. These foci were first described in trisomy 18 and in children with Wilms' tumor,[17] although the condition may be seen in other malformation syndromes such as Beckwith-Weidemann syndrome or as an isolated finding at autopsy.

NEPHROBLASTOMA (WILMS' TUMOR)

Nephroblastoma is now known to be excessively rare in the neonatal period, although fatal metastasizing nephroblastoma has been adequately documented in this age group.[18] Most cases of congenital nephroblastoma are now recognized as one of the *infantile congeners of Wilms' tumor,* a term that includes mesoblastic nephroma, monomorphic epithelial nephroblastoma and the nodular renal blastema–nephroblastomatosis complex.[19–21] This recognition may well account for the high survival rate quoted in previous series of nephroblastoma diagnosed within the first year of life.

The inter-relationships between teratology and oncology that are reflected in congenital tumors are discussed further in Chapter 8.

RENAL PELVIS AND URETERS

The ureters and renal pelvis develop from the metanephric duct: the ureters develop from the unbranched caudal portion and the pelvis and calyces are formed by coalescence of the first generations of branching of the cranial portion.

URETERIC ANOMALIES

Some degree of duplication of pelvis and ureter is a common type of malformation. Duplication may involve a bifurcation of the renal pelvis opening into a single ureter, duplication of the upper ureter with junction to form a single lower ureter opening into the trigone, or duplication of the entire pelviureteric system. These anomalies are ascribed to premature division or duplication of the ureteric bud. In most instances they are asymptomatic, but occasionally there is obstruction of part of the system with development of hydronephrosis or urinary infection. In cases of complete duplication, one of the ureteric openings may be ectopically located in bladder, seminal vesicle, urethra, vagina or rectum.

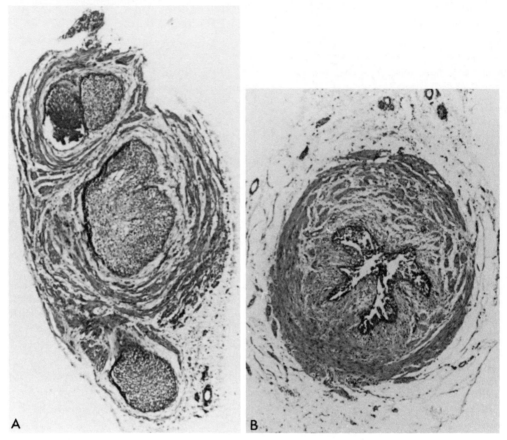

Figure 17–13. Ureters of a case of severe renal cystic dysplasia. H and E × 30. *A*, Right ureter is malformed with multiple solid epithelial cores but no lumen. *B*, Left ureter is narrow but has a lumen.

CALIBER OF THE URETERS

The ureters of the newborn infant normally appear dilated relative to those of the adult. The pathologist should be aware of this when assessing the significance of caliber variation. Hydroureter and hydronephrosis may result from partial obstruction at the ureterovesical junction or from obstruction to bladder outflow. The presence of threadlike ureters provides good evidence for lack of urine production (Fig. 17–13).

URINARY BLADDER AND URETHRA

DEVELOPMENT

The primitive urogenital sinus becomes separated from the cloaca by development of the urorectal septum during the seventh postconceptional week. The anterior part of the cloacal membrane becomes the urogenital membrane. The bladder develops from the upper part of the urogenital sinus, the membranous (and in the male the prostatic) part of the urethra develops from a narrow pelvic part of the urogenital sinus, and the penile urethra develops from the lower definitive urogenital sinus (Fig. 17–14). During division of the cloaca the caudal part of the mesonephric ducts becomes absorbed into the bladder to form the trigone. The ureters, originally branches of the mesonephric duct, gain their own

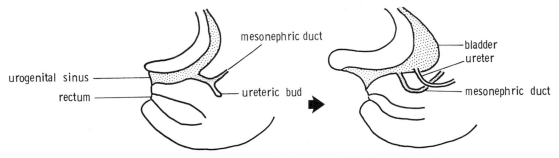

Figure 17–14. Diagram to illustrate development of bladder and urethra.

entry into the bladder. In the male, the mesonephric ducts persist to form the ejaculatory ducts entering the prostatic urethra. In the early stages of development the upper part of the bladder continues into the allantois, but the lumen of the allantois later becomes obliterated to leave a fibrous cord, the urachus, connecting the apex of the bladder to the umbilicus.

CONGENITAL ANOMALIES OF THE BLADDER

These anomalies include agenesis, extrophy, duplications and septation. Agenesis is exceedingly rare except in association with anomalies involving the rest of the urogenital system. Bladder, ureters, kidneys, rectum and anus are all missing in cases of sirenomelia. References to cases of bladder agenesis as an isolated entity are given by Glenn.[22] Bladder duplications of various types can occur.[23] Complete duplication may be associated with duplication of the urethra. Associated rectal and genital anomalies are common. Various forms of partial duplication and septation have been described.[8]

Extrophy of the bladder is one end of a spectrum of anomalies that result from failure of midline fusion of the mesodermal elements of the lower anterior abdominal wall. These structures include the anterior wall of the bladder and urethra, the genital tubercle and the pubis. Bladder extrophy is thus associated with separation of the pubic bones and epispadias or apparent duplication of the penis or clitoris. Associated bowel anomalies are common. Simple epispadias is the mild end of this spectrum of anomalies.

BLADDER OUTLET OBSTRUCTION

Prune-Belly Syndrome. This condition of deficient abdominal musculature and bladder outlet obstruction is described in Chapter 7.

Posterior Urethral Valve Obstruction. Most textbook descriptions of this condition quote and illustrate the series of diagrams published by Young and McKay depicting different types of valvular obstruction of the posterior urethra in male infants.[24] The normal male posterior urethra has a pair of mucosal folds passing down and laterally from the lower end of the verumontanum to the lateral urethral wall (Fig. 17–15). The most frequent variety of posterior valve obstruction is said to involve an accentuation of these folds to form valves that partially obstruct the urethra and lead to bladder hypertrophy, hydroureter and hydronephrosis, often with cystic renal dysplasia (Potter type IV). However, in infants who die shortly after birth, the type of obstruction I have seen most often is that illustrated in Figure 17–16, in which the upper part of the urethra appears to end as a blind pouch and there is a pinhole orifice on the verumontanum leading into the distal part of the urethra. This kind of obstruction was not described or illustrated by McKay and Young, although it has been mentioned as a variant by

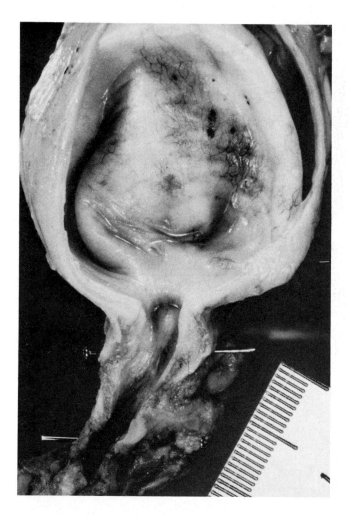

Figure 17–15. Bladder and normal posterior urethra in newborn male infant.

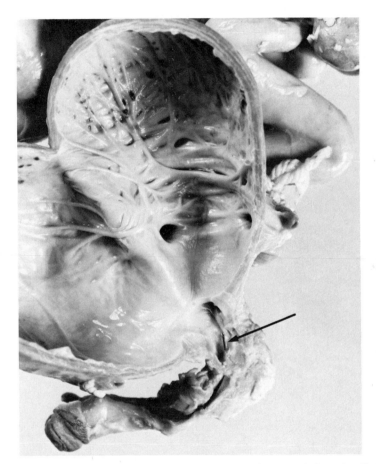

Figure 17–16. Valvular obstruction of the posterior urethra in a term infant who died at 13 hours of age. The bladder and posterior urethra have been dissected from the left side to show a pinpoint orifice leading to the penile urethra. An arrow indicates the tip of a probe protruding from this orifice. In my experience this is the most frequent appearance in infants who die in the perinatal period without being subjected to instrumentation in life.

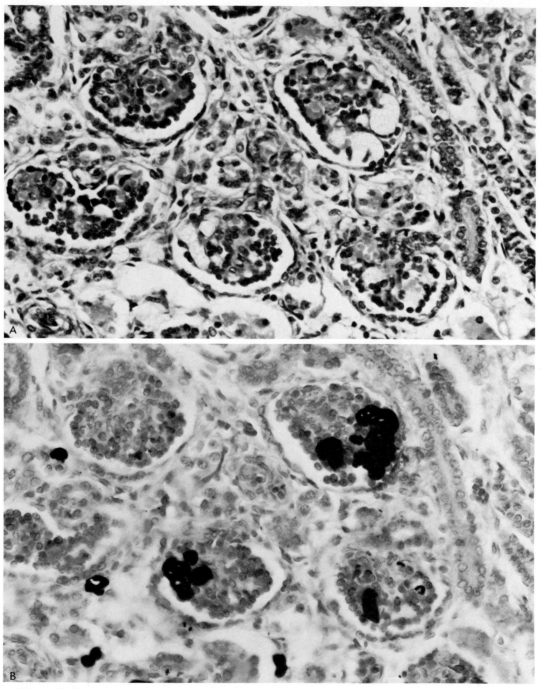

Figure 17–17. Intralipid emboli within the renal glomeruli of an infant of 30 weeks' gestation who died at 37 days of age after being maintained on intravenous feeding. *A*, H and E × 400. Intralipid shows up as foamy areas within the glomerular capillaries. *B*, Sudan black stain on an adjacent section showing positive lipid staining as intense black areas.

Rattner et al.[25] The passage of a catheter through the urethra in life or slitting up the urethra from the anterior aspect at autopsy will transform this type of malformation into one apparently showing the classic posterior urethral valves. Infants who die with the condition in the early neonatal period usually have evidence of almost total urinary obstruction with oligohydramnios and hypoplastic lungs. The obstruction seen at autopsy in this group may not be typical of lower urinary tract obstruction in surviving infants. However, the concept that urinary outlet obstruction in male infants is usually caused by valvular folds partly occluding an otherwise normally formed urethra is probably incorrect.

EFFECTS OF MANAGEMENT ON THE URINARY TRACT

As with other organs, including the heart and brain, the ability to maintain a sick preterm infant alive for a prolonged period allows development of renal lesions to a later stage than would otherwise be the case. The advanced stages of cortical and medullary necrosis illustrated in this chapter thus represent lesions that have been modified by management. A number of lesions are more directly attributable to methods of management. Intravenous feeding with Intralipid may be associated with Intralipid embolization in the renal glomeruli (Fig. 17–17). There have been several reports of infection localized to malformed kidneys following prolonged intravenous feeding. Infection with indwelling umbilical arterial catheters may cause damage to the urinary tract. The umbilical arteries are closely applied to the bladder. Damage to one of these vessels may result in hematoma formation involving the bladder wall. Renal artery thrombosis is a further hazard of umbilical artery catheterization. The complication may result from spread of a mural thrombus of the aorta to involve the renal artery orifice or from infusion of hypertonic solutions through a catheter with its tip situated near the renal arteries.

REFERENCES

1. Potter, E. L., and Craig, J. M.: Pathology of the Fetus and the Infant, 3rd ed. Chicago, Year Book Medical Publishers, 1976, pp. 434–475.
2. Hutchinson, D. L., Kelly, W. T., Friedman, E. A., and Plentl, A. A.: The distribution and metabolism of carbon-labeled urea in pregnant primates. J. Clin. Invest. *41*:1745–1753, 1962.
3. Fantel, A. G., and Shepard, T. H.: Potter syndrome: Nonrenal features induced by oligoamnios. Am. J. Dis. Child. *129*:1346–1347, 1975.
4. Fetterman, G. H., and Habib, R.: Congenital bilateral oligonephronic renal hypoplasia with hypertrophy of nephrons (oligoméganéphronie). Am. J. Clin. Pathol. *52*:199–207, 1969.
5. Osathanondh, V., and Potter, E. L.: Pathogenesis of polycystic kidneys: Type I due to hyperplasia of interstitial portions of collecting tubules. Type II due to inhibition of ampullary activity. Type III due to multiple abnormalities of development. Type IV due to urethral occlusion. Arch. Pathol. *77*:459–509, 1964.
6. Blyth, H., and Ockendon, B. G.: Polycystic disease of the kidneys and liver presenting in childhood. J. Med. Genet. *8*:257–284, 1971.
7. Bernstein, J.: Hereditary disorders of the kidney. Part I. Parenchymal defects and malformations. *In* Rosenberg, H. S., and Bolande, R. P. (eds.): Perspectives in Pediatric Pathology, vol. 1. Chicago, Year Book Medical Publishers, 1973, pp. 117–146.
8. Risdon, R. A.: Diseases of the kidney and lower urinary tract. *In* Berry, C. L. (ed.): Paediatric Pathology. Berlin, Springer Verlag, 1981, pp. 395–450.
9. Sotelo-Avila, C., and Gooch, W. M.: Neoplasms associated with the Beckwith-Wiedemann syndrome. *In* Rosenberg, H. S., and Bolande, R. P. (eds.): Perspectives in Pediatric Pathology, vol. 3. Chicago, Year Book Medical Publishers, 1976, pp. 255–272.
10. Fitzhardinge, P. M.: Complications of asphyxia and their therapy. *In* Gluck, L. (ed.): Intrauterine Asphyxia and the Developing Fetal Brain. Chicago, Year Book Medical Publishers, 1977, pp. 285–292.

11. Dauber, I. M., Krauss, A. N., Symchyck, P. S., and Auld, P. A.: Renal failure following perinatal anoxia. J. Pediatr. *88*:851–855, 1976.

12. Nagington, J., Wreghitt, T. G., Gandy, G., Roberton, N. R. C., and Berry, P. J.: Fatal echovirus 11 infections in outbreak in special-care baby unit. Lancet *2*:725–728, 1978.

13. Chrispin, A. R.: Medullary necrosis in infancy. Br. Med. Bull. *28*:233–236, 1972.

14. Porter, K. A., and Giles, H. M. C.: A pathological study of five cases of pyelonephritis in the newborn. Arch. Dis. Child. *31*:303–309, 1956.

15. Kissane, J. M.: Hereditary disorders of the kidney. Part II: Hereditary nephropathies. *In* Rosenberg, H. S., and Bolande, R. P. (eds.): Perspectives in Pediatric Pathology, vol. 1. Chicago, Year Book Medical Publishers, 1973, pp. 147–187.

16. Bolande, R. P.: Congenital mesoblastic nephroma of infancy. *In* Rosenberg, H. S., and Bolande, R. P. (eds.): Perspectives in Pediatric Pathology, vol. 1. Chicago, Year Book Medical Publishers, 1973, pp. 227–250.

17. Bove, K. E., Koffler, H., and McAdams, A. J.: Nodular renal blastema. Definition and possible significance. Cancer *24*:323–332, 1969.

18. Wexler, H. A., Poole, C. A., and Fujacco, R. M.: Metastatic neonatal Wilms' tumor: A case report with review of the literature. Pediatr. Radiol. *3*:179–181, 1975.

19. Bove, K. E., and McAdams, A. J.: The nephroblastomatosis complex and its relationship to Wilms' tumor: A clinico-pathologic treatise. *In* Rosenberg, H. S., and Bolande, R. P. (eds.): Perspectives in Pediatric Pathology, vol. 3. Chicago, Year Book Medical Publishers, 1976, pp. 185–223.

20. Rous, S. N., Bailie, M. D., Kaufman, D. B., Haddy, T. B., and Mattson, J. C.: Nodular renal blastema, nephroblastomatosis, and Wilms' tumor. Different points on the same disease spectrum? Urology *8*:599–604, 1976.

21. Bolande, R. P.: Developmental pathology. Am. J. Pathol. *94*:627–684, 1979.

22. Glenn, J. F.: Agenesis of the bladder. JAMA *169*:2016–2018, 1959.

23. Abrahamson, J.: Double bladder and related anomalies: Clinical and embryological aspects and a case report. Br. J. Urol. *33*:195–214, 1961.

24. Young, H. H., and McKay, R. W.: Congenital valvular obstruction of the prostatic urethra. Surg. Gynecol. Obstet. *48*:509–535, 1929.

25. Rattner, W. H., Meyer, R., and Bernstein, J.: Congenital abnormalities of the urinary system. IV. Valvular obstruction of the posterior urethra. J. Pediatr. *63*:84–94, 1963.

Chapter Eighteen

The Reproductive Organs

The problems of development of the reproductive organs and the abnormalities that may be observed in relation to them are inextricably related to those of sex determination. In fact, the major clinical problem related to the reproductive organs in the neonatal period is accurate determination of sex in infants with ambiguous genitalia.

PROBLEMS OF SEX DETERMINATION

The normal development of a male or female genital tract is primarily dependent on chromosomal constitution but may be modified by endocrine influences. The normal female karyotype comprises 44 autosomes and 2 X chromosomes, while the normal male karyotype is 44 autosomes with X and Y chromosomes. Individuals with a single X chromosome (45 XO, Turner syndrome) have gonadal dysgenesis and other anomalies (Chapter 7), but a high proportion of embryos with this karyotype are aborted at an early stage. At least one X chromosome seems to be essential for fetal development, as the YO karyotype is unknown.

Differentiation of the genital tract into the male form is determined by the presence of a Y chromosome. Male differentiation will occur even if there are two or more X chromosomes (e.g., Klinefelter syndrome, 47 XXY).

Most abnormalities of sex chromosome number result from nondisjunction of the sex chromosomes during gametogenesis, although true hermaphroditism may be associated with failure of disjunction of sex chromosomes during the first meiosis of the ovum, leading to mosaicism.

Development of both primary and secondary sexual characteristics depends on hormonal secretion irrespective of chromosomal constitution. Thus deficient androgen secretion in the normal XY male results in pseudohermaphroditism. Androgen production by the fetal adrenal (congenital adrenal hyperplasia, Chapter 16) or exogenous administration of androgenic steroids may cause virilization of a chromosomally normal female fetus.

DEVELOPMENT OF THE REPRODUCTIVE ORGANS[1]

GONADS

The gonads appear initially as a pair of longitudinal ridges, formed by proliferation of the coelomic epithelium and condensation of the related mesenchyme. During the sixth week the primordial germ cells (derived from yolk sac endoderm) invade the genital ridges and induce development of the primitive sex cords to form an indifferent gonad. During the seventh week sexual differentiation of the gonad takes place. Under the influence of the H-Y gene of the Y chromosome, there is development of the medullary sex cords to form a testis, while in the female the medullary sex cords degenerate and cortical cords develop to form an ovary.

DUCT SYSTEM

Both male and female embryos initially have two paired genital ducts, the mesonephric (wolffian) ducts and the paramesonephric (müllerian) ducts. The latter arise as invaginations of coelomic epithelium with an opening into the coelomic cavity at the cranial end and close proximity to the opposite paramesonephric duct near the midline caudally.

Both the duct system and the external genitalia develop under the influence of circulating hormones. Inhibition of the paramesonephric duct system occurs in the male under the influence of an anti-müllerian hormone. Testosterone from the fetal testis induces development of epididymis and ductus deferens from the mesonephric duct and also stimulates development of penis and penile urethra, fusion of the scrotal swellings and development of the prostate and seminal vesicles. In the female, in the absence of androgens and the anti-müllerian hormone, the mesonephric ducts degenerate and the paramesonephric ducts develop into uterus, fallopian tubes and upper third of the vagina. The lower two thirds of the vagina develop from the urogenital sinus.

EXTERNAL GENITALIA

At 6 weeks the external genitalia comprise paired urethral folds around the urogenital membrane, which unite anteriorly to form the genital tubercle. A pair of genital swellings develop laterally to the urethral folds (Fig. 18–1).

In the male, under the influence of androgens secreted by the testis, the genital tubercle rapidly elongates during the second and third months to become the phallus. The urethral folds are pulled forward to form the walls of a urethral

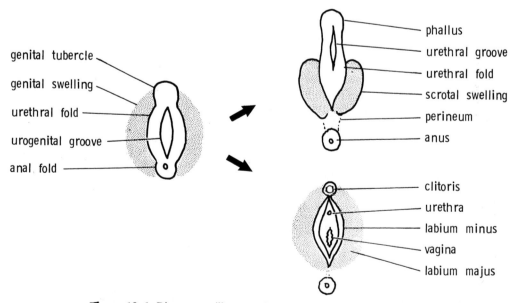

Figure 18–1. Diagram to illustrate development of external genitalia.

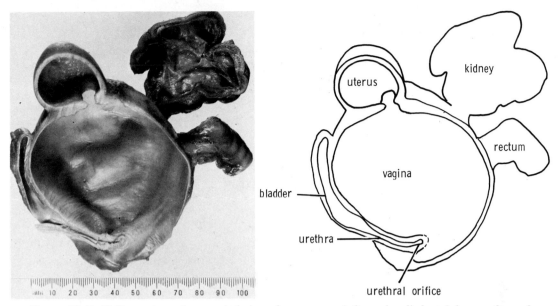

Figure 18–2. Malformation of urogenital sinus from a term infant who died at 2 hours of age from pulmonary hypoplasia. The specimen has been dissected to show how the urethra opens into the vagina and has caused massive distension of both vagina and uterus. The urinary obstruction has also resulted in distension of the bladder and hydronephrosis. The urethra and vagina connect via a pinhole orifice with the lower end of the rectum.

groove and later close to form the penile urethra. The genital swellings fuse in the midline to become the scrotum.

In the female, development of external genitalia is under the influence of maternal and placental estrogens. The genital tubercle slightly enlarges to become the clitoris, the urethral folds form the labia minora and the genital swellings form the labia majora. The urogenital groove remains open as the vestibule.

FEMALE SEX ORGANS

MALFORMATIONS

Malformations of uterus and vagina may involve (1) incomplete fusion of the lower part of the paramesonephric ducts (e.g., uterus didelphys); (2) partial or total atresia of the lower part of one or both paramesonephric ducts (uterus with rudimentary horn, vaginal atresia); and (3) persistence of a uterovaginal septum after fusion of the ducts.

Such anomalies may be found incidentally by the pathologist in the perinatal period but are of more importance in the otherwise normal girl and will not be considered here.

Occasionally the urethra opens into a vagina that is closed at the lower end, with resultant massive dilation of vagina and uterus by urine during fetal development (Fig. 18–2). This form of anomaly is likely to result in neonatal death due to associated pulmonary hypoplasia.

A range of malformations of uterus and vagina is illustrated in Potter and Craig,[2] and the subject is discussed by Risdon.[3]

OVARIES

In the normal fetus the ovary contains oocytes and primordial follicles. Some of the follicles may undergo cystic dilation up to 1 cm or more in diameter in late pregnancy. Such cystic ovaries are a relatively common incidental finding at necropsy in the perinatal period (Fig. 18–3). Ovarian hypoplasia (streak ovaries) is recognized in Turner syndrome (Chapter 7). Follicles and oocytes are lacking on histological examination of the ovary in this condition. A form of ovarian dysgenesis characterized by reduction in germ cells and primordial follicles resulting from necrobiosis and the presence of mesothelial clefts and abnormal masses of stromal cells is seen in cases of trisomy 18 and several other karyotype abnormalities.[4]

MALE SEX ORGANS

MALFORMATIONS

Total absence of external genitalia occurs in sirenomelia (Chapter 19). Absence of the penis is uncommon in infants with normally developed lower limbs but is illustrated in Potter and Craig.[2] The urethra in such cases may open into the rectum, or there may be absence of the bladder with opening of the ureters into the intestine or other complex urogenital malformations.[3, 5]

Hypospadias results from failure of fusion of the urethral folds during the eleventh to twelfth postconceptional weeks. In the mild form of glandular hypospadias the urethral meatus is on the lower surface of the glans penis. In more severe forms the urethral opening may be located on the shaft of the penis, at the scrotal-penile junction or in the perineum. The latter types of hypospadias are associated with penile hypoplasia and abnormal scrotal development. Complete hypospadias with a vulviform appearance of the scrotum and failure of testicular descent is one of the most common forms of ambiguous external genitalia.

Epispadias, in which the urethral opening is on the dorsal surface of the

Figure 18–3. Uterus (dissected), fallopian tubes and ovaries of a term infant who died at 4 weeks age, showing a large follicular ovarian cyst.

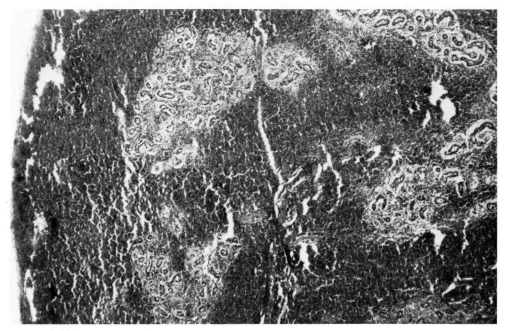

Figure 18–4. Hemorrhagic infarction of testis of obscure origin in an infant of 36 weeks' gestation who died at 36 hours of age. H and E × 30.

penis, is less common than hypospadias. The most severe form of the condition is that associated with extrophy of the bladder (Chapter 17). Congenital urethral obstruction may occur at any level from the prostatic urethra to the meatus. The effects are described in Chapters 7 and 17.

Absence of the testis may rarely accompany renal agenesis but is otherwise extremely rare.[3] Failure of descent of the testis is common in association with severe urogenital and anorectal anomalies.

LESIONS OF SCROTUM AND TESTIS IN THE PERINATAL PERIOD

Several lesions of the scrotum and testis may be recognized in the perinatal period by the pediatrician or pathologist.

Scrotal congestion and edema result from vaginal breech delivery and may be associated with extreme congestion and interstitial hemorrhage affecting the testis. Congestion and edema have been suggested as a possible cause of male infertility.[6] However, autopsy has revealed interstitial hemorrhage, and even infarction, of the testis in infants delivered spontaneously by the vertex or by cesarian section, so the relationship of the lesion to trauma remains unproven.[7]

Patency of the processus vaginalis, particularly in preterm infants, allows direct communication between the peritoneal cavity and the scrotum. Thus peritoneal bleeding (e.g., ruptured subcapsular hematoma of the liver) is sometimes associated with a distended blood-filled or clot-filled scrotum; ascites may be associated with hydrocele and pneumoperitoneum with pneumatocele.

Confusion may arise between a clot-filled scrotum and testicular infarction. The latter condition can develop as a result of torsion of the spermatic cord but is often of obscure etiology (Fig. 18–4).[2, 7]

MAMMARY GLANDS

Mammary glands develop from a band-like thickening of epidermis, the mammary line or ridge, which appears during the sixth postconceptional week and extends on each side of the body from the axilla to the inguinal region. Most of the mammary line disappears, leaving a small persistent thoracic portion that penetrates the underlying mesenchyme and gives rise to a number of epithelial sprouts from which the lactiferous ducts develop. In the term fetus the glands are firm masses of about 1 cm diameter with an acinar structure; the acinar lumens contain desquamated cells and may be dilated with secretion. Engorgement of the breast with secretion of a colostrum-like fluid, "witch's milk," often occurs in the newborn, and neonatal breast abscesses are described.[2]

In the preterm infant the breast tissue is inapparent. However, it is important to remember that the scarring caused by insertion of a drainage tube through the breast tissue in a newborn girl may cause deformity of the breasts, which becomes apparent at adolescence (Fig. 1–8).

REFERENCES

1. Pelliniemi, L. J., and Dym, M.: The fetal gonad and sexual differentiation. *In* Tulchinsky, D., and Ryan, K. J. (eds.): Maternal-Fetal Endocrinology. Philadelphia, W. B. Saunders Co., 1980, pp. 252–280.
2. Potter, E. L., and Craig, J. M.: Pathology of the Fetus and the Infant, 3rd ed. Chicago, Year Book Medical Publishers, 1976, pp. 476–499.
3. Risdon, R. A.: Diseases of the kidney and lower urinary tract. *In* Berry, C. L. (ed.): Paediatric Pathology. Berlin, Springer Verlag, 1981, pp. 395–450.
4. Russell, P. R., and Altshuler, G.: The ovarian dysgenesis of trisomy 18. Pathology 7:149–155, 1975.
5. Campbell, M. F.: Clinical Pediatric Urology. Philadelphia, W. B. Saunders Co., 1951, pp. 698.
6. Dunn, P. M.: Testicular birth trauma. Arch. Dis. Child. 50:744–745 (Abstract), 1975.
7. Emery, J. L., and Mitchell, R. J.: Interstitial haemorrhage and infarction of the testes in the newborn. J. Pathol. Bacteriol. 74:413–417, 1957.

Chapter Nineteen

The Skeletal and Integumentary Systems

Specific disorders of the skeletal tissues and skin that the pathologist encounters in the perinatal period are individually uncommon but require accurate diagnosis for purposes of genetic counseling. Secondary lesions such as septic foci or hemorrhages in cases of perinatal infection are rather more frequent.

Of more general significance to both clinician and pathologist is the way in which development of the framework tissues of the body is influenced by factors such as alterations in nutrition or neuromuscular function of the fetus and infant.

Changes to be observed at the macroscopic level include regional or generalized alterations in muscle bulk, stiffness and distortion of joints, variations in times of appearance of ossification centers and the form of the rib cage. At the histological level the pattern of the osteochondral junction may provide evidence of preceding stress. The pathologist who is able to interpret such features may gain useful clues as to the nature of the underlying disorder, which might range from anoxic-ischemic damage to the central nervous system in utero through chronic uteroplacental ischemia to prolonged leakage of amniotic fluid.

THE SKELETON

DEVELOPMENT

All the skeletal tissues, including muscle and bones, develop from the undifferentiated mesenchyme derived from the mesodermal cell layer. Bone formation occurs by two separate processes, membranous and endochondral ossification. Both processes involve an initial condensation of the mesenchyme. Membrane bone typical of the bones of the cranial vault and of the frontal, parietal and squamous occipital bones is formed by direct transformation of the mesenchymal cells into osteoblasts with production of a network of bone spicules radiating from the ossification center.

Of more importance from the point of view of the perinatal pathologist is the process of endochondral ossification and development of the long bones. The site of the shaft of each bone is marked by the appearance of a cartilage model within the condensation of mesenchyme (Fig. 19–1). The perichondrium around the cartilaginous core undergoes differentiation into osteogenic tissue and thus becomes periosteum. The cartilage cells within the center of the primitive shaft

377

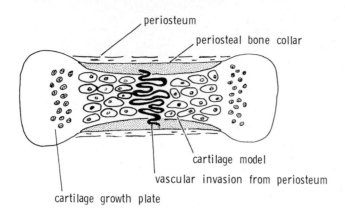

periosteum

periosteal bone collar

cartilage model

vascular invasion from periosteum

cartilage growth plate

Figure 19–1. A schematic diagram to show initial development of ossification in a long bone.

become enlarged, develop vacuolated cytoplasm and eventually die, leaving a network of lacunae within the cartilage matrix. Calcification of the matrix walls within the center of the shaft represents the primary "ossification" center, which appears in the major long bones at 6 to 8 weeks of postconceptional age. Subperiosteal calcification followed by ossification results in development of a periosteal bone collar, the first true bone of the shaft. Vascular channels and accompanying osteoblasts and osteoclasts from the periosteum invade the shaft center and lead to formation of the medullary spaces, which become filled with the embryonic bone marrow. The original lacunar calcified matrix walls become remodeled into bony trabeculae.

At each end of the bone an organized region of cartilage growth becomes established, the cartilage growth plate. Division of the chondrocytes, predominantly in the long axis, results in the formation of longitudinal columns of cartilage cells. These columns undergo an orderly sequence of changes involving progressive hypertrophy and vacuolation followed by cell death with calcification of the intervening matrix. Vessels and osteogenic cells invade the spaces left by the dead cartilage cells and transform the calcified matrix walls into bone trabeculae. The epiphysis of each long bone becomes vascularized and develops a secondary ossification center in the latter part of fetal life.

The physiological mechanisms involved in the process of bone induction and development have been reviewed by Royer[1] and will not be discussed here.

The time of appearance of some of the ossification centers in fetal life may be of some value to the pathologist in confirming gestational age, particularly if postmortem radiography is performed as a routine. The primary center in the calcaneum is usually present by 26 weeks' gestation and that in the talus by 28 weeks.[2] The ossification center of the lower femoral epiphysis normally appears at about 36 weeks' gestation and that of the upper tibial epiphysis by 38 to 40 weeks.[3] However, the time of appearance of these centers is considerably influenced by nutritional variations. In growth-retarded infants the centers may appear several weeks later than the times given here.[2–4] Ossification may be more advanced in female infants than in males and may also be advanced in anencephalics. The presence of an ossification center at the lower femoral epiphysis is helpful in confirming that an infant has reached a maturity of 36 weeks or so, but absence of this center could only be taken to indicate immaturity if the infant was well nourished.

Costochondral Junction During Development

The importance of study of the costochondral junction as an aid to analysis of perinatal deaths has been emphasized by Emery and Kalpaktsoglou.[5] In a survey of over 5000 ribs from perinatal and pediatric autopsies, these workers found that the costochondral junction of the fifth and sixth ribs provided a sensitive histological indication of alterations in growth rate during the perinatal period.

The normal fetal rib increases its length by some 0.43 mm per day, and it may be calculated that a column of about 16 cartilage cells in depth must be replaced daily. Growth arrest due to acute or chronic prenatal or perinatal stress interrupts this process and causes a number of recognizable changes (Figs. 19–2 and 19–3). The cartilage cells tend to lose their regular columnar alignment and become piled up in disorderly groups. Within the marrow space the trabeculae may be absorbed almost up to the cartilage face. The junctional line becomes irregular, and a band of matrix often intervenes between the cartilage cells and the bone cavity. When growth resumes, the matrix bands may persist as transverse ossified bands within the bone shaft.

These changes will be found to a varying extent in a very high proportion of perinatal deaths. They are of particular value in distinguishing between cases of genuine sudden accidental death during delivery and those in which death was preceded by clinically unrecognized stress. The documentation of such changes constitutes part of the profile of a perinatal death that the pathologist needs to build up if he is to provide the clinician with information to aid in future management.

CONGENITAL ANOMALIES OF THE SKELETON

Generalized skeletal anomalies are individually uncommon. Those that are of major importance to the perinatal pathologist present as short-limbed dwarfism. The largest group of such conditions comprises the lethal neonatal chondrodysplasias. Death in most of them is caused by pulmonary hypoplasia associated with thoracic dysplasia.

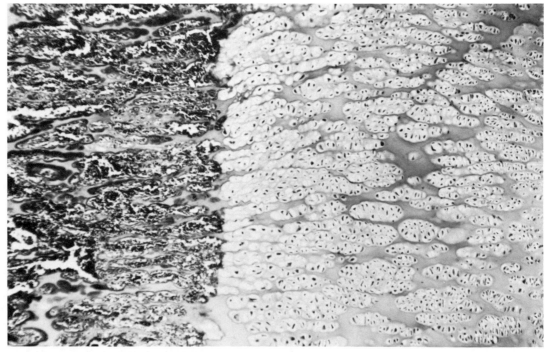

Figure 19–2. Normal costochondral junction from a normally developed infant who suffered acute intrapartum asphyxia and was stillborn at term. H and E × 60.

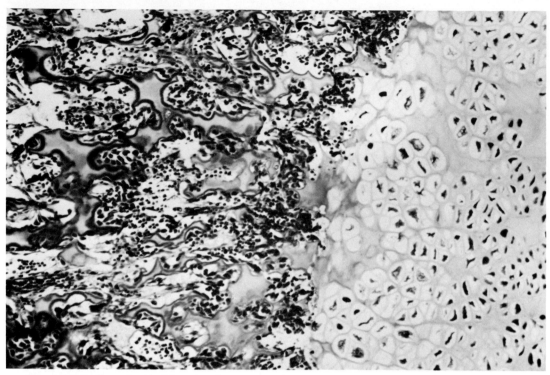

Figure 19–3. Costochondral junction from a growth-retarded infant who suffered intrapartum asphyxia and died at 2 hours of age. H and E × 150. Note the irregularity of cartilage columns and bone trabeculae as compared with Figure 19–2.

LETHAL SHORT-LIMBED CHONDRODYSPLASIAS

These are listed in Table 19–1. These conditions will not be described in detail here, as some of them are exceedingly rare. The reader is referred to the excellent review by Yang et al.[6] and other works that discuss these conditions.[7, 8]

Achondrogenesis. This is the severest form of chondrodysplasia and is of autosomal recessive inheritance. There is extreme micromelia with absence of ossification in vertebrae and pelvis, severe disturbance of endochondral ossification and reduced osteoblastic and osteoclastic activity. Most of the affected infants are stillborn, and there is often maternal polyhydramnios. Type 2 differs from type 1 in showing normal cranial ossification, and there are other slight radiological and morphological differences.

TABLE 19–1.   LETHAL SHORT-LIMBED CHONDRODYSPLASIAS

Achondrogenesis	Type 1
	Type 2
Homozygous achondroplasia	
Thanatophoric syndrome	Type 1—classic
	Type 2—with cloverleaf skull
Asphyxiating thoracic dystrophy	(Jeune syndrome)
Chondroectodermal dysplasia	(Ellis–van Creveld syndrome)
Chondrodysplasia punctata	(Two types, not necessarily fatal)
Camptomelic syndrome	
Short-rib polydactyly syndrome	Majewski type
	Saldino-Noonan type

Homozygous Achondroplasia. The classic heterozygous form of achondroplasia is inherited as an autosomal dominant, is not associated with histologically abnormal endochondral ossification and is compatible with normal survival. Infants with homozygous achondroplasia born to achondroplastic parents all have severe limb shortening (rhizomelia) with a small thorax, large head with frontal bossing, depressed nasal bridge and a small foramen magnum. The infants die in early infancy with respiratory difficulty. There is severe disturbance of endochondral ossification with minimal proliferation of chondrocytes and lack of column formation.

Thanatophoric Dwarfism. This is the most common form of lethal short-limbed dwarfism. It was first differentiated from achondroplasia by Maroteaux et al. in 1967[9] and is of sporadic occurrence. The infants have a large head, gross micromelia and a narrow thorax and die in the early neonatal period with severe respiratory difficulty (Fig. 19–4). Diagnostic radiological features include severe platyspondylia with markedly widened disc spaces, small ilia with narrow sacrosciatic notches and curved appendicular bones with telephone receiver–like femora. Histological examination shows severely retarded endochondral ossification with irregular chondrocytes and lack of column formation (Fig. 19–5).

It is claimed that homozygous achondroplasia can be differentiated from thanatophoric dwarfism because there is not such extreme shortening of long bones, the femora do not have the telephone receiver–like form and there are abundant PAS–positive intracytoplasmic granules in the chondrocytes in achon-

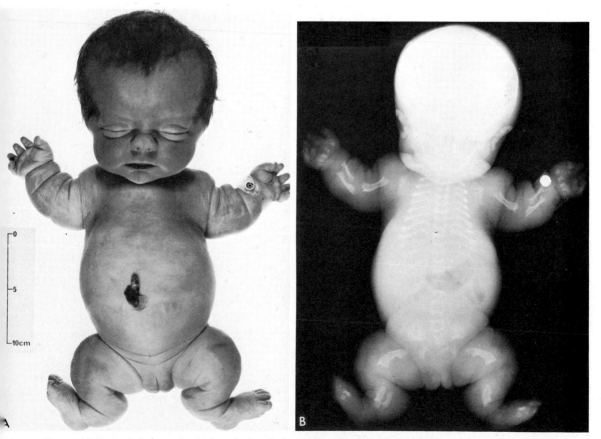

Figure 19–4. *A*, A thanatophoric dwarf who died at 12 hours of age. *B*, X-ray of the same infant showing the telephone receiver–like femora, narrow sacrosciatic notch, short ribs and narrow vertebral bodies with wide intervertebral disc spaces which together characterize this condition.

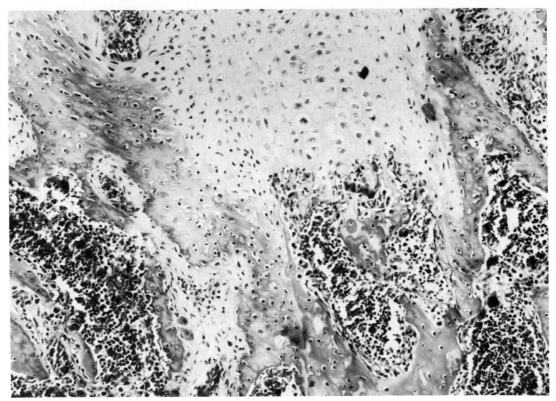

Figure 19–5. Costochondral junction in thanatophoric dwarfism. H and E × 150. Compare with Figure 19–2. There is lack of cartilage column formation and gross irregularity of the osteochondral junction with distorted trabeculae.

droplasia. There is still much confusion in the literature between the two conditions; many of the published descriptions and illustrations of achondroplasia relate to cases of thanatophoric dwarfism.

Cases of thanatophoric dwarfism with cloverleaf skull have been separated into a type 2 by Yang et al.[6]

Asphyxiating Thoracic Dystrophy (Jeune Syndrome). The main feature of this condition is severe chest narrowing. On radiology the thoracic cage can be seen to have short horizontal ribs, which are widened anteriorly. The pelvis is small and distorted, but the skull and spine are normal. Some infants have accessory digits, and cystic renal disease may be seen. The disorder is of autosomal recessive inheritance. Endochondral ossification may show patchy or diffuse disorganization.

Chondroectodermal Dysplasia (Ellis–van Creveld Syndrome). This syndrome comprises small size with irregularly short extremities and polydactyly with hypoplastic nails and a narrow thorax, which resembles that of asphyxiating thoracic dystrophy. Many of the infants have a cardiac anomaly, most often atrial septal defect. Retarded and disorganized endochondral ossification has been reported in some instances, or there may be islands of poorly calcified cartilage in the spongiosa. Death is common in early infancy owing to cardiac and respiratory problems. The condition is of autosomal recessive inheritance.

Chondrodysplasia Punctata. This condition is characterized by myxoid and cystic degeneration of cartilage with focal calcification. Two types are described.

Camptomelic Syndrome. The infants with camptomelic syndrome have marked anterior bowing of the tibia with minor bowing of the long bones, a small thoracic cage, hypoplastic or absent scapulae and a flat face with micrognathia. Death occurs in early infancy from respiratory difficulty associated with tracheobron-chomalacia. Cerebral abnormalities may be present. There is defective prolifera-tion and maturation of chondrocytes with dense mineralization of the provisional zone of calcification and osteoporosis within the diaphysis.

Short-Rib Polydactyly Syndrome. This syndrome comprises thoracic dysplasia, narrow thorax and polydactyly with dwarfism and internal malformations, includ-ing pulmonary, cardiac, intestinal and genitourinary anomalies with cystic kidneys. Two types are described, the Majewski type with severe thoracic dysplasia and disproportionately short tibiae, and the Saldino-Noonan type with severe short-ening of extremities and abnormal pelvis. Abnormalities of endochondral ossifi-cation have been described. Both forms are fatal in the neonatal period and are of autosomal recessive inheritance.

OTHER CONGENITAL SKELETAL ABNORMALITIES

Osteogenesis Imperfecta Congenita. This disorder is characterized by fragile bones and by the presence of blue sclerae and development of otosclerosis in survivors. Infants with the autosomal recessive form of the condition die at, or soon after, birth. They are underweight and may show hypoplastic lungs. Multiple old and recent fractures of ribs and long bones are seen with evidence of healing in the form of masses of callus. The legs are curved, and the calvarium comprises a fibrous membrane containing small islands of bone or a mass of small bones separated by multiple sutures. Cartilage structure is normal, but there is decrease in number and size of bone trabeculae and an excessively thin cortex. A paucity of osteoblasts is associated with reduction in the total mass of bone.

Abnormalities of collagen synthesis,[10] or of noncollagen bone matrix pro-teins,[11] have been found on study of patients who survive with the less severe autosomal dominant form of the disease (osteogenesis imperfecta tarda).

Osteopetrosis (Albers-Schönberg Disease, Marble Bone Disease). The character-istic feature of osteopetrosis is markedly increased bone density. A severe auto-somal recessive variety of the condition can be recognized radiologically in utero or soon after birth and may prove fatal in early infancy. All bones are affected, and there is expansion of the metaphyses of the long bones. On histology there is dense cortical bone and extensive replacement of the marrow cavity by dense bone trabeculae. Abnormally wide zones of proliferating cartilage are seen at the bone ends. The condition is believed to be an abnormality of endosteal remodeling, possibly due to a defect of osteoclastic activity.[12]

Bone marrow transplantation has been claimed to have some success in treatment of the lethal recessive form of osteopetrosis, presumably by restoring normal resorptive activity.[13] The dominant form of osteopetrosis becomes appar-ent only in later infancy and childhood.

Hypophosphatasia. This inborn error of metabolism is of autosomal recessive inheritance and is associated with deficiency of alkaline phosphatase in blood and tissues.[14] Severely affected infants may at birth be seen to have a soft calvarium and short, bowed limbs. The costochondral junctions are prominent and laterally displaced, with short ribs resulting in reduced thoracic volume and respiratory distress. The long bones are soft and susceptible to fracture. Radiology shows poor bone mineralization, and histological examination reveals widening of carti-lage growth zones with disorganization of the matrix. Hypercalcemia results in early development of nephrocalcinosis. Milder cases may become manifested in later infancy by changes similar to those of rickets.

Rickets. Bone disease caused by vitamin deficiency develops relatively fre-quently in very low birth weight infants maintained in neonatal intensive care units. Features of rickets, including expanded costochondral junctions giving the classic rachitic rosary of the thorax, may develop despite administration of vitamin supplements (Fig. 19–6). The soft rib cage results in such cases showing features of late respiratory distress.[15] On histological examination the widened osteochondral junctions show large masses of cartilage with deficient calcification, irregularity of the junctional line, deficient capillary ingrowth and excessive osteoid formation within the metaphysis. It has recently been suggested that neonatal rickets may be caused by hypophosphatemia rather than vitamin D deficiency; the changes seen on histology include osteoporosis with decreased osteoblastic activity.[16]

Other Inborn Errors of Metabolism That Affect the Skeleton. These include the mucopolysaccharidoses, Gaucher's disease and Niemann-Pick disease. These conditions may not be recognized at birth and do not often present to the pathologist within the perinatal period. The advent of antenatal diagnosis for these conditions means that affected fetuses may be available for study by the perinatal pathologist at an early stage of development. In Gaucher's disease and Niemann-Pick disease, which may prove fatal in early infancy, the characteristic lipid-laden cells may be found within the bone marrow. Skeletal x-ray and bone histology of an infant with a very rare storage disorder (β-glucuronidase deficiency, MPS V11) diagnosed postmortem at Hammersmith recently are shown in Figure 19–7. This infant presented as a case of nonimmunologic hydrops; a similar presentation has been reported in Gaucher's disease, generalized gangliosidosis (GM$_1$ disease) and sialidosis.

INFECTION

OSTEOMYELITIS AND PURULENT ARTHRITIS

Osteomyelitis and purulent arthritis can occur in newborn infants with generalized sepsis but are relatively uncommon.[17] Most reported cases are caused by staphylococcal or streptococcal infections, although there are occasional instances of bone or joint infection due to gram-negative organisms, including *E. coli,* Proteus sp., *Klebsiella pneumoniae,* Pseudomonas sp. or Salmonella.

Hematogenous infection of the long bones commences in the metaphysis, but the vascularity and spongy structure of the bone cortex in the newborn allow the infection to spread rapidly to the subperiosteal space rather than to the marrow cavity. Sequestra are uncommon, and rapid formation of new bone with remodeling of the shaft occurs when the infection is treated.

LOCALIZED SKELETAL ANOMALIES

There are many patterns of localized skeletal anomaly and nonlethal forms of generalized or localized limb shortening. These are illustrated in textbooks on malformation syndromes and in Potter and Craig.[18] Sirenomelia (mermaid fetus) is a lethal condition occasionally seen by the pathologist. Fusion of lower limbs, or a single limb (Fig. 19–8), is associated with renal agenesis and the external facial features of oligohydramnios. The infant dies soon after birth from lung hypoplasia.

ANOMALIES OF THE FACE AND MANDIBLE

A variety of developmental anomalies may affect the face and mandible. These are described and illustrated in texts such as that of Potter and Craig,[18] and only a few points will be made here.

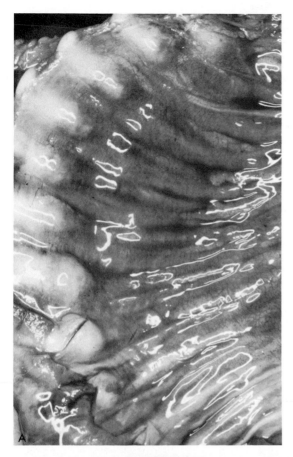

Figure 19–6. *A*, View of costochondral junctions from within thorax in an infant of 30 weeks' gestation who died at 5 months of age showing expansion of the costochondral junctions due to rickets. *B*, Histologic appearance of a costochondral junction from the same case. H and E × 30. There is lack of normal alignment of cartilage columns, grossly irregular costochondral junction, failure of normal capillary ingrowth, poor formation and calcification of matrix and increased osteoid formation.

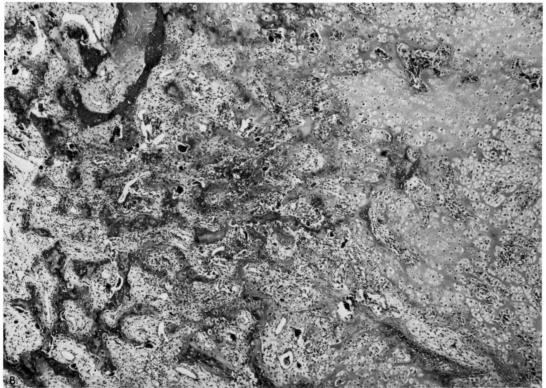

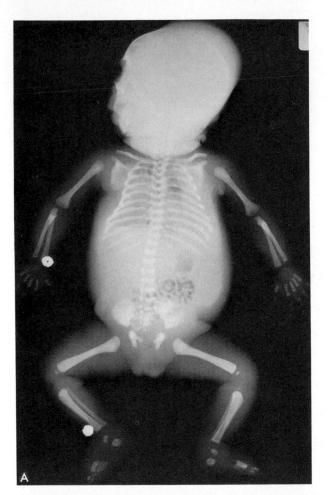

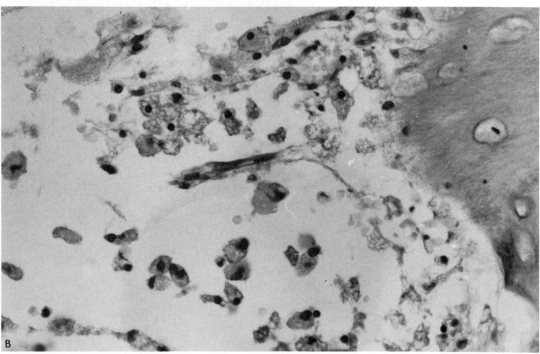

Figure 19–7. Mucopolysaccharidosis VII presenting as hydrops. *A,* Whole body x-ray. The ribs appear thick and there is poor development of the vertebral bodies. *B,* Bone marrow showing foamy storage cells. H and E × 300.

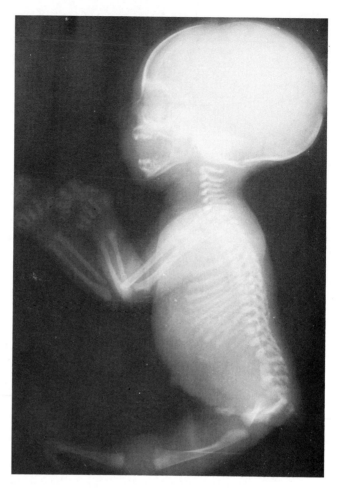

Figure 19–8. Lateral x-ray of mermaid fetus.

Anomalies of mandibular and maxillary development have been related to disturbance in development of the first branchial arch.[19] Such anomalies include the Pierre Robin syndrome, which comprises micrognathia with glossoptosis, mandibular hypoplasia and cleft palate, and Treacher Collins syndrome, in which malformation of the internal and external ear is combined with hypoplasia of facial bones and mandible and an antimongoloid slant to the palpebral fissure. The concept of a branchial arch abnormality has the merit of emphasizing that both bony and related soft tissue and special sense organ structures are involved in malformations of this region. Thus in cases of extreme mandibular hypoplasia there is gross hypoplasia of the tongue, which is of similar derivation from the first branchial arch (Chapter 13).

The associations of various facial and mandibular anomalies with chromosomal defects are referred to in Chapter 7.

MUSCLE AND CONNECTIVE TISSUES

CONGENITAL NEUROMUSCULAR DISORDERS

A number of congenital neuromuscular disorders may be manifested in the neonatal period as the floppy infant syndrome (Table 19–2). Diagnosis in most instances demands muscle biopsy with enzyme histochemistry supplemented in some cases with electron microscopy. These rare conditions will not be discussed

TABLE 19–2. PARALYTIC CONDITIONS WITH HYPOTONIA THAT MAY PRESENT IN THE NEONATE

1. Spinal muscular atrophy (Werdnig-Hoffmann syndrome)	
2. Congenital myopathies a. Structural	Myotubular myopathy Nemaline myopathy Mitochondrial myopathy Congenital fiber type disproportion
b. Metabolic	Glycogenosis Type II and III
3. Other neuromuscular disorders	Congenital myotonic dystrophy Congenital muscular dystrophy Neonatal myasthenia (maternal myasthenia) Congenital myasthenia (nonmyasthenic mother)

Adapted from Dubowitz, V.: Muscle Disorders in Childhood. Philadelphia, W. B. Saunders Co., 1978.

here; they are fully dealt with in texts such as that by Dubowitz.[20] However, it should be remembered that some of them may affect the fetus in utero and can lead to stillbirth or early neonatal death. Congenital myotonic dystrophy is associated with polyhydramnios, and the infant frequently dies from respiratory failure in the neonatal period. Excessively thin ribs and hypoplasia of the diaphragm have been described in this condition.[21] The condition is of autosomal dominant inheritance, and on examination the mother will show signs of dystrophia myotonica.[22]

Congenital muscular dystrophy can become apparent at birth with muscle wasting and limb distortion (arthrogryposis). In the case illustrated in Figures 19–9 and 19–10, the abnormal tone caused by muscle disease probably rendered the infant susceptible to trauma sustained during breech delivery (Chapter 6). The abnormal respiratory muscles would be expected to impair fetal breathing by the mechanism discussed in Chapter 10 and lead to the observed lung hypoplasia.

The possibility of a primary congenital neuromuscular disorder should be considered by the pathologist in any infant who has muscle wasting and limb distortion (see later discussion).

ARTHROGRYPOSIS

Arthrogryposis comprises joint stiffness caused by fibrous muscle contractures developing in utero. The distortion indicates a failure of development of normal function, which may occur in several different ways. There may be a failure of normal muscle development within the limbs, damage to already developed muscles, lack of neural function, or physical prevention of limb movement. Some of these mechanisms are inter-related. As normal skeletal muscle development beyond the myotube stage requires motor innervation, damage to anterior horn cells of the fetal spinal cord results both in failure of normal muscle growth and in lack of limb movement. Experimental injury to the spinal cord in the fetal rabbit may cause typical arthrogryposis in addition to lung hypoplasia (Chapter 10). In two infants described and illustrated in Chapter 7, the limb distortion and pulmonary hypoplasia were associated with histological evidence of old anoxic-ischemic damage in the CNS. These infants may be regarded as the naturally occurring human counterpart of our experimental rabbit fetuses. As mentioned earlier, primary muscle disorders such as congenital dystrophy may have similar effects.

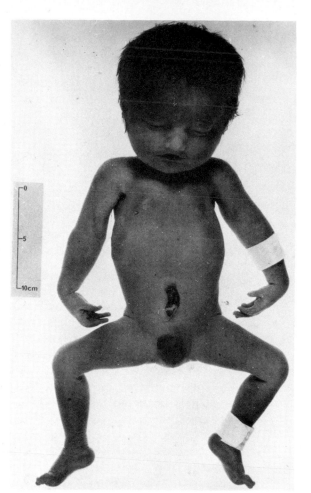

Figure 19–9. Congenital muscular dystrophy. This infant had breech delivery and suffered birth trauma with bilateral fractures of the humerus (see Chapter 6). There was severe lung hypoplasia.

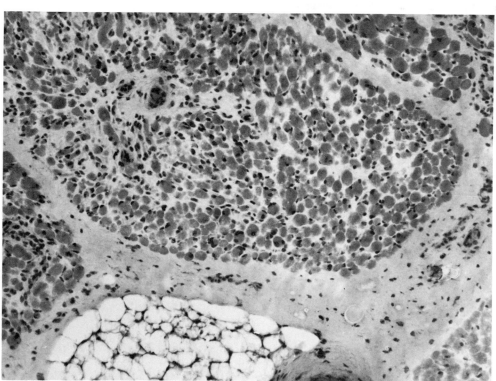

Figure 19–10. Muscle in congenital muscular dystrophy. Cryostat section, H and E × 150. This is from the same case illustrated in Figure 19–9. There is marked disproportion in fiber size and many fibers show central nuclei.

The limb distortions resulting from prolonged oligohydramnios represent the effects of prevention of movement in an otherwise normally developed limb.

The recognition by the pathologist of arthrogryposis does not therefore constitute an adequate diagnosis, but should prompt the initiation of studies to determine an underlying cause within the CNS, muscle tissues or fetal environment.[23]

PRUNE-BELLY SYNDROME

This condition is described in Chapter 7.

SPECIFIC FORMS OF JOINT AND LIMB DISTORTION

Many forms of joint and limb distortion may be seen in the perinatal period and are illustrated in texts such as that by Potter and Craig.

Congenital dislocation of the hip is of importance to the pediatrician because normal development of the hip joint depends on maintenance of the normal relationship between the head of the femur and the acetabulum. Early diagnosis of an actual or potential hip dislocation allows appropriate treatment to encourage normal joint development. Dislocation of the hips at birth may be seen in infants with severe neuromuscular disorders. In such cases the affected leg is externally rotated and shortened. Dissection of a congenitally dislocated hip joint in an infant who dies in the perinatal period will show that the head of the femur is unduly small and the acetabulum flat and poorly developed.[24]

A characteristic severe form of club foot (talipes) is seen in cases of spina bifida, whereas the upper limb equivalent, fixation of the hand in a varus position, is associated with absence of the radius. Figure 19–11 illustrates a fetus in which both forms of abnormality were present.

The talipes seen in the oligohydramnios sequence is characteristic in that the feet can be folded up together; talipes equinovarus of one foot is often associated with talipes calcaneovalgus of the other. The different form of deformity in left and right feet confirms that external compression is responsible rather than an intrinsic imbalance of neuromuscular function.

SKIN

DEVELOPMENT

The epidermis becomes segregated from other ectodermal tissues during the process of neurulation in the fourth postconceptional week. By the beginning of the second month the epidermis is a two-layered structure with a superficial layer of flattened cells, the periderm, lying on the basal or germinative layer. The periderm is an independent structure maintained by mitotic activity of its own cells and is believed to play an important part in metabolic exchange between the developing epidermis and amniotic fluid.[25] Intermediate cell layers within the epidermis appear during the third month, and the melanocytes and Langerhans' cells are present by 12 weeks. By term the epidermis has well-developed spinous, granular and horny layers. The dermal papillae develop during the third and fourth months, and the pattern of dermal ridges is well established by the end of the fifth month. Development of hair follicles commences in most areas during the fourth month, and sebaceous glands are active from the end of the sixth month. Sweat glands appear relatively late during the fifth month and only become functional near term.[26]

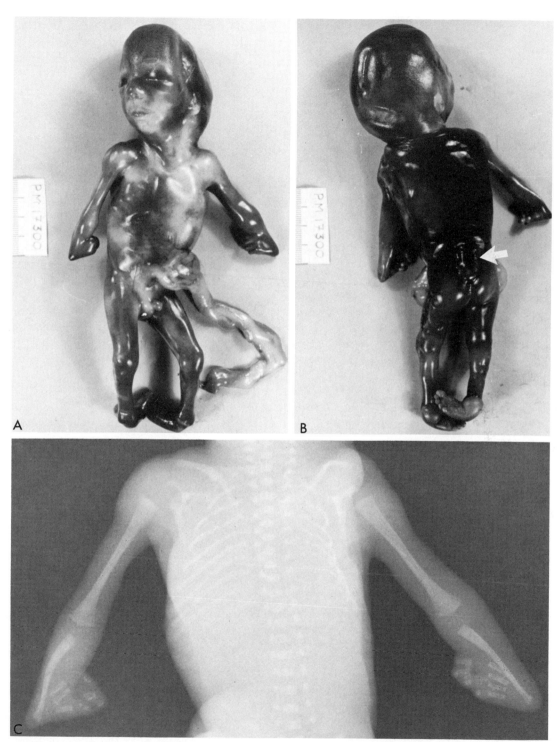

Figure 19–11. A fetus aborted at 19 weeks' gestation when amniotic cell culture demonstrated trisomy 18 in association with a raised amniotic α-fetoprotein level. *A*, Anterior view showing severe bilateral talipes and a similar distortion of the hands, in addition to a small omphalocele. *B*, Posterior view showing a lumbosacral myelocele (arrowed). *C*, X-ray showing bilateral absence of the radii.

The nails first appear toward the end of the third month, but nail growth in utero is very slow and the free margin seldom reaches the tip of the digit before term.

CONGENITAL ANOMALIES OF THE SKIN

Localized skin defects are seen occasionally. They occur most frequently over the vertex of the head and present as round lesions with punched-out margins.[18]

AMNIOTIC BAND SYNDROME

Connections between the body of the fetus and the amnion are seen rarely at term but more frequently in fetuses aborted in the second trimester. The bands may run between mesodermal tissues such as the pericranium of the skull and the amnion and are often associated with constriction rings around the extremities or amputation of digits (Fig. 19–12). Evidence was presented by Torpin that these deformities are caused by amniotic rupture early in pregnancy.[27] This evidence is further supported by recent reports of occurrence of the syndrome following amniocentesis.[28]

DERMAL AND PILONIDAL SINUSES

A congenital sinus tract over the spine may communicate with the spinal canal and can lead to meningitis. The external orifice is often surrounded by long hair. Pilonidal sinuses are located lower down over the sacrum and do not penetrate into the spinal canal, although they may be a site of development of local infection.

MALFORMATION OF THE NAILS

Abnormalities of nails, including hypoplasia or aplasia, occur in a number of malformation syndromes such as nail patella syndrome, hereditary ectodermal

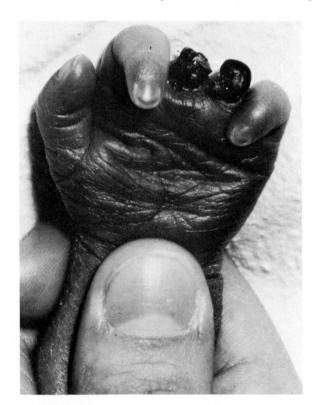

Figure 19–12. Intrauterine amputation of two digits by amniotic bands. (Courtesy of Dr. H. Gamsu, King's College Hospital, London.)

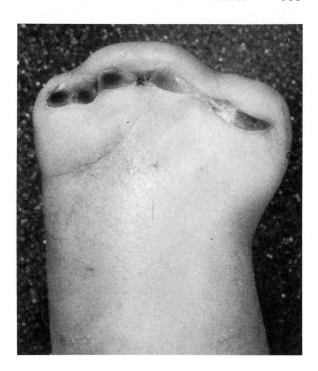

Figure 19–13. Fusion of digits and nails of the hand in Apert syndrome.

dysplasia and Ellis–van Creveld syndrome (see descriptions in Smith[29] and Salmon.[30]) In acrocephalosyndactyly (Apert syndrome) the digits are fused and the nails form a single band (Fig. 19–13).

BULLOUS LESIONS OF SKIN

EPIDERMOLYSIS BULLOSA

A number of varieties of epidermolysis bullosa are recognized.[31] In the most severe form, epidermolysis bullosa hereditaria letalis, the stratum granulosum comes away from the basal layer of the epidermis on the slightest friction, resulting in development of multiple fluid-filled bullae soon after birth. The epidermis can be loosened by rubbing (positive Nikolsky's sign), the nails may be loose and the buccal mucosa may become ulcerated. Death usually occurs as a result of secondary infection at several weeks of age but some infants now survive.[32] In a case seen some years ago, shedding of the nails at birth was the first indication of abnormality (Figs. 19–14 and 19–15).

TOXIC EPIDERMAL NECROLYSIS (SCALDED SKIN SYNDROME), RITTER'S DISEASE)

Toxic epidermal necrolysis occurs in the newborn as a toxic reaction to coagulase-positive staphylococci of phage group 11.[33] A scarlatiniform rash is followed by desquamation of large areas of skin associated with a positive Nikolsky's sign. There is necrosis of the superficial portion of the granular layer with development of bullous lesions and shedding of the superficial epidermis. The staphylococci responsible can sometimes be cultured from the skin, but the primary infective focus may be elsewhere in the body. The disorder responds well to treatment with an appropriate antistaphylococcal antibiotic. After the neonatal period toxic epidermal necrolysis may result from many causes, including drug sensitivity.

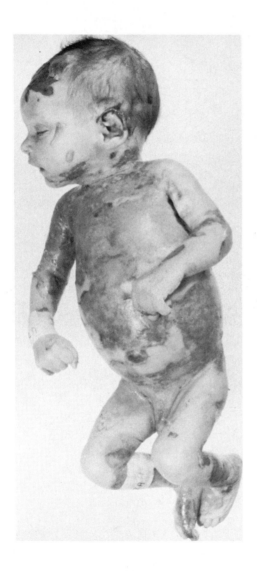

Figure 19–14. Epidermolysis bullosa hereditaria letalis in an infant who died at 5 weeks of age. (From Brain, E. B. and Wigglesworth, J. S.: Developing teeth in epidermolysis bullosa hereditaria letalis. Br. Dent. J. *124*:225–260, 1968.)

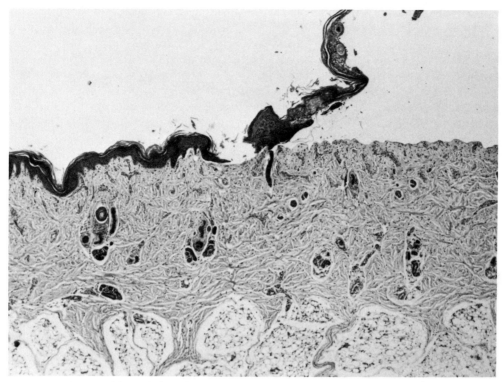

Figure 19–15. Epidermolysis bullosa. Section of skin from case shown in Figure 19–14. H and E × 30. There is a separation at the dermal-epidermal junction.

HYPERKERATOSIS

ICHTHYOSIS CONGENITA

The ichthyosiform dermatoses constitute a large group of conditions, most of which do not present until after the neonatal period.[34] The two varieties of ichthyosis congenita that are recognizable at birth are both rare inherited abnormalities: lamellar ichthyosis, which is of autosomal recessive inheritance, and an X-linked recessive variety. The most severe form of lamellar ichthyosis, ichthyosis congenita gravis (harlequin fetus), is incompatible with survival. The infant is born with thick, horny plaques covering the body and separated by fissures. Ectropion of eyes and mouth is common. Successful prenatal diagnosis by fetal skin biopsy has been reported.[39] Several milder varieties compatible with survival are recognized and are discussed by Potter and Craig.[18] In the mildest form, collodion baby, the infant has a parchment-like surface covering that desquamates within a few days after birth. This outer layer is thought to be derived from the fetal periderm. Indeed, it is suggested that the more severe forms of ichthyosis are also caused by persistence and abnormal keratinization of the periderm.[25] X-linked ichthyosis is sometimes recognizable at birth as a collodion baby but may not become apparent for several months.

INFECTIONS

Toxic epidermal necrolysis has been mentioned earlier. Nonspecific maculo-papular rashes may occur with a variety of bacterial or viral infections. Cellulitis, erysipelas and impetigo can all be seen in newborn infants, usually caused by streptococcal infection, although impetigo may be caused by staphylococci.[17] The common and harmless erythema toxicum of the newborn may be mistaken for an infective rash, but a smear of the "pustular" lesions reveals masses of eosinophils.

Vesicles, although typically associated with infection of herpes simplex and varicella-zoster viruses, may sometimes be seen in the early stages of skin infection caused by *S. aureus* or *P. aeruginosa*. Pustules are commonly due to staphylococcal infection. Ecthyma gangrenosum is caused by *P. aeruginosa*. The lesion begins as a vesicular eruption on an erythematous base. Following rupture of the vesicles an indurated black eschar appears and a circumscribed area of necrosis develops. Organisms are present in large numbers within the lesions (Chapter 9).

Purpura is an important indication of possible infection in the newborn: it is a frequent manifestation of the TORCH group of congenital infections but may also develop in cases of bacterial sepsis.

EDEMA

Edema is a relatively common phenomenon in the newborn and may be localized or general in distribution.

LOCALIZED EDEMA

The most frequent form of localized edema is the caput succedaneum caused by pressure in the region of the presenting part during birth. Abnormal presentation may result in development of a caput at an unusual site (Fig. 19–16). This cause of localized edema should always be considered and excluded before looking for unusual causes.

Localized edema of varying degrees of severity may result from abnormalities of lymphatic development. These vary from cystic hygromas and localized areas of lymphangiectasia to generalized lymphangiomatosis.

SCLEREMA AND SCLEREDEMA

Sclerema neonatorum is a condition of hardening of the skin and subcutaneous tissues that begins usually on the legs of ill neonates and may spread to involve most of the body surface. Affected areas are smooth, hard and cold to touch and do not pit on pressure. The term scleredema is applied to patients with doughy edema rather than mere hardening of the tissues. The latter change is perhaps more frequently seen these days in preterm infants submitted to intensive care. Examination postmortem shows no specific findings in sclerema and a nonspecific tissue edema in cases of scleredema.[18]

GENERALIZED EDEMA

Generalized subcutaneous and tissue edema is usually associated with ascites and serous effusions in pleural and pericardial sacs. In some infants serous effusions are more prominent than tissue edema.

The most frequent cause of generalized edema in the newborn in Europe and North America has until recently been hydrops fetalis due to Rh isoimmunization.[35] The advent of prophylactic treatment with anti D globulin has so reduced the incidence of this condition that the other disorders listed in Table 19–3 will usually need to be considered when an edematous infant is seen by the pediatrician or pathologist. Features common to many of the conditions listed in Table 19–3 are fetal heart failure, anemia and hypoalbuminemia. There have been a number of papers reviewing this topic.[36–38]

Figure 19–16. Caput over buttocks in an infant with renal agenesis delivered by breech. A uterine constriction ring developed during labor.

TABLE 19–3. CAUSES AND ASSOCIATIONS OF GENERALIZED EDEMA AND ASCITES IN THE NEWBORN

1. Hematological (Ch. 20)
   Rh isoimmunization (classic hydrops fetalis)
   Homozygous α-thalassemia
   Twin-twin transfusion (recipient or donor)
   Chronic fetomaternal transfusion

2. Cardiovascular (Ch. 11)
   Some congenital anomalies (premature closure of foramen ovale or ductus
       arteriosus; Ebstein's anomaly
   Disorders of fetal myocardial function
           Endocardial fibroelastosis
           Paroxysmal supraventricular tachycardia
   Large angiomas with a-v shunting in fetus or placenta

3. Pulmonary (Ch. 10)
   Cystic adenomatoid malformation of lung
   Pulmonary lymphangiectasis

4. Renal (Ch. 17)
   Renal vein thrombosis
   Congenital nephrotic syndrome
   Lower urinary tract obstruction—primarily abdominal distension and ascites

5. Intrauterine infections (Ch. 9)
   Particularly TORCH group (CMV, toxoplasmosis, syphilis).

6. Miscellaneous
   Fetal neuroblastomatosis
   Storage disorders (Gaucher's disease, GM, gangliosidosis)
   Achondrogenesis*

7. Unknown

*Hydropic infants with this condition probably account for the inclusion of "achondroplasia" in most lists of causes of nonimmunologic hydrops.

REFERENCES

1. Royer, P.: Growth and development of bony tissues. *In* Davis, J. A., and Dobbing, J. (eds.): Scientific Foundations of Paediatrics, 2nd ed. London, William Heinemann, 1981, pp. 565–589.
2. Pryse-Davies, J., Smitham, J. H., and Napier, K. A.: Factors influencing development of secondary ossification centres in the fetus and newborn: A postmortem radiological study. Arch. Dis. Child. *49*:425–431, 1974.
3. Russell, J. G. B.: Radiological assessment of age, retardation and death. *In* Barson, A. J. (ed.): Laboratory Investigation of Fetal Disease. Bristol, John Wright & Sons Ltd., 1981, pp. 3–16.
4. Scott, K. E., and Usher, R.: Epiphyseal development in fetal malnutrition syndrome. N. Engl. J. Med. *270*:822–824, 1964.
5. Emery, J. L., and Kalpaktsoglou, P. K.: The costochondral junction during later stages of intrauterine life, and abnormal growth patterns found in association with perinatal death. Arch. Dis. Child. *42*:1–13, 1967.
6. Yang, S.-S., Heidelberger, K. P., Brough, A. J., Corbett, D. P., and Bernstein, J.: Lethal short-limbed chondrodysplasia in early infancy. *In* Rosenberg, H. S., and Bolande, R. P. (eds.): Perspectives in Pediatric Pathology, vol. 3. Chicago, Year Book Medical Publishers, 1976, pp. 1–40.
7. Sillence, D. O., Horton, W. A., and Rimoin, D. L.: Morphologic studies in the skeletal dysplasias. Am. J. Pathol. *96*:811–870, 1979.
8. Hwang, W. S., Tock, E. P. C., Tan, K. L., and Tan, L. K. A.: The pathology of cartilage in chondrodysplasias. J. Pathol. *127*:11–18, 1979.
9. Maroteaux, P., Lamy, M., and Robert, J.-M.: Le nanisme thanatophore. Presse Med. *75*:2519–2524, 1967.
10. Penttinen, R. P., Lichtenstein, J. R., Martin, G. R., and McKusick, V. A.: Abnormal collagen metabolism in cultured cells in osteogenesis imperfecta. Proc. Natl. Acad. Sci. USA *72*:586–589, 1975.
11. Dickson, I. R., Millar, E. A., and Veis, A.: Evidence for abnormality of bone matrix proteins in osteogenesis imperfecta. Lancet *2*:586–587, 1975.
12. Shapiro, F., Glimcher, M. J., Holtrop, M. E., Tashjian, A. H., Brickley-Parsons, D., and Kenzora, J. E.: Human osteopetrosis. J. Bone Joint Surg. *62*:384–399, 1980.
13. Ballet, J. J., Griscelli, C., Coutris, C., Milhaud, G., and Maroteaux, P.: Bone marrow transplantation in osteopetrosis. Lancet *2*:1137, 1977.
14. Gorodischer, R., Davidson, R. G., Mosovich, L. L., and Yaffe, S. J.: Hypophosphatasia: A developmental anomaly of alkaline phosphatase? Pediatr. Res. *10*:650–656, 1976.
15. Bosley, A. R. J., Verrier-Jones, E. R., and Campbell, M. J.: Aetiological factors in rickets of prematurity. Arch. Dis. Child. *55*:683–686, 1980.
16. Oppenheimer, S. J., and Snodgrass, G. J. A. I.: Neonatal rickets: Histopathology and quantitative bone changes. Arch. Dis. Child. *55*:945–949, 1980.
17. Klein, J. O., and Marcy, S. M.: Bacterial infections. *In* Remington, J. S., and Klein, J. O. (eds.): Infectious Diseases of the Fetus and Newborn Infant. Philadelphia, W. B. Saunders Co., 1976, pp. 747–891.
18. Potter, E. L., and Craig, J. M.: Pathology of the Fetus and the Infant, 3rd ed. Chicago, Year Book Medical Publishers, 1976.
19. McKenzie, J.: First arch syndrome. Arch. Dis. Child. *33*:477–486, 1958.
20. Dubowitz, V.: Muscle Disorders in Childhood. Philadelphia, W. B. Saunders Co., 1978.
21. Bossen, E. H., Shelburne, J. D., and Verkauf, B. S.: Respiratory muscle involvement in infantile myotonic dystrophy. Arch. Pathol. *97*:250–252, 1974.
22. Dubowitz, V.: The floppy infant, 2nd ed. Clinics in Developmental Medicine, No. 76. London, William Heinemann, 1980.
23. Wynne-Davies, R., and Lloyd-Roberts, G. C.: Arthrogryposis multiple congenita. Search for prenatal factors in 66 sporadic cases. Arch. Dis. Child. *51*:618–623, 1976.
24. Dunn, P. M.: The anatomy and pathology of congenital dislocation of the hip. Clin. Orthopaed. *119*:23–27, 1976.
25. Moynahan, E. J.: Developmental biology of the skin. *In* Davis, J. A., and Dobbing, J. (eds.): Scientific Foundations of Paediatrics, 2nd ed. London, William Heinemann, 1981, pp. 721–741.
26. Schwartz, V.: The development of the sweat glands and their function. *In* Davis, J. A., and Dobbing, J. (eds.): Scientific Foundations of Paediatrics, 2nd ed. London, William Heinemann, 1981, pp. 741–744.
27. Torpin, R.: Amniochorionic mesoblastic fibrous strings and amnionic bands: Associated constricting fetal malformations or fetal death. Am. J. Obstet. Gynecol. *91*:65–75, 1965.
28. Moessinger, A. C., Blanc, W. A., Byrne, J., Andrews, D., Warburton, D., and Bloom, A.: Amniotic band syndrome associated with amniocentesis. Am. J. Obstet. Gynecol. *141*:588–591, 1981.
29. Smith, D. W.: Recognizable Patterns of Human Malformation. Philadelphia, W. B. Saunders Co., 1982.
30. Salmon, M. A.: Developmental defects and syndromes. Aylesbury, H. M. & M. Publishers, 1978.
31. Bauer, E. A., and Briggaman, R. A.: The mechanobullous diseases (epidermolysis bullosa). *In* Fitzpatrick, T. B., et al. (eds.): Dermatology in General Medicine, 2nd ed. New York, McGraw-Hill, 1979, pp. 334–347.

32. Pearson, R. W., Potter, B., and Strauss, F.: Epidermolysis bullosa hereditaria letalis. Arch. Dermatol. *109*:349–355, 1974.
33. Shinefield, H. R.: Staphylococcal infections. *In* Remington, J. S., and Klein, J. O. (eds): Infectious Diseases of the Fetus and Newborn Infant. Philadelphia, W. B. Saunders Co., 1976, pp. 979–1019.
34. Esterly, N. B.: The Ichthyosiform dermatoses. Pediatrics *42*:990–1004, 1968.
35. Macafee, C. A. J., Fortune, D. W., and Beischer, N. A.: Nonimmunological hydrops fetalis. J. Obstet. Gynaecol. Br. Cwlth. *77*:226–237, 1970.
36. Turski, D. M., Shahadi, N., Viseskul, C., and Gilbert, E.: Nonimmunologic hydrops fetalis. Am. J. Obstet. Gynecol. *131*:586–587, 1978.
37. Etches, P. S., and Lemons, J. A.: Nonimmune hydrops fetalis: Report of 22 cases including three siblings. Pediatrics *64*:326–332, 1979.
38. Machin, G. A.: Differential diagnosis of hydrops fetalis. Am. J. Med. Genet. *9*:341–350, 1981.
39. Elias, S., Mazur, M., Sabbagha, R., et al.: Prenatal diagnosis of harlequin ichthyosis. Clin. Genet. *17*:275–280, 1980.

Chapter Twenty

Hemopoietic and Lymphoreticular Systems

Common disorders involving the hemopoietic system in the perinatal period include Rh isoimmunization and glucose 6-phosphate dehydrogenase deficiency, although their frequency varies in populations of different genetic constitution. Most other conditions that involve the hemopoietic or lymphoreticular systems at a primary level in the perinatal period are individually rare. However, abnormalities such as jaundice, anemia or hemostatic failure may play a significant role in many perinatal disorders that the pathologist may be asked to investigate post-mortem, particularly if death has occurred before a diagnosis could be established. Similarly, although direct involvement of the lymphoreticular system in pathological processes is uncommon, reactions such as lymphoid depletion of the thymus, which can be recognized postmortem, may help in establishing the time course of a perinatal illness.

I. Hemopoietic System

DEVELOPMENT

Embryonic hemopoiesis begins in the area vasculosa of the yolk sac by about 19 days after conception. The initial blood-forming cells are hemocytoblasts, which mainly differentiate into primitive megaloblasts containing hemoglobin, although some also differentiate into histiocytes.[1] The embryonic generations of red cells are large and nucleated, and the hemoglobin structure differs from that contained within the later fetal red cells. During the second and third months the sinusoids of the liver gradually become the main site of formation of red cells: hemopoietic activity develops within the bone marrow at the end of the fourth month. Polymorphonuclear leukocytes are formed from about 7 weeks in connective tissue in sites such as the meninges and mesentery. Circulating leukocytes are sparse until formation begins within the bone marrow. Megakaryocytes are formed in the liver from about 6 weeks and in the bone marrow from 10 weeks. By the time of birth the bone marrow has become the major site of production of both red and white cell series.

Erythropoiesis-stimulating factor (erythropoietin) is found in plasma during fetal life in higher concentration than in neonates.[2] Erythropoietin levels are raised in infants with Rh isoimmunization and in fetal lambs made acutely anemic.[3] Such observations suggest that red cell production is controlled by red cell mass in late fetal life.

NEONATAL JAUNDICE

BILIRUBIN FORMATION AND METABOLISM

The breakdown of the hemoglobin of effete red cells involves opening of the macro-ring of heme under the influence of the enzyme heme oxygenase present in the liver, spleen, kidney, bone marrow and macrophages of lung and peritoneal cavity.[4] The opening of the heme ring yields biliverdin, which is in turn reduced to bilirubin by the enzyme biliverdin reductase. The rate-limiting step in this process appears to be the activity of heme oxygenase. Bilirubin, which is fat soluble but relatively insoluble in water, passes to the liver in combination with plasma albumin, which has a high affinity for it. The presence of specific bilirubin-binding proteins such as ligandin may also be important. Within the liver cell bilirubin is conjugated with glucuronic acid under the influence of glucuronyl transferase to form the water-soluble bilirubin diglucuronate and secreted into the biliary system.

Several stages of this process are poorly developed in the newborn, particularly the preterm newborn infant. Bilirubin formation occurs readily in the fetus, and the unconjugated bilirubin is transported readily across the placenta. Uptake of bilirubin by the liver cells may be impaired if plasma albumin levels are low or other compounds, such as certain drugs, are present that compete with bilirubin for albumin-binding sites. The ease with which bilirubin uptake can be interfered with may perhaps partly be a result of low hepatic ligandin levels.

The ability of the hepatic cell to conjugate bilirubin is defective in the preterm newborn infant at birth, and lack of glucuronyl transferase activity may often be the limiting factor that leads to development of unconjugated neonatal hyper-bilirubinemia. Glucuronyl transferase activity is induced within a few days of birth but the trigger mechanism remains obscure, although it is known not to involve glucocorticoids.

Although the mechanisms of secretion of bilirubin by the hepatic cell are not well understood, excretion by the biliary system is largely dependent on bile flow, which is in turn mainly controlled by the osmotic drive produced by secretion of bile acids.[5] Within the bile ducts there is modification of the canalicular bile by the addition of other solutes with chloride and bicarbonate, under the influence of secretin.

A variety of factors may contribute to the susceptibility of the newborn infant to development of cholestasis.[5] Coincident with the loss of the placenta as a route of metabolism, profound changes occur in the hepatic circulation. Enteral feeding needs to be established to promote the secretin-dependent component of bile flow, and there is a low intraduodenal concentration of bile salts and low total bile salt pool in preterm infants. In addition, at least two of the products of bile salt metabolism, lithocholic acid and 3-β-hydroxy 5 cholenic acid, are known to cause cholestasis and hepatocellular damage experimentally and may be found in the meconium of preterm infants.[6, 7]

CAUSES OF JAUNDICE IN THE NEONATAL PERIOD

From the preceding discussion it can be seen that jaundice in the newborn, as in the adult, is related to problems in uptake, conjugation and secretion of conjugated bilirubin by the hepatic cells. However, the limited ability to perform these functions in the preterm newborn infant means that the development of jaundice in the early neonatal period is more likely to be caused by overloading an imperfectly developed system than by primary liver disease. Therefore, jaundice may result from (1) excessive breakdown of red cells, (2) impairment in transport of bilirubin to the liver, (3) impaired uptake of bilirubin by the liver, (4) impaired conjugation of bilirubin, or (5) impaired excretion of bilirubin via the biliary system.

Jaundice of early onset in the neonatal period is most often unconjugated and involves one of the four mechanisms labeled A to D in Table 20–1. Some of the conditions are mild and are often not associated with liver disease. Persistent jaundice (e.g., severe blood group incompatibility) may involve an increasing component of conjugated bilirubin, and most forms of jaundice developing after the first few days of age are associated with conjugated hyperbilirubinemia.

The newborn infant is particularly susceptible to development of cholestatic jaundice, as indicated by the large number of conditions listed under E in the table. Liver pathology of these conditions is described in Chapter 14.

ANEMIA

Anemia in the newborn may be due to blood loss, blood destruction by hemolysis or inadequate red cell production.

Site and Timing of Hemorrhage Resulting in Neonatal Anemia

A number of characteristic forms of hemorrhage occur before, during or after birth and are listed in Table 20–2.

INTRAUTERINE BLOOD LOSS

This may be caused by transplacental (fetomaternal) hemorrhage, may occur from torn vessels on the fetal surface of the placenta or may result from twin-twin transfusion.

Fetomaternal Hemorrhage. Some fetal cells enter the maternal circulation in about 50 per cent of all pregnancies, and in about 1 per cent the loss has been said to exceed 40 ml.[8] Procedures such as diagnostic amniocentesis and external cephalic version may increase the frequency and extent of fetomaternal hemorrhage.[9] Direct laceration of vessels on the fetal surface of the placenta may occur during amniocentesis. Bleeding in this case takes place into the amniotic sac and between amnion and chorion.

Twin-Twin Transfusion. The mechanism of development of this condition, which occurs in 15 to 20 per cent of all monochorial twin pairs, is discussed in Chapter 4. The donor twin is usually smaller than the recipient and may show marked pallor in contrast to the polycythemia of the recipient (Fig. 20–1). The problems of the recipient, which include respiratory distress and hyperbilirubinemia, may be at least as great as those of the donor.[10] A difference in cord hemoglobin level of 5 g per dl between the twins is usually taken as indicative of twin transfusion syndrome, but in the absence of other evidence of the syndrome does not exclude the alternative possibility of fetomaternal bleeding from the anemic twin.

TABLE 20–1. CAUSES OF NEONATAL JAUNDICE

UNCONJUGATED HYPERBILIRUBINEMIA				CONJUGATED HYPERBILIRUBINEMIA
A Excessive Red Cell Breakdown	*B* Impaired Transport	*C* Impaired Uptake	*D* Impaired Conjugation	*E* Impaired Excretion
Blood group incompatibility	Hypoxia and acidosis	Poor hepatic perfusion (cardiac anomalies, etc.)	Breast milk jaundice	GENERAL
Hemorrhage (cephalhematoma, intramuscular in breech delivery, etc.)	Hypoalbuminemia (preterm)		Hypoglycemia	Low intestinal obstruction or meconium retention
Red cell abnormalities (G6PD deficiency, hemoglobinopathies, spherocytosis)			Hypothyroidism	Blood group incompatibility (late effect)
			High intestinal obstruction	Sepsis
			Crigler-Najjar syndrome	Infections involving liver (bacterial, viral, fungal)
Polycythemia (placental transfusion, twin-transfusion)			Physiological jaundice	Drugs
Sepsis			Drugs (novobiocin, chloramphenicol)	Parenteral nutrition
Drugs				Extrahepatic biliary atresia
				Paucity of intrahepatic bile ducts
				Choledochal cyst
				METABOLIC ABNORMALITIES
				Galactosemia
				Fructose intolerance
				α-antitrypsin deficiency
				Tyrosinemia
				Wolman's disease
				Niemann-Pick disease
				Zellweger syndrome
				Gaucher disease
				OTHER GENETIC DISORDERS
				Cystic fibrosis
				Familial and recurrent forms of cholestasis
				Chromosomal disorders (i.e., trisomy 18)

TABLE 20–2.   TIMING AND TYPES OF HEMORRHAGE LEADING TO ANEMIA IN THE NEWBORN

TIMING	TYPE
Intrauterine	Fetomaternal
	Twin-twin transfusion
	Traumatic (fetus or placenta)
Intrapartum	Abnormalities of cord or fetal vessels (e.g., vasa praevia)
	Placenta praevia
	Abruptio placentae
	Trauma to placenta
Neonatal	EXTERNAL
	Bleeding from umbilicus
	Bleeding from intestine
	Traumatic
	INTERNAL
	1. Cranial
	Cephalhematoma
	Subaponeurotic hemorrhage
	Subdural and subarachnoid hemorrhage
	Intraventricular/intracerebral hemorrhage
	2. Other sites
	Intramuscular (e.g., breech)
	Retroperitoneal
	Subcapsular hematoma of liver
	Any site subject to trauma (e.g., rupture of umbilical artery during catheterization)

INTRAPARTUM HEMORRHAGE

This usually results from damage to fetal placental vessels during labor or delivery. The classic form of such injury is tear of an abnormal umbilical vessel during birth of the baby through a velamentous insertion of the cord related to the internal os (torn vasa praevia). Other possibilities include rupture of a varix or aneurysm of the cord, avulsion of the cord, fetomaternal or retroplacental hemorrhage occurring during labor, or accidental incision of the placenta during cesarean section.

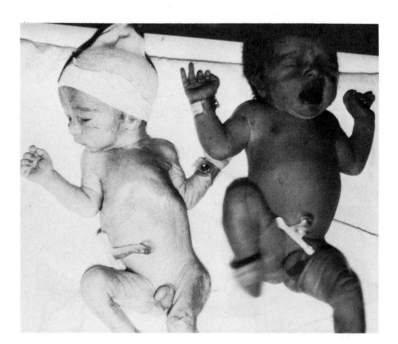

Figure 20–1. Donor and recipient twins in twin-transfusion syndrome.

The clinical differentiation of an infant who has suffered acute hemorrhage during birth from one suffering the effects of acute intraparatum asphyxia is an urgent problem in life. Occasionally an infant who has sustained an acute intrapartum hemorrhage may come to the pathologist undiagnosed. In such a case the pallor of the internal organs may allow the condition to be recognized at autopsy (Fig. 20–2).

Although examination of the placenta in a case of intrapartum hemorrhage may reveal a torn fetal vessel, there is often no obvious abnormality. In such cases fetal bleeding from villous vessels may have occurred, resulting in a retroplacental or revealed accidental hemorrhage or a fetomaternal hemorrhage. If the condition has not been suspected clinically, the pathologist may reasonably suggest that an attempt be made to confirm the diagnosis by demonstrating fetal red cells in the maternal circulation by the Kleihauer acid elution technique.

NEONATAL HEMORRHAGE

Significant sites of hemorrhage are shown in Table 20–2. Most of the traumatic causes are discussed in Chapter 6. Nontraumatic causes of neonatal bleeding are listed in Table 20–4 and are discussed later (p. 409).

HEMOLYTIC ANEMIA IN THE NEWBORN

Causes of hemolysis that may present as anemia in the newborn are shown in Table 20–3. Detailed discussion of most of these conditions is outside the scope of this book. The reader is referred to works such as those by Oski and Naiman,[11] Lanzkowsky[12] and Zipursky[13] for further information.

Rh ISO-IMMUNIZATION

This was one of the major causes of neonatal jaundice and anemia in Western countries until the advent of prophylactic treatment with Rh immunoglobulin.

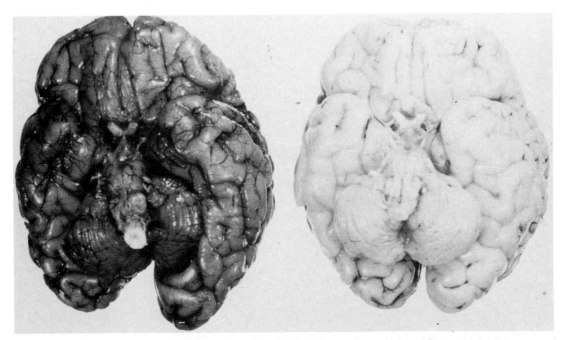

Figure 20–2. Brain of a term infant who suffered a fatal hemorrhage during delivery (right) is compared with that of an infant who died of birth asphyxia (left). The fetal hemorrhage was misdiagnosed as maternal antepartum hemorrhage.

TABLE 20–3.   NONHEMORRHAGIC CAUSES OF ANEMIA IN THE NEWBORN*

A. HEMOLYTIC ANEMIAS Congenital red cell defects	1. *Membrane defects* Hereditary spherocytosis Hereditary elliptocytosis Infantile pyknocytosis 2. *Hemoglobin defects* α-thalassemia α,β-thalassemia Unstable hemoglobin (Hb Köln, Zurich) 3. *Enzyme defects* Embden-Meyerhof glycolytic pathway (pyruvate kinase) Hexose-monophosphate shunt (G6PD)

Acquired red cell defects	1. *Immune*
	Rh isoimmunization
	ABO and minor group
	    incompatibilities
	2. *Nonimmune*
	Infections (TORCH group)
	Disseminated intravascular coagulation
	Drugs and chemicals
	    Synthetic vitamin K analogues
	    Maternal thiazide diuretics
	    Antimalarials
	    Sulfonamides
	    Naphthalene
	    Aniline dye marking ink
	    Penicillin
	Vitamin E deficiency in preterm
	    infants
	Metabolic disease (galactosemia)

B. RED CELL APLASIA	Congenital hypoplastic anemia

*Some of the conditions listed (e.g., DIC) are also associated with hemorrhage (Table 20–4) but may cause anemia *without* hemorrhage.

The condition develops when an Rh-negative woman becomes sensitized to her Rh-positive fetus.* Maternal immunization occurs in 20 per cent of Rh-negative mothers following a transplacental hemorrhage of 0.25 ml of Rh-positive blood from an ABO-compatible fetus, a degree of hemorrhage that occurs in about 20 per cent of all deliveries. Larger hemorrhages resulting in a higher incidence of immunization may be caused by procedures such as manual removal of the placenta, external cephalic version, amniocentesis, cesarean section or spontaneous or therapeutic abortion. The observation that most of the transplacental bleeding occurred during, or shortly before, delivery and that immunization did not occur in ABO-incompatible pregnancies (in which fetal cells reaching the maternal circulation would be rapidly lysed) provided the rationale for prophylactic treatment of Rh-negative mothers with Rh immunoglobulin in the early puerperium.[14]

The clinical picture in the infant varies according to the severity of immunization. There may be death in utero with delivery of a macerated fetus, birth of a stillborn or liveborn hydropic infant or birth of a liveborn infant with a variable degree of anemia, hepatosplenomegaly and jaundice.

Hydrops, comprising severe edema of subcutaneous and connective tissues and effusions into serous cavities, is characteristic of severe Rh isoimmunization. Hydrops is usually associated with severe anemia but is not directly related to the Hb level. It is probably related to the level of serum proteins and nonprotein

---

*Rh-positive is taken to mean positive for the D antigen.

oncotic pressure of the plasma and may also be influenced by development of fetal heart failure or by raised venous pressure associated with fetal asphyxia.[13]

Severely affected infants may have ascites and pleural effusions without gross tissue edema, and the liver and spleen are both markedly enlarged (Fig. 20–3). The adrenals are characteristically large, with lipid streaking of the cortex. In cases with pleural effusions the lungs are usually undersized. Evidence of a bleeding diathesis occurs in life in some infants. At autopsy this may be evidenced by multiple petechiae within connective tissues and muscles. Convexity hemorrhages are sometimes seen over the brain, and there may be hemorrhage into the lungs. The serum bilirubin rises rapidly after birth so that affected infants who die after the first 12 hours will show severe jaundice. The thymus and lymphoid tissues are very poorly developed. Placental changes are described in Chapter 4. On histology there is a massive extramedullary hemopoiesis distorting the architecture of the liver (Chapter 14). The spleen shows poor development of follicles and masses of hemopoietic cells within the pulp (Fig. 20–4). Iron stains usually reveal positive hemosiderin deposits within both liver and spleen.

Severely affected infants who survive for 4 to 5 days or more may develop a conjugated hyperbilirubinemia. If such an infant comes to autopsy, the liver shows changes of cholestasis superimposed on those of erythroblastosis.

OTHER CAUSES OF HEMOLYTIC ANEMIA IN THE NEWBORN

Among the causes of hemolytic anemia given in Table 20–3, those that may be seen by the pathologist in the neonatal period include homozygous α-thalassemia (in the form of hydrops in infants of Asian parentage), infections of the TORCH group and other forms of neonatal sepsis (Chapter 9), disseminated intravascular coagulation and reactions to drug therapy.

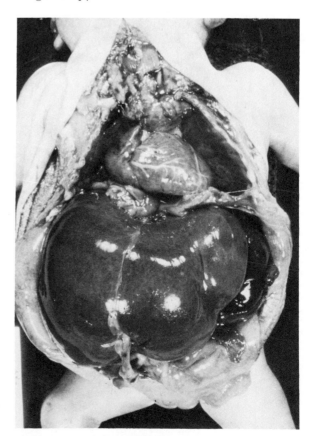

Figure 20–3. Gross enlargement of liver and spleen in an infant who died shortly after birth of severe Rh isoimmunization.

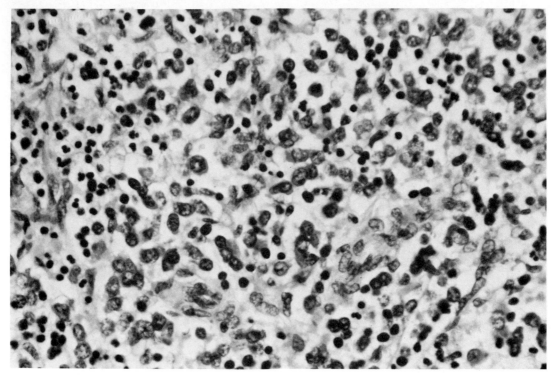

Figure 20–4. Spleen in Rh isoimmunization. H and E × 350. Normal pattern obscured by loss of lymphocytes and presence of large numbers of immature hemopoietic cells.

Congenital Hypoplastic Anemia (Blackfan-Diamond Syndrome)[15]

This uncommon condition occasionally is seen with anemia at birth and in one third of cases is associated with congenital defects, including dwarfism, neckwebbing, skeletal anomalies, cardiac defects and anomalies of the urinary tract. The infants are often born prematurely. Red cell precursors in the bone marrow are markedly reduced, although platelet and leukocyte production remains normal.

HEMORRHAGIC DISORDERS AND THROMBOCYTOPENIA IN THE NEWBORN[11, 12]

Causes of nontraumatic hemorrhage in the newborn are given in Table 20–4.

Congenital plasma factor deficiencies are an occasional cause of bleeding in the newborn. Vitamin K deficiency is associated with low levels of prothrombin (factor I) and factors VII, IX, and X. Hemorrhagic symptoms usually develop at 2 to 4 days of age, particularly in breast-fed infants, with gastrointestinal bleeding as a characteristic feature. The condition is normally prevented by routine administration of vitamin K after birth. A similar condition may follow maternal ingestion of oral anticoagulants and anticonvulsants such as phenytoin, primidone and phenobarbital.

Hepatic disease in the newborn may result in inability of the liver to synthesize coagulation factors despite administration of vitamin K. Hemorrhagic phenomena may be seen on this basis in a range of disorders varying from infections to circulatory collapse or metabolic disease. An overlapping series of conditions including infections, perinatal hypoxia and hypothermia may induce disseminated intravascular coagulation with resultant hemolytic anemia, red cell fragmentation,

TABLE 20–4. CAUSES OF NONTRAUMATIC HEMORRHAGE IN THE NEWBORN

A. Congenital plasma factor deficiencies (factor VII, factor VIII)
B. Acquired plasma factor deficiencies
  1. Vitamin K responsive
    Spontaneous: classic hemorrhagic disease of newborn
    Secondary to maternal drug ingestion (anticoagulants, anticonvulsants)
  2. Vitamin K nonresponsive
    Hepatic dysfunction: infection, hypoxia, hypoperfusion, metabolic disease
    Disseminated intravascular coagulation
C. Thrombocytopenia
  1. Normal or increased megakaryocytes
    a. Immune disorders with passive transfer of platelet antibodies
      Maternal idiopathic thrombocytopenic purpura
      Maternal drug-induced thrombocytopenia
      Maternal systemic lupus erythematosus
    b. Isoimmunization—platelet group incompatibilities
    c. Drugs—thiazides given to mother
    d. Disseminated intravascular coagulation
    e. Inherited thrombocytopenias (sex-linked or autosomal)
  2. Decreased or absent megakaryocytes
    Congenital megakaryocyte hypoplasias (associated with bilateral absent radii–TAR syndrome)
    Rubella syndrome
    Trisomy syndromes
    Bone marrow infiltration—congenital leukemia

thrombocytopenia and prolonged prothrombin, partial thromboplastin and thrombin times. Fibrinogen, factor V and factor VIII levels may be low and levels of fibrin degradation products raised.

A history of bleeding or signs of localized or widespread hemorrhage may thus be a feature of many infants who come to the pathologist in the neonatal period.[16, 17] It will only be possible to determine the underlying cause of bleeding (e.g., to differentiate between hepatic damage and disseminated intravascular coagulation) if full coagulation studies have been instituted in life.

A giant hemangioma is an occasional site of disseminated intravascular coagulation (Kasabach-Merritt syndrome).[18]

ABNORMALITIES OF WHITE BLOOD CELLS IN THE NEWBORN

A number of forms of congenital neutropenia are known. Differential diagnosis is a hematological problem that needs to be sorted out in life. The most severe form of white cell defect is reticular dysgenesis (congenital aleukocytosis), in which there is congenital absence of granulocytes and decrease in numbers of circulating lymphocytes. The bone marrow shows lack of myeloid cells, and the thymus and spleen lack lymphocytes (see p. 413). The infants suffer multiple infections and die in the neonatal period.

Other causes of neutropenia in the newborn include isoimmunization or autoimmunization and overwhelming sepsis.[12]

CONGENITAL LEUKEMIA

Congenital leukemia is rare but may be recognized in stillbirths (Dr. Elizabeth Gray, personal communication), may be present at birth in liveborn infants or may develop in the first month. Acute myelogenous leukemia is the most frequent variety. Features resemble leukemia in older infants, but slate-colored nodular skin infiltrations are common in the newborn. Hepatosplenomegaly and a hemorrhagic diathesis are common, and anemia may develop within a few days after birth. A high proportion of affected infants have congenital anomalies, particularly chromosomal anomalies, of which Down syndrome is the most common. However, congenital leukemia has also been reported in trisomy 13 and Turner syndrome.[19]

It may be difficult to differentiate the condition from other myeloproliferative disorders such as the dysmyelopoietic syndrome seen in many infants with Down syndrome. Criteria suggested for the diagnosis of congenital leukemia include presence of immature lymphoid or myeloid cells in the bone marrow and peripheral blood, infiltration of nonhemopoietic tissues by these cells and absence of hemolytic disease, congenital infection, or another malignancy (e.g., disseminated neuroblastoma).

Congenital leukemia responds poorly to therapy and is usually rapidly fatal.

II. Lymphorecticular System

DEVELOPMENT

The thymus develops from the third pharyngeal pouch and appears during the sixth postconceptional week. The main portion of the gland migrates caudally and medially to fuse with its counterpart from the opposite side. The tail of the gland may persist within the neck, and small portions of thymus often remain attached to the thyroid. The parathyroid derived from the same pouch descends toward the thorax with the thymus. Lymphocytes appear in the thymus at 7 to 8 weeks.[1] At about 8 weeks the mass of epithelial cells becomes divided into lobules by vascular invasion from the surrounding mesenchyme. Hassall's corpuscles develop as small aggregates of epithelial cells with eosinophilic and granular cytoplasm at about 9 to 10 weeks. Ultrastructural studies of the thymus have confirmed that Hassall's corpuscles carry out digestion of lymphocytes from an early stage of development.[20]

The histological appearance of the thymus alters through gestation. At an early stage the gland is predominantly epithelial. By the end of the second trimester there is dense infiltration of lymphocytes in the outer part of the lobule, giving a well-marked cortex and medulla (Fig. 20–5). Toward term the lymphocyte component becomes more pronounced, and the clear demarcation of zones is lost (Fig. 20–6).

The spleen develops as a condensation of mesenchyme within the dorsal mesogastrium during the sixth postconceptional week. Subdivision of the organ by trabeculae occurs at 8 to 9 weeks, and hemopoietic activity is present by 12 weeks. Follicles develop during the second trimester at about 22 to 24 weeks.

The lymph nodes appear by 8 postconceptional weeks and in the early part of gestation may be a site of hemopoiesis,[1] but by 10 weeks they contain lymphoid cells only. However, lymphopoiesis in the fetus is slow in all tissues other than the thymus.

DEVELOPMENT OF B AND T LYMPHOCYTES

The development of the two major classes of lymphocytes is outlined in Figure 20–7. Both B and T lymphocytes are derived from the pluripotent

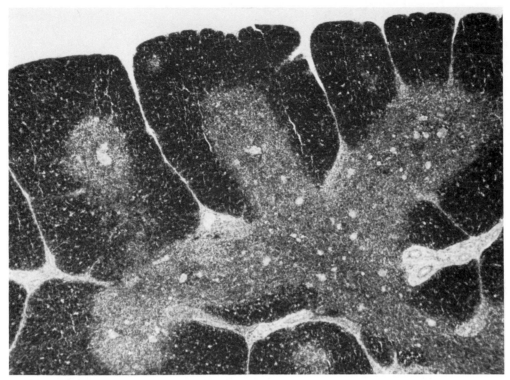

Figure 20–5. Thymus at 26 weeks' gestation. H and E × 30. There is a clear demarcation of cortex and medulla.

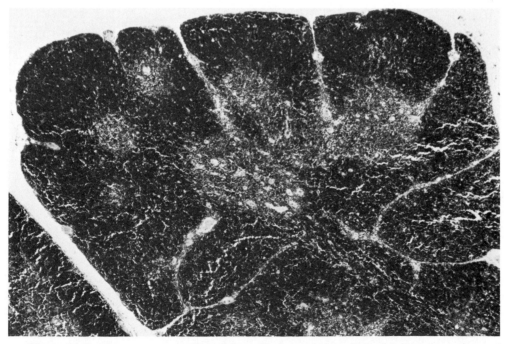

Figure 20–6. Thymus at term. H and E × 30. Loss of clear distinction between cortex and medulla seen at earlier stage.

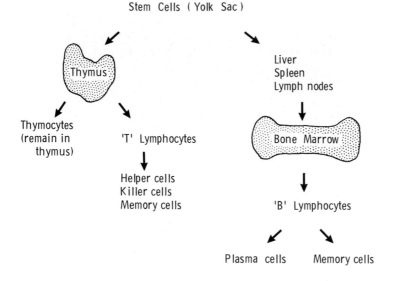

Stem Cells (Yolk Sac)

Thymus

Thymocytes (remain in thymus)

'T' Lymphocytes

Helper cells
Killer cells
Memory cells

Liver
Spleen
Lymph nodes

Bone Marrow

'B' Lymphocytes

Plasma cells   Memory cells

Figure 20–7. Diagram to illustrate development of major classes of lymphocytes.

T Cell Development   B Cell Development

hemopoietic stem cells, which also give rise to myeloid, megakaryocytic and erythroid cell lines.[21] Pre-B cells categorized by their ability to synthesize cytoplasmic IgM can be recognized in the fetal liver by 8 weeks after conception. By 15 weeks the fetus has an adult proportion of B lymphocytes expressing different immunoglobulin classes and capable of responding to a wide variety of antigens.[22] T cells, recognized by their ability to form rosettes with sheep erythrocytes, are present in the thymus by 11 weeks' gestation. Between 12 and 20 weeks, 95 to 100 per cent of thymocytes are differentiated T cells. The timing of further differentiation of T cells into helper, suppressor and cytotoxic cells has yet to be determined. By 20 weeks' gestation the B cells can respond to infection such as syphilis and toxoplasmosis by formation of plasma cells, but the antibodies produced are mainly of the IgM class. By this time the other elements of the immune response such as the components of complement are all present in normal proportions.

At birth the cellular immune system has been described as anatomically intact, antigenically inexperienced and functionally deficient.[23] There is evidence that qualitative and quantitative deficiencies in antibody responses of the newborn as compared with the adult reflect immaturity of regulatory interaction between B cells, T cells and macrophages rather than absence of B cells capable of responding to an antigenic stimulus.[22, 24] Lack of helper T cells may be a major factor.

CONGENITAL ANOMALIES OF THE LYMPHORETICULAR SYSTEM

THYMUS

THYMIC AGENESIS (DiGEORGE SYNDROME)

Thymic agenesis is an abnormality of third and fourth pharyngeal pouches in which absence or hypoplasia of the thymus is associated with a variable hypoplasia or absence of the parathyroids, and in many cases, anomalies of the aortic arch or conotruncal region of the cardiovascular system. The frequency with which right aortic arch and interrupted aortic arch are found in this syndrome has prompted the suggestion that the etiology may lie in an interruption of the primitive blood supply to the third and fourth pouches during organogenesis.[25] Associated features include facial abnormalities such as micrognathia, short philtrum, small palpebral fissures, and malformed ears, hypoplastic spleen and lymphoid depletion of thymic-dependent areas of the lymph nodes. Absence of the parathyroids leads to hypocalcemic tetany in the neonatal period. Humoral immune function is usually well preserved, but functional tests in life reveal severe defects in T cell activity. This fact confirms that the primary defect is failure of normal development of the thymus anlage, which prevents normal processing of stem cells to T cells.[26] The condition is often encountered incidentally at neonatal autopsy in infants who die with congenital cardiac anomalies.

RETICULAR DYSGENESIS

Reticular dysgenesis is a rare condition in which the thymus lacks lymphocytes and there is little or no development of peripheral lymphoid tissue. There is lymphopenia, agranulocytosis and agammaglobulinemia.[27] The condition appears to result from failure of normal development of the precursors of the lymphocyte and granulocyte cell populations, as red cells and platelets are present. The infants die of infection in the neonatal period.

THYMIC DYSPLASIA

This is an abnormality of development of the thymic epithelium comprising absence or severe reduction in number of Hassall's corpuscles associated with severe lymphocyte depletion (Fig. 20–8).[28] The abnormality is seen in a number of immunological deficiency syndromes, including combined immune deficiency, defective cellular immunity with normal circulating immunoglobins, and Wiskott-

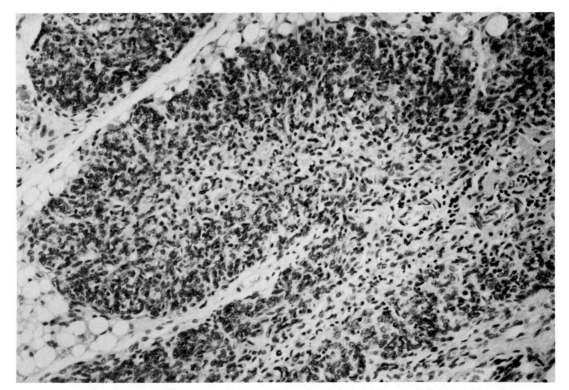

Figure 20–8. Thymic dysplasia in an infant with severe combined immune deficiency. H and E × 150. There is severe lymphocyte depletion and absence of Hassall's corpuscles.

Aldrich syndrome. Lymph nodes may be absent or poorly differentiated, and the spleen shows poor development of lymphocyte cuffs around the penicillar arteries.

Thymic dysplasia will rarely be seen in the newborn because the immune deficiency syndromes do not usually become apparent until after the first month of life, when maternally derived IgG levels decrease. However, the pathologist should be aware of the possibility that a small thymus in an infant who has died soon after birth may be associated with an undiagnosed immune deficiency syndrome and should retain other lymphoid tissue for examination in such cases. If autopsy is performed within 12 hours after death it may be possible to carry out tests of lymphocyte function on cells from thymus, lymph nodes and bone marrow. Such studies will be appropriate only in cases in which there is a high index of suspicion of immunological deficiency. Usually a small thymus will be found merely to show lymphoid depletion caused by a stress reaction. Prenatal diagnosis of combined immune deficiency has recently been reported.[31]

SPLEEN

Accessory masses of splenic tissue, splenunculi, are found in 10 to 15 per cent of neonatal autopsies, and are of no pathological significance. Polysplenia, a condition in which multiple splenunculi occur in place of a normal spleen, is associated with a central liver, malrotation of the intestine and situs ambiguous of left lung type (Chapter 11). Asplenia (Ivemark syndrome) is also associated with anomalies of intestinal position, central liver and situs ambiguous of right lung type (Chapter 11). As mentioned earlier, a hypoplastic spleen is often found in cases of DiGeorge syndrome.

OTHER PATHOLOGY OF THE LYMPHORETICULAR SYSTEM IN THE PERINATAL PERIOD

THYMUS

The thymic lesions most frequently encountered at perinatal autopsy are cortical hemorrhages and evidence of reaction to stress.

Petechial hemorrhages in the thymic cortex are common in infants who suffer an acute anoxic death such as that associated with abruptio placentae, and are of significance only as an indication of the mode of death. The occasional occurrence of large thymic hemorrhages is discussed and illustrated by Larroche.[29]

Lymphocyte depletion in the thymus is a useful indicator of the time course of preceding illness in an infant who dies in the perinatal period. The earliest change comprises focal loss of lymphocytes in the thymic cortex, giving a "starry sky" appearance to the organ (Fig. 20–9). As the thymic cortex becomes progressively depleted of lymphocytes, the medulla may retain its cellularity with an apparent reversal of the normal pattern (Fig. 20–10). Finally, as there is almost complete loss of lymphocytes throughout the organ, the lobules appear small and shrunken with wide bands of intervening connective tissue, and the Hassall's corpuscles are crowded together and appear more numerous than normal (Fig. 20–11). Evidence of lymphocyte destruction within Hassall's corpuscles is variable: in some cases they are markedly enlarged and contain masses of cell remnants and polymorphs. An exaggeration of this effect was known in the older literature as Dubois abscess; it was thought at one time to be specific for syphilis.

Lymphocyte depletion within the thymus does not occur on a consistent time scale in all perinatal illnesses. In my own experience the changes appear to develop

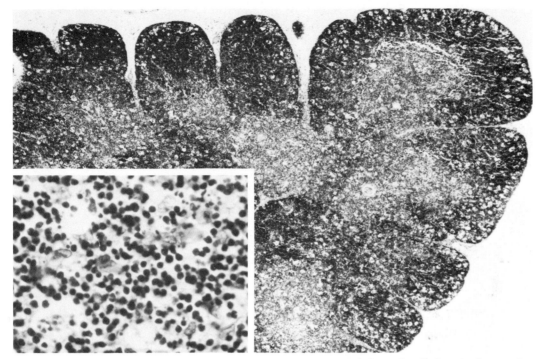

Figure 20–9. Thymus showing "starry-sky" appearance in a term infant who died at 21 hours of age following severe birth asphyxia. H and E × 40. Inset (H and E × 350) to show pyknotic remnants of lymphocytes within the clear areas.

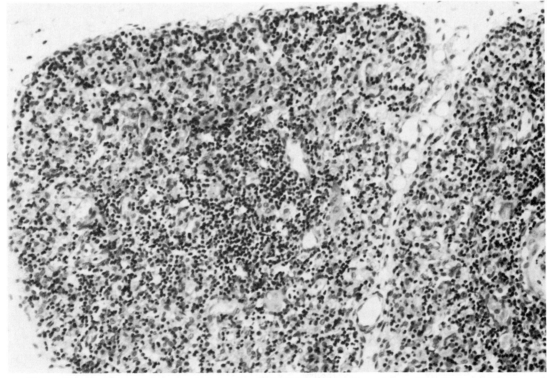

Figure 20–10. Thymus from an infant who died of sepsis at 4 days of age. H and E × 150. There is extensive loss of lymphocytes from the cortex, but they persist within the medulla to give a reversal of the normal appearance. Nuclear remnants are present within the Hassall's corpuscle at the right hand margin.

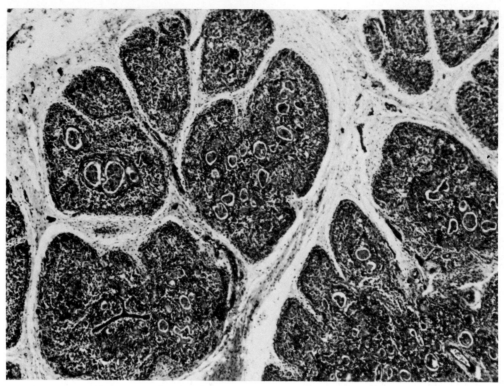

Figure 20–11. Thymus in a preterm infant who died at 21 days of age following prolonged neonatal intensive care. H and E × 40. There is extreme depletion of lymphocytes and the Hassall's corpuscles are crowded together.

more rapidly and consistently in cases of severe infection than in conditions such as respiratory distress syndrome. Advanced lymphocytic depletion of the thymus is seldom seen in infants subjected to prolonged intrauterine stress (e.g., fetal growth retardation in maternal pre-eclampsia), but the thymus may be relatively small in such cases with a poorly developed, rather thin, obviously depleted cortex. Despite the variability of response, demonstration of a well-developed starry sky pattern in the thymus indicates an acute stress that has developed at least 24 to 48 hours before death, and advanced depletion implies stress dating for at least 5 days. Such times are based on appearances of the thymus in infants who have died at varying ages after acquiring an acute infection (e.g., β-hemolytic streptococcus of group B) during birth.

SPLEEN

The spleen may occasionally suffer traumatic rupture during birth (Chapter 6) or be punctured during paracentesis performed for relief of ascites in cases of hydrops. Splenic damage was sometimes seen when intrauterine transfusion was needed frequently for management of severe Rh isoimmunization.[30] Splenic infarction is one manifestation of splanchnic ischemia in infants who require intensive care (Chapter 13).

Splenomegaly is seen in many of the conditions in which hepatomegaly occurs, including chronic intrauterine (TORCH) infections, blood group incompatibilities, a number of inborn errors of metabolism, and congenital neoplastic disease such as leukemia and histiocytosis (Letterer-Siwe disease).[19] The appearance of the spleen in Rh isoimmunization has been described previously (p. 407). Metabolic disorders in which typical storage cells may be recognized within an enlarged spleen include Gaucher's disease, Niemann-Pick disease and Wolman's disease.[26]

REFERENCES

1. Gilmour, J. R.: Normal haemopoiesis in intra-uterine life. J. Pathol. Bacteriol. *52*:25–55, 1941.
2. Halvorsen, S.: Plasma erythropoietin levels in cord blood and in blood during the first weeks of life. Acta Paediatr. *52*:425–435, 1963.
3. Finne, P. H.: Erythropoietin production in fetal hypoxia and in anaemic uremic patients. Ann. N.Y. Acad. Sci. *149*:497–503, 1968.
4. Isherwood, D. M., and Lathe, G. H.: Newborn jaundice: Bile pigment metabolism in the fetus and newborn infant. *In* Davis, J. A., and Dobbing, J. (eds.): Scientific Foundations of Paediatrics, 2nd ed. London, William Heinemann, 1981, pp. 138–160.
5. Rushton, D. I.: Fetal and neonatal liver disease. Diagn. Histopathol. *4*:17–48, 1981.
6. Palmer, A. K., and Heywood, R.: Pathological changes in the rhesus fetus associated with the oral administration of chenodeoxycholic acid. Toxicology 2:239–246, 1974.
7. Back, P., and Ross, K.: Identification of 3 beta OH5 cholenoic acid in human meconium. Hoppe-Seyler's Zeitschrift für Physiologische Chemie *354*:83–89, 1973.
8. Cohen, F., Zuelzer, W. W., Gustafson, D. C., and Evans, M. M.: Mechanisms of iso-immunisation. 1. The transplacental passage of fetal erythrocytes in homospecific pregnancies. Blood *23*:621–646, 1964.
9. Woo Wang, M. Y. F., McCutcheon, E., and Desforges, J. F.: Fetomaternal hemorrhage from diagnostic transabdominal amniocentesis. Am. J. Obstet. Gynecol. *97*:1123–1128, 1967.
10. Pochedly, C., and Musiker, S.: Twin-to-twin transfusion syndrome. Postgrad. Med. *47*:172–176, 1970.
11. Oski, F. A., and Naiman, J. L.: Hematologic Problems in the Newborn, 3rd ed. Philadelphia, W. B. Saunders Co., 1982.
12. Lanzkowsky, P.: Pediatric Hematology—Oncology. New York, McGraw-Hill, 1980.
13. Zipursky, A.: Hemolytic disease of the newborn. *In* Nathan, D. G., and Oski, F. A. (eds.): Hematology of Infancy and Childhood. Philadelphia, W. B. Saunders Co., 1974, pp. 280–314.
14. Freda, V. J., Gorman, J. G., and Pollack, W.: Rhesus factor in prevention of iso-immunisation in clinic trial on mothers. Science *151*:828–830, 1966.
15. Diamond, L. K., Allen, D. M., and Magill, F. B.: Congenital (erythroid) hypoplastic anemia. Am. J. Dis. Child. *102*:403–423, 1961.
16. Chessells, J. M., and Wigglesworth, J. S.: Secondary hemorrhagic disease of the newborn. Arch. Dis. Child. *45*:539–543, 1970.
17. Chessells, J. M., and Wigglesworth, J. S.: Coagulation studies in preterm infants with respiratory distress and intracranial hemorrhage. Arch. Dis. Child. *47*:564–570, 1972.
18. Shim, W. K. T.: Hemangiomas of infancy complicated by thrombocytopenia. Am. J. Surg. *116*:896–906, 1966.
19. Dehner, L. P.: Neoplasms of the fetus and neonate. *In* Naeye, R. L., Kissane, J. M., and Kaufman, N. (eds.): Perinatal Diseases. Baltimore, Williams & Wilkins, 1981, pp. 286–345.
20. Pinkel, D.: Ultrastructure of human fetal thymus. Am. J. Dis. Child. *115*:222–238, 1968.
21. Adinolfi, M.: The development of lymphoid tissues and immunity. *In* Davis, J. A., and Dobbing, J. (eds.): The Scientific Foundations of Paediatrics, 2nd ed. London, William Heinemann, 1981, pp. 525–544.
22. Lawton, A. R., and Cooper, M. D.: B cell ontogeny: Immunoglobulin genes and their expression. Pediatrics *64*(suppl.): 750–757, 1979.
23. Stiehm, E. R., Winter, H. S., and Bryson, Y. J.: Cellular (T cell) immunity in the human newborn. Pediatrics *64* (suppl.):814–821, 1979.
24. Hayward, A. R., and Lydyard, P. M.: B cell function in the newborn. Pediatrics *64* (suppl.):758–763, 1979.
25. Robinson, H. B.: DiGeorge's or the III-IV pharyngeal pouch syndrome: Pathology and a theory of pathogenesis. *In* Rosenberg, H. S., and Bolande, R. P. (eds.): Perspectives in Pediatric Pathology, vol. 2. Chicago, Year Book Medical Publishers, 1975, pp. 173–206.
26. Berry, C. L., and Revell, P. A.: Spleen, lymph nodes and immunoreactive tissues. *In* Berry, C. L. (ed.): Paediatric Pathology. Springer Verlag, 1981, pp. 535–569.
27. Gitlin, D., Vawter, G., and Craig, J. M.: Thymic alymphoplasia and congenital aleukocytosis. Pediatrics *33*:184–192, 1964.
28. Berry, C. L., and Thompson, E. N.: Clinico-pathological study of thymic dysplasia. Arch. Dis. Child. *43*:579–584, 1968.
29. Larroche, J. C.: Developmental Pathology of the Neonate. Amsterdam, Excerpta Medica, 1977.
30. Valdes-Dapena, M.: Iatrogenic disease in the perinatal period as seen by the pathologist. *In* Naeye, R. L., Kissane, J. M., and Kaufman, N. (eds.): Perinatal Diseases. Baltimore, Williams & Wilkins, 1981, pp. 382–418.
31. Levinsky, R. J., Linch, D. C., McLellan, K., et al.: Antenatal diagnosis of severe combined immunodeficiency (SCID). Arch. Dis. Child. *58*:649, 1983 (Abstract).

Chapter Twenty-one

Unexpected Death in Infancy

It has not been customary to consider unexpected death in infancy as a perinatal problem, and the subject has received little or no mention in previous texts on perinatal and infant pathology. The problem for the pathologist, in cases of sudden infant death syndrome (SIDS), is similar to that in many perinatal deaths in that he is presented with a dead infant with relatively little clinical history or diagnostic information. Moreover, when gross unrecognized illness has been excluded as a cause of death, the pathologist may need to assess the evidence for long-term recurrent minor illness or stress to form a profile, in the same way as he may do in cases of perinatal death. In addition, an increasing number of recent studies have provided evidence that many SIDS cases have their origin in the perinatal period, with changes denoting chronic or recurrent hypoxemic damage in cerebrum, brain stem and pulmonary vascular bed.

This chapter is not designed as a general review of the subject, which has been well covered in recent publications,[1-3] but to indicate how the pathologist may reasonably approach the problem in practical terms.

DEFINITION OF SIDS

SIDS is defined as a sudden and unexpected death of an infant in which a thorough postmortem examination fails to reveal an adequate cause of death. The diagnosis cannot logically be made until autopsy has excluded all known causes of death. In practice many infants who die in these circumstances may still be examined (in Great Britain) by pathologists who have little knowledge or experience in perinatal or pediatric pathology and who diagnose SIDS, or their own favored alternative (such as viral pneumonitis), on the basis of a hurried examination without the aid of histology or other ancillary investigations.

The pathologist who is asked to perform an autopsy on an infant who has died unexpectedly is in effect asked to disprove the hypothesis that this is a case of SIDS. The cases finally accepted as SIDS will depend both on the skill, experience and time available to the pathologist and on what he considers to be an adequate explanation of cause of death.

CHARACTERISTICS OF INFANTS WHO DIE UNEXPECTEDLY[1-3]

Age at Death. The most frequent age at death is 1 to 4 months. Some authors exclude deaths within the first 2 weeks of life, but in practice sudden unexpected death is relatively common in the neonatal period. Relatively few cases are seen after the first year, although the upper age limit is usually taken as 2 years of age.

Birth Weight and Gestation. Sudden unexpected death occurs significantly more frequently in infants of low birth weight and short gestation than in mature infants, but most infants who die unexpectedly are of normal birth weight and gestation length.

Feeding. Some surveys have shown a significantly greater risk of SIDS in formula-fed infants than in those entirely breast-fed, but other studies have failed to confirm this association and breast feeding clearly does not prevent SIDS.

Time of Year. Unexpected death occurs more frequently in the winter months than in summer.

History of Recent Illness. A history of recent minor illness, such as symptoms of an upper respiratory tract infection or a mild gastrointestinal upset with slight diarrhea, is very common. Parents have often sought medical advice within the week before the infant died.

Time of Day. Sudden unexpected death may occur at any time of the day or night. The most frequent time of discovery of a dead infant is at attempted waking for the first morning feeding.

Socioeconomic Condition. Sudden unexpected death occurs in all social groups but is more common in socially disadvantaged racial groups or families. Many studies have recorded associations with parental poverty, very young or unmarried parents, large families or abuse of drugs or smoking.

Sex. Male infants are found unexpectedly dead more often than female infants, but the difference in some series is no greater than that found in explained deaths.

Incidence. There is considerable variation in reports from different countries and in different population groups within countries. Incidence in the United States alone varies from 0.51 per thousand live births (Asians) to 5.93 per thousand (American Indians).[3] The average incidence is 1 to 2 per thousand live births.

PATHOLOGICAL INVESTIGATION OF UNEXPECTED INFANT DEATHS

PURPOSE OF AUTOPSY

The pathologist investigating an unexpected infant death must have a clear idea of the purpose of his examination. There are a number of very different requirements that need to be satisfied.

The legal and administrative requirement is that the pathologist should establish the cause of death, mainly for the purpose of excluding a violent or unnatural death. In the case of an infant who has died unexpectedly and fails to show abnormalities in any of the internal organs that would be accepted as a cause of death at any other age, the legal requirement can pose a problem for the pathologist. In the United Kingdom it has only recently become permissible for the pathologist to record SIDS as a "cause" of death. Previously it was necessary to record the deaths as caused by bronchopneumonia, gastroenteritis or some condition related to whichever organ might show a minimal abnormality. For epidemiological research purposes it is obviously important that the sudden and unexpected nature of the death be recorded on the death certificate irrespective of the precise pathological findings.

The second requirement of autopsy in sudden unexpected deaths is to provide maximum information for the clinician advising the parents and for the parents themselves. The need is similar to that already discussed in Chapter 1 in relation to perinatal deaths. The shock and grief of the parents who lose an apparently normal infant unexpectedly at several months of age may, of course, be considerably greater than that resulting from loss of an infant in the perinatal period. Counseling will be aided by the availability of a detailed postmortem report.

The third requirement in cases of sudden unexpected death is research. This is not one of the main purposes of autopsy in this situation but is an aspect that will concern many pathologists, particularly pediatric pathologists who work in academic centers.

TECHNIQUES OF EXAMINATION

Postmortem examination in cases of unexpected death should be performed in such a way as to satisfy the aforementioned requirements. A number of special techniques may appropriately form part of the study of cases of unexpected death in infancy.

X-Rays. A whole body x-ray taken before beginning the autopsy may sometimes show unexpected skeletal pathology, including evidence of possible child abuse.

Vitreous Humor. Study of vitreous humor electrolytes may be useful and has formed the basis for recognition of hypernatremia as a significant finding in some deaths.[4] It is usually possible to obtain 0.5 ml fluid through a 19-gauge needle passed into the eyeball at the outer canthus. The collapsed globe can be refilled with water. The sodium chloride and urea concentrations of vitreous humor remain relatively stable for 24 hours or more after death, and glucose is stable for 6 to 12 hours. Potassium levels rise quite rapidly.

Cerebrospinal Fluid. Examination of the CSF (microscopy and culture) may reveal evidence of early infection at a stage when it is not apparent as a frank meningitis. A sample of CSF may also be frozen in case the possibility of an inborn metabolic error is raised by the findings in the internal organs.

Middle Ear Cavity and Nasal Sinuses. Examination of the middle ears by a technique such as the one described in the Appendix should be performed in cases of unexpected infant death. Some pathologists also study the nasal sinuses.[2]

Microbiology. Bacteriological study is usually performed on swabs from the respiratory tract and middle ear, and blood cultures are taken.

Viral studies are undertaken on lung, heart, kidney, spleen, liver and contents of the large intestine.

Histology. A wide range of organs should be sampled for histology. One group of workers, for instance, has advocated the selection of 44 standard blocks (J. L. Emery, personal communication). Blocks should in all cases be taken from each of the lung lobes, main airways and larynx, heart, liver, spleen, kidneys, adrenals, pancreas, costochondral junction, thymus and brain.

The extent and precise pattern of tissue sampling does in practice depend on workload and local research interests, since the exploration of all suggested etiologies for SIDS could render the postmortem examination a completely open-ended commitment.

It is in planning the routine protocol for such cases that the pathologist needs to be sure of the purpose underlying the examination. For most pathologists not actively engaged in research into SIDS it will be regarded as satisfactory to perform an autopsy that excludes major bacterial or viral infection or unsuspected anomalies or metabolic disease and determines whether there is evidence of significant preceding stress or long-standing illness.

Many other types of study may be performed as research investigations, and most pathologists will be happy to collect data and specimens that may be needed for soundly based research projects in this area.

PATHOLOGICAL FINDINGS IN CASES OF SUDDEN INFANT DEATH

Although a variable proportion of infants who die unexpectedly are found to have pathological lesions characteristic of a specific disorder at postmortem examination, the majority of them, in most series, present a number of features that are not normal but do not fit into a disease pattern sufficient to account for death. Various changes have been reported as typical for different organs but only a selection of them is likely to be found in any one case.

External Appearances. These are not distinctive. Sometimes the infant is found with blood-stained froth or mucus exuding from the mouth and nostrils.

Upper Respiratory Tract. An acute or subacute rhinitis may be present if sought, and a round-cell or mixed inflammatory cell infiltrate may be present at any level of the upper airways, including epiglottis, larynx and trachea. Ulceration of the vocal cords or fibrinoid necrosis beneath an intact epithelium is a frequent finding.[5, 6]

Lungs. These are commonly bulky, congested and edematous. The edema, although widespread, tends to be of irregular distribution, and affected regions may be interspersed with areas of collapse. Small hemorrhages are often present over the pleural surfaces and may also be seen deep in the parenchyma (Fig. 21–1). However, many of these infants have been subjected to vigorous resuscitation

Figure 21–1. Lung of an infant found unexpectedly dead at 4 months of age showing congestion and small surface hemorrhages.

attempts by parents, ambulance drivers and hospital medical staff, so the lung pathology may have been modified postmortem.

On histological examination the patchy pulmonary edema is confirmed, and there is often a moderate histiocytic reaction (Fig. 21–2). Lymphocytic infiltration may be seen around the walls of bronchi and bronchioles and within the alveolar septa. There is often desquamation of bronchial epithelium, and prominent lymphoid aggregates are sometimes present (Fig. 21–3). The latter finding has been interpreted as evidence of preceding infection.

Heart. Surface petechiae are common. A mild endocardial fibroelastic thickening of the left ventricle has been described as a relatively frequent finding.

Thymus. Petechial hemorrhages are often present. The thymus is usually of normal size and thus seems very large in comparison with that seen in infants who have suffered prolonged illness. On histology, however, there is often evidence of a stress reaction in the form of cortical lymphocytic depletion with a "starry sky" picture (Chapter 20).

Brain. A number of pathological findings have been reported as characteristic over recent years. These include the presence of lipid-containing cells within the corpus callosum,[7] a significant incidence of periventricular leukomalacia,[8] and abnormal proliferation of astroglial fibers in the brain stem.[9] All these changes have been interpreted as evidence of episodes of hypoxia or of a chronic hypoxemia that preceded the terminal event and may have dated from early in the neonatal period.

Other Tissues. Some infants show evidence of a mild enteritis.[2] There is often

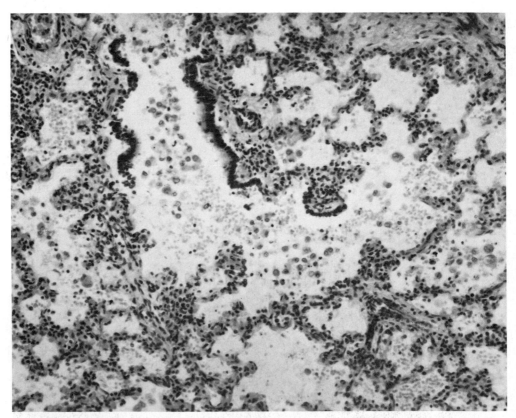

Figure 21–2. Lung of an infant born at 26 weeks' gestation who survived the neonatal period but was found unexpectedly dead at 6 months of age. H and E × 150. There is edema with histiocytes and red blood cells within respiratory bronchioles and alveoli.

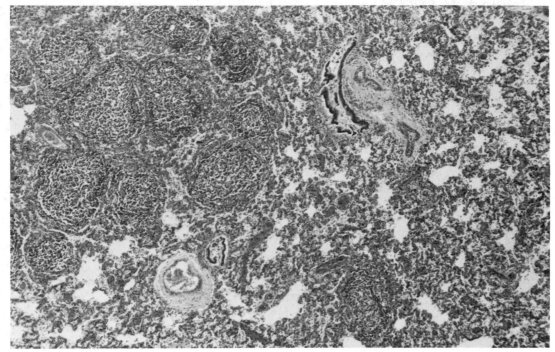

Figure 21–3. Lung of an infant found unexpectedly dead at 4½ months. H and E × 30. There are prominent lymphoid aggregates.

evidence of growth arrest at the costochondral junction (Chapter 19).[10] Many of the infants show fatty infiltration in the liver, and some show hemopoietic cells within the sinusoids. The latter appearance has been interpreted by Naeye as evidence of chronic hypoxemia, as has an abnormal retention of perirenal brown fat.[11]

The adrenals usually appear very small. This is assumed to be attributable to the age at which the deaths commonly occur, 1 to 4 months, a time when the fetal adrenal cortex has fully involuted, but the definitive cortex remains relatively small in bulk. Occasional cases of sudden infant death have been reported in association with significant adrenal hypoplasia.[12]

Evidence of impaired development of renal glomeruli may be seen in some cases as a further evidence of significant preceding illness (Fig. 21–4).

QUANTITATIVE ABNORMALITIES

In addition to glial proliferation in the brain stem, Naeye has presented a number of other "tissue markers for hypoxemia," which he has found in about 50 per cent of SIDS cases. These include an increase in the muscle within the small pulmonary arteries, increased mass of the right ventricle and a decrease in total mass and size of individual glomus cells of the carotid body.[11] In a few cases there may be hyperplasia of the carotid body glomus tissue.[13] The latter change would be compatible with chronic hypoxemia. Study of the spleen by a different group has shown an increased quantity of lymphatic tissue and germinal center tissue, suggesting a high exposure to antigenic stimulation.[14]

ATYPICAL FINDINGS IN CASES OF SUDDEN INFANT DEATH

In any series of cases of unexpected death in infancy the pathologist will encounter a range of interesting pathological findings that help to explain a number of the deaths.

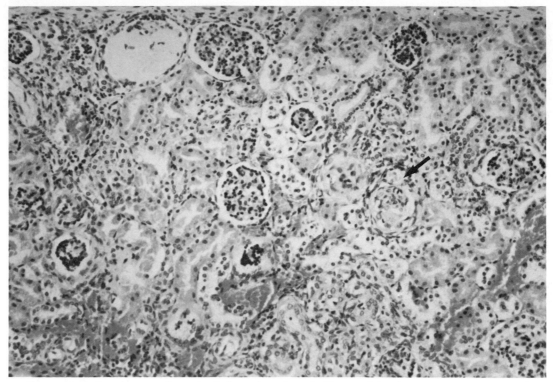

Figure 21–4. Renal cortex from the infant whose lung is illustrated in Figure 21–2. H and E × 150. Impairment in renal development is indicated by the presence of small glomeruli of immature form with masses of closely packed nuclei, particularly at their periphery. Several old sclerosed glomeruli are also visible (arrowed).

One infant was found unexpectedly dead at 4 days of age. (Death in infants at this age is not considered to be genuine sudden infant death by many authors.) The findings comprised a congested, swollen brain with early periventricular infarction, massive microvesicular fatty infiltration of hepatic parenchymal cells (Fig. 21–5) and fatty infiltration of the cells of the proximal tubules of the kidneys. These changes were considered typical of Reye syndrome. In another infant who died suddenly at 6 months of age, one of triplets, autopsy revealed an accessory lung lobe that was located behind the trachea and was the seat of acute pneumococcal pneumonia (Fig. 21–6). It was postulated that the swollen lung lobe had caused obstruction to the lower trachea.

THEORIES OF CAUSATION[1, 3]

Innumerable theories have been advanced as to "the" cause of crib death. Some of the more important ones are mentioned here.

INFECTION

As unexpected death occurs most often in the winter months in an infant with a preceding history of mild respiratory or gastrointestinal symptoms, it is logical to suppose that infection may play a significant role in many of the deaths. Viral infections seem the most likely candidates and could be involved in a variety of ways. An acute rhinitis might obstruct the nasal passages, or a laryngotracheobronchitis might cause obstruction of lower airways. Lack of host defenses or

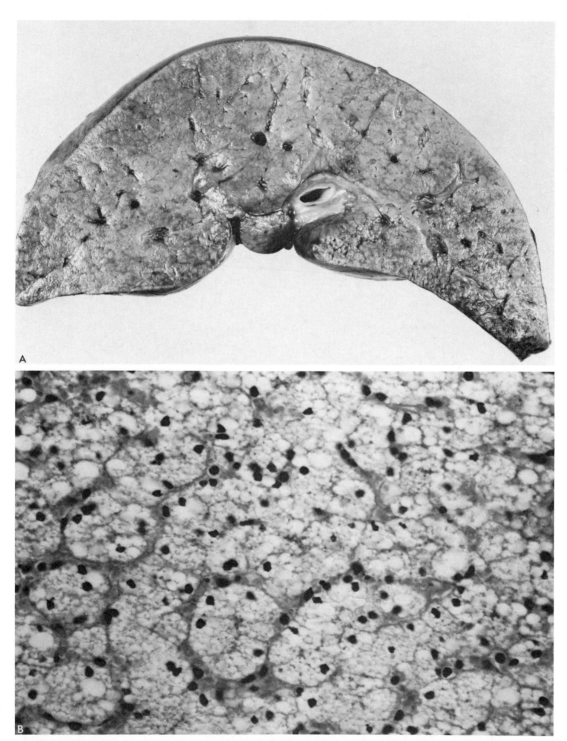

Figure 21–5. Liver of an infant found unexpectedly dead at 4 days of age. *A*, Macroscopic appearance showing pallor due to massive lipid infiltration of parenchymal cells. *B*, Histologic appearance. H and E × 300. The cells have a foamy appearance due to massive microvesicular fatty infiltration.

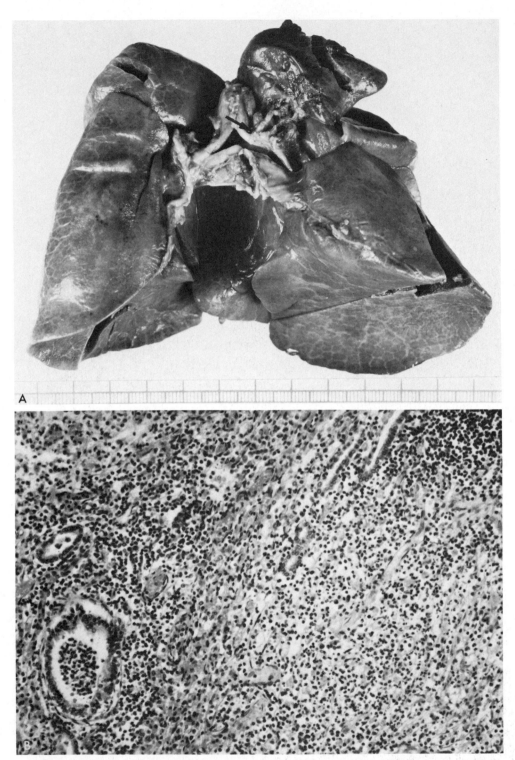

Figure 21–6. *A*, Posterior aspect of the lungs of an infant found unexpectedly dead at 6 months of age. An accessory lobe, originally located behind the trachea has been displaced to show the blind-ending bronchus (arrowed). *B*, Histologic appearance of the accessory lobe showing acute pneumonia. H and E × 150. *S. pneumoniae* was cultured in pure growth.

prior sensitization might result in abnormal response to infection. A mild infection might cause fatal expression of a previously occult metabolic abnormality.

ABNORMAL RESPIRATORY PHYSIOLOGY

Abnormalities of respiratory control are a major current area of investigation.[1, 3, 15] An abnormal cry, abnormal respiratory patterns or episodes of spontaneous apnea have been observed in "near miss" SIDS cases (infants who did not die during an observed severe apneic episode, although they may have died on a later occasion).

Some infants have been shown to be obligate nose breathers and unable to respond to nasal obstruction by opening their mouths to breathe. The possibility that recurrent apneic episodes might themselves damage the respiratory center and produce a vicious circle effect is suggested by the demonstration of gliotic changes compatible with chronic hypoxemia in the brain stem of some infants who die unexpectedly, as mentioned earlier in conjunction with other "tissue markers" of hypoxemia.

ACUTE ASPHYXIA

Accidental or deliberate suffocation or aspiration of gastric contents has frequently been suggested to account for varying proportions of cases of unexpected death in infancy.

METABOLIC ABNORMALITIES

Suggestions have included hypernatremia from hyperosmolar formula feedings, hypocalcemia, hypoglycemia, hypoadrenalism, hyperpyrexia[16] or abnormal pulmonary surfactant composition.[17]

IMMUNOLOGICAL MECHANISMS

An anaphylactic response to aspirated cow's milk following previous sensitization is one suggested mechanism; another is an immune complex disease related to viral infections.[18]

CARDIOVASCULAR SYSTEM

Abnormalities of cardiac conduction have been proposed as one possible cause and structural abnormalities of the conducting tissue have been described.[19]

TOXIC MECHANISMS

Botulism has been incriminated in a few cases of unexpected infant death.[20]

AN APPROACH TO THE CAUSATION OF UNEXPECTED INFANT DEATH

From the preceding section it would seem that there is a plethora of theories on the etiology of SIDS from which anyone may choose. Although some of the theories put forward have found little support when tested by other workers, there is evidence that many of the mechanisms do account for death of some infants. Thus mechanisms as diverse as hypernatremia and botulism may at various times and places have been responsible for sudden infant death. A few infants are undoubtedly asphyxiated by their parents.[21] Other apparently disparate causative factors may interact. Infection, abnormal respiratory control patterns, metabolic abnormalities and immunological reactions could be involved in almost any combination.

In my view one of the most characteristic features is the age at which unexpected death occurs. I prefer to think of the factors involved as acting against the background of normal neonatal development. For whatever reason the period of greatest vulnerability appears to be at the 1 to 4 month age period. Disorders that would be insufficient to cause death at any other time of life may do so during this particular time. Clearly it would be nice to know the factors that might confer vulnerability at this age period. Endocrine or immunological mechanisms could well be involved. Even without such knowledge the idea of a vulnerable age allows one to view the different postulated "causes" for SIDS as alternative possible pathways leading to death rather than as competing and mutually exclusive hypotheses.

A group of workers in Sheffield, England, has repeatedly pointed out that infants coming to autopsy who have died unexpectedly show a wide range of pathology. Of infants coming to autopsy in one series, 40 per cent proved to have congenital malformations or serious undiagnosed disease (i.e., death was pathologically explained even if sudden and unexpected).[10] A further 40 per cent had evidence of reactions to mild infection such as tracheitis, mild gastroenteritis or otitis media. In most of the remainder there were morphological alterations of thymus, costochondral junction or liver, which suggests some long-standing disorder. These findings are what one might expect on the basis of a "vulnerable age" hypothesis.

I suspect that investigations of normal physiological development in the first year of life may provide more information on the causation of SIDS than studies on dead infants or a search for particular abnormal physiological mechanisms in supposedly vulnerable subgroups of the infant population.

REFERENCES

1. Valdes-Dapena, M.: Sudden infant death syndrome: A review of the medical literature 1974–1979. Pediatrics 66:597–614, 1980.
2. Althoff, H.: Sudden infant death syndrome (SIDS). Progress in Pathology, vol. 114. Stuttgart, Gustav Fischer Verlag, 1980.
3. Shannon, D. C., and Kelly, D. H.: SIDS and near-SIDS. N. Engl. J. Med. 306:959–965 and 1022–1028, 1982.
4. Emery, J. L., Swift, P. G. E., and Worthy, E.: Hypernatraemia and uraemia in unexpected death in infancy. Arch. Dis. Child. 49:686–692, 1974.
5. Valdes-Dapena, M.: Sudden death in infancy: A report for pathologists. In Rosenberg, H. S., and Bolande, R. P. (eds.): Perspectives in Pediatric Pathology, vol. 2. Chicago, Year Book Medical Publishers, 1975, pp. 1–14.
6. Keeling, J.: Sudden infant death syndrome. In Berry, C. L. (ed.): Paediatric Pathology. Berlin, Springer Verlag, 1981, pp. 671–678.
7. Gadsdon, D. R., and Emery, J. L.: Fatty change in the brain in perinatal and unexpected deaths. Arch. Dis. Child. 51:42–48, 1976.
8. Takashima, S., Armstrong, D., Becker, L. E., and Huber, J.: Cerebral white matter lesions in sudden infant death syndrome. Pediatrics 62:155–159, 1978.
9. Naeye, R. L.: Brain stem and adrenal abnormalities in the sudden infant death syndrome. Am. J. Clin. Pathol. 66:526–530, 1976.
10. Sinclair-Smith, L., Dinsdale, F., and Emery, J.: Evidence of duration and type of illness in children found unexpectedly dead. Arch. Dis. Child. 51:424–429, 1976.
11. Naeye, R. L.: The sudden infant death syndrome—A review of recent advances. Arch. Pathol. Lab. Med. 101:165–167, 1977.
12. Russell, M. A., Opitz, J. M., Viseskul, C., Gilbert, E. F., and Bargman, G. J.: Sudden infant death due to congenital adrenal hypoplasia. Arch. Pathol. Lab. Med. 101:168–169, 1977.
13. Naeye, R. L., Fisher, R., Whalen, P., and Ryser, M.: Carotid body in the sudden infant death syndrome. Science 191:567–569, 1976.
14. Barzanji, A. J., and Emery, J. L.: Quantitative study of the lymphatic tissue and germinal centres in the spleen in infants dying from expected and unexpected causes (cot deaths). Histopathology 1:445–449, 1977.

15. Steinschneider, A.: Prolonged sleep apnea and respiratory instability: A discriminative study. Pediatrics 59(suppl.):962–970, 1977.
16. Denborough, M. A., Galloway, G. J., and Hopkinson, K. C.: Malignant hyperpyrexia and sudden infant death. Lancet 2:1068–1069, 1982.
17. Morley, C. J., Hill, C. M., Brown, B. D., and Barson, A. J.: Surfactant abnormalities in babies dying from sudden infant death syndrome. Lancet 1:1320–1322, 1982.
18. Urquhart, G. E. D.: Sudden death in infancy—Studies in virology and immunology. *In* Robinson, R. R. (ed.): SIDS 1974. Canadian Foundation for the Study of Infant Deaths, pp. 107–115.
19. Anderson, R. H., Bouton, J., Burrow, C. T., and Smith, A.: Sudden death in infancy: A study of cardiac specialized tissue. Br. Med. J. 2:135–139, 1974.
20. Arnon, S. S., Midura, T. F., Damus, K., Wood, R. M., and Chin, J.: Intestinal infection and toxin production by *Clostridium botulinum* as one cause of sudden infant death syndrome. Lancet 1:1273–1276, 1978.
21. Emery, J. L.: The "gently battered" child. Arch. Dis. Child. 57:798–799 (Abstract), 1982.

APPENDIX

Technique for Removal of the Newborn Middle and Inner Ear

Contributed by:

DR. PETER KELEHAN

Consultant Pathologist
Regional Pathology Laboratory
Regional Hospital, Galway, Ireland

The middle ear of a newborn at term is about the same size as in the adult, with anteroposterior and vertical diameters of about 1 cm and transverse diameters of 6 mm at the roof, 2 mm at midpoint and 4 mm at the floor.[1,2] The tympanic membrane is 1 cm in diameter and cone shaped, projecting inward to reduce the midtransverse diameter. The mastoid antrum is well developed, but the mastoid process and mastoid air cells are as yet unformed.

The ossicles are adult size from the sixth month of fetal life. The oval window at 2.5 by 1.5 mm and round window at 2 mm are the same size in the newborn as in the adult.

The bony and membranous labyrinths of the inner ear are almost equal to those of the adult in size and proportions.

Unlike the adult external acoustic meatus, the inner third of which is an osseous extension outward of the tympanic bone, the inner third in the neonate and in the child up to about 3 years of age is composed of fibrous tissue. Therefore, it can be dissected off the tympanic bone to yield a clear view of the tympanic membrane when a thin rim of fibrocartilage is removed from the circumference of the eardrum and vernix caseosa, obscuring the detail of the tympanic membrane, is removed by spatula.

The tympanic membrane is slanted by more than 60 degrees from the vertical in the premature neonate and by 50 to 60 degrees in those in the postneonatal period. Because of this, it is best viewed and photographed and the middle ear inspected and explored following the removal of the intact petrous bone. Removal is easily achieved with a strong scissors because the petrous and squamous parts of the temporal bones in the neonate are usually partially separated by the petrosquamous fissure and the squamous parts are soft and thin. Following the removal of the brain in the usual way, the scalp incision is carried out behind the ear and a skin flap is dissected over the ear, keeping the scalpel blade close to the temporal bone to avoid buttonholing the skin.

431

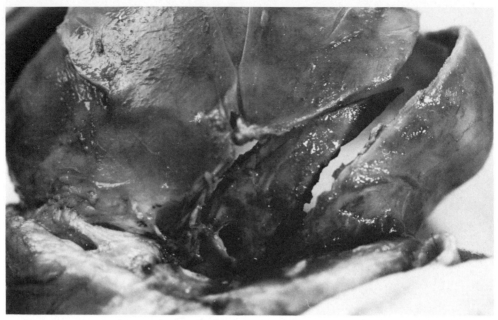

Figure 1. A stage in the dissection of the middle and inner ear showing the lines of incision through the squamous temporal bone. The occiput is to the right.

The roof of the external auditory meatus is opened to reveal the longer floor and tympanic membrane. Following lateral extension of the dissection to provide better exposure, the floor is divided by scalpel incision, and the styloid fossa is entered by further dissection.

The lambdoidal suture is opened by scissors and cuts are made in an arc in the squamous bone along the petrosquamous fissure (Appendix Fig. 1). The wing thus formed in the squamous bone (long wing to identify left, short for right petrous bones) is grasped, and the petrous bone is removed by further cuts anterior, posterior and inferior through the styloid fossa.

The complete auditory apparatus removed in this way can be trimmed and examined immediately or after fixation (Appendix Fig. 2). In the stillborn infant and the infant who has died early in the neonatal period, the drum has a gray translucent appearance. Air bubbles entering the middle ear confer a steel-blue appearance after about 6 hours of postnatal life. A straw-colored fluid can often be aspirated by needle through the drum in the sick neonate at 2 to 3 weeks, especially from the epitympanic recess and mastoid antrum. This fluid on cytological examination may contain mucus, meconium, inflammatory cells and desquamated respiratory epithelium and occasionally foreign body giant cells and squames.

The remarkable funnel-shaped concavity of the drum in the neonate may give a false impression of retraction. This concavity may persist with severe suppurative otitis media, the drum tending to bulge around the outer margin only. There is increased vascularization of the drum in otitis media, in association with congenital pneumonia and chorionamnionitis, whether congenital or acquired later. Up to midtrimester the fetal middle ear contains a pale brown gelatinous and viscous fluid.

Following a short decalcification the squamous parts are trimmed from the petrous bone, and the block may be processed and embedded in two parts, the

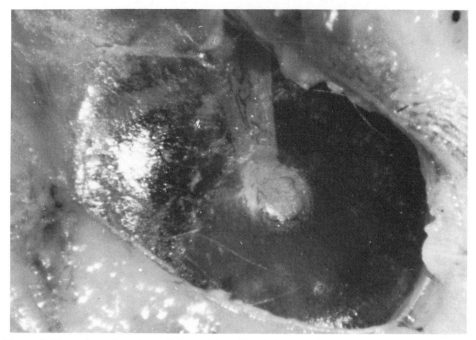

Figure 2. Normal eardrum in an infant with sudden infant death syndrome at 3 months of age.

petrous bone being divided by a longitudinal cut parallel to the drum into a middle ear block containing auditory tube, ossicles and mastoid antrum and an inner ear block containing cochlea and semicircular canals.

REFERENCES

1. Crelin, E. S.: Functional Anatomy of the Newborn. New Haven, Yale University Press, 1973.
2. Crelin, E. S.: Anatomy of the Newborn: An Atlas. Philadelphia, Lea and Febiger, 1969.

INDEX

Italics indicate illustrations and t denotes tables.

MAJOR PROBLEMS IN PATHOLOGY

MAJOR PROBLEMS IN PATHOLOGY (MPP)—
A series of important monographs focusing on significant topics of current interest. Unsurpassed in clarity and depth of coverage, each hardbound volume in the series is superbly illustrated, and covers a specific issue or disease, a recent advance in clinical therapeutics, or a newly developed diagnostic technique. Each title is written and edited by carefully selected experts of widely recognized ability and authority. In fact, MPP's list of authors is a virtual "Who's Who" of pathology.

Join the MPP Subscriber Plan. You'll receive each new volume in the series upon publication—one to three titles publish each year—and you'll save postage and handling costs! Or you may order MPP titles individually. If not completely satisfied with any volume, you may return it with the invoice within 30 days at no further obligation.

Timely, in-depth coverage you can count on . . . Enroll in the Subscriber Plan for MAJOR PROBLEMS IN PATHOLOGY today!

Available from your bookstore or the publisher.

Complete and Mail Today!

✔ YES! Enroll me in the MAJOR PROBLEMS IN PATHOLOGY Subscriber Plan so that I may receive future titles in the series immediately upon publication, and save postage and handling costs! If not completely satisfied with any volume, I may return it with the invoice within 30 days at no further obligation.

Name_____

Address_____

City_____State_____Zip_____

☐ Credit my
  salesman

Printed in USA.   283   PM2416E   Postage & handling additional outside USA.